THE
EAST INDIA MILITARY CALENDAR;

CONTAINING THE SERVICES OF

GENERAL AND FIELD OFFICERS

OF THE

INDIAN ARMY

BY THE EDITOR OF THE ROYAL MILITARY CALENDAR

VOL. III

The Naval & Military Press Ltd

Published by
The Naval & Military Press Ltd
Unit 10, Ridgewood Industrial Park,
Uckfield, East Sussex,
TN22 5QE England
Tel: +44 (0) 1825 749494
Fax: +44 (0) 1825 765701
www.naval-military-press.com
www.military-genealogy.com

© The Naval & Military Press Ltd 2007

In reprinting in facsimile from the original, any imperfections are inevitably reproduced and the quality may fall short of modern type and cartographic standards.

Printed and bound by Lightning Source

THE EAST INDIA MILITARY CALENDAR.

MAJOR-GENERAL JOHN ARNOLD, C. B.

(Bengal Establishment.)

This officer commenced his military career the 9th of March, 1778, as a Cadet on the Bengal Establishment, and was attached to the grenadiers of the 3d European regiment: he was appointed Ensign, 4th June 1778; Lieut., 16th Nov. 1780; Capt., 7th Jan. 1796; Major, 13th July 1803; L.-Col., 19th Oct. 1805; Brevet-Col., 4th June 1813; Brigadier, 2d Jan. 1815; B.-Gen., 14th Sept. 1817; succeeded to a regiment, 5th July 1819; and was promoted to M.-Gen., 12th August 1819.

In 1778, he was in the field with the 1st European reg. at Caunpoor, then the frontier station of the field army, to act against the Mahrattas. In 1780, he was Adjutant to the 1st European reg., and commanding the company of Cadets in Fort William. In 1783, he was appointed Aid-de-Camp to Col. Hampton, Commandant of Fort William, and subsequently commanding the 2d brigade at Burhampoor. In 1788, he served as Aid-de-Camp, and as Persian interpreter, to Col. John White, commanding a brigade at Dinapoor; and subsequently the frontier station of the army at Futtyghur and Anoopsheher.

In 1796, he served as Capt. in the 1st batt. 9th N. I. in command of various detachments in the Gooruckpoor jungles, after marauders; on the successful termination of which service, he was selected, by M.-Gen. Sir James Craig, to take charge of, and place in an efficient state of defence, the fort of Sandie, in the Newaub Vizier's dominions of Oude; also, to sink and construct granaries, as a depôt for the army Gen. Craig was leading against Zemaun Shah.

In 1800, he was removed to the 1st. batt. 1st. N. I. at Midnapoor, having the temporary command of the battalion, and commanding detachments at Beerbhoom and Pateoom. During the inclement season of the rains in the Pateoom district, the mortality was so great, that one half of the detachment fell a prey, in six weeks, to the jungle fever.

In 1803, this officer, after a continued service of 25 years in the army in India, and 27 in the country, never having applied for leave of absence, or been reported sick, repaired to Europe on furlough.

In 1806, he sailed in the Lady Burgess, Indiaman, Capt. A. Swinton, for Bengal, and was shipwrecked in the passage, losing a moderate fortune, many letters of approbation from M.-Gen. Sir James Craig, and other officers high in rank, valuable plans, routes, &c. collected during a long service.

In 1807-8, he was employed in reducing several forts, ghauts, and strong holds in Bundlecund; viz. fort of Sehleehoo, Mekheewa, Joudpore, Sahnugger, Ramghurra, Roreesingpore, Deewghur, Birsingpore, and Ummooah, with the ghaut of Gunge Mahoodra.

The following are among the public testimonies for service rendered at this period:—

Extract of a Letter from J. Richardson, Esq. Agent to the Gov. Gen., to L.-Col. J. Arnold, commanding the detachment.

"Camp, Mooreareh, the 20th Dec. 1807.

"SIR,—Sensible as I am of the zeal, activity, and prudence, manifested by you in promoting the objects government has in view, by employing the detachment under your command on the present service, and of the exemplary good conduct of the officers and troops composing the detachment, it is with sincere pleasure, I have the honour to annex an extract of a letter from Mr. Secretary Edmonstone, received yesterday."

Extract of a Letter from N. B. Edmonstone, Esq., Secretary to Government, in the Secret and Political Department, to Mr. J. Richardson, Agent to the Governor-General, dated the 30th Nov. 1807.

" I am directed to acknowledge the receipt of your letters of the 12th, 14th, and 15th instant. The Right Hon. the Gov.-Gen. in Council highly applauds the activity manifested by L.-Col. Arnold, and the detachment under his command, in proceeding against the fort of Sehleehoo Gunge, in consequence of the unexpected flight of Gopaul Sing, and in the success which attended that measure, and laments the casualties which occurred on that occasion. The Gov.-Gen. in Council observes, that the enterprize appears to have been conducted and executed in a manner highly creditable to L.-Col. Arnold, and the officers and troops under his command."

Extract of a Letter from N. B. Edmonstone, Esq., Secretary to Government, to Mr. J. Richardson, Agent to the Governor-General in Bundlecund, dated 7th Dec. 1807.

" The operations against the rebel Gopaul Sing, described in these despatches, are extremely satisfactory to government, and reflect great credit on the zeal and activity of L.-Col. Arnold, and the officers and men under his command."

Extract of General Orders issued by the Commander-in-Chief.

" *Head Quarters, Fort William, 28th Jan. 1808.*

" *General Orders by the Right Hon. the Governor-General in Council. Fort William, 25th Jan. 1808.*

" The Right Hon. the Gov.-Gen. in Council has observed with great satisfaction, from the official reports communicated by His Ex. the Com.-in-Chief, that the service on which the detachment in Bundlecund, under the command of L.-Col. Arnold, has been recently engaged, is brought to a successful termination, by the full and complete accomplishment of all the objects to which, under the orders of government, the operations of the detachment have been directed. The Gov.-Gen. in Council avails himself of this occasion, to express his most marked and distinguished approbation of the eminent zeal, talent, and exertion, manifested by L.-Col. Arnold in the command of the detachment, through every period of its operations.

" The bravery, discipline, and good conduct of the officers and men composing the detachment under the command of L.-Col. Arnold, are entitled to the warmest thanks and commendations of government, and His Lordship in Council has peculiar satisfaction in distinguishing the conduct, gallantry, and exertion of Captains Leadbeater and Shower, who led the successful and well-concerted attacks on the rear of the insurgents at the Gunge Mahoodra Ghaut, on the morning of the 25th Dec., and the spirit, regularity, and laborious efforts of the officers and men of their divisions, who executed that service, and obtained that decisive advantage. The great exertion of the artillery and sepoys, who at the same period of time, under the immediate command of L.-Col. Arnold, ascended the steep ghaut in front, with two guns and their tumbrils, on most irregular and unfavourable ground, have been also noticed by His Lordship in Council, with most particular approbation.

" The Gov.-Gen. in Council, has the most cordial pleasure in requesting His Ex. the Com.-in-Chief, to convey these sentiments to L.-Col. Arnold, and to the officers and sepoys of the detachment under his command."

Extract.—General Orders by the Right Hon. the Governor-General in Council.
" *Fort William*, 20th *Feb*. 1813.

" Ordered, that the following paragraph of a general letter, received from the Hon. the Court of Directors in the Military Department, under date the 9th Sept. 1812, be published in General Orders.

" *Account of operations of a detachment employed under the command of L.-Col. Arnold, for placing Rajahs Bukht Bullies, and Kissore, in their possessions above the Ghauts, &c.*

" Par. 10.—We are much gratified with the success attending the operations of the detachment employed under L.-Col. Arnold, and with the military ability, zeal, and spirit displayed by L.-Col. Arnold, Capt. Leadbeater, and the other officers and soldiers under his command."

In 1809, L.-Col. Arnold commanded a battalion, as a *corps de reserve*, with Col. G. Martindell's* force at the capture of the fort of Adjeeghur, after the attack of the Ruggoulee hills. In 1810,

* Services, vol. i. p. 406-8; vol. ii. p. 562-3.

he commanded a brigade with Col. G. Martindell's army at Terrie and Khemlassa. In 1811-12, he commanded the fort and district of Allyghur. In 1812-13-14, he commanded the post of Hansie, in Hurriana, and was nominated to the command of a brigade with M.-Gen. D. Marshall's * army employed against the forts of Ullewur; and subsequently commanded a force to reduce the fort of Iheend, which capitulated. About this period Sir George Nugent †, Com.-in-Chief, being on his tour of inspection, was pleased to express his approbation of the discipline maintained by the Lieut.-Col. at Hansie, in the following terms:—

Extract of General Orders by the Commander-in-Chief.
"*Head Quarters, Camp Iheend, 4th January,* 1813.

" The Com.-in-Chief has seldom, on any similar occasion, derived greater satisfaction than from the review of the 1st batt. 19 N. I., and Capt. Skinner's corps of irregular cavalry; the whole under the orders or L.-Col. Arnold, commanding at Hansie. The performance of the battalion was, throughout the course of the review, distinguished by a facility, justness, and precision of movements, which the Com.-in-Chief has seldom seen surpassed; and his Excellency remarked, with particular approbation, the very correct and prompt execution of every point which depended on the personal conduct of the commanding officers of companies, and mounted officers of the corps.

" Of Capt. Skinner's corps, the Com.-in-Chief considers it but justice to that officer, thus publicly to declare, that the size, condition, and figure of the horses, and the arms, clothing, and appointments of the men, are of a superior description to those of any other class of irregular cavalry that have yet fallen under his Excellency's observation. Acting in brigade, their movements indicated such a knowledge of European tactics, as would enable the corps to combine, whenever required, its movements with those of regular troops, while its separate performance of the various movements, more particularly appropriate to and characteristic of irregular horse, satisfactorily demonstrated the superior excellence of the corps for that particular line of service, which is more immediately the object of its maintenance by government.

" The Com.-in-Chief requests L.-Col. Arnold and Capt. Skinner will ac-

* Services, vol. i. p. 395-7. † Services, Royal Military Calendar, vol. i. p. 394-9, 3d edit.

cept his best thanks, for having, by their individual and united exertions, rendered the two corps at Hansie so highly disciplined and efficient."

In 1814-15, Col. Arnold served as second in command under M.-Gen. Ochterlony*, during the Ghoorka or Nepaul war, at the reduction of the fort of Naldghur, and the line of stockaded positions near Ramghur, after which, he was detached, as Brigadier, to gain the heights of Tulsooree, by which the enemy's communication with Belaspore and his supplies would be cut off; and, ultimately, to closely invest the fortress of Maloun on the north-west: he retained the command until the capture of that place, and consequent expulsion of the Ghoorka forces from the country. The following acknowledgment appeared in the orders of M.-Gen. Ochterlony, about the conclusion of the campaign:—

Extract of Division Orders, by M.-Gen. Ochterlony, Commanding.

"*Camp Buttoo*, 18*th April*, 1815.

"The M.-Gen. cannot close this public testimony of his thanks and approbation, without expressing his acknowledgments to Brig. Arnold, for his cordial assistance in promoting the objects in view; and particularly for strengthening the right column of division, from his own force, when the Seik auxiliaries, intended and ordered for the service, did not appear."

In 1817-18, this officer was selected Brigadier-General, and second in command under M.-Gen. Sir D. Ochterlony, commanding the 8th Brigade in the Reserve, and the Reserve Division during the absence of Gen. Ochterlony, in Rajpootana. The following is an extract of Sir David's orders on re-assuming the command of the Reserve:—

Extract of Reserve Orders, by M.-Gen. Sir David Ochterlony, Commanding.

"*Head Quarters, Camp Meenda*, 12*th April*, 1818.

"The M.-Gen. cannot conclude without offering his thanks to Brig.-Gen. Arnold, for his ready acquiescence in his views and wishes, though expressed in a private form; and for his obliging attention in giving shape and form to suggestions, which, from distance, hurry, and other circumstances, could only have been vague and indefinite."

* Services, vol. i. p. 379-87.

In 1818, he served as Brigadier-General, commanding the 3d division of the army at Kurnaul, and was selected to command an army to reduce the forts of Futteabad, Sirsah, and Ranneea, in the Bhuttee country, which had successfully resisted a detachment, and to subjugate the district. After the performance of this service he entered the Bickaneer Desert, and regained the forts of Seedmook, Dudrera, Jaheereea, Chooroo, Surcilla, Soluckneer, and Buhul, delivering them over to the Rajah of Bickaneer, to whose territory they belonged.

Extract of a Letter from C. T. Metcalfe, Esq., Resident at Delhi, dated 23d September, 1815, to Brig. Arnold, commanding the Field Force.

"Sir,—I have the honour to acknowledge the receipt of your letters, noted in the margin, and beg leave again to congratulate you on the successful result of your judicious operations, by the satisfactory completion of the service for which the force under your command entered the Bickaneer country."

Extract of a Letter from C. T. Metcalfe, Esq., Resident at Delhi, dated 12th November, 1818, to Brig. J. Arnold, &c. &c., Kurnaul.

"I have great pleasure in communicating to you the accompanying extracts from letters from the Chief Secretary to government, and beg leave to congratulate you on their contents."

Extract from a Letter from the Chief Secretary, dated 26th Sept. 1818.

"The conduct of Brig. Arnold, in the execution of the former service, in the Bhuttee country, to which alone your despatches now acknowledged refer, has given his Lordship in Council entire satisfaction; and his Lordship doubts not that the further proceedings of that officer, will be equally prudent and successful. The Gov.-Gen. in Council's approbation of Brig. Arnold's conduct, will be conveyed to his Excellency the Commander-in-Chief."

Extract of a Letter from Col. J. Nicol. Adj.-Gen. of the Army.—Presidency of Fort William, the 24th of October, 1818, to Brig. Arnold, commanding 3d Division Field Army.

"Sir,—I am directed by the Com.-in-Chief, to express to you his Excellency's entire concurrence in the sentiments expressed by government, of your conduct, during the late operations in the Bhuttee country, as conveyed in the annexed extract from a letter, to my address, from Mr. Secretary Adam:"—

Extract of a Letter from J. Adam, Esq., Chief Secretary to Government, to L.-Col. Nicol, Adj.-Gen.—Dated the 26th *September,* 1818.

" The Gov.-Gen. in Council considers the conduct of Brig. Arnold to have been marked with much judgment and prudence; and his Excellency the Com.-in-Chief is requested to convey this sentiment to the Brigadier, on the part of his Lordship in Council."

Extract of a Letter from the Chief Secretary, dated 17th *October,* 1818.

" The Gov.-Gen. in Council, has derived great satisfaction from the rapid and successful completion of the service entrusted to Col. Arnold. The whole of that officer's proceedings are considered to deserve much commendation, and you are requested to communicate to him, the approbation of the government."

In 1819-20, this officer commanded the district of Rohilcund; and in 1823, was appointed on the General Staff of India, to command the Saugor division of the army in Central India.

MAJOR-GENERAL JEREMIAH SIMONS.

(Madras Establishment.)

In 1781, this officer entered the Hon. Company's service as a Cadet: he arrived at Madras about the end of March 1782, when he was promoted to the rank of Ensign. The first active service on which he was employed, was in 1783-4, against the Zemindar of Nozeed, in the northern Circars.

In 1792, he served under the late Marquess Cornwallis, at the storming of Tippoo Sultaun's lines before Seringapatam, on the 6th of February in that year, and during the siege. He was also present at the siege and capture of Pondicherry, in 1793; and, on the breaking out of the last Mysore war, he was appointed to the command of Pylny, on the borders of the Mysore country, in the district of Dindigul; and finding the enemy, who held the hill fort of Chuckergery, sending out parties at night to plunder the Company's districts, and otherwise alarming the inhabitants, this officer, on receiving a small reinforcement from Major Adam Lindsey, who commanded a detachment near Daraporam, went against the place, took it, and recovered all the cattle previously plundered, amounting to several thousand heads.

After this service, he was removed to the Hyderabad force, and on his joining the 1st-11 reg. N. I. he was appointed to the command of a grenadier battalion, and detached, under the command of Cols. Bowser and Stevenson, against the rebel Doondia Waugh.

He served the whole of the Mahratta war, commencing in 1803, under Col. Stevenson and the Hon. Col. Wellesley, and was on the night attack with L.-Col. Kenny, near Barramgaum, on the 9th September, 1803; also at the battle of Argaum, on the 29th November following; and at the siege and storming of the hill forts of Asseerghur and Gawilghur. In October 1804, he served with Col. Wallace, who commanded the force after the departure of the Hon. Col. Wellesley, and was, by his orders, sent against the fort of Lassligaum; an attempt to take it by a force under the command of Capt. Brown, who was killed, having failed. He succeeded in capturing this place, and for his conduct obtained both the public and private approbation* of Col. Wallace. He next served at the siege and taking of Chandore and Gaulnah: the latter place was afterwards established as a depôt for grain and military stores for the army, and this officer was selected for the command of the same.

On the 26th November 1817, he was appointed to the command

---

* *Private.*

"My dear Simons,—I congratulate you on your success, and the prompt manner in which you have executed the service that you were entrusted with.

"9*th Oct.* 1804." (Signed) "W. Wallace."

Public.—" *To Major Simons, Commanding Detachment.*

"Sir,—L.-Col. Wallace received this evening your letter, giving an account of your successful attack on the small fort of Lassligaum. He requests that you will accept his thanks for the prompt and effectual manner in which you carried his orders into effect, and that you will express to those under your command his sense of their good conduct on the occasion.

(Signed) "P. Vans Agnew, Dept.-Adj.-Gen."

" *Camp at Chandore, 9th Oct.* 1804."

of the Ganjam district, which had a short time before been the scene of Pindarry excursion; and in 1818, the war being at a close, and after having served the Hon. Company during a period of nearly 38 years, and arrived at the command of a regiment, he, in 1819, returned to Europe.

LIEUTENANT-COLONEL WILLIAM MILES.
(Bombay Establishment.)

THIS officer is the son of an officer who passed his life in His Majesty's service. He was appointed a Cadet in the Hon. Company's service, in February 1799, sailed from England in June 1800, and arrived at Calcutta in January 1801.

After remaining a short time in that city, he embarked for his presidency, Bombay; at which place he arrived in April or May 1801. The battalion to which he was appointed (the 2d batt. 1st reg.) being on service in Egypt, he was ordered to join it; and after a voyage to Mocha and Kosseir, he crossed the Desert in two days to Kine, and thence proceeded down the Nile to Giza, and ultimately to Aboukir, near Alexandria, where his corps was encamped.

On the evacuation of Egypt by the British troops, this officer's corps was ordered to Demanhour, and afterwards to Boulac, a suburb of Grand Cairo; from which place it marched across the Desert to Ainmoosa, or Moses' Wells, near Suez; and embarked thence for Bombay, where it arrived in July 1802.

Soon after Lt. Miles's arrival at Bombay, his battalion was ordered to Guzerat, to form part of a force assembled there under the command of Col. Woodington*, and destined for the expulsion of a

---

* Mention of this officer will be found in Vol. i. pp. 355, 414-16, and other parts of this work. The following General Order was issued on his return to Europe:—
" *General Order.—Bombay Castle, Feb.* 4, 1808.
" The Hon. the Gov. in Council is pleased to permit L.-Col. Woodington to proceed to

large body of Arabs in the service of the Guicawar, who had usurped his authority and held his person in restraint.

For this purpose, in January 1803, the siege of Baroda was formed, and his battalion took a distinguished part in its operations, which terminated with complete success, although not without considerable loss. The Arabs were expelled, and the Guicawar released from his confinement. Guzerat, however, still continuing in a disturbed state, many of the Arabs and mercenary soldiery of that province having joined Canojee, a factious brother of the Guicawar,

---

Europe on furlough, with the option of eventually retiring from the service, conformably to the existing regulations.

" The Gov. in Council will have great satisfaction in communicating to the Hon. the Court of Directors, the high sense entertained by government of the professional deserts of L.-Col. Woodington, as manifested during the long course of his meritorious service in India.

" The earlier instances thus referred to have already attracted the notice of the Hon. the Court of Directors, who were pleased, in the 46th paragraph of their general letter, dated the 8th of April 1789, to direct that some staff situation should be conferred on that officer, in consideration of the severe wound he had sustained in their employ. Since his last return to India, L.-Col. Woodington has further established his claims to the approbation of his employers, by a series of distinguished and important services, equally promotive of the welfare of his country, and conducive to the increase of his own military reputation. The siege of Baroda, in 1803, afforded the most satisfactory proof of the judgment, exertion, and professional talents of the L.-Col.; which, in the same year, were again highly distinguished in the reduction of the valuable fortress of Broach, an event that, viewed in reference to the smallness of the detachment employed upon the occasion, sufficiently bespoke the abilities that directed, and the gallantry that achieved the conquest; whilst the subsequent and rapid reduction of the strong hill fort of Pawanghur, and of Champneer, closed this officer's active career in the last war on this side of India.

" The record of these memorable occurrences stands severally marked by the most respectable testimonies of approbation, bestowed on the conduct of L.-Col. Woodington, by the distinguished authorities, who, at the periods in question, exercised a control over the operations of the field army of this presidency, the present government of which coincide entirely in the opinions expressed by M.-Gens. Jones and Bellassis, that the Bombay establishment will sustain a loss in the departure and eventual retirement of this excellent officer, whose exemplary and conciliatory conduct, in command of the subsidiary force in Guzerat, during periods when such attentions were absolutely necessary, forms another very laudable part of the Colonel's conduct, such as the Gov. in Council will not omit to make due and creditable report of to the Hon. the Court of Directors, inclusive of the several other occurrences above adverted to."

and a pretender to his *gudi*, or throne, and who had assembled a considerable force to attain his object, Lieut. M.'s battalion, with some others, (among which were the 75th and 86th regiments) under the command of Major Holmes*, were ordered to march and attack him.

This service, which required long marches, and unceasing exertion, was performed in the hottest season of the year; and after several engagements, of which that at Sewree, or Seora, on the eastern bank of the river Mihie, was the most important (a great loss having been sustained by the British troops, particularly the 75th reg. from the bravery and skill of the Arabs, although the former were completely victorious), Canojee's force was broken and retired from Guzerat.

In August 1803, the war with Scindia commenced, and the troops in Guzerat were placed under the command of Sir A. Wellesley. After the storm and capture of Broach, by Col. Woodington, the 2d batt. 1st reg. joined that officer, and assisted in the siege of the almost impregnable hill fortress of Pawanghur.

On the capture of this fort, Lieut. M. was left, with a small detachment, to garrison the city of Champneer, which is situated at the foot of Pawanghur, and remained there a few months, when he was attacked by the fever, prevalent in that peculiarly unhealthy part of the country, and was obliged to proceed to Baroda for medical aid, and where he arrived at the point of death. On his recovery, he rejoined his corps, then forming part of the army, which, at the commencement of the war with Holkar, in 1804, advanced to Oogein, under the command of Col. Murray †.

He accompanied this army from Oogein to Kotah, and thence towards Bundlecund. His battalion being under the command of Col. Holmes, was, at that period, detached to the frontier of Guzerat, to convoy treasure and stores thence to the army. It may be proper to remark here, that this was a very difficult and desperate

* The late M.-Gen. Sir George Holmes, K. C. B. Services, vol. i. p. 408-21.

† Now Lt.-Gen. Sir John Murray, Bart. Services, Royal Military Calendar, vol. ii. p. 227-9, 3d edit.

service, the intervening country being filled with the troops and partizans of Holkar, and the greater part under his immediate authority.

The battalion, on its march, passed the Mokundra defile without molestation, but from that pass it was incessantly followed and harassed by Holkar's cavalry to the river Mihie.

On the first day they made their appearance, it was Lieut. M.'s good fortune to be in command of the rear-guard, which consisted of 100 men. The battalion under Col. Holmes and Col. Murray, had marched on to the distance of 4 or 5 miles, leaving the intermediate space covered with the baggage and stores of the corps; a subaltern (Lieut. Robertson) and 12 men, had, however, been appointed for its regulation on the march, and part of these, with their officer, afterwards joined the rear-guard. The country over which the rear-guard had to pass, was open, but uneven, the road leading alternately through low ground, and over small rocky eminences.

The enemy, under Gungaram Kothari, one of Holkar's most enterprising officers, consisted of upwards of 1000 excellent horse; these had previously defeated a body of 250 auxiliary cavalry, attached to the battalion under Lieut. Bowen, who was wounded on the occasion.

Holkar's chief being aware, after the defeat of the auxiliaries, that the battalion could afford the rear-guard no relief, immediately surrounded it, advancing both on its rear and in front; Lieutenant M. was therefore obliged to halt, to form his men 4 deep, and make the 3d and 4th ranks face outwards, having placed a few of the beaten auxiliary horse, who had sought refuge with him, on his flanks.

Holkar's horse advanced with great steadiness; some individuals charging up to the bayonets of the men, who reserved their fire until the mass arrived within about pistol shot, when they were saluted with a smart independent fire, which brought down several of their foremost men, (among whom was one of their standard bearers) and the horses of these men getting loose, and causing much confusion, they pulled up. The shot, however, still falling thick among them, they at last broke and fled, having sustained a considerable loss in killed and wounded, the infantry pursuing them.

A short time after this, a party detached from the battalion to assist the rear-guard, joined it, and they proceeded together to Mundeseir, (where the battalion had encamped) without seeing any more of Holkar's horse.

Notwithstanding the bad fortune which had attended the first essay of Holkar's troops against the battalion, they for many days never quitted it, while on the march, but, with the exception of cutting up a few stragglers, never made the least impression.

A day or two after, from the hostile appearance of the people and garrison of a small fort and town belonging to Holkar, near the fort of Jowra, Col. Holmes was obliged to attack them, and possession was obtained of both places with a very trifling loss. On the return of this battalion and the 2d-9th, with the treasure and stores towards Hindostan, to rejoin the army, then under M.-Gen. Jones, they were met near the river Mihie, by Kassy Rao Holkar (the brother of Jesswunt Rao), with a force estimated at 8000 horse and foot; the 2d batt. 1st reg. formed the rear-guard on this occasion, and had the honour to stand the brunt of the action. Kassy Rao's troops were received by them with such spirit, that they soon retired in great confusion, and with considerable loss. The effect of this action was such, that the battalions and convoy remained unmolested from that time until their arrival at Bhurtpoor, where they joined the army under Gen. Lord Lake.

At the peace with Holkar in 1805-6, Lieut. Miles returned with his corps to Guzerat, and was cantoned at Kaira. From thence he was detached, with a small body of cavalry and infantry, to the banks of the Mihie, to repress the depredations of a Desye of Neriad, who had rebelled and plundered part of that district.

In this service, having fallen in with a party of the rebels, he defeated them with the loss of some men and horses, and succeeded in making them abandon entirely that part of the country.

During the whole of this service, which lasted without remission six years, and throughout which Lieut. Miles was continually in the field, he never ceased to prosecute the study of the native languages, and he was in consequence, in 1807, appointed interpreter to his battalion. In the years 1808-9-10 and 11, the corps was stationed at Baroda, Poona, and Bombay.

In 1812, Lieut. Miles was placed in command of the escort attached to the Assistant to the Resident at Baroda, and employed in that division of Guzerat, called the Mahiekaunta. In the course of this service, he was present at an attack made by the Guicawar troops on Bhoyen, a strong Koolie village near Ahmedabad; and in 1814, on his promotion to a company, he was appointed to command the British guards in the fort and Poora of Baroda, under the Resident, Capt. J. R. Carnac *.

In Sept. 1817, immediately preceding the war with the Peishwa, he was deputed, in a political capacity, to settle the disputes which had occurred at Pahlunpoor, a Mahomedan state in the north-western part of Guzerat. The causes of these disputes were briefly, that in 1813, Shumsheer Khan, chief of Deesa, had been constituted guardian to his nephew or kinsman Futteh Khan, the chief recognized by government, but then a child.

In 1816, it was discovered that Shumsheer Khan had usurped the chief authority, that he had in a manner expelled his nephew from his own possessions, and it was even said threatened his life: he had, moreover, for some years delayed to pay his tribute to the Guicawar. Under these circumstances, Capt. Miles was deputed to expel Shumsheer Khan from Pahlunpoor, and restore the authority usurped by him to Futteh Khan.

It happened peculiarly unfortunate, that previous to his arrival at Seidpoor, either from some misunderstanding of the object of government, or the intrigues of Shumsheer Khan, Futteh Khan, notwithstanding, by his continual complaints and representations, he had been the sole cause of the interposition of government in his

* Services, vol. ii. p. 477-81.

favour, with the inconsistency and perfidy of the native character, made up his quarrel with Shumsheer Khan, and joined him in a determination to resist the aid he had for several years abjectly solicited.

The force destined to proceed to Pahlunpoor, and which joined Capt. Miles at Seidpoor, consisted of 100 men of the 8th regt. under Lieut. Holland, and in all about 900 Guicawar horse and foot, with 2 small guns, or rather jinjals, 2-pounders.

After negotiating for some time with little or no effect, being convinced nothing would be determined while he remained at a distance, on the 10th Oct. 1817, Capt. Miles marched his small force from their encampment near Seidpoor to Pahlunpoor.

On the arrival of the Guicawar troops at Pahlunpoor, they found Shumsheer Khan and Futteh Khan with a body of from 2 to 3,000 horse and foot, forming a semicircle round the town to the South and S. E. and about one mile distant from it; these commenced their fire as soon as the Benee or Guicawar advanced guard came within shot of them.

It may be proper here to observe, that Pahlunpoor is a large walled town with a deep ditch, and well provided with cannon, and that the soldiery of this part of the country are esteemed the bravest in Guzerat; that the ground in front of this town on the South and S. E. sides is much broken, deep excavations having been made in former times to supply bricks for the building of the town and fort; that some of these hollows contain gardens, the enclosures of which form excellent cover for infantry, and which indeed were, on this occasion, filled with them. The cavalry, about 800, mostly covered with chain armour, paraded as usual about the place, and they had with them several small field guns, which were adroitly managed, and fired with great precision.

Capt. Miles being informed that these hollows were occupied as above mentioned, forbore to charge them immediately, as the cross fire of the concealed infantry must have occasioned him considerable embarrassment, and the action continued with much loss to the

Guicawar troops, who were entirely exposed, while their enemies had every shelter and advantage.

During this time, however, knowledge of the ground having been obtained, and a favourable point for an attack observed at the left of their line, Capt. Miles assembled there a body of cavalry, one gun, (the other having broken down) and the 100 regular infantry, and observing their flank become unsteady at this movement, immediately charged them.

The charge was attended with the happiest effect; their cavalry were routed and dispersed, and their infantry retiring, were driven into the ditch of the fort with great loss. Many were also taken prisoners, but after being plundered by the Guicawar troops, were allowed to escape.

An outwork at the south gate, said to have contained 300 men. however, still held out; it was therefore assaulted by the infantry and taken with the gate adjoining, and in consequence, the whole of the town immediately fell into the hands of the assailants.

The trophies of this day's work were not inconsiderable. They consisted of a pair of nagaras or kettle-drums, 2 cavalry standards, 6 infantry do., a great number of horses, (the capture of the majority of which were, however, atthat time concealed by the Guicawar officers and people, from the fear that they would be obliged to give them up), 2 elephants, the town and property in it, and 40 or 50 pieces of artillery, mounted and dismounted.

Of all the advantages attained, the greatest, however, was, that this success freed the force (about 2500 regular troops), under Col. Elrington[*], (then within a few days march of Pahlunpoor,) from all occupation in this quarter, and left the government at liberty to employ it in services of greater importance, the war with Holkar and the Peishwa.

The loss of the Guicawar troops on this occasion, was 107 killed and wounded, and about 80 horses; that of the enemy was never

---

[*] Services, Royal Military Calendar, vol. iv. p. 462, 3d edit.

precisely ascertained, but it is supposed to have been very considerable, as a number of their wounded died in Pahlunpoor after the place was taken.

For this service Capt. Miles was complimented in District Orders*, by Sir E. Nepean, Gov. of Bombay, and appointed to the political superintendence of the whole of the north-western frontier of Guzerat; he also received the thanks and acknowledgments of the Guicawar government.

* *District Orders.*—"*Camp, Oonjah, 31st Oct.* 1817.

"Lt.-Col. Elrington has the highest satisfaction in announcing to the detachment the fall of Pahlunpoor, which was taken by storm on the 10th inst., after a smart action, by the Guicawar force and a detachment of the 2nd batt. 8 regt., whose behaviour on the present occasion, merits the highest praise.

"The prompt and gallant conduct of Capt. Miles of the 2nd batt. 1st. regt., Lieut. Holland, 2nd batt. 8th regt., and Yarrow, Jemedar, commanding his Highness the Guicawar's force, reflects the greatest honour upon the officers and the troops under their command.

(Signed)   "E. STANNUS, D. A. G."

"*Bombay, 28th October,* 1817.

"SIR,—I have the honour to enclose a copy of a letter from the Chief Secretary to Government to the Resident at Baroda, regarding the capture of Pahlunpoor, which his Ex. the Com.-in-Chief desires you will communicate to the parties concerned; and to express at the same time, his Excellency's entire approbation of the conduct of Capt. Miles, Lieut. Holland, and all the troops employed in the attack on Pahlunpoor, and throughout the operations against Shumsheer Khan.

(Signed)   "D. LEIGHTON, Adj.-Gen. of the Army.

"To Col. J. W. Morris, Commanding the Field Force, Baroda."

Extract of a Letter from the Chief Secretary.—Dated 22d *August,* 1817.

"1st, I am directed by the right hon. the Gov. in Council, to acknowledge the receipt of your letter, dated the 14th instant, with its enclosures, from Capt. Miles, announcing the capture of Pahlunpoor, by the detachment of the Hon. Company's and Guicawar's troops, under his orders; and detailing the circumstances which led to that event, and his subsequent proceedings.

"2d, the Gov. in Council concurs in the sentiments of approbation expressed by Col. Elrington, in the general order which accompanied your despatches, of the conduct of Capt. Miles, Lieut. Holland, of Yarrow, Jemedar, and of the whole of the detachment; and notices particularly, the judgment and decision which have marked the character of Capt. Miles, throughout the whole of his proceedings; of which you will be pleased to acquaint that officer, apprizing him that the Gov. in Council has been pleased to confide in him the political charge of the affairs of Pahlunpoor, until further orders.

"You will be pleased, also, to communicate these sentiments of approbation to the Officer Commanding the Field Force, that they may be announced to Lieut. Holland, and the detachment which he commanded, and to the Guicawar government, in order that they may be made known to Yarrow, Jemedar, and the Guicawar troops under his command."

Capt. Miles afterwards accompanied the force from Baroda under Col. Elrington, which arrived a few days after, to Hauttédra and Veerumpoor, towns situated to the north-east among the hills, in a very strong country, and to which Shumsheer Khan and Futteh Khan had retired; these were taken with a very trifling loss.

In the course of these operations, Futteh Khan, having of his own accord, returned to his allegiance to government, in consideration of his youth and inexperience, they were pleased to overlook his misconduct, and re-seat him on the *gudi* of his ancestors. Shumsheer Khan having also surrendered, was sent to Baroda.

From this period to 1819 Capt. Miles remained at Pahlunpoor, for the regulation of the affairs of that state, and, indeed, those of the whole of the frontier.

In 1819, the ravages of a tribe of wild Bullooches, called Surrais and Khosas, who had for many years infested and plundered the province of Marwar, and the north-western districts of Guzerat, attracted the attention of government, and measures were suggested for their suppression and expulsion from those parts.

Previous to describing the operations against this tribe, it may not be irrelevant to mention, that they had been expelled from Sindh, about 40 years before, for their depredations and irregularities, and had occupied the Desert dividing Sindh from Marwar, and the country in the vicinity of the Run' and river Looni, most of which had become tributary to them. In 1819 and 1820, besides ravaging the country to a great extent, they had attacked, and plundered the town of Radhanpoor, and the fort and district of Dhunnera, depending on Pahlunpoor. Infinitely superior to the Pindarries in personal appearance and courage, they were, like them, famous for the extraordinary length of the marches they made to obtain their booty, and the impenetrable secrecy attending their movements; these advantages secured them success in all their expeditions, and as they had never sustained any material check or loss from the troops of native chiefs employed against them, it at last became a confirmed opinion, that no force in the country, except that of the Honourable Company, could repress their excesses.

In 1819, therefore, the British government determined to employ a force in the suppression of these freebooters, and Capt. Miles was appointed to conduct the political details connected with its operations.

The difficulties opposing themselves to the success of this expedition, were numerous and great. The Desert on which the Khosas in general resided, was well enough qualified for their mode of life. Originally, inhabitants of the deserts of Bulloochéstan or Mukran, and encamped in small parties with their herds, at a considerable distance from each other, the wells all known to them, or in their possession, they appear to have been completely at home. For the rest, the Desert is, in most parts, a loose sand; and, except in the rainy months, bare of forage, and almost entirely destitute of water; the few wells on it being at great distances from each other, and from 200 to 300 feet deep.

It is easy to understand, therefore, from this description, that the existence, much less the movement, of a considerable body of troops and their followers, in such a barren waste, was impossible, without innumerable precautions. To add to these difficulties, it happened that the whole of the habitable country on the border of the Desert was entirely desolated, by the dreadful famine which occurred in these parts in 1812-13.

Independent of these formidable obstacles to the success of this service, others presented themselves.

1. From the difficulty of assembling the troops, the expedition, which should have proceeded immediately after the rains had ceased, did not reach Radhanpoor, from which place the operations commenced, until the beginning of the month of February 1820.

2. Although it was well known these marauders were encouraged and even supported by the government of Sindh, still, all measures likely to give umbrage to that state, were, from political motives, prohibited, and notwithstanding the whole of the dependents of

Sindh on this frontier were notoriously identified and associated with the Khosas in all their excesses, yet it was the opinion of government that the objects of the expedition had better remain unattained, than that they should be molested, or any war or dispute arise in consequence.

Notwithstanding these difficulties, the force moved on and arrived at Sooi Gaum, a village on the eastern bank of the Run, on the 12th February, and a party of about 200 horse, under Mr. Richards, an officer in the Guicawar service, who was detached across the country from Deesa to Thuraud, was the first engaged; this party defeated a body of about 300 of these freebooters, with considerable loss.

The force, although the followers were exposed to many privations for want of grain, proceeded by the eastern bank of the Run, to Bhoyatra, a village situated at the disemboguement of the river Looni into that extraordinary Salt Lake; and then wheeling to the left, moved on by rapid marches to Parkur, a kind of island in the midst of the Run and Desert, and the head-quarters of the Khosas, although dependent on Sindh.

On entering this island, which is, comparatively, fertile and populous, (containing 50 or 60 towns and villages) it was discovered that the whole of the inhabitants had made common cause with the Khosas, and had abandoned their villages and retired to Nuggur, the chief town of this district. This is situated under a high range of mountains, called Kalinjur, which extend across the whole of the island.

In this strong position, it was reported, they had determined to make a stand. The orders of government, however, being precise regarding interference with the subjects of the Sindh state, it was not intended to molest the town, unless it could be clearly established that the chiefs had actually harboured these plunderers; and as the Rana of Parkur had sent vakeels to camp, and, however guilty, denied that he had either harboured or participated in the excesses of the Khosas, there remained no pretence for such a measure.

The force under Col. Barclay*, therefore, marched from Bhodesur to Nuggur, without any suspicion being entertained that they would meet opposition there; they had, however, no sooner approached the town, than they were fired on, and several men killed and wounded; the Colonel was therefore obliged to form them for the attack, which was soon after commenced with great spirit.

The troops having first occupied the town, driving out their opponents, gallantly ascended the mountain in two columns, under a heavy and incessant fire, crowning all its heights, and penetrating into its inmost recesses and defiles; and notwithstanding the difficulties of the ascent, and the brave resistance made, they soon dislodged the Khosas, Bheels, and Rajpoots opposed to them, and very few escaped. The town was also plundered during the attack.

Although the action continued the greatest part of the day, and under the greatest disadvantages, the loss of the British troops was not severe; that of the Khosas and predatory tribes of Parkur, was, however, very great.

This success had a great effect in the surrounding country, as it was generally supposed the town of Nuggur, and the heights of Kalinjur, if well defended, were impregnable.

* The late L.-Col. Robert Barclay, of the Bombay establishment, entered the Hon. Company's service as an Ensign in 1791; was promoted to Lieut. in Dec. 1795; to Capt. in Dec. 1799; to Major in Aug. 1809; and to L.-Col. (by brevet) on the 4th June 1814; and regimentally, in Dec. following. He served for upwards of thirty years, and was employed in almost every war which took place during that period, having been but one year absent from duty, occasioned by sickness, and only one year in garrison. The following notice of this gallant officer's decease, was issued by the Governor of Bombay:—

"*Bombay Castle, 7th June,* 1822.

"Information having been received of the death of L.-Col. Barclay, of the 1st regt. of cavalry, on board the ship Castlereagh, on the 18th of April, the Hon. the Gov. in Council in announcing this lamented casualty, considers it due to the memory of an old and meritorious officer, to record the sense he entertains of his merits, and of the loss which the service has in consequence sustained, after an uninterrupted career in it of thirty years; during which L.-Col. Barclay was ever distinguished for zeal, activity, and professional gallantry, until reluctantly compelled to relinquish the command of the troops in Kattywar, by severe ill health, which terminated in death, and has deprived the public of an officer warmly attached to his profession, and anxiously disposed to uphold the reputation of the corps he commanded, and of the army to which he belonged."

The force had now been for some time separated from all supplies, and the difficulty of provisioning the followers became so great, that Col. Barclay determined (as none were procurable, except a limited one, by the plunder of the town) to recross the Run*; and two days after, he accordingly marched towards Berana, a town on the western edge of the Run opposite to Sooi Gaum.

Another motive for returning, was, that in the event of falling in with any of the Sindh troops, reported to be about to advance, hostilities in all probability would have commenced, and this would have involved the British government in negotiation, and perhaps a contest, which they appeared most anxious to avoid.

The force under Col. Barclay, after crossing the Run, marched north, along the eastern bank of the river Looni, into the Nyere, or country of the Chowhans (a very fertile and populous district, before

---

* The width of the Run, from Berana to Sooi Gaum, is upwards of 30 miles; 13 to 14 coss, or 20 miles, from Berana; and nearly in the centre of the Run is an island, called Nurra Bate: this produces forage, and has some pools of brackish water, scarcely drinkable, in it.

As this was, perhaps, the first attempt ever made to cross so wide a branch of the Run, with so large a force, it may not be irrelevant to attempt a brief description of this salt desert.

The Run, by tradition, was formerly an arm of the sea. It is now a plain of immense extent; but in many parts continually overflowed with water, and in those parts entirely impassable, being a bog, or swamp, ingulfing every thing entering it.

The outlines of the Run are as follows: the circumference, at a moderate estimation, is upwards of 450 miles; it commences from the sea, at the junction of the province of Cutch and Kattywar, near Mallia, and extends west to Bujjana, about 70 miles. It then takes a direction north by Radhanpoor and Vauw to Bhoyatra in Marwar, near 130 miles. From Bhoyatra it stretches S.W. to Parkur, about 50 miles, and thence west, about 200 miles more, to the sea, where it forms a junction with the southern branches of the Indus, near Shah Bunder. Its breadth varies throughout this space, from 10 or 12 miles to 70 or 80. It entirely surrounds the province of Cutch on three sides, and with the sea westward, makes it a perfect island.

The surface of the Run, not under water, is covered with a thick crust of salt, and except a few islands furnishing brackish water, and a little forage, it is destitute of every kind of vegetation.

It is remarkable, that after the sun has risen, the glare, called by the Persians and Arabs *surab*, makes it assume the appearance of the sea, or an extensive lake.

The only animals seen in this vast and dreary space, are droves of wild asses, and aquatick birds, with a few antelopes.

its occupation and desolation by the Khosas) to Ihab and Gurra, in Marwar, to free that part of the country from the marauders.

During these operations, information having been received, that a body of this tribe still remained at a village, called Guddra, on the border of Parkur, an expedition was undertaken against them, from Bhoyatra; the distance being 30 coss, about 45 miles.

Accordingly, about 250 Guicawar horse, commanded by a Jemedar, under Capt. Miles, moved off from Bhoyatra on the evening of the 24th March, 1820, and arrived at Guddra, about day-break the next morning. Not finding any Khosas there, and hearing they were at Holingra, about 7 coss distant, it was decided to follow them; and notwithstanding the troops were a good deal fatigued, having marched the whole of the night, they pushed on.

About 5 coss from Guddra, it became necessary to cross a branch of the Run, full of water, 2 coss in breadth, and nearly 3 feet deep; this completed the exhaustion of the men and horses, and it was with great difficulty they got over; however, on their reaching the opposite side, they were recompensed by the complete surprisal of the Khosas, who appear to have had no intimation of their approach, and a number of them were taken with their cattle, without opposition. On the troops, however, advancing to another village, named Dedeevera, a party of them, aided by the inhabitants, made a vigorous resistance, and two Jemedars of the Guicawar horse were killed, and the chief Jemedar dismounted; at this time also, a considerable body of Khosas and Bheels, well armed, and keeping up a continual and well-directed fire, appeared in the plain, at a short distance, and seemed desirous to attain the village, which being situated on a rocky eminence, and extremely well qualified for defence, if occupied by them, would in all probability have exposed the troops to great loss, and rendered all further attempt to subdue them abortive.

Capt. Miles therefore, under these circumstances, determined, if possible, to cut them off from the village; but as the Guicawar horse without their Jemedar (who remained in the rear) were very bashful, it was with the greatest difficulty he prevailed upon about 50 of them to try the effect of a charge on these new assailants.

Having assembled his small party, he formed them into two divisions, and directed one to make a small detour to the right, to distract the attention of the Khosas, while he proceeded himself with the other to attack them in front; the horse led in this manner, soon closed with the Khosas, and they were entirely cut up, with the exception of a few who laid down their arms, and cried out for mercy.

In this affair 23 of the enemy were taken, and about 60, among whom were 7 chiefs of the freebooters of Parkur, who had joined the Khosas in their excesses, were killed. The loss of the Guicawar troops was 8 men killed and wounded, and 16 horses.

The water at Holingra being brackish, and insufficient in quantity for the troops, they were obliged to retrace their steps, or in other words, to re-wade through the water of the Run, and encamp at Pethapoor, a village above 3 coss distant.

It was afterwards discovered that the Guicawar Jemedar had allowed two Khosa chiefs, with their women, to escape, and that, during the whole of the action, his conduct had been very equivocal and discreditable.

The troops sent to Ihab having been recalled, by the order of government, to make a further incursion into the Desert in pursuit of the Khosas, they again advanced to Veera Vauw, and from this place, as reports were received that the Khosas had again assembled in Parkur, a joint expedition was arranged by Capt. Miles, to scour the whole of that district, and again clear it from these pests.

On the 2d of April the troops marched; Col. Barclay, with his regulars, round the western side of the Kalinjur mountains, whilst the Guicawar troops, under Capt. Miles, proceeded round the eastern extremity of that range.

On the 3d, in the evening, a letter was received from Col. Barclay, stating, that on his march on the 2d, he had received information that a considerable body of Khosas were encamped in the

Desert, (at a place called Bhakee, 12 coss from his encampment at Bhodesur) and that he had marched in the evening, and surprised them, killing about 100, including several of their chiefs. Col. Barclay was wounded in this affair.

No Khosas having been discovered on the eastern side of Parkur, the troops returned to Veera Vauw, and were afterwards withdrawn, by the orders of government, to Bhoyatra, on the east side of the Run; at which place, soon after, vakeels arrived from Sindh, and a long negotiation with Capt. Miles ensued, the terms of the conclusion of which were highly approved by government.

The barbarous government of Sindh, however, notwithstanding the negociations of its vakeels, irritated at the defeat of their countrymen, the Khosas, whose depredations they had so many years encouraged and supported, at this very time directed a party of their troops to make an attack on Cutch.

A British force was therefore assembled in Cutch to invade Sindh.

While this was in operation, Capt. Miles had made arrangements with the whole of the Rajpoot and Mahomedan states on the east bank of the Run, (viz. Radhanpore, Thuraud, Vauw, Morewara, Deodur, Chowraur, Warye, Terewara, Sooi Gaum, and a tract of country extending from the southern extremity of the Radhanpore territory to the river Looni, upwards of 100 miles in length, and from 60 to 70 in breadth, and nearly the whole of which was formerly occupied by the Khosas,) providing for their future independence and security, and for the payment of an annual tribute to the British government to defray the expenses of the protection which government has now secured to them, by a strong chain of posts on that frontier*.

---

* It is satisfactory to add, that these measures have been completely successful, the country from a desert having become covered with re-peopled towns and villages, and promising, at no very remote period, to constitute a valuable possession to the British government, and do honour to those who suggested and carried into effect its recovery and improvement.

It may be further remarked, 1st. That this part of the country, which is the chief and almost only practicable road for the conveyance of merchandize between Guzerat and Hin-

These arrangements having been completed, and sanctioned by the actual inspection and confirmation of the Hon. the Governor of Bombay, who visited these districts in 1820-21, in the commencement of the latter year, Capt. Miles was ordered to take temporary charge of the political agency, in the Mihie Kaunta division of Guzerat, and measures for the reduction or suppression of a band of near 1000 mercenary Arabs, Mukranies, and Sindhies, who, with the refractory Rajpoot chief of the town of Titooee, had laid the whole of that part of the country under contribution: for this purpose he was ordered to Morasa, a town near Edur, where a small body of infantry and cavalry subsequently joined him.

In these operations, by a display of his small force and conciliatory measures, he, after some negociation, induced them and their chief to surrender, and on their being paid a small sum claimed by them from the chief as their arrears, they dispersed, and returned to their homes; the chief also, by a written engagement, agreed to make good all the damage he had done.

In the course of this service, the force under Capt. Miles's political charge also attacked and took some of the most considerable refractory villages in that wild and hitherto insubordinate part of the country, the Mihie Kaunta.

In June 1821, he was relieved by the officer originally appointed to this charge, and returned to Pahlunpoor.

For these services, Capt. Miles received many very honourable testimonials of the approbation of government, and the officers and individuals with and under whom he served.

It may be remarked in conclusion, that L.-Col. Miles has served

dostan West, and which, from the depredations of the Khosas, had been not only abandoned by its inhabitants but totally deserted by commerce, has now attained a degree of prosperity not known for the last century; innumerable droves of camels and bullocks, laden with the productions of Europe and Asia, incessantly passing and re-passing by this route. 2d. That the Khosas, whose name was once so terrible in this part of the country, have been so completely dispersed and annihilated as a body, that they are no longer heard of, except in the recital of their former exploits.

nearly 25 years in India without a furlough, or a day's leave of absence from his duty, except in cases of ill health, and that even then, he has never left his station.

MAJOR SAMUEL R. STROVER.
(Bombay Establishment.)

IN 1800, this officer was appointed a gentleman Cadet for the artillery, and joined the academy for extra cadets, on Shooter's Hill: he filled a vacancy at the Royal Military Academy, at Woolwich, at the latter end of the same year, passed all examinations, and embarked for India in June 1802: he arrived at Bombay 25th November 1802, and was appointed Acting Adjutant of the Bombay artillery, and in 1803, Adjutant of that corps.

In 1807, he volunteered and commanded a detachment of artillery upon an expedition to the gulf of Persia; in 1809, in consequence of severe illness, he was ordered by the faculty to England, for change of climate: he returned to Bombay in 1812, and was immediately appointed to command the artillery, at Surat.

In 1813, he was ordered to the Deccan; and in May of that year, proceeded to Bombay, upon being appointed Deputy Commissary of ordnance. In 1814, he marched with the army in the field under the command of Maj.-Gen. Sir George Holmes, K. C. B.* In 1816, he was appointed to the charge of the Ordnance Department, Poona division of the army, then in the field under Maj.-Gen. Sir Lionel Smith, K. C. B.† In the same year he was appointed to the charge of the general arsenal at Bombay, which he held nearly a whole year.

In 1818, he volunteered to serve with the force against the

* Services, vol. i. p. 408-21.   † Services, Rl. Mil. Cal. vol. iv. p. 45, 3d edit.

Peishwa, commanded by Colonel Prother, C. B.,* and conveyed the battering train, ammunition, and stores, from Bombay to the top of the ghauts: he served in the batteries at the reduction of several hill forts, and was afterwards appointed to take charge of the general arsenal at Bombay.

In 1819, he went with the force in the field in Cutch, commanded by Maj.-Gen. Sir William Keir Grant, K. C. B.†; and was at the taking of Bhooj; and upon the service being accomplished, took charge of the ordnance and stores, and conveyed them to Bombay: soon after which he proceeded to Baroda, in Guzerat, being appointed to the charge of the Ordnance Department, with the Guicawar subsidiary force; and twice commanded the troops at the station of Baroda. Upon his promotion to a Majority, 11th September 1820, he was ordered to join the head-quarters of his regiment at Bombay, to command the 2d battalion of artillery; and at this period he also commanded the artillery cantonments at Bombay.

In 1824, he volunteered to command the artillery ordered from Bombay to join the force against the Burmese, under Brig-Gen. Sir Archibald Campbell, K. C. B.‡

In February 1825, he was ordered to Guzerat, to command the artillery in that province, and also the troops composing the garrison of Surat.

LIEUTENANT-COLONEL WILLIAM FORREST.

(Bengal Establishment.)

In 1798, this officer was appointed a Cadet of infantry on the Bengal establishment: he proceeded to India in the following year, and was permanently posted to the 1st batt. 2d regiment, which

---

* Services, vol. i. p. 304-7.   † Services, Rl. Mil. Cal. vol. iii. p. 267-9, 3d edit.
‡ Ibid. vol. iv. p. 236-8.

formed part of the force employed against the forts of Sasnee, Bejighur, Catchoura, and Tatteah.

During the operations against the above-mentioned forts, this officer was appointed Assistant Field Engineer, and on their reduction, he rejoined his battalion, with which he again took the field, in 1803, when he was selected by Gen. the late Lord Lake, and appointed by his Lordship to the corps of pioneers, with which he served the campaigns of 1803 and 1804, against the Mahratta states.

He was present at the taking of the fort of Allyghur, at the battle of Delhi, at the fall of the fort of Agra, at the battle of Laswarree, at the taking of the forts of Gwalior and Rampoora, and finally, at the taking of Deeg, on the storming of which fortress he lost an arm, and received upwards of 22 severe wounds.

Lieut.-Colonel Forrest's dates of commissions, are as follow :— Ensign, 26th September 1799; Lieutenant, 28th October 1799; Captain, 30th September 1808; Major, 11th July 1823; and Lieutenant-Colonel, 7th Nov. 1824.

The following are honourable testimonials of this officer's services:

Extract of a Despatch from the Com.-in-Chief to the Gov.-Gen. the Marquess Wellesley.

" MY LORD,—My despatch of the 24th and 25th inst., will have informed your Lordship of the complete success of our operations against the town and fort of Deeg, &c. &c.

" The corps of pioneers, under the orders of Capt. Swinton *, command my warmest praise for the cheerfulness with which they performed their laborious duties, and particularly for the alacrity they displayed on the night of the 22d instant.

" Too much praise cannot be bestowed on Capt. Swinton, who on this and every former occasion, has been most zealous and active. I am sorry to add that this excellent officer is severely wounded, as is Lieut. Forrest of the same corps, whose conduct was equally meritorious."

" *Camp at Deeg, Dec. 26, 1804.*"   (Signed)   " G. LAKE.

* Services in this volume.

Extract of a Letter from the Adj.-Gen. to Government, July 4, 1805.

" Lieut. Forrest, exclusively of the loss of an arm, received 22 other wounds at the assault of Deeg, which have rendered him unfit for the duties of the line."

Extract.—Military Letter from Bengal, dated Dec. 24, 1813.

" Par. 62. We beg leave to represent to your Hon. Court, that Capt. Forrest has not been less distinguished by active gallantry in the discharge of his professional duties, while serving with his corps against the enemy, than his services have since proved beneficial to the public, from his good management and attention to economy in the responsible situation in which he was placed by government, at the recommendation of the late Lord Lake, as a reward for sufferings almost unexampled in the annals of military history."

LIEUTENANT-COLONEL ALEXANDER CUMMING.

(Bengal Establishment.)

This officer arrived in Bengal the 15th of Feb. 1797: he was appointed to a Cornetcy of cavalry, and joined the 3d reg., commanded by Col. Black. He marched to Caunpoor in Nov. 1798, and proceeded to Anoopsheher with the army under Sir James Craig.

In 1799, he served under the late L.-Gen. Sir Ewen Baillie, in Oude, and in the following year was removed to the 6th light cavalry, at Ghazeepore. In 1802, he commanded a troop in the Governor-General's escort; and at the latter end of that year, was present at the capture of the forts of Sasnee, Bejighur, and Catchoura. At the latter place his horse was shot under him, whilst attending Major Robert Nairne, on a reconnoitring party; and on the night of the 12th of March, he commanded the picquet that charged the enemy on their evacuating the fort. This body of the enemy amounted to 600, and Major Nairne was unfortunately killed.

In August 1803, the 6th cavalry joined the army under Lord

Lake, at Delhi, on the Jumna, and Lieut. Cumming was present at the surrender of Agra, and battle of Laswarree; and in 1804, returned to Europe, in a bad state of health, having been promoted to Capt.

In Sept. 1806, Capt. Cumming again landed at Calcutta, and joined the 7th light cavalry as senior Captain: he served under M.-Gen. Gregory* and Col. O'Donnell† in Oude, in 1807-8, and was wounded before Petre Serai. In 1811, Capt. C. commanded two squadrons of cavalry in the Nepaul country, and was present at the capture of Kalunga, where M.-Gen. Gillespie was killed. He was promoted to Major in 1812, and commanded a brigade of cavalry at the taking of Hattrass, on which occasion he received the thanks of Sir Dyson Marshall. On the breaking out of the late war, in 1817, Major Cumming, with his regiment, joined the grand army under the immediate command of the Marquess of Hastings, and was shortly after detached in command of the 7th light cavalry, five companies of light infantry, and the whole of the dromedary corps, for the protection of the district of Bundlecund, against Pindarry ‡ incursion.

* Services, vol. ii. p. 441-7.   † Services, vol. i. p. 51-5.

‡ In a note to vol. i., p. 302-3, the character of the Pindarries is given, and we are enabled, from Sir John Malcolm's Memoir of Central India, briefly to sketch the history of these plunderers.

Ever since the dissolution of the Mogul power, Central India has been, more or less, the prey of innumerable disorders, from the wars of petty chiefs, for the territorial revenues of the country. But after death had withdrawn the directing genius of Alia Bhye from the scene, these disorders grew to a height; and the confusion arising from the contests among the Mahratta powers, and the minor feudatories and chieftains, who were left in the possession of lands, had nearly extinguished all known rights. The country had become one common arena of contention for daring and ambitious spirits, where might constituted right, and where, in the general convulsion, every man seemed to rise to the level of his capacity or courage. Power, held by no legitimate title, was seized as the natural prey of usurpers, and thus was Central India kept in continued trouble. The long continuance of these commotions at length engendered a disposition to anarchy and violence, which nothing could check. No usage or right was respected—no tie held sacred; and society seemed to be threatened with a dissolution of all its ancient bonds. The Mahratta confederacy, while it subsisted, presented some principle of national union, however imperfect; if it did not prevent, it set some bounds to flagrant excess and violence. But all these sanctions, however consecrated by usage, by law, or religion, were now thrown down, and the country became one disgusting scene of plunder, burning, and massacre. The different chiefs fought with each

Major Cumming afterwards formed part of the force under Sir Dyson Marshall, and was at the reduction of several strong forts other for the privilege of pillaging their wretched subjects. Their soldiers had degenerated into a licensed banditti, the destroyers of the country: they now ranged over India in bands, fierce and mutinous, for want of pay, and in this state they were frequently let loose on the defenceless inhabitants. At other times, the rulers of the country replenished their exhausted treasuries, from the same unhappy source. In this case, advancing unexpectedly on some wealthy town, and surrounding it with troops, they commenced, in a systematic manner, the work of pillage; and the excesses to which these plundering expeditions gave rise, exceed all belief.

In consequence of these continued commotions, it happened that a great portion of the population of Central India were inured to habits of disorder and military licence; and as fresh troubles arose, this class gradually received new accessions. Many of the peaceable inhabitants, driven from their homes, were compelled to plunder others for a subsistence to themselves. New adherents thus daily flocked to the standard of anarchy; its bands increased in union and strength, and they were at length regularly organized and disciplined, for the trade of robbery and murder. The name of Pindarries occurs in the history of India, in 1689, but it is only of late years, that from obscure freebooters, they rose to be the auxiliaries of the Mahratta powers, by whom their leaders were rewarded with lands. Plunder being their sole object, they were suitably trained and equipped. The policy was not to fight, but to fly—to escape as quickly as possible from the vengeance which pursued them, after securing their prey. Their force consisted, accordingly, of a light species of cavalry trained to long marches, and hard fare: they were armed with a bamboo spear, from twelve to eighteen feet long, a formidable instrument, either for attack or defence, as was experienced by the unfortunate Capt. Darke, who, rushing to the single combat of a Pindarry, basely declined by one of his soldiers, was laid low by this powerful weapon, in a skilful hand. Every fifteenth man carried a matchlock: of every 1000, about 400 were well, and 400 indifferently mounted; the remaining 200 consisted of slaves and camp followers, riding on wild ponies, and keeping up with the main body as they best could. These hordes of plunderers, in 1809 and 1812, penetrated the lines of posts established by the British, for the defence of their dominions at different points, and returned untouched, and enriched with spoil. In 1815 and 1816, they repeated their visit, and, marching in one day 38 miles, plundered 92 villages, with every circumstance of unheard-of cruelty. Next day, they plundered 54 villages; and it was ascertained, that in the course of the 12 days they remained in the Company's territories, they had put 182 persons to a cruel death, severely wounded 505, and put 3603 to different kinds of torture. The patience of the British government being exhausted by their repeated inroads, it was resolved, not only to attack and extirpate the Pindarries in their remotest haunts, but to put down that system of misrule and violence which had so long desolated India. The success of the war which took place in consequence, is well known: the Pindarry force, hemmed in by the British, were intercepted at all points; they were either destroyed or forced to submit, and were followed by most of their chiefs, who bargained only for their lives. But this decisive success was not the only fruit of the war—the secret and hostile combination formed by the Mahratta powers against the British was entirely broken. The Rajah of Nagpoor was driven from his dominions and throne; the Peishwa, the head of the Mahratta empire, was also dethroned, and

towards the Nerbudda river, particularly at the siege of Mundela, which was carried by assault; and Major C. had the honour to command the cavalry at a point where the enemy endeavoured to effect their escape, in which they completely failed, and great numbers were cut to pieces, and many prisoners made. At the termination of this service, Major Cumming was sent to Husseinabad, and served under Brigadier Adams, who entrusted him with the command of a detachment, consisting of 1 regiment of cavalry, 2 battalions of infantry, 1 troop of horse, and 1 brigade of foot-artillery, into the Batool district, which was, at that time, in a most disturbed state. The forts of Amburah and Moultye were taken after a protracted resistance, and several large bodies of Arabs were defeated on various occasions, and ultimately compelled to quit the country.

Great sickness having prevailed in this detachment, and the whole of the country to the northward of the Nerbudda river having been reduced to obedience, the Bengal troops were recalled, and Major Cumming returned to cantonments at Kritah, in Bundlecund; having received the thanks and approbation of Brigadier Adams, and Mr. Jenkins, Resident at Nagpore, for his services on this occasion.

At this time Major Cumming's health was so much impaired as to make it necessary for him to return to Europe. In the following year, August 1822, he was promoted to Lieut.-Colonel of cavalry.

LIEUTENANT-COLONEL JOHN MONCKTON COOMBS.

(Madras Establishment.)

In 1800, this officer arrived at Madras as a Cadet on the Madras establishment. He joined the cadet company, commanded by that excellent officer Capt. Charles Armstrong, at Chingliput, and was

now lives as a prisoner on the bounty of the British, who assign him £100,000 per annum for his maintenance. Holkar fell from the rank of an independent prince; and Scindia is, in reality, in the same condition.

promoted to Lieutenant on the 15th of July 1800, and appointed to the 1st regt. N. I. and 1st batt., which he joined (at Seringapatam) in April 1801; from the head-quarters of which he was shortly afterwards detached in command of three companies, to form the Native infantry part of the escort under L.-Col. Shee, attending the Mysore princes and families to the Carnatic, on which occasion the conduct of Lieutenant Coombs received the approbation* of the Commandant of the escort.

On his return to Seringapatam, Lieut. Coombs was appointed, under the orders of the Hon. Col. Wellesley, to the command of the honorary escort attached to his Highness the Rajah of Mysore, which charge he held, until his corps took the field with the division of the army under Col. Wellesley, against the Bullum Rajah. He was present, in command of the light infantry of his corps, at the assault and capture of Arakerry.

In 1802, this officer was appointed Acting Adjutant of his corps, and in June 1804, Adjutant to the 1st extra battalion, commanded by Capt. George Martin; and in Nov. following, on the augmentation of the army, he was appointed Adjutant of the 2d batt. 23d regt. In Dec. 1806, he was promoted to Captain, and in June 1807, on the recommendation of the Com.-in-Chief, L.-Gen. Sir John Cradock†, Lieut. Coombs was apointed Deputy Judge Advocate to the Mysore division of the army; and on L.-Gen. Hay Macdowall's succession to the chief command of the army, in October of the same year, this officer was placed on his personal staff as Aid-de-camp.

---

* *Copy of Detachment Orders, by L.-Col. Shee, of H. M. 33d Regiment, Commanding a Detachment.*

" *Camp, near Bangalore, 3d July,* 1801.

" The three companies of the 1st batt. 1st regt. being relieved by Capt. Macpherson's detachment, Lieutenant Coombs will be so kind as to return to Seringapatam, with the companies under his command, as soon as he may find it convenient. The Commanding Officer of the detachment feels happy in expressing his entire approbation of the conduct of Lieut. Coombs and his detachment on all occasions, since he has had the honour of commanding them."

† Now Lord Howden. Services, Royal Military Calendar, vol. ii. p. 12-14, 3d edit.

Capt. Coombs remained with L.-Gen. Macdowall until his departure for Europe, when he assumed charge of the office to which he had been previously appointed, Assistant Quarter Master General* to the Mysore division of the army; and was in the active fulfilment of its duties, when, consequent to the disturbances in the army, he was ordered to join his corps; on which occasion he received the approbation† of the Quarter Master General of the army.

Upon joining his corps in the ceded districts, Capt. Coombs was immediately employed in the command of a detachment sent out to expel some freebooters who had recently infested the districts, and to protect the borders against their incursions; a service he executed to the satisfaction of the authorities ‡ by whom he was employed.

* *Extract of a Letter from L.-Gen. Hay Macdowall to M.-Gen. Gowdie.*

"Captain Coombs, Assistant Quarter General in Mysore, has acted as my Aid-de-camp since I assumed the command of the army. He is a young man of very fair promise, and possesses great quickness, application, and intelligence. I beg to recommend him especially to your notice."

† *Copy of a Letter from L.-Col. Munro, Quarter Master General of the Army, to Captain Coombs.*

"I have had the honour to receive your letter, under date the 10th inst., which absence from the Presidency has prevented me from answering at an earlier period of time. For the reasons of your removal from the situation of Assistant Quarter Master General, I must refer you to the general orders of the 1st May, as it is not in my power to state them; but I must conclude, that those reasons are entirely unconnected with the manner in which your duties in this department have been executed; for I can state with truth, that they have been performed with a diligence, activity, and zeal, that deserve the fullest approbation.

(Signed) "J. MUNRO, Quarter Master General of the Army.
"*Quarter Master General's Office, Fort St. George, 30th May,* 1809."

‡ *From the Assistant Quarter Master General in the Ceded Districts.*

"*Bellary,* 4*th June,* 1810.

"SIR,—On withdrawing the detachment under your command, from the banks of the Toombuddra, the officer commanding in the ceded districts has directed me to convey to you his entire approbation of your conduct in the charge of this detachment, and the execution of your instructions, which M.-Gen. Croker observed with much satisfaction, has been marked with every attention, and has met that full success which was expected to result from the object of employing the force committed to your guidance.

(Signed) "W. V. CAMPBELL, Assistant Quarter Master General.
"To Capt. Coombs."

Capt. Coombs afterwards joined the other battalion of his regiment in the southern division of the army, and was selected by M.-Gen. Wilkinson, commanding it, to officiate as Judge Advocate at several general courts-martial, held in that division; for which service he received the approbation * of the Major-General.

On the nomination of the Hon. William Petrie to be governor of Prince of Wales Island, in 1812, he offered Capt. Coombs the appointment of Aid-de-camp and private secretary; in which situation Capt. Coombs accompanied him, and was, soon after his arrival, appointed Town-Major, which situation he continued to hold, under the re-appointment of three succeeding governors, until August 1825; when, having obtained promotion to a Lieutenant-Colonelcy, on the new organization of the army of the 1st May, he returned to Europe, for the benefit of his health.

In 1814, Captain Coombs being the senior officer on the island, on the departure of Col. Shuldham for Bengal, held, for several months, the command of the troops.

In 1817, he was selected by the government of Prince of Wales Island for the charge † of a political mission to the state of Acheen, then under the agitation of a recent revolution, and in a state of great misrule and anarchy. Capt. Coombs was directed to proceed

---

* *From M.-Gen. Wilkinson, Commanding the Southern Division of the Army.*

"*Trichinopoly*, 10*th March*, 1812.

"My dear Sir,—A ruling principle in my conduct during my services in the army, has always been, to search for merit, and to the extent of my power, to bring it into public view, and reward it; I shall consider myself as fortunate, if I am always as correct in that practice, as I have been in the late appointment of you to act as Judge Advocate.

"Yours faithfully,

"To Captain Coombs."   (Signed)   "W. Wilkinson.

† *Extract of a Letter from the Hon. Colonel Bannerman to the Marquess of Hastings.*

" I have selected Capt. Coombs, who on my arrival I re-appointed town-major, to confide this missson to; and I beg to assure your Lordship, that in employing this gentleman, I have been solely influenced by a sense of public duty.

" His character I have long been intimately acquainted with, and I have unlimited confidence in his integrity, his temper, and zeal for the public interests; and I shall feel greatly satisfied if my selection, and his future conduct, shall meet your Lordship's approval."

to Bengal, and submit his reports and the result of his mission to the Supreme Government; and was honoured by very flattering approbation * from that high authority; and was again deputed, under the immediate authority and orders of the Governor-General, in concert with Sir Stamford Raffles, and as joint agent with him, to adjust all future relations of the British government with the state of Acheen, and to remain as Resident with the King, in the event of negociating a treaty with that state.

On quitting Prince of Wales Island, in August 1825, Lieut.-Col.

---

* *Extract of a Letter from the Secretary to Government in the Political Department, to Captain Coombs.*

"Sir,—I am directed to inform you, that his Lordship in Council has determined to send a mission directly, on the part of the Supreme Government, to Acheen, and to commit that duty jointly to Sir Stamford Raffles and yourself.

"2. You will accordingly be pleased to hold yourself in readiness to proceed in the execution of this service, in company with Sir Stamford Raffles, under the instructions which I shall have the honor to communicate to you, by his Lordship's command.

"3. Those instructions (which will be addressed jointly to Sir Stamford Raffles and yourself) will embrace every point connected with the proposed mission.

"4. The special purpose of the present letter is to refer to your report of your proceedings during your late deputation to Acheen, under the orders of the Governor in Council of Prince of Wales Island.

"5. Such observations regarding the recent state of that country, and our future relations with its government, as have been suggested to the Gov.-Gen. in Council by the perusal of your report, will be adverted to, in the instructions under preparation, or in a despatch addressed by the Governor-General in Council to the Hon. the Governor in Council of Prince of Wales Island.

"6. The Hon. the Gov. in Council will be requested to communicate to you those parts of the letter to his address that are expressive of the Gov.-Gen. in Council's opinion on your proceedings generally, and his Lordship's sense of the very satisfactory manner in which you executed the duty assigned to you by the government of Prince of Wales Island.

"7. His Lordship in Council is desirous, however, of conveying to you directly, the sense he entertains of your services on that occasion, and of assuring you, that the accurate, minute, and extensive information collected by you, regarding the condition and affairs of Acheen, is considered to be extremely valuable, and to display a very creditable spirit of industry, observation, and inquiry. I have further to notify, that the temper, judgment, and address, which governed your conduct throughout your mission, have entitled you to the recorded approbation of the Gov.-Gen. in Council.

(Signed) "J. Adam, Chief Sec. to Gov.

"Council Chamber, the 31st October, 1818."

Coombs received the following public compliment from the government*, and was gratified by a very kind testimonial of personal regard and esteem from a number of his friends, in the presentation of an address and an elegant piece of plate.

MAJOR-GENERAL THOMAS MARRIOTT†.

(Madras Establishment.)

This officer was educated for the royal artillery, having been appointed, by the Duke of Richmond, a Cadet in 1789: in 1790, his father (to serve a younger son) accepted of a cadetship for him to Madras, where he landed the 29th May, 1791, having been promoted to an Ensigncy in 1790.

On joining his corps (25th battalion) he was detached with the light company and 30 men to the assault of Ahtoor: in the same year, 1791, he was detached with the flank companies to join Col. Cuppage's detachment to clear and take possession of the Coimbetoor country, and to collect grain for the grand army under Lord Corn-

---

* "*Fort Cornwallis,* 15*th July,* 1824.

"The Hon. the Gov. in Council is pleased to comply with an application from L.-Col. Coombs, Town and Fort-Major of Fort Cornwallis, for permission to proceed to Europe on furlough, *via* China, subject to the confirmation of the government of Fort St. George. The leave to commence from the date of his departure from this Presidency.

"The Gov. in Council would, on the present occasion, he feels, ill discharge the duties of his station, or those more immediately personal, were he not thus publicly to express the just appreciation he entertains of the talents, zeal, and integrity possessed, and ever willingly and actively exercised by L.-Col. Coombs, for the benefit of the public service, not only as principal staff at this Presidency, but in other confidential situations under this government, during a period of twelve years; and while rendering to L.-Col. Coombs this fair tribute to his merits, the Gov. in Council tenders to this valuable officer, his cordial acknowledgments and assurance of notifying to the government of Fort St. George, the high sense entertained of his long and faithful services at this Presidency."

† Third son of Randolph Marriott, Esq., of the Leases, in Yorkshire, formerly a member of council in the Supreme Government of Bengal.

wallis, then besieging Seringapatam. On the completion of this service he was placed in command of one of the captured forts (Denaickencota), and on the peace of Seringapatam, in 1792, was commissioned to exchange certain frontier fortresses with Tippoo Sultaun's officers. In 1792-3, he was employed, under Col. Maxwell, in quelling the rebellion of the Southern Polygars; having, on the 3rd Oct. 1792, been promoted to a Lieutenancy.

In 1793, he marched with his corps, under Gen. Floyd*, to invest Pondicherry, and during the siege was appointed to serve in the engineer corps. In 1794, he was made Adjutant to the 22nd battalion. In 1795, he was appointed, by Lord Hobart †, to the government and command of Namcul, a frontier fortress. In Oct. 1796, on the new formation of the army, he was appointed Adjutant and Quarter-Master (in one person answering to Brigade Quarter-Master) to the battalions of the 1st Native regiment. In June 1797, he was nominated Brigade Quarter-Master and Assistant under the Quarter-Master-General on the Manilla expedition, under Sir James Craig. In July 1798, he was appointed Brigade-Major to the cantonment of Wallajahbad. The 2nd Jan. 1799, he was appointed Aid-de-Camp and

---

* Services, vol. ii. p. 330-3.

† *The following Address from the Army to this Nobleman, on his quitting India, shews the sense entertained of his Lordship's government.*

"My Lord,—We, the undersigned Officers of the Coast Army, deeply sensible of the national advantages which attended your Lordship's public exertions in this country, lament that your sudden and unexpected departure, deprived us of the opportunity of expressing jointly with our brethren at the Presidency, our esteem and respect for your person and character, and our sincere regret at your retiring from power in India.

"Owing to the wisdom and ability of your Lordship's plans, and the confidence reposed in them by all ranks, those conquests were achieved, which have proved no less beneficial to the general interests of the British empire, than reflective of new lustre on the reputation of this army; while the Native troops, firmly relying on your good faith and uniform attentions, have embarked for foreign service with a zeal and alacrity which have no example. To these sentiments, which grow out of the feelings of gratitude and justice, we are induced to add an earnest and anxious hope, that in critical times like these, your country may avail herself of that integrity and those talents which so admirably qualify your Lordship for the most arduous public trusts."

(Signed by 524 Officers.)

Deputy Persian Interpreter to the Commander-in-Chief, General Harris[*]. On the fall of Seringapatam, he was made Military Secretary to the Commander-in-Chief. He was employed in the revenue department at Seringapatam to collect materials for forming the partition treaty of Mysore; and also in the political department, and put in charge of the Mysore Princes [Vide Marquess Wellesley's despatches to the Court of Directors, &c.] On the 10th Dec. 1799, he was promoted to Capt.-Lieutenant, and on the 7th May 1800, to Captain of a company in the 1st Regiment of Native Infantry. He remained in the Hon. Col. A. Wellesley's family, and in political charge of the Mysore families, until their final removal to Velore; when, in Jan. 1803, he was appointed Town Major of the fortress of Velore, and Deputy in charge of the Mysore Princes. The 4th April 1804, he was promoted to the rank of Major; and the 22d Jan. 1805, appointed, in the political department, to the full charge of the Mysore Princes. The 17th Oct. 1805, he obtained the rank of Lt.-Colonel.

After the mutiny at Velore, Lieut.-Col. Marriott was sent by the government of Madras in charge of the seven senior Mysore Princes to Bengal, on board H. M.'s ship Culloden. He returned to Madras; and in May 1807, reached Calcutta by land with the junior Princes and families, after a march of five months from Velore. He received on this occasion the thanks of the supreme government, and a present of 5000 rupees.

The 29th Oct. 1807, he sailed for England on furlough; and the 10th Sept. 1811, returned to his duty at Madras.

On the 4th June 1814, this officer was promoted to Brevet-Colonel, and the 8th July 1814, appointed by government to the command of the fort and cantonment of Bangalore. The 1st Feb. 1815, he was appointed to command the Light Brigade with the army on the Toombuddra, under the personal command of Sir T. Hislop[†], Commander-in-Chief.

The 14th Oct. 1815, Col. Marriott was appointed by government to command a field force for the reduction of the fort and province

---

[*] Services, vol. ii. p. 385-6.   [†] Services, Roy. Mil. Cal., vol. ii. p. 333-40, 3d edit.

of Kurnool, also first commissioner for the settlement of the affairs of the same.

On the 14th Dec. the batteries opened, and on the 15th the usurper and garrison surrendered at discretion. For this service he received a present of 1000 pagodas (£400) from the East India Company.

On the 31st Aug. following, he resumed the command of Bangalore; and on the 16th Jan. 1820, sailed for England on furlough. The 6th Aug. 1820, he was appointed Colonel Commandant of a regiment: and the 19th July 1821, on His Majesty's coronation, promoted to the rank of Major-General.

LIEUTENANT COLONEL WILLIAM BLACKBURNE.

(Madras Establishment.)

In 1782, this officer was appointed a Cadet on the Madras establishment; Ensign, in 1783; Lieutenant, in 1790; Captain Lieutenant, in 1799; Captain, in 1800; Major, in 1807; Lieut.-Col. in 1813; and Lieut.-Col.-Commandant of a regiment, in 1824.

He arrived at Madras in June 1783, and joined the 24th battalion of Sepoys, serving in the southern army, under the command of Lieut.-Col. Fullarton.

After the peace with Tippoo Sultaun, in 1784, the 24th Battalion was employed in the reduction of certain refractory Poligars in the southern provinces, and on the successful termination of the service, in 1785, was ordered into garrison at Trichinopoly. In the following year a great reduction of the army took place, and Ensign Blackburne was removed to the 1st battalion of Sepoys, in garrison at Tanjore.

Ensign Blackburne had already acquired a competent knowledge of the Hindostanee language, and applied his leisure at Tanjore to the study of the Mahratta. The Rajah of Tanjore, Tuljajee, died in

1786, and the Governor of Madras, Sir Archibald Campbell, proceeded, in 1787, to Tanjore, to enquire into and determine the right of succession. In these enquiries, and in the subsequent negociation of a treaty of alliance with the Rajah of Tanjore, Amer Sing, Sir A. Campbell availed himself of the services of Ensign Blackburne, and expressed a flattering approbation of them; and, on his return to the presidency, rewarded them still further by a present of 500 star pagodas, and the appointment of Mahratta Interpreter at Tanjore.

Ensign Blackburne discharged the duties of this office to the entire satisfaction of the Resident at Tanjore, until war broke out again between the British government and Tippoo Sultaun; soon after which, he obtained the permission of the government of Madras to join his corps in the field, and served with it until the termination of hostilities, in 1792, when he returned to Tanjore, and resumed the office of Mahratta Interpreter.

In June 1793, Lieut. Blackburne proceeded to England, in consequence of ill health, and in the latter end of 1798, he was re-appointed Mahratta Interpreter at Tanjore, and received a commission to enquire into and settle a serious dispute between the Rajah of Tanjore, and a large body of his discontented troops; on which occasion the Company's civil and military authorities at Tanjore, had taken different views of the question, and ranged themselves on opposite sides. Lieut. Blackburne's settlement of the dispute was fully approved of by the government, and carried into execution.

Lieut. Blackburne continued at Tanjore as Mahratta Interpreter, and was very actively employed in the negociation of the treaty of 1799, between the Company and the Rajah, and received the approbation of the Resident, and of the Governor in Council, for his services on the occasion.

In March 1801, the Resident, Mr. Torin, resigned his appointment; which was immediately conferred on this officer, then a young Captain in the army, unknown personally to the Governor, Lord Clive, and without his making any application to his Lordship.

In June 1801, a serious rebellion broke out in the southern provinces of India, and an invasion of the province of Tanjore was threatened and soon undertaken by the rebels. Captain Blackburne, within twenty-four hours after receiving intelligence of the insurrection, took the field, at the head of his own escort, and the disposable part of the forces of the Rajah of Tanjore. His force was speedily augmented by a large body of irregulars raised by the Rajah, by the Collector of Tanjore and by himself, and by the junction of the two flank companies of His Majesty's 94th regiment. During this campaign, which lasted five months, Captain Blackburne repelled two invasions by the rebels of the province of Tanjore, recovered from them the province of Ramnad, which they had occupied, and co-operated in various ways with the army under the command of Lieut.-Col. Agnew. His services on this occasion were highly approved of by the Governor in Council at Madras, the Governor-General in Council at Calcutta, and by the Court of Directors.

After the extinction of the rebellion, Captain Blackburne returned to Tanjore, and continued in the performance of the duties of his civil station, accompanying the Rajah on a pilgrimage through the province of Tanjore, and subsequently to Pylny.

In 1804, Captain Blackburne charged the whole of the Native officers and servants employed in the revenue, judicial, and police departments of the province of Tanjore, with embezzlement, fraud, exaction, and oppression; and, after an investigation, which was continued uninterruptedly through a period of five months, succeeded in establishing by proof, and ultimately by the unanimous confessions of the accused, the truth of every charge.

The consequences of the discoveries thus made, were a total change in the system of revenue, attended by an increase of one-third; the recovery of one hundred and twenty thousand pagodas, from the confessed embezzlement of three hundred thousand; and the substitution of arrangements in all the civil departments of Tanjore, which have gradually raised that important and valuable province, to a state of high prosperity and happiness.

Rajah Tondiman Behauder, a native chief, dependant on the British government, and ruling his own extensive province with absolute authority, died in 1806, leaving two sons, the elder 10, the younger 9 years of age; and a most factious and turbulent nobility, exercising despotic power upon their own estates, and ready and eager to decide their pretensions to the administration by an appeal to arms. Captain Blackburne having since his appointment as Resident at Tanjore been charged with the communications between this dependant Native Prince and the British government, interposed, maintained the public tranquillity, and was subsequently appointed by the government of Madras, the guardian of the minors, and placed in charge of the administration of all their affairs. He continued in this charge until the majority of the present Rajah, Tondiman Behauder; paid off a very large debt which was contracted in the former reign; suppressed the various abuses which prevailed; established courts of justice, till then unknown in the province; and a regular system of revenue; directed and superintended the education of the young Princes; and acquitted himself generally, of his trust, in a manner which obtained for him the repeated approbation of his own government, and the warm gratitude of the chief himself, and of every description and class of his subjects.

During the government of Sir George Barlow, Lieut.-Col. Blackburne was twice sent to Travancore, with a commission, on the first occasion, to endeavour to prevent hostilities, which were threatened, and which actually took place before he was able to obtain an interview with the Rajah. On the second occasion, he was appointed to succeed the Resident, Colonel Macauley, who had intimated his desire to retire, but afterwards was permitted to withdraw his application.

The public services above alluded to may be considered as foreign to and independant of the regular duties of a political resident at Tanjore. It may suffice to state that these duties were performed and sustained during twenty-three years, at the court of a most wayward Prince, in a manner, as will be seen by the annexed documents, which commanded the uniform and warm approbation of the successive governors who administered the affairs of the Company at Madras during that period. And that his Highness, the Rajah of Tanjore, although thwarted unavoidably in all his favourite projects of ambition and aggrandizement, by the immediate agency of the Resident at his court, gave a most remarkable proof, in India unprecedented, of the high estimation in which he held the honor and integrity of that officer, by personally soliciting him to remain a year longer at Tanjore, and to take charge, uncontroled and absolute, of his Highness's only son, his family, and all his affairs, public and private, during the absence of his Highness on a pilgrimage to Benares. The government at Madras yielded to the request of the Rajah, and on his Highness's return from the pilgrimage, after an absence of twenty months, he expressed to that government the warmest gratitude for the manner in which the Resident had performed the trust reposed in him.

During the course of this officer's service, as Resident at Tanjore, he was frequently employed on committees of revenue and police, and on investigations of various description. He was commissioned also, in the governments of Lord W. Bentinck and Sir George Barlow, to watch and counteract the proceedings of the French agents and emissaries, at the Danish settlement of Tranquebar, and to maintain a private and confidential, as well as public communication, with the governors of that settlement.

L.-Col. Blackburne resigned his appointments at Tanjore, and embarked for England on the 4th March, 1823. After his departure the Gov. in Council at Fort Saint George, recorded his sentiments of the public services of the Lieut.-Colonel: a copy of which instrument, as well as the accompanying correspondence *, justly appertain to this memoir.

* The Editor has very great satisfaction in presenting this correspondence to the Indian Army, as whilst it reflects high honor on L.-Col. Blackburne, it at the same time adds lustre to the characters of the distinguished individuals who have so nobly supported and approved

From Lieut.-Colonel Agnew to Captain Blackburne.

"Sir,—The seizure and execution of the chief rebels having happily restored this district to subordination, I deem it no longer necessary to detain you from the important duties of your station at Tanjore, or to require the services in the Marawah districts, of the detachment under your command. You have therefore my permission to return, with your detachment, to the Tanjore country, where you will make such arrangements for the distribution of your force, as to you may seem proper. You will direct the persons provisionally appointed to the management of the Shevagunga Talooks, on your taking possession of them, to render a just account of their administration to the managers named by the Zemindar of Shevagunga; and you will have the goodness to take the necessary precautions to prevent plunder on the part of the irregulars of your detachment, from whose habits acts of this nature may be expected on their evacuating the district.

"I cannot allow your detachment to quit the limits of my command, without requesting you to present to the officers and men composing it, my warmest thanks for the activity, zeal, and courage, which they have displayed on several occasions of difficulty, in which they have rendered the most important service to the public interest. And I beg you, personally, to accept my acknowledgments for the able assistance I have derived from your operations, the readiness and energy with which you, on every occasion, co-operated with me, and the judgment with which you, on every occasion, marked your determination and movements. To these I attribute the security of the Tanjore country; and much of the success which followed the capture of Caliarcoil, I am happy to attribute to the promptitude of your march to occupy the station I had pointed out to you as the probable retreat of the chief rebels, and the magazine of their ammunition and grain.

(Signed) "P. V. AGNEW, L.-Col., Commanding Southern Detachment.
"*Camp, 24th Oct.* 1801."

his conduct. Of the amiable and talented Lord William Bentinck, this correspondence is a further proof to the many already before the public, of his fitness for command in India, and of the importance his further services might be to the Hon. Company, and to the British government. It is a matter of regret with every friend of the Indian Government, that such distinguished characters as Lord William Bentinck and Sir John Malcolm, are, at a period so critical as the present, absent from a country with which, as well as the characters of the people, they are so intimately acquainted, and so able to direct.

From J. Webbe, Esq. Chief Secretary of Government, to Capt. Blackburne, Resident at Tanjore.

Par. 1. "Sir,—I have received your several letters, and am directed to transmit to you the orders of the right hon. the Governor in Council, on the points which require his Lordship's determination.

2. "The Governor in Council has felt the greatest degree of satisfaction, in observing the uniform spirit of zeal and activity, which has distinguished your exertions to protect the frontier; and to assist the operations of the force under the command of L.-Col. Agnew. The vigilance with which you have watched the rebels, and the promptitude with which you have moved to frustrate their designs, are entitled to the approbation of his Lordship in Council; while the success of your arrangements for conciliating the minds of the well-affected Poligars, is a convincing proof of your qualifications to discharge the duties of your important situation. I am directed, therefore, by the right hon. the Governor in Council, to express to you his Lordship's entire approbation of your conduct in the command of the detachment, and to inform you that the Governor in Council has communicated to the Hon. the Court of Directors, his Lordship's sentiments of the services, which he considers you to have rendered to the Company.

3. "The Governor in Council also feels great satisfaction at the manner in which the troops of His Excellency the Rajah of Tanjore, have acquitted themselves of their duty in this service; and the personal conduct of His Excellency is entirely conformable to the principles of the alliance established between him and the Company. It is the intention of the right hon. the Governor to express to His Excellency his Lordship's sense of his conduct on this occasion; in the meanwhile, you will assure the Rajah of his Lordship's entire approbation.

4. "The Governor in Council approves the attention observed by you to the Poligar Worja Tewer, and the advance of money paid by you, for the defrayment of his expenses. Orders have been transmitted to the department of audit, for the adjustment of the amount.

5. "The Governor in Council also approves the rate at which you have authorized batta to be paid to the troops of Tondiman.

6. "The Governor in Council confirms the rate of pay stated in your letter of the 27th July last, for the Colleries, whom you have engaged for the service, and will expect your report on the amount of pay to be fixed for Mootoosingen.

7. "On a re-consideration of your letter, dated the 24th July last, to the collector at Tanjore, on the subject of the pay of the Sibbendy sepoys, the Governor in Council authorized their pay to be fixed at one pagoda and twenty-four fanams per month, during the time they may have been actually engaged on service.

8. "The success which has attended the operations of L.-Col. Agnew's force, appears to have rendered the return of your detachment immediately practicable; if therefore no objection should exist to that measure, of which the Governor in Council is not aware, his Lordship directs you to resume your situation at Tanjore, and to discontinue, as soon as may be practicable, the field charges of the detachment under your command, and of the Sibbendies and Colleries attached to it.

(Signed) "J. WEBBE, Chief Secretary to Government.
"*Fort St. George, 21st Oct.* 1801."

Extract.—Military Letter from the Government at Fort St. George, dated 15th Oct. 1801, *to the Hon. the Court of Directors.*

67. "The southern districts of Tanjore, being menaced at the same period of time, by a part of the rebellious force, the Resident at Tanjore, Capt. Blackburne, acting with great zeal and promptitude, assembled such a force as could be collected from His Excellency the Rajah's guard, from the irregular Sibbendy, and from the well-affected Poligars of the country.

68. "The progress of affairs having rendered it expedient to augment the force under the command of Capt. Blackburne, measures were taken for that purpose; and instructions were transmitted to that officer, to employ it for the protection of the Tanjore country; to confirm the confidence of Tondiman, and to obtain the co-operation of as large a portion of his irregular force, as might be practicable.

74. "We have great pleasure in acquainting your Hon. Court, that the equipment of the force under the command of Capt. Blackburne, has been attended with very beneficial consequences. The zeal and activity of that officer, and his extensive communication with the chieftains of Tanjore, and of the neighbouring provinces, have been successfully employed in confirming the attachment of the well affected; in bringing the whole force of the Poligar Tondiman into useful action; in detaching from the cause of the Murdoo, those who had submitted to his influence from motives of fear; and in employing his force, when the employment of military force was

practicable, with great spirit and judgment. We, therefore, consider Capt. Blackburne to have rendered important services in the situation in which he has been placed, and we recommend his conduct to your favourable notice."

Extract of a Letter to the Right Hon. Lord W. Bentinck, Governor in Council, Fort St. George.

" *Tanjore, 3d August,* 1804.

" After dispatching the report of the Committee, Mr. Wallace proceeded to Trichinopoly, and I arrived at Tanjore yesterday. We shall not probably return to Combeconum until we receive your Lordship's commands on the subject.

" No public inconvenience can result from our absence. The Committee has never exercised any control over, or interference in the current business of the revenue department.

" I earnestly hope that your Lordship may be of opinion that I have redeemed the pledge I gave, and proved the truth of all my charges. I have proved embezzlement and fraud in every receipt and disbursement of the collector; exactions from every description of private property; bribes for the perversion of justice; the falsification of the treasury accounts; the robbery of the cash chest; perjury universal; and every intended check established by the collector, from the Circuit Cutcherries of his assistants to the Hircarrah examinations, converted into additional instruments of plunder and extortion. Barefaced villany has been every where triumphant, and those who had the courage to attempt to check its progress, have been baffled, punished, and disgraced.

" Your Lordship will perceive that the Committee has declined, for reasons sufficiently obvious, the inquiry into the cause and effect of these extraordinary and disgraceful scenes. But as your Lordship has a right to expect my private opinion of the actual state of the department, I will give it without hesitation, although not without reluctance.

" The Cutcherry and the province at large, are in a state of extreme disorder. The balances are considerable, some of them cannot, and some ought not to be collected. The landholders are in a state of great alarm, in consequence of a little re-action of the old servants and their numerous adherents.

" The complaints of the merchants are serious, and the appeals against decisions obtained by palpable bribery and false witnesses, are numerous and urgent. A very able, vigilant, and steady hand is required to restore regularity and order, to redress grievances which are urgent, to re-establish the authority of government, and to give confidence to the inhabitants.

(Signed)   "W. BLACKBURNE."

Copy of a Letter from Lord W. Bentinck, Governor in Council.

"*Fort St. George, 29th Sept.* 1804.

"Sir,—I send you the letters which it is my wish to record according to the intention, and for the reasons expressed in my last letter. There are no parts which do not appear to me perfectly proper to meet the public eye, and calculated to do you very great honour. But I request, that in your answer, you will consult only your private feelings. My wish is certainly to record the whole. I can do in no other way equal justice to the sentiments and principles by which you have been actuated throughout. My feelings have been much interested in this transaction. My desire is, that the government should act decidedly and consistently, both in its punishments and in its rewards. With regard to yourself, I wish it was in my power to do more than to express (as strongly as I feel) to those superior in authority, whose approbation we value; the zeal, the disinterestedness, the patriotism, exhibited in your public conduct; with you lies the whole merit of the original discovery, and of the successful conduct of the disclosure of that abominable train of villany and mal-administration. I beg leave to offer you the most sincere assurances of my private respect and public gratitude.

"I beg you will repeat the recompense which you thought should be given to Appooviah and to Annapien. I shall enclose in another paper a petition lately presented to me by that unfortunate man Trivadateyenger. What compensation can be made to him? He is certainly entitled to some amends. I forgot to say, that I remarked in Mr Harris's report, reflections cast upon the honesty of Appooviah and Annapien, as having been implicated with all the rest of the Meerassidars, in the general embezzlement. Is this the case?

"I remain, my dear Sir, with sentiments of the most sincere regard,

(Signed)   "W. BENTINCK."

Copy of a Letter to the Right Hon. Lord W. Bentinck, Governor in Council.

"*Tanjore, 5th Oct.* 1804.

"MY LORD,—I have had the honour to receive your Lordship's letter of the 29th ult. I am penetrated with the deepest sense of the generous consideration and uncommon delicacy of your Lordship's conduct. You cannot but be sensible, my Lord, that to obtain the private regard and the public approbation of a man like your Lordship, is to accomplish every just object of laudable ambition, and to secure a perpetual spring of the purest pleasures. I dare not add more on this subject than that I am well aware of the conditions on which alone I can preserve your Lordship's favorable opinion, and that I am confident of fulfilling them.

" I have the honour to return the papers which accompanied your Lordship's letter. I cordially acquiesce in your Lordship's wish to record my letters. I have not altered nor expunged any part of them, although if I had intended them to be public, I should probably have omitted to specify any particular instances of Mr. Harris's severity to accusers and complainants. In all my letters to your Lordship, I have been influenced by the most sacred regard to truth; and I have endeavoured, carefully, to guard against the operation of local or temporary prejudices.

" I return also Trivadatayengar's petition to your Lordship. The facts stated in the petition are, I believe, true, and do not appear to be exaggerated. As a public officer of the government, I should be ashamed to meet Trivadatayengar until his injuries are redressed. The mode of redress is not very material; the sentence of his banishment being reversed, he may receive a sum of money as a compensation for his injuries, or a place under the collector, as an acknowledgment of his innocence.

" In regard to Appooviah and the other men employed by me, or rather united with me, in the detection of the numerous and distinct frauds, peculations, and embezzlements, committed by the revenue servants; it is certain that embezzlements of grain were carried on in the villages, in which they possess property, although they commenced considerably later than in the other villages of the same Talooks. Your Lordship may recollect that I stated this fact, generally, in my letter of the 7th May, pointed out the step which I took in consequence, and praised the prompt obedience of these men and of the Rajah's servants, in delivering their true revenue accounts; thus setting an example to the country, which must have had a powerful effect. None of these proprietors resided upon their estates; their refusal in the first instance, to accede to the plan of the revenue officers, was followed by vexations innumerable, and by the destruction of a considerable part of their crops from the detention of water, the delay in giving permission to reap, and other similar oppressions. Many of the native inhabitants of Madras possess land in Tanjore. They were all compelled, sooner or later, to give their sanction to the embezzlements. Mr. Wallace's head servant is a landholder in Tanjore. He was obliged to authorize his manager to agree to the embezzlement in order to save his crop, but he informed his master of it. Mr. Wallace communicated this fact to me, near a month before I proceeded to Combeconum. I stated this to your Lordship before. I mention it now to draw an inference in favour of Appooviah. The considerations which prevented Mr. Wallace from acquainting Mr. Harris of this villany, must have operated, but with tenfold force, on Appooviah, to prevent him from volunteering a charge against the revenue officers. The cause which induced Mr. Wallace's head servant at Trichinopoly, and many other proprietors at a much greater distance from Tanjore, to consent to the embezzlements, was the same that influenced Appooviah, the fear of serious injury, if not utter ruin, if they refused.

"It is in my power to prove that an offer of an indefinite sum was made to Appooviah by a dependant of Ramchander, to induce him to withhold his assistance from me. Another offer of 20,000 chuckrams was made to Appooviah and my head servants, by a great and opulent landholder, to induce them to accept of false accounts of the embezzlements in his villages, and to abstain from compelling the disclosure of the particular connexion between him and Ramchander.

"If I appear too earnest on this point, I entreat your Lordship to pardon me. I own I am very anxious that Appooviah should receive some mark of public approbation, not merely because his services deserve to be rewarded, but because it is necessary to reconcile him to himself, to elevate his mind above the feelings which now depress it considerably, from having acquired the resentment and reproaches of all his friends and connexions, and gained the goodwill of no individual but me; for even the Rajah and Dettagee are deeply offended with him for his inflexibility in the execution of his duty, and for his refusal to recommend for offices some dependants of the palace whom he did not think worthy of confidence.

"If your Lordship shall think proper to express your approbation of Appooviah's services, it will be very flattering to me to be permitted to be the channel of the communication to him.

(Signed) "W. BLACKBURNE."

Copy of a Letter from the Right Hon. Lord W. Bentinck.
"*Fort St. George*, 15*th October* 1804.

" I have the pleasure of sending you a minute, which is the winding up of the affairs of the Committee, and is the only part which has been really satisfactory to me. My feelings tell me that I have done you but imperfect justice. But the acts require not the colouring of my poor eloquence, and speak most clearly and decidedly for themselves. It is my intention to send a copy of the enclosed officially to the Governor-General. I need not say that all the propositions have passed council unanimously. You will, of course, receive a copy of the minute from the public Secretary; but till that arrives, the records of government should remain secret, which has been the cause of the words written at the head of the other page. I trust that the rewards ordered for Appooviah and Annapien will meet with your approbation. (Signed) " W. BENTINCK."

" I stated in my minute of the 21st September, my intention to record my sentiments upon the conduct of Capt. Blackburne with respect to the late investigation in Tanjore.

" The proceedings of the Committee have already shewn the discovery to have originated with that gentleman, and I believe it may be stated, without taking away from the merit which is justly due to the zealous and cordial co-operation of Mr. Harris, that to Capt. Blackburne's indefatigable perseverance, ability, and temper, the complete and successful result is to be attributed.

" Nothing but the strongest impression of public feeling could have induced an individual to leave the path of his ordinary duty, and to engage in a service invidious, uncertain, and laborious. He must have been fully aware of the doubtful issue of the attempt, from the artifice, union and general strength of the conspirators. He must have known that an inquiry, extending to every talook, and almost to every individual in the province, must prove a work of great personal fatigue.

" He must also have felt that an officer arraigning the administration of a gentleman, belonging to a different branch of the service, must be necessarily exposed to that dissatisfaction which common fellow-feeling alone is disposed to create, and in case of failure, to general odium, and to the general charge of impertinent officiousness. None of these considerations appear to have deterred Capt. Blackburne from his object, and the event has proved most honourable to himself and most advantageous to the Company.

" The accompanying letters were written to me in my public capacity, prior to the inquiry and during its progress. I did not then make them public, because I was desirous that the exertions of Capt. Blackburne should not have the appearance of being directed rather to the accusation of the collector, than to the detection of the peculation of his servants. The sentiments expressed in some of those letters, might lead to such an idea. It is due to him now to record the best proofs, as they were written at the time, of the principles by which that gentleman was actuated.

" Honourable acts, impelled by honourable motives for the good of the state, are entitled to its proudest rewards.

" I should feel myself wanting in my duty if I did not point out this servant of the Company as being entitled in the strongest manner to the approbation of the Court of Directors. He has saved to the Company revenue to a very great amount; he has stopped the system of peculation, to which, without his interference, no probability of termination appeared; he has done much more, in my opinion, in delivering the country from oppression, and in rescuing the character of the British administration from disgrace. If a subject can be entitled to public gratitude, for extraordinary civil services, no man more justly deserves it than Capt. Blackburne.

" I beg leave also to record a letter from Capt. Blackburne, in answer to a letter from the Chief Secretary of the 4th September. I was influenced by the same reasons in withholding this as well as the other letters of Capt. Blackburne. It is strongly corroborative of the necessity which existed of a reform in the administration of affairs in Tanjore.

" I must beg leave also to mention to the Board, Appooviah and Annapien, who were principally instrumental, particularly the former, in aiding the detection of the embezzlements. While I have recommended the strongest examples being made of all those who have been convicted of guilt, I think the same policy, and the same justice requires, that our rewards should be commensurate with our punishments. The only mode of reclaiming that province from the debasement into which it is sunk, will be by steady good government, by the marked encouragement of virtue, and discouragement of vice. Appooviah has been particularly mentioned to me by Capt. Blackburne. I recommend that 4000 pagodas and a palanquin be presented to Appooviah. I recommend that 2000 pagodas be presented to

Annapien. I recommend sums to this extent, because the former refused a bribe of 10,000 pagodas from Ramchunder Row, to prevent the investigation. Rewarding handsomely the agents of the present discovery, will be an effectual check against any similar combination in future.

"I recommend that these marks of the approbation of government, shall be bestowed through the Resident in Tanjore.

"I consider it an act of justice also, as connected with the present subject, to lay before the Board a petition from Trivadatayengar. His case has been already stated at great length by the Committee. He has been one of the unfortunate victims of Mr. Harris's servants.

"I neither condemn Mr. Harris nor the Board of Revenue. They could only determine upon the evidence before them. The innocent individual, however, who has been severely flogged, banished from his country for two years, and branded with public infamy, is entitled to satisfaction from government.

"I recommend that the order of banishment be taken off, that he receive 1000 pagodas, and that he be mentioned to the collector, as a person in whose future welfare the government will feel a concern.

"*Fort St. George, October* 12, 1804."

Extracts.—Fort St. George, Revenue Consultations, 6th September, 1805.

The Right Hon. the President delivers the following minute, with an enclosure from Bengal.

"Having always considered the conduct of Capt. Blackburne, in standing forward to detect the revenue peculation in Tanjore, to have proceeded from the most honourable and disinterested motives, from an anxious regard for the reputation of the British character, and from a proper and just sense of his duty to the Hon. Company, I felt it my duty to solicit, in a particular manner, the attention of the supreme government to that transaction. The Governor-General's sentiments are contained in the accompanying letter, which I request may be recorded. I beg to propose that a copy of it be sent to Capt. Blackburne, for his information and satisfaction.

(Signed) "W. BENTINCK.

"*Fort St. George, Sept.* 1, 1805."

From the Governor-General to Lord W. C. Bentinck.

"MY LORD,—Having perused the different statements submitted to your Lordship by Captain Blackburne, regarding the condition of affairs in the province of Tanjore, I consider it to be my duty to signify to your Lordship my entire approbation of the zeal and honourable spirit which have marked the conduct of that respectable public officer, in the discharge of the duties entrusted to him by your Lordship. I request your Lordship will be pleased to communicate to Captain Blackburne, in such manner as you may deem most expedient, this testimony of my favorable opinion of his useful and meritorious services under your Lordship's government.

(Signed)   " WELLESLEY.

" *Fort William, July* 20, 1805."

From the Rt. Hon. Lord W. Bentinck.

" *Fort St. George, Sept.* 29, 1807.

" MY DEAR SIR,—Embarking in an hour, I must be brief, and I have only therefore to leave with you my best wishes, and to assure you that there exists no man in India, of whom I entertain a higher respect and regard than of yourself. I enclose the copy of a minute which I have recorded regarding the Rajah's jurisprudence. Believe me, my dear sir, very sincerely your's.

(Signed)   " W. BENTINCK.

" Major Blackburne."

Extract of a Letter from Sir George Barlow, Governor in Council of Fort St. George, to the Court of Directors in the Political Department, dated 6th February, 1810.

185. " We derived much satisfaction from the great degree of attention which Major Blackburne appears to have devoted with such beneficial effects, to the general administration of the affairs of the Tondiman country, subsequently to the demise of the late Vejaya Ragonath Tondiman, and during the nonage of his minor successor.

186. " We particularly observed and approved the system and method which he substituted in room of the gross defects of the former scheme of the revenue economy of that province, his measures for assigning to the cultivating inhabitants an increased share of the produce, for appointing carnums and revenue officers, for keeping and rendering regular accounts; measures which have already had a salutary operation in augmenting the resources of the country, and especially in improving the condition of the people.

187. " We also expressed our approbation of his successful arrangements

for liquidating the debt of the late Rajah, by which a large portion had been discharged in the first year, and of his judicious suggestions and directions for facilitating the distribution of justice and the administration of the police."

To the Chief Secretary to Government.

"*Fort St. George.*

"Sir,—I have the honour to inform you, that in the course of a visit which I made lately to Rajah Tondiman Behauder, at Poodoocottah, his desire to address a letter to the Honourable the Governor to congratulate his honour's arrival at Madras, and to offer his own grateful acknowledgements for the protection and kindness which have been extended to him, was mentioned, and received my entire approbation.

"I have now the honour to transmit a letter in the Mahratta language, addressed to the Hon. Governor, by Rajah Tondiman Behauder, and a translation of it by Captain James Michael, and I take the liberty of adding an original letter to me, in English, which accompanied the letter to the Governor.

"The Mahratta letter is the composition, unaided in any material degree, of the Rajah Behauder, and in his usual handwriting. In the composition of the English letter he was assisted by his English teacher, but the writing is his own, and is not superior to his ordinary penmanship.

"In former times, the Persian language was employed in the communications by letter between the Governor at Madras and the Chief at Poodoocottah. This custom, originating in the dependance of the latter on the Nabob of the Carnatic, appears to have been continued as a matter of indifference after the superiority and rights of the Nabob were transferred to the British government. Since that transfer the Persian language gradually became obsolete, and is now nearly extinct at Poodoocottah. As much was required to be done, in a short time, in the education of the sons of the late Rajah Behauder, I decided against attempting to impose upon them a foreign language, which was a matter of curiosity only, not of use, and which could not be acquired and kept up without extraordinary labour and expense; but I did not oppose their desire to learn the Mahratta language, as that language was capable of serving as a medium of direct communication between them and me, and of being useful to them also in the administration of their affairs, in all the departments of which were to be found Mahratta Brahmins, distinguished by their talents and learning. I restrained, however, the impatience of the young men to begin the study of Mahratta, until they had acquired a very competent knowledge of the Gentoo and Tamul languages; the former, the language of their family, the latter the vernacular tongue of the province. They were then allowed to apply to the Mahratta language, and it speedily became the medium of our intercourse and communications, whether personal or by letter, whether of a public or a more familiar description. It became, in consequence, a favorite language, was pursued with augmented zeal and ardour, and a degree of perfection attained in it, which very few natives of this part of India can boast of.

" I have entered into this explanation in the hope that it may induce the Honourable the Governor in Council to acquiesce in the Rajah Behauder's wish to substitute the Mahratta language for the Persian, in the correspondence which may take place between them.

"The late Rajah Tondiman Behauder, in his last illness, recommended his two sons to my care in the most pathetic manner, and so did their mother before she threw herself into the flames to accompany her husband in death. The boys were old enough to understand the greatness of their loss, and the solemn injunctions of their dying parents, which will never, I am confident, be effaced from their memories, or cease to influence and regulate their conduct. These injunctions were to maintain the ancient fidelity and attachment of their ancestors to the British government, and to confide implicitly in the Resident at Tanjore, as the representative of the Governor.

" From the death of their natural parents, the orphans have addressed me invariably as their father, and although I was aware that this mode of address might originate in the flattery of some of their attendants, I was not inclined to object to it decidedly, for it appeared to be calculated to render their dependance on me more pleasing and confiding to themselves, and to give additional weight to the advice which I might offer, and to the measures which I might adopt with a view to their improvement and advantage. I have not been deceived by the hopes which I indulged.

" The circumstances above stated, and my desire that the Honourable the Governor in Council should see the style and writing of Rajah Tondiman Behauder, in their usual and natural state, not altered or embellished, will excuse me, I trust, for making no change in the customary mode of address.

" Rajah Tondiman Behauder completed his twenty-third year in the month of August last. He has one son. Ragonath Tondiman is eleven months younger than his brother, and has two daughters. At the father's death, the elder son was nine and a half years of age. Until that event, the brothers had been confined to the interior of the palace; no attempt had been made to improve their minds, and they were unable to read a word in any language. Since that period they have studied, successively, the Gentoo, Tamul, and Mahratta languages, and acquired a very considerable knowledge of each. They have studied also and still attend to the English language, in which their progress has been more slow, unavoidably, from the want of an European teacher, English society, and of the means even of associating with the natives of the country conversant in the language. It has been attempted to provide a remedy for the last inconvenience, by establishing an English school at Poodoocottah, where the pupils are instructed at the expense of the Rajah Behauder and to which the Sirdars of the Durbar are encouraged to send their sons. Rajah Tondiman Behauder and his brother have learnt to speak Hindostanee, but do not write it. They have studied with success Hindoo jurisprudence, a subject to which I have urged their continual attention, and they are quite familiar with the practice of the court at Poodoocottah. They are perfectly well acquainted with the civil institutions of their country, and with all the varieties of its revenue arrangement.

" At the beginning of my superintendence over the affairs of Tondiman Behauder, I caused occasional communications to be made to him of the principal circumstances which occurred in the Cutcherrie, and subsequently in the court of justice. These communications were gradually extended, and assumed at length the form of daily reports, and after a certain interval, every measure of importance was submitted to the Rajah Behauder, discussed in his presence by the managers, and was not adopted until he understood and sanctioned it. Every decision of the court of justice was read and explained to him, and it was made his especial duty to enforce the speedy execution of decrees. In cases of appeal from the decision of the court, he decided on the appeal, assisted by his principal officers, and he held a court of equity, once a month, or more frequently when the case required it, for the trial of all causes, aborigine, which were not specifically provided for in the books of Venganeshwar and Chundrika. His faculties expanded with the exercise which they received, and habits of application and reflection were established, which, I confidently trust, will adhere to him through life.

" In the prosecution of the plan which I had adopted, I gradually extended the sphere of the Rajah Behauder's personal superintendence and direction of his affairs, until by degrees, scarcely perceptible to himself, he was placed in the command of the whole administration, three or four years ago. I did not renounce my right to interpose if it should be necessary, but excepting in instances, sufficiently numerous, when my advice or opinion has been solicited by the Rajah Behauder, I have rarely had occasion to offer either. I have not neglected to observe most carefully his proceedings and conduct, and I have rejoiced to see the principles of truth and justice, of mercy and kindness—the grand objects of my tuition—operating unequivocally, and promising to him a reign of honour, and to his people a rule of wisdom and beneficence.

" The Rajah Behauder, and his brother Ragonath, would be regarded as extraordinary instances of brotherly love and union in any part of the world. From their infancy till their marriages, they slept in one room, took their meals together, had the same masters, pursued the same studies, performed together their religious ceremonies and their manly exercises, and appeared to acquire in each pursuit, the same degree of eminence. They were married on the same day, advanced gradually to mature age, and each became the father of a family, but their perfect harmony has never been interrupted. In disposition they resemble each other strongly, but the Rajah Behauder is, as might be expected, a little more serious and reflective than Ragonath.

" The observations which I propose to take the liberty of submitting to the Hon. the Governor in Council, on the province of Poodoocottah, and its relations internal and external, shall form the subject of another communication to you.

(Signed) " W. BLACKBURNE,
Resident at Tanjore.

" *Tanjore, 21st Feb. 1821.*"

Translation of a Letter, in the Mahratta language, from Rajah Tondiman Behauder, to the Hon. the Governor of Madras.

" To the Hon. Sir Thomas Munro, K. C. B., Governor, Behauder (may the Almighty preserve him in health) Rajashree Rajah Vejaya Ragonath Raey Tondiman Behauder presents his compliments.

" To the very kind and affectionate friend, the discriminator of worth, be it known, that we are all well here, and beg the favor of him to write us the pleasing accounts of his own welfare.

" Having heard some time since, that such an excellent, respectable, and honourable person as yourself, whom we look up to as the protector of our persons and honour, had been appointed by the unparalleled, just, and charitable Company, to whom our ancestors have ever been faithful, and in whom they have placed implicit confidence, acting always with fidelity towards them, thereby meriting their favour, and being ever considered the most faithful of their allies, for whose prosperity we are constant in our prayers to the Almighty; we request you will receive our letter of congratulation, which we have taken upon ourselves to write at a favorable opportunity.

" From the time of Major Lawrence at Trichinopoly, till the rebellion of Murdoo, our late father and ancestors continued constantly faithful to the Hon. Company, and assisted them to the utmost of their power, in all emergencies: in like manner we pray for an opportunity of shewing our fidelity and devotion.

" In the records of the government, our late father's and ancestors' services will be fully shewn,—they cannot be related within the compass of such a short letter as this, and as I have no doubt but you are acquainted with them, I will not now give you the trouble to dwell upon them, but confine myself to the subject of my present circumstances, and for the trouble, I beg you will pardon me.

" Ever since the death of our father and mother, in our infancy, until now, their intimate friend, the fatherly Lieut.-Col. W. Blackburne, Resident, has carefully superintended our household and durbar affairs, and treated us with the affection and kindness of a parent, and from our infancy, he has had my younger brother and myself carefully educated, and completely taught four different languages, paid off all the debt contracted by our late father, married us both according to our established customs, with all the splendour and forms requisite, and attended the ceremonies himself. He built for us a new city, as an ornament to the country, and for the comfort and health of the inhabitants. Great part of our country was covered with jungle, some had become desert from neglect; at present it is under cultivation, in consequence of his exertions to improve it.

" He established a court of justice, and appointed to it Durma Shastrees, and Pandits of such worth and respectability, who are so strict in their inquiries, and so just and impartial in their decisions, that all our subjects live in security and tranquillity: the poor, fearing no oppressions from the rich or powerful, pass their days in peace and comfort. And by his means we have acquired the reputation of being just.

" He has constantly advised us to act in a manner which has ensured the order and well management of the affairs of our household and durbar, which has gained for us the confidence of our subjects, as we have treated them with all the kindness and civility which lay in our power, and have thereby gained the favour of the Hon. Company. He has, with great care and trouble, occasionally examined minutely into our conduct, with the view of ascertaining if we had acted according to his advice. In short, we are unable to express the extent of the obligations we lie under to him.

" We and our ancestors have gained the favour of the Hon. Company in consequence of our unshaken fidelity, and taking this into your consideration, we beg you will do us the favour to fulfil our wishes of being promoted to greater power, honour, and respectability. We constantly pray to the Almighty for the prosperity of you, the universal benefactor.

" Our father-like Lieut.-Col. W. Blackburne, the Resident, will write you at large about our circumstances and desires, and from his account you will become acquainted with them all.

" What more need be written?   (Signed)
" RAJAH VEJAYA RAGONATH RAEY TONDIMAN BEHAUDER.
" *Poodoocottah,* 15*th February,* 1821."

From the Governor of Fort St. George to Rajah Vejaya Ragonath Raey Tondiman Behauder.

Par. 1. " I have received your letter of the 19th December 1822, and I had before received your address under date the 15th February 1821.

2. " You represent your grateful sense of Lieut.-Col. Blackburne's kind attention to your affairs, and to the education of yourself and of your brother, during the period of your minority, as also of his exertions for the improvement of your country, and of its institutions; and mindful of his continued solicitude for your welfare, you now express the regret, which you had experienced on being made acquainted with his intention to return to Europe.

3. " The reports which I have received from Lieut.-Col. Blackburne, of your acquirements, of your disposition, and of the regularity with which you apply yourself to the business of your Sumastanum, are exceedingly satisfactory to me; and it has afforded me a further pleasure to learn that his endeavours to qualify you for the station to which you were destined, have

been correctly estimated, and are thankfully acknowledged by you. The prosperous state of your country attests their success, and justifies the confidence with which Lieut.-Col. Blackburne had, at an early period, charged you with the administration of its affairs. Your proceedings and conduct in the discharge of that trust are stated to afford a promise of much happiness to your people, and honour to yourself. Go on, and prosper.

4. "I am also informed by Lieut.-Col. Blackburne, of the perfect harmony and union which subsist in your family. I trust that you will still continue to set an example to your people of that brotherly concord, which is so delightful in the relations of life, and cannot fail to be productive of beneficial consequences to your state.

5. "Lieut.-Col. Blackburne having now embarked for England, I have appointed Col. Robert Scott, C. B. to succeed that officer as Resident in Tanjore. As my agent with your Sumastanum, it will be his aim to follow, in all respects, the steps of his predecessor; giving the same attention to your affairs whenever they demand it, and conducting his communications with the public officers of the neighbouring zillas, according to the usage which has been established by Lieut.-Col. Blackburne. I am persuaded that you will find in Col. Scott, the same anxious desire to consult your happiness, and to promote the welfare of yourself and of your people.

"What more?

(Signed) "THOMAS MUNRO.

"*Fort St. George, 7th March* 1823."

"POLITICAL DEPARTMENT.

"*To the Right Hon. the Court of Directors for the affairs of the Hon. the United Company of Merchants of England trading to the East Indies.*

"HONOURABLE SIRS,

Par. 1. "L.-Col. W. Blackburne having proceeded to Europe on board the Hon. Company's ship Warren Hastings, we have the honour to bring to the notice of your Hon. Court, a minute of our proceeding in this department, on the receipt of his resignation of the office of Resident at Tanjore, which it will be in the recollection of your Hon. Court, had been filled by that officer for a period of twenty-two years.

2. "Our President, in the minute recorded on the occasion, to which we beg leave to request your attention, has noticed the various important duties with which the Lieutenant Colonel had been charged, during a residence of

thirty-five years in India. We had great pleasure in bearing our testimony to L.-Col. Blackburne's useful and honourable career of service under this government, and estimating highly his claims to our acknowledgments, we beg to submit our sense of his merits to your approving judgment.

3. " We have appointed Col. Robert Scott, C.B., to succeed L.-Col. Blackburne, as Resident at Tanjore.

(Signed)

" Fort St. George,
25th March, 1823."

" Thomas Munro.
" A. Campbell.
" G. Stratton.

" *The President records the following Minute.*

" *7th March, 1823.*

"Minute,—L.-Col. Blackburne, late Resident at Tanjore, having embarked for England, after a service of forty years, of which thirty-five were actually spent in India, it is no more than a just tribute to his character, that government should record the high sense they entertain of his conduct, in the discharge of the various important duties with which he was entrusted, during that long period.

" In 1799, he was sent to Tanjore to settle a serious dispute between the Rajah of Tanjore and a large body of the Native officers, which he effected to the entire satisfaction of the government. In 1801, he was appointed Resident, and gave the first intimation of the impending insurrection of the Murdoos, took the field unauthorised, with the Rajah's troops, his own escort, and the irregulars raised by the collector, repelled the invasions of Tanjore, by the Poligars, and recovered the province of Ramnad. In 1804, he discovered a system of fraud and embezzlement in the revenue department; charged the whole of the collector's servants and every Mirasdar in the province with being concerned in it; proved his charges; and received the thanks of government. The amount embezzled was three lacs of pagodas, of which one lac and twenty thousand were actually recovered. In 1808-9, he was entrusted by government with a commission to endeavour to reconcile the misunderstandings which then prevailed in Travancore, but he was prevented from acting, by the breaking out of the insurrection, while he was upon his journey to that province. On the termination of the insurrection, he was again ordered to Travancore, to receive charge of the Residency from Col. Macauley; but that officer having withdrawn his resignation, he was employed as a Commissioner to investigate charges of abuses in the factory at Anjengo. He had the entire management of the district of Poodoocottah for a period of twelve years, during the minority of the Rajah Tondiman Behauder, and by the manner in which he executed this trust, he secured the affectionate gratitude of the young chief. But the value of Col. Blackburne's services is not to be estimated merely by the particular duties on which he was employed, but by the whole tenor of his public life. During the long course of twenty-two years, that he was Resident at Tanjore, his judicious, temperate, and upright conduct, secured the confidence of the different branches of the royal family, and tended mainly to attach the great body of the Rajah's followers, and of the people, to our government, and to impress them with respect for the national character.

(Signed) "THOMAS MUNRO."

"The Board, under date the 3d Dec. last, recorded their regret that L.-Col. Blackburne should be under the necessity of relinquishing his situation at Tanjore, where they had still hoped to have the benefit of his experience and his services. Concurring entirely in the sentiments expressed in the foregoing minute, and considering the Lieutenant-Colonel's honourable and useful career of service under this government, to claim for him the tribute of its acknowledgments, the Board will have great satisfaction in submitting to the Hon. Court the high sense which they entertain of his conduct on various important occasions, during a residence of thirty-five years in India, including a ministry of twenty-two years as British Agent at the court of the Rajah of Tanjore; and they trust, that their estimation of his merits will receive the stamp of the confirmation of the Hon. the Court of Directors."

LIEUT.-COLONEL COMMANDANT JAMES LIMOND.

(Madras Establishment.)

IN 1792, this officer was nominated a Cadet for the artillery corps. He sailed from England in June 1794, and arrived in India in Feb. 1795. He was appointed Lieutenant fireworker, 24th Sept. 1793; promoted to Lieutenant, 28th Sept. 1797; to Captain-Lieutenant, 14th June 1801; to Captain of a company, 21st Sept. 1804; to

Major, by brevet, 4th June 1813, and regimentally, 21st Oct. 1814; to Lieutenant-Colonel, 13th May 1821, and to Lieutenant-Colonel Commandant, 26th July, 1824.

In 1797, he was first detached from the artillery head-quarters, on service to Ceylon: he was Adjutant to the artillery at Trincomallee, and in that situation perfected the greatest part of H. M.'s 80th reg. of foot in artillery exercise. He returned to the coast towards the end of 1798, and was, unsolicited, appointed to command the horse artillery attached to H. M.'s 19th dragoons, preparing for the Mysore war. He was at the battle of Malavilly, siege of Seringapatam, and accompanied Gen. Floyd's detachment to Sedaseer, to bring up the Bombay army to the siege, and also Gen. Brown's detachment from Coimbetoor; and was present in occasional skirmishes during the war.

In 1800, an expedition was arranged to proceed against Manilla, and for this service, Lieut. Limond was expressly ordered, by the Commander-in-Chief: it was, however, countermanded, and at the close of the same year, the expedition to Egypt was directed: on this service, Lieut. Limond was also ordered*, and was on the artillery staff with the Indian force, under General Baird. While absent from India on this expedition, he was appointed Adjutant to the 1st batt. of Madras artillery.

In 1802, Capt. Limond returned to India, and in the same year was ordered into the field for the Mahratta war. He joined the army under Gen. Stuart on the Toombuddra, and was detached from the grand army, in command of the artillery, with a detachment under Col. Irton, which was sent on a special service, to secure the succession of the present Nizam, Secunder Jah, on the expected death of his father. The detachment arrived at the Hyderabad capital, at

* It may here be noticed, that the Company's ship Rockingham, in which, with the artillery, this officer embarked, struck with great violence on a rock in the Red Sea, when she immediately made 9 feet water an hour, and which, with excellent chain-pumps, required the united exertions of every officer and man on board to keep under, until her arrival in Judda harbour; when the troops removed to another ship, and sailed for the rendezvous at Kossier.

the most auspicious moment, and but for its seasonable presence, a revolution would have been attempted in favour of the second son: the guns were brought up to the gates, to blow them open, and the troops in column, in readiness to advance, when the garrison, seeing these preparations, opened the gates; the force proceeded direct to the palace, and the ceremony of placing his Highness on the musnud was performed. The force, however, had to remain in the palace gardens for nearly a month, until the government, under the new prince, was established.

After the battle of Assaye, an express was received by the Hyderabad resident, from Gen. Wellesley, calling for every artilleryman that could be procured. In 24 hours, Capt. Limond marched with the artillery, having also under his command, 2 companies of infantry, a detail of the Nizam's troops, and in charge of 13 lacs of rupees, for the use of the army. After a march, which was effected with a degree of celerity beyond expectation, he joined Gen. Wellesley's army under the fortress of Gawilghur, and had the melancholy satisfaction, on entering the camp, of seeing the storming party advancing up the hill to the storm of the place.

The army now proceeded after the Boonslah towards Nagpoor, but on the second day's march the vakeels (ambassadors) from that prince, came into camp, and a treaty of peace was concluded. Not long after this, Scindia* sent his vakeels, when Gen. Wellesley had

---

* The following picture of this turbulent leader is not without interest:—

"As we passed back round the fort, we were fortunate enough to meet Scindia returning from the chase, surrounded by all his chiefs, and preceded or followed by about 700 horse. Discharges of cannon announced his approach, and a few light scattered parties of spearmen were marching before the main body. We stopped our elephants just on one side of a narrow part of the road, where the Rajah and chiefs, with his immediate escort, must pass.

"First came loose light-armed horse, either in the road, or scrambling and leaping on the rude banks and ravines near; then some better clad, with the quilted pashauk, and one in a complete suit of chain armour; then a few elephants, among them the hunting elephant of Scindia, from which he had dismounted. On one small elephant, guided by himself, rode a fine boy, a foundling protegé of Scindia, called the Jungle Rajah. Then came, slowly prancing, a host of fierce, haughty chieftains, on fine horses, showily caparisoned; they darted forward, and all took their proud stand behind and around us, planting their long

also the gratification of concluding a favourable peace with that powerful prince.

The army having wintered in a standing camp, in the Lowghur valley, again took the field under Col. Wallace, for the reduction of the strong forts belonging to Holkar, in Candeish: Captain Limond was present with this force during the whole of its operations, and at the sieges of the strong forts of Chandore and Gaulnah.

So early as this year, 1805, Capt. Limond commanded the artillery with a light force, under Col. Doveton, in pursuit of a body of 20,000 Pindarries, of the same hordes that called for the decided measures of Lord Hastings in 1817: on this occasion the force saved the opulent city of Omrawatty from being plundered and destroyed, the Pindarries having nearly forced the strong barricades of the city, when the British approached it. The wonderful celerity of the Pindarries in movement was proved in this pursuit; the British force was com-

---

lances on the earth, and reining up their eager steeds, to see, I suppose, our salaam. Next in a common native palkee, its canopy crimson, and not adorned, came Scindia himself: he was plainly dressed, with a reddish turban, and a shawl over his vest, and lay reclined, smoking a small gilt or golden calean. We stood up in our howdah, and bowed; he half rose in his palkee, and salaamed rather in a courteous manner. At this there was a loud cry of all his followers near, who sung out his titles, and the honour he had done us, &c.; and all salaamed themselves profoundly.

" I looked down on the chiefs under us, and saw that they eyed us most haughtily, which very much increased the effect they would otherwise have produced. They were armed with lance, scymitar, and shield, creese and pistol; wore, some shawls, some tissues, some plain muslin, or cotton; were all much wrapped in clothing, and wore, almost all, a large fold of muslin, tied over the turban top, which they fasten under the chin, and which, strange as it may sound to those who have never seen it, looks *warlike*, and is a very important defence to the sides of the neck. How is it that we can have a heart-stirring sort of pleasure in gazing on brave and armed men, though we know them to be fierce, lawless, and cruel—though we know stern ambition to be the chief feature of many warriors, who, from the cradle to the grave, seek only fame, and to which, in such as I write of, is added avarice the most pitiless? I cannot tell, but I recollect often before, in my life, being thus moved. Once, especially, I stood over a gateway in France, as a prisoner, and saw file in several squadrons of *gens d'armerie d'élite*, returning from the fatal field of Leipsic. They were fine, noble looking men, with warlike helmets of steel and brass, and drooping plumes of black horse hair; belts handsome and broad, heavy swords—were many of them decorated with the cross of the Legion of Honour. Their trumpets flourished, and I felt my heart throb with an admiring delight, which found relief only in an involuntary tear. What an inconsistent riddle is the human heart!"—See *Sketches of India, written by an officer, for Fireside Travellers at Home,* p. 260, 264.

posed of the cavalry, the flank companies of the corps formed into a light battalion, and a brigade of well-equipped artillery. A month's pursuit forced the Pindarries to disperse through the Gawilghur range of hills; but although the British marched every day from morning to night, they invariably kept the distance of a village in advance.

Captain Limond remained in the field in the Mahratta country until 1806, having been under a tent since the end of 1802. On the return of the troops to garrison, Captain Limond was appointed Commissary of ordnance in Malabar and Canara. In 1810, he was ordered in charge of the battering train on the expedition against the Isle of France, and was present at the surrender of Port Louis.

On his return to Madras, he was selected by the Com.-in-Chief, Sir S. Auchmuty*, to conduct the arrangement and embarkation of the ordnance equipment for the Java expedition. On this service he was appointed Aid-de-camp to the Commander-in-Chief, and Chief Commissary of ordnance to the expedition. He was present at the battle of Weltevreeden, capture of Cornelis, surrender of Fort Sodowick and Souraboya, and different other affairs. On the final reduction of Java, he was appointed Chief Commissary of ordnance, and had the arrangement of the whole department on the island and its dependencies; and on his return to India, a general order was issued by the Governor in Council, from which the following is an extract:—

"The Hon. the Governor in Council deems it incumbent to express, at the same time, his favourable sentiments on the zeal, correctness, and ability, with which Capt. Limond has performed the important duties of his office, and on the services rendered to this government by that officer."

The Rajah of Palembang having inhumanly and treacherously murdered the whole members of a Dutch factory, in his capital, an expedition was formed under the commander of the forces, Gen. Gillespie, and Major Limond was ordered by that gallant officer, to accompany the

* Services, Royal Military Calendar, vol. ii. p. 263-93, 3d edit.

force in command of the artillery. The features of this expedition were of no common nature, having, in armed and flat-bottomed boats, to ascend a noble river, defended with most formidable batteries and fire-rafts. The name of Gillespie was in itself a host: the expedition succeeded in every thing, but the capture of the immense treasures, which were removed from the Krattan, just before the troops got up to it: they had even the mortification to see the war prows, deep laden with the treasure, proceed up the river with a rapidity that set pursuit at defiance. This immense treasure, in specie, reputed to be 10,000,000 of Spanish dollars, was buried at a place up the river, known only to the Rajah and his eldest son, the prince Pangerang Rattoo, and it was confidently asserted, that 200 men employed in burying the treasure, were immediately after murdered, to preserve the secret.

On the return of this officer to the coast, he was appointed to command the artillery, with the Hyderabad subsidiary force. In 1816, his health obliged him to proceed to sea, and ultimately, in 1817, to repair on sick furlough to England. Having returned to his duty in 1820, he remained in command of his corps, the 1st batt. of artillery, until 1822, when the Governor in Council appointed him to the responsible office of Principal Commissary of ordnance in charge of the arsenal at Madras. Being now (1826) senior officer of the corps in India, he has the honour to fill the office of Commandant of Madras artillery.

MAJOR GEORGE M. STEUART.

(Madras Establishment.)

This officer was appointed a Cadet of infantry, on the Madras establishment, in 1802: early in 1803, he embarked for India, and arrived at Madras in June. He joined the cadet company at Trippassore, and remained there till the end of the year: he was promoted to Lieut., 16th Nov. 1803, and joined the 1st batt. 1st regt. N. I.

at Madras. In 1804, he served with five companies of his corps, (one of which he commanded,) with Col. Moneypenny's detachment, against the Poligars in the Chitore country. In 1806, the 1st regt. was stationed at Velore. Early in that year, four companies were ordered on detachment to Chitore, and were directed to parade at three o'clock in the morning, and to commence their march at four. Few of the men, and none of the Native officers, made their appearance before 7 o'clock; the commanding officer in consequence placed several of the Native officers in arrest, but on their making some excuse, they were released at the end of the first day's march: it was afterwards ascertained that they had been employed the whole of the preceding night in organizing their plans for the destruction of all their European officers, and that those concerned in the plot had taken a solemn oath to support their comrades at Velore, where the insurrection was to commence. On the 11th July following, reports were brought to Chitore, that the sepoys had killed all the Europeans in the garrison of Velore. This naturally excited a considerable degree of anxiety and alarm in the European community at Chitore, and Lieut. Steuart volunteered his services to ride over to Velore, and ascertain the truth of these reports. The commanding officer approving of this proposal, he proceeded there, and found that the 2d batt. 23d reg., with the 6 companies of the 1st regiment, had thrown off their allegiance* to the British government

* The following interesting remarks on these events are from a Biographical Memoir of the late Maj.-Gen. Sir R. R. Gillespie, K. C. B.

It is, beside, our purpose here to enter into a minute detail of the various causes which combined in producing the insurrection and catastrophe that now took place; but no doubt can be entertained, that the alterations in the dress of the Native troops were no more than a mere pretext for the discontent and mutiny. Certain it is, that the business had a much deeper foundation, and a more extended line of operations, than appeared at the time; for though the military regulations might have been, in some degree, calculated to excite fears in the prejudiced minds of the Natives, who naturally felt apprehensions of further innovations, civil and religious, still these jealousies were nothing more than convenient matter, upon which the designing were enabled to act, and convert to another object. The sepoys and the lower classes of the people were only instruments in the hands of crafty, ambitious, and intriguing men, who, in their hatred of the English, hoped by this opportunity to suc-

(having been instigated to do so by the sons of Tippoo, who were confined there), and endeavoured in the middle of the night to murder all the

ceed at once in annihilating our dominion in that quarter. With this view, it was resolved, by a general massacre, at the same time to distract the attention and to render the efforts of the Europeans of no avail, by a rising at once in different places, waiting for the success of that at Velore, as the signal to spread the work of carnage and desolation through the three presidencies: the scheme was planned upon a scale so extended, and with such a superiority of skill in the direction, as to prove clearly that it had been long in contemplation, and that it was under the management of those, who to great intellect and inveterate malignity, added the powerful means of riches and numbers. Velore was pitched upon as the centre of operations, on account of its local advantages, and because it afforded a rallying point, in being the spot selected by our government for the residence of the sons of Tippoo. From the turbulent state of the Native chiefs, and the natural jealousy of foreigners, it was anticipated by the authors of this formidable conspiracy, that the whole mass of population would be so favourable to the insurgents, as to withhold all assistance from the objects of their fury.

This was the critical period when the Lieut.-Col. (the late M.-Gen. Sir R. R. Gillespie) took the command at Arcot, where he learned, with great satisfaction, that his old companion in arms, Col. Fancourt, with whom he had served in St. Domingo, under Gen. Simcoe, was at the head of the neighbouring garrison of Velore. On the 9th July, Col. Gillespie had appointed to dine with his friend and family; but just as he mounted his horse for the purpose, some letters arrived from the government, which requiring immediate answers, compelled him to relinquish his visit, and to send an apology to Col. Fancourt for his unavoidable absence. There was a visible interposition of Divine Providence in this disappointment, since, had it not been for the imperative circumstance of duty which detained him at Arcot, Col. Gillespie would, in all probability, have shared the melancholy catastrophe of his brave and unfortunate acquaintance. The troops which at this time garrisoned Velore, were six companies of the 1st batt. 1st reg. N. I. and four complete companies of H. M. 69th regiment.

The confederates intended that all who were brought to join in the insurrection should act upon a preconcerted plan, which had been digested and privately circulated by some of the Marawa chiefs; and in connexion with them were some Frenchmen disguised as Fakeers, who went about the country inveighing every where against the English, as robbers and tyrants. Unhappily, the splendour which the sons of Tippoo were enabled by our liberality to keep up, and the liberty which they enjoyed of holding an intercourse with a continual influx of strangers, contributed to strengthen the conspiracy, and facilitate the desperate resolution of those who formed it. They were, however, as it seemed, too precipitate, and the very day that Col. Gillespie was to have dined with his friend, happened to be the one which the insurgents pitched upon as the most opportune for their diabolical purpose, encouraged thereto, in all likelihood, by the unsuspecting deportment of our officers, and the extreme mildness of the government. It was, indeed, to many valuable men, a fatal supineness; for, while they were enjoying, in complete confidence, social harmony, neither apprehensive of evil designs in others, nor meditating oppression themselves, the murderers plot was ripening into action. About 2 o'clock in the morning of the 10th

Europeans: they had partly succeeded in this, having killed 15 officers of the different regiments, about 80 men of H. M.'s 69th, and wounded

July, just as the moon had risen above the horizon, the European barracks at Velore were silently surrounded, and a most destructive fire was poured in at every door and window from musketry, and a six-pounder, upon the poor defenceless soldiers, who being taken by surprise, fell in heaps. At the same moment, the European soldiers with those on the main guard, and even the sick in the hospital, were inhumanly butchered; after which the assassins hastened to the houses of the officers, where they put to death all who fell into their hands. Col. M'Kerras, who commanded one of the battalions, was shot while haranguing his men on the parade-ground; and Col. Faucourt fell in like manner, as he was proceeding to the main guard. Lieut. Ely, of the 69th, with his infant son in his arms, was bayoneted in the presence of his wife; and this scene of barbarity continued till about 7 o'clock, when two officers and a surgeon, whose quarters were near to the European barracks, contrived to get in, and take the command of the remains of the four companies. These few men made a sally from the barracks, and gained possession of the six-pounder: they fought their way desperately through their assailants, till they succeeded in reaching the gateway, on the top of which Serjeant Brodie, with his European guard, continued most gallantly to resist the whole body of the insurgents.

Such was the state of things at Velore, when Lieut-Col. Gillespie, totally ignorant of the confusion that raged there, mounted his horse at six o'clock in the morning, with the intention of riding over to breakfast. At the instant he was about to set out, the dismal tidings came of the tragic fate of his friend, and the horrors that were still prevailing. No time was to be lost; and, therefore, collecting immediately about a troop of the 19th dragoons, and ordering the galloper guns to follow with all possible speed, he hastened forward with the utmost eagerness. So anxious indeed, was he to reach the place, that he was considerably in advance of his men all the way; and on his appearance, Serjeant Brodie, who had served with him in St. Domingo, instantly recognized him, and turning to his drooping comrades, he exclaimed, "If Col. Gillespie be alive, he is now at the head of the 19th dragoons, and God Almighty has sent him from the West Indies, to save our lives in the East!" It was, indeed, in all respects, such a display of Divine goodness, as could hardly fail to kindle, in the most thoughtless mind, a ray of devotional gratitude, while hope was painting out a prospect of deliverance. Urged on by the noblest of all motives, that of saving his fellow-creatures, the Colonel, regardless of his own safety, and in the face of a furious fire, poured upon him from the walls, pushed towards the bastion, where a chain, formed of the soldiers' belts, being let down by the serjeant, the latter had the indescribable satisfaction of welcoming a leader, from whom he knew every thing might be expected that energy and perseverance could accomplish. Immediately, on assuming the command, the Lieut.-Col. formed the resolution of charging the mutineers with the bayonet; which he carried into effect, and thus kept them till the arrival of the galloper guns, when orders were given to blow open the gate, which, being promptly done by the dragoons, a short, but severe conflict ensued. The sepoys were encouraged to make a severe stand by their officers, but after losing about 600, who were cut in pieces on the spot, the rest fled in all directions. A considerable number escaped through the sally-port; but many hun-

many others; the dead were lying in heaps on the parade. The 19th dragoons having arrived from Arcot, under the command of the gallant Col. Gillespie, blew open the gates with their galloper guns, entered sword in hand, and cut up several hundreds of the sepoys. The 1st reg. had four officers killed and one wounded; three of them were murdered with the most savage barbarity. Finding they could make no resistance against such numbers, they hid themselves in a bath. The sepoys, upon discovering their retreat, first fired at, then rushed forward and bayoneted them, and afterwards collected straw and other combustibles, and set fire to them; when found, they were so disfigured, it was impossible to distinguish one from the other. Lieut. Steuart gallopped back to Chitore, and gave the commanding officer an account of this melancholy affair, who took immediate steps to prevent a similar occurrence at that station, by taking all the ball ammunition from the men, and keeping a sharp look-out after their motions. It was afterwards ascertained, by a court of inquiry, that the same scene of butchery was to have taken place at Chitore; but the sepoys got alarmed, on hearing the success of the 19th dragoons.

In 1808, Lieut. Steuart was employed, in command of a party, escorting treasure from Masulipatam to Hyderabad. In 1809, he commanded a small field detachment of 100 men, for some months, in the Rajahmundroog jungles, against the plunderers who infested that part of the country, and succeeded in capturing a noted freebooter,

---

dreds were taken in hiding places, and imprisoned. The standard of Tippoo had been hoisted on the palace soon after the dreadful business commenced, which left no doubt of its being projected with the knowledge of the princes. So well assured, indeed, was the Lieut.-Colonel of this fact, that in the first emotions of indignation occasioned by the death of his friend, and the shocking spectacle which presented itself on all sides, he would have consented to the demands of the enraged soldiers, who were bent upon entering the palace. But the entreaties of some persons who had the care of the princes prevailed; and though the Colonel could not be persuaded of their innocence, he condescended to take them under his protection, and sent them soon after with a guard to Madras. Thus it may be truly said, did the prompt and decisive spirit of one man put an end to this dangerous confederacy; for, had the fort remained in the possession of the insurgents but a few days, they were certain of being joined by 50,000 men from Mysore.

with some of his followers. He served the campaign of 1812-13 and 14, in the southern Mahratta and Concan countries, during the greater part of which he commanded the pioneers. At the end of 1814, he accompanied Col. Thompson's detachment going on the expedition to Candy, in Ceylon, attached to the pioneers, but after marching as far as Trichinopoly, the force was recalled to Madras; when finding his constitution a good deal impaired, from the fatigues he had undergone with the pioneers, in the Mahratta country, he went to Europe on sick certificate.

On the 19th of Jan. 1816, he was promoted to Capt.-Lieutenant, and on the 28th Nov. 1817, to a company. He returned to India in 1817, and served the Mahratta campaign of 1817-18, with the 1st division of the army of the Deccan, attached to the rifle corps. On the 14th Jan. 1818, the Com.-in-Chief nominated him to act as Major of brigade to the 1st infantry brigade, which situation he held till the army of the Deccan was broken up, when he was appointed Brigade Major to the troops forming his Excellency's escort. He accompanied Sir Thomas Hislop* over land to Bombay: he thence went to Madras by sea, and arrived there in Sept. 1818, where he was ordered to remain, and recruit for the rifle corps.

In Jan. 1819, six extra battalions were ordered to be raised, to be commanded each by a captain, with an European adjutant. The Com.-in-Chief, Sir Thomas Hislop, nominated Capt. Steuart to the command of the 2d extra battalion, to be embodied at Trichinopoly, to which place he immediately proceeded, and in the short space of four months and six days, he completed his corps to 900 men, for which he received the thanks of the Com.-in-Chief: in four months after, the battalion was reviewed by Gen. Dyce†, commanding the southern division of the army, who was much pleased with its appearance and performance. Shortly after, the following order was published to the army :—

" The Com.-in-Chief performs a gratifying duty in expressing his approba-

* Services, Royal Mil. Cal. vol. ii. p. 333-40, 3d edit.   † Services, vol. ii. p. 283-8.

tion in general orders, of the distinguished zeal and unremitting attention evinced by Captain G. M. Steuart, commanding 2nd, Captain J. Nixon, commanding 4th, and Captain Baker, commanding 5th extra battalions. These officers have, in a few months, recruited and disciplined their respective battalions in so satisfactory a manner, as to call forth the unqualified praise of officers commanding divisions, who have inspected and reported to head-quarters, that the interior economy, as well as precision in the field movements of those battalions, is not inferior to old and long established corps."

Capt. Steuart's battalion being ordered to Travancore, arrived at Quilon in June 1821, without losing a single man by desertion: he there received the thanks of the new Com.-in-Chief, as expressed in the following letter to the officer commanding at Travancore, from the Deputy-Adjutant-General :—

"Sir,—I have the honour to convey to you, by order of the Com.-in-Chief, the observations which his Excellency has made on the perusal of the confidential report, made by M.-Gen. Dyce, at the review of the 2nd extra battalion, previous to that corps being removed to Travancore. It is particularly gratifying to his Excellency Sir Alexander Campbell, K.C.B., to have received such a favourable report of the discipline and interior economy of this young corps. Captain Steuart's zeal and abilities must have been very judiciously directed in forming the battalion, and the report made by the reviewing general of the zeal and alacrity with which the duties were carried on by the adjutant, during the absence of Capt. Steuart on leave, is very creditable to Lieutenant Agnew, and gives a fair prospect of that young officer proving an ornament to his profession. His Excellency the Com.-in-Chief requests you will be pleased to communicate his thanks and applause to Capt. G. M. Steuart and Lieutenant Agnew."

Towards the end of 1821, the country being in a very quiet state, there was no further occasion for the services of these extra corps, and orders were received to draft volunteers to other regiments, and to discharge the rest: this was done, and Captain Steuart marched with the volunteers for his own corps, 2d batt. 1st reg. to Trichinopoly, and joined it in Jan. 1822, and shortly after, being the senior officer present, he obtained the command.

In March 1823, he was ordered to return to the Travancore country, in command of the 2d batt. 1st reg., and one company of European artillery, and arrived with his detachment at Quilon, on the 16th of April. In June, he was appointed by the governor, Sir Thomas Munro*, to the situation of Secretary to the clothing-board at Madras, which he held till promoted to a Majority, 14th October 1823, when he obtained the command of the 1st. batt. 1st reg., then at Madras. On the new organization of the army in May 1824, he was appointed Major of the 17th reg. N. I. (late 2d batt. 1st reg.) which he again joined in Travancore, and took the command.

LIEUT.-COL. COMMANDANT JOHN GREENSTREET.

(Bengal Establishment.)

This officer was appointed Ensign in the Bengal army, 22d Nov. 1796; Lieut., 30th Oct. 1797; Captain-Lieut., 29th Oct. 1804; Captain, 10th Jan. 1805; Major, 25th April 1810; Lieut.-Col., 25th Jan. 1815; and Lieut.-Col. Commandant, 2d May 1824.

He was present at the skirmish before Coel, 29th Aug. 1803; at the siege and capture of Allyghur, 4th Sept. 1803; at the battle of Delhi, 11th Sept. 1803; the storming the heights and ravines of Agra on the 10th †, and up to its surrender on the 18th October

---

* Services in this volume.

† An incident occurred on this day tending to illustrate the character of the Native soldiery, and that of the illustrious commander who so well knew how to appreciate and cherish their attachments and professional emulation.

At the attack of the ravines under the walls of Agra, the life of Col. Worsley (services, vol. i. p. 130-9) may be said to have been saved, under Providence, by the courage and fidelity of a non-commissioned officer.

On ascending a height on which was posted a party of the enemy, whom we almost surprised just at the break of day, having for a moment looked back, calling to the leading section to push forward, Col. Worsley observed, in turning round again, an officer of the enemy with his tulwar (broad-sword) uplifted, in the act of advancing to make a blow at him: on which he directed the attention of a havildar, who was by his side, who instantly charged the enemy with his pike, on which he received the stroke of the sword, and at the same time, a severe wound in the hand of his extended arm, by which he lost the use of three fingers. We took a stand of colours from the enemy, and Col. Worsley sent them

1803; at the battle of Laswarree, 1st Nov. 1803; battle of Deeg, 13th Nov. 1804; and siege and taking of Deeg, 25th Dec. 1804; and at the siege of Bhurtpoor. He also served in the Nepaul campaign of 1814-15, to its conclusion at Muckwanpoor, where he was in command of the 2d battalion 15th regiment N. I.

At the siege and capture of the fortress of Hattrass*, he com-

the next day to the Com.-in Chief, Lord Lake, by the hands of the havildar, with a note to the Adjutant-General respecting his good conduct.

The Com.-in-Chief expressed himself much pleased at the opportunity of noticing such behaviour, and in the general orders of that day, promoted the havildar to the rank of a commissioned officer.

* The author of a tour through the Upper Provinces of Hindostan, gives the following account of the siege of the fort of Hattrass:—

At the time our troops attacked the fort of Hattrass, it was defended by five hundred pieces of artillery, with an outer fort, in which were twenty immense bastions, surrounded by a ditch ninety feet broad, seventy-five feet deep, and containing six feet of water.

The town is a rectangular work, about seven hundred and fifty yards from the fort. In form it is nearly square, five hundred by four hundred and eighty yards, with nine circular bastions, and a pretty deep ditch.

The attack was made upon the fort at half-past eleven o'clock at night, March 2d, 1817. On the preceding evening all our batteries were advanced within a hundred yards of the glacis, and by sun-rise next morning, we had forty-three pieces of heavy cannon ready to bear upon it. The General who commanded, gave the Rajah until nine o'clock, to decide whether he would stand a siege or surrender. He chose the former. Accordingly, at the hour appointed, all our batteries opened, and kept up an incessant firing until five o'clock the next evening; at which time one of the shells fell upon his principal magazine, containing six thousand maunds[1] of gunpowder, and caused a terrible explosion. It was the most awful and beautiful scene that could be imagined: the earth trembled as if shaken by an earthquake. This was immediately followed by a stunning crash, which even deadened the sound of our batteries. The fort was instantly enveloped in a thick black cloud, which gradually rose in the form of a regular and beautiful tree, growing rapidly, yet majestically out of the ground, at the same time preserving its exact proportions. The panic caused by this occurrence it is impossible to describe, each party supposing that the other had sprung a mine. All was, for a moment, silent horror and breathless expectation! The firing, which had been kept up without intermission for eight hours, ceased as if by magic. Every one seemed transfixed to the spot, too much astonished to speak; for lo! they were in total darkness! which continued for more than eleven minutes. This so sudden change from a fine clear sky, with the sun shining forth in all its splendour, to impenetrable darkness, was sufficient to strike the firmest mind with dread. The darkness subsided by degrees, and our people soon discovered what had been the cause; upon which, our batteries again

[1] A maund is 80 lbs. weight.

manded the 2d batt. 15th reg. N. I.; and at the siege and capture of Asseerghur, he served as Brigadier, being detached to aid in the operations with fifteen companies of the 15th reg., a squadron of cavalry and train of artillery from the Nagpoor field force.

This officer acted as Adjutant to the 1st batt. 15th reg. in the battles of Allyghur, Delhi, Agra, and Laswarree, and was Adjutant and Quarter-Master to a brigade in the battle of Deeg, in which latter engagement his horse was shot under him.

LIEUT.-COL. COMMANDANT JOHN L. RICHARDSON.
(Bengal Establishment.)

In 1780, this officer was appointed a Cadet on the military establishment at Bengal. He arrived at Madras the 10th Jan. 1781, where the Bengal and Madras cadets being formed into a cadet company, he carried arms till the May following, when, with the rest of the gentlemen appointed to Bengal, he proceeded to Calcutta.

About the latter end of 1782, being desirous of actual service, he volunteered and proceeded to join the Bengal detachment, under Col. Pearce*, serving in the Carnatic, and was present at the siege and battle of Cudalore, in 1783. On peace being concluded, he re-

---

opened with redoubled vigour, the Rajah's answering them feebly, and only now and then, from which it appeared evident, that there was much confusion within the fort. We kept it up, however, until eleven o'clock, when the Rajah, being fairly burnt out, contrived with two hundred of his best horsemen to effect his escape. They were all, as we afterwards learned, himself not excepted, clad in chain armour. The destruction occasioned by the explosion of the magazine in the fort was dreadful; scarcely a man or animal within, but was wounded by it, and the greater part of the buildings were laid in ruins. The Rajah and his party made a dash through a picquet of the 8th dragoons, and a regiment of Rohilla horsemen, whose swords made no impression. During the night there had been just sufficient moonlight to distinguish the fort, over which our shells were seen to mount in air, then rolling over each other like so many balls of fire, eight or nine at a time, they sunk majestically down. It was afterwards understood that the Rajah, Diah Ram, had taken refuge with the Bhurtpoor Rajah, another Jaut chief, to whom he was nearly related.

* Services, vol. ii. p. 247-50.

turned over land with the detachment to Bengal, where, soon after his arrival, the corps to which he belonged was employed in various services against outlaws and rebellious Zemindars, till the Mahratta war broke out, the latter end of 1802, during which the corps was detached under Col. Burn*, and in the campaign of 1804-5, defended the city of Delhi against the combined forces of Holkar and the Mahrattas; after which, the corps was sent to drive the Seiks † out of the Dooaub, which they had entered, and were burning and plundering during the siege of Delhi. On this service, it was their good fortune to stop the progress of Holkar, by the defence of Shamlie, where, being surrounded by the enemy, they held out, although in the utmost distress for provisions, till the arrival of Lord Lake with the reserve from the main army, whom they accompanied in pursuit of Holkar, as far as Meerat; whence they were again detached with augmented force, and obliged Ameer Khan to retire from Bundlecund; and having driven the Seiks out of the Dooaub, crossed the Jumna, and punished them by taking several of their principal places, particularly the city of Karnaul; after which the corps joined the main army, with which it continued till the end of the war.

During the course of L.-Col. Richardson's services, he was twice compelled to repair to Europe for the recovery of his health: at length, being promoted to the command of a regiment in 1823, he returned to England.

* Services, vol. ii. p. 495-517.

† The Seiks now occupy by far the most valuable part of that extensive territory, which constituted the Mogul empire in its proudest days. From latitude 28° 40' to 32° N., and even further; they inhabit the whole of that extensive and fertile country, which is watered by the five branches of the Indus, a part of the province of Multau, and almost all that tract of country which lies between the Jumna and the Sutlej; touching the territories of the king of Cabul on the one side, and those of the English on the other. Their importance in the population of India, therefore, is sufficiently obvious. If a conqueror, indeed, had the choice of a spot in which he might establish an empire which might domineer over the whole of India, from the Himmalaya mountains to the Sacred Bridge, he would probably select the very ground which is now covered by the Seiks. When the productive qualities of the soil, and the health and strength of the inhabitants are taken into account, there is, probably, no portion of India which deserves to be compared with it.—See *Ed. Rev.* vol. 21.

The following are the dates of this officer's commissions: Ensign, Jan. 1781; Lieutenant, Aug. 1781; brevet Captain, in 1796; regimental Captain, in 1800; Major, in 1807; Lieut.-Colonel, in 1812; and Lieut.-Colonel Commandant, in 1823.

LIEUTENANT-COLONEL T. A. S. AHMUTY.
(Madras Establishment.)

This officer arrived at Madras the 9th Jan. 1797, and was appointed to a detachment of the 2d batt. 3d N. I., under the command of the late L.-Col. Oram, stationed at Sankledroog, and embarked with that corps, under the command of L.-Col. Oram, in the proposed expedition against Manilla, which was recalled in consequence of the hostile preparations made by the late Tippoo Sultaun against the British possessions, and which led to the Mysore war. He served with the late Col. Read's* force during the war, till the capture of Seringapatam, in command of a detachment of Europeans, composed

* In the campaign of 1799, L.-Col. Read being invested by the Marquess Wellesley with the same extensive powers which had been delegated to him by the Marquess Cornwallis, in the former war, was appointed to superintend and collect the revenues of such of the enemy's districts, as might, in the course of the campaign, submit to the British power. In this manner Col. Read had been so successfully employed, after the capture of Bangalore in 1791, that before the peace of 1792, he had actually paid into the Company's treasury, a sum not less than one lac of pagodas, collected in districts between Bangalore and the Carnatic, from which, in their then unsettled state, little or nothing was to have been expected. This proof of his zeal and ability, added to the practical knowledge he had acquired in matters of revenue since that period, pointed him out as the fittest person that could be selected for so important a duty. Although the rapidity of the conquest of Mysore rendered Col. Read's labours, in the settlement and collection of revenues unnecessary, yet they proved highly serviceable in the still more essential object, of collecting supplies of grain and cattle for the army. He had delivered to L.-Gen. Harris, before he entered Mysore, above one month's allowance of rice, at half a seer per day, for 30,000 fighting men, besides 1,500 bullocks, laden with rice and other grain, sufficient for the maintenance of 40,000 followers, for one month. Exclusive of this immediate supply, he had also entered into engagements, on the part of government, with the head Brinjarries, for the delivery of 52,377 bullock loads of grain, which they were to bring, at stated periods, into the Bara-mahal;

of details of H. M.'s regiments, and was at the taking of several hill forts in Mysore, and wounded at the storm of Sooligheri. In 1800, by the augmentation and re-organization of the Madras army, he was removed to the 1st-8th N. I., commanded by L.-Col. P. Desse, and served with the force against the late Doondia Waugh. In 1801, he repaired to England on sick certificate, and returned to India in 1804. He was appointed, in 1805, Quarter-Master of brigade to the Travancore subsidiary force, and Assistant Quarter-Master-General to that force during the war in Travancore, and was in the actions of the 15th and 25th Jan. and 21st Feb. 1809, the latter the storming of the enemy's batteries.

In May 1810, he was appointed Store-keeper and Paymaster to the Goa subsidiary force, and on that force being withdrawn, in 1813, he was appointed Paymaster to the Mysore division, which he vacated in consequence of his promotion to a Majority, in the 1st-8th reg. This corps he commanded, with the exception of a few months, till March 1819, when he was promoted to L.-Col., and appointed to raise the 1st-25th reg., which was completed and re-

and which, added to the depôts at Coorga and Kisnagheri, would have formed so ample a supply, as to leave no apprehension of any scarcity of grain, even if the war had been prolonged to a second campaign.

Whilst the Brinjarries were drawing towards the Bara-mahal from the most remote parts of the Deccan, L.-Col. Read was employed in reducing the country to the northward of Ryacotah. He took the strong hill fort of Sooligheri by storm, and Pedanaigdurgum, another hill fort, by capitulation. His operations were intended to have embraced a wide range, when the more urgent service of conveying to the army the large supplies provided in the Bara-mahal, made it necessary for him to change the direction of his march, and to proceed to the vicinity of Covriporam, for the purpose of collecting at that place, the numerous Brinjarries, and their supplies, intended for the army.

L.-Col. Read having summoned the fort of Covriporam, situated at the entrance of the pass of that name, it surrendered to him without resistance, on 22d of April. Here he collected his supplies for the army, and leaving them under the protection of the fort, proceeded with his detachment to clear the pass, which proved a most arduous service. For, although he marched from Covriporam on the 23d, he did not reach Marenhully, or the head of the pass, until the 27th April; and with every exertion which he could make, it was the 6th May before the supplies got through the pass. On the 13th May, L.-Col. Read arrived with his convoy at Seringapatam.—See M.-Gen. Beatson's *View of the Origin and Conduct of the War with Tippoo Sultaun.*

viewed in a year. In 1821, he was removed to the 1st batt. 1st reg. at Bellary, which he commanded for a few months, previous to his return to England on furlough in Jan. 1823, and retired from the service in 1824.

The following are the dates of this officer's commissions: Ensign, 1796; Lieut., Oct. 1797; Capt., 21st Sept. 1804; Major, Oct. 1813; L.-Col., 28th Feb. 1819.

MAJOR CHARLES MARRIOTT*.
(Madras Establishment.)

This officer, the youngest of six sons, five of whom were in the army or navy, went out a Cadet to Madras, where he landed 3d Dec. 1797. He was appointed Ensign, 12th April 1796; Lieut., 29th Nov. 1797; Adjutant, 19th May 1801; Capt.-Lieut., 26th May 1804; Capt. of a company, 27th June 1804; brevet Major, 4th June 1814; and Major in the regiment, 14th April 1817.

The 26th Dec. 1797, he joined the 1st batt. 1st N. I. at Pondicherry, and was with it at Wallajabad and Madras in 1798. He joined the army proceeding against Seringapatam early in Feb. 1799; and was present with his battalion at the battle of Malavilly, 25th March; at the attack on Tippoo's advanced post, on the 5th and 6th April; and with Gen. Gowdie's brigade and the cavalry, in bringing in Cols. Read and Brown's detachments. He assisted another officer and thirty men, in the surprise, by night, and disarming a lawless band of 500 men, attached to a man called the Jungle Nabob; who was sent prisoner to Seringapatam on the same night. He commanded the light company, which attacked and were beaten off the stockaded village of Sambraney, and obliged to retire till the rest of the corps came up, when the place was carried, and 200

---

* Brother to M.-Gen. Thomas Marriott. Services, p. 39, in this volume.

Mahrattas driven out and put to the sword by 2 troops of cavalry. He afterwards commanded 2 companies at Soopah, on the confines of the Portuguese territory at Goa.

In Jan. 1800, he was appointed to the 2d batt. 5th reg. and joined at Ryacotah. In the same year, he marched into the Coorgh country, and on the ceded districts being made over to the Company, the corps of this officer was the first to take possession of them. On Christmas-day 1800, he was placed with a company in command of a hill fort of Gaujecottah: the 19th Jan. 1801, being ordered out to storm two ghurries, he escaladed one, and killed and wounded 26 of the garrison; he then marched against the other, before daybreak, but the enemy had taken the alarm, and were off.

In May 1801, he was appointed Adjutant of his battalion, and in 1802, was sent with two flank companies to escort treasure from Gooty towards Hyderabad. He joined the army in 1803, collected on the Toombuddra under Gen. Stuart, and marched together with the 2d batt. 10th reg. to Hyderabad. His battalion took possession of the city on the death of the Nizam, and almost every officer of the corps had detachments to camp under Gen. Wellesley, except the Adjutant. In 1804, he was promoted, and in 1806, appointed assistant to his brother, Col. Thomas Marriott, in charge of the Mysore princes. Three months afterwards the mutiny broke out, and this officer was shot in the side whilst addressing the mutineers. In 1807, on his brother's return to England, Major Marriott was confirmed in his charge; and in 1815, he took some of Tippoo's grandchildren round by sea to Bengal, and returned over land.

In Jan. 1816, he received charge of the captive king of Candy and his family. In Dec. 1819, he resigned his appointment, after completing 22 years service; the 15th Jan. 1820, sailed from Madras; landed in England, 27th May following, after an absence of 23 years; and retired from the service, 13th March 1822.

LIEUTENANT-COLONEL JOHN LINDSEY.

(Madras Establishment.)

In 1796, this officer was appointed a Cadet on the Madras establishment; Ensign, 15th Sept. 1797; Lieut., 12th Oct. 1798; Capt., 29th Oct. 1804; Brevet-Major, 4th June 1814; Major of the 24th reg., 19th Feb. 1819; L.-Col. of the 48th reg., 1st May 1824. He was present at the battle of Malavilly and siege of Seringapatam, in 1799, and received the honorary medal for Seringapatam. He was several times employed after the Poligars, and served seven years with the pioneer corps.

MAJOR EDWARD HINDLEY.

(Madras Establishment.)

This officer arrived at Madras as a Cadet of cavalry, 26th July 1801, and was promoted to Cornet, and appointed to the 5th reg. light cavalry, on the 21st July in that year. He joined his regiment in the field in Feb. 1802; and in Feb. 1803, joined M.-Gen. Wellesley's division at Hurreehur, and proceeded to Poona: he was present during the whole of the Mahratta campaign of 1803; at the reduction of the town and fortress of Ahmednugger, 8th Aug.; and at the battle of Assaye, 23d Sept., on which occasion his commanding officer put on record his approbation of his conduct.

Extract from Regimental Orders, by Major Leonard, dated Camp at Assaye, 28th Sept. 1803.

" Cornet Hindley having led on the 3d troop most gallantly to victory on the 23d inst., is appointed to the command of that troop."

Cornet Hindley was present at the battle of Argaum, 29th Nov. 1803; at the siege of Gawilghur, in Dec. following; and was promoted to Lieutenant on the 21st of the latter month.

In 1804, he served in the campaign of the Deccan, with the Poona subsidiary force, under the command of Col. Wallace, and was present at the sieges of Chandore and Gaulna, in Oct. 1804.

In Aug. 1806, he was appointed Adjutant of his regiment. He served in the campaign of 1812, against the southern Mahrattas, and in Nov. 1814, took the field with the Hyderabad subsidiary force, under Col. J. Doveton. He acted as Major of Brigade to the right brigade of cavalry, commanded by Col. Patrick Walker*, during the greater period of the Pindarry war. In June 1816, the 5th regiment of cavalry was transferred from the Hyderabad subsidiary force to the Nagpore subsidiary force, under Col. P. Walker, and this officer's situation of Major of Brigade ceased in consequence, when he was appointed Deputy-Judge-Advocate to the Nagpore subsidiary force, but subsequently Deputy-Paymaster and Postmaster to a division, under the command of Col. H. S. Scott, C.B. † at Nagpore. He was present at the battle of Seetabuldee, on the 26th and 27th Nov. 1817; at the battle on the plains of Nagpore, 16th Dec. 1817; and at the reduction of that city. He was appointed Paymaster to the Nagpore subsidiary force, in March 1818; and attained the brevet of Captain, 8th Jan. 1816. He was appointed Capt. of a troop, 8th May 1819; and promoted to Major, 20th March 1822. In Sept. 1823, he returned to England, on furlough, having completed the regulated period of 22 years actual service in India.

THE LATE LIEUT.-GENERAL CHARLES REYNOLDS.

(Bombay Establishment.)

The general orders by the Bombay government, and the extract of a letter to the Court of Directors, which accompany this statement, bear evidence of this officer's enterprize and merits in their service,

---

* Services, vol. i. p. 425-60. † Services, vol. ii. p. 525-7, and in this volume.

while many surviving friends, who lament his loss, unite in heartfelt testimony to the excellent qualities which distinguished a character combining strength and ardour of mind, with indefatigable perseverance in every duty or pursuit that claimed or attracted his attention; quick discernment of capacity in agents unavoidably required for objects in view—steadiness in attachment—generosity to all beneath his influence—warmth of heart—liberality of sentiment, with a manliness of expression, and conduct which claimed the confidence of his countrymen, as well as the natives of India.

The magnitude of his geographical undertaking is most creditably noticed by his liberal employers, and that eminent leader in similar exertions, Major Rennell; but the difficulties which this feeble sketch had to encounter well deserve consideration. Had his general map of Hindostan appeared at an earlier period, before the late fortunate and well-earned success of British valour laid open that extensive field to minute survey, his accuracy, or even approximation to such accuracy, would have been considered wonderful as the achievement of one man. He had to fight his way through territories which now acknowledge British sway, while others were totally inaccessible to Europeans or any avowed agent;—he had to study the completion of his design by selecting and training natives, qualified in various disguise, to fulfil his instructions, and penetrate where he could by no means advance;—he had to watch their fidelity and progress with anxious vigilance, and munificently to reward every fortunate effort to serve him, which he undeniably did to the exclusion of self-interest. Throughout these regions, to him otherwise inaccessible, British government, or acknowledged influence, now prevails, to the facility of open and deliberate surveys; and had General Reynold's life been prolonged, an interesting map of topographical information, accumulated by him through intricate means, would probably have appeared, and furnished additional proofs of the ardour and intellect which marked his career amidst such obstacles to overcome.

Arriving in India about the age of fourteen, when the rudiments of science are barely attainable under advantages of the most favoured education, he qualified himself for an astonishing attempt, and struck out a path towards its accomplishment, (pronounced by Major Rennell to belong to the true system of geographical research,) not seated amidst extensive libraries, or encouraged by learned instructors, but through the tedious labours of unassisted acquirement.

In fine, the following extracts testify his public merits; and justice to his memory warrants the assertion, that his private friends considered him an ornament to society, of which they will mourn the deprivation till they shall cease to exist:—

Extract of a Letter to the Hon. the Court of Directors, dated 25th Feb. 1807.

Par. 16.—" We take this occasion to advise your Hon. Court, that having had an opportunity of viewing the Map, as drawn out on the largest scale by Col. Reynolds, we have no doubt of the work's being honoured with the approbation of your Hon. Court, and doing credit to the ability and unwearied labour of Col. Reynolds in its construction: neither when the very great scope of this unparelleled undertaking is considered, need perhaps the time required in its completion excite surprise; the main object for appreciation is, whether the work be well performed, as we trust will be admitted, by professional judges more competent to pronounce on its execution and accuracy than we pretend to be; and in that case Col. Reynolds (and from his labours the Presidency of Bombay) will derive the, to him, well-earned reputation of exhibiting the first General Map of India, and of having achieved the most enlarged and important geographical undertaking ever probably attempted by one man. We have also the honour to refer to the general orders we have published on the occasion of Col. Reynolds' embarkation for Europe, as evincing the sense we entertain of the general merits of that officer."

General Order by Government.

" *Bombay Castle, 10th Feb.* 1807.

" Upon the occasion of the return to England of Col. Reynolds, the Governor in Council feels a satisfaction in expressing his very favourable sense of that officer's long and distinguished services. Entering immediately after his arrival in India, in the year 1772, on active service, he continued during the course of the twelve following years in the honourable discharge of his professional duties, including those of an engineer, on the various field operations of that period, against the Mahrattas and Tippoo Sultaun, from the reduction of Broach till the attack on Duboy, in 1780, at which he was wounded; and thereafter, on service with General Goddard, at the reduction of Ahmedabad, the siege of Bassein, and the capture of Arnauld; and on the occasion of that General's memorable retreat from the ghauts to Panwell, at which arduous crisis Col. Reynolds was attached to the rear-guard of that army, and was twice wounded; and having subsequently proceeded, in command of a detachment of six grenadier companies of N. I., to join Brig.-Gen. Mathews on the service of 1783-4, in the province of Canara, had thence the opportunity of bearing a very creditable share in the lengthened and gallant defence of Onore*, which was not given up till the peace of 1784.

" During the next hostilities with Tippoo Sultaun, Col. Reynolds was attached, in the year 1792, to the staff of the late M.-Gen. Hartley†, in the capacity of Quarter-Master-General, and in the confidential charge of the Intelligence Department; his able and useful services in which, gained to this meritorious officer the approbation and thanks of that eminent military commander and accomplished statesman, the late ever-to-be-lamented Marquess Cornwallis.

" Between the years 1784 and 1792, and since the conclusion of the peace of Seringapatam, Col. Reynolds has, in his official station of Surveyor-General, been chiefly engaged, by the extensive surveys of himself and Native assistants, in the sedulous acquisition and arrangement of the most accurate materials for the construction of a General Map of India on the most extensive scale‡, the result of which he is now returning to offer to his honourable employers and to his country, in a work that (to say the least of it) will, for magnitude of conception and extent of geographical information, be, if ever equalled, not easily surpassed.

(Signed)   " FRANCIS WARDEN, Sec. to Government."

* *Vide* services of Major Torriano, vol. ii. p. 117-206. This distinguished veteran, and most amiable character, died in 1825.

† Services, vol. ii. p. 102-17.

‡ A manuscript map, now suspended at the East India House, constructed by this officer from his own surveys: those of many officers employed under him; and from the information of many Natives whom he instructed and sent in all directions to gather information; is on a scale, as to magnitude and filling up, rarely equalled by the labours of any individual. It is, indeed, a splendid monument of his industry, science, and taste.

CAPTAIN THOMAS MARTIN*.

(Bengal Establishment.)

THIS officer was appointed a Cadet of the season of 1794, on the presidency of Bengal. On his voyage to India in 1796, in the Lord Camden, Capt. Dance, Cadet Martin volunteered, at the Cape of Good Hope, against the Dutch fleet, captured in Saldhanna Bay.

On his arrival in Calcutta, early in 1797, by an introduction from Col. Ironside†, he was most hospitably received by Capt. W. B. Davis‡, commanding the Calcutta militia, who procured the appointment of Ensign Martin to the 1st European reg. at Caunpoor, commanded by L.-Col. Edward Clarke, with which, in that year, he marched to Lucknow under Sir James Craig, forming part of the force, which, under Sir John Shore, and Sir A. Clarke, displaced Vizier Ally, and placed Sydaat Ally on the musnud of Oude. The next year, 1798, his regiment took the field under Sir J. Craig, against Zemaun Shaw, who had threatened an invasion of our provinces from Lahore, but from which he was deterred by the encampment of our army for some weeks near Anopsheher. In 1799, on regimental rank taking place, Lieut. Martin was posted to the 14th N. I., commanded by L.-Col. W. Burn§, which he joined at Dacca, and soon after, with half of the 2d battalion, the colonel, and colours, proceeded to Chittagong, where he was appointed acting Adjutant and public officer. In 1800, the battalion being ordered to Bareitch, Lieut. Martin proceeded on leave to the presidency, and, for some time, was ordered to do duty with the Marine battalion at Barrackpore, under Capt. Lewis Thomas‖, and in the latter end of

---

* Although the military career of Capt. Martin was closed at a very early period, the distressing situation to which he was reduced, by the loss of both his eyes, by one shot from the enemy, of which he furnishes a solitary instance, entitles it to be herein commemorated, more especially as accompanied by the flattering testimonials of his conduct, from the high authorities of Sir David Ochterlony, M.-Gen. Burn, and Lord Lake, and confirmed by the Bengal government, in their military correspondence with the Court of Directors.

† Services, vol. ii. p. 452-3.   ‡ Now a Lieutenant-Colonel on the retired list.
§ Services, vol. ii. p. 495-517.   ‖ Services, vol. ii. p. 306-8.

1801, joined his battalion at Bareitch, from which he was detached as acting Adjutant to five companies, which he afterwards for some time commanded, to assist the Aumil in his collections. The station proving most unhealthy, losing Lieuts. Shelden and Arrowsmith, and six European artillery-men out of eleven, with all the officers sick, and half the battalion in the hospital, in 1802, the battalion was ordered to Futtyghur; from whence he was again detached as acting Adjutant to five companies, under Capt. J. L. Richardson*, ordered against the fort of Tutteah, possessed by a refractory Zemindar. On their arrival before the fort, they found Col. Guthrie, at the head of his battalion, had expelled the Rajah, but with much loss, including that of his own life, which he lost in the most gallant performance of his duty. Lieut. Martin was afterwards ordered on command with his company, as an escort to Mr. Claud Russel, appointed to the collection of the district of Coel, from which he joined his battalion at Saharunpoor. The war now raging with the Mahrattas, in 1804, the battalion was called, by Col. Ochterlony, the Resident, to Delhi, for its defence against Holkar, who besieged it for some time, and at this period Capt.-Lieut. Martin had an opportunity of manifesting his zeal on active service, as he had ever before in his public duties, to the entire satisfaction of his superiors. Holkar decamped from before Delhi, on Gen. Lake coming up to its relief, and Col. Burn was ordered back to re-occupy Saharunpoor; and as it was not expected the Colonel would have any enemy to contend with there, Gen. Lake allowed Capt.-Lieut. Martin to join five companies commanded by Capt. W. Nichol†, with the grand army; but as information was received that Runjeet Sing, the Lahore chief, had joined the Mahratta confederacy, and had made an incursion into the Dooaub, and demolished the cantonments at Saharunpoor, Gen. Lake permitted him to rejoin Col. Burn's battalion, which, with a Tallinga battalion, commenced its march against Runjeet Sing.

Holkar, with all his cavalry, pursued the detachment, and on the

---

* Services in this vol. p. 80-2. † Services, vol. ii. p. 517-21.

second day harassed its rear, and the day after completely surrounded it. Nevertheless, the detachment, though it failed in its attempt to get possession of Shamlie, forced its way into the fort, close to the town.

Col. Burn's detachment, consisting of about 1,500 men, with not more than a dozen officers, (not one being of the artillery) with an 18, a 12, and four 6-pounders, camp followers, cattle, and baggage of all description, had been penned up for about six days in the fort of Shamlie, which might be computed at about 80 yards square, with a bastion at each angle, separated from the town, in possession of the enemy, by a road of about 8 or 10 yards wide; when, on the morning of the 2d November 1804, Capt-Lieut. Martin being the officer on duty in command of the detail of the garrison, finding the enemy had raised themselves during the night, by a scaffolding, erected in the inside, to the top of the gateway of the town, through which they had bored loopholes, commanding the very centre of the fort, and from which they were picking off the men very fast, even as they were laying at their repose, he determined to bring a 6-pounder, which had been mounted on an outer bastion, and was facing outwards, round to an embrasure, to bear upon the gateway of the town, to drive the enemy from it; and was hastening the performance of this service, the enemy keeping up a brisk fire upon him, wounding some of his men, and particularly a Golandauze, through his right arm, who was pointing the gun close to Capt.-Lieut. Martin's left, and if language can be spoken with the eyes, made him understand a shot was intended for him. He did not feel this the time to shrink from his duty, but, in assistance to the Golandauze, dropping on his knees to be able to cast his eye along the gun, to see that it bore on its proper point, he at that moment received a wound through both his eyes, when rising and seizing a pistol he had in his sash, it was wrenched from him, and he was hurried from the bastion giving the word of command to fire, which effected the purpose, the enemy quitting the gateway.

This was the last act of Capt.-Lieut. Martin's duty: it sealed his fate, and closed his military career.

The Governor-General in Council, in recompense for the services and sufferings of Capt.-Lieut. Martin, recommended him to his late Majesty for promotion to the rank of Captain of a company, which was granted, under date 16th June 1806, and the Governor-General in Council, by general orders, dated July 22, 1806, transferred Capt. Martin to the Invalid establishment, and posted him, from that date, to the 2d company of European infantry invalids.

It is only necessary in proof of the estimation in which this officer was held, by those who had the best opportunity of appreciating his merits, to subjoin the following documental testimonials of his services and misfortune:—

"*To his Excellency the Most Noble the Marquess Wellesley, Gov.-Gen.*

"*Delhi, March* 1805.

"My Lord,—In an appeal to your Lordship's benevolence, any apology would be improper: I, therefore, without doubt or hesitation, venture to recommend to your Lordship's notice, and humane consideration, Capt. Martin, of the 14th reg., whose zeal, activity, and gallantry, I had an opportunity of witnessing, during the siege of Delhi; and whose exertions at Shamlie, under Col. Burn, out of his immediate line of duty, subjected him to the calamity which, I am fully persuaded, will claim your Lordship's benign consideration, and every indulgence which can be granted to a misfortune so uncommon.

(Signed) "David Ochterlony."

Col. Burn's Certificate of Capt. Martin's misfortune.

"*Bareilly, in Rohilcund, July* 1, 1806.

"In justice to a brave, and once very promising officer, Capt. Thomas Martin, of the 2d batt. 14th reg., who, for upwards of five years, served under my personal command, I feel it my duty to make known his merits, and the zeal which he has displayed on several instances of arduous service, greatly to his own credit, and to the advantage of his country. During the siege of Delhi, and whilst my small detachment was surrounded by the troops of Holkar at Shamlie, when all were so distinguished, his conduct was conspicuously meritorious; but his fate has been greatly unfortunate. Instead of enjoying the fruits of distinguished merit, his ardour, in the discharge of his duty, has subjected him to the most deplorable of all misfortunes, having, at Shamlie, received a wound by a musket ball through both his eyes, which has rendered him for ever blind.

  (Signed)   "W. BURN, Colonel, Commanding the station."

"I perfectly agree in Col. Burn's statement of the meritorious services of Captain Martin.

          (Signed) "LAKE."

Extract.—Military Letter from Bengal to the Hon. the Court of Directors, dated 7th August 1806.

"We beg leave earnestly to solicit the attention of your Hon. Court to the case of Capt. Thomas Martin, of the Invalid establishment at this presidency. Capt. Martin suffered the severe misfortune of being deprived of both his eyes by a musket shot, whilst gallantly performing his duty with a detachment of your forces, which was surrounded and attacked by a numerous body of horse, commanded by Jeswunt Rao Holkar in person, during the late war in Hindostan. The detachment to which Capt. Martin belonged, after resisting, with distinguished valour, every attack of an enemy, greatly superior in numbers, forced its way into the fort of Shamlie, where it maintained its position, against every effort of the enemy, until the approach of the Right Hon. the Commander-in-Chief obliged Jeswunt Rao Holkar and his forces to seek their safety in flight. During the performance of this gallant service, Capt. Martin received a wound from a matchlock ball, which, passing through both his eyes, instantly deprived him of sight, and all hope of ever rising to that rank in his profession, or of obtaining those honourable marks of distinction, which, but for the calamity which had befallen him, in the gallant performance of his duty, he had every reason to expect, would have been the reward of his courage, his talents, and his attachment to his profession. In this melancholy situation, Capt. Martin having expressed his anxious desire of being permitted to return to Europe—for the purpose of passing the remainder of his days with his relations and family, whose humane attention, and affectionate concern, he hoped, might in some degree, soften the severity of his calamity—we have permitted him to return to Europe on furlough; and we earnestly recommend that your Hon. Court will permit Capt. Martin to continue there during his life, and to draw, either in England or in this country, as to your Hon. Court may appear most advisable, the same allowances which he would have been entitled to receive, had he remained in this country as a Captain in the Invalid establishment. This measure will occasion no additional expense to the Hon. Company; and as a case so peculiarly unfortunate and distressing as that of Capt. Martin, is not likely again to occur, the precedent which may be established by your Hon. Court, in granting to him the indulgence we have recommended, will not be attended with any inconvenience."

LIEUTENANT-COLONEL ALEXANDER HAY.

(Bombay Establishment.)

In 1798, this officer obtained a Cadetship on the Bombay establishment, and after five years service, was appointed, by the Hon. the Governor in Council, Military Auditor-General. The Court of Directors disapproved of his being nominated to so important a situation, on the ground of his short standing in the service. He was, in consequence, superseded in the appointment, but was afterwards restored to it by the Bombay government, and eventually confirmed in it by the Court of Directors.

The approbation of official superiors, constitutes the most pleasing reward that a public officer can receive for a faithful discharge of his duty: it has been the good fortune of this officer to have been honoured, on different occasions, with the approbation of the Bombay government, and also of the Court of Directors, as will be seen by the accompanying extract of a letter from the Court of Directors (Military Department) to the Hon. the Governor in Council, dated the 17th Jan. 1810; and also by an extract from general orders, on his leaving India.

It may be proper to mention, that when Sir John Mac Gregor Murray* (then captain) was appointed Military Auditor-General, on the Bengal establishment, the Court of Directors conferred on him the

* Services, vol. ii. p. 461-3.

rank of Colonel in the army, transmitting at the same time, the orders published on the occasion, to Bombay and Madras, with instructions to confer the rank of Lieut.-Colonel on such Auditors-General as might distinguish themselves in the department. On the ground of this order the rank of Lieut.-Colonel in the army was conferred upon Capt. Hay, by the government of Bombay.

Extract of a Letter from the Court of Directors (Military Department) to the Government of Bombay, dated 17th Jan. 1810.

167. "We highly approve of your zealous and successful endeavours to reduce the military expenses of your presidency, in which we observe, with much satisfaction, that you have been most cordially and ably assisted by your Military Auditor-General, Capt. Hay, and the members of your Medical Board, Dr. Helenus Scott and Dr. William Sandwith; and we desire that you will signify to those officers the high sense we entertain of their laudable and upright discharge of their duties, as conscientious servants of the Company*.

Extract from General Orders, Bombay, Saturday, 23d Nov. 1811, by the Hon. the Governor in Council.

"Bombay Castle, 19th November, 1811.

"The Hon. the Governor in Council is pleased to permit L.-Col. Alexander Hay, Military Auditor-General, to proceed to Europe on sick certificate, agreeably to the regulations, and regrets that that officer is thus compelled to relinquish a situation which he has for several years filled with acknowledged advantage to the public service, and to the great satisfaction of government."

CAPTAIN JAMES FRANKLIN†.

(Bengal Establishment.)

In 1805, this officer was appointed a Cadet of cavalry, and during his passage out to India, was employed, with the rest of his fellow

---

* The government of Bombay, in a letter to the Court of Directors, dated the 31st July 1807, state that annual savings in military expenditure had been effected, on L.-Col. Hay's suggestions, to the amount of several lacs of rupees.

† Brother to the enterprizing Capt. Franklin, the commander of the Arctic land-expedition.

cadets, in the capture of the Cape of Good Hope. He arrived in India in March 1806, and was sent to Barraset, which at that period was a military institution, for the purpose of enabling the cadets to acquire a knowledge of oriental languages, and also of their duty. He availed himself of the opportunities afforded by this institution to lay a good foundation for his future studies of the oriental languages, and afterwards experienced the advantage of having done so *. He obtained the highest academic prizes of this institution, viz. 1200 rupees, and a valuable sword, and, at the first general examination, was reported qualified to join his regiment.

In consequence of this report, he quitted the Barraset institution, and was appointed a Cornet of the 1st regiment of cavalry, which regiment he joined in 1808, and was shortly afterwards appointed Adjutant to it.

In 1809, he was appointed Field Secretary to Colonel (now Major General Sir Gabriel Martindell †), who commanded the division of the Bengal army, acting in co-operation with a division of the Madras army, against Meer Khan; and in 1810 and 11, he served as Principal Staff to a detachment of light troops under Col. (now M.-Gen. Sir Thos.) Brown ‡, employed in pursuit of a noted marauder, named Gopal Sing, who had for years baffled every attempt to subdue him. This active service led the troops into parts of the country which till then were almost altogether unknown, and were considered as impracticable, and Adjutant Franklin availed himself of the opportunity thus afforded of collecting much information respecting it, and the light he threw on its geography and localities occasioned his being afterwards appointed to conduct an extensive survey§ throughout the whole of the states of Bundlecund, situated on the S. W. frontier.

* Much of this officer's success may be fairly attributed to the early foundation he laid at Barraset, and a subsequent consistency of action, in availing himself of opportunities to be useful as they occurred. And as the military service of India affords those opportunities in a proportion, at least equal, if not greater than other services, the career of Captain Franklin may be regarded as an instructive lesson to young officers.

† Services, vol. i. p. 406-8, and vol. ii. p. 562-3. ‡ Services, vol. i. p. 253-8.

§ It is worthy of remark, that the very liberal encouragement given both by the Court of Directors and India governments, for obtaining exact surveys of Southern India, and the

In 1812, he was appointed to the survey above mentioned, which is one of the most extensive of its kind that has been completed by one individual, comprising an extent of 18,000 square miles, including 25 separate states, with their boundaries and dependencies, and the whole line of the British frontier from Allahabad to the Chumbul river.

These states are governed by chiefs or rajahs, who are independent with regard to their own internal regulations and management; but are, nevertheless, under the agency of British interference, so far as relates to quarrels or disturbances amongst themselves: thus they enjoy British protection against foreign enemies, and are on terms of close alliance with the British government. At the period when the survey commenced, these states were not so well settled as they are now, and it required no small degree of tact and skill, to manage the prejudices and humours of the several chieftains with sufficient address to prevent them from throwing obstacles in the way. Captain Franklin, however, succeeded in establishing a complete series of triangulation throughout the whole of them, in the following manner. He measured an extent of 11 miles 5 furlongs and 218 yards, with great care and precision, at an elevation of 1200 feet above the level of the sea; this, therefore being reduced by the usual process, became the base line of his operations, and from it a series of primary triangulation was extended, until it terminated with another base line of verification of 9 miles 2 furlongs and 210 yards in extent, measured with the same scrupulous exactness. Intermediately, as opportunities offered, or occasion seemed to require, base lines of smaller extent were measured for the purpose of probation, as a check upon incipient error; and thus, aided by daily astronomical observations, the series finally spread over the area comprised within 81° 26′ 45″ east long., and 25° 8′ 30″ north lat., and 77° 51′ 25″ east

ceded provinces, bespeak the interest entertained of these extensive acquisitions, already yielding revenues greatly exceeding those derived under the Native governments. The many highly-educated young men, now yearly proceeding to fill the various branches of the service of the Company's civil and military establishments, will speedily add to that extensive stock of historical and statistical information already before the public.

long., and 25° 39′ 5″ north lat., including in depth the parallels of 26° 36′ 0′ north lat., and 24° 20′ 0′ north lat.

The secondary triangulation formed the network of the above process, and was necessarily connected with and dependent upon the points established by the primary triangles; it is, of course, from this series that the topography and geographical positions were laid down, and the sides of the triangles were consequently so regulated as to command a perfect view of the area to be surveyed, so that nothing could escape observation, whilst every object was fully within the capacity of the angles which determined its position. The result of this process (passing over the great points), is, that every minute village, hamlet, hill, or streamlet has been inserted, and an accurate delineation of the topography of the country obtained.

The maps were accompanied with a copious memoir, containing the history, political and statistical, and also the localities and productions of the whole tract, collectively, and of each state separately, so that the survey is complete in all requisite information for the civil or military branches of the service; and the maps of it were arranged accordingly on the scales of one mile to an inch, and of four miles to an inch, both of which are deposited in the office of the Surveyor-General of India, at Calcutta.

This survey was characterized in the following terms by the late Lieutenant-Colonel Lambton*:—

* The late Lieut.-Col. William Lambton. As the military services of this officer are inserted in the Royal Military Calendar, vol. v, 3d edit., it will be sufficient in this place briefly to sketch his operations in India. He entered the army in 1782, and commenced his services in India in 1797, at which period he was a Lieutenant in H. M.'s 33d regiment, of which corps the present Duke of Wellington was then Lieutenant-Colonel. In 1798, he was appointed by Sir A. Clarke, Brigade-Major of the King's troops on the coast of Coromandel. In the same year, the 33d reg. was ordered to the coast, and he accompanied it. In 1799, the army took the field, and this officer, as Major of Brigade to the King's troops, was attached to the 1st European brigade, commanded by Sir David Baird, in whose family he served the whole campaign. He attended him at Malavilly, at the siege of Seringapatam, and finally in the storming of that capital, when chance threw him in the way of taking an active part on the north rampart, the whole of the officers of the leading companies of that attack being either killed or wounded. The leading men being opposed by a considerable body, with the Sultaun at their head, fell back twice, but Lieut. L. was able to rally them, and a confused, hurried, and furious struggle took place for about 15 minutes, when the

" Your survey is precisely of that description which I wish to connect with my operations, and you may rest assured, if I live to extend my mea-

enemy gave way, chiefly on account of a party of the King's 12 regiment getting over the ditch; and the supporting troops closing upon the rampart, all opposition ceased, and a dreadful carnage ensued.

The following anecdote of this officer, whilst in the family of Gen. Baird, appeared in a biographical sketch, by Mr. John Warren, read before the Asiatic Society of Calcutta:—

" On the 4th of April, 1799, Gen. Baird received orders to proceed, during the night, to scour a tope, where it was supposed that Tippoo had placed an advanced post. Lieut. Lambton accompanied him as his Staff, and after having repeatedly traversed the tope without finding any one on it, the General resolved to return to camp, and proceeded accordingly, as he thought, towards head-quarters. However, as the night was clear, and the constellation of the Great Bear was near the meridian, Lieut. L. noticed that instead of proceeding southerly, as was necessary for reaching the camp, the division was advancing towards the north, that is to say, on Tippoo's whole army; and immediately warned Gen. Baird of the mistake. But the General (who troubled himself little about astronomy) replied, that he knew very well how he was going, without consulting the stars. Presently the detachment fell in with one of the enemy's out-posts, which was soon dispersed; but this at last led Gen. Baird to apprehend that Lieut. Lambton's observation might be correct enough; he ordered a light to be struck, and on consulting a pocket compass, it was found (as Capt. Lambton used humorously to say), 'that the stars were right!'"

The fall of Seringapatam, and the death of the Sultaun, opened a vast extent of territory to be traversed by the British armies, and of course an extensive field for geographical investigation.

The scientific labours of this eminently-gifted character, are well known to the learned of every country. The Asiatic Reseaches, and the Transactions of the Royal and other learned Societies, contain ample evidence of their extent and importance; and their general utility, as far as the geography of India is concerned, has been too universally felt to need any illustration. We may be permitted, however, cursorily to notice those parts of his works which are justly denominated scientific, and, as such, have made the Deccan and Central parts of India, objects of classic interest throughout the civilized world. The original object of the Marquess Wellesley in establishing the trigonometrical survey, was to unite the east and west coasts of the peninsula, so as to connect the latter with the government observatory at Madras, upon precisely the same principles as those which had been adopted by the French and English philosophers, in connecting the observatories of Greenwich and Paris. The noble Marquess's choice fell on Lieut. William Lambton; and it appears that the powers of discrimination, which characterized the whole of that distinguished nobleman's administration, were here exerted with their wonted effect; for the mild, easy, and affable demeanour of Lieut. Lambton, did not conceal from the piercing eye of his Lordship, the great and grasping intellect, the high powers of reflection, and the uncontrolled perseverance, which never viewed a difficulty or embarrassment, but with a steady determination to surmount it.

In the progress of his labours, Lieut.-Col. Lambton found that a noble field was laid open, for adding to the scientific data respecting the figure of the earth, by carrying a series of triangles down that meridian which passes through the southern promontory of India;

surement towards the point I contemplate, I shall not fail to connect it when I pass through the field of your useful labours."

for, as the extent of the same meridian was limited on the northern side, by the boundary of the British territories only, there was obviously an opportunity of measuring a meridional arc of nearly 26° in amplitude, which would be almost thrice as great as that which had occupied the French geometricians, Mechain and De Lambre, between the Balearic Isles and Dunkirk. Such a boon to science could not escape the notice of Lieut.-Col. Lambton; the difficulties, however, of attaining it were such as would, perhaps, have appalled any man of moderate capacity, though with him they seemed merely to enhance the value of the prize; and the result has exceeded the most sanguine expectations of its projector. Already had the meridional series been brought to Takoorkera, 15 miles S. E. from the city of Ellichpoor, which gave an amplitude of more than 12° of latitude; and in spite of his advanced age, the active mind of the philosopher still contemplated the extension of it to Agra, in which case the meridian line would have passed at short distances from Bhopal, Seronge, Nurwur, Gualior, and Dolpore. At his advanced age he despaired of health and strength remaining for further exertion, otherwise it cannot be doubted that it would have been a grand object of his ambition to have prolonged it through the Dooaub, and across the Himalaya to the 32nd degree of north latitude. If this vast undertaking had been achieved, and that it may yet be completed is not improbable, British India will have to boast of a much longer unbroken meridian line, than has been before measured on the surface of the globe.

Though the measurement of the arc of the meridian was the principal object of the labours of Col. Lambton, he extended his operations to the east and west, and the set of triangles covers great part of the peninsula of India, defining with the utmost precision, the situation of a very great number of principal places in latitude, longitude, and elevation, and affording a sure basis for an amended geographical map. The triangulation also connects the Coromandel and Malabar coasts in numerous important points, thus supplying the best means of truly laying down the shape of those coasts, and rendering an essential service to navigation.

It was the Colonel's intention to have himself carried the meridian line as far north as Agra; and he detached his first assistant, Capt. Everest, of the Bengal Artillery, to extend a series of triangles westward, to Bombay; and when that service should be completed, eastward, to Point Palmyras, and probably to Fort William; by which extensive and arduous operation, the three presidencies of India would be connected, and several obvious advantages gained to geography and navigation.

With a degree of vigour and fire which would have done credit, even to his earlier years, Lieut.-Col. Lambton embarked for the continuation of his arduous career from Hyderabad, in the middle of January 1823; but Providence willed it otherwise. On his arrival at Hingham Ghaut, 50 miles south of Nagpoor, on the 26th of January, he fell a victim to a catarrh, which had long threatened his existence, and which, being ultimately attended with fever, put a period to his life.

Thus, in an obscure village of Central India, died, at the age of 75, one of the most highly-endowed philosophers and mathematicians who ever trod on her shores; a man whose name will ever be dear to science; one of the sacred few, who have tended to raise the fame of England, in the intellectual scale, with the civilized world. He died not ingloriously: his

In 1814, he was promoted to Lieutenant, and in 1817, on the formation of the Quarter-Master-General's department, this officer was appointed to it, and in the same year, was selected for the duties of the Quarter-Master-General's department of the centre division of the grand army, under the personal command of the Marquess Hastings. At the outset of this service he superintended the construction of a bridge of boats across the Jumna river, which, for its magnitude, solidity, and the rapidity with which it was executed, obtained for him, and those in co-operation with him, the marked approbation of the Commander-in-Chief, expressed in general orders; and this officer was further honoured with his approbation of the whole of his professional conduct, whilst employed in the duties of his Lordship's camp.

In the same year, he was selected for the duties of Deputy Assistant Quarter-Master-General, Field Secretary, and Persian Interpreter, to Major-Gen. Sir Thomas Brown, on the occasion of his being detached from the centre division of the grand army, in pursuit of the Pindarries. The operations of this division have been strongly characterized by Col. Blacker[*], in his memoir, who resembles them to the flight of a rocket, carrying consternation wherever they were directed, from the rapidity of its movement, and the decision of its attack.

Gen. Browne's division was detached from the centre division of the grand army by the Com.-in-Chief, lightly equipped, and with almost carte-blanche instructions, for the purpose of moving with rapidity, and without restraint, in pursuit of the Pindarries, a large body of whom had for some time hovered near Poree, in the hopes of assistance or protection from Scindia; this body, however, having been dispersed, before Gen. Brown could come in contact with it, he resolved not to waste time in fruitless pursuit of the small

labours will ever be viewed with interest by the votaries of science; and it may be a proud boast of the East India Company, that it has been the beneficient patron, and steady protector of an undertaking, which confers more practical benefit, in the solution of the grand question of the figure of the earth, than the efforts of all the world besides.

An account will be found in the 7th vol. of the Asiatic Researches, p. 312-35, of Lieut.-Col. Lambton's method for extending a geographical survey across the peninsula of India.

[*] Services, vol. i. p. 321-5.

parties into which the Pindarries had divided, but pushed on towards the scene where Holkar's army was then in force, and on his route, receiving intelligence of the battle of Mehidpoor, and also of the flight of the insurgent chieftain, with a large portion of artillery, to Rampoora, a strongly fortified town belonging to Holkar, he immediately resolved on annihilating this body, and accordingly altered the direction of his route, and marched forthwith to Rampoora, which sudden movement enabled him to take the enemy completely by surprise. The arrangement for the attack was, that a part of the troops (the cavalry) should push on rapidly and take up positions opposite the gateways, to prevent the escape of the enemy, whilst the main body, (the infantry) with the aid of two 12-pounder galloper guns should storm the principal gateway; it happened, however, that a party of the enemy's horse were on the look-out at a short distance from the town, on the arrival of our troops at day-break, and a vigorous pursuit being made after them, they fled towards the town, where the panic became so great that the pursuers and pursued entering together, a conflict ensued within the walls of the town, which was soon decided by the entrance of the remainder of the troops. This affair may, in some measure, be considered as a following up of the blow which had been struck at Mehidpoor*, as the result of it was the

* The President of the Board of Controul, Mr. Canning, noticed this important battle in his speech, in the House of Commons, of 4th March, 1819, in the following language:—

" This brings me to the battle of Mehidpoor, the only great general action which occurred in the course of the campaign. Of this battle I feel myself incompetent, even if it were necessary, to enter into the military details; the gazettes furnish a more perspicuous account of it than I could pretend to offer. But I may be permitted to say, that more determined gallantry, more inflexible perseverance, or greater exertion of mind and body on the part of every individual engaged, were never displayed, than in the battle of Mehidpoor. The result was, the defeat and dissolution of the army of the enemy, though not without a loss on our side deeply to be deplored. This victory recommends to the gratitude of the House the name of Sir Thomas Hislop, by whose conduct, and under whose auspices, it was won; and that of Sir John Malcolm, second in command on that occasion, second to none in renown, whose name will be remembered in India as long as the British tongue is spoken, or the British flag hoisted throughout that vast territory. The result of this battle, as it was the complete dissolution of the army of Holkar, so it was that of the confederacy among the Mahratta powers, which had been long secretly formed, and which an unprosperous, or even a doubtful issue of our first action, would unquestionably have brought into full play. A treaty of peace was forthwith negociated with Holkar, by which were ceded to us all his possessions on the south side of the river Nerbudda; and the remainder of the campaign, so far as this member of the hostile confederacy was concerned, consisted in collecting for the British government the scattered fragments of dismembered chieftainship."

capture of all their guns, 13 in number, one of their chiefs, who was made prisoner, and the total annihilation of the hopes of this turbulent faction.

From Rampoora, Gen. Brown proceeded to Jawud, a strongly fortified and walled town belonging to Scindia, the chief place and residence of Jeswunt Rao Bhow, one of his relations, and a kind of viceroy over this portion of his dominions. The conduct of this chief had excited suspicion, on account of his known attachment to the Pindarries, and strong representations had been made to him by the political agent of the British government, without effect: he had assembled a large body of troops and artillery, which were encamped at a short distance from the town, and matters assumed a very hostile appearance.

On the arrival of the division of General Brown, it was resolved to bring matters to a crisis, if he continued to persist in the same line of conduct. The political agent, accordingly, temporarily resigned his powers into the hands of the general, and a message was sent to the chief, calling upon him to adhere strictly to the treaty which had been concluded between Scindia and the British government; and informing him, that any deviation from it, would be treated as an act of hostility. The reply to this message was evasive, and a body of his troops moved in defiance from the camp, with their guns, and took up a menacing position under the walls of the town; whereupon, a reconnoissance was immediately made, and a squadron of cavalry ordered to watch their motions. The veil was now withdrawn at once, and their hostile intentions evinced by their opening a fire upon our troops; there required nothing more than this act to authorize a summary chastisement, which was accordingly inflicted forthwith. The whole line was ordered under arms. The infantry and artillery, which consisted of galloper guns, under the personal command of General Brown, moved to the attack of the troops who had taken post under the walls of the town; and on their dispersion, the grand gateway of the town was blown open, stormed, and carried at the point of the bayonet. A smart conflict ensued in the town, when the chief and his adherents fled out at the opposite gateway, closely pursued by the 3d reg. of cavalry, who cut up a number of them.

Whilst these operations were going on in the town, the 4th reg. of cavalry, and a party of Rohilla horse, under the command of Capt. E. J. Ridge*, and conducted by Lieut. Franklin, attacked and carried the entrenched camp of the enemy, posted a short distance from the town, which consisted of 10 guns and 2000 men: and thus, in the short space of an hour, a blow was struck which annihilated the hostile spirit of Scindia's government in favour of the Pindarries, and destroyed the last hope of those freebooters, whilst the example of summary chastisement thus inflicted, had an immediate and salutary effect on the surrounding fortresses, by inducing them to surrender on the first summons.

For Lieut. Franklin's services on the above occasion, he received the unqualified thanks of the Major-General commanding, and was further honoured with the approbation of the Commander-in-Chief, for his conduct at the storming of Jawud, by mention in general orders.

On the close of the campaign of 1817-18, Lieut. Franklin returned to Bundlecund, to complete his survey. He was promoted to Brevet-Capt. in 1819; and in 1820, his health becoming delicate from constant service, he proceeded to Calcutta, where he was employed for a short time under the orders of government, in collecting and arranging geographical and other documents relating to the late campaign, which were disposed in various offices and other public departments; and having discharged this duty, to the satisfaction of government, as conveyed to him in their secretary's letter, he obtained permission to take a voyage to Singapore on account of his health; and whilst at Singapore, finding no survey in existence, he made a survey of that island, together with the old and new straits, and prepared also a series of points, to serve as a basis for a large harbour

---

* Services in this volume, and with which will be found the general order issued on this occasion.

chart, which is highly expedient and necessary for a harbour likely to be so much frequented as that of Singapore.

From Singapore Capt. Franklin returned to Bengal in 1822, and was appointed to conduct a survey of about 60,000 square miles; but finding his health not thoroughly re-established, he proceeded to England on furlough.

At the time he left India, Capt. Franklin was Assistant Quarter-Master-General of the Bengal army, and brevet Captain of the 1st cavalry; but in consequence of the new organization of the Indian army, he became a regimental Captain of the 1st reg. of light cavalry, since 1st May 1824.

MAJOR WILLIAM RICHARDS.

(Bengal Establishment.)

IN 1793, this officer was nominated a Cadet on the Bengal establishment; and on his arrival at Fort William, in 1794, he was appointed a subaltern of artillery. In 1796, he was ordered up to the field station of Caunpoor, where he remained doing duty with the artillery until 1797, when he was ordered down to Fort William, to join the detachment of artillery destined to serve with the force proceeding to the south, under the command of Gen. Erskine*; and marched to the capital of his Highness the Nizam of Hyderabad.

During the years 1797-8 and 9, this officer was employed in the Hyderabad subsidiary force, against the French force in the service of the Nizam, and was present at their surrender. In 1799, he

---

* The late M.-Gen. John Erskine, of the Bengal establishment, entered the army in 1764, and rose by gradation to the rank of M.-Gen. in 1798. He was an excellent officer, and possessed, from his long residence in India, considerable information on the manners, politics, and languages of India, and was highly regarded by every branch of the service.

The M.-Gen. had never been innoculated, and entertained a strong presentiment that he should die of the small-pox; and which, it is believed, befel him before the introduction of the vaccine virus into Bengal.

marched with the subsidiary force to join the grand army employed against Tippoo Sultaun, and was in the whole of that war. He served in the division of the army, commanded by Col. Wellesley, at the siege and storming of Seringapatam; and was afterwards employed against the chief, Doondia Waugh.

The Bengal troops being ordered to return home, this officer proceeded with the artillery and 10th N.I., *via* Hyderabad, through the interior of India to Caunpoor. On his arrival, the company of artillery to which he was attached, was ordered down by water to Fort William. In 1802, he was ordered, in command of a detachment of artillery, to the station of Midnapoor, where he remained one year. In 1803, he was ordered up with the annual relief of artillery to Allahabad; and was soon after employed with the artillery ordered to join the army destined for the conquest of the province of Bundlecund. He was present at the battle of Kopsa, and served at the siege and surrender of the fortress of Gwalior, when he received a severe wound. He returned to Fort William in 1804, on his promotion to the rank of Captain.

In 1807, Capt. Richards was ordered with a detachment of artillery for the service of Prince of Wales Island, where he remained, in the command of the artillery, for the space of three years. In the end of 1809, he was ordered to return to Bengal, where he continued with the artillery at the presidency until 1811, when he was directed to join the army forming for the conquest of the island of Java. He was present at the capture of Batavia; and severely wounded when in command of the grand battery of twelve 18-pounders, erected against the works of Cornelis.

At the end of 1811, Capt. Richards returned to Bengal, when he was appointed to take charge of the field depôt magazine at Allahabad, as Commissary of ordnance. He remained in this staff situation for two years, when, his constitution being much impaired by wounds and climate, he was obliged to proceed to England. In that year, he obtained the rank of Major; but not recovering his health sufficiently to return to India, he was compelled to retire from the service; and has retired on the half-pay and pension for wounds, which has been granted him, after a service in the Bengal artillery of above twenty years.

LIEUTENANT-COLONEL HERBERT BOWEN.
(Bengal Establishment.)

This officer served as a Midshipman in his Majesty's navy in 1793, 1794, and 1795, and was present in several actions, particularly in that by the squadron under the command of Admiral Cornwallis with the French fleet on the 15th, 16th, and 17th June 1795.

In 1795, he entered the military service of the East India Company; was appointed Ensign, 17th Nov. 1796; Lieutenant, 30th Oct. 1797; Captain, 30th Oct. 1806; Major, 30th Oct. 1817; and Lieut.-Col., 29th April 1823.

He was present at the defence of Futtehghur on the 15th and 16th Nov. 1804, against the army under the personal command of Jeswunt Rao Holkar; at the capture by assault of the fortified town of Adaulut Nuggar, between Agra and Bhurtpoor, on the 1st May 1805; at the capture, by assault, of the enemy's camp and guns on the banks of the Chumbul, by a detachment under his command, from the troops under Lieut.-Col. Bowie*, in June 1805; at the capture, by assault, of the palace of Delhi, on the 10th August 1809, during the residency of Mr. Seton; and at the capture, by assault, of the fortified town of Bhowanny, on the 29th August 1809, under Lieut.-Col. Ball†.

---

* The late Lieut.-Col. Robert Bowie, of the Bengal establishment, was a Cadet of 1778. He proceeded to the coast with the 26th Bengal Native battalion, forming part of Colonel Pearse's detachment, and served in all the campaigns of Sir Eyre Coote. He subsequently served in Lieut.-Col. Cockerell's detachment, and afterwards under the late Lieut.-Gen. Popham. In the war with Holkar, he commanded a subsidiary force of three battalions and artillery, for the protection of the Rana of Gohud, and the province of Agra; during which command he died, after a period of twenty-nine years of almost constant service in the field.

† Services, vol. ii. p. 355-7, 563; and in this volume.

He served with the expedition to Java, under the late Gen. Sir Samuel Auchmuty*, and was present in the engagement at Weltervreeden on the 10th, and in the capture, by assault, of Fort Cornelis on the 26th August 1811.

The battalion which this officer commanded formed part of the 5th division of the army of the Deccan; and he was present with it at the capture, by assault, of the fortified town of Sirree Nuggur, on the 5th January 1818.

This officer led, with the grenadiers of his corps, the successful assaulting columns on three of the above occasions, and was the first man who entered the enemy's works; and obtained the thanks and approbation of his commanding officer.

In consequence of the imminent danger to which the East India Company's territorial possessions were exposed, by the irruption of a Burmese force of about 10,000 men into the neutral provinces of Cachar, (in alliance with the British) a strong detachment, including Lieut.-Col. Bowen's corps, was collected at Buddapoor in the months of Nov. and Dec. 1823. In Feb. following, our troops broke ground, and in a few days penetrated into the interior of Cachar.

The Burmese had erected strong and extensive stockades at the several passes, which they defended with much coolness and bravery, but from which they were (with one exception, evacuated during the night) successively driven; and by the end of that month, the province was entirely freed from the enemy. L.-Col. Bowen was wounded during the latter service.

LIEUTENANT-COLONEL ALEXANDER LINDSAY.

(Bengal Establishment.)

This officer arrived in India in 1804, and was promoted, on the 14th August in that year, to the rank of Lieutenant, in the Bengal artil-

---

* Services, Royal Military Calendar, vol. ii. p. 268-93, 3d edition.

lery. He left Calcutta 15th March 1805, with a detachment for the Upper Provinces, and, arriving at Caunpoor early in July, was posted to a company of artillery attached to the subsidiary force, under the command of L.-Col. Bowie*, in Gohud and Gwalior, which he joined about the end of Sept. He was present at the siege of Gohud, in Feb. 1806: in the storm of the outwork of that place, two officers were killed and several wounded, and about 150 sepoys killed and wounded; but a practicable breach being made in the town-wall, the place surrendered.

The subsidiary force being no longer required, it was broken up. The artillery marched to Agra, and soon afterward to Caunpoor, where it arrived about the beginning of June, from whence this officer was detached to Lucknow, to command the artillery (a detail with four 6-pounders) at that station. He was promoted to Capt.-Lieut. 28th Feb. 1806, and removed to another company, which he joined at Agra, in October.

Lieut. Lindsay was present at the memorable, but unfortunate siege of Cummonah, (a small mud-fort in the Allyghur district;) at the storming of which place our troops were beat back with a heavy loss of officers and men. The artillery being few in numbers, and insufficient to furnish a relief, they continued in the batteries during the whole siege, which lasted a month. The fort, at last, being evacuated, the army proceeded to Gunnowrie, (also in the Allyghur district,) which, after a fortnight's siege, was also evacuated. The army was then broken up, and this officer returned to Agra in Jan. 1808.

In July following, Lieut. Lindsay was detached with five companies of sepoys, and two 6-pounders, against some petty forts in the Candoulee district. These being soon evacuated, and others given up, the detachment returned. In Nov., he marched to Muttra, where he continued, in command of the artillery (a detail with eight 6-pounders), till Oct. 1809, when he marched to Futtehghur, and remained there, in command of the artillery, till Nov. 1812, when he rejoined the head-quarters of the regiment at Dum Dum, on the 1st

---

* Services, p. 109.

Jan. 1813, and obtained the rank of Captain on the 26th March following.

Capt. Lindsay was removed to another company on the breaking out of the Nepaul war in 1814, and with it joined the Dinapoor division of the army forming under M.-Gen. Marlay. He marched with the division from Dinapoor into the Turraye in Nov. Little or nothing was done this season; and in May following, the army broke up, part returning to Dinapoor; the remainder, with which this officer served, continuing to protect the frontier in a temporary cantonment at Amowah.

A new army being formed, by that of the preceding year being about trebled, the whole moved on to the frontier, under Sir David Ochterlony, and then separated into three columns. Capt. Lindsay was in command of the artillery, with the right column under the command of Brigadier Kelly, of H. M.'s 24th foot. He proceeded with it through the forest bounding the Turraye and the Cheriaghatty range of hills by the Luckundie pass without opposition, until arriving close to Hurreehurpoor, a hill fort near the Bhaugmutty river. Capt. Lindsay having reconnoitered the place, (as acting field-engineer, there being none with the division,) and observing a good situation for a battery, he recommended it being occupied. This was done on the following morning without loss, the small party left for its defence retiring on the approach of the British; but it being of great importance, a sally was made from the fort by a strong force under Runjoor, a chief of considerable celebrity, who had that morning arrived, and assumed the command of the fort. The attack was persevered in till about 2 P.M., having lasted about eight hours, when they were forced to retreat: the British loss, in killed and wounded, amounted to about 150: five officers were wounded, but none killed. Capt. Lindsay was wounded by a musket-ball, which shattered the fore-finger and thumb of his right hand, and entered his right hip close to the joint. During the night the place was evacuated.

Peace being concluded, the brigade marched back to Amowah; and the army being broken up, moved off in different directions.

Capt. Lindsay proceeded to Dinapoor in May 1816; to Allahabad in August; and to Caunpoor in Jan. 1817, where a force, with a large train of artillery, was collecting for the reduction of the strong fort of Hattrass. He accompanied it; and after reducing the pettah, and a very considerable advance had been made in the approaches, which had nearly reached the foot of the glacis, the fort was bombarded by forty-two mortars and a rocket-battery, from 9 o'clock in the morning till midnight, when (every place which could be being burnt, and a large powder-magazine having been blown up* about sun-set) the enemy sallied out, but were driven back by the troops in the trenches, who followed them up, and took the fort. The remaining forts having surrendered, the army was broken up.

Capt. Lindsay returned to Caunpoor, and was appointed, in Sept. 1817, superintendent of half-wrought materials for gun-carriages, &c.; but the army being about to take the field, he obtained permission to accompany one of the divisions. He marched from Caunpoor, 30th Sept., in command of the artillery, with the left division, and accompanied it through Bundlecund; ascended the Bisramgunge Ghaut; proceeded by Huttah and Saugor to Seronge; thence northwards towards Gwalior, as far as Nya-Serai; where, leaving the heavy guns and a part of the army, the troops advanced in pursuit of the Pindarries, and after marching forty-two miles, (halting only for a few hours,) came up with their rear-guard, which the cavalry pursued several miles, killing a few.

The pursuit was continued for three days, but without success. The division then returned to Nya-Serai, and from thence to Bairseah, where it remained encamped for nearly two months.

In Feb. 1818, the division being reinforced by several more battalions, and a battering train under Major Hetzler †, it proceeded against several forts, most of which surrendered at once. The fort of Dhamoony, a large fort built of stone, held out till a breach was nearly completed, and then gave in.

* *Vide* note, p. 79.   † Now Lieut.-Colonel, and C. B.

The division next received orders to proceed against Mundelah, a strong fort on the Nerbudda river, distant two or three hundred miles, a great part of which was over a difficult hilly country, where no wheel-carriage had probably ever gone before. This place was besieged, and carried by storm, on the 30th April, with a very trifling loss on the side of the British, but a very heavy one on the part of the enemy.

The division then marched against Chowragurh, a strong hill-fort several marches to the southward of the Nerbudda, which surrendered on the troops arriving within a march of it. They then returned to Saugor, which place they reached in the beginning of June, when cantonments were ordered to be built.

The services of the division being brought to a close, Capt. Lindsay quitted it, and returned to Caunpoor, and from thence, by water, to the presidency, where he took charge of his appointment in the beginning of October.

The 12th August 1819, he obtained the brevet of Major: in November following, he was appointed to superintend the telegraphic department, and in Oct. 1820, agent for the manufacture of gunpowder at Allahabad, in which charge he continued till June 1824, when the augmentation of the army of the 1st May bringing him in as a Lieut.-Colonel, he was removed from that situation. On the 22d Sept. he re-joined the head-quarters of the artillery regiment at Dum Dum, and was appointed by the Com.-in-Chief to command the artillery on the Chittagong frontier.

LIEUT.-COLONEL COMMANDANT HENRY ROOME.

(Bombay Establishment.)

This officer arrived in India and was appointed Ensign 30th Sept. 1795, and posted to the 2d battalion (old establishment) commanded by Capt. James Romney. He proceeded with that corps from Bombay to Paulghautcherry, the then frontier station of Malabar. On his arrival he remained at head-quarters about six months. He was employed on various detachment duties during the years 1796 and 1797. He was promoted to Lieutenant in 1796. In 1798, he was employed on the frontier betwixt Paulghautcherry and Coimbetoor, to keep in check Coonjee Atcheen and other freebooters from the enemy's (Tippoo's) country, who were constantly making irruptions into the Company's territories, plundering and murdering the inhabitants.

In 1799, this officer joined the field-army assembled at Cannanore, for the invasion of Tippoo Sultaun's dominions. He served and was wounded at the battle of Seedaseer, 6th March 1799. He also served at the siege and capture of Seringapatam, stormed on the 4th May 1799. In 1801, he joined the field-army assembled at Surat for service in Guzerat; and was present at the battle of Kurree, 17th March 1802. He was promoted to Captain on the 19th of the latter month.

Capt. Roome was again wounded at the storming of the Pattan battery and Kurree lines, 30th April 1802. He was present in July following at the siege and capture of Sunkina; and carried the poorah by storm, (commanding the storming party), from which the fort was breached; and, upon the breach becoming practicable, it surrendered.

Capt. Roome commanded at the reduction of Bursood in Nov. 1802, and at the siege and capture of Baroda in Dec. following.

In 1803, he commanded a field detachment on the frontier of Guzerat; in 1805, in the Atteveessy; and reduced and took possession of the fort of Futty Broach; and in 1806, a field detachment assembled for the expulsion of the Bheels, who had invaded and were laying waste the Company's newly-acquired territories. In 1807, he was appointed to the command of the corps of Bombay cavalry, and joined the field force in Kattywar. He was present at the siege and capture of Kundoorha in Nov. 1807. In 1809, he was on field service in Kattywar, and present at the siege and capture of Mallia, stormed 6th July 1809. In 1810, he commanded a field detachment against the Pilwie Rajhpoots; and in 1811, a field detachment against the Coolies, and reduced them both to subjection. In 1812, he commanded a field detachment on the frontier of Guzerat, to prevent the incursion of the Pindarries.

He was promoted to Major, 2d Oct. 1813; and commanded a field detachment in the Atteveessy, to prevent the further irruption of the Pindarries into that province. In 1815, Major Roome joined the field force assembled on the frontier of Guzerat. In 1816, he joined the Deccan division of the army, commanded by M.-Gen. Lionel Smith; and was present, in 1817, at the battle of Kirkee, 5th Nov., commanding the 2d batt. 6th reg.; which corps he also commanded at the attack and defeat of the Peishwa's army at Poona, on the 16th and 17th November following.

This officer was promoted to Lieut.-Col. 1st Jan. 1818; and to Lieut.-Col. Commandant 1st May 1824.

LIEUT.-COL. COMMANDANT GEORGE MACKONOCHIE.

(Bombay Establishment.)

THIS officer was nominated a Cadet in 1796; and arriving at Bombay on the 4th Sept. in that year, he was appointed to an Ensigncy, and posted to the 2d batt. 4th N. I. then stationed at Bombay.

In Sept. 1797, he obtained a Lieutenancy, and was removed to the 2d. batt. 2d N. I. stationed at Paulghautcherry. On the breaking out of the war with Tippoo, he was ordered with 150 men into the Coimbetoor district, to co-operate with Lieut.-Col. Brown* of the Madras establishment, and where he remained until after the capture of Seringapatam, when he returned to his station at Paulghautcherry.

In 1800, he was posted to the 1st or grenadier battalion, which he joined in May, and was immediately ordered to take the command of a detachment that formed part of a force against Jemaulabad.

In 1802, he served with Sir William Clarke at the taking of

---

* Services, vol. ii. p. 207-15.

Kurree; and in the same year at the siege and capture of Baroda, under Lieut.-Col. Woodington*. In 1803, he was at the siege and storm of Broach; also at the siege and capitulation of Pawanghur, both under the command of Lieut.-Col. Woodington. He served the campaigns of 1803-4 and 5 with Col. Murray and M.-Gen. Jones, and was present at two of the storms of the fortress of Bhurtpoor.

In 1808, he served the campaign in the Deccan under Col. Wallace; in 1809, in the campaign in Kattywar; and was at the siege and storm of Mallia under Lieut.-Col. Walker †; in 1812, in the campaign in the Deccan under Col. Montresor ‡.

In 1815, this officer was removed from the grenadier battalion to the 2d batt. 1st reg. stationed at Baroda; and in the beginning of 1816, he was ordered with that battalion to reinforce Lieut.-Col. Kenny at Bearah, where he was posted to prevent the Pindarries from entering the Atteveessy district, and from thence he was ordered to Poona.

In October 1817, about the breaking out of the Mahratta war, he was obliged, from ill health, to give up the command of his battalion, and return to England; in consequence of which the command devolved on the late Lieut.-Col. Staunton §, who distinguished himself so conspicuously at Corygaum.

Lieut.-Col. Mackonochie again returned to Bombay, in Oct. 1819, and was posted to the 2d batt. 6th reg. at Poona; and in March 1820, his battalion, and the 1st batt. 8th N. I., were formed into a brigade, and he was ordered to Sholapoor, to form a new cantonment.

In Nov. 1820, he was ordered with his battalion to Guzerat: and in May 1822, he was removed to the Marine battalion at Bombay. In Feb. 1823, he was appointed to the command of the field force in Cutch; and in Jan. 1825, he embarked at Bombay for England.

This officer obtained his Captaincy in August 1804; his Majority in Dec. 1812; Lieut.-Colonelcy in 1818; and was appointed Lieut.-Col. Commandant in May 1824.

* Services, p. 10. † Services, vol. i. p. 147-58.
‡ Services, Royal Military Calendar, vol. iii. p. 313-14, 3d edit.
§ Services, vol. i. p. 95-106, and in this volume.

MAJOR HENRY EVANS DOWNES.

(Madras Establishment.)

This officer was a Cadet of 1799, and promoted to Lieutenant, 15th July 1800. He joined the 1st batt. 11th reg., serving with the Hyderabad subsidiary force, in March 1801, and was engaged in the campaigns against the Mahratta confederates in the years 1803, 4, 5, and 6, during which time he was present at the following affairs: siege and fall of Jaulnah, Asseerghur, battle of Argaum, siege and storm of Gawilghur, storm and fall of Lasslighaum, siege and fall of Chandore, and siege and fall of Gaulnah.

He was employed surveying in Candeish during part of the years 1804 and 5, in which period he commanded 3 companies of infantry, with 500 irregular horse, convoying a large supply of provisions from Surat to the army, in Bawen Berar.

He acted as Adjutant to the 1st batt. 11th reg. one year on field service, and received the thanks of the officer comanding the Hyderabad force, for particular conduct during the agitations that prevailed in 1806.

In 1810, he served in the expedition against the French islands, and was appointed Assistant-Quarter-Master-General to the forces: he accompanied the flank battalion in two attacks, viz. on Saint Denis and Saint Paul. He was permanently appointed Assistant-Quarter-Master-General, by his Excellency Lieut.-Gen. Abercrombie, and for several months had charge of the signal and barrack departments. For his conduct he received the thanks, in general orders, of his Excellency Major-Gen. Warde*, as also the following letters on his departure and return to India:—

" *Port Louis, December 7th,* 1811.

" Sir,—Capt. Downes, of the Madras establishment, late Assistant-Quarter-Master-General to the forces, serving on the island of Bourbon, being on the point of returning to India, I beg you will have the goodness to submit to his Ex. the Commander of the Forces, the sense I entertain of

---

* Services, Royal Military Calendar, vol. ii. p. 294-5, 3d edit.

the zeal and ability which Capt. Downes has uniformly shewn during the time he has been employed in the department, and his exertions upon all occasions to forward the public service: and I shall feel myself particularly obliged, if his Ex. Gen. Warde will have the goodness to bring these circumstances under the favourable notice of his Excellency the Commander in Chief at Madras.

(Signed)   " H. EDWARDS, Dep.-Quarter-Master-General.

" *To Capt. Molloy, Military Secretary.*"

" *To his Excellency Lieut.-General Sir S. Auchmuty, Com.-in-Chief.*

" SIR,—I have the honour to transmit for your Excellency's notice the copy of a letter from the Deputy-Quarter-Master-General to my Military Secretary, and I have great pleasure in adding my confirmation of the praise bestowed on Captain Downes by Major Edwards.

(Signed)   " HENRY WARDE, Major-General.

" *Mon Plaisir, Isle Mauritius, 8th Dec.* 1811."

In March 1812, he rejoined the 1st-11th reg. at Paulcondah, in the northern Circars, where the corps was employed, under Col. Fletcher, against refractory Zemindars. In 1813, he commanded detachments from the 11th and 20th regiments at Palaveram and in the hills in the Rajahmundry district. In Oct. 1814, he was appointed to the 1st battalion of pioneers, and marched in command of 500 men of that corps towards Ceylon, with Col. Thomson's detachment.

In Feb. 1815, he marched with the pioneers and magazines under Col. Dalrymple to the army of reserve, under Sir T. Hislop, on the banks of the Toombuddra river. In Nov. following, he marched in command of pioneers with a detachment under Col. Marriott* for the reduction of Kurnool, and was at its siege and surrender.

In May 1816, he was removed to the 2d battalion of pioneers, and joined a detachment of that corps, serving with the Poona subsidiary force at Seroor. In Dec., he marched with the Poona force, under Col. Smith, towards the frontiers near Chandore; and in Feb. 1817, he returned with the pioneers towards Seroor, to complete basons for

* Services in this volume, p. 39-42.

flying bridges over the Gore river. In April, he marched with the Poona subsidiary force to the southward after the ex-minister Trimbuckjee; returned to Poona, which was invested on the 8th May, and a treaty made with the Peishwa.

On the 8th Oct. 1817, he marched with the Poona subsidiary force (now the 4th division of the army of the Deccan) under B.-Gen. Smith, towards the frontiers of the Mahratta country, for the purpose of attacking the Pindarries. The force halted near Chandore, and returned, on the 9th Nov., to Seroor, on the way towards Poona, in consequence of the Peishwa breaking out and attacking the residency and cantonment.

Major Downes continued with this force until February 1818, when he was obliged to proceed to sea on account of ill health, and eventually to Europe. In June 1821, he returned to Madras, and joined the 2d batt. 11th reg. at Velore. In Feb. 1822, he was appointed Deputy-Judge-Advocate-General to the Hyderabad subsidiary force; and on his promotion, 10th April 1824, to the rank of Major, he rejoined the 21st, (late 1st-11th reg.) having vacated his appointment, in conformity to the late regulations of the service.

MAJOR WILLIAM MORISON.

(Bombay Establishment.)

IN 1801, this officer was appointed a Cadet on the Bombay establishment. He reached India in July, and was immediately attached, as an Ensign, to the 1st or grenadier battalion (his rank not having then arrived from England), at Sadashewghur*, or Carwar, with which corps he proceeded to and remained at Goa †, attached to

* This is the popular name: it would classically be written Sida-Sivagheri, the hill of the holy Siva.

† In consequence of the French having entered Portugal, and fearing their influence would extend to India, it was judged advisable by the British government, to have, for a time, possession of Goa; and as the British envoy, Sir William Clarke, was apprehensive

the grenadier battalion, till February 1802, when his rank in the Company's army having arrived, he was promoted to a Lieutenancy, 17th October, 1801, and permanently posted to the Bombay European regiment, which corps he joined at Cananore, in April.

Lieut. Morison continued with his regiment, without any thing particular occurring, till the declaration of war against the Nairs, in Cotiote, occasioned by a surprise of an outpost, and murder of two British officers and many sepoys, and the escape of the Pyche Rajah's nephews, (accompanied by a few of our Native troops) from confinement in the fort of Cananore. The corps left Cananore for Tellichery the next morning, and proceeded, on the following day, to Cotaparambah, 9 miles inland, where they remained, the then heavy monsoon not allowing them to commence active operations in the field: here they were joined by a part of the regiment which had been stationed at Cochin, and employed in detached parties in pursuit of the enemy for some time, till they finally formed part of a force under the command of Colonel Montresor*, and were employed marching about the districts of Coonnanaad, Curtinaad, and Wynaad, sometimes enduring extreme privations, engaged with the enemy†, and carrying fire and sword in every direction.

---

resistance would be made to such (in all appearance) an unjustifiable demand, it was deemed necessary to have troops to overawe the Portuguese. The above regiment was ordered to form part of a force destined, in case of emergency, to act against Goa, and accordingly embarked from Sadashewghur on board H. M.'s frigate, La Chiffon, in the latter end of the above year; arrived off Fort Alguada, which commands the entrance into the river, on which the city stands; cast anchor about eleven o'clock the following day; and immediately disembarked, without any opposition from the numerous Portuguese garrison. The day after their arrival, a demand was made by Sir W. Clarke, to be allowed to take possession of a fort called Gasperdees with British troops, which was at first refused, but the Governor and his council, finding Sir William firm and peremptory, and perceiving large bodies of troops had arrived, of which they pretended to have been totally ignorant, and that military preparations were making by the English to seize Goa by force, the Viceroy, as he said, to prevent the effusion of blood, gave up his right to govern, and the British quietly took possession of Gasperdees, which was garrisoned by the 3d batt. N. I., under the command of Capt. Lloyd.

* Services, Royal Military Calendar, vol. iii. p. 313-14, 3d edit.

† An idea of the character of the enemy may be formed by the following account of an

Lieut. Morison remained with the European regiment the whole of 1802 and 1803, but on the 9th N. I. being raised, he was transferred to that corps. In Feb. 1804, he embarked from Tellichery for Bombay, to join the 1st battalion, then forming part of a large army destined to act against Jeswunt Rao Holkar. Col. Murray's* force was then stationed at the village of Cupperwanjee, 24 miles S.E. of Ahmedabad, so that he had to travel, principally at his own expense, not less than 750 miles. After a tedious and unpleasant voyage to Bombay and Surat, Lieut. Morison reached Col. Murray's army on the 1st of April, and as war was then declared against Holkar, the army marched† towards Oogein, the capital of Dowlut Rao Scindia.

Near the Lunawarra pass, and not a great distance from a town of the same name, Lieut. Morison was detached on a foraging party, with 200 Native infantry, and 60 irregular horse, about 10 miles from camp: he was attacked by 500 Bheels, the aborigines of Guzerat, and after a smart contest, succeeded in repulsing them, with nearly

---

affair in which this officer was personally concerned. After the force under the command of Col. Montresor had advanced as far as Pullinyaul and Monontody, it descended the Kallyary ghaut, and marched to the south in the direction of Cotaparamba. A few of the Europeans straggled into an unfrequented part of the country to the right of the line of march, and were fired on by a numerous body of the enemy, there stationed under the command of one of the Rajah's relations, for the purpose of attacking the whole force under Col. Montresor, who, it was expected, would take that road. Three of the poor fellows fell, and the others made their escape. On the business being made known to Col. Montresor, he ordered 30 Europeans and 100 sepoys, to proceed and bring off the bodies of the wounded or dead men. Being first for duty, Lieut. Morison was of the party. Guided by the men who had escaped, they soon came in sight of the bodies, and found that the savages had opened their heads, taken out their brains, torn their shirts, wrapped the brains within, and placed the same in the hands of the dead soldiers! they were also in other respects most horribly mangled. While in the act of securing the bodies, the party received the full fire of the enemy, and lost several more men: they succeeded, after enduring a very warm fire for about half an hour, in carrying off the killed and wounded, and rejoined the force.

* Services, Royal Military Calendar, vol. ii. p. 227-9, 3d edit.

† At this period the thermometer ranged as high as 110° in the tents, and 10 or 12 men were daily struck down: an elephant in going through the Lunawarra pass, in Guzerat, died on the spot, from the effects of a noon-day sun; and in a forced march of a detachment commanded by Major, the late Sir George Holmes, not less than 30 men of H. M.'s 65th reg. died from the same cause.

equal loss, 10 men killed and wounded. The enemy, however, showed a determination to cut him off, if possible, and availed themselves of their local knowledge of the country, and kept hovering on the flanks of his detachment, sniping his men, till within a very short distance of camp, where he found a brigade of Native infantry, with guns, ready to march to his assistance, Col. Murray having received information from some fugitives, that the Bheels had been successful in their attack upon his little band. On this occasion Lieut. Morison received the personal thanks of Col. Murray.

The troops continued their march towards Oogein, and soon after, passing the frontiers of Guzerat, at Dhouad, they were led to believe they were on the way to co-operate with a force under Col. Monson, advancing from Lord Lake's army, in the Bengal provinces, towards the town of Mundooseer: this belief gained ground, and they were in expectation of active service, when, on reaching a small village, two marches from the N. E. bank of the river Mihie, they heard that Col. Monson had arrived at Mundooseer, and that he had there been intercepted by a large force, under the personal command of Jeswunt Rao Holkar, and was in full retreat towards the grand army, commanded by Lord Lake. To this discouraging information a further disappointment was experienced, as they found they were also going to retrogade; and early next morning Col. Murray marched, and reached the banks of the Mihie, which the army had crossed two days before. Here he deemed it necessary to take up a strong defensive position, as it was rumoured a considerable army of Holkar's was in full march to attack him.

The army remained in this situation till it was ascertained none of Holkar's troops were in that part of the country, when, on the requisition of the British resident at the court of Scindia, they again advanced towards Oogein, which they reached a little after the commencement of the heavy rains, in 1804.

It must be in the recollection of officers who were present with Col. Murray's army, what hardships were experienced during the rainy months in the above year; when, after an advance to Holkar's capital, Indore, they encamped, on their return, within a few miles of Oogein, on the banks of the river Siprah, which in the course of a very few hours, rose in such a manner as to fill the minds of all with fear and consternation, and exposed them to numerous perils; and, such was the belief, had the river continued to rise, the whole force would have perished in another day, as it would have joined, in the midst of the camp, a small but rapid stream, directly in the rear of Col. Murray's tent. During the period the army was stationed in this horrid spot, nothing was to be seen but human misery in all its shapes;—men, women, children,—horses, camels, and every kind of animal,—lying dead, and dying.

At this time, Lieut. Morison was stationed in Oogein in command of 100 sepoys, as a protection to military stores; and on the falling of the river, he was ordered across to get instructions from Col. Murray, which having received, he was returning, when he found his boat crowded with poor wretches of both sexes, anxious to avail themselves of such an opportunity to avoid another dreadful night, and rendered desperate from hunger. The boat was so crowded, that dire necessity compelled the crew to strike the unfortunates on the fingers, so as to oblige them to let go their hold, and sink under the boat to rise no more. Such are the effects of a monsoon campaign in India.

Lieut. Morison was relieved from his charge at Oogein, on the following day, by Lieutenant, now Lieut.-Colonel Thatcher.

The army continued near Oogein till October when it broke ground, and marched to the northward, in the direction of Mundooseer. On arriving at Kotah, it quitted the original line of march, and directed its route to Shawabhad, about four days' journey to the eastward, a place of considerable size and strength, belonging to Holkar; and again the troops were in expectation of soon coming into contact with the enemy, but a second time they were disappointed, as on taking up their ground on the third day, M.-Gen. Jones* arrived in camp to supersede Col. Murray in his command.

* This officer has now arrived at the rank of Lieut.-General, and is a Knight Commander

The enemy halted a few days, and then retraced their steps to Kotah, from thence crossed the Chumbul, marched through the

of the Order of the Bath. The following extracts, from general orders, afford a just compliment to the Bombay army, and at the same time furnish a sketch of the services of Sir Richard Jones:—

Extract from General Orders, by the Commanding Officer of the Forces.

"L.-Gen. Nicolls has great satisfaction in publishing to the army of this presidency, a copy of His Excellency the Com.-in-Chief's letter of the 14th Dec. 1805, expressing his entire approbation of the conduct of the division of the Bombay army, under the immediate command of M.-Gen. Jones, co-operating with the army under the personal command of his Excellency Lord Lake, to which L.-Gen. Nicolls is happy to add, a copy of the favourable sense the Hon. the Governor in Council entertains of the Major-General's conduct, as well as that of the corps of His Majesty and the Hon. Company, in the late campaign under the command of M.-Gen. Jones."

By Government.

"*Bombay Castle, 21st Jan.* 1806.

"In publishing the following letter from His Excellency the Right Hon. the Com.-in-Chief in India, dated the 14th of Dec. 1805, the Hon. the Governor in Council, impressed with the duest sense of the important services rendered by the division of the Bombay army, under the command of M.-Gen. Jones, will take an early opportunity of bringing those services under the notice of the Hon. the Court of Directors.

"The Gov. in Council has, on every occasion when the services of the Bombay army have been called into action, had cause to express his approbation of the meritorious and exemplary manner in which their duty has been performed; and it is with particular satisfaction that, to his own sentiments, he has now to add, the professional sanction of so competent a judge as the present distinguished Commander-in-Chief of his Majesty's and the Hon. Company's troops in India.

"The Commanding Officer of the forces is accordingly requested to convey to M.-Gen. Jones, the thanks of this government, for the very able manner in which he has discharged the arduous duties incident to the command of the division of the Bombay army of Hindostan.

"The judgment and talents which that officer has displayed in the exercise of that important trust, have fully established, in a manner the most creditable to his reputation, his claims on the confidence of his employers, both at home and abroad.

"Gen. Nicolls will also be pleased to direct M.-Gen. Jones, to convey the thanks of the Governor in Council to the officers, non-commissioned officers, and privates of His Majesty's and of the Hon. Company's forces, composing this division of the Bombay army, for the perseverance, steadiness, and spirit they have evinced, during the distant and extended series of honourable duties in which they have been so long engaged."

"*To the Hon. Jonathan Duncan, Governor of Bombay.*

"Sir,—The division of the Bombay army, under M.-Gen. Jones, being on its return to the province of Guzerat, I deem it proper to convey to you the high sense I entertain of its conduct and services since it has been employed in this quarter of India.

"In the course of its very long and arduous march to Hindostan, it evinced a perseverance under severe fatigue, and a patience under the privation of many of its comforts, which I con-

Boondie pass to Rampoora, whence, after halting a few days, they proceeded towards Bhurtpoor, then besieged by the grand army

sider in the highest degree exemplary, and which afford the most decisive proof of the high discipline it possessed, and of the honourable zeal by which it was actuated.

"On its junction with my army, the valour, steadiness, and spirit, which it displayed, under circumstances of the greatest difficulty, obtained my warmest approbation; and, subsequently to that period, its conduct in the performance of every service in which it has been employed, has been in the highest degree meritorious.

"The judgment and ability of M.-Gen. Jones have on all occasions been eminently displayed, and entitle that officer to every possible testimony of praise. The activity with which he prosecuted those objects entrusted to him, and his zealous exertions in all situations to promote the public service, have afforded me the utmost satisfaction, and in a high degree justified the confidence reposed in him by the government, when he was selected for so important a command.

"In expressing to you my approbation of M.-Gen. Jones, and of the officers and men under his command, I indulge an earnest hope, that the government of Bombay will withhold no mark of its gratitude and applause which may be due to their very meritorious services.

(Signed) "LAKE."

General Orders by the Hon. the Gov. in Council.

"Bombay Castle, Oct. 2, 1809.

"It is not without considerable and very sincere sentiments of concern, that the Governor in Council sees himself on the eve of being deprived of the able and very grateful co-operation and assistance which, for the two years past, government have not ceased to derive from the military experience, professional talents, and cordiality of manners, so conspicuously manifested during the latter period of M.-Gen. Jones holding the chief command of this army; such as will not fail to be brought to the notice of the Hon. the Court of Directors, in addition to the favourable sentiments which the Gov. in Council has already had more than once occasion to express of the uniformly acceptable eminent services, which the General has rendered to the Hon. Company and his country, during the period of his extended military career in India.

"Under these impressions, the request of M.-Gen. Jones to proceed to England in the Taunton Castle, is complied with; at the same time, that, should that ship be ultimately ordered to join the Madras convoy at Point de Galle, General Jones will, in due attention to his rank, and deference to his professional merits, be allowed to retain the command till the ship's leaving, or passing that station."

M.-Gen. Jones' farewell Orders to the Bombay Army.

"In a period of near forty years in the Hon. Company's service in the Bombay establishment, M.-Gen. Jones has had opportunities most ample to ascertain the character and conduct of the Bombay army; and from experience in every rank in the service, he is enabled

under Lord Lake, and arrived in sufficient time to hear the roar of cannon and musketry on the night Jeswunt Rao Holkar attacked the trenches, at the head of a numerous body of chosen men.

The engineers belonging to Lord Lake's army having reported the breach practicable, his Lordship again determined to storm, on the 20th Feb., Bhurtpoor; to make a diversion which, it was hoped, would have withdrawn the attention of the enemy from the principal assault, and also to attack a fortified village, afterwards called Grant's Post. Orders were accordingly issued for the whole to move down; the storming party to the trenches, and the others to march off the parade at 3 o'clock in the afternoon. Col. Don[*], of the Bengal army, commanded the storming party; Lieut.-Col. Taylor, Bombay division, the party destined to blow open the gate, (to create a diversion); and Captain Grant, H. M.'s 86th reg., to command against the fortified village. On this occasion Lieut. Morison was a volunteer, and directed to take charge of eight scaling ladders. Lieutenant, now Major Charles Garraway, of the 17th N. I., also received an equal number, and they were attached to Col. Taylor's command.

When Col. Taylor waited on Lord Lake to receive his final instructions, his Lordship said, he had given him good guides, who

to declare, with the most sincere and heartfelt gratification, it has been uniformly most honourable.

"In the field, it has been gallant and brave, and patient in fatigues and hardships, that reflect the highest merit on the army as soldiers.

"In garrison, the army has been zealously active and obedient,—truly loyal to their King and Country,—possessing a stern fidelity that has never been shaken; all of which qualifications combine to make them worthy of the highest commendation as soldiers, as men and citizens.

"With these sentiments of sincere approbation of the conduct of officers and men, M.-Gen. Jones takes leave of the Bombay army; and while it will be his duty to communicate his opinion of their well-earned and well-established merits before his superiors, he begs leave to assure them, it will ever be his pride and his pleasure to uphold their good name, and they will ever have his warmest wishes and support, on every occasion, where their interests and welfare are under consideration."

[*] Services, vol. ii. p. 527-60.

would bring him under the walls of the fort without observation. The guides accordingly arrived; and at the hour appointed, they marched off the ground to the attack. Their fire was to be the signal for the storming party to move out with celerity from the trenches, Capt. Grant at the same time making his destined attack. Col. Taylor followed his guide, who, however, proved a most treacherous rascal, and instead of taking the detachment a circuitous route, directly led them down to the town, so that they soon experienced the consequences, as they perceived, long before they saw the walls of the town, being then in an open jungle, a very large body of the enemy's horse, at least 2000, who drew near, and evidently shewed a disposition to attack them. They were, therefore, obliged to open a line of fire to check them; it attained the object, but at the same time frustrated the design they were intended for, discovered them to the enemy, and caused the main attack to commence too soon. A very little time after the dispersion of Holkar's horse, they were saluted, when advancing, with a most tremendous enfilading fire from the town, which laid many low. The instant the Native pioneers who carried the ladders found some of their companions were killed, and that there were likely to be many more, down they fell, ladders and all, and the utmost exertion was insufficient to get them to rise; Lieut. Morison and Lieut. Garraway were therefore obliged to leave them to their fate, and follow (with what ladders remained) the detachment, which was pushing on with great rapidity to the gateway they were sent to seize, and which was discovered full of matchlockmen, who fired, retreated to load, and again fired. At this time many officers and men were killed and wounded; but still Lieut. Morison was in great hopes of succeeding, when, as he was running, and would have been in a few steps so near the wall that no cannon-shot could have hurt him, one struck him on the joint of the left knee, and shattered it to pieces. He dropped; and immediately after Col. Taylor, whose age and health would not carry him through the day so actively as a young officer, came up to the head of the line, and thinking, from the force of the enemy, and the fatigued and reduced state of his detachment, there were no hopes of success, ordered a retreat.

The detachment was in full retreat, and at least one hundred yards from Lieut. Morison, when two brave brother officers, Captains Tolcher and Waddington, both now no more, left their divisions and returned, exposed to the heavy fire from the town, attended by a few gallant sepoys from his old regiment, the grenadier battalion, and carried him off in the best way they could; and on reaching his tent the limb was amputated.

After a hard struggle of upwards of two hours, and dreadful loss in men and officers, the main assault on Bhurtpoor* failed; and the storming party having executed as much as men could perform, were obliged to retire to camp. Capt. Grant was more successful, indeed completely so, as he carried the fortified village in a most gallant style; in which he found some guns which Holkar had taken from Col. Monson in his memorable retreat. Notwithstanding the discomfiture of the troops on the 20th, Lord Lake determined again to storm the breach; and after every effort, and with hundreds killed and wounded, our brave fellows were compelled again to retire.

Shortly after, all the wounded were directed to be sent to Agra, under escort of a very strong detachment, commanded by Colonel Macan† of the Bengal cavalry, which, being a good opportunity, Lieut. Morison availed himself of it to quit camp. In April he proceeded to Futteghur, and thence embarked in a budgeroe for Calcutta. On his passage down the Ganges to Caunpoor, in the afternoon of the 2d day, a most severe storm of hail, accompanied by tremendous thunder and lightning, came on from the N. W. The boat was driven with great fury down the river, and Lieut. Morison had just time to commit himself to the water, and the

* See Memoir of the gallant Lord Lake, in this volume.
† The late Major-General Macan, of the Bengal establishment, was appointed a Cadet in 1769. He served under Brig.-Gen. Goddard, and proceeded to the coast with Lord Cornwallis. He was subsequently at the head of the four brigades of Bengal cavalry, and also upon the general Staff of the army, and after his tour of duty had expired, embarked, greatly impaired in his constitution, for England, but died of a fever on the passage.

river being shallow, he gained the shore, where he underwent, from the hail, most acute pain, as his back was exposed to it, which quite exhausted him: he then laid himself down on his stomach, with his head resting on his hands, expecting every minute the river would rise and carry him off. He continued in that position till the storm subsided, when some of his people, who had thrown themselves also from the boat, came to him, by whose assistance he was conveyed to a small village about a mile off, which could afford him no sustenance. His poverty saved him from robbery, and perhaps murder, as in that part of Bengal the inhabitants are wild and ferocious; several times during his stay with them, they held consultations amongst themselves, but as he had nothing but a pair of loose trowsers and shirt on, they did not think it worth while to pilfer him. He spent the night in the midst of these people, in the open air, round a large fire, and in the morning dispatched his hamauls (palanquin bearers) to learn something about his boat. They returned with the intelligence, that it was stranded in the middle of the river, and that all his baggage was swept away; he however got on board the boat, and that evening arrived at Caunpoor. After experiencing many difficulties, he reached Calcutta, on the 1st July; sailed for Bombay on the 1st September, and arrived there on the 1st November, 1805.

Lieut. Morison was appointed Barrack-Master in Guzerat, and proceeded, in February 1806, to take charge of his situation at Baroda, to which was soon added that of Commissay of Bazars at that station, where he remained till the establishment of the Commissariat in 1811, when he was appointed to the command of Bancoote, 60 miles to the south of Bombay, which office he assumed in September of the same year. On the 8th January, 1816, he was promoted to a company.

In 1817, war was declared against Badjee Rao, and as it was considered an object of some moment, by the Bombay government, to deprive him of his strong holds on the coast, a small force* was sent

* Hon. Company's cruizer, Prince of Wales, Lieut. Robson, dead; Hon. Company's

from Bombay, and placed under the orders of Capt. Morison, to take the fort of Severndroog, 16 miles from Bancoote, or Fort Victoria, said to be garrisoned by a large body of brave men. He embarked on board the Company's cruizer, Prince of Wales, and arrived within cannon-shot of the enemy's fort, at 5 o'clock on the evening of the 30th November 1817; passed within pistol shot of Severndroog, and each vessel, as it did so, opened a heavy fire upon the fort, which was returned by guns of large calibre, but the vessels were so close the enemy could not sufficiently depress their guns, and all but two shots, which struck the rigging of the Prince of Wales, passed over them without doing any injury. The transports having sailed past the S. W. angle of Severndroog, found a heavy fire opened on them from fort Kunkah, a most formidable battery, which Capt. Morison had been led to believe, previous to quitting Bancoote, was nothing more than a gurree or breast-work, in possession of 12 or 15 men, and he had, agreeably to the information received, made his disposition of attack; but the fire of such a strong place completely overturned all his plans. He therefore, as soon as the ships had anchored, caused a signal to be thrown out for the officers to come on board, when he represented that notwithstanding the account of fort Kunkah was very different to what it actually proved to be, still he intended to make an immediate landing, and an attempt to take it, as he conceived, with his small force, there would be much danger in delay, particularly as the enemy could easily and speedily be reinforced by the garrisons from the interior; and if the force could capture the most formidable of the three, by storm, it would strike an effectual damp upon the men, within the other two; and, probably, be the means of an immediate surrender. He was opposed by all, as, in their opinion, there was not the slightest chance of success. He therefore reluctantly gave an order for the immediate landing of the men, not to storm fort Kun-

---

ship, Sylph, Lieut. Dominicity, dead; 2 gun boats, Engineer, Lieut. Dashwood; Company of Artillery, Lieut. Stevenson; 400 Sepoys, Captains Campbell (dead) Soppitt; Assistant-Surgeon, Dr. Purnell.

kah, but to take up an encampment on the beach; the sequel, however, will shew, that had he been guided by his own judgment, he would, probably, have carried fort Kunkah.

The troops disembarked in the evening, and took up a position favorable to landing stores from the ships, about 150 yards from the shore; in the rear of which was a very high hill, within musket-shot from the tents. The enemy being in great numbers, determined on a night-attack. Accordingly, when dark, they detached a strong party from fort Goa, the principal gate of which was towards the north, and washed at high water by the sea, and completely secured from the view of the British, the town being between the camp and fort. In the middle of the night the enemy commenced a sharp fire from the hill, which they had gained by a circuitous footpath; every ball came into camp, but as the British were in tents, and the enemy were ignorant of the exact quarter where the piquets and guards were stationed, the fire did little injury.

On the 1st November, Capt. Morison directed Lieut. Stevenson of the artillery to cause two eight and a half inch howitzers to be carried and planted in a commanding position over the village, as he conceived a bombardment of the fort, to which the Mahrattas were entirely unaccustomed, would have a good effect, and produce either the abandonment of the three forts or the delivery of the same into his hands. Agreeably to instructions, therefore, that officer, with those under him, Lieutenants Miller, Osborne, and Lyons, accompanied by a body of infantry, as a covering party, under Captain R. Campbell, used every exertion to meet his orders. The howitzers continued to play all day upon Goa, and the enemy, at times, returned the fire with spirit. Finding, however, the bombardment towards the afternoon did not answer the desired object, and considering the detachment under his command to be too divided if he allowed the artillery to continue on the hill, in addition to which, he was apprehensive the enemy would again attempt their camp during the night, he ordered Capt. Campbell and Lieut. Stevenson to abandon their situation for the present, and at night-fall, to return within the line of sentries. And to frustrate any design which the enemy might form to annoy them, he sent Capt. Soppitt, with a strong party, to remain concealed in the hills during the night, all which was performed by the respective officers with promptitude and the utmost alacrity, and the camp remained quite undisturbed.

On the 2d December, Capt. Morison was determined, if possible, to make an attack upon the walls of fort Goa, with artillery, and sent a party into the village and in the neighbourhood, to collect as much coarse cloth as possible to make sand bags; he at the same time reconnoitred from a hill, for the most eligible spot on which to erect a battery, and fixed on a piece of ground about 300 yards from the walls, certainly exposed to a cross fire from the other two forts, but being at the same time a spot where there was a little cover for the troops; he resolved to move down as the moon disappeared at 12 o'clock, but this plan he was also obliged to abandon, as the parties returned without cloth, the inhabitants of the villages, on their approach, having abandoned their homes.

Every attempt to take Severndroog having hitherto proved abortive, Capt. Morison began to apprehend that the troops were insufficient for the purpose, and to think only of keeping his ground till the Bombay government could send reinforcements. On the 3d, therefore, they remained quiet in camp, but on the 4th he ordered Lieut. Stevenson to plant 2 twelve-pounders in front of the encampment, and to open a fire upon the works of fort Kunkah, which was returned with spirit and precision by the garrison. Capt. Morison found his shots fell somewhat short of the range of the enemy's works, and directed the guns to be withdrawn, at the same time every shot from the enemy's guns was thrown into the midst of the camp, and rendered it expedient to remove. Capt. Morison immediately seized the opportunity, and determined to attempt the capture of fort Goa, at all hazards; but he was anxious to avail himself of the services of volunteers, as he felt quite certain it would be an attack of great danger; and having considered the several modes of taking forts, he finally came to the resolution of storming it that afternoon at 3 o'clock*.

Accordingly he asked the Commander of the Prince of Wales, if he would lead the seamen to the assault, which he declined: he then asked Lieut. Dominicity the same question, who consented with pleasure: and Capt. Campbell also gave him his services, on the occasion. The storming party† with ladders, were directed to quit camp at half past three o'clock. The artillery under Lieut. Stephenson and officers of his detachment, were again sent to the rising ground to fire upon the two forts, to keep them employed whilst the party were engaged with Kunkah: the signal to advance, being a single gun fired from the howitzer battery.

The gun was fired precisely at three, on which the storming party pushed most gallantly across the rocks which separate Kunkah from the continent, covered by the fire of howitzers and musketry from the party stationed within musket shot, to prevent the enemy from making their appearance on the walls, or to discover the weakness of the stormers. On gaining the intended place of escalade, Capt. Campbell and his brave men, found it very formidable and defended by numerous matchlock-men; that, however, did not lower the spirit of his brave companions, who immediately placed the ladders and ascended; which, when the enemy, three times their number, perceived, they moved quickly to the end of the works, threw down their arms, and called for mercy. This was granted, but not before our men had fired a volley in amongst them. The fort being taken, the guns were turned against the two others, the fire of which, directed by British artillery-men, very soon rendered useless those mounted

---

* In India the natives dine immediately after noon, and retire to rest, never dreaming of an attack in open day; consequently only few guards are kept to protect works, who also often fall asleep. This consideration greatly influenced Capt. Morison, knowing also that a day-attack had succeeded at Broach, in 1803, and at Mallia in 1809.

† Capt. Campbell, 60 men; Lt. Dominicity, 80 seamen; 1 Native officer, with a covering party, 50; and scaling ladders. Total, rank and file, 190.

on Severndroog, and, with the assistance of the howitzers, nearly silenced the fire of fort Goa.

Previous to Capt. Campbell quitting camp, Capt. Morison had directed him, if successful in the attack on fort Kunkah, to give his men rest, to get all their muskets cleaned, and when the moon went down, to proceed and storm Goa: fearing, however, he might not recollect the order, Capt. Morison penned him a few lines from the howitzer battery, agreeably to which he moved out, planted his ladders, and mounted the walls, when he found the place was totally deserted, the garrison having made their escape at dusk; and in the morning, a flag of truce was perceived waving in the wind from the strong island fort of Severndroog, which was soon taken possession of with many prisoners.

Thus, in the short space of four days, fell very unexpectedly the three strong forts, Severndroog, Goa, and Kunkah, generally called Hurne by the Mahrattas, after a trifling loss on the part of the British, and not a heavy one on that of the enemy. 320 guns of various calibres, four large pirate vessel, several boats, quantities of grain, ghee, and sundry stores, fell into the hands of the captors.

Severndroog was the first place of strength taken by the British in the war of 1817, consequently, Capt. Morison indulged an honest pride in firing a royal salute on its fall, which was repeated, by order of government, at Bombay, and the hon. Governor in council returned thanks to the detachment for their bravery and conduct during the siege.

On the evening of the 5th December, Major Bond*, of the Bombay artillery, sent down by the government to assume the conduct of the siege, arrived, but, fortunately, Captain Morison had saved him the trouble. He delivered over charge to Major Bond, and, on the morning of the 6th, returned, to assume his command at Bancoote†.

* Services, vol. i. p. 335-9.

† About ten miles to the S. E. of Bancoote, there is a strong hill fort, called Muddenghur, which then belonged to the Peishwa, and was garrisoned by a considerable body of men, who it was suspected used to issue out at night, and attack one of his outposts. Captain Morison, therefore, wished to dislodge them, and offered to the Bombay government, if 300

A strong detachment, under Lieut.-Col. D. Prother*, having been formed to take the hill forts belonging to the Peishwa, that officer took Loghur, Pallie, and several other places, and advanced to a large village called Mahar, at the head of the Bancoote river, from whence Captain Morison received a letter to join him with every man he could spare from his command.

On the 26th April 1818, the night Capt. Morison arrived at Mahar, at 11 o'clock, a strong detachment, commanded by Major Hall, H. M.'s 89th reg. marched from camp to attack a stockade, which protected the approach to the pettah of Ryghur, defended by a considerable body of Arabs. The party arrived at the stockade as the day broke, and met with a warm reception, but soon caused the enemy to retreat; many were killed in the attack and retreat, and the pettah fell into our possession.

On the return of Major Hall's detachment, Col. Prother determined to march next morning to invest Ryghur, a fort till then considered by the Natives impregnable. The troops took up their ground about three miles from Ryghur, plainly seen from the camp. The pioneers were immediately set to work, to make a road for guns, which were sent up in the evening, and put in battery.

At day-break on the morning of the 28th April, Col. Prother and staff, to which Capt. Morison was attached, proceeded to superintend the opening of the batteries, and having done so, proposed breakfasting in the pettah. When they arrived at the batteries the Colonel was told by Maj. Bond, that the enemy had burned a work outside, and had either retreated within the fort, or had abandoned it altogether, as they had not molested the covering party or tried to prevent the erection of the battery. The Colonel, however, gave the word to commence firing on the works: the first and second round of spherical

---

men were placed under his command, to take the fort; he received an answer from the Adjutant-General of the army, saying, that the contents of his letter had been laid before the Com.-in-Chief, that his services would have been accepted, but as a senior officer had been ordered to command at Severndroog, and to take the forts in the Concan, out of delicacy to him, they must be declined.

* Services, vol. i. p. 304-7.

case were received in silence by the enemy, but on the third fire they opened their guns so suddenly as made our troops know they were within, and determined to defend the place. When the Colonel saw the batteries were opened, and that every thing was going on in a regular manner, he and his staff returned to breakfast, and had got a considerable way back, when the gay mouldings of his palanquin attracted the attention of the enemy, who commenced a fire at it, which was continued whilst within range of the guns. On reaching the pettah where the Colonel had desired his servants to prepare breakfast, it was ascertained they had misunderstood his orders, and gone to a village between the fort and pettah. It consequently became necessary, either to return or go without breakfast; the former alternative was adopted, and the Colonel and his staff retraced their steps, and found their breakfast-table secure from the view of the enemy, only by an old ruined house, and completely under fire. Notwithstanding which, and in momentary expectation of having their table upset by a cannon-ball, for they could hear them crashing the trees around them, the morning air and exercise gave the officers so good an appetite that all made a hearty meal, occasionally passing jokes, at the want of precision of the enemy's gunners. After breakfast they returned to the pettah and expected to run the gauntlet again, but whether the garrison thought they were too far off, or were themselves sufficiently employed in returning the fire from the British batteries, they did not molest the staff.

By the time they reached the pettah, the troops, with the exception of the 1st of the 9th, (now 17th), commanded by Capt. Soppitt, which remained on the old ground as a protection to all the stores, were encamped near it. Thirteen half-inch mortar batteries* were

* On the batteries opening, the enemy seemed to treat them with disdain; as the artillery officers, to get a proper elevation, gradually threw the shells from the mortars, till they completely got the range of the highest part of the rock. The garrison, therefore, on the shells bursting short of them, thought they were perfectly safe, and boldly for the first day came to relieve their guards; but on the mortars being gradually elevated, they became more cautious; and when they perceived that the shells from the three batteries were crossing each other, and bursting with a tremendous explosion on every part of the hill, their terror became

soon after formed on the E. and S. W. faces of the fort, which commenced their fire that evening, and continued, as also the grand battery, to throw shells into the place, till the final surrender of Ryghur, on the 10th May.

Seven days after the commencement of the siege, the enemy threw out a flag of truce, and vakeels, or ambassadors, from the fort came down to negotiate. Their terms of surrender were such, however, as to render them inadmissible, and an order was given to re-commence the bombardment, which continued all the night of the 7th and day of the 8th. Towards evening of the latter, a shell from the S. W. battery, commanded by Lieut. Jacobs of the artillery, set fire to one of the principal magazines, which was rapidly destroyed, and obliged them again to sue for terms. It was, however, too late then to send down people from the fort, and a cessation of hostilities took place during the night.

In the morning, nearly all the troops marched down close to the bottom of the rock on which the fort stands, the place appointed for negotiation, where the Colonel and his staff breakfasted, and soon afterwards two respectable brahmins from the enemy, made their appearance. The Colonel, however, soon ascertained, they were as extravagant in their terms, as those who first came down to camp for that purpose. He demanded unconditional surrender; they requested that the Killedar should be allowed to keep one-third of his private property, and the Arab garrison the honours of war, which broke off the negotiation.

---

evident. It was their constant practice to relieve all guards on their works at 12 o'clock at noon, their hour of dinner. The artillery officers used to watch their opportunity, and when any body of men were seen descending, they always sent a few shells in amongst them, which on bursting, carried confusion and dismay, and effectually prevented them from descending with their usual regularity and boldness: on the contrary, when they were obliged to come to the relief, they were seen creeping down the hill on the side of deep ravines covered with bushes, which in some degree secured them from view, and by which they held; this, however, did not save them from the well-directed fire of our officers, as a shell generally before they reached their post found its way in the midst of them. They also, when discharging the guns upon their works, spunged, loaded, fired, and retreated with the utmost precipitation, not only on account of a return from the batteries, but also fearing their ordnance would burst.

The vakeels finding Col. Prother quite inexorable, requested he would suspend the operations of the siege till one o'clock, when they promised to try and prevail upon the garrison to give up the place on his terms, which he agreed to do, and the brahmins returned into the fort.

At the expiration of the hour, Col. Prother perceiving no signs of the vakeels, ordered Capt. Miller, of the artillery, to open his batteries, when a few minutes afterwards, two men were seen vaving a white cloth from the top of the rock, on which the fire ceased, and they were allowed to come down, but to the surprise of the Colonel, they acquainted him that the terms offered by him would not be acceded to. The batteries therefore recommenced, which was instantly answered from the fort, and from a direction the Colonel little expected; for it appeared, that during the time the brahmins were in negociation with him, and the cessation of hostilities from ten to one, the enemy had been making excellent use of it. An Arab jemedar who commanded, had caused a few guns to be brought from a distant part, and directly planted above the position of the staff, but which could not be sufficiently depressed to injure them materially. The fire, however, effectually roused them, and made them quit the house they were in. At this time, they were awkwardly situated, being a full mile from their batteries, the road to which was broad, open, and enfiladed the whole way; many shots struck the ground close to them, as they were moving away, but did no mischief. This treacherous act on the part of the enemy, would have precluded them from the future advantages of favourable terms, but the fort was strong, and could not be stormed without losing many men, added to which, the monsoon was at hand. The Colonel, therefore, under such circumstances, deemed it best, when terms were again sued for, to grant the garrison those offered before, and Ryghur* was taken possession of on the morning of the 10th May 1818.

* Soon after the declaration of the Mahratta war, the Peishwa had sent his wife and some treasure to Ryghur, conceiving it a place of such strength, that it would never be taken, but British prowess reversed the opinion. The Ranee was in the fort when it was

Thus fell Ryghur, and immediately after Cangooree, another strong hill fort belonging to the Peishwa, the garrison of which was so intimidated, that an immediate surrender took place without their firing a shot.

A few days subsequent to the accomplishment of the above services, Capt. Morison left Col. Prother's force, which soon returned to Bombay, and proceeded to join his station at Bancoote, where he remained without any thing further occurring till May 1819, when, after a sojourn in India of 18 years, and finding his constitution on the decay, he was under the necessity of repairing to England.

Capt. Morison returned to Bombay in April 1822, and joined his regiment at Dapoolie, 9 miles inland from Severndroog, in the southern Concan, but soon after was ordered to Bombay, and appointed Barrack-Master, a Member, and then President of the Committee of Survey at the presidency. These situations, and Acting Staff to the Commandant and Brigadiers at the presidency, he held till the 9th October 1824.

He was promoted to a Majority on the 1st May 1824; and as his regiment, now the 18th, was ordered in Sept. following, to form part of a brigade, and to proceed against a very strong hill fort, called Pawanghur, in Guzerat, he determined to take the command of it. They did not, however, go upon this service, but were ordered into Cutch. Capt. Morison resigned his appointments, and embarked with the corps for Mandavie, in Cutch, 16th Oct., and arrived at Bhoog on the 1st Nov., where the regiment formed part of a brigade commanded by L.-Col. Commandant Dyson.

On the 29th March 1825, information was received by the resi-

---

surrendered: she was treated with every kindness; not an article of value was withheld from her, and she was safely escorted to her native town, Wye, on the top of the Ghauts, by a company of the 1st batt. 9th Reg. under Capt. Soppitt. The Arab garrison, amounting to about 1500 men, marched out with colours flying and drums beating, and were allowed to go wherever they pleased. Considerable booty in money was found by the captors, but it would have been much greater, had not the Arabs been allowed to go unsearched: this was afterwards ascertained, as the collector of Poona seized 10 lacs of rupees, on behalf of the Company, which had been carried away from Ryghur.

dent at this court, that a numerous band of plunderers, called Menahs, a caste of Musselmen in Cutch, had crossed the Run, which divides Cutch from Sindh, and were burning and plundering the villages in every direction, within 16 miles of the capital. Their force was described to be about 4000 men: their object was to release Bharmajee, the Ex-Rao, who was in confinement under a British guard in the city, and to put to death Luckmadass, an obnoxious minister. It was even said, the young Rao, a boy about 14 years of age, was to share the same fate, and that they intended to compel the regency to grant them the grass lands on the borders of the Run, free of all taxation, which they had enjoyed previous to the deposition of the Ex-Rao, but which Luckmadass had taken away from them, and reduced them to very great distress.

Colonel Dyson, commanding the Cutch brigade, would have taken immediate measures to suppress the disturbance, but understanding from spies, that their force was very considerable, and that they expected the English would send out a detachment to attack them, when they intended to make a desperate effort by outflanking it, to march directly on Bhoog, plunder it, carry into effect the object they had in view, and retire before our troops could return; that officer deemed it necessary to put the hill fort in as good a defence as possible, cover the city, take every measure for the protection of his camp, and wait till a reinforcement of men arrived from other stations. All this was accordingly done, and the ladies retired to the hill fort, to which place the Ex-Rao was also removed.

The brigade, what with a strong detachment in Wagur, guards in the city and fort, and camp, could not at this time face the enemy with more than 800 men, and 3 guns. In this situation they remained under arms every night, until the detachment commanded by Capt. Soppitt, arrived from Waugur, and a squadron of Native cavalry from Dookerwarra on the northern side of the Run, under Capt. Sandwith. Col. Dyson, thinking it would give the enemy too much confidence, and depress the minds of the subjects of the Rao were he longer to delay the march of the troops, ordered a light detachment* to quit camp at 11 o'clock, P. M., which after an arduous march of 16 miles, arrived before a small ruined fort situated on the top of a high hill, called Ballara, said to be defended by a large body of men. The gallant little band, however, after the artillery had fired a few rounds, although opposed to a heavy fire, rushed with impetuosity up the hill, took a gun, and drove the enemy at the point of the bayonet from their strong position, and caused them to fly in every direction †.

Having been successful in this attack, the detachment returned to camp, men and officers being completely fatigued, having marched with but little rest and food, (besides going in pursuit,) a distance of not less than 32 miles, most of the time exposed to a hot burning sun.

Although the enemy were in some degree dispersed, a large body of them, about 1000 of their best men, had previously gone away to plunder Anjar, a very considerable town belonging to the Rao, about twenty-four miles from Ballara, and situated ten miles from the gulf of Cutch. They were, however, repulsed in the attack, by some Arab infantry, and lost upwards of 100 men. Col. Dyson was most anxious to intercept them on their return, but his men were so dreadfully harassed, and fearing they would make an attack on camp, or Bhooj, during his absence, he hastened back to cover both. When, however, it was actually found, that the enemy were on their return from Anjar, with considerable booty, which they had taken, notwithstanding the gallant defence of the town by the Arab garrison, the brigadier, on the requisition of the British resident, resolved to use

---

* Col. Dyson, Commandant; Capt. Falconer, artillery; Capt. Leighton, Brigade-Major; Capt. Waite, Staff; Lieut. Burns, Brigade Quarter-Master; grenadier company, 18th reg.; light do., 18th reg.; 100 men, 21st reg.; 2 guns; one troop of Native cavalry, Capt. Sandwith; and Lieut. Wilks, 1st light cavalry.

† All officers who have seen service in India must have observed, that the enemy invariably fire too high: such was the case on the present occasion, and therefore the trifling loss sustained must be attributed to the enemy's want of steadiness and aim, as the detachment had only one officer, Capt. Soppitt, who led the assault, and four sepoys wounded. The enemy's loss could not be ascertained, as they carried off their killed and wounded.

every means in his power to intercept them. He accordingly privately issued orders for a detachment* of 300 men, and a detachment of cavalry, to march at a moment's notice.

The troops quitted their bivouac at 11 o'clock, on the night of the 7th April, and after a tedious dispiriting journey of 30 miles, they were recompensed for all their anxiety and trouble, by coming, on the morning of the 8th, upon the enemy, numerously and strongly posted on the heights of Joorun, near a village of that name, situated upon the borders of the Run, at the bottom of an extensive range of hills. However, in defiance of their being five to one, and occupying such ground that the cavalry were entirely useless, Col. Campbell advanced his small force immediately to the attack; and although the enemy received the fire of the detachment with shouts and music, keeping up a smart contest for a little time, yet British discipline caused it to slacken. From the perpendicular height of Joorun hill, it was impossible for Col. Campbell's excellent officers to push straight up it: some time, therefore, was necessarily lost before Lieuts. Cavaye and Clark could ascend by another side of the position, (for road there was none), so as to open a fire upon the Menahs; this however, was accomplished, when, after standing a few rounds from our men, the enemy were compelled by our superior fire and rapidity to fly in every direction, many taking along the ridge of the adjoining hills, pursued by Lieutenants Cavaye and Clark, others descending the plain, and entering upon the Run, where they were overtaken and cut down by Lieut. Wilks.

Colonel Campbell having fully accomplished the object of his march, returned to camp with his detachment on the morning of the 10th, and a few days after his arrival, information was received, that with the exception of a few stragglers, the Menahs had fled the country, and returned to Sindh. Every thing then resorted to its

* Colonel D. Campbell, 21st reg., commanding; Lieut. C. C. Rebenack, 18th reg. line, adjutant; 100 men, 21st reg., Lieuts. Cavaye, Wyllie, and Clark; 12 men, 4th reg., Lieut. Chalmers; 200 men, 18th reg., Lieut. James and Ensign Wade; one troop of Native cavalry, Capt. Sandwith, and Lieut. Wilks, 1st light cavalry.

usual state; all guards were reduced, the ladies returned to camp, and the Ex-Rao is now again a prisoner in his palace within the city. Rumours, however, prevailing of another invasion, Major Morison was ordered, on the 14th of May, to command a detachment* in Waugur, head-quarters, at the village of Doodye, 32 miles from Bhoog.

COLONEL MARTIN FITZGERALD.

(Bengal Establishment.)

In 1782, this officer was appointed a Cadet on the Bengal establishment. He arrived in India in 1783, and joined, in that year, the 3d European regiment, then under orders for the field. He marched with the corps, and remained with it until 1785, when he became a supernumerary Ensign on reduced allowances. The 1st Feb. 1790, he was promoted to a Lieutenancy, and posted to the 31st battalion N. I., then in the field; from which corps he was removed, in 1795, to the 30th battalion. Lieut. Fitzgerald partook of the services on which these corps were employed.

The 7th Jan. 1796, he obtained the rank of Captain; and the 1st June following, was removed from the infantry to the 1st regiment of light cavalry, then serving on the frontier.

Early in 1797, Capt. Fitzgerald marched with the army under M.-Gen. Robert Stuart into Rohilcund, to quell the Rohilla chiefs, and remove the family of Golam Mahomed to Lucknow. In the same year, he accompanied the army under the Com.-in-Chief, Sir Alured Clarke, to depose Vizier Ally, the pretended Nabob of Oude. In 1798, he marched with the field army under Sir James

* Major Morison, 18th reg., commanding; Lieut. C. C. Rebenack, 18th line, adjutant; 125 men, 18th reg., Lieuts. Pelly, Rebenack, and Ensign Wade; 100 men, 21st reg., Lieut. Clark, Ensign Whichelo; 100 men, 16th reg., Lieut. Lukin, Ensign Landon; one troop of light cavalry, Lieuts. Fawcett and Vardon.

Craig to give check to Zemaun Shaw, king of Cabul, then advancing into Hindostan, in favour of Tippoo Sultaun. Shortly after the army had reached its destination at Anopsheher, intelligence being received of Vizier Ally's rebellion, and the massacre at Benares, the field army retrogaded and marched to Lucknow, from which place the 1st light cavalry was one of the corps sent in pursuit of Vizier Ally and his adherents.

In 1800, this officer was removed to the 2d reg. light cavalry. In 1803, he joined the grand army under the personal command of Lord Lake, and was present at the siege and fall of Agra: he was also on the advanced guard at the battle of Laswarree, 1st Nov. 1803, where the enemy were completely defeated with the loss of 75 pieces of cannon; on which occasion, this officer had one horse shot under him, and another wounded.

In June 1804, the corps returned to cantonments, when Capt. Fitzgerald left it on medical certificate.

In 1805, he rejoined the corps, and was present at the attack at Bhurtpoor; also at the beating up of Holkar's camp, near Bhurtpoor, on the 29th March 1805; and, on the 2d April, the camp of Ameer Khan, joined by Holkar. At the conclusion of the campaign, Capt. Fitzgerald was appointed Staff to M.-Gen. Palmer*, commanding at Burhampoor. The 25th April 1808, he obtained the rank of Major; in 1810, he was ordered to officiate as Secretary to the Board of Superintendence for the improvement of the breed of cattle; and in 1812, he was appointed a member of the Board.

The 4th June 1814, he was promoted to Lieut.-Colonel; and in the same year, he proceeded to England on account of bad health. In 1818, he returned to India; and in Dec. of that year, he was appointed to the command of the 1st reg. light cavalry, then stationed on the Agra and Muttra frontier, and commanded the troops at the latter station for near two years; during which time the family of Dowlut Rao Scindia visited the station in great state, and remained there six weeks.

* Services, vol. ii. p. 451-2.

On the 1st May 1824, he was appointed Lieutenant-Colonel Commandant of the 7th regiment light cavalry.

Col. Fitzgerald, in 1824, again returned to Europe, on medical certificate, for the recovery of his health.

MAJOR WILLIAM LLOYD.

(Bengal Establishment.)

This officer was nominated a Cadet of infantry on the Bengal establishment, for the year 1799. He arrived at Calcutta early in Dec. 1800, when being posted to the 2d batt. 5th reg., he joined that corps at Barrackpoor. In August 1803, he volunteered for foreign service, and took down with him from Midnapoor to Calcutta, the Native volunteers of his battalion, who were attached to the 2d batt. Bengal volunteers. Severe indisposition prevented Lieut. Lloyd going with the battalion to Ceylon, which, however, was of no moment, as he soon had an opportunity of being actively employed. In March, 1804, he volunteered to serve, in command of the marines, on board the Bombay frigate; and on the 3d April, sailed to the southward with some homeward-bound Indiamen. During the month of July the frigate and some other ships were employed against the seaport town of Muckee*, on the western coast of Su-

* The following account of the operations of this small expedition, cannot be read without interest:—

" *To John Shaw, Esq. Secretary to the Marine Board.*

" Sir,—I have the honour to state for the Board's information, that I quitted Bencoolen road, agreeable to my intimation from thence by the Commissioners' despatches of June last, conveyed in the Clyde, and proceeded along the west coast of Sumatra, conformably to their commands; in our way up I looked into the following ports, all of which are known and visited by the French, *viz.* Port Chinco, Padang, Tappanooly, Poolo Doa, Tampatoan, Muckee, Laban Hadgee, Talapan, Sooso, and Analaboo, but without meeting with any of their cruizers.

" It is necessary for me to particularize the port of Muckee, as the inhabitants of that place have been, in the first instance, brought to the notice of his Excellency, the Most Noble the Gov.-Gen. in Council, for barbarous treatment of the crew of the English ship

matra; and after this service was completed, the Bombay continued her cruise along the coast, and around its northern extremity, to Crescent, and confiscation of her cargo, in violation of humanity and the law of nations; and, in the second instance, for an atrocious attempt to assassinate the expedition sent there by the Commissioners of Fort Marlbro', under his Excellency's sanction, to demand a reasonable and just satisfaction for the original outrage and insult offered to them and the British nation. This latter act of perfidy, cruelty, and treachery, appears to be unparalleled in the history of the world, as it was attempted and partly executed, (many of our countrymen being inhumanly butchered), after the existing parties had entered into a solemn treaty with our government, and delivered up hostages as pledges of their good faith and for our security; in consequence thereof, the barbarians possessed themselves of the guns and other government property, which the few survivors were obliged to abandon in their precipitate retreat from the intended general massacre, whereby the evil was one-hundred fold increased, instead of being eradicated or assuaged. On the 19th of June, the remainder of this unfortunate expedition arrived at Marlbro', during my presence there, which inclined the Commissioners to represent the affair personally to me, in such a manner as to lead to a determination not to pass that port without asserting, and fully establishing the superiority of his Excellency's government, over the daring and lawless courses of these formidable, cruel, and sanguinary savages; and in fixing such determination, I deemed myself strongly urged by the Board's commands, which clearly and distinctly enjoin every aid and protection in my power, to be given for the general security of commerce; and, I trust, it will appear, that I have followed up the spirit of their instructions, with an energy that will impress upon the minds of the most savage tribes, upon the west coast of Sumatra, in future, a due respect, deference, and consideration for government, as well as the rights and privileges of those trading thither, under its countenance and protection. In continuation, I beg leave to state, that the country ship, Phœnix, fitted out for the first expedition, by the Commissioners of Fort Marlbro', joined us off Port Loa, to the northward of Passage Island, with William Grant, Esq. H. C.'s civil service, who was employed at the head of the former, or original project. This respectable gentleman accompanied me in the frigate, and had under his charge 40 sepoys, with two small tenders, the Alert and Providence, likewise to attend the present enterprise. On the 26th, we anchored in Muckee bay, 2 P. M.; soon after which a seid came on board, to treat, as he said, (but it appeared afterwards to deceive), in order to satisfy government, if possible, for the injuries and insults offered by the Muckee people, as aforementioned. I sent him back with Lieut. Burghall, and a flag of truce, to state, that I would enter into terms with the chiefs only in person, after being put into possession of one of their forts on shore, the H. C.'s guns and other property; but whether these preliminaries were accepted or not, I would instantly land the next forenoon, and do that justice to the cause of my honourable employers, which my duty pointed out as my first consideration. After repeatedly receiving many evasive projects, merely to gain time, I finally returned this deceitful treacherous priest, at 9 A. M. next morning, and then made the signal for the divisions to embark in boats for storming the place. They had scarcely formed near the off side of the frigate, when the faithless barbarians opened their fire upon her from three batteries abreast, and within half a mile of us. I immediately caused a heavy cannonade to com-

Prince of Wales Island, and finally to Bengal, where she arrived the 26th September.

mence from the frigate, drawn up by a spring for the purpose, and was seconded by the Phœnix, in like order, for three-quarters of an hour, when I put myself at the head of the corps, and pushed on shore, which we gained without loss: the enemy, on our rapid approach, abandoned their strong works, and fled in every direction: thus, in one hour, we gained complete possession of the whole, without accident of any kind, a rare instance of good fortune altogether unexpected, considering the ferocious banditti we had to contend with, and dislodge from very strong positions. After gaining the enemy's works, I secured them by posting the Bengal Volunteers, under Lieut. Nott, on the right, in the battery containing the heavy guns, and most exposed; the Bombay Marines, under Lieut. Lloyd, in the centre; and Malbro' Volunteers on the left, or ground battery. During the afternoon of this day, I withdrew the guns and troops from the right to the centre battery, and gave the command of the whole on shore to Lieut. Nott, of the Bengal establishment, when I re-embarked the two divisions of seamen belonging to the frigate and the Lord Castlereagh. On leading up the advance after landing, to the grand battery, I came within forty paces of the rear of the enemy, but from motives of humanity, desisted from firing at them: upon this occasion 46 pieces of cannon, from 18 to 4lbs. calibre, fell into our hands, besides a large quantity of shot, some few shells, and various other articles adapted for the support and defence of the place: one wounded prisoner was brought in; him I sent off for medical aid. The number of killed we could not ascertain, as it is a sacred custom with these barbarians to carry off the bodies of the slain, that they may be buried with their ancestors. Death has no terrors for these savages, but the dread of having their bodies exposed is insupportable; not only to the person affected, but every one of his connexions. The next morning, at 9 A. M., I marched with the major part of the forces (the Bombay Marines, commanded by Lieut. Lloyd) employed in capturing Muckee, to destroy the enemy's posts in the interior, and completely succeeded, notwithstanding they made a vigorous resistance, at different stations, from many pieces of small ordnance and small arms, wherewith every one of their strong holds were defended. In fact, every chief's residence was a complete fortress, only assailable by an European force. On this occasion we captured about 20 pieces of small cannon from 3 to 16lbs. calibre, 13 of which we brought off without any loss on our side, although the corps sustained a heavy fire from the enemy, in the performance of their duty. The enemy's loss has been irreparable, at least for years, if not utterly irreparable, as we reduced every description of building to ashes, and cut down all the plants producing the necessaries of life, which escaped the general conflagration: many of the barbarians must have fallen during the conflict, but for the reasons aforementioned, added to our pursuit, which was incessant in the prosecution of the main object, only five dead bodies came within our observation. During the next day we shipped off the ordnance, &c. and in the evening embarked the troops, leaving the enemy's works, &c. at Muckee, under total conflagration and destruction.

" I take the further liberty to state, that this important service to government, and the British interest in general, was performed in 48 hours space of time, by a handful of men, in opposition to a numerous host of daring ferocious banditti, well equipped and secured by a succession of works, rendered so strong by nature and art as to set at defiance the at-

In Nov. following, Lieut. Lloyd was detached from Fort William to Hazareebaugh, with stores for the troops assembled there; and when the camp broke up, he was ordered to take post at Ootaree, on the frontier of Talamow. Early in May 1805, his little detachment joined the camp forming at Shughatty; and, some time afterwards, went with those troops to Benares, where they remained encamped till August, when they proceeded by water to Calcutta.

In Nov., the escort of the resident at the court of the Rajah of Berar was formed of volunteers from the different regiments at Barrackpoor, and marched, under Lieut. Lloyd's command, for Nagpore, early in Jan. 1806. The route lay through a wild, unfrequented country, but little known to Europeans, which induced Lieut. Lloyd to survey that part of it which lies between our western frontier and the Mahratta capital, a distance of 600 miles. The government subsequently directed him to continue his geographical* inquiries, whilst he might remain attached to the embassy.

tempts of every other nation if defended by Britons. Sixty-five pieces of ordnance, in all, fell into our possession; fifty-seven of which we embarked on board the Phœnix; the remaining eight were rendered useless, and abandoned. To conclude my detail, I humbly commend the gallant officers and men, of every description, acting under my personal command, upon this arduous enterprise, to the consideration of the Board, for whose justice and liberality I have the highest veneration.

(Signed) " JOHN HAYES.

" Hon. Company's frigate, Bombay,
 Sooso Roads, August 3d, 1804."

* " *To the Hon. M. Elphinstone, Resident at Nagpore.*

" SIR,—I am directed to acknowledge the receipt of your letter of the 14th ultimo, referring to the second part of Lieut. Lloyd's survey of his route to Nagpore, which has also been received.

" 2nd. On the receipt of your letter of the 27th Sept. 1806, transmitting the first part of the survey, that document was referred to the Surveyor-General, with a view to obtain his opinion on the merits of the work, previously to determining on the question submitted by you respecting the remuneration to be granted to Mr. Lloyd. The report of the Surveyor-General being very favourable to Lieut. Lloyd's execution of the survey, and Lieut.-Col. Colebrooke having also expressed a favourable opinion of that officer's general qualifications as a surveyor, the Gov.-Gen. in Council has great satisfaction in authorizing you to communicate to Mr. Lloyd the Gov.-Gen. in Council's approbation of his useful work, and to signify to him, that the Gov.-Gen. in Council has been pleased to grant him the usual

On the 15th Dec. 1810, a small detail of cavalry, under Capt. Lloyd's command, attacked and defeated a body of Pindarry horse-

allowances received by officers acting as surveyors in similar cases, to commence from the date on which Mr. Lloyd commenced his survey. The necessary orders will be issued through the proper officers in the military department, respecting this additional allowance.

" 3d. The Gov.-Gen. in Council has derived satisfaction from your reports of the attention which you have paid to the object of obtaining accurate information of the geography of a country so little known as the territory of the Rajah of Berar. The attainment of such information is, in the opinion of the Gov.-Gen. in Council, extremely important, both as an accession to geographical science, and as an object of political interest. The advantage of intrusting the superintendence and conduct of these geographical inquiries, and the arrangement of the information collected, to a person qualified by mathematical and practical knowledge, to execute the duty with accuracy and skill, are obvious; and the Gov.-Gen. in Council being fully satisfied of Lieut. Lloyd's qualifications for the performance of that duty, is pleased to authorize his being employed in the manner suggested by you. The Surveyor-General will be apprised of the service assigned to Mr. Lloyd, and will be directed to furnish herewith such instructions for his guidance as may appear to be requisite and proper; and Mr. Lloyd will, of course, conform to such directions as he may receive from Lieut.-Col. Colebrooke, and will communicate to that officer, and to the resident at Nagpore, the result of his inquiries and labours.

" 4th. The Gov.-Gen. in Council is pleased to authorize Lieut. Lloyd to continue to draw the same allowances, as those above referred to, during his employment on this duty, and to charge, in a contingent bill, such extra expenses as may be necessarily incurred by him in the progress of the work.

" 5th. You will be pleased to communicate to Lieut. Lloyd, such parts of the preceding observations and instructions as are necessary for his information and guidance.

" 6th. Any small increase of the number of hircarrahs at present employed by you, which may be rendered necessary, will be sanctioned; you will be pleased to submit a note of such extra hircarrahs, for the previous sanction of government.

" 7th. The Gov.-Gen. in Council relies on your discretion and care, to prevent the occurrence of any circumstances, connected with the service referred to in this letter, which may occasion jealousy or distrust, however unfounded, on the part of the government of the Rajah.

(Signed)   " N. B. EDMONSTONE, Sec. to Government.
" *Fort William, 8th Jan.* 1807."

" *To George Swinton, Esq. Secretary to Government.*

" SIR,—Captain Lloyd, the officer commanding my escort, having received permission to proceed to the presidency, preparatory to embarking for Europe; I beg to bring to the notice of government, his claims to some remuneration for his merits and services as a surveyor.

" To this situation, he was appointed, on Mr. Elphinstone's recommendation, in 1807; and the deficient knowledge then possessed regarding this country, gave great scope to his abilities

men; and in June 1813, the escort marched, in the rainy season, to Poona, returning to Nagpore early in Jan. 1814. At this period, the Deccan was annually overrun by large bodies of Pindarries, so that Capt. Lloyd was forced to march and encamp with the precautions usual in an enemy's country, and even found it necessary to augment his force, by additional troops from the principal military stations on the route.

The Nagpore escort bore a distinguished share in the Mahratta war of 1817, and particulary at the battle of Seetabuldee*, in which Capt. Lloyd was four times wounded. The events which immediately preceded, and led to that memorable engagement, are as follows:—

On the 23d Nov. 1817, the Rajah made known to the Resident his intention of receiving, on the following day, a khelut, or honorary dress, which had been sent to him by the Peishwa, and requested he

and assiduity, of which, as the records of the Surveyor-General's office will testify, Capt. Lloyd fully availed himself. Nor was the information obtained by his exertions of mere general use, as accessions to geographical knowledge, though, in that respect, it has not been devoid of value. He has at various periods of public exigency, afforded both to the resident and to every commanding officer of troops at Nagpore, routes and sketches of considerable moment to the prosecution of military operations. He furnished the late Sir Barry Close with a map, in 1809, when Meer Khan threatened the Rajah of Nagpore's dominions; the late Colonel Walker drew largely upon him in the same branch, in 1816, when the Madras troops took up a defensive position for the first time, on the line of the Nerbudda; General Doveton, in the year 1817, at Nagpore, received a good deal of topographical information from him, as did Colonel Adams, in his operations against Chanda, the Peishwa, and Appa Sahib, in the hills; and his maps have been extremely useful to me, in tracing the movements of the Pindarries, and counteracting their measures, and especially in the various military operations which it fell to my lot to direct, during the insurrections and disturbances excited by Appa Sahib, in 1818 and 1819.

"The only allowance which Capt. Lloyd has drawn on account of these labours, has been the trifling salary of 100 rupees per month, which is, I believe, granted to all officers who march on a new road with a perambulator; and although I do not feel myself qualified to suggest any specific amount of reward, for services that have proved so generally and extensively beneficial to the public interests; yet, I trust, that government will consider Captain Lloyd entitled to some remuneration for them, and confer upon him, such pecuniary compensation, as may in its wisdom appear proportionate to his merits.

"*Nagpore Residency, 24th Dec. 1822.*" (Signed) "R. JENKINS, Resident.

* The general orders issued upon this occasion, will be found in this volume.

would honor the ceremony with his presence, or if indisposed, depute some other person: he also expressed a wish, that a salute should be fired in the British cantonment on the occasion. As, however, the British government was at this very time at war with the Peishwa, it was clear the representative of that government could not possibly accede to the Rajah's wishes; and considering the friendship then existing between the Company and the state of Nagpore, it was equally plain, the Rajah in accepting a khelut from the Peishwa, would shew a deference to him, which might prove highly offensive to the British government: this view of the measure the Rajah was about to adopt, was officially notified to him by Mr. Jenkins, the Resident at his court.

On the 24th Nov. the disposition of the Rajah was decidedly hostile. In direct opposition to the advice of the Resident, he proceeded to follow the course of policy recommended by those of his ministers who were inimical to the English. He caused himself to be publicly invested with the honorary dress sent him by the Peishwa, Bajee Rao, and also accepted a commission from Poona, creating him Commander-in-Chief of the Mahratta armies: then, mounting his elephant, he addressed his principal sirdars, telling them, his honour was now deposited in their hands, and that he placed his trust in them alone. Surrounded by his troops, he proceeded to the camp at Suckurdurra in great state; the zireeputka, or royal standard, was displayed; the army drawn up; salutes fired from the artillery stations around the camp; and, in short, nothing was omitted which could add to the pomp of the ceremony.

On the morning of the 25th, all communication between the residency and the city was prohibited; the Resident's hircarrahs were refused permission to carry a letter to the durbar; the markets were shut against the English troops and followers; and it seemed probable the difficulty of obtaining intelligence of what was going on in the Mahratta camp, would render the precautions taken to prevent a sudden attack on the residency of no avail; still it was judged best to delay taking any decisive measure as long as possible.

Towards noon a body of about 2000 of the Rajah's horse left their camp at Bokur, five miles N. W. of the city, and approached the residency. The cavalry, commanded by Gunpatras, subadar, got under arms, and reports were spread abroad that the Pindarries were in the neighbourhood, and threatened Nagpore. The city now became a scene of consternation, confusion, and alarm, not that the inhabitants believed that there was any danger from the Pindarries, but because the Rajah's design of attacking the British and driving them out of his dominions, was publicly talked of and universally credited. The alarm had now spread to the market, frequented by the people of the residency, which soon became almost deserted, and indeed all classes, both rich and poor, removed their families and property from the vicinity of Seetabuldee.

From all these circumstances, and perhaps many other considerations not publicly known, the Resident very justly apprehended an attack on the residency. At half-past 2 o'clock P. M. he sent orders to Lieut.-Col. Scott*, to march immediately from his cantonments at Telincary, three miles off, and post himself on the Seetabuldee hills with the whole of the British force: the troops at the residency, under Capt. Lloyd's command, got under arms at the same time, to prevent the enemy seizing the position, before the arrival of the troops from the cantonments: these amounted to about 400 men, and consisted of the Nagpore escort, two field pieces, and about 200 men, commanded by Lieut. Bayley.

Between 3 and 4 o'clock, it was reported to the latter officer, that a body of Arabs were marching to Seetabuldee, and he, apprehending an attack, took possession of the tombs on the east end of the large hill. At this period, L.-Col. Scott was in full march with three troops of the 6th reg. Bengal cavalry, two 6-pounders, and two weak battalions of infantry, followed by the camp followers of the force: fortunately the enemy did not harass the line of march, but allowed the British to encamp on the two hills of Seetabuldee, in full sight of the Mahratta army. This bold movement, being quite un-

* Services, vol. ii. p. 525-7, and Addenda in this volume.

expected, must have astonished the Rajah; he saw the British in quiet possession of the strongest ground in the vicinity of his capital before the day had closed.

Early in the morning of the 26th, the troops had their several stations allotted them for the defence of the hills, and an attempt was made to strengthen the small hill, though to little purpose. The enemy employed himself in drawing his numerous artillery around the hills, in which operation they were not molested, though if the British had thought proper to commence hostilities, every gun might have fallen into their hands with ease, for they were not supported by troops. About sun-set the whole of the enemy's preparations were finished, when the Rajah sent two of his ministers to Mr. Jenkins, to represent his grievances, and whilst they were in close conference, the action began, accidentally, it is believed, and not with the knowledge of the ministers deputed to the residency.

The British right rested on the large hill of Seetabuldee, the left upon the smaller one, four hundred yards distant, directly north, and connected with Seetabuldee by a curved ridge. Both hills are elevated about one hundred feet above the level of the surrounding country. Their summits have very different forms: Seetabuldee is flat, covered with mausoleums and tombs, and 280 yards in length, from east to west, the breadth varying between 120 and 50 yards. The small hill is peaked, the top being only 100 feet long by 17 feet broad: this hill slopes gradually to the north, south, and west; the eastern side at 30 yards from the summit is scarped away by the formation of a deep and extensive quarry. The slopes of Seetabuldee are likewise easy of ascent, excepting to the south, where it is abrupt, but nevertheless practicable for infantry; considerable portions of the eastern face are quarried at distances of from 80 to 100 yards from its brow. The lines of the Nagpore escort ran along the base of the small hill on the western side; and to the northward and eastward beyond the quarry, it is embraced by the suburbs of the city. On the eastern side, the base of Seetabuldee hill is covered with huts: an extensive village stretches along the foot of it to the south, and the houses of the gentlemen of the residency occupy the bottom of the western face. The city of Nagpore lies on the east of these hills, with the Mahratta camp beyond it, extending from the east around to the south, and distant about three miles from the British position.

From this detail of the localities of the British position, it will be perceived, that the small hill on the left was their weak side, and that the force was much too small to take every advantage the ground offered.

The 1st batt. 24th, with two 6-pounders, formed on the northern slope of the small hill: the line extended from east to west, with Telpooree, a village joined to the suburbs of the city, not more than 60 or 80 yards in front. The 1st batt. 20th regiment and a company of the 24th drew up on Seetabudlee, facing the south and east, and 100 men of the Nagpore escort, with one 6-pounder, occupied the western end of the same hill; the remaining gun was placed at the opposite extremity. Those men of the Nagpore battalion who had arms, the remainder of the escort, and a small detachment of the 20th, were disposed of in the Resident's house, the houses belonging to the gentlemen of the embassy, and burying-ground: and the three troops of the 6th Bengal cavalry went out into the fields nearest the enemy.

The action began by a smart fire of musketry from the enemy's huts and quarries on the east side of Seetabuldee, accompanied by a brisk cannonade, and shortly afterwards they opened a destructive fire of musketry from the huts in front of the 24th, on the left of the British position: the battle thus became general.

As it was not probable the point on which the escort was posted would be attacked, Capt. Lloyd took away a detachment of his men, and went to the eastern extremity of the hill, and joined the troops defending it: here he witnessed considerable confusion at different times; the sepoys would not keep their ranks, but crowded together many deep; some were running for refuge amongst the tombs in the rear, the fire of the Arabs was incessant, and to complete the disorder, the 6-pounder limber blew up about half-past 9 o'clock, illuminating both hills, and conveying destruction to every thing within the sphere of the explosion: another gun was dragged to this point, and brought to bear on the enemy, and a constant fire of musketry being kept up, they would not venture out of the huts and quarries.

Capt. Lloyd's party remained here till past midnight; they were but little exposed, from being retired just enough to see over the brow of the hill, and ordered to sit down.

The left of the position was all this time defended by the 1st batt. 24th reg. with particular gallantry: the Arabs who occupied the huts in their front, fired from this cover, at one time, with decided effect, occasioning a great number of casualities; the sepoys returned it with equal determination, and being aided by the two 6-pounders, managed to set the place on fire not long after the action began: the enemy, however, again occupied the huts, and fired with as much spirit as before, but not with like effect, as Capt. Charlesworth, who assumed the command when Capt. Sadler fell, ordered the battalion to fall back a few paces and sit down. This movement was extremely judicious; it placed the swell of the small hill between him and the village, which screened his men very much; it was, nevertheless, deemed necessary to reinforce the 24th, with the grenadier company of the 20th, under Lieut. Dunn, and by 1 o'clock A. M., this admirable corps had suffered so severely, that it was determined to withdraw it to the right of the position.

About 10 o'clock P. M. large bodies of the enemy's cavalry with guns, arrived from the Mahratta camp, and took up positions to the north, south, and west, forming the segment of a large circle[*];

---

[*] At this time the corps was surrounded by at least 10,000 cavalry, 6000 infantry, and 35 pieces of artillery, independent of the troops that remained in the enemy's camp with the Rajah. All communication with the surrounding country was cut off; the camp followers, including the wives and children of the sepoys, and also the families of the European officers, in the Resident's house, were exposed to the enemy's shot; the supplies were only sufficient for a few days, and even ammunition was far from being plentiful. Under these circumstances, it was of the utmost importance to make known their situation to Lieut. Col. Gahan advancing from Hoossinjabad with a battalion of sepoys and 3 troops of cavalry, and to Major Pitman's detachment in Berar; the task was hazardous, but was

they did not, however, attempt to close with our cavalry, but confined their operations to a cannonade and skirmishing: at intervals they threw rockets, whose long luminous tracks, crossing the horizon in various directions, produced an effect highly picturesque.

At midnight it was determined to withdraw the troops from the left; they had sustained a heavy loss both in officers and men, were fatigued, and unable to dislodge the Arabs from the strong cover they fought in. One hundred men of the Nagpore escort, and 50 men of the 20th regiment were therefore ordered to relieve them.

It took some time to collect and form this detachment, so that they did not reach the southern slope of the small hill, before 1 or half-past 1 o'clock. They found two 6-pounders on the summit of the hill; the battalion of the 24th on the northern slope, engaged with the enemy, and the commanding officer, Capt. Macdonald, who had succeeded to the command when Capt. Charlesworth was wounded, superintending the construction of a slight breast-work of bags of grain, but so much down the slope of the hill, that independently of other inconveniences, there was not a sufficient number (which circumstance Capt. M'Donald was not aware of) to form so entensive an enclosure, or time to complete it before daybreak: the little which had been done was to be undone, as Capt. Lloyd had determined to confine the enceinte to the top of the hill, and nothing more.

The huts occupied by the enemy were not more than 150 yards off, and they fired from them with great vivacity and good aim; but with Capt. Macdonald's assistance, the work had made some progress by half-past 2 o'clock, when he marched to the right flank with the 24th, and detachments of the 20th, with one 6-pounder. The enemy perceiving this movement, came out from the huts with shouts and every mark of exultation, and extending their front under shelter of the fall of the ground between the British and the village,

undertaken by two of Capt. Lloyd's personal servants, and a sepoy of the Nagpore escort, who all passed through the enemy's horse unnoticed.

kept up a continued fire on the position of the latter, now confined to the single point.

A reserve, divided into three parties, consisting of 50 men of the 20th, and a couple of sections of the escort, had already been posted in rear of the hill on the south side, which secured the sepoys and pioneers, who worked with uncommon coolness and great labour; for the bullocks with the bags of grain, aware of their danger, could not by any means be brought to the top of the hill, but threw down their loads at some distance from it: there were two or three exceptions that excited admiration.

By day-break, the summit of the hill was crowned with a breast-work, (if it could be so termed) three feet and a half high, inclosing a space barely sufficient to contain 100 men: all were obliged to sit down close to the parapet, and, unfortunately, the breadth (17 feet) and not the length of the top of the hill, pointed to the enemy, consequently, not more than ten men could have fired upon them in a direct line, if a six-pounder had not been in the way; as it was, the direct fire of the British was reduced almost to nothing.

A little before day-break, Cornet Smith brought up his troop to the rear of the hill at Capt. Lloyd's request, but being discovered as he approached, could do nothing. The Arabs ran into the huts and would not come out again until he had gone away, and although he only remained a short time, two of the troop-horses were killed and three wounded by canon-shot, besides two more with match-lock-balls.

The British now, for the first time, had a distinct view of the number and position of the Mahratta army. The cavalry mounted and drew nearer, not in lines and columns, but in large irregular masses. Many of their guns were drawn to more favorable points, supported by infantry. The Arabs were more than usually active, so that by 7 o'clock the British troops had to sustain a better directed and heavier firing than at any previous period of the battle.

Between 8 and 9 o'clock, the enemy had 9 pieces of artillery playing upon the small hill, and of these, 2 were with the Arabs, not more than 80 or 100 yards from the summit: had it not been for the elevation of the hill, the British must have been swept away in a quarter of an hour: the casualties now became serious; 2 men were killed by one cannon-shot, a third had his turban knocked off without sustaining any injury, and, in short, the enemy had got the range so exactly, that unless the British could seize the two nearest guns, the most serious consequences were to be apprehended, for the slight breast-work of bags of grain would not withstand the effects of artillery.

Capt. Lloyd ordered his small reserve to make a dash at these guns, but, by some mistake, 30 of the sepoys had gone away, and the remainder were unequal to such an undertaking. At his requisition, however, Captain Brooke, with the light company of the 20th, came to execute this duty; the opportunity was gone: the Arabs, guessing what was about to take place, drew back their guns amongst the huts. Capt. Brooke, in the most gallant manner, offered to make the attempt, but the Arabs were in such force, and so strongly posted, that it was judged necessary for him to withdraw again to the right. Before he left, however, Capt. Lloyd begged he would mention to the commanding officer, that the post was untenable unless measures were taken to dislodge the Arabs from the cover in front, the breast-work being too weak to resist ordnance, and the six-pounder being quite useless from its exposed situation.

Between 9 and 10 o'clock, the artillery officer represented to Capt. Lloyd the necessity of retiring the gun to the rear of the post, as he was apprehensive it would soon be dismounted where it then was; and Capt. Lloyd being of the same opinion, the measure was immediately carried into effect. The enemy had, by this time, set fire to the lines of the Nagpore escort; and seeing the field piece going to the rear, they supposed the British were about to abandon the post, and made a rapid charge on their front and both flanks. The charge was so instantaneous, that no arrangement could be made to repel it: Capt. Lloyd had only time to order the men to fire, and expecting to be followed, jumped over the parapet to meet the Arabs: not a man came out of the work to support him, although almost in contact with the enemy; a matchlock ball grazed his left arm, and, to complete the disaster, the reserve, instead of charging the enemy, fired a few scattered shot, and retreated very precipitately towards the hill, on the right of the position. The game was up: officers and men rushed out of the work together, closely pursued by the Arabs, who used both sword and dagger. The British twice attempted to make a stand: it was useless; a few of the bravest men turned, but the panic was too general to be remedied, except by a prompt advance of fresh troops, and the escort were fairly forced to the right.

From midnight to this period of the action, the attack on Seetabuldee had been continued with great vigour by the enemy on the eastern side; and in the morning they occupied the village on the south side also, from whence they kept up a smart fire, which was returned by the 1st battalions 20th and 24th, with great animation; they did not, however, attempt to carry this hill sword in hand, but confined their attack to small arms and a cannonade, which had little effect on account of the elevation and flat surface of the hill. The enemy being now in possession of the key of the British position, took instant advantage of his good fortune. The field-piece he had taken he turned on Seetabuldee, and fired with great effect. Lieut. Clarke and Assistant Surgeon Niven were both killed by the same shot: both had their heads carried off; and at this time, Mr. Sotheby was mortally wounded by a cannon-ball. Three or four Arabs, more daring than the rest, planted their standards within 70 yards of the British, and the main body occupied the lines or cantonments of the Nagpore escort, and the space between them and the small hill.

The whole of the enemy's cavalry, elated at the success of the infantry, pressed forward from the westward towards Seetabuldee, when Capt. Fitzgerald*, animated with that spirit which entitles a

* The well-timed charge of Captain Fitzgerald stands conspicuous amongst the many

man to distinction, charged them with the cavalry, whilst Lieut. Hearsay, with half a troop, made a dash at two of their guns: both attacks succeeded; Lieut. Hearsay turned the captured guns upon the enemy's horse with effect, and, being joined by Capt. Fitzgerald, they returned to the residency, bringing with them the trophies of their victory.

The infantry on Seetabuldee hill witnessed this brilliant exploit: emulating the cavalry, they opened a galling fire upon the Arabs, which drove them into the cover afforded by the lines of the escort. At this moment the limber of their field-piece on the small hill blew up; nothing could have been more fortunate for the British: the escort, with perhaps an equal number of men of the 24th and 20th regiments, rushed forward to the attack. The space they had to pass over being 400 yards, the compact order they set out in could not long be preserved, and the mass was changed into an irregular column, of small front. The Arabs kept their standards on the summit of the hill until the British were ascending it, and within a few paces of them: here Capt. Lloyd was shot through the right shoulder, and Lieut. Grant, of the 24th, was killed; fortunately the former was not struck down, and the men being greatly animated, they passed rapidly over the breastwork and burning ammunition barrels, charging the enemy, and resolved to terminate the battle by driving him out of the village, from which he had annoyed them so much during the whole action. Capt. W. Stone, of the 24th reg. had formed the like resolution, for both at the same time passed the enemy's two brass field-pieces on the slope of the hill, and entered the village together. The Arabs could not stand this vigorous attack; they fled in all directions. In crossing a lane, in the village, Capt. Lloyd was shot through the body: the sepoys con-

brilliant exploits achieved in the campaign. It was generally allowed to have given the turn to the tide of success on this day; and, consequently, to have mainly contributed to the salvation of our interests within the Nagpore dominions; to say nothing of the effect on public opinion, that would have been felt throughout India, even to Nepaul, had Appa Sahib succeeded in cutting off this brigade."—PRINSEP's *Narrative of Political and Military Transactions in India*, p. 259.

tinued to do their work handsomely, and in a short time drove their opponents out of the place at the point of the bayonet. The affair did not end here: Capt. Stone, with a small party of the 24th, turned back towards Seetabuldee, and joining another party of sepoys, under Lieut. Ritchie of the 20th, who was accompanied by Surgeon J. Gordon, captured and spiked two heavy brass guns. Capt. Lloyd was now exhausted, could exert himself no longer, and walked back to the right for assistance, the sepoys at the same time dragging with them the two brass captured guns to a place of safety.

By these operations the small hill and village in its front were left nearly without troops: the Arabs observing this, began to re-assemble and occupy the huts again, when Capt. Moxon, of the escort, who now commanded on this point, took his measures so well that they durst not venture out of cover; and before they had time to re-establish themselves firmly, Cornet Smith came up with a troop of cavalry, charged through the village, pistolled between twenty and thirty of the enemy, and forced them to abandon this strong hold altogether.

It was now noon. The Arabs being completely beaten at all points, the cavalry retired to a respectable distance from the hills; the fire of their artillery slackened, and by half past 2 or 3 o'clock ceased entirely.

Thus terminated the battle of Seetabuldee, which was, perhaps, one of the most important in its consequences, of any fought in India for many years.

By an oversight in the orders of the 29th Nov. 1817, issued by the commanding officer, the services of the Nagpore escort* were

---

* It is true they lost the small hill for a time, but then the artillerymen, pioneers, and a party of the 20th reg., with two small sections of the escort, composing the reserve, and perhaps a dozen more in the centre and rear of the work, quitted it before the great body of the escort. On the other hand, the escort bore a very conspicuous part in retaking, not only the hill and two field-pieces, but the village in front, and in retaining this important post, under Capt. Moxon, when threatened by the enemy: a considerable detachment of this corps was engaged on the large hill, on the right, from 7 P.M. of the 26th till midnight. It must not be forgotten also, that the escort defended the key of the position, from

omitted, and also in the report* of the battle to Sir T. Hislop; and as the thanks of the Com.-in-Chief of the army are founded upon the

about 2 o'clock A. M. till 10 of the 27th, and that a battalion and one 6-pounder more than they had, only performed the same duty before them, and that too in the dark, whilst they, the escort, laboured many hours under the double disadvantage of fighting in the day, and with an enemy elated at having caused the first troops, who defended the point, to be withdrawn: the sight of 10,000 cavalry, ready to take any advantage, was an awful spectacle. The escort were, besides, cooped up in a small space, with a slight breastwork, not cannon-proof, and from which they could not fire in a direct line.

* The importance of this battle, and respect to the brave officers whose names are introduced in the report, render the insertion of that document necessary.

Report.

" SIR,—Having done myself the honour to report for the information of his Excellency the Com.-in-Chief, on the 26th instant, that the troops under my command, had left their cantonments the day before, at the requisition of the Resident, they took post on the hill of Seetabuldee, which overlooks the residency and the city of Nagpore, at the same time taking possession, with the 1st batt. 24th reg. N. I., of a hill about 300 yards on the left of this position, and to retain which was of the utmost consequence to our retaining possession of Seetabuldee. Having made all the arrangements that I thought necessary during the 26th, at 6 P. M. of that day, when posting sentries, accompanied by Capt. Bayley, on the face of the hill, and in front of the Arab village, at the foot of the hill, and into which we had, during the day, observed large bodies of Arabs, with five guns, to be sent to reinforce a party of the Rajah's infantry, who had been previously posted there; the Arabs in the village opened a fire on this small party, although previously informed that it was merely a matter of military precaution customary with us, and to which they had assented; and that it was not my intention to molest them. Seeing their determination to commence hostilities, and the small party with me having shewn the utmost forbearance, and until this time not having fired a shot, I directed them to fire a volley, and retreated to the top of the hill, under the fire of all the troops posted in the village. The action immediately commenced on both sides, and continued, incessantly, until 12 o'clock the following day, when it ceased. Having, in consequence of their great loss and fatigues, found it necessary to withdraw the 1st batt. 24th reg., together with a party of the 1st batt. 20th reg. by whom they had been reinforced during the night, at 5 A. M. of the 27th instant, and confine the defence of the hill on our left, which had been strengthened during the night, by a breast-work of bags of grain, to the immediate possession of the top, for which purpose I had detached Capt. Lloyd, with 100 men of the Resident's escort, and 50 men of the 1st batt. 20 reg. N. I., under a European officer. A body of Arabs gained possession of this post at 8 A. M., by the charge of an overwhelming force up the face of the hill, after Capt. Lloyd had displayed the utmost gallantry, in endeavouring to keep his men to their duty, and to maintain the post. At this moment Capt. Fitzgerald, reinforced by a Native officer and 25 troopers of the Madras body-guard, charged an immense body of the enemy's best horse, and having captured their guns, which were immediately turned upon them, he remained in possession of the plain, covered in every direction with the

report and orders issued in the first instance by the officer in command during an action, Sir T. Hislop, in his orders of the 14th Dec. 1817, makes no mention of the escort. This oversight occasioned a representation to the proper authorities, and produced a letter from Lieut.-Col. Conway* to the British resident at the court of Berar,

flying enemy. Whilst waiting for spikes to send to Capt. Fitzgerald, to spike the enemy's guns, it being my intention to recall him to support an attack of the infantry on the hill, in the possession of the Arabs, an explosion was observed to take place in the midst of them, and the troops, with one accord, rushed forward to the attack; it having been with the utmost difficulty they were prevailed on to wait the cavalry; and I found my utmost exertions necessary to prevent the hill we were on being deserted. On the near approach of our troops the Arabs fled, leaving two guns. Capt. Lloyd took possession of the hill, supported by Captains Moxon and J. M'Donald, Lieuts. Watson, W. Macdonald, and Campbell. Lieut. and Adjutant Grant, 1st batt. 24th reg. N. I., who had been twice wounded during the night, in the defence of the hill, was here killed. And I beg leave to offer my tribute of praise, and to express my regret for the loss of a most gallant officer. Shortly after the Arabs beginning to collect in considerable numbers in front of the hill, and the cavalry having by this time returned with their captured guns to the residency, a charge of a troop of cavalry, led by Cornet Smith, round the base of the hill, in which he cut up numbers of them, which seemed so totally to dispirit them, that from this time their attacks in every quarter began to slacken, and at 12, entirely ceased.

" I can never sufficiently express my admiration of the conduct of the troops on this occasion, and to Major Mackenzie, second in command, and to every officer and individual engaged, I have to offer my thanks, which are feebly expressed in my orders issued on the occasion, and of which I inclose a copy, as also copy of a letter from Mr. Jenkins, resident, who was present during the whole of the action, and whose animating conduct tended, in a very considerable degree, to excite the troops to their duty. I have to deplore the death of Mr. Sotheby, his first assistant, a gallant gentleman, who had also been present from the first, and exposing himself, in every situation, was severely wounded towards the close of the action, and died in the course of the day.

" I shall, by to-morrow's toppaul, forward regular returns of killed and wounded, which, I am sorry to say, are considerable, amounting to 14 officers, and 333 killed and wounded of all other ranks.

(Signed) " H. S. SCOTT, Lieut.-Col. Commanding at Nagpore.
" *Camp, Nagpore, 30th November,* 1817."

' P. S.—From the best information I can obtain, and my observations, the enemy opened upwards of 35 guns upon us. The number of their cavalry is said to amount to 12,000, and their infantry to 6000; 3500 of which are Arabs, from whom we met our principal loss.

(Signed) " RICHARD TAYLOR, Brigade-Major."

* *Extract of a Letter from Lieut.-Col. Conway, Adjutant-General of the Army, to Mr. Jenkins, dated Feb. 20th,* 1818.

" I am further directed by his Excellency the Com.-in-Chief, to express the conviction

dated 20th Feb. 1818, which conveys the thanks of His Excellency the Com.-in-Chief to the Nagpore escort. This letter, however, came late, was not published to the army, and although gratifying to the escort, could not fix the eye of the public on the corps in the distinguished light it merited *.

In 1820, the Nagpore escort was disbanded, but the government permitted Capt. Lloyd to remain attached to the embassy.

The nature and importance of the military services performed by this escort, are shewn by the following letter from the British resident (Mr. Jenkins†) at the court of Berar, to Captain Lloyd :—

" Sir,—On the occasion of the approaching departure of the Nagpore escort to Hoossinjabad, to be disbanded there, agreeably to the orders of government, I cannot withhold the expression of my regret at parting with a body of men who have for so long a period been attached to me as a personal guard, and who, from the ties of long acquaintance and habit, as well as from the uniform satisfaction which I have derived from their good conduct and discipline as soldiers, have established so many claims on my regard, both in a public and private point of view. It has not, indeed, been the lot of the

---

he feels, that the Nagpore escort, as well as the Rajah's regular battalion, participated most fully in the honour and glories of the memorable 26th and 27th Nov.; and his Excellency requests, that you will cause these his sentiments to be expressed to them, with an assurance that, as they merited, so they have his high approbation and commendation."

* The casualties of the gallant 1st batt. 24th reg. amounted to 149 killed and wounded; but of the Nagpore escort, consisting of only 124 individuals, its loss was 43 killed and wounded, which is greater in proportion to the strength of each corps.

† " At Nagpore, as at Poona, an attack was suddenly made on the British residency, while the attention of the Gov.-Gen. was supposed to be exclusively occupied with the Pindarry war. A similar resistance was successfully opposed to this attack, by the resident, Mr. Jenkins, who affords another instance of the happy union of military qualifications with diplomatic skill, and whose courage and constancy had been heretofore displayed under very trying circumstances, when, after the former Mahratta war, he held the office of resident at the court of Scindia. The few troops stationed at Nagpore, under Lieut.-Col. Scott, made a gallant stand against the superior numbers of the enemy, a superiority sufficient to surround and overpower the British force, even if the attack had been foreseen. Instances of individual heroism, displayed on this occasion, are deservedly recorded in our military annals."—The President (Mr. Canning) of the Board of Controul's Speech, in the House of Commons, 4th March, 1819.

Nagpore escort only to do the duties commonly expected from the body-guard of a public minister at a foreign court. From the disturbed state of the country, for a period of ten years out of the fifteen that have elapsed since their arrival at Nagpore, there has been constant occasion for their alertness and steadiness as a military body, and not unfrequently for the more harassing duties which are usually considered as peculiarly the lot of troops of the line in time of war. At all times I have viewed the cheerfulness with which they have submitted to these fatiguing duties, and the spirit and bravery which they have shown when occasionally called to more active service with unqualified approbation. If such have been their merits during so long a period previous to the late war, no terms can express my high sense of their bravery and devotedness in the memorable battle of Seetabuldee. No praise, indeed, which I could offer to them, or to yourself, whose distinguished gallantry on that occasion set before them so noble an example, would be valuable after the eulogium which has been pronounced by the highest military authorities on the occasion. I shall, therefore, only add my warmest wishes for the future prosperity and reputation of those individuals of the Nagpore escort who may embrace a more extensive line of service, as well as for the ease and happiness of those who may retire; and in requesting you to communicate the general sentiments and good wishes contained in this letter to the corps, I must beg to express my high satisfaction with your conduct throughout the long period during which you have commanded it; and further, to offer my thanks to Lieut. Smith, for the favour of his services since the removal of Captain Moxon.

(Signed) " R. JENKINS, Resident.
" *Nagpore, 17th August,* 1820."

In Jan. 1821, Capt. Lloyd proceeded to Hurdwar, through the north-western provinces, under the Bengal government; and in 1822, made a second tour, which embraced the whole scene of the military operations between the rivers Jumna and Sutlej against the Nepaulese, and extended to the Borendo Pass, leading across the parent ridge of the Himalaya mountains to the Chinese frontier: the highest point attained in this tour was 16,096 feet above the level of the sea. In 1823, he returned to England, by sea, on furlough.

The following are the dates of this officer's commissions: Cadet of infantry, 1799; Ensign, 6th Nov. 1800; Lieutenant, 16th Nov. 1802; Capt.-Lieut. 3d Dec. 1813; Captain, 16th Dec. 1814; Major, 7th Nov. 1824.

CAPTAIN MATTHEW RANDLE FORD.

(Bengal Establishment.)

This officer left England on the 24th May 1795, as a Cadet for the Bengal infantry, and arrived at Calcutta in Sept. following; he was promoted to Ensign, and ordered to join the 6th battalion of Europeans at Caunpoor. In the latter end of 1796, he was promoted to Lieutenant, and posted to the 3d reg. N.I.; shortly after, he was removed to the 13th reg., at Chunar. He volunteered with two companies to join the Madras army, about to take the field against Tippoo Sultaun, and embarked, with the 2d battalion of volunteers, in Dec. 1798, for Madras. After staying a short time at the Mount, under the command of the late Lieut.-Gen. Popham*, they marched to join the army, assembled in the neighbourhood of Ryacotah, under the command of Gen. (now Lord) Harris. Lieut. Ford was present at the battle of Malavilly, in March 1799; and at the whole of the operations of the campaign, including the march to Periapatam, under Gen. Floyd, to join the Bombay army under Gen. Stuart, which ended in the capture of Seringapatam.

Lieut. Ford was at the first pursuit of Doondia, under Col. Wellesley. At the conclusion of this service, the Bengal volunteers formed part of the troops selected to garrison Seringapatam, where they remained till December, when they were ordered to Madras, with as little delay as possible, for the purpose of being re-embarked for Bengal; but, upon their arrival at Madras, they were ordered to march through the northern sircars, towards their own presidency. On reaching Masulipatam, their services were required

* Services, vol. ii. p. 93-100.

to reduce a refractory zemindar in the neighbouring hills; and, as soon as steps could be taken for the purpose, they were relieved, resumed their march, and reached Midnapoor, the frontier station of Bengal in that quarter, in July 1800. Here they found orders for the formation of the three volunteer battalions, into the 18th and 19th regiments; Lieut. Ford was appointed to the 12th reg. and proceeded to Chunar, to join his corps.

In 1803, Lieut. Ford was at the assault of the town of Agra, the 11th Oct. when the place was carried; and soon after, the fortress of Agra capitulated; on both occasions the whole of the troops employed, received the thanks of Lord Lake, the Commander-in-Chief. Lieut. Ford was at the battle of Laswarree, 1st Nov., when the enemy were completely defeated, and the whole of their artillery captured.

On the 16th April 1804, Lieut. Ford marched with his regiment, and the troops under Col. Monson, for the purpose of joining a detachment of the Bombay army; the detachment received orders to retreat* from Jeswunt Rao Holkar's army: and during this retreat, Lieut. Ford received a severe wound in the forehead from a matchlock, which in a few days occasioned a paralytic affection of the whole of one side, and disabled him from further services.

In the autum of 1804, he was promoted to the rank of Captain: and was obliged to repair to England on account of his health, and

---

* See Narrative of the retreat, vol. ii. p. 540-60. Lackerie Pass, through which Brigadier Monson retreated, is noted for the action which took place between Scindia and Holkar. After the reduction of Hindostan, by the Mahrattas, Scindia and Holkar quarrelled about the partition, which gave rise to the battle of Lackerie, in 1792, when the forces of Scindia and Holkar were opposed to each other, to decide the contest and end the contention, who should solely govern the Mahratta conquests in Hindostan. Madajee Scindia had the two brigades of De Boigné, and 20,000 horse. Holkar had the four battalions of Dudrenec, and 30,000 horse; but Holkar had taken possession of the pass of Lackerie, and Scindia was compelled to drive him from it. De Boigné commenced the attack with his battalions and 500 Rohillas; the narrowness of the pass would not admit of more troops being brought into action; but De Boigné gained the day, took Dudrenec's guns and camp, and drove Holkar to a precipitate retreat of fifteen coss. Every European officer in Dudrenec's detachment, was killed or wounded, and he himself narrowly escaped. This battle decided the doubtful contest between Scindia and Holkar, and Scindia became, without further struggle, the sole master of the Mahratta acquisition in Hindostan.

his medical advisers having certified that he ought not to return to India, he was compelled to retire on half-pay.

CAPTAIN THOMAS GRANT.

(Bombay Establishment.)

This officer commenced his public career at the early age of twelve, as a midshipman in the Royal navy. He was in the signal action between the Nymph and Cleopatra, in the war with France in 1793; also in the same ship, commanded by Sir Edward Pellew, (now Lord Exmouth) when she attacked and ran a ship on shore at St. Malo, though exposed to a heavy fire from the fort. He was likewise at the capture of a national brig, after a long chase, and had a narrow escape from being taken by a French line-of-battle ship, that approached the British during the chase. He next sailed with Capt. (now Admiral) Sir Israel Pellew, in the Squirrel, conveying supplies to the Duke of York's army in Holland, which they were obliged to land over the ice. Returning from a cruize to Denmark, the Squirrel struck on a reef about fifteen leagues from Elsineur, and after working all night in throwing the guns and heavy stores overboard, and on the point of cutting away the masts, a ship that heard the guns of distress came to her assistance; and having anchored off in deep water, the crews succeeded, after springing two messengers, in heaving the Squirrel off the shoal by a purchase on the other ship's mainmast.

In 1795, Mr. Grant obtained an Ensign's commission in the North Devon militia, commanded by Earl Fortescue, and joined that corps when encamped at Berry Head.

In 1797, his friends being desirous that he should make another attempt to complete his time as a Midshipman, in order to pass for a Lieutenant, he resumed his station at sea, though rather against his inclination, as he never could get the better of sea-sickness, and was nominated to the Glory, line-of-battle ship, commanded by Capt. Bryant, and attached to the grand fleet under the command of Lord Bridport, where he was appointed Signal-officer.

He was on deck, at Spithead, when the general signal was made to get under weigh, at which signal every ship in the fleet mutinied: they turned out such officers as were disliked, and refused leave of absence to those they allowed to remain on board, unless they took an oath to return to the ship again, and not divulge any thing that had passed. Mr. Grant asked for leave to go on shore; but as they tendered the oath to him, he declined taking it, and remained on board till all was again quiet. He was frequently ordered to attend the delegates in the boat, when they had occasion to visit other ships, and happened to go with them on board the London, (which ship had several men killed, and the crew attempted to hang the marine officers) where he found Admiral Sir John Colpoys in close confinement in his cabin.

The men having obtained a redress of their grievances, order was restored, and the fleet put to sea; shortly after which, the crew of the ship in which this officer was serving, mutinied, about 10 o'clock at night; but the officers fortunately had a seasonable hint given them, by one who happened to hear of their intentions to murder the officers, and take the command of the ship. At the appointed hour at night, the crew began to assemble on the main deck and forecastle, and attacked one of the boatswain's mates, who received a serious blow on the head; and observing all the officers together on the gangway, the men on the forecastle run in the gun, and pointed it to the spot where the officers were standing; but the man with the match was knocked down by one of the master's mates, who escaped himself unhurt. At the same instant they were informed, that orders had been given to the marines to fire, and charge forward to the bows of the ship; first offering protection to those who chose to come off; and many of the crew having joined the officers, the rest were afraid to act, and went below.

In 1798, from his dislike to continue in the navy, and his friends having obtained for him a Cadetship in the Company's service, Mr.

Grant was appointed to the Bombay establishment, and arrived at that presidency 21st Sept. 1798, when in consequence of his producing a satisfactory certificate from Lord Fortescue, of having served under his command, he was immediately appointed to the grenadier battalion, and directed by General Stuart to lodge his Lordship's certificate in the Adjutant-General's office; the General at the same time promising, that he should have precedence of all other cadets for the season. Gen. Stuart returned to England soon after, and this officer did not obtain the rank he was entitled to, by the Company's regulations.

In 1799, on the breaking out of the war with Tippoo, the grenadier battalion composed a part of the force sent from Bombay, under Col. Little *, to co-operate with the Mahrattas, which force was, however, obliged to retire very suddenly from the Mahratta territories. The grenadier battalion embarked at Jaeghur, for Cannanore, and proceeded by forced marches to the Poodecherum Ghaut, to join the grand army under General, now Lord Harris. They halted at Sedapoor, on the Cavery, in the Coongah country; and on the capture of Seringapatam †, returned to Malabar with Gen.

* Services in this volume.

† The following account of the capture, is from the journal of an officer, in possession of the Editor:—The forces under Gen. Harris, amounted to 45,000 men, out of which number, 8000, commanded by Gen. Baird, composed the storming party, and an officer, serjeant, and forty-two men, turned out for the forlorn-hope. About one o'clock in the day, 4th May 1799, all being ready, three cheers were resounded along the trenches, and the whole of the party moved on to the storm. Tippoo headed his troops himself, and twice repulsed our storming party, with a heavy loss; but our brave fellows rallied again, and in less than an hour, were in possession of the fort; when the regimental bands, with every drum and fife, struck up the grenadier's march, while Tippoo's broken ranks were flying in all quarters. Crowds of the terrified inhabitants rushed to the sallyports and gateways, all under a dreadful destructive fire from their own guns, which our troops had now turned upon them. Some of our regiments next proceeded to Tippoo's palace, which was strongly fortified, and commanded by one of his own chiefs: at first they refused to surrender; however, upon Gen. Baird coming up, and threatening to blow the gateway open, the chief and Tippoo's two youngest sons surrendered the palace, and gave themselves up prisoners. The palace contained the whole of Tippoo's family and confidential servants; and, including some of his father's wives, and other ladies, and all Tippoo's own female establishment, with their attendants, there were six hundred and fifty females in the zenana. A search was now made for the body of Tippoo, which, after a considerable time, was found in the north sallyport, under a vast heap of others, shot in several places, and disfigured with blood and dust:

Stuart, and were immediately employed in taking possession of Mangalore, in the province of Canara, and at the siege of Jemaulabad.

Ensign Grant commanded for some time, one of the captured forts, Deckel, and had a narrow escape from the treachery of a Native non-commissioned officer, Timnaick, a rebel well known to the Bombay army. He came to the outer gateway of the fort, with a large party of unarmed recruits, who, with himself, had very recently entered the

it was placed upon his palanquin, and carefully conveyed to the court of the palace. Tippoo first received a ball in his right side, and, shortly after, another close to it: his horse was shot under him; his attendants raised and placed him on his palanquin, on one side of the gateway, where he lay for some time faint and exhausted, till our troops entered. One of our soldiers seized Tippoo's belt, which was richly studded with jewels: he attempted to pull it off, and Tippoo, who still had his sword in his hand, made a cut at the soldier, with all his remaining strength, and wounded him about the knee; upon which, the soldier shot him through the temple, when he instantly expired. Such is the exact account of this great man's death, as related by one of his attendants, who was with him the whole time. A thousand men were killed under this one gateway, where Tippoo fell. A number of his women fell with him, and one of superior rank and beauty, was taken out from this heap of dead and dying; nothing but her head could be seen; and, upon her being taken out, it was found she had not received any wound whatever. She was close to Tippoo when he fell. The enemy's loss was about 11,000; ours, not more than 900 killed and wounded. The next day, the body of Tippoo was taken from the palace, and buried in his father's mausoleum, situated in the Loll Bang gardens, with all military honours, and with the greatest pomp, attended by thirteen of his sons, and the chief of his household. Scarcely had his remains been committed to the earth, when a most tremendous storm of thunder and lightning commenced, such as had hardly ever been before witnessed or remembered, and continued its violence for some hours. A great many lives were lost in our camp, by the lightning; two officers of the 77th reg. were killed by it, and the nephew of Gen. Bellasis, had every one of his servants, all his horses and dogs, killed close to him, and he himself received a severe shock. A prize-committee was soon appointed to arrange all the captured treasures. The state-durbar, audience chambers, and a great many ranges of immense stone houses and galleries, were filled with gold, silver, jewels, rich and valuable stuff, and an endless variety of all kinds of the most beautiful articles, that were ever produced. Muslins, cambrics, and shawls, alone, in the palace, were reckoned at the enormous amount of 500 camel loads. Tippoo's throne was raised about four feet from the ground, on the back of a tiger; the steps to it were all solid silver, and every other part gold: the throne, about eight feet long, and five feet wide: no person could be found to judge the value of this throne, and as there was no possibility of ever getting a purchaser, it was broken up in presence of the commissioners and prize-agents. Tippoo generally slept in a small apartment just behind the throne, in a bed made of wood, with short silver legs, but suspended by the four corners from the ceiling, so as to hang about ten inches from the ground, in order to prevent rats or any other vermin from getting upon it. The gold coins and jewels were valued at one million five hundred thousand pounds: about 1000 guns were taken in the fort, brass and iron, and about 130,000 small arms.

Company's service from Tippoo's army, and requested admittance to the fort, to rest themselves: the sentinel immediately apprized the main guard, and the havildar on duty, reported it to Ensign Grant, who directed him to admit the officer, but not the party: he came in, and produced a passport, signed by Major Baird, stating that—" The bearer, Timnaick, a havildar, had leave for the purpose of recovering some deserters, and requesting that every assistance might be given him." He observed, that there were many deserters in a village only a few miles from the fort, and that if Ensign Grant would furnish him with arms and ammunition, that he could easily take them: the Ensign answering, that he had not a spare musket in the fort; he then pressed hard, that his men might be allowed to come in and rest themselves for the night, and in the morning he would return to Mangalore: but this request was also refused, from the circumstance of there not being sufficient room for them; and Timnaick then left the fort, somewhat chagrined. Ensign Grant had no suspicion of the passport being forged, which afterwards turned out to be the case; but his orders were, not to admit strangers into the fort, and he could not consider a body of raw recruits, just enlisted from the enemy's corps, in the same light as the Company's troops.

Timnaick next proceeded to Jemaulabad, where he succeeded and took possession of the fort, the officer being at the time in the pettah *.

* The officer commanding at Jemaulabad, was, in consequence of the upper fort being very unhealthy, permitted to reside in the pettah, with his detachment, leaving only a small guard in the fort. Timnaick with his party entered the village of Jemaulabad about 10 or 11 at night, with lighted torches, and made directly for the officer's quarters. The sentry at his house, challenged, and was answered in the usual manner, " Friends," and was almost immediately knocked down. Lieut. Allen, hearing the scuffle, came to the door, and received a desperate wound, and was immediately secured: they next made towards the sepoys' huts, and succeeded in murdering many of them, and got possession of the barrack of arms with ease. Towards morning, Timnaick desired Lieut. Allen to order the party in the upper fort to surrender; observing, it was useless to make any resistance, as Tippoo had not fallen, as was supposed, in the defence of Seringapatam; that he was in great force; and all the British troops in Mysore, Malabar, and Canara, had been cut up: Lieut. Allen positively refused to give any such orders, and three days after the surprise, he was tied to

Regimental rank having taken place in the Indian army in 1800, this officer was appointed a Lieutenant in the 1st batt. 3d reg. N. I. and joined the battalion at Cundapore, from whence he was detached to Bilghie*, Bednore, &c. He commanded at the latter place for some time, in consequence of the commanding officer having been obliged to proceed to the sea-coast for the benefit of his health.

On the receipt of an express from Seringapatam, announcing the escape of the Bilghie Rajah from confinement in that fortress, and from the supposition that he had fled to his own country, Lieut. Grant was directed to proceed to Bilghie in search of him; and after several forced marches, he reached the house of the Rajah's father (situated in the jungle many miles from Bilghie) before day light, and surrounded it with his detachment: but the Rajah was not there;

a tree, and shot at as a mark. Preparations were immediately made to retake this place; and Timnaick and his party managed to escape from the upper fort at night, by means of an iron chain: he was, however, shortly afterwards, found concealed in a house in the pettah at Deckel, and conveyed to Mangalore, where himself, and a great number of his party that had been taken in the jungle near Jemaulabad, were tried by a general court martial and sentenced to suffer death. Timnaick was himself blown from a gun at Mangalore, and the rest of his party distributed and hung at the Company's stations on the coast of Malabar and Canara: eight were executed on one gallows at Cundapore.

* Lieut. Grant had many difficulties to encounter on his route to this place, having proceeded alone through a strange country, in the severest part of the monsoon. After many fatiguing marches, and drenched with rain, it was with difficulty he reached the house of a Brahmin, near the top of Bilghie Ghaut, where he remained two days to recruit, having from the loss of blood, occasioned by leeches that had fastened themselves to him, in consequence of his boots and stockings being in such a state before he had walked one-third of the way up the ghaut, that he might as well have been without them. The first time he observed the leeches was about half-way up the ghaut; when, finding himself excessively fatigued and sleepy, he laid down for some time by the road side, expecting to be refreshed by a little sleep, but on awaking he felt as weak and languid as ever: perceiving the blood running from both his feet, which he at first thought was owing to a scratch or cut from some substance in the stream he had to pass through in many parts of the ghaut, he, on searching for the wound, discovered many dozen leeches on his feet and legs, which he began to take off; but finding that removing them forcibly occasioned the blood to issue from the wounds very fast, he desisted, and made the best of his way to the house of the Brahmin, from whom he received the greatest hospitality and kindness. The Brahmin first proceeded to remove the leeches by touching them with chunam; he then washed his legs, and closed all the wounds by applying some kind of paste: he afterwards prepared some rice for his dinner, brought him milk to drink, provided him with a bed made with some mats, &c. &c.

and on Lieut. Grant's return to Bilghie, he was satisfied, from the information of some Natives with whom he was well acquainted, that the Rajah had not arrived in that part of the country; he therefore made his report to the commanding officer at Bednore, and the same day received an order to return to that garrison, as the Rajah had been retaken at Seringapatam.

Lieut. Grant served at Goa in 1801-2, under the command of Sir William Clarke. He accompanied the detachment under Col. Murray, that proceeded with the Peishwa from Bassine, to reinstate him at Poona; and was at the taking of Kurnella. In 1803, he was detached to command the post at Karlie, and had the direction and superintendence of conveying the battering train and various stores for Gen. Wellesley's army, up the Bhore Ghaut, which service proved fatal both to men and cattle. A considerable number of men died from fever; and out of 900 head of cattle, attached to the pontoon establishment, and employed in the ghaut, there were not 200 left when the service was completed*.

Lieut. Grant repeatedly received the most gratifying communications from the Brigade-Major to the forces at Poona, assuring him of the commanding officer's high opinion of his zeal for the service, by the unexpected and rapid progress he had made in forwarding the guns and stores to Poona †.

* Lieut. Grant received considerable assistance from Lieut. David Davies, of the artillery, who had charge of the store-department at Panwell, and whose zeal for the service entrusted to him, induced him to pay the most unremitting attention to all Lieut. Grant's routes. The success of the latter officer, in getting through the passes of the Bhore Ghaut the heavy guns, was, in a great measure, owing to Lieut. Davies' promptness in forwarding the various stores he had occasion to demand of him. This gentleman is now Collector of His Majesty's customs at Swansea, where he is highly respected, and considered a zealous and most efficient officer.

† *Extracts from Letters addressed to Lieut. Grant, during his command at Karlie and the Bhore Ghaut, by the Brigade-Major to the Forces at Poona, in* 1803.

" Your progress in bringing up the heavy guns exceeds any thing we could expect, from the numerous obstructions and impediments you have to encounter. Col. Coleman approves much of the arrangements and steps you have taken; and Capt. Powell will forward you an ample supply of ammunition, in lieu of what you have expended. A Native doctor, with a supply of wines and medicine, shall be immediately sent you, and doolies to

Lieut. Grant served at the taking of Poonadur and Lowghur. In 1804, the regiment to which this officer belonged marched from Poona to Surat. From the latter place he was detached to Broach and Baroda; and thence ordered, in June, to conduct about 1400 head of cattle, and several hundred carts loaded with provisions for the army, through the Bheel country, upwards of two hundred miles, to Oogein; and, from the difficulties he had to encounter, he did not reach Oogein till the 16th August. He had only a few men killed; but his detachment suffered much from sickness, plunder, and loss of cattle. He was fortunately joined by a detachment at Oarwarra from Lunawarra, or he must have been cut up. At Dohud, he had a strong reinforcement, and the whole was commanded by Col. Capon, who directed Lieut. Grant to undertake the arrangement of the duties on the march, under the authority of his line-adjutant. At Dohud, Lieut. Grant was robbed of 600 rupees by a Native servant*, who absconded; and having, in company with

bring your sick to the general hospital; and you will direct the bearers to return to you again without delay, as they are in future to be attached to your party. Lieut. Armstrong having arrived, you will give him over charge of his company, with accounts, &c.; but you are to order such escorts from that detachment as you have occasion to call for, either for this camp, or to be detached to any other part of the country. Two hundred coolies left this in the morning, and more will follow this afternoon.

" The bearer is the classie, with two carpenters and two smiths; and I wish you would acquaint me, by him, what day you expect to get the other 12 and 18-pounders to the top of the ghaut, that I may send a party to escort them to this place, as the commanding officer does not wish to harass your detachment in coming so far as Tellegaum again."

" I am directed by Col. Coleman to acquaint you, that he has every reason to be satisfied with your conduct in your late command, and particularly from being able to keep on such good terms with the Natives. I have now to observe to you, that the subadar of the Conkan, who has charge of the district of Vizapoor, has lately acquainted the Resident at Poona, that the inhabitants of that district are sometimes incommoded by persons belonging to the British troops who pass to and from Panwell. It is, therefore, expected that you will at all times hear and inquire into any complaint that may be lodged against any officer, soldier, or follower of our army; and it may have a good effect to acquaint the inhabitants of the neighbouring villages, that you are not only disposed to hear and attend to their complaints, but ready also to redress them as much as lies in your power."

* The author of "Fifteen Years in India; or, Sketches of a Soldier's Life," gives the following anecdote of the thievish dexterity of some of the Natives of India:—

" Colonel Blackburne related to me an amusing anecdote of the inhabitants of Seringa-

an officer of the 84th foot, pursued him, they narrowly escaped being captured by the Bheels.

The health of Lieut. Grant, owing to the numerous difficulties he had to encounter on his march to Dohud, with a detachment too small to defend the large convoy he had in charge, being continually harassed by the Bheels, and sleeping on the ground, became, for a time, much impaired. He was daily obliged to select the strongest position for encampment, and make a barrier with the carts and provision-packages; but the Bheels always took advantage of heavy rain to attack; and though he caused the priming of the fire-arms to be changed very often during the night, yet half the pieces missed fire in a storm.

pettah. Some years ago, a detachment of the King's artillery intending to halt there for the night, was advised of the thievish propensity of the Natives, and recommended to be well on their guard against it. The two officers in charge of the detachment, as well as the men, ridiculed and scorned the idea of these poor wretches (such as they seemed to be) being able to rob the King's artillery, but took the precaution of placing sentries over all the tents, and a double one at that of the quarter-guard, with orders, rendered unnecessary by the awakened pride of the sentries themselves, to be more than usually watchful. The inhabitants, through the means of the Native servants, heard that their skill in thieving was set at nought, and their vanity was proportionably piqued. Next morning, the officers rising early, missed nothing, and began to exult in their security, when one of the serjeants arrived, with shame and dismay pictured on his countenance, and informed them, that the whole of the arms belonging to the main-guard were missing, and that all the Natives had abandoned the village. Every search, though undertaken instantly, was in vain, and the detachment was compelled to march away unarmed, and fully aware of the reception they would be likely to meet with from their corps, when their disaster became known. The manner in which this dexterous theft was achieved long remained unknown; but many years afterwards, when the circumstance was almost forgotten, the villagers themselves voluntarily surrendered the arms to the authorities of the country, and delared they had taken them merely because their skill in thieving had been called in question; and observed, in confirmation of this, that they had not taken a single article with the exception of the arms, which they now restored. Being asked how they had contrived to steal them from the centre of the tent, the guard sleeping around them, and two sentries outside, they gave the following account:—Several of them stripped themselves naked, and oiled their bodies over, that, if caught, they might not be easily held: they then approached that part of the tent where the sentry in the rear was posted, who, as usual, was walking about twenty paces, backwards and forwards. The night was dark, and the most bold and dexterous among them advanced obliquely towards the tent, creeping on his belly, lying still while the sentry was pacing towards him, and only moving on, slowly and cautiously, when his back was turned. In

Lieut. Grant accompanied the army from Oogein to Indore*. In returning from the latter place, a tremendous storm of wind and rain, which continued some days, had caused such a flood, that the army was obliged to halt between two branches of the Siprah, during which time no provisions were procurable, as the communication with Oogein was completely cut off, and they could not retreat on account of the river in their rear. None but the best private tents could stand the severity of the storm, and men and cattle were dying fast from starvation, and exposure to the severity of the weather †.

The river had overflown, and a body of water was collecting be-

---

this way he arrived at the tent, and his black body was, in the dark, invisible to the sentry. He now, with the utmost adroitness, lifted up a part of the side of the tent, having carefully removed one peg, and soon found that all the guard were asleep, relying on their double sentries. By this time the other villagers had followed their leader, and were all lying in the same posture, with the head of each touching the feet of the one who had preceded him. In this way the arms, being slowly removed, without the slightest noise, by the most advanced thief, were, with equal caution, passed along from one to another, until the whole were secured, and the thieves retired as they came, unseen and unsuspected."

* Scindia, with 11 battalions of De Boigné's brigade, commanded by Col. Sutherland, and six of Falozé's party, assisted by 18 or 20,000 cavalry, advanced to Oogein, in Oct. 1801, to avenge the cruel destruction of his capital, the loss of seven of his battalions, and 35 pieces of cannon. Holkar was tempted to try the contest on the plains of Indore. The two armies met here in October. Holkar commanded his own. Scindia staid with his baggage, and sent Col. Sutherland, with 10 of De Boigné's battalions, 4 of Falozé's, and 10,000 horse, to the field.

Holkar had 10 battalions, 5000 Rohillas, and above 25,000 cavalry. After an obstinate contest, Col. Sutherland gained a complete victory, drove Holkar and his troops from the field, and took 98 pieces of cannon, 160 tumbrils, his baggage, and his capital, which was pillaged, and great part of it raised to the ground by Scindia's horse.

Had Scindia followed up the victory of Indore, Holkar would not have had time and opportunity to collect fresh forces, seize the Peishwa's artillery at Poona, cut off Capt. Dawes' party, oblige the Peishwa to fly from Poona, and throw himself on the British government for protection and assistance. In short, had Scindia pursued Holkar immediately after the battle of Indore, the subsequent war with the British government would not have taken place, but Scindia from inertness, and his ministers from venality, lay idle for six months.

After the battle of Indore, Falozé, who commanded a brigade, cut his throat at Oogein. The reasons given for his suicide were, that he had carried on a treacherous correspondence with Holkar previous to the battle, which correspondence had been intercepted by Scindia.

† See a further description, p. 123-4.

tween the line and left picquets, but the storm fortunately subsided before the flood was knee-deep on the ground of encampment.

The wind and rain having considerably abated, and the rivers become passable for boats, the corps of pioneers were employed in removing the dead bodies, so as to make a way for the army to march off the ground; and men, women, and children, dead and dying, were to be seen in heaps on each side of the road. On the return of the army to Oogein, they found the flood had burst the walls of the city, soaked the foundation of several houses, which fell, and buried whole families in the ruins.

The army marched from Oogein on the 18th Oct. 1804, and joined the Bengal army at the siege of Bhurtpoor, the 11th Feb. 1805.

On the 25th January 1805, the Bombay army reached Rampoora, and as Lieut. Grant had for some time been suffering from a severe fever, he was left in this fort, with the heavy guns and stores. On his recovery he acted as a volunteer at the taking of several forts in this part of the country, under the orders of Capt. Hutchinson, of the Bengal artillery, who commanded the garrison of Rampoora, consisting of one company of artillery, the 2d batt. 8th reg., and four companies of the 2d battalion * 21st reg. Bengal N. I.

The garrison of Rampoora, which had long been in a very sickly state, and harassed by an enemy that cut off their supplies, until the approach of the Bombay army, being now sufficiently reco-

* Captain Francis Heron, Bengal establishment, was Adjutant to this distinguished battalion, when its conduct was so conspicuous on the heights of Muckwanpoor; where its charge, at the head of a column upon the enemy, at the close of that hard contested day, proved so overwhelming and decisive, in front of their capital, that an immediate peace, advantageous and honourable to the British interest in India, was the result.

Previous to this service Capt. H. volunteered, with the quota of volunteers from the 8th, on the expedition against the Mauritius, in 1811, and was present at the reduction of the Isle of France, for which services the Native troops, in conjunction with the British, got the thanks, not only of the Indian government, but of the Houses of Parliament. He was subsequently employed throughout the Nepaul war, in that division of the army, under Sir David Ochterlony. Unfortunately, the course of Capt. H.'s services brought on a disease that compelled him to quit India, and eventually to retire from the army.

vered to admit of sending out parties to reduce some of the neighbouring forts, a detachment, which Lieut. Grant accompanied as a volunteer, proceeded, about the middle of February 1805, to the attack of Bomongaum, a fort about 16 miles from Rampoora, and after several attempts, during the first day and night, it was found impossible to succeed with brass guns. Lieut. Grant accordingly returned alone to Rampoora, and having had some narrow escapes from the enemy on the road, he brought up the iron 18-pounders and a supply of ammunition on the following day; and after a loss of only seven or eight men, the detachment succeeded in getting possession of the fort.

From Bomongaum the detachment proceeded to Kurawal, a large fortified town, garrisoned by 2000 men: here they formed a battery within 200 yards of the fort, and having completed a good breach* by 8 o'clock in the evening, Lieut. Grant led the storming party of 250 men, and in less than half an hour after, the troops were in possession of the fort, having lost not more than 10 men from the first attack of the place.

Capt. Hutchinson next ordered a detachment, under the command of Lieut. Nugent, to attack the fort of Darrarah, which place very unexpectedly proved to be remarkably strong, and garrisoned by a set of brave fellows, who had sent all their families out of the fort, and were determined to make a desperate defence. Lieut. Nugent's party was repulsed with a severe loss, and from his known bravery, it was feared that he would again attempt it with an inferior force. Capt. Hutchinson, (whom Lieut. Grant accompanied) therefore, immediately proceeded with a reinforcement to his assistance. Upon reconnoitring, it was found that the fort, though small, was surrounded by a deep ditch, and so covered by the glacis, that it was impossible to make a breach without erecting a battery within

---

* When the breach was about half finished, a flag of truce came out from the fort, and was conducted to the commanding officer in the battery: it was an offer to surrender, if two days were allowed them to remove their private property. His answer to this was, that he would cease firing for two hours, as he required that time to cool his guns; and if they did not then surrender, he should renew the attack, and which he accordingly did.

20 yards of the ditch. The consequence of this was, that the detachment sustained a very heavy loss, being within musket-shot of the fort.

Darrarah was considered the strongest place in this part of the country, and never had been taken, and Colonel Holmes' detachment being then on its march to join the grand army, Capt. Hutchinson requested a reinforcement of cavalry, which was immediately granted.

Having made a very fair breach by noon, the storming party moved out under a heavy fire from the fort. At this time, Lieut. Grant was serving the howitzers in the battery against the gateway. From the difficulty the storming party met with in getting into the ditch, and exposed to a heavy fire, nearly the whole of the front division were either killed or wounded, and the rest retired into the battery. The commanding officer being apprehensive the enemy would take advantage of this critical moment, and make a sally from the fort, several of the artillerymen quitted their guns, and joined the storming party, who immediately rallied, and ascended the breach, and at the same moment Lieut. Grant moved one of the howitzers, from the battery, and planted it within 10 yards of the gateway, where a large party of the garrison had assembled; and he succeeded, after a few rounds, in making his way in. The enemy were then between two fires, as the storming party had by this time arrived at the second gateway, pursuing the enemy to the outer gate, at which Lieut. Grant had entered. There his party suffered severely, as the attack was so close that the powder set fire to the men's clothes, from the burning of which, and explosion of their cartouch-boxes, added to the excessive fatigue, and effects of a scorching sun at mid-day, and not a breath of air stirring, they became much exhausted before they got possession of the fort, which was not till they had killed upwards of 70 of the enemy after the storming party had entered the fort *.

* The enemy fought most desperately, and were at one time so intermixed with the

Having proceeded to Agra, on leave of absence, Lieut. Grant was directed, at the latter end of July 1805, to take charge of the men recovered from their wounds, on his return to Tonk. He consequently proceeded from Agra to Futtehpoor, where he waited the arrival of Col. Polhman's* detachment from Muttra, which was ordered to escort supplies for the army to Tonk. Col. Polhman's detachment consisted of 2 battalions of Scindia's regular infantry, commanded by Capt. Grant and Lieut. Bruce; 1 battalion of najeebs, (matchlock-men), commanded by Ensign M'Culloch; and 1400 Hindostany horse, under the command of various rossildars, besides Col. Polhman's own body-guard, of 250 Mogul horse.

The day the detachment encamped at Khooshalghur, a violent storm of wind and rain set in, and obliged them to halt 12 days; the men were deserting fast, and an attack † was daily expected from Holkar, who was encamped a few marches off.

Col. Polhman having made known the particulars of the situation of the detachment to head-quarters, two parties of horse were detached from Tonk, to take post between the detachment and the enemy, and a battalion of infantry sent to reinforce Col. Polhman;

---

detachment, that an officer of the latter unfortunately killed a man of his own company, having mistaken him for one of the enemy.

Lieutenants Nugent, Yates, and Lane, particularly distinguished themselves at the attack of this fort. Lieut. Yates was severely wounded, having received two shots in his thigh.

* This officer, a German, was chief in command of all Scindia's regular troops; and from his declining to act against the British at the battle of Assaye, was taken into the Company's pay, with the regiments that accompanied him. The Colonel was an exceedingly cheerful and entertaining character. He lived in the style of an Indian prince; had his seraglio, and always travelled on an elephant, attended by his whole body-guard of Moguls, all dressed alike in purple robes, and who marched in file, in the same order as the British cavalry.

† The whole of this force would, in the event of an attack from Holkar, have been under Lieut. Grant's command, from the circumstance of Col. Polhman and his officers, although in the Company's pay, having no rank in the army, which Col. P. was fully aware of, and invariably paid Lieut. Grant the compliment of consulting him upon all matters relating to the service, although the Lieutenant declined to interfere with any arrangement respecting the Colonel's own troops.

and with the exception of many camels and horses, which were plundered by the Meenahs, the detachment reached Tonk in Sept. without any other material loss.

From Tonk this officer proceeded with the army to Jeypoor, and returned to the Deccan, and was stationed at Seroor with the subsidiary force, under the command of Col. Wallace. From thence he was appointed to the command of the fort of Ahmednuggur, (taken by Gen. Wellesley, in 1803), where he continued for some time after the army returned to Bombay.

He returned to England * on account of ill health, in 1810; was subsequently promoted to the rank of Captain; and 23d Dec. 1812, placed on the retired list, the state of his health not admitting of his return to India. He has the honour of wearing the Seringapatam medal.

Capt. Grant has, for some years, been in the civil service of government, as a Collector of His Majesty's customs.

MAJOR THOMAS PIERCE.
(Bombay Establishment.)

This officer arrived at Bombay, 26th May 1800, and did duty as Ensign for eleven months with the 1st batt. 5th N. I.: he was promoted in the same year to Lieutenant, and joined the 2d batt. 3d N. I., commanded by Lieut.-Col. Lawrence†, in 1801, with which

---

* In this country he has been chiefly the means of light-houses being erected in the north of Devon, for the safety of lives and property, and which has turned out to be a very great benefit to the shipping interest. He has also taken some pains about local improvements, such as roads, enclosing land from the sea, &c. The Trinity-house have placed the light-houses on the Devon coast under his management, and complimented him for his attention to their service at Lundy, during the erection of a light-house in that island. A few years since Capt. Grant converted a ship water-cask into a life-preserver, for which invention the Society of Arts presented him with their large gold medal. See their *Transactions*, vol. xxxvi. p. 63.

† Now Lieutenant-General. Services, vol. ii. p. 481-2.

corps he served during the Cotiote war in 1802-3 and 4, and was severely wounded. He was present at the reduction of the island fort Severndroog; and next served with the same regiment against a body of Bheels, on which occasion he was slightly wounded. Lieut. Pierce was six years Adjutant to the 2d batt. 3d reg. In 1815 he was present with it, forming part of a field force for the protection of the Atteveessy against the Pindarries. He was promoted to Captain on the 1st November 1817, and, in consequence of great debility, he then took his furlough to England.

In 1821, he returned to Bombay, and was ordered to join the field force in Kattywar, and to take the command of the 2d batt. 3d reg. N. I. After the breaking up of this force, he proceeded with his regiment to Bombay; and on his arrival, the state of his health was such, that he was recommended by his medical attendants to return to England, as the only chance of saving his life. He left Bombay for Europe, on the 7th May 1822, on sick certificate, and was promoted to Major the 14th July following.

The following is Lieut-Gen. Lawrence's testimony of this officer's services:—

"Major Thomas Pierce, of the 3d reg. N. I., Bombay establishment, having been obliged to revisit England on account of serious indisposition, and that officer having applied to me for a certificate touching his services while under my command in India, I feel, in justice to him, and for the honour of the army to which I belong, bound to afford such statement as I am enabled to give from personal observation.

"Major Pierce, in the first instance, came under my command as a subaltern, in the 2d batt. 3d N. I., stationed in the province of Malabar, and at the time of the Cotiote war, when this corps had to share in the fatigues and hardships of that campaign. It was on this occasion, and particularly on my march to Pyche, that I had an opportunity of witnessing the good conduct and bravery displayed by Major Pierce, when he received a severe wound through the body, from the effect of which, I fear, he suffers to this day; added to continued relapses of a fever, caught while on service with me against the Bheels, when he was again wounded. In fact, I have no hesitation in declaring, that while in command of the 2d batt. 3d reg. N. I., the conduct of Major Pierce was always correct and officer-like; while he supported his duty on active service with a gallantry most worthy of my admiration.

(Signed)   " H. P. LAWRENCE.

" *Sydenham-Lodge, Harefield, 15th Dec.* 1822."

MAJOR EDWARD J. RIDGE, C. B.

(Bengal Establishment.)

THIS officer went out as a Cadet, and reached India in the year 1798; he was appointed, on his arrival, Cornet in the 4th reg. Bengal cavalry, which corps he joined at Benares, in January 1799. In May 1800, he obtained a Lieutenancy; in August 1810, was promoted to Captain, and to a Majority in July 1819.

The 4th regiment was actively employed during the Mahratta campaigns, under the late Lord Lake, and this officer was with it during the whole period, never having quitted the corps until 1809, when he was obliged to repair to England for the recovery of his health, which had suffered severely from the effects of the climate. He returned to India, and reached Calcutta in November 1813, and joined the 4th reg. at Kietah, in Bundlecund, the 15th January, 1814, where the corps remained till the end of 1815, when it changed its cantonments to Purtaubghur, and returned again to Kietah in the beginning of 1817.

On approaching Kietah, this officer was detached with the right squadron of the 4th regiment, to join Major Alldin at Lohorgong. His proceedings against the Pindarries on the 11th April 1817, are detailed in the following general orders:—

General Orders, by the Commander-in-Chief.
" *Head Quarters, Calcutta, April* 26, 1817.

" The Commander-in-Chief has directed, that the following report from Capt. Ridge, of the 4th Native cavalry, to his immediate commanding officer be published in general orders, not only with the view of giving publicity to the applause which His Excellency bestows on Capt. Ridge's conduct, but as furnishing a most encouraging example for the army.

"This affair, and the gallant exploit antecedently performed by Capt. Caulfield, of the 5th Native cavalry, evince what incalculable superiority is possessed by troops, confident in their own discipline; while both instances show, how much may be achieved by the determined bravery of even a handful of men. The disproportion on this latter occasion, was so enormous, that an opportunity could not have been more completely fashioned by fortune, for displaying the judicious and intrepid decision of the leader, as well as the admirable courage of the Honourable Company's troops; nor should the perseverance of the squadron, in the effort to overtake the Pindarries, be put out of view by the more brilliant circumstances of the final contest. An exertion, continued for 45 miles at this season, is a proof of both ardour and patience, best to be appreciated by the lamented event of its having actually caused the death of that most valuable officer, Captain Howorth.

"In expressing his praise of the zeal and energy manifested by Capt. Ridge and Capt. Caulfield, the Com.-in-Chief desires them to communicate to the officers and men, whom they commanded, His Excellency's warm approbation of their distinguished behaviour.

(Signed) "JAS. NICOL, Adj.-Gen. to the Army."

"*To Major Alldin, Commanding.*

"SIR,—Agreeable to your instructions, on the 11th inst., I have the honour to report to you, that I left the camp about a quarter past two, P. M., and after marching about sixteen miles, at a trot and gallop the whole way, I came in sight of three goles of Pindarries, I should conceive of about 1500 each, to whom I immediately gave pursuit; on which, they separated, and took different directions: but I am happy to say, after a chase of about eight miles, I had the good fortune to come up with a body of them, of whom about 250 were killed: the engagement occurred about half-past four P. M.: the number of wounded, it was impossible to ascertain. I had no sooner driven this body across the Bearmee river, when another gole was observed, advancing on my right: those I pursued, but from the obstacles, such as deep ravines, and broken ground, could not come up with the main body, but about fifty or sixty stragglers were shot in the jungle, where they had taken refuge: this body fled across the Bearmee. At this time my horses were so fatigued, having been mounted from half-past eight the preceding evening, until half-past seven the following evening, during which time we had marched forty-five miles, and since having gone twenty-four miles in little more than two hours, I deemed it advisable to discontinue my pursuit, and halt for a short time to refresh my men and horses; during this, the third body was observed advancing in my rear: these I kept off for a short time with my skirmishers, when I determined to make a third attack, which the enemy perceiving, took flight in the direction the two above bodies had gone: my horses were now so much fatigued, that I could not have proceeded two miles with any prospect of success. I have particularly to regret the smallness of my force, for had I had 500, instead of 190 men, I have not the smallest hesitation to assert, that of the enemy, which I conceived to amount to about 5000, the greatest part would have been destroyed, as it will be perceived, that it was impossible from my small force, to detach any part to intercept their retreat.

" I am sorry to say, my loss has been severe, particularly in horses: this I attribute to the dreadful bad ground we had to pass over, not only in pursuit, but before we came in sight of the enemy. The whole of the fugitives, after being driven across the Bearmee, appeared to take the direction of Huttah.

" I beg leave to express my satisfaction, at the assistance I received from Lieut. King, in keeping the men together, as I had a great many recruits who had never before seen a shot fired, but whose eagerness to attack the enemy, frequently caused them to quit the ranks: the conduct of the Native commissioned and non-commissioned officers and privates, afforded me the highest satisfaction: every individual is entitled to my warmest thanks, for their gallant conduct on the afternoon of the 11th. I beg leave to inform you, that Capt. Kennedy, 5th reg. Native cavalry, who was waiting for an escort to enable him to join his regiment with the Nagpore force, volunteered his services with the squadron, and did me the honour of accompanying me throughout the afternoon of the 11th, in pursuit of the Pindarries. I feel the greatest pleasure in offering Capt. Kennedy my warmest thanks, for the assistance I received from his presence; and I shall ever remember the flattering compliment he paid the squadron I have the honour to command, in accompanying it as a volunteer.

" I have now to perform the most painful part of my duty, in reporting to you the melancholy fate of my lamented friend, Capt. H. Howorth, of the 6th reg. Native cavalry, whose zeal for the service induced him to volunteer, to serve with the squadron under my command, notwithstanding the very bad state of health in which he then was. After accompanying me in pursuit of the Pindarries for some distance, he became so completely exhausted, that he fell from his horse, and expired on the spot, in the arms of one of my troopers.

"I have now only to add, that I hope the conduct of the European and Native commissioned and non-commissioned officers and privates, belonging to the squadron of the 4th reg. Native cavalry, has merited your approbation.

(Signed) " E. J. RIDGE, Capt.-Lieut. Commanding squadron, 4th reg. C.

" P. S.—I have the honour to enclose a return of the killed and wounded."

Major W. Elliot, C. B. (since dead) then commanding the 4th reg., being obliged to quit it on account of ill health, Capt. Ridge was ordered down to Kietah to take the command. In August following, he marched and joined the force under the command of Major-Gen. Sir Dyson Marshall, K. C. B.* destined to act against the Pindarries. He afterwards, towards the end of the year, joined a light force under Major-Gen. T. Brown†; and commanded the attack on the enemy's camp on the outside of Jawud‡, at the time the Major-General stormed that town, the success of which is detailed in the following general order of the Commander-in-Chief.

* Services vol. i. p. 395-7.
† Services, vol i. p. 253-8; and see p. 105 of this volume.
‡ Capt. John Paterson, of the Bengal establishment, now employed on the East India Company's recruiting service, in England, distinguished himself on this occasion. He was then a Quarter-Master of Brigade, and voluntarily accompanied the party ordered to blow open a gate with a gun; was among the first who entered the fort through the crevice, (the gate being but partially blown open after a third explosion from the gun) and was for some time personally engaged on the ramparts by the side of a gallant young officer, Lieut. Paton, of the Dromedary corps, who was severely wounded. Capt. Paterson's hat was cut from his head by a blow from a tulwar (sword), and he was instrumental in saving the life of Lieut. Paton, by tumbling a fellow, who was aiming another stroke at him, off the rampart, by a violent thrust with his shoulder, having himself previously spent his blow upon the turban of another opponent. Lieut. Paton and this officer had, in the heat of action, advanced too far, and were entirely unsupported. Capt. Paterson, being altogether out of place in this storm, (his proper station being in the rear of his brigade) his name could not, with propriety, appear in the public despatch, although his gallantry was fully appreciated.

General Orders by the Commander-in-Chief.

"*Head-Quarters, Camp, Kunjowlee, 7 Feb.* 1818.

" The Com.-in-Chief has received with sentiments of admiration, the official details of the successful attack made by the troops under the command of Major-General Brown, on the town of Jawud, and the troops of Jeswunt Rao Bhow, on the 29th of January.

" In the details before his Lordship, the prominent features are those of clear and decided judgment in the conception, and of the most energetic gallantry in the execution of the several operations, which were so deservedly crowned with brilliant success.

" On the one hand, a strongly fortified town was stormed by the 1st batt. 1st N. I., after their blowing open the gate: on the other, the camp of Jeswunt Rao Bhow was attacked and carried by the 4th cavalry and a detachment of the 2d Rohilla horse, though defended by cannon, and the approach to it presenting great natural difficulties and impediments on all sides; an enterprize in which Capt. Ridge, Lieut. Franklin, and Lieut. Turner, appear to have highly distinguished themselves. In both attacks, the order and bravery of the British troops succeeded without a check. The enemy was driven from the town and from their camp, with great loss, and fled in every direction.

" The Com.-in-Chief requests Major-Gen. Brown's acceptance of his applause, as well as of his best thanks; and desires that the same may be conveyed to every officer and man engaged in the spirited and well-conducted affair.

(Signed) " W. L. WATSON, Acting Adj.-Gen. of the Army."

In May 1818, after the campaign was terminated, the 4th reg. marched into cantonments at Muttra, where it remained until the end of 1819, when it marched to Neemuch, a cantonment in Central India. In Sept. following, the regiment was called into the field to put down the refractory Rajah, Kishor Sing, who had assembled a large force in Horrowtee. The commanding officer, Lieut. Col. W. G. Maxwell, after finding all offers of accommodation fruitless, determined on attacking the Rajah's position, which he did on the 1st Oct. 1821. The enemy immediately retired, when Major Ridge was ordered to pursue them with two squadrons. He soon came up with a body of horse, of about 5 or 600, moving slowly on, and determined to defend their master, the Rajah. He charged them; and the result is thus stated by Lieut.-Col. Maxwell, in a letter of the same date, to the Adjutant-General of the army:—

"Major Ridge, with two squadrons 4th light cavalry, soon came in sight of the powerful body of the enemy's cavalry, under the Maharoo in person.

"He immediately formed, and charged with the greatest promptitude; but I am deeply concerned to add with the loss of two brave, enterprising young officers, Lieut. Read, and Adjutant Clark, who nobly fell in the service of their country. Major Ridge was severely, though not dangerously, wounded, by a sabre in his head; and, much as all those who admire his distinguished gallantry must be concerned at his sufferings, yet considerable consolation arises from the assurance of its not being likely to keep him more than a few days from the able discharge of his duty."

Major Ridge was at this time in so bad a state of health, that it was deemed absolutely necessary that he should return to England for his recovery, and where he arrived in January 1823.

This officer was never absent from his corps when it was employed on any kind of service, from the time he first joined it in 1798. He retired from the service 3d November 1824.

For his services, this officer has been appointed a Companion of the most honourable Order of the Bath.

LIEUTENANT-COLONEL HENRY FAITHFULL.

(Bengal Establishment.)

This officer received, at the Royal Military Academy in Woolwich Warren, a military education, and qualified himself for the engineer and artillery branches of the service. The demand for officers caused him to be posted to the artillery on his arrival in Bengal, in the year 1801; and the 14th Feb. 1802, he was promoted to Lieutenant.

At the commencement of the Mahratta war, in 1803, he was detached from the cantonment of Dinapoor to command the artillery of the field force, assembled at Mirzapore, under the command of M.-Gen. George Deare. This army, instead of acting in advance, as was expected, became one of observation, owing to the rapid success of Lord Lake, and of the British armies generally.

From the camp at Mirzapore he was detached, in the latter part of 1803, to command the artillery of a small force for the reduction of the fort of Chowkundee, bordering on the province of Allahabad. The enemy, after having foiled our troops in one attempt to storm by a breach, evacuated the fort, under cover of a dark night; but not before the breach had been so enlarged and lowered, as to render the place untenable. The parapets and bastions being destroyed, the troops returned to Mirzapore, and the army there, shortly after, went into fixed cantonments.

In 1805, this officer was again in command of a detachment of artillery, with a small force encamped at Mirzapore, to protect the town of that name from a body of Mahrattas.

On his promotion to the rank of Captain, in 1806, he rejoined the head-quarters of his regiment at Fort William.

In 1810, he was detached, with the Bengal artillery, serving on the expedition for the capture of the island of Java.

In 1813, he was appointed to the department for the construction of gun-carriages in Bengal, and continued on that duty until the year 1822, when he succeeded to the situation of Principal Commissary of ordnance in Fort William, where he remained until loss of health obliged him, in Dec. 1824, to leave India, and to return to England.

The 4th June 1814, he obtained the rank of Major; and the 1st May 1824, that of Lieutenant-Colonel.

MAJOR WILLIAM GORDON.

(Bombay Establishment.)

In 1802, this officer arrived in India, and was appointed to a Lieutenancy in the following year. He was employed, with the 1st batt. 6th reg., under Col. Anderson*, in covering Surat, the Mahratta forces being then in the field above the ghauts. In the rains of 1803, he was Line-Adjutant to a force under the same officer, assembled for the reduction of the fort Purneire. In 1804, he was ordered to join the 2d batt. 6th reg., then with Col. Murray's army at Oogein: he served the campaigns under that officer and M.-Gen. Jones, and joined Lord Lake's army. He was at the siege of Bhurtpoor, and the affairs in the neighbourhood. In 1806, he returned to Surat, and found himself appointed Adjutant of the 1st battalion, which formed part of the auxiliary force at Goa, and subsequently the subsidiary at Poona. He was at the taking of Anja, under Colonel East*.

In 1816, having been promoted to a company, on the 8th Jan. in that year, he joined the light battalion of the Poona subsidiary force, and was actively engaged after the Pindarries, till the war broke out at Poona, in November 1817. Having been sent thither by Sir Lionel

---

* The late Lieut.-Gen. Anderson. He bequeathed the bulk of his fortune, amounting to about 70,000*l.*, for the purpose of establishing two institutions in Elgin. One for the reception of indigent natives, of upwards of 55 years of age; the other, for the education of poor children. He died in 1824.

† The late Col. William East, C. B. of the Bombay establishment. The following notice of the death of this officer was issued by the Bombay government:—

"August 30th, 1817.—It is with deep concern, that the Right Hon. the Governor in Council announces the death of Colonel William East, Companion of the most Honourable Order of the Bath, Commanding Officer of the force subsidized by his Highness the Guicawar, and of the force assembling in Guzerat for the field. It is not necessary that the Governor in Council should enter, upon this mournful occasion, into a recapitulation of those important services which Col. East rendered to the government, during an uninterrupted period of 36 years. The most decisive testimony that can be afforded to the merits of that valuable officer, is an appeal to the distinguished honor that had been conferred upon him by his Sovereign."

Smith on a particular duty, he was fortunate in acting as Staff to the late L.-Col. Burr *, during the action at Kirkee, 5th November.

He rejoined the flank battalion, and was at the affair of Achten, when the Suttah Rajah and family were taken.

In the rains of 1818, Capt. Gordon commanded a light detachment in pursuit of Trimbuckjee Dhanglia: in November, he was appointed to Sholapore, by Sir Lionel Smith; and soon after, by the present Hon. Governor, Mr. Elphinstone, Inspector of forts in the Deccan; from which situation he was called, in Jan. 1823, to the command of his regiment (now the 11th,) which he gave over to Capt. F. Hickes, in Dec. 1824, preparatory to his proceeding to Europe on furlough. He was promoted to a Majority 21st May 1824.

LIEUTENANT-COLONEL JAMES MORSE.
(Bombay Establishment.)

THIS officer arrived in India 26th May 1804, and joined the 2d batt. 7th (now 14th) regiment at Brodra, in Nov. following, as junior Lieutenant. In 1807, he was posted to the grenadier company, and continued in charge until 1814, when he was obliged to return to England in consequence of ill health, brought on by a *coup de soleil*, received in July 1809, when marching with the flank companies of his regiment, commanded by Capt. (now Lieut.-Colonel) J. Cunningham, with the field force under the late M.-Gen. (then Lieut.-Col.) Sir G. Holmes †.

In 1810, he volunteered his services with the 1st batt. 7th (now 13th) reg. then at Siroor, and marched with the field force under Colonel Montresor ‡.

In 1811, he volunteered his services to accompany the expeditions

---

* Services, vol. i. p. 350-65. † Services, vol. i. p. 408-21.
‡ Services, Royal Military Calendar, vol. iii. p. 313-14, 3d edit.

to Java, but which were refused by Lieut.-Gen. Wilkinson, then Com.-in-Chief of Bombay, on the plea, that the Bombay troops were not to be employed on that occasion.

In 1812, he marched with the 2d batt. 7th reg. from Siroor, with the force under M.-Gen. Montresor; and in 1813, he was detached, in command of 4 battalion companies of his reg., to Tannah. In Oct. of the latter year, he embarked from Bombay with the detachment, to join the regiment at Malwan. Early in 1814, he marched with the regiment, then commanded by Lieut.-Col. Webb, against the fort of Raree; and on being joined by the 32d reg. of Madras infantry, and the regiments being formed into a brigade, this officer, was, in consequence, for a short time, in the command of his regiment. In Aug. 1814, his health obliged him to return to England, and from the then existing regulation, regarding officers obtaining sick certificates to Europe, he was compelled to take advantage of his furlough.

In May 1818, he returned to India, and arrived at Bombay in Sept. following: in Nov. of that year, he joined the 1st battalion (now 13th reg.) at Siroor; and in February 1819, marched from that cantonment in command of the light-battalion companies of the regiment, with the field force under Lieut.-Col. Cosby. In April of the latter year, M.-Gen. Sir Lionel Smith, appointed this officer Brigade-Major to the 2d Poona brigade; and in June following, he was appointed by government, to the command of Fort Victoria, Bancoote. On his promotion to a Majority, he joined and took charge of the 1st batt. 7th reg., at Bhewndy, northern Concan, and remained in command of that district until March 1823, when he marched with his regiment to Ahmedabad. In Oct. following, he was again compelled by ill-health, to return to England.

The following are the dates of this officer's commissions: Ensign, 1st May 1804; Lieutenant, 3d Oct. 1804; Capt.-Lieut., 1st Jan. 1817; Captain, November, 1817; Major, 19th April 1822; and Lieutenant-Colonel, 19th March 1825.

THE LATE LIEUT.-COLONEL WILLIAM COWPER.

(Bombay Establishment.)

In 1791, this officer entered the corps of Bombay engineers, with the advantage of an education at the Military Academy at Woolwich, which had previously been closed against young men destined for the East India Company's service. He soon attracted the notice of government, by the earnest he gave of the talent, which afterwards placed him, unaided by interest, in situations which it seldom falls to the lot of an individual to fill. He was, in consequence, appointed Assistant to Capt. (now Colonel) Johnson, C. B.[*], who was employed in surveying the coast and interior of Malabar, with whom he continued for several years, until obliged to relinquish the situation from ill health.

He then took the usual routine of duty, distinguishing himself by the correctness and highly-finished style of his plans and surveys, and particularly by the accuracy of his estimates, till 1804, when he was called to the field as Chief Engineer to the army, which, under the command of the present Lieut.-Gen. Sir Richard Jones, effected a junction with the Bengal army before Bhurtpoor.

A complete survey of that portion of Hindostan Proper which was for the first time traversed by a British army, was the recreation of his active mind, and was gratuitously presented to the government, as he had neither the establishment nor the allowances usually granted to officers employed in the Survey department.

Soon after the return of this force to garrison, he was selected for the national work, which will perpetuate his fame, along with that of the naval glory of Great Britain, with which it is so intimately connected. The commanding sea-force which it was deemed necessary to keep afloat, during the late apparently interminable war, naturally turned the serious attention of government to the means of securing an adequate supply of timber, for the enormous expen-

---

[*] Services, vol. i. p. 220.

diture which threatened to desolate our forests; whilst the increasing influence of the French emperor, deprived us of the usual resources on the continent. In this dilemma, the extensive regions of our Indian empire, with its inexhaustible stores of durable teakwood, appeared to provide an ample remedy against the approaching evil, and to avail ourselves of its magazines with the fullest effect, it was determined to have docks constructed in India, capable of building vessels of eighty guns.

The local advantages of the island of Bombay, pointed it out as the best adapted for applying the resources of the east to the exigencies of the parent state. But the difficulties which attended the commencement of the undertaking, had nearly caused its abandonment, when Col. Cowper was requested by the government to superintend it. After a short deliberation, he accepted the charge; but it was not till after he had commenced his labours, that he was himself aware of the numerous and unexpected difficulties with which he had to contend: to the world they will remain unknown; but it may be observed, that the ordinary studies of a military engineer, are not directed to such structures; and that, without the means of reference to scientific experience, or to books, and wholly dependant on untutored artificers, whom he was obliged personally to instruct, it is solely to the resources of his powerful mind, that the British empire is indebted for one of her most durable and magnificent monuments.

After the completion of this splendid achievement, he was selected by the Com.-in-Chief, Sir John Abercrombie, to organize and consolidate the Commissariat department of the army, the duties of which had previously been dispersed in a variety of confused channels, naturally producing disorder and inefficiency; the ill consequences of which, were seriously felt in all military equipments. The success which attended his arrangements as Commissary-in-Chief, which was the designation of his new office, was as complete as that which attended every measure intrusted to his judgment and abilities.

He returned to his native country with an impaired constitution, in 1817, and retired from the service in the following year. Respected by the whole army, esteemed by his numerous acquaintance, and loved by the few who enjoyed his intimacy, and who alone could fully appreciate the unassuming virtue, honourable feelings, and zealous friendship, which distinguished his character through life: he finished his career at the early age of fifty, leaving a widow* and three young children—too young, alas! to be sensible of their irreparable loss.

CAPTAIN RICHARD LANGSLOW.

(Bengal Establishment.)

THIS officer arrived at Calcutta as a Cadet, in 1801, and was appointed to do duty with the 2d batt. 4th N. I., at Seetapore Oude, then commanded by his uncle, Lieut.-Col. Robt. Phillips, (now a senior Lieutenant-General, residing at Shrewsbury).

Being permanently posted as 5th Ensign to the 1st batt. 7th N. I., under the late Col. James Morris, he had scarcely joined that corps, at Futtehghur, when his company was detached to aid in the collections of the Bareilly district. The Zemindars were refractory; the rainy season commenced, and this officer had an early opportunity, then 16 years of age, of witnessing hostile demonstrations, and encountering a jungle fever. At the expiration of ten weeks, the company got back to cantonments; and at the general relief of corps, this officer accompanied his battalion to the presidency, under the temporary command of Capt., the late Lieut.-Col. Bartlett Kelly.

In consequence of the Mahratta war, the 22d and 23d N. I., were raised towards the end of the year, and this officer was removed to the former, as 20th Lieutenant, and joined it early in 1804, at Futtehghur. The rains were not over, nor the boy recruits perfected in

* Lieut.-Col. Cowper married, in 1819, the eldest daughter of Dr. Richard Reece.

the drill, when the 2d battalion was called forth to aid in staying the career of the victorious Holkar, who was pursuing the remains of Col. Monson's detachment, to the gates of Agra. The battalion reached that fortress by hurried marches, on the 16th August, but it was not until September, that, by the junction of Col. (now Sir Sackville) Brown's brigade, and other troops, the British were in sufficient force to take up a position on the plain of Secundra, three miles from the city; and so elated were the enemy by recent success, that they scoured the country, and actually cut off many supplies and camp followers, between the British encampment and the town.

It was at this epoch that Holkar turned his thoughts to the capture of Delhi, employing his numerous horse and Pindarries to annoy and impede the formation and progress of the British army. Lord Lake, however, having joined with the Caunpoor and other divisions, the troops advanced to Muttra on the 3d October, and the enemy relinquished that place without resistance.

Several fruitless efforts were made to bring the enemy in contact with the British cavalry; but to obstruct and plunder were their only objects, in trying to effect which, they got occasionally very roughly handled. The particulars of these skirmishes on the march to the relief of Delhi; the gallant and extraordinary defence of that capital; the subsequent pursuit and destruction of Holkar's horse at Futtehghur, have already been stated in this work. We shall, however, advert to the successes of the infantry division, under Gen. Frazer, H. M.'s service, on the 13th Nov., on the glacis of the fort of Deeg, where, though early deprived of their valued leader, with a long list of brave companions, yet one hundred captured pieces of the enemy's artillery, announced their heroic deeds, and consoled their surviving friends.

The fortress of Deeg, which had quietly regarded the early part of the conflict, in anticipation of the annihilation of the British, opened its tremendous fire upon the victorious, but thinned columns, as they were finishing the glories of the day, by the capture of the third and last tier of ordnance, ranged completely under cover of the guns of the fort. British valour could alone have persevered against such dispiriting odds; but the artillery from the walls proved as unavailing, except in augmenting mortality, as that of the 130 pieces well served upon the plain below. The Jauts were justly punished for this perfidious attempt, in the capture of their fort and city, on the 24th Dec. following, by the same gallant regiments, which had experienced their baseness.

The sequel of the proceedings against the enemy, in which the 2d-22d bore a part, were not equally fortunate, from causes beyond the control of the British general. As the failure of the four assaults on Bhurtpoor have already been adverted to, and will be found particularly noticed in the memoir of Lord Lake, in this volume, it is here sufficient to observe, that the 2d-22d was actively employed in three of them; and when the enemy had the audacity to make a sortie on the British trenches, their repulse cost this battalion upwards of 80 killed and wounded. In the general list of casualities before Bhurtpoor, will be found the major part of the names of officers of this battalion who were present, viz. Capt. Hugh Griffiths, (now Lieut.-Col.) with a Java medal; Lieut. L. H. Davy, (now a retired Captain); Lieut. J. F. Blackney, (subsequently killed in Nepaul); Adjutant R. A. C. Watson*, (died lately, a Lieut.-Colonel); and Lieuts. Titcher and Pollock, (now dead).

Lieut. Langslow was appointed to act as Adjutant, during Lieut. Watson's cure, and in the performance of this duty, under occasional trying circumstances, he gave satisfaction to his superiors.

In April the army changed its position to the banks of the Chumbul to keep in check Dowlut Rao Scindia, who had advanced to that neighbourhood, and seemed to contemplate a coalition with Holkar and the Rajah of Bhurtpoor. The object of this movement being perfectly attained, towards the end of May the troops began to separate for different cantonments, and Agra fell to the lot of the 2d-22d, when the rains commencing with violence before they were halted, produced considerable sickness in their ranks.

* Services, vol. ii. p. 365-6.

The rains of 1805 had scarcely terminated, when the battalion was dispatched to the Rewarry district, to form part of the division under Lieut.-Col. George Ball*, in quest of Holkar's remaining force; but it did not fall to their lot to encounter it: and they finally took up a position near the town of Rewarry, where they remained, occasionally taking the Delhi duty in turn, until the general relief of corps in 1807-8, whereby the 2d-22d was transferred to more congenial quarters, at Seetapore Oude.

Orders were about this time issued for the formation of a light company in each battalion of Native infantry, and Capt. Langslow was appointed to command that of the 2d-22d. Every facility was afforded him in the selection of the men, and when, in Oct. 1808, he marched the company to Caunpoor, to join the light battalion embodied under Major Mansell, H. M.'s 53d, no company there was found to exceed it in efficiency or appearance.

Capt. Langslow was not long destined to hold this gratifying command; the liver disease, which had first shewn itself at Bhurtpoor, now assumed so serious an aspect that he was obliged to repair to the presidency on sick certificate, and eventually to England, where he arrived in 1810, and shortly after assumed the duties of a captain, in the 1st Somerset militia. In this regiment, under the late Earl Powlett, he served for four years, and his constitution became so much improved, that he was enabled, in 1814, again to repair to India.

The first news that greeted this officer on his arrival, was the disaster of his own battalion in Nepaul; the left wing had been nearly annihilated, and Capt. Blackney and Lieut. Duncan, were among the slain. He immediately proceeded to Dinapore, and thence to Bettiah, where he found Capt. R. A. C. Watson employed in restoring and giving efficiency to the remains of the battalion: they had little leisure at this post, till the division under Sir George Wood, K. C. B., separated, to take up positions for the hot and rainy seasons near the Nepaul hills. The battalion, now united under the com-

* Services, vol. ii. p. 355-7, 563; and in this volume.

mand of Lieut.-Col. Goddard Richards *, was posted at Amowa, in brigade with H. M.'s 24th foot, commanded successively by Colonels Chamberlain and Kelly.

It was not till October that the Gov.-Gen. of India, seeing the futility of further forbearance with the Goorkhas, summoned Sir David Ochterlony † from the upper provinces, and placed the political and military affairs with the Nepaulese, under his management. Sir David, uniting the shrewdness and experience of diplomacy with consummate military skill, lost no time in discovering the aim of the Goorkha emissaries, and soon brought the long-pending negociation to this point: That in failure of the appearance in camp of the treaty, fully ratified by a given day, the army would move forward. The ratification came not; and the troops were not tardy in traversing the Saul forest.

During the 14th, 15th, and 16th Feb., a movement was made by the troops, the direction of which would alone have served to rank the gallant general with the most skilful of the day. After unwearied research and investigation, an obscure and almost perpendicular path, penetrating the hills, was discovered, only known to smugglers, and believed to be totally impracticable for troops: Sir David thought otherwise; and by the aid of ropes, in the hands of the light company of the 87th, the General himself was one of the first who appeared on the summit of the Chowriaghatte pass.

The above extraordinary operation was attended with most beneficial effects in the prosecution of the war; but it terminated Capt. Langslow's active career; as, in effecting this manœuvre, he had the misfortune to sustain a bodily injury—that time cannot remove, nor emolument compensate for. He had almost gained the top of the

* Services, vol. ii. p. 358-9.

† Services, vol. i. p. 379-87: see also Addenda of this volume. This distinguished officer died at Meerut, on the 14th July 1825. The Bombay Gazette observes,—" As a public character, we are not aware of his parallel in the annals of British India. During a most active service of forty-seven years, in the double capacity of statesman and soldier, his unremitted exertions and unerring judgment, contributed largely to the stability of government, and the prosperity of the country."

pass, when the roots to which he clung giving way, and at the same time his feet slipping, he was on the point of being precipitated to the bottom; and he only avoided such a catastrophe by a sudden and extraordinary effort, whereby his whole weight became supported by a shrub caught by one hand alone. Life was saved; but the infirmity produced by the sudden wrench, rendered the boon scarcely worth acceptance. Hopeless of cure, he obtained his transfer to the Invalid establishment, with the promise, that a suitable provision should be made for him in that department of the service; but even that modification was denied him by the return of his original malady, abscess in the liver, brought on by want of that exercise to which he had always been accustomed, and from which his recent misfortune entirely excluded him. He sailed from Calcutta in 1817, as great a martyr to the service and the climate, as ever quitted India alive.

The Marquess of Hastings took upon himself the benevolent task of recommending, in his own hand, the favourable consideration of this officer's case, to the Chairman of the East India Company; and the Court of Directors were, in consequence, pleased, with their usual liberality, to decree him, in addition to his half-pay, the regulated pension as for the loss of an eye or a limb.

BRIGADIER ALEXANDER KNOX.

(Bengal Establishment.)

In 1780, this officer arrived in Bengal: he was appointed to a Cornetcy, 6th Oct. in that year; promoted to Lieutenant, 4th Aug. 1781; to Captain, 7th Jan. 1796; to Major, 1st May 1804; to Lieut.-Col. 15th Aug. 1809; to Col. 12th Aug. 1819; and to Col. Commandant, 16th August, 1822.

He served a campaign against the Mahrattas; and was at the taking of the fort of Culpee, in March 1781. He next served the campaign against the Rajah, Cheyt Sing, and was present during the siege and capture of the fortress of Bidzighur (Benares), in Nov. 1781. He was employed with his corps, in the years 1782-3 and 4, in reducing the refractory Zemindars in Bogelcund and Bundlecund; and was present at the storm of the fort of Khytul, in March 1783, and at the siege and reduction of Chowkundee, in May 1783.

He marched from Futtehghur in Dec. 1789, for the Coromandel coast, with Colonel Cockerell's* detachment; served the whole of the campaign with the centre army, and was present with the grand army during the siege and storm of Bangalore, in March 1791. He was also present in the general action against Tippoo's whole army, 15th May 1791; at the siege, and of the storming party, in the column commanded by Sir David Baird, at Severndroog, Dec. 21st 1791; at the capture, by assault, of Ootradroog, Dec. 24th 1791; and of the party who stormed Tippoo's fortified lines before Seringapatam, 6th Feb. 1792. He served the whole of Lord Cornwallis's campaigns on the coast. He was in the battle of Cutterah, on the 23d Oct. 1794; and served from the commencement to the close of the campaign, against the Rohillas, under Sir Robert Abercrombie. He was at the siege and reduction of the forts of Sasnee and Bejighur, in the Doouab, in Jan. and Feb. 1803; and at the siege and taking of Catchoura, by storm, in March 1803, under Lord Lake; in the action before Allyghur, 29th August; and the capture of Allyghur, by storm, 4th Sept. 1803; in the battle of Delhi, 11th Sept. 1803, (when the enemy was completely defeated, with the loss of all his guns); and had a charger killed under him. The regiment, the 2d light cavalry, on this occasion received an honorary standard. He also served at the siege and taking of Agra, 18th Oct. 1803; at the battle of Laswarree, Nov. 1st, 1803, (when he had a second charger disabled under him by a cannon shot); at the battle of Deeg, and taking of the whole of Holkar's guns, 13th Nov., 1804; at the siege and capture, by storm, of the fort of Deeg, Dec. 23d, 1804; at the siege and four assaults of Bhurtpoor, from Jan. to April 1805; during the

* Services, vol. i. p. 114-16.

whole of Lord Lake's campaigns against the Mahratta confederates and Jeswunt Rao Holkar; and in several other attacks and skirmishes.

This officer commanded the 4th cavalry brigade attached to the reserve, consisting of the 2d light cavalry and Skinner's horse (3000 strong), and was detached by Sir David Ochterlony, in April 1817, with the cavalry brigade, 3 battalions of infantry, and ten 6-pounders, to compel the Newaub, Jumshere Behauder, (son-in-law to Meer Khan, and his principal Sirdar), to give up his guns, which he refused to do, though repeatedly demanded by Sir David Ochterlony. After three forced marches, he overtook the Newaub on the banks of the Sambur lake, with his army of 10,000 men drawn up for action, and took the whole of his artillery, (44 guns, with a proportion of tumbrils) The following orders were issued on this occasion:—

"*Detachment Orders by Brigadier Knox.*

"*Camp, near Sambur, 7th April,* 1818.

"Brigadier Knox has the pleasure of congratulating the detachment under his command, on the successful termination of their exertions since quitting the reserve, in the unconditional surrender of the Newaub, Jumshere Khan's guns this morning. The cheerfulness with which the troops sustained the fatigue and privations incident to a rapid, though short, series of forced marches, and the alacrity and precision with which the columns were formed on the expected hostile approach of Jumshere Khan, has given the Commanding Officer the most favourable impression of their discipline and intrepidity. Brigadier Knox requests that the Commanding Officers of corps, and the officers and men generally, will accept his best thanks for their diligence and good conduct, whilst under his command, which it will be a pleasing part of his duty to bring to the notice of his Excellency the most Noble the Commander-in-Chief.

"In issuing this order, the Brigadier feels it particularly incumbent on him, to acknowledge the great assistance he has derived from the exertions of Capt. E. Barton, Assistant Quarter-Master-General, the promptitude and certainty of whose intelligence has contributed much to the success of the detachment."

Reserve Orders by Brigadier-General Arnold*, C. B.
"*April 8th*, 1818.

" An express received this morning from Brigadier Knox, commanding the detachment sent on special service, detailing the spirited address, and soldier-like manner, in which the Brigadier demanded and obtained 44 guns, with tumbrils, at the point of the sword and bayonet, in front and within 50 paces of the troops drawn up by Jumshere Khan, demands from Brigadier-General Arnold, his most sincere thanks and acknowledgments to Brigadier Knox, and the detachment under his command."

Reserve Orders by Major-General Sir D. Ochterlony.
"*12th April*, 1818.

" On re-assuming the command of the division, it is the first wish, as it is the most pleasing duty of Major-Gen. Sir D. Ochterlony, to offer his best thanks to Brigadier Knox, and generally to the officers and men composing the detachment placed under his orders, by Brigadier-Gen. Arnold, on the 4th instant.

" The Major-Gen. has read with the greatest satisfaction, the detail transmitted to him, and he is fully persuaded he is not misled by the partiality of friendship, when he expresses his confidence, that the judgment, decision, and energy, evinced by the Brigadier in his instantaneous rejection of all correspondence with the vakeels of Jumshere Khan; the moderate, but firm and decided tone, in the subsequent interview with the Khan himself; the order of advance to his columns of attack; and ultimately, the intimation sent him of his determination, if he longer refused the fulfilment of his promises; will not fail to attract the notice, and ensure the approbation of the most Noble the Com.-in-Chief, whose feelings will be gratified in hearing, that every object which could have been hoped from the most decided victory, has been obtained by the Brigadier's firm and judicious conduct without a contest."

"*To Lieut.-Col. Knox, Commanding a Detachment.*

" Sir,—I am directed by the Com.-in-Chief to acknowledge the receipt of your letter and enclosures of the 7th inst., and to convey his Excellency's high approbation of the judgment and zeal evinced in the performance of the service, on which you have lately been employed.

" His Lordship requests you will accept his sincere thanks, and offer the

---

* Services, p. 1-8 of this volume.

same to the officers and men of your detachment, whose admirable discipline during the march, justly entitled them to the handsome order issued on the occasion; and whose steady and cool behaviour, in presence of Jumshere Khan's troops, no doubt intimidated them, and produced the successful result, in the unconditional surrender of the guns; a circumstance of importance at the present juncture.

   (Signed)   "Jas. Nicol, Adjutant-General of the Army.
" *Head-Quarters*, 19*th April*, 1818."

In June 1818, the Brigadier was directed, by Sir David Ochterlony, to proceed against Ajmeer, and had with him six battalions of infantry, 2d reg. of light cavalry, 2d and 3d regiments of Rampoor horse, and a suitable battering train. On the surrender of the town and fort, with 73 pieces of cannon, the following order was published:—

   Detachment Orders by Brigadier Knox.
          " *Ajmeer*, 3*d July*, 1818.

" In offering his congratulations to the troops under his command, on the surrender of the strong fortress of Tarraghur, Brigadier Knox feels it peculiarly incumbent on him, to express his belief, that the successful issue of the affair is principally to be attributed to the zealous and spirited conduct of the detachment employed in the operations of the 1st instant. The close and attentive reconnoissance of the town and fort of Ajmeer, executed by Lieut. Hall of the Quarter-Master-General's department, and Ensign E. Garstin, of the engineers, appears to have led to the immediate evacuation of the former, and to the consequent occupation of positions by our troops, of the greatest importance to our ultimate success; whilst the decisive effect on the minds of the defenders of the fort, caused by the battery which had been planned by the latter of these officers, affords the best test of its position having been judiciously chosen.

" To Major Butler, who voluntarily undertook the superintendence of the artillery detail; to Capt. Arden of the 27th infantry; Lieuts. Pringle and Aire of the pioneers; and, generally, to all the officers and men employed on this occasion, the Brigadier begs leave to offer his best thanks. The facility with which, during a very stormy night, and in spite of great natural obstacles, the battery was erected by the pioneers, clearly shews, how much may be expected from the services of this valuable corps.

"In the judicious and successful application of the labour of the public servants and cattle on this occasion, Lieut. E. C. Sneyd, of the Commissariat department, has established an additional claim to that approbation on the part of Brigadier Knox, which his former conduct, on the expedition to Sambur, had so justly excited."

"*To Brigadier Knox, Commanding a Detachment.*

"Sir,—I am directed by the Commander-in-Chief to acknowledge the copies of your despatches to M.-Gen. Sir D. Ochterlony, dated the 29th ult. and 3d inst., reporting your being in possession of the fortified city of Ajmeer, and of the fort of Tarraghur, with the circumstances which led to the early acquisition of the latter important place. The Com.-in-Chief has viewed with approbation the measures adopted by you to awe the factious garrison of Tarraghur into speedy submission, or in the event of that being refused, to commence operations against it without delay: and the early success which placed you, without loss of lives, in possession of so strong a fortress, gives you a fresh claim to the thanks which His Excellency has more than once had the gratification of offering to you, for the decision and conduct you have displayed. His Excellency warmly concurs in the applause which you have bestowed on the officers and troops under your command, and especially on those whose conduct has been particularly mentioned by you, though the Com.-in-Chief doubts not, had opportunity occurred for actively employing them, that the whole would equally have merited your approbation.

(Signed) "J. Nicol, Adj.-Gen. of the Army.
"*Fort William, 24th July,* 1818."

In March 1823, the Brigadier received orders from Sir D. Ochterlony, to proceed against the fort of Lamba, in the Jeypoor territory: after a fruitless negotiation of some days, in which it at length appeared evident, that the enemy were insincere in their promises of surrender, and only anxious to gain time, the batteries were opened on them, on the morning of the 17th March 1823, when, after the short space of four hours' playing, the garrison, consisting of 500 men, evacuated the fort in rapid flight, and the Brigadier took possession of it.

On this occasion, the following orders were issued:—

Division Orders by Brigadier Knox.

"*Camp, Lamba,* 17*th March,* 1823.

"Brigadier Knox takes the earliest opportunity to offer his cordial thanks to the whole of the troops he has had the honour to command before Lamba. The fatiguing service so alertly and perseveringly performed, by the 3d reg. light cavalry, in closely and successfully patrolling round the place, night and day, reflects high credit upon Captain Smyth, and the whole of the officers and men of that efficient corps. To Major Baines*, and the 1st batt. of the 18th reg. N. I.; Capt. W. Skeene, with the flank and light companies of the 1st batt. 25th and 2d batt. 29th regs., the Brigadier feels much indebted, for the cheerfulness with which so small a body carried on the extensive trench and town duties; but, to Capt. C. H. Bell, and the artillery, the Commanding Officer's highest praise is due; to the quickness and precision of its fire, the Brigadier feels well assured, the service owes the almost unexampled unconditional evacuation of so strong a fortification, by a numerous and boasting garrison, in the short space of four hours open batteries. In thus recording such happy results, the Commanding Officer conceives he does the merits of Capt. Bell and his detachment no more than justice, by the most unqualified expression of his approbation. Capt. Pringle and the pioneers have performed their arduous and fatiguing duties, with their wonted indefatigable zeal, and claim that high applause which has ever distinguished that corps: Capt. Pringle is further entitled to the Brigadier's best thanks, for the skill and activity with which he discharged the important duty of engineer to the detachment, during the siege. It would be a dereliction of duty to omit the exertions of Capt. James Wilkie, who escorted four mortars from Ajmeer to camp, a distance of 43 miles, in the almost incredible time of seventeen hours. The zeal and activity of Capt. F. H. Sandys, Dep. Assist. Quar.-Mas.-Gen., has been conspicuous, and is entitled to the Brigadier's highest approbation; and his best thanks are also due to Capt. C. Taylor, Major of Brigade, and Lieut. J. G. Burns, Commissariat officer. The Commanding Officer is so deeply indebted to the zeal and able advice of Capt. Hall, Political Agent, that he is at a loss to express, in appropriate terms, his acknowledgments of that valuable officer's eminent services; he must, therefore, trust to Capt. Hall to do justice to the Brigadier's feelings on this occasion, when he offers him *only* his sincere thanks."

* Services, vol. ii. p. 361.

Division orders by Maj.-Gen. Sir D. Ochterlony, commanding Western Division of the army.

"*Head-quarters, Camp, Ajmeer, 19th March,* 1823.

"The Major-General having received the reports of Brigadier Knox, and a copy of his orders, has only to intimate his own entire concurrence in the sentiments expressed by the Brigadier, and to request the several officers, who have been honoured with his approbation, will accept his warm acknowledgments and thanks. Though the Major-General feels, no doubt, that the merits of the Brigadier will be felt and acknowledged by higher authority, he cannot refrain from expressing his high sense of the moderation, lenity, and forbearance, which marked his earlier proceedings, and his admiration of the skill, spirit, and decision, which characterized his subsequent operations."

MAJOR-GENERAL GEORGE PROLE.

(*Bengal Establishment.*)

This officer was appointed a Cadet on the Bengal establishment, in 1776; Ensign, 12th March 1777; Lieutenant, 9th August 1778; Captain, 28th October 1794; Major, 14th July 1799; Lieut.-Colonel, 30th June 1802; Colonel, 4th June 1811; and Major-General, 4th June 1814.

He arrived in Bengal on the 12th September 1776, carried a musket eight months in the Cadet company, and was selected, with another cadet, to do duty as Ensigns (officers in that capacity being wanted) previous to their promotion. In 1778, he volunteered for foreign service, with the Bombay detachment under Gen. Goddard*: he served in all the campaigns of that corps, in the infantry, and, occasionally, in the engineer corps as a volunteer, until he was severely wounded, at the siege of Ahmedabad. He recovered after eight months, and rejoined his corps, but was again wounded in General Goddard's retreat from the Bhore ghaut.

* Services, vol. ii. p. 414-29.

This officer was next appointed Paymaster to the Bombay detachment, with which he returned to Bengal.

In 1790, he again volunteered for service on the Coromandel coast, under Lieut.-Col. Cockerell*. He served, as a subaltern, under Gen. Medows †; and was present in all the campaigns of the Marquess Cornwallis, in Mysore; sometimes in command of two or three companies, at others, in command of a battalion of volunteers; and his conduct did not escape the favourable notice of his Lordship.

In 1792, this officer returned to Bengal with the detachment. He next served in the Rohilla war of 1793-4, under Sir Robert Abercrombie, and at this period was promoted to Captain.

In January 1796, he repaired to Europe, on furlough, and in December 1798, returned to Bengal.

Captain Prole volunteered his services for the expedition to Egypt, but was ordered to remain and discipline a regiment, to the command of which he had been appointed by Sir Alured Clarke ‡, the Commander-in-Chief, soon after his promotion to a Majority.

* Services, vol. i. p. 114, *et seq.*

† Lieut.-Colonel (now Lieut.-Gen. Lord) Harris (Services, vol. ii. p. 385-6) accompanied Gen. Sir W. Medows to Bombay, in 1788, as his private Secretary. He was appointed to the head of a department then denominated Commissary-General, which has since been changed to the more appropriate title of Auditor-General. Major George Hart, then of the 75th reg. also accompanied Gen. Medows to Bombay, as his Aid-de-Camp. He was appointed Adjutant-General of the Bombay army, and by his admirable turn for military arrangement and detail, he wrought a most desirable reform and improvement in that army, which, before his time, was a strange heterogeneous compound; in which, however, bravery and fidelity had long been conspicuous ingredients. This distinguished officer has arrived at the rank of Lieut.-General, is the Colonel of a regiment, and member of Parliament for Londonderry.

‡ The following address from Sir Alured Clarke, Commander-in-Chief, to the army of India, prior to his departure for Europe, should be recorded in a work intended to uphold the honour and interests of that army.

"*Fort William, Feb.* 16, 1801.

"The Commander-in-Chief, before his final departure from India, esteems it not more an act of justice to the army that has served under his immediate orders near four years, than a tribute due to his own feelings, to publish his sentiments of its merits and deserts.

"He reflects with heartfelt satisfaction, that, throughout the whole period of his command, the zeal and attention which have been invariably manifested by the officers of all ranks to the duties of their profession, have not had stronger claims on his public approbation, than

Major Prole finally served in the Mahratta war, in the army of Lord Lake, and under the command of Brigadier Martindell*, in Bundlecund, and whom he succeeded in the command of that province, and was honoured by the approbation of Lord Lake, through the Adjutant-General, Col. Worsley†.

In the end of 1809, he was ordered by his Excellency Gen. Hewitt, Commander-in-Chief, to assume the military command of the districts of Delhi, Rewarry, and Hurrianah; in which command he continued as Lieut.-Colonel, and from 1811 as full Colonel, until Sir George Nugent‡ was appointed Commander-in-Chief, who obtained for this officer the rank and allowances of a Brigadier.

In Nov. 1814, he obtained permission to resign his command, and to return to England on furlough, and this permission was accompanied by an acknowledgment on the part of government of his long and diligent services.

---

the cordial support and personal attention he had uniformly experienced, entitle them to his warmest thanks. The Commander-in-Chief must ever cherish the sentiments of gratitude with which his mind is impressed, for men endeared to him by the spirit of honour, propriety, and disinterestedness, that have distinguished their public and private conduct: and he shall be happy, on all occasions, to bear ample testimony to the collective and individual merits of this army, and with real approbation, embrace every opportunity to promote its interest. Where the Commander-in-Chief has had so much reason to express his approbation generally, it might seem difficult to discover cause for particular praise; but the peculiar situation in which Major-Gen. Sir James Craig has been placed in the field, having occasioned the greatest part of the army to be at different times under his immediate command, and the discipline of the whole having received essential benefit from his unremitted exertion, knowledge, and care, the Commander-in-Chief cannot resist the impulse he feels in this public manner, to offer his hearty thanks to the Major-General, for those and his other important services, during the period of his command in the field, which he hopes he will be pleased to accept."

* Services, vol. i. p. 406, *et seq.* and vol. ii. p. 562.
† Services, vol. i. p. 130-9; and Addenda of this volume.
‡ Services, Royal Military Calendar, vol. i. p. 394-9, 3d edit.

THE LATE COLONEL GRANGER MUIR*.

(Bengal Establishment.)

This officer commenced his military career by serving under his father, Major Muir, of His Majesty's army, at the sieges of Pondicherry, in 1747 and 1748. He remained at Madras until 1752, when the Court of Directors nominated him a writer on the Bengal establishment. On his arrival at Calcutta, he was appoined to an office; but disliking the inactivity of the situation, he obtained, in 1754, the Governor in Council's permission, to resign it, and received an Ensign's commission in its place.

In 1756, when Surajah Dowlah took the fort of Calcutta, Ensign Muir was stationed with twenty men, at the factory of Jugdia, under the orders of Mr. Amyat, the chief, with Messrs, Pleydell, Verelst, Smyth, and Hay, of the civil service: they were directed by the Governor and Council, to quit the factory, and repair to Futta, where the dispersed English were collecting, under the protection of some of the Company's ships, just arrived from Europe.

On the arrival of Col. Clive and Adm. Watson with reinforcements from Madras, the army took the field, when Mr. Muir was promoted to Captain, and as such, commanded a company at the battle of Plassey, as he did in the other actions, during the year 1757.

In 1758, Capt. Gowen, of the Bombay establishment, came round

---

* He was the son of a respectable officer in His Majesty's service, who was one of the Majors sent out, in 1747, in command of twelve independent companies, in Admiral Boscawen's fleet, to recover, if possible, Madras, and some other settlements, which had been taken from the Company, the year before, by the French: and Mr. Muir, then a youth of about fourteen, accompanied his father. The Admiral arrived at Fort St. David the latter end of the year, and, with the assistance of the garrison of that place, invested Pondicherry; but the monsoon setting in, and some mismanagement having existed in the engineer department, he was obliged to raise the siege, with considerable loss. He sat down against it a second time, in 1748, but had made little progress, when accounts were received from England of a general peace. Madras being restored by the treaty, the troops moved from Pondicherry to take possession of it, when Major Muir died in the following year.

to Bengal, and being an old officer, Col. Clive presented him with a Majority in this army. This gave so much dissatisfaction to the Bengal army, that eight captains*, including Capt. Muir, resigned their commissions in one day.

Capt. Muir returned to England, and in Jan. 1760, obtained a Lieutenancy in the 94th reg., with which corps he served in America, during the remainder of the seven years' war. In 1763, the 94th was disbanded; but accounts having reached England at the latter end of the same year, of the war with Cossim Ally, and the destruction of the Patna detachment, (see p. 74 and 81, vol. ii.) proposals were made to some of the disbanded Lieutenants, to raise men for Bengal, on the Company's bounty, five guineas, and those who could enlist 125 men were to have Captains' commissions. Many offered their services, and amongst the rest, Lieut. Muir, who soon completed his company, and with it embarked for India; but having a long passage, did not arrive in Bengal until early in 1765, and immediately after joined the army.

Capt. Muir rose to the rank of full Colonel, and head of a brigade†,

---

* Captains Rumbold (afterwards Sir Thomas), Alexander Grant, Muir, Carstairs, Campbell, and three others; the two last named were subsequently restored to the service, but with loss of rank.

† That eccentric, but clever character, Capt. Ralph Broome, was at this period Persian interpreter to Colonel Muir. The Captain subsequently annoyed Mr. Edmund Burke and his phalanx by a diurnal poetical report, in "Simkin's Letters," of their proceedings before the House of Lords, in the impeachment of Warren Hastings, containing much wit and sarcasm on their movements, during their celebrated prosecution of that distinguished public character. In volume ii. p. 243-6, we have given a memoir of Mr. Hastings. The following eulogy is from Mr. Forbes's Oriental Memoirs, vol. ii. p. 462:—"A venerable Brahmin told me, he had lived under different governments, and travelled in many countries; but had never witnessed a general diffusion of happiness, equal to that of the Natives, under the mild and equitable administration of Mr. Hastings, at that time Governor-General of Bengal. I cannot forget the words of this respectable pilgrim: we were near a banian tree, in the durbar court, when he thus concluded his discourse: ' As the burr-tree, one of the noblest productions in nature, by extending its branches, for the comfort and refreshment of all who seek its shelter, is emblematical of the Deity; so do the virtues of the Governor resemble the burr-tree,—he extends his providence to the remotest districts, and stretches out his arms, far and wide, to afford protection and happiness to his people: such, *saheb*, is Mr. Hastings!' Yet, this is the man, who, by the violence of faction, intended for patriotic zeal,

and for a long time, commanded a field force in the Mahratta country, having succeeded, in 1781, to Lieut.-Col. Camac's command, soon after that officer's brilliant attack on Scindia's camp: and, in October of that year, he concluded a separate treaty with the Mahratta chief, which was speedily followed by a general peace with all the Mahratta states.

On the field force being broken up, Col. Muir embarked for England, but died on the passage.

CAPTAIN THOMAS BLAIR.

(Bengal Establishment.)

In 1769, this officer received his commission as Ensign in the Bengal army, and was shortly afterwards appointed to a sepoy battalion, stationed at Allahabad: in 1773, he was promoted to Lieutenant, and removed to the 2d European regiment, and soon after again to a sepoy battalion. In 1779, he was appointed Adjutant and Quarter-Master to the troops in the Midnapoor district, that province being threatened by the Beraker Rajah, who had assembled a considerable force at Cuttack, under Chumnagee: he continued at Midnapoor till his promotion to the rank of Captain, in 1781, and was appointed to the command of the 1st batt. 6th N. I., which corps he joined at Chunarghur, a short time prior to the rebellion of Rajah Cheyt Sing.

On taking the command of his corps, he found them in great want of arms; one-third of the men were exercised with bamboos, instead of muskets; and those in the possession of the corps were very defective and old. On the day of the breaking out of the rebellion, and the massacre of the guards which had been placed over Rajah Cheyt

and conducted by a flow of eloquence, seldom equalled, was arraigned for crimes, the most foreign to his benevolent heart, and doomed to a trial of seven years' duration: a scene unparalleled in the annals of mankind!"

Sing, Capt. Blair arrived from Chunar at Benares: the Governor-General, Mr. Hastings, requested to see him immediately, to learn, if, in the state of insurrection into which the country was thus suddenly and unexpectedly thrown, he considered it practicable to proceed to Chunarghur, and march his battalion to the vicinity of Ramnagur, the residence of Rajah Cheyt Sing, on the opposite bank of the Ganges to Benares, to which place he had made his escape after the massacre of the guards placed over him.

Having obtained orders for a complete equipment of arms, &c. Capt. Blair undertook this dangerous journey, rendered so by the hostility of all the inhabitants, and accomplished it late on the same evening; his battalion being on duty, was relieved the following morning. Having received new arms, ammunition, &c. by 2 o'clock, he marched and arrived that same evening in the vicinity of Ramnagur, where they continued encamped, till Major Myaffre, on the 18th August, joined with a detachment of artillery, the European corps of rangers and Capt. Sparks' sepoy battalion. The following morning, Major Myaffre having previously assumed the command, marched to the attack of Ramnagur; and the troops, after a very heavy loss, were beat back from the town. The enemy firing from the houses, did great execution: Major Myaffre and Capt. Doxet were killed, and three other European officers wounded.

Having collected the troops as they arrived outside the town, a very singular request was made by the European officers, and acquiesced in by Capt. Sparks, the then senior officer, that Capt. Blair would assume the command. On ascertaining that it was the unanimous wish of the troops, he complied with the request, gave the necessary orders for completing the men's ammunition, and sending forward the wounded, the baggage, and camp-followers, commenced their march to the neighbourhood of Chunar. The enemy made several attempts to harass and impede the march of the troops, without success, and a shot from a six-pounder with the rear-guard, kept them in check. The following general orders were issued on this occasion:—

"*General Orders, Chunarghur, 26th August*, 1781.

" The Gov.-Gen. having this day received the returns of all the killed and wounded in the late attack upon the town of Ramnagur, and circumstantial reports from the proper officers, finds the greatest alleviation to his sorrow for the unhappy issue of that event, in the testimonies which those reports exhibit, of the bravery and firmness displayed by the officers and troops, both Europeans and Natives, after they were compelled to retire from the town, with so considerable a loss. The Gov.-Gen. remarks, with particular satisfaction, the spirited and judicious conduct of Capt. Sparks and Capt. Blair, in effecting a retreat; and to the latter gentleman, especially, without derogating in the least from the approved and acknowledged merit of Capt. Sparks, the highest acknowledgments are due, for the skill and resolution with which he extricated the troops from their dangerous situation in the streets of Ramnagur, until their junction with Capt. Sparks' battalion. The Gov.-Gen. considers the officers engaged in this unfortunate action, entitled to his warmest thanks and applause, for their gallant behaviour, and requests they will please to convey to the troops, under their command, his entire approbation of their courage and discipline; particularly to the corps of rangers, who so eminently distinguished themselves throughout the whole attack and retreat, and whose loss, with his own, on the death of their unfortunate companions, he justly laments."

On the 3d Sept. 1781, Major Popham*, who had been appointed to the command of the troops, selected Captain Blair to command the detachment to attack the Rajah's troops, consisting of 4000 of his best infantry and more than 500 cavalry and 6 field-pieces, encamped in front of Pateeta, a fortified town. This hazardous service was attended with complete success: the steady gallantry of this small body of men, consisting of the remains of Capt. Blair's sepoy battalion, the grenadiers of the 35th sepoy reg. that escaped the massacre of Benares, and two 6-pounders, in all barely 550 men, defeated the enemy, and captured 4 of their guns. The loss of the detachment was severe, suffering particularly from the enemy's artillery, which was well served, and bravely defended. Capt. Blair was highly indebted to Lieuts. Birrell, Murray, and Fallon, who exe-

* Services, vol. ii. p. 93-100.

cuted his orders, in charging with the bayonet, and capturing two guns that were mowing down the ranks: the enemy's artillerymen were several of them killed at their guns, which were immediately turned on them, and greatly contributed to their defeat.

In elucidation of this action, which was dearly purchased, and held in high estimation, the report thereon, the general orders issued by the Gov.-General, his letters to the Vice-Gov.-Gen., and to Col. Morgan, are here inserted:—

" *To the Hon. Warren Hastings, Esq. Governor-General, &c.*

" SIR,—I have the honour to congratulate you on the success which Capt. Blair has this morning met with. I shall do myself the pleasure of waiting on you as soon as the detachment returns to camp, which I expect in half an hour or so.

" What I gather of this business is, that our people advanced under a severe fire at first, but the enemy soon gave way, and left us three of their guns; one of those is the gun Capt. Myaffre lost. Mr. Murray and four Europeans are scorched, by the explosion of a gun-cartridge, and several sepoys killed and wounded.

" *Camp, 3d Sept.* 1781." (Signed) " W. POPHAM.

" *To the Hon. Warren Hastings, Esq. Governor-General, &c.*

" SIR,—The third instant, at night, Major Popham did me the honour to mention his wish of surprising the enemy, then encamped near Pateeta, with an offer to me of commanding the party, which was to perform that service. I most gladly accepted it; and at 1 o'clock in the morning, marched off with the greater part of my own battalion, the grenadiers of the 35th regiment, in all about 550 men, and two 6-pounders. I took my route by the left of our present encampment, to avoid their out-posts, which I was so fortunate to pass unobserved, and expected to have arrived by the first appearance of day-light; but was retarded in my march by the badness of the gun-bullocks and drivers. The enemy were first alarmed by some firing on the west-side of Chunar; nearly at the same time they must have received information of my march and intentions; for I found them regularly drawn up on an extensive plain, more than a mile to the eastward of their former station, and in numbers about 4000, including 400 cavalry tolerably well mounted, and six pieces of ordnance. They commenced the cannonade about 5 o'clock in the morning, distant about three-quarters of a mile. I continued to advance, and so soon as our round shot would take effect, I fired upon their line, and continued doing both, their infantry and artillery firing very smartly, and their cavalry having surrounded us, but which were deterred from charging our line, by a shot from our guns now and then. The fire of our artillery and sepoys, which was very quick, obliged their infantry to fall back; and to get possession of their guns, was immediately necessary at this critical moment; convinced of it, I ordered the whole of the grenadiers to advance for that purpose, which they did with such impetuosity as overcame all opposition, and seized two guns, which were immediately turned upon the enemy. The grenadiers were led on by Lieuts. Fallon, Birrell, and Murray. I must beg leave to mention them in the warmest manner, for their gallant steady conduct. The enemy began to give way in every part immediately after; a very smart fire from all the guns and line, completed out success. About six, or a little after, the enemy observed no regularity; every man appeared to be guided by his own fears, and ran away to the town and fort of Pateeta, which was in the rear of their left flank. Another gun was about this time taken by a party which I detached for that purpose; in another part, one of the enemy's standards was taken, and soon after, a fourth gun. Our guns were well pointed, and served by Lieut. Baillie, the officer of artillery, to whom I am much obliged for his activity and conduct during the whole of the action.

" Taken from the enemy four brass guns with limbers and tumbrils, with a very large quantity of ammunition of every kind, and of the very best materials: one of each sort I have taken the liberty of sending for your inspection. It appears evident to me, from the quantity and quality, to have been all prepared long before your arrival at Benares, and at a very considerable expense, part of it being of European materials. I was under the necessity of blowing up a tumbril and two limber-boxes full of ammunition, a large quantity of powder, and leaving upwards of 1500 round shots and one gun shotted and spiked for want of any means to bring them off.

" Three brass guns, one tumbril, and one limber-box of ammunition, I brought with me. The sepoys offered their services to draw them, which I thankfully accepted, and made them a small recompense for their readiness.

" I now collected my wounded men, which were very considerable, and much dispersed, occasioned by the distance I had advanced. I provided them with palanquins, officers horses, doolies, and every thing which could be collected. Mr. Laird, the surgeon, was very diligent and active in giving his assistance on this occasion, as well as during the action. About 8 o'clock I was joined by Lieuts. Wade and Malcolm with one gun, the rangers, and 100 sepoys. The rangers made an offer of dragging the enemy's guns, which I accepted, and employed them with the sepoys, who had before made the like application, and were much fatigued.

" Having accomplished the service, and I believe the intention of my being detached, though I could not surprise the enemy's camp, owing to their early intelligence, I judged it most proper to return to our present station, which I did, the enemy not choosing to give me any further trouble. I take the liberty to mention Lieut. Birrell's conduct during the whole of the action, as deserving the highest praise from me; also every officer and soldier I had the honour of commanding.

(Signed) " THOMAS BLAIR.
" *Camp, near Chunar, 4th Sept. 1781.*"

" *To Edward Wheeler, Esq., Vice-Governor-General.*

" SIR,—Yesterday morning Major Popham detached Capt. Blair with his battalion and two companies of his own grenadiers, and two guns (6-pounders) to attack the enemy collected at Pateeta. They were prepared to receive him, and made a very spirited resistance. After a very severe action, the fortune of the day was happily turned in our favour, by a bold, but well-judged manœuvre. Capt. Blair detached his grenadier companies to attack two guns, which were posted on the flank, and galled his troops exceedingly. The attack succeeded, and the two guns were turned upon the enemy, who were soon after totally routed. Capt. Blair brought off three of their guns, and spiked the fourth, the carriage of which was disabled. He brought away also one of their tumbrils, and also his own, loaded with their ammunition. Three more of their tumbrils, with much loose powder, were blown up on the field, Capt. Blair having no means of bringing them away. He was also obliged to leave about 1500 of their shot piled in a village. The enemy's numbers are reputed 8000 or 9000 men, though Capt. Blair judges them, from appearance, to be only 3000 or 4000. They were their prime men. Our loss, which I add with regret, is 105 men killed and wounded: their's must be proportionably more, though unknown. It is remarkable that the enemy's artillery and cartridges made at Ramnagur, are almost equal to our's; their cartridges and port-fires compounded with equal skill, and their powder much better. This is the second instance in which the service is signally indebted to the collected and intrepid gallantry of Capt. Blair. Other praises are due which cannot be noticed in this.

(Signed) "WARREN HASTINGS.

"*Chunar, 4th Sept.* 1781."

"*General Orders, Chunar, 8th Sept.* 1781.

"The Gov.-Gen. desires to express publicly the sense which he entertains of the gallant behaviour of the officers and troops in the attack made upon the enemy's camp near Pateeta, on the 4th inst. The Gov.-Gen. considers Capt. Blair as entitled to his warmest approbation for the resolution and conduct which he evinced in defeating a force so much superior in number, nor wanting, as it has appeared, in personal bravery.

"The spirit exerted by Lieuts. Fallon, Birrell, and Murray, who led the grenadiers; the service performed by the artillery under charge of Lieut. Baillie; and, in general, the steadiness and attention of every officer in his station, materially contributed to the success of the action, and give them a claim to the highest commendations.

"The Gov.-Gen. also highly commends the care and activity of Mr. Laird, in his attention to the wounded during the action.

"It is with great satisfaction that the Gov.-General gives the praise which has been represented to him as due to the distinguished behaviour of the grenadiers of the detachment.

"*To Edward Wheeler, Esq.*

"SIR,—I have advised you in triplicate of the success gained by Captain Blair, on the 3d. It was dear, but decisive. With 550 men, opposed to more than 4000, he completely routed them, took all their guns (4), tumbrils (4), and ammunition immeasurable.

(Signed) "WARREN HASTINGS.

"*Chunar, 11th Sep.* 1781."

"*To Colonel Morgan, Commanding the field station of Caunpoor.*

"SIR,—I have written to you the news of the 3d. On that morning, Capt. Blair with five battalion companies, and two companies of Major Popham's grenadiers, with two 6-pounders, attacked the enemy, encamped in a body of more than 4,000 men at Pateeta, and after a very severe and doubtful conflict, in which we lost 105 men, killed and wounded, he obtained a most decisive victory, taking all their guns and ammunition, viz. four guns, four tumbrils, and of ammunition an incredible quantity, &c.

(Signed) "WARREN HASTINGS."

Rajah Cheyt Sing, with his principal forces, continued to occupy Luttufpoor, a fort situated at the foot of the passes leading to Bidzighur, defended towards the plain by thick jungles and entrenchments. Ramnagur, Benares, and all the districts, remained faithful to him, and continued to supply new levies of men. At this period Major Popham was preparing to bombard Ramnagur and Benares: his plan of prosecuting the war presented many causes of delay: supposing the capture of Ramnagur and Benares to take place at the shortest period, Luttufpoor remained the head-quarters of the Rajah! Strong objections to this procedure presented themselves to Capt. Blair, who, from his knowledge of the country, his inquiries and intercourse with intelligent Natives, enabled him to submit to the Gov.-Gen. a plan for marching by a road hitherto considered impracticable for regular troops, or any kind of artillery, to attack Luttufpoor from the passes behind, where the difficulties of approach, and the defences of the fort, were less formidable. The Gov.-Gen. gave his unqualified approval, and promised Bundoo Khan, a Native then in Capt. Blair's employ, who principally furnished the information of the roads and passes, to reward his services. Major Crabb, with 1800 infantry and artillery, were ordered on this important service; and the Gov.-Gen. made a personal request to Capt. Blair to accompany and consult with Major Crabb, placing much dependence, as he was pleased to express himself, in his information and conduct, &c. After some days marching, by a route presenting constant difficulties, the troops encamped within a few miles of the head of the pass leading to Luttufpoor. The enemy, consisting of about 2000 infantry, some cavalry, and artillery, had taken post to defend the pass. On the following morning the detachment marched, and found the enemy drawn up to the best advantage: the action commenced with the artillery; they were defeated, and their guns captured; and on the news of this defeat reaching the Rajah, he evacuated Luttufpoor, and fled, by another road, to Bidzighur, where his family and treasures were. Luttufpoor was plundered and deserted in the night; and the following morning, Major Crabb found the gates open. The artillery fired a royal salute from the guns on the ramparts, and which gave the earliest information of the capture.

As it had been anticipated, this capture and dispersion of the Rajah's troops was the immediate cause of the whole country returning to submission, with the solitary exception of the strong hill fort of Bidzighur. Bundoo Khan was rewarded with a village and lands in Jaghire. Captain Blair received the personal thanks of the Gov.-Gen., and his assurance, that he might consider and find him his best friend as long as he continued in the government.

The following document more fully explains the above operations:—

" *To Lieut.-Colonel Blair, Commanding at Chunarghur.*

" It is with much satisfaction, that I now give you an account of our arrival at Luttufpoor, after a most fatiguing march, as ever troops experienced, over hills, rocks, rivers, and through jungles. It does much credit to the abilities and knowledge of Bundoo Khan, his being able to conduct us by such a road, without losing our way. The only circumstance in which he has been deceived, is the length of the coss, each of which are at least four miles. We, yesterday, were opposed, at Lora Suckroot, by a body of the Rajah's troops, something less than 2000 men in number, and three pieces of ordnance, whom we dispersed, and took their guns. Their guns, tumbrils, and ammunition, for want of means to bring with us were destroyed, excepting one small gun and limber, we have now with us. The quantity of ammunition, found in Luttufpoor, is considerable. The place, in consequence of our success yesterday, was evacuated by the Rajah in the evening: the people who did not attend him, remained only to plunder his house, which they have done, and destroyed what was valuable, and of no use to them. I do not believe, there was one man in the fort, when Major Crabb marched in. The intention of our march, in the main point, has, I hope, answered the Governor's expectations,—the expelling the Rajah from a place of strength, and preventing his taking possession of the ghauts leading to Bidzighur. Under his present alarm, it appears to me, that if measures are speedily taken to invest that place, little resistance will be made. I was, during the whole march, under much concern for the success of the expedition, as I considered myself partly answerable for the consequences, though I had not the command; and I shall be much pleased to find it has met with the approbation of the Governor, who, I hope, will do me the justice to believe, I have done all in my power to forward the expedition. I have to request you will mention Bundoo Khan to the Governor. I am much fatigued, and have hurt my foot a good deal by walking, otherwise in perfect health. I will refer you to Bundoo Khan for the particulars of our expedition, till I have the pleasure of seeing you.

(Signed) "THOS. BLAIR.

"*Camp at Luttufpoor, 21st Sept. 1781, at Night.*"

"*To the Hon. Warren Hastings, Esq. Governor-General of India, &c.*

"SIR,—In compliance with the wishes you were pleased to express, I have the honour herewith to furnish you with the journal of the march of the troops, to attack the fort of Luttufpoor: the impediments to artillery frequently obliged us to leave the more direct road, consequently increased the distances, and occasioned some delay; but in all the principal points, it corresponds with the original plan and route I had the honour to submit for your consideration. The success has completely fulfilled all the anticipated expectations of my plan, and I trust you will do me the justice to believe, I felt as anxious during the march, as if I had commanded the detachment, as it was originally intended I should do. I may be permitted to mention, that during the march, I found Major Crabb on every occasion most cordially disposed to receive every information I had the means of offering, and the unwearied zeal of Bundoo Khan to afford intelligence, does him much credit. Any indulgence you may be pleased to afford him, will be highly valued.

(Signed) "THOS. BLAIR.

"*Luttufpoor, 29th Sept. 1781.*"

Journal of the march of the troops to attack the fort of Luttufpoor, from the hills and passes, and to secure the ghaut or pass leading to the strong hill fort of Bidzighur.

"*To the Hon. Warren Hastings, Esq. Governor-General, &c.*

"SIR,—The following troops, Major Crabb's regiment of sepoys, Captain Thomas Blair's battalion, Lieut. Polhill's corps, being part of the Vizier's body-guard, in all about 1700 sepoys, six guns, two tumbrils, and one howitzer, being ordered on detachment under the command of Major Crabb, to attack the fort of Luttufpoor from the hills and pass to the eastward of it—we began our march from the encampment, in the neighbourhood of Chunar, about 10 o'clock in the evening of the 15th instant, crossed the Jurgau Nullah, in which there were three feet water, the banks of that part being steep, which detained the troops till past eleven, before the whole crossed. From thence the detachment proceeded to cross the first hills by the Foolwauree Ghaut; ascent not very steep, but the large stones and broken ground retarded the guns very much. With the assistance of the officers and sepoys, the whole of the ordnance and tumbrils were got to the top of the hill by day-light. The descent to the plain is very little; for some distance, the road level; small villages at a distance from each other, the inhabitants of which fled on our approach to the hills. Passed the village of Dowan on our left, which is about two coss from Chunar; some small jungles and broken ground. Proceeded on to Byrah about one coss. It is a small village, with a little round brick tower, on the bank of the Goordowr river, where the troops should have crossed; but on examination, finding it unfordable at that part, turned to the left through a tope, and marched to Putpur Ghaut. The road, part of the way, very bad: the passage might be defended by a few men against the whole detachment. The guns were obliged to be unlimbered, and the tumbrils unloaded, to bring them over the river: the rocks at the bottom of it very large; from the east side of it, thick jungles for two miles. When the troops came opposite to Byrah village, the distance round to cross at Putpur Ghaut, about two coss out of the direct road. Encamped about five o'clock in the afternoon at Bulleeah-Ghaut, below Suttusgur hills, on a spot pretty clear of jungle, distant from Chunar about fourteen miles. The hill fort of Suttusghur from our camp, distant about one mile and a half.

"September 17.—At day-light marched by the right tolerable road, a small nullah now and then, no villages to be seen for two coss; Ponsillah Ghaut: the hill neither high, nor difficult to ascend; a small village to the right named Nicarcaw; all the way jungle, not very thick; distance three coss. Came upon the plains, passed Koradee, which is two coss; marched to Cersee village, which is about two coss; and encamped at 6 o'clock in the evening. Left Simraw, a large village on the right; the country flat, and well cultivated. From Bulleeah Ghaut to Cersee is about eight coss.

"September 18.—At daylight crossed the field, and entered the Borriah jungle; several nullahs and broken ground, some small villages, the road bad till out of the jungles, near to Borriah, where the country is open and cultivated. At the edge of the jungle, surprised Sobaw Sing, a relation to Cheyt Sing; encamped for the day; distance from Cersee two coss.

"September 19.—Marched at daylight, to avoid some water and bad ground, went out of the direct road two coss; encamped in the afternoon in a clear spot of ground, at a small village, named Butt, distance, in a direct road from Borriah, about three coss. The troops marched about six coss this day. In the evening saw several of the enemy's horsemen, mounted as our troopers; from my hircarrahs received intelligence of the enemy being at Lora, with three guns, and about 2000 men.

"September 20.—Marched by the right; two guns in front of the body-guard, one in front of the 7th reg., one gun and one howitzer in the centre, one gun in the rear of it, one gun in the rear of the 1st batt. 6th reg. The enemy were drawn up across the road leading to Luttufpoor, upon ground free from jungle, but divided by some ditches, &c. The cannonade commenced on their side. The detachment formed in their front in the same order as they marched; the guns, as they came up, returned the fire. Soon after the whole was formed we advanced on the enemy, who fired smartly from their guns and small arms, till the line was within twenty or thirty paces of their guns, when they ran away. Their guns were immediately taken. Three companies of the Rajah's sepoys and some matchlock-men, retreated behind a tank, opposite the centre of Capt. Blair's battalion, who opened and marched round two sides of it, and gave them fire, which did great execution, and totally dispersed the enemy, who no longer made any stand, but ran as fast as possible; the troops pursued the enemy some way. Halted to collect the dead and wounded; the latter were provided with palanquins, doolies, &c.: when we marched on to Suckroot, about one mile and half from the field of battle, and encamped for the day. The Rajah's troops were commanded by Myher, the commandant of his sepoys, and Sewpursaud Sing. The former rode to Luttufpoor in great haste, threw himself at his master's feet, and entreated him to make his escape immediately; that a very large force with artillery was close in his rear, and would inevitably take him alive. He at the same time accused the Rajah of having deceived him, or being so himself, respecting the English force which he went against. It appears, the Rajah's people had no certain information of the destination of the detachment, prior to its arrival at Koradee, or of its strength, till the engagement commenced. Their hircarrahs seeing the advanced guard followed by two guns, concluded it was the whole force, and the followers of the camp were taken for some of Owsan Sing's people, whose head the Rajah had ordered to be brought to him, and the others to be killed and left, as if of no consequence. The Rajah received the melancholy account of the defeat of his troops before noon, and evacuated the fort before three. He was followed by numbers; some continued all night to plunder, and left the place the next morning.

"September 21.—Major Crabb marched with his regiment, three guns and the howitzer, at 4 o'clock. At 6 o'clock, Capt. Blair's battalion, Lieut. Polhill's corps, with the remaining guns, tumbrils, &c. followed. The road good till we came to Tarrapatill, where there are large stones and broken ground; from thence the road very good, through trees, till we came to Supdur Ghaut; which, from the precipitous declivity and large stones, is exceedingly difficult for guns to pass. Came to a small village of about ten huts; crossed the Gurreah Nullah, no water in it. The road to the fort, through bamboos and other thick jungles; arrived at Luttufpoor. The gate being open and the place evacuated, Major Crabb took possession of it about 10 o'clock. The remainder of the detachment arrived soon after, when two of our guns were brought into the fort, and light cartridges taken out of the Rajah's magazine: a royal salute was fired, and the union flag hoisted on the highest part of the works. Three guns were found on the hill, which overlooks the fort, and had been placed there to prevent an enemy from possessing themselves of a spot which gives them every advantage over the fort, which is commanded from it.

"I shall be glad if the foregoing account of our march is sufficiently correct to convey a general idea of the roads, rivers, and passes. The distances are right, so far as I am able to judge without having measured them. Troops marching by that route without guns, would find the distances, probably, less than I have made them, as we were frequently obliged to leave the direct road, to avoid stones, broken ground, and other impediments to artillery.

(Signed) "THOMAS BLAIR.

"*Luttufpoor, 29th September, 1781.*"

In 1786, Capt. Blair was appointed Secretary and Persian Interpreter to the commanding officer of the field station at Caunpoor, which office he continued to hold till the relief of the troops in 1788, when he proceeded to Calcutta; where finding no prospect of active employment, being a period of profound peace, and his health having suffered, he obtained leave of absence, and returned to England in the year 1789.

THE LATE MAJOR EDWARD ROUGHSEDGE.

(Bengal Establishment.)

This officer was nominated a Cadet in the East India Company's service in 1794. He arrived in India in 1797, and was appointed to an Ensigncy, on the Bengal establishment, 17th Nov. 1795; promoted to Lieutenant, 30th Oct. 1797; to Captain, 21st Sept. 1804; and to Major, 4th June 1814.

He was raised, when a very young man, to the command of an important corps, and placed in a very responsible and confidential situation, frequently calling for the exercise of extensive civil, as well as military powers; and invariably conducted himself with wisdom, probity, and humanity. In a long course of years, and amidst various clashing interests, and open and concealed enmities, he managed the affairs of the numerous small principalities on the south-west frontier with approved integrity and judgment; and in the settlement of all their disputes, whether arising amongst themselves, or with the government, evinced a sound discretion, great personal purity, and the most even-handed justice. His affability with the Natives, both high and low,—his thorough knowledge of their customs and language,—his undeviating kindliness of feeling, and attention to their prejudices, wishes, and interests, had gained him such an ascendancy over them, that his name was a password for every thing just and honourable; and his order ranged undisputed over a tract of country extending several hundred miles, and comprising many different tribes and classes of men. In 1813, when our provinces were threatened with an invasion by the Pindarries, he was entrusted with the important post of defending the frontier between the Soam and Cuttack*; and, about 1819, the unlimited confidence which government had long reposed in him, was crowned, and the importance of his situation enhanced, by his nomination as political agent,—an appointment, the duties of which he had, in fact, long virtually exercised†.

* See Extracts from the correspondence of Major Roughsedge with Capt. Sinnock,—following statement of Services.

† The following extract from a letter, written in 1820, and with reference to a part of this officer's services, is not without interest:—

"It is rather remarkable, that at no great distance from Calcutta, there should exist a warlike tribe, almost unknown beyond their own mountains, until the arrival of Major Roughsedge (commanding Ramghur battalion, and Gov.-General's agent on the south-west frontier) among them. They are called Lurkas, and inhabit a part of Singhboon, named after them, Lurkacole. About sixty years ago, a Rajah attempted to subdue the Lurkas, but he was repulsed with great slaughter. This inspired their neighbours with such dread of them, that no Native has ever since ventured near them with any authoritative claims; and they are now quite independent of the rajahs and zemindars, to whom they pay no tribute, or mark of submission of any kind.

"Major Roughsedge, after settling his business in the civilized part of Singhboon, entered Lurkacole on the 20th of March. The country is described to be very populous and flourishing, and full of large villages. At first it was thought that matters would proceed smoothly, and that our troops would be permitted to pass unmolested through the country; especially as the head men had come in, in a way that promised well. On the 25th, however, an event happened which terminated all amicable relations for the time being, and called loudly for prompt and signal punishment. The inhabitants of a large village near Major Roughsedge's camp, wantonly murdered some of his followers, undeterred by any fear of the troops in their close neighbourhood. Other unequivocal indications of hostility appeared also. The Major immediately attacked the insurgents, who were in number about 300, all armed with bows and arrows, and battle-axes. They made for the hills; but Lieut. Maillard, with a troop of Rohilla horse, pursued, and overtook them. The Lurkas, on seeing the near approach of Lieut. Maillard's party, turned round, drew up in line, and received them with a discharge of arrows. Seeing, however, that no great impression was made by these weapons, they, with the utmost impetuosity and blind courage, rushed on the charge of the Sewars, battle-axe in hand, seemingly seeking rather to kill the horses than their riders, probably from an idea that by dismounting the latter, they should find them an easy prey. It need only be mentioned, in proof of the violence with which they attacked the horses, that they killed two of them with single blows of battle-axes. At last they were

As a soldier, Major Roughsedge had frequent opportunities of shewing that he combined all the principal virtues of military life; daring courage, intrepidity, utter carelessness of self, kind consideration for his officers and men, protection of his friends, and clemency to his enemies. He successively subdued various refractory chiefs, without cruelty or oppression; and on every occasion shewed the utmost desire to avoid hostilities, and spare blood.

In private life, Major Roughsedge was not less estimable. His unsparing hospitality has been experienced, at one time or other, by half of his brother officers, and was, indeed, proverbial throughout India. To the officers of his corps he so demeaned himself, that he was held by them in the light of an elder brother. He possessed great sweetness of disposition and amiability of temper; so that those who lived with him for years never saw him angry, or even ruffled. He had carefully cultivated a naturally very superior understanding by extensive reading, and was, in conversation, unassuming, amusing, and instructive.

Major Roughsedge died at Soanpore, sixty miles south of Sumbhulpore, on the 13th Jan. 1822, of a fever, which had harassed him about three months.

---

completely routed, leaving half of their number dead on the field; and another party, about sixty in number, who stood over the bodies of the murdered camp-followers, fought with the most desperate obstinacy till *every one of them was sabred!*

" Major Roughsedge now having got intelligence that a dawk had been cut off, and that attempts were made on his supplies, ordered a party into the rear, against the offending village; the inhabitants of which, reinforced by their neighbours, were found all drawn up ready for action. This they commenced with repeated discharges of arrows, by which ten men of Lieut. Maillard's party were wounded (two of them mortally). At length it became necessary to fire the village; upon which the Lurkas (their arrows being nearly expended) rushed furiously upon their foes, armed with battle-axes and large stones, by one of which Lieut. Maillard, who behaved very gallantly on the occasion, was nearly killed. The majority fought most desperately, until they fell. Very few deigned to ask for quarter; but such as did, received it. One of those who was spared, was dispatched to the main body in the mountains, to warn them that an attack would be made upon their position, unless they restored the dawk they had intercepted with the least possible delay. This threat was principally meant to intimidate them from holding out; for Major R. felt unwilling to push matters to further extremities, since enough had been done, for example, against these ignorant and savage, but brave mountaineers. He was, accordingly, pleased to find his warning

CAPTAIN HENRY SINNOCK.

(Bengal Establishment.)

This officer joined the Bengal army, in 1801, and was appointed to the 6th, now the 3d, Native infantry, in 1802. After serving five years with the 6th reg., he was directed, in 1807, to join, and do duty with, the Ramghur battalion. In that year he was sent, in command of two companies, to Bancoora, to relieve a party of the same strength, which had refused to perform the (to it new) duties incident to that station, and which evinced such symptoms of insubordination, as to render their discharge from the battalion and service an act of necessity. This officer succeeded, but not without difficulty, in reconciling the men of his own detachment, to the discharge of those duties, and was favoured with the thanks of his commanding officer on the occasion.

He rejoined the head-quarters of the battalion, in 1808, in Toomar, and was present at the attack on the strong hold of Jargo Cocha; whence, after possession of the place was obtained, he was detached into Chota Nagpore, in pursuit of two rebel Jageer Dars, and several of their relations and sirdars, proclaimed outlaws, whose persons he succeeded, after a long and tedious correspondence, with the Rajah of Chota Nagpore, in securing. On that occasion, also, he received the late Major Roughsedge's warmest thanks *, and

---

produced the desired effect; for they returned the dawk packets in the most humble manner. A peace was concluded between both parties."

* *Extracts of two Letters from the late Major Roughsedge, dated Camp, 14th and 30th March,* 1808.

 "I have just been favoured with your letter of the 12th inst., and most sincerely regret that so much zeal and activity, as have distinguished your conduct on the fatiguing, and I may say, unexampled march to Soondaree, should have failed of its merited success.

 "In the apprehension of the wives and family of Decary Sahy, however, I consider a great point gained, as it will, probably, tend to prevent his quitting the country entirely, and I am not without hopes, considerably facilitate his ultimate seizure.

 "I did not answer your most acceptable letter (which the man was more than two days

he was, moreover, subsequently honoured with the thanks of the Court of Directors*, the late Lord Minto †, and Gen. Hewett. A thousand rupees were offered for the apprehension of each of those Jageer Dars, and 500 for each of their relations and principal sirdars.

In 1813, this officer again obtained the thanks ‡ of Major Roughsedge, for his conduct when detached from camp, in Chota Nagpore, against Mundul Sing (a disaffected Jageer Dar), who had rendered himself obnoxious to the civil power, by the commission of several serious crimes, and by refusing to obey the orders and precepts of the magistrate of Ramghur.

In 1816, he was detached from camp in Sirgoojah, with two companies and a party of Gardner's horse, to the Purguna of Bogree, and placed under the orders of the commissioners, Messrs. Oakley and Barwell, with whom he remained actively employed about nine months, and of whose approval of his conduct, he received repeated assurances.

---

in bringing) sooner, because I knew you were pushing on to join me; allow me now, however, to congratulate you most sincerely on the brilliant success of your expedition, which I have reported to government in the terms it deserves."

* *Extract from the public letter of the Honourable the Court of Directors, dated 9th Sept.* 1812.

" Par. 11.—The gallantry, activity, and ability, displayed by Capt. Roughsedge, as well as by Lieuts. Fountain and Sinnock, and the other officers and men engaged in the service, detailed in these paragraphs, (267-8) are extremely creditable to them; and we desire that you will communicate to the officers and men employed on that occasion, our entire approbation of their meritorious and successful exertions."

† *Extract of a Letter from the Chief Secretary to the Government to Capt. E. Roughsedge, commanding the Ramghur Battalion.*

" His Lordship in Council has also observed with satisfaction, the testimony borne by you to the zeal and ability manifested by Lieut. Sinnock, in the performance of the duty committed to him by your orders.

" *Council Chamber, 6th March* 1813."

‡ " *Camp, Chittra, June* 13*th*, 1813.

" I cannot relieve you from your situation without expressing my entire approbation of your conduct during your command.

(Signed) " E. ROUGHSEDGE."

At the expiration of the above period, he was remanded to Hazareebaugh; whence, after a temporary residence there, of about three months, he marched into Palamow with the commissioners, the late Major Roughsedge and Mr. Lindsay, under whose orders he continued to act, in the joint capacity of Commandant of the troops, and Translator of the proceedings of the commission, until October, when he joined the late Major-General Sir W. Toone's division, with a body of irregular horse, raised for the purpose of patrolling in his front and on his flanks.

During his command in Palamow, he succeeded in seizing all the rebel Jageer Dars but one, who fled into Rewar, and most of their followers, and he was repeatedly favoured with the approbation* of

* *Extracts of Letters from the late Major Roughsedge.*

" A just confidence in your zeal and experience, renders it superfluous to issue any instructions to you, as to the internal management of your detachment.

" *Camp, 24th March,* 1816."

" Having received the commands of the Gov.-Gen. to provide a party of irregular horse, to serve as patrols with the force under the personal command of Brigadier-Gen. Toone, and to send to that gentleman's camp an officer acquainted with the country, and its chief inhabitants, I have, under a just confidence in your zeal, experience, and ability, selected you for this important and delicate duty.

" *Hazareebaugh,* 1817."

Extract of a Letter from the late Major Roughsedge to Major J. Nicol, Adjutant-Gen.

" I have great satisfaction in acquainting you, for the information of his Excellency, that Capt. Sinnock, whose services have frequently called for the approbation of the Com.-in-Chief, has already succeeded in the apprehension of two Sirdar Chooars; the importance of whose capture has been very handsomely acknowledged by Mr. Commissioner Oakely.

" *Camp, Sirgoojah, 3d June,* 1816."

Extract of a Letter from the late Commissioners in Palamow, Major Roughsedge and A. D. Lindsay, Esq.

" The Commissioners consider themselves fortunate in the opportunity the apprehension of Poorun Sing, and so many other persons deeply concerned in the late insurrection, will afford, of representing to government the great benefit your residence in command of the troops in Palamow, has already caused to the public service."

Extract of a Letter from the late Major Roughsedge.

" I embrace this opportunity of respectfully drawing his Excellency's attention to Capt. Sinnock, and of soliciting that a salary may be granted to him, for the duty of superintending the irregular horse with Gen. Toone, from the 15th Oct. 1817, to the 1st of April 1818. I can bear testimony to the arduous nature of the task confided to him: the whole

the commissioners, as well as with that of Gen. Toone*, on the separation of his division, consequent to the successful termination of the campaign of that year.

In June of the same year, he was nominated to the civil and military charge of the district of Sirgoojah, which had just been ceded to the British government by the Berar Durbar: he remained in Sirgoojah more than 16 months, during which period he was actively employed against the powerful and refractory Jageer Dars, who had expelled their late sovereign, and refused to acknowledge and submit to the British government. Before he left the country, however, he apprehended all of them except one, and brought the district into a state of tranquillity; and the Governor-General was pleased to honour his services, both in Bogree and Sirgoojah, with his approbation.

Captain Sinnock's operations in this quarter are noticed in the following extracts of letters:

Extract of a Letter from Major Roughsedge, Political Agent.

" Although your exertions for the apprehension of Monohur Sing have not been crowned with the success to which they were entitled, you have abundant sources of consolation in the reflection that your operations on the whole, have been attended with a result more fortunate than within my remembrance it has fallen to the lot of any officer employed in a similar service to obtain.

" The benefit which must arise to the public interest from the appre-

line of frontier posts, and the general superintendance of what was going forward in the adjacent districts, exclusively of the controul of the internal discipline of a species of force not very easily managed, being in his hands."

* " *To Major Roughsedge, Commanding Rhamgur Battalion, &c. &c.*

" Sir,—Capt. Sinnock having left me this morning, I feel it a pleasing part of my duty, to express to you my warmest approbation of the zeal and attention evinced by that officer while under my command.

" His readiness, on all occasions, reflects on him the greatest credit, and I feel much obliged by your having detached that officer in command of the irregular horse, as none would have conducted that trust more to my satisfaction. I cannot omit to add, his indefatigable zeal, in ascertaining all that was going on in his vicinity, is highly praiseworthy.

" *Camp, Outaree, March* 10, 1818." (Signed) " W. Toone.

hension and punishment of so many dangerous and refractory individuals, is not inconsiderable; and being convinced, that to your zeal, judgment, and ability, is alone to be ascribed the uncommon success of your exertions, it will be my duty to submit to the government my opinion that you have established for yourself a peculiar claim to its favour and approbation."

Extracts of a Letter from Major Roughsedge to C. T. Metcalfe, Esq., Secretary to Government.

" I now have the honour to submit extracts and copies of Capt. Sinnock's reports to me, and my replies, as per margin, which will afford full information of the principles on which the affairs of Sirgoojah have been conducted, and of the fortunate result of that officer's zealous and able management of the important and delicate duties committed to his charge.

" Capt. Sinnock, after a judicious arrangement for the combination, in his operations against Ramcola, of the faithful Jageer Dars of Jilmillee Chandnee Pall, &c. and, on the north, with Rajah Odwant Sing, of Singrowla, marched to attack Gumbheer Sing, on the 14th Dec.; his attempt to surprise him, though ably managed, did not succeed; but, notwithstanding the extraordinary strength and local difficulties of the country which he has described in detail, Capt. Sinnock found means, in a very few days, to reduce Gumbheer Sing to the necessity of attempting to quit the Purgunnah; when, with his whole family, he was seized and delivered up to that officer, by Rajah Odwant Sing, of Singrowla, whose attachment to the state, and former services, will be recollected."

" After settling the Purgunnah in the manner which at the time appeared most advisable, and providing comfortably for the subsistence of the females and infant children of Gumbheer Sing, and his brother Bene Sing, Capt. Sinnock proceeded to the south-western extremity of Sirgoojah, in pursuit of Lal Gudraj Sing and Lal Isseree Sing, who were reported to have taken refuge in Khurgowa, a purgunnah in the southern extremity of Khowreea, and lying between Pahar, Barilla, and Ruttunpoor. There appeared, at the time he reached the frontier, little prospect of success, for the meditated combination, with a force from Chutteesgurh, was no longer practicable; and the Zemindar of Khurgowa was nearly related to Gudraj Sing. The decided tone, however, judiciously taken by that officer, and the excellent conduct of Rajah Gureeb Sing, of Khowreea, lately transferred by Mr.

Molony to my superintendance, smoothed all difficulties, and this dangerous rebel, with a relation of nearly equal notoriety, named Sheoraj Sing, were brought, on the 6th of March, into his camp."

" Be this as it may, all Capt. Sinnock's efforts to induce him to return, or secure his person, proved fruitless, and he directed his views to the apprehension of Joynant Sing, his able, though gradual, accomplishment of which, is detailed in his reports, as per margin. I would especially point out to the commendation of government, the admirable accuracy of his information, shewn in the 3d para. of his letter of the 8th May, which secured the attainment of his object; because, in jungle service in general, and where he was in particular, the grand difficulty is a want of good intelligence."

" I cannot conclude this despatch without expressing the high sense I entertain of the active, zealous, and able conduct of Capt. Sinnock, during the period in which the management of the district of Sirgoojah has been confided to him ; the result has been, the establishment of tranquillity every where, but in Cooreea, and a manifest improvement in the condition of the inhabitants of the country: many of the Khalsa villages, depopulated in consequence of the depredations of the rebel Jageer Dars, have been resettled, and no instance of murder, on pretext of sorcery, or of any other heinous crime, has occurred for some months ; it is indeed already obvious, that the assumption of the government of Sirgoojah has proved an important blessing to these new subjects of the British empire."

The very anxious duties on which this officer was employed in Sirgoojah, together with the dreadfully unhealthy climate of that province, brought on a severe jungle fever, which obliged him to quit his station, and repair, in search of health, to the Cape of Good Hope, and subsequently to England.

THE LATE MAJOR C. W. YATES.

(Madras Establishment.)

THIS officer was appointed a Cadet on the Madras establishment in 1802 ; and shortly after his arrival in India, 23d Sept. 1803, succeeded to the rank of Lieutenant. He was employed in various staff situations, particularly in Malacca, till about the year 1809.

His services at the capture of Banda by the British forces, in the year 1810, appear to have been very conspicuous; they are mentioned in the following terms in Capt. Cole's despatch to the Governor in Council, at Fort St. George, dated 22d Oct. 1810, announcing the reduction of that place:—

"The services rendered by Capt. Nixon, of the Madras European regiment, and Lieut. C. W. Yates, doing duty with the artillery, were of a nature to command my warmest approbation, and I beg leave particularly to recommend them to your notice."

The importance of these services is further corroborated by the Governor-General in Council, in his letter to the Court of Directors, dated 15th December, 1810.

"Your Honourable Court will observe, that Capt. Cole has expressed, in the strongest terms, his obligations to the detachment of the Hon. Company's troops, which co-operated with the naval force in the reduction of Banda, and especially to Capt. Nixon, who commanded the detachment, and to Lieut. Yates and Ensign Allen, whose services on this occasion, we have great satisfaction in bringing under the notice of your Honourable Court."

After the reduction of Banda, Lieut. Yates was appointed, by the general orders of the 1st, 11th, and 13th August, to the following not unimportant offices of trust:—"1st, one of the committee for taking an account of the public stores which fell into the hands of the captors; 2d, Paymaster and Commissary of provisions; and 3d, to take charge of the engineer department.'

The unhealthy nature of this climate is well known, and the constitution of Lieut. Yates was not proof against its baneful influence. He was compelled to return to England, on sick certificate, in the year 1815.

On the 29th Sept. 1817, he obtained the rank of Captain-Lieutenant, and on the 1st January 1819, that of full Captain. In the month of April of the same year, he returned to India, and shortly after his arrival, was placed under the orders of the Resident at Hyderabad, and nominated to a command in the Nizam's service. In this station he continued till the breaking out of a war, which was destined to add laurels to his brow.

On the 20th June 1824, he was raised to the rank of Major, posted to the 26th N. I., and called upon to take the command of that regiment, under the orders of Sir Archibald Campbell, against the Burmese. The post of honour which he had to defend was that of Kemmendine, which was attacked by a body of nearly 20,000 of the enemy; to which mass, Major Yates had no greater force to oppose than his own regiment, the 26th, and about 75 Europeans, with a few pieces of cannon *.

* The following interesting despatch from Major Yates to the Deputy Adj.-Gen, contains so many traits of noble and disinterested feeling, and is so honourable both to the writer and to the distinguished individuals whose names are therein mentioned, that its insertion in this place cannot be otherwise than acceptable to the Indian army:—

"*To Lieut.-Col. F. Tidy†, C. B. Deputy Adjutant-General.*

"SIR,—For the information of Brigadier-Gen. Sir A. Campbell, K.C.B. and K.T.S., I have to report that the important post of Kemmendine, which he did me the honour to place under my command, was attacked by the enemy at half-past 4 o'clock on the morning of the 1st inst. Having distributed my force of infantry, consisting of 58 rank and file of the Madras European regiment, and the whole of the 26th regiment of Madras N. I. into three divisions, and a covering party of 35 rank and file from the 26th regiment, for the guns which I had appropriated to the defence of the western or river front, and every officer and man under my command being acquainted with his post, and the duties I expected of them at the moment of attack, the attempt to surprise, on the part of the enemy, would have been unavailing and impossible. The strongest division was destined for the defence of the eastern front of my stockade, which, from the nature of my defences, and the approach to them, I was well aware would be the position in which the enemy would most strongly invest himself, and offer to me the most formidable attacks, against which I should have to operate. Confidently impressed with this assurance, I could not for a moment hesitate to confer this important trust on that vigilant, gallant, and zealous officer, Capt. Robson, of the 26th reg.; and now that a siege of seven days has ended in the precipitate flight of the enemy, I have to congratulate myself and the service on my choice having fallen on an officer who, through the whole of this arduous struggle, has gone hand and heart with me in every difficulty. The command of the 2d division, or that appropriated to the defence of the Northern front, was conferred by me on Capt. Rehe, of the 26th reg., who proudly

† Services, Royal Military Calendar, vol. iv. p. 456-8, 3rd edit.

The highly meritorious and gallant conduct of Major Yates maintained the high opinion I had formed of him, in the collected and gallant manner in which he received the first dreadful rush of the enemy, which was made on his division, and under cover of a large fire-raft, sent down the river with a double view of hurling destruction among the shipping, and covering the advance of the enemy with their ladders to escalade. The appearance of this attack before day-light was awfully sublime; but so collected and undaunted was Capt. Rehe, that he inspired a confidence and courage in his men which rendered the attempt fruitless against our land defences, though it deprived me of the services which I had expected from the Hon. Company's cruizer Teignmouth, and exposed the defence of the western, or river front, solely to the little band of European and Native artillery, (with only two 6-pounder guns, and one 12-pounder cannonade) under the command of Lieut. Aldritt of the Madras artillery. The gratitude I owe to Lieut. Aldritt —the admiration with which his conduct and his skilful application of his science have inspired me,—are of a nature so exalted, that I feel quite inadequate to their expression. The glorious fact, that with these small means alone he kept at bay the innumerable war-boats of the enemy, will convey a higher eulogy to the comprehensive mind of Sir A. Campbell, than any tribute to his valuable services which I am conpetent to offer. During the whole of this arduous day and night, the enemy's charges, with the view to escalade, were so frequently repeated, that the stockade was one continued blaze of fire. On the north-east angle the enemy got so many gingalls to bear, that, exposed as the situation was, I felt myself compelled to run a 12-pounder cannonade up to the top of an old pagoda: to effect this, under the galling and incessant fire of the enemy, was so daring and dangerous a service, that I called for volunteers to execute it, and myself encouraged them by mounting the pagoda with them, and giving, in person, the necessary directions for the accomplishment of my views. This object once attained, its advantages were palpably evident to all, though even when in the act of answering a question from me, I had the painful mortification of seeing Serjeant Bond, of the Madras European regiment, shot dead. A braver, or more willing soldier, never graced the British uniform! Almost at the same moment, and before sand-bags could be got up, private Thomas Chamberlain, (since dead) of the artillery, was grazed in the shin, though not returned among the wounded, by a shot which passed through his trowsers, and indented the gun-carriage. I beg leave earnestly to recommend this meritorious soldier to the consideration of Sir A. Campbell, for his indefatigable exertions in the battery during the whole of the siege. The morning of the 2d was ushered in by another fire-raft floating down the river, and a repetition, on the northern and eastern fronts of the stockade, of a desperate charge for escalade. The steady, rapid fire of my brave soldiers mowed down these invaders in multitudes, yet, nevertheless, with a daring intrepidity highly creditable to them, their attempts to escalade, throughout this day and night, were repeated so soon as their slain could be removed, and their troops could rally. Until about 1 o'clock on the 2d, when the enemy's trenches not being completed, every energy was exerted towards an overthrow by escalade, I was left solely to my own land resources. At this critical juncture, Lieut. Kellett, of H. M.'s ship Arachne, came to my aid with a gun-brig and four gun-boats. Never was assistance more seasonable; and never did any officer of the British navy more gallantly, or more ably, afford it. To recapitulate the various services I received at the hands of Lieut. Kellett, is impossible. By the extremely judicious distribution made by Lieut. Kellett of his force, I was enabled

throughout this arduous service, obtained him the highest commen-

to remove great numbers of my men from the 2d and 3d to the 1st division, which, without this addition to its strength (and which could not have been yielded without the aid of Lieut. Kellett) I am really of opinion that my eastern front could not have held out against the repeated and impetuous charge of the enemy. In addition to these extraordinary exertions of Lieut. Kellett, I owe him a debt of gratitude, which never can be forgotten or repaid, for the salvation, through his intrepid valour and seaman-like conduct, of thirty out of fifty men of the Madras European regiment, sent out to replace deficiencies by sickness, killed, and wounded, in my detachment from that corps. Owing to the excessive darkness occasioned by the smoke from the incessant fire kept up by ourselves and the enemy, and the extreme rapidity of the tide, these poor fellows were carried past Kemmendine, and anchored by the cowardly Native crews of their boats immediately under a heavy battery of the enemy. The boatmen hid themselves in the bottom of the boats, and these unfortunate soldiers, ignorant of the tides or the management of boats, had inevitably fallen a sacrifice to the vengeance of the enemy, but that the gallant Kellett, alive to compassion, and careless of danger or of death, boldly run his own vessel under the guns of the enemy, and at the imminent risk of his own life, and to his eternal honour, preserved the lives of thirty of his countrymen. In this daring enterprise Lieut. Kellett was seconded by Mr. Valentine Pickey, a midshipman on board of H. M.'s ship Arachne, and from whose services throughout the siege I have derived so great advantage, that I confidently trust Sir A. Campbell will confer on me the favour, and on the service the justice, of bringing the highly-valuable and meritorious conduct of these two gentlemen to the favourable consideration of the naval Commander-in-Chief in India. At about three o'clock on the morning of the 3d, H. M.'s ship Sophie anchored off Kemmendine, and although it were presumption in me to offer an eulogy, or even an opinion, on the conduct of Capt. Ryves, yet, as I should outrage my own feelings were I not to acknowledge my lasting gratitude to him for his masterly assistance and generous aid upon all occasions, I feel no hesitation in trusting to his liberal mind to pardon this slight tribute of my unfeigned obligations and gratitude. On the morning of the third, the enemy had so completely entrenched himself in all directions around me, and kept up so continued and galling a fire on my eastern front, and particularly from a heavy battery of guns and gingalls in front of the gateway, that I was induced to make a sortie on this battery, in the hope of wresting from him his mounted ordnances. In this dangerous service I feel deeply indebted to Capt. Page, of the 48th regt., for the gallant manner in which he stepped forward and volunteered to command a party of 40 Europeans and 40 natives. Ensign Weir, of the Madras European regt., and Ensigns Reynolds and Smith of the 26th regt. also came forward in the most valorous manner, earnestly entreating me to avail myself of their services in this daring enterprize. The position of the enemy was, however, found to be so excessively strong, and his defences so extensive, that I lament to say, this little band were driven back with the loss of two Europeans killed, and the gallant Ensign Smith and two Europeans severely wounded. The enemy, discomfited by the dreadful slaughter with which his men were driven back from every attempt to escalade, had recourse to a never-ceasing fire from his guns, his almost innumerable gingalls, and his enormous force of musketry from various intrenchments and batteries which he had constructed during the fourth and fifth days of the siege. On the

dation of the officer commanding the forces. From Sir Archibald evening of the fifth day, the enemy, reinforced by immense numbers who had been driven by a sortie, under the command of Major Walker, from their intrenchments at the foot of the Great Pagoda at Rangoon, again rushed with impetuous fury to escalade the southern and eastern fronts of the stockade. Again, however, he was driven back, and again he rallied and returned to the charge, but to be again routed with dreadful slaughter. On the morning of the sixth day of the siege, Capt. Chads, of H. M.'s ship Arachne, conferred on me the honour of a visit, and in the handsomest and most flattering manner offered me additional succour to that which had already proved so eminently valuable to me in my defence of this important post; and in the evening sent up the Powerful, bomb vessel, with a serjeant major of the Bombay artillery, whose nicety of precision in throwing shells over the stockade and into the enemy's batteries, was eminently serviceable to me. During the whole of this night the guns of H. M.'s ship Sophie, and the war-boats, with the mortars of the Powerful, and the guns on shore, played over and around the stockade in the most beautiful and masterly manner, hurling destruction on the enemy, while it excited emulation and confidence in the troops. Throughout the whole of the sixth and seventh days the enemy continued to fire upon us from his trenches; but again reinforced by the multitude who had been driven from their trenches by another sortie on the eastern wing of the enemy's line of intrenchments against Rangoon, two more most desperate attempts were made to escalade by the eastern, northern, and southern faces of the stockade. The efforts, however, though supported by multitudes, were fruitless as the former, under the incessant and well-aimed fire of my sturdy band, which, again supported, as on the preceding evening, by the naval force, and aided by the guns under the ever-vigilant and gallant Aldritt, hurled destruction on the disheartened foe, who, at about half past four o'clock on the morning of the eighth day, terminated the siege of Kemmendine in a precipitate retreat, leaving many of his intrenching apparatus, his spears, some powder, and vast numbers of musket and gingall balls, behind him. The killed of the enemy, until the last day, had been carefully removed; but in these last desperate charges, his loss had been so great, and his flight was so precipitate, that many were left as they fell, and the remains of immense numbers are so lightly covered, that the smell all around us is absolutely dreadful. On the last day of the siege, and in one of their charges on the eastern front, I have reason to think a chief of high rank was slain, as no less than five several attempts, by bands of six or eight each, were made to rescue a body which lay close in by the stockade, and was covered by a cloth; and in each attempt three or four of their people were shot dead, and the body, in consequence, remained till dark. Since the retreat of the enemy, one grave, widely differing from all others, has been perceived, and it is covered over with a very thick teak board. I have also heard that the Commander-in-Chief of the Burman army fell in one of the desperate charges made during the first night of the siege. The intrenchments of the enemy, which, since the retreat, I have myself examined, are really of a nature so wonderfully strong and so immensely extensive, that I cannot but attribute them to the incessant labour of many thousand individuals.

" Where each officer under my command evinced every proud qualification of the soldier, it is impossible to bring to Sir Archibald Campbell's notice the individual merits of all, but I may at least be permitted to observe, that every officer and man, both European and Native, under my command, has gained to himself my gratitude and my admiration. Lieut. and Quarter-

Campbell's official letter, dated Rangoon, the 9th December 1824, we extract the following passages:

"Early in the morning of the 1st instant, the enemy commenced his operations, by a smart attack upon our post at Kemmendine, commanded by Major Yates, and garrisoned by the 26th Madras N. I. One division of the enemy opened a distant fire upon the shipping; another immediately broke ground in front of Kemmendine; and for six successive days, tried, in vain, every effort that hope of success and dread of failure could call forth, to drive the brave 26th, and a handful of Europeans, from this post; while tremendous fire-rafts, and crowds of war-boats, were every day employed in the equally vain endeavour to drive the shipping from their station off the place. The attacks upon Kemmendine continued with unabating violence, but the unyielding spirit of Major Yates, and his steady troops, although exhausted with fatigue and want of rest, baffled every attempt on shore."

Master Gordon, though labouring under much present illness and great debility, persevered nevertheless (even against my advice) in the active discharge of his duties. To Lieut. and Adj. Eastment I owe a large debt of gratitude, for a perseverance in that zealous ardour for the public good which shone conspicuous in his gallant bearing at the battle of Mehidpore, and has eminently marked his conduct ever since he has been under my command. Of Mr. Assist. Surgeon Bright I cannot speak in terms of too high eulogy, for never, during any siege, were energy, humanity, and skill, more eminently conspicuous than in him throughout the whole of this arduous contest. From the commencement of the attack every sepoy of the 26th regt. who was in the hospital, and who could possibly carry a musket, entreated permission to lend his aid in the general struggle; and, in consequence, after eight nights and seven days, without either officer or man having scarcely entered a house or changed his clothes, the enemy had not retreated many hours before the hospital list increased 140, and very many more, I fear, must shortly be added to it. I have the honour to enclose a list of the killed and wounded, and of the expenditure of ammunition during the siege, and beg leave to conclude this despatch with an act of justice to determined merit and dauntless valour, by earnestly recommending to Sir Archibald Campbell, that corporal John Lucas, of the Madras European regt. (since dead), who served during the whole of the siege in the battery in which the gallant Serjeant Bond fell, and who himself had a shot through his cap, should succeed to the rank of serjeant, vacant in the regt. by the death of his lamented comrade, the gallant Bond.

(Signed)   " C. W. YATES, Major, Commanding Kemmendine.
" *Kemmendine, Dec.* 9, 1824."

" KILLED—1 jemadar and 12 sepoys of the 26th regt.—WOUNDED—1 Ensign and 69 Natives; of the latter, 20 since dead.

" Daily expenditure of musket cartridges, average 22,000 rounds. Ordnance ammunition I forget, but an immense expenditure.

We cannot resist extracting, from the same despatch, Sir Archibald's eulogy on his brave companions in arms.

" Of my troops, I cannot say enough ; their valour was only equalled by the cheerful patience with which they bore long and painful privations. My Europeans fought like Britons, and proved themselves worthy of the country that gave them birth; and, I trust, I do the gallant sepoys justice when I say, that never did troops more strive to obtain the palm of honour, than they to rival their European comrades in every thing that marks the steady, true, and daring soldier.

The gallant and important services of Major Yates, on this occasion, are further noticed by Sir A. Campbell, in his general orders, dated 12th December :—

" The defence of Kemmendine was the only part of the operations not conducted under the immediate eye of the Commander of the Forces. He considers himself, therefore, bound to express his thanks to Major Yates, for his persevering and gallant defence of so important a post, which he requests the Major will convey to the officers and men of the 26th Madras N. I. as also to the detachments of Madras artillery, and Madras European reg., who so nobly supported him through a week of almost unprecedented fatigue and exertion."

Recently, the Commander-in-Chief has directed, that in future the 26th regiment should bear upon its colours the word " Kemmendine".*

But Major Yates was not destined long to enjoy the honours thus nobly won. He had reached Serwah, on the Sarawuddy, in pursuit

* " Fort William, January 21, 1825. The Right Hon. the Governor-General in Council, is pleased to publish in General Orders, the following resolution of the Supreme Government, passed in the Secret Department under this date.

" Resolution.—In testimony of the exemplary valour and steadiness displayed by the 26th reg. of Madras N. I. under the command of Major C. W. Yates, in the defence of the post of Kemmendine, near Rangoon, against the furious and reiterated attacks of vastly superior numbers of the enemy, by day and night, during the period between the 1st and 9th December; the Right Hon. the Governor-General in Council, is pleased to resolve, that the corps shall be permitted to bear the word ' Kemmendine', inscribed on their colours, as a perpetual record of their distinguished and persevering gallantry on that occasion."

of the Bundoolah, when he was attacked by the cholera, and died on the 12th March 1825.

Of the merits of Major Yates, as a soldier, the reader will already have formed his opinion; it only remains for us to add, that, from his brother officers down to the sepoy, all united in bearing testimony to the goodness of his heart, and the general kindness of his disposition. Of his domestic virtues we cannot speak too highly; whether we regard him in the character of a son, a brother,* a father, or a friend.

---

* The following is extracted from a communication made to the Editor in June 1825, by Capt. Langslow, (Services, p. 197 in this volume) a companion in arms of a gallant brother of this officer.

"Amongst those we lost at this period, (during the rains of 1804-5) fell one, whose private and military virtues it devolves on my humble pen to record, for they well deserve a place in the archives of the *East India Military Calendar*.

"George Yates, the son of a respectable London merchant, and educated at the Charter-House, through the interest of his relative, the late Sir Walter Farquhar, was placed in a Regimental Staff situation soon after his arrival in Bengal, 1797-8. On the formation of the 22d N. I. he was removed to it from the 13th N. I. as Quarter-Master, with the then emoluments of 1000*l.* per annum; and the credit he had previously acquired in Bundlecund, was fully supported by his conduct as a Brigade Quarter-Master, in all the successes and reverses of 1805. Though of most liberal habits, generous to a fault, he could not be charged with selfish extravagance, or prodigality; being never guilty of either, but to assuage the distresses of others, his main object in life. Many felt and knew his worth, both in England and India; but few now survive who can conveniently bear witness to it. Twenty years have revolved since this amiable and gallant soldier fell a victim to a sensibility too acute, operating on a frame, the energies of which were impaired by recent excessive fatigue and exposure, in an arduous campaign and debilitating season. About to lose, by promotion to Captain, the ability he had some years enjoyed of administering to the wants of his fellow beings, the contrast presented by the curtailment of his finances, preyed upon his spirits, and doubtless hastened his end. His medical attendants were unable to name any specific disease, as the cause of his death; indeed his soul appeared to quit its mortal abode without either a pang or a struggle, leaving but few kindred ones behind it.

"To Captain Walter A. Yates, of the Bengal Commissariat, Major Charles W. Yates†, of the Madras establishment, and Mr. Frederick Yates, our admirable Comedian, this slight tribute to the virtues of their gallant and amiable brother, (cut off at the early age of four and twenty) will not be unacceptable, particularly from the hand of a brother officer, on whom devolved the melancholy duty of commanding the funeral escort of his friend, on the plain of Nowmilah."

† His death was not known in England, at the date of this communication.

THE LATE LIEUT.-GENERAL THOMAS MARSHALL.

(Bombay Establishment.)

This officer entered the service of the East India Company in 1775; he was promoted to Lieutenant 6th Sept. 1778; and in 1783, was appointed Town-Major * of the garrison of Bombay. In June 1784, he, and nearly thirty others of the senior Lieutenants of the Bombay army, were made Brevet-Captains †.

* Many officers still of the Bombay army will hold in pleasing remembrance the kindness of Lieutenant and Captain Marshall's demeanour to them while Cadets and Ensigns, during the period of his Town Majorship, and many others, the elegant hospitality of his cheerful table, then, and after his attainment of higher rank. Although not within the strict boundary of a military memoir, a few points illustrative of the private character of this officer, may not be unacceptable. He possessed, in an eminent degree, a talent for the stage. On a parade, or indeed any where off the stage, no one, it is believed, could have excited less suspicion of the possession of such a talent: but on the boards, there were, and are very few, who could act the parts of Sir Anthony Absolute, in the Rivals; the Old Citizen, in the farce of that name; and many others in that range of character, with greater humour and appropriate effect, than the steady, grave, Town-Major. The performances at the Bombay theatre were then, and perhaps still are, entirely by Amateurs.

† This, although a measure promotive of the interests and views of many of the best and most deserving officers of that army, was still bottomed in injustice and partiality; since it originated in the view of giving the rank of Captain in a manner before unprecedented, and thereby giving an equivocal qualification to the command of battalions of sepoys, to the prejudice of older claimants, and, indeed, possessors; some of whom were actually displaced to make room for the newly promoted. This occurred about the time when the rage for the newly-invented balloons was prevalent in England; and a variety of articles just then imported into Bombay by the ships of that season, were distinguished and recommended by that epithet prefixed. We had balloon-buckles, balloon-buttons, balloon-hats, &c. &c. It was almost a matter of course that the newly-made Captains should also share in the distinction; and they were accordingly denominated "balloon-captains"—an appellation which they retained for many years. The promotion stopped precisely at a near relation of one of the members of Government, to whom a battalion of sepoys, the only thing then in the service worth having, was immediately given, affording a reasonable clue to the object of Government in making the promotion adverted to. It is not denied but that the army and service benefited by the objectionable measure. The injured parties petitioned the Court of Directors, and redress to some extent was awarded. Several other of the balloon-captains also obtained battalions; but Capt. Marshall was not among them. He continued to hold the office of Town-Major until 1788, when he was appointed to the command of the 12th battalion. He was succeeded as Town-Major by Lieut. (afterwards Col.) Woodington. Services in this vol. p. 10.

In the year 1798, he was Lieut.-Colonel, commanding the 2d batt. 2d reg. N. I., and had charge of the Aujarrypur district, in Malabar, at which place his own corps was then stationed. Here he continued in command, until early in the following year, when he was ordered to join the army assembling at Cannanore, to which quarter he immediately repaired with the selected portion of his regiment, to the number of 700 rank and file, with a due proportion of officers. Soon after reaching Cannanore, Lieut.-Col. Marshall marched along with the forces collected there under the command of the late Gen. James Stuart, for the purpose of entering the Mysore country and commencing operations against the troops of Tippoo Sultaun. On the progress of the army towards Seringapatam, the 2d batt. 2d reg. N. I. was unexpectedly and suddenly ordered, a little after midnight, between the 3d and 4th March, to separate from the army, and proceed, without a moment's delay, to the post of Stoney river, at the foot of the Poodicherrum ghaut, and reinforce the party stationed as a guard over the depôt of stores and provisions in that quarter. The cause of this forced march arose from information received that an armed banditti had meditated an attack on the depôt; and the small party (only 20 or 30 men, with one officer) placed as a guard there, could afford no effective opposition should an attack be made before assistance reached them. Lieut.-Col. Marshall, who was always on the alert in the hour of emergency, instantly carried the order into execution, and by extraordinary efforts succeeded in gaining the top of the ghaut the same evening.

By this time, however, the greater part of the regiment, from the excessive fatigue they had undergone, were unable to advance further, and a detachment of the most effective men, to the number of 200, was selected, with Lieut. Lock (late Major) and Ensign Marshall*, (now a retired Captain), and placed under the command of Captain (the late Colonel) Heath, with instructions to proceed as speedily as possible to the station at the foot of the pass, and reinforce the party

---

* Services in this volume, p. 250.

there. But before the arrival of this detachment the depôt had unfortunately been attacked by the banditti, who cruelly butchered every one of the guard and plundered the stores. (See p. 252.) The painful employment of disposing of the dead had not well terminated when the detachment was directed to re-ascend the mountain, and join the regiment, which had been ordered to return to the army, without loss of time, in consequence of some prospect of an engagement with Tippoo's troops. The regiment under Col. Marshall made this counter movement with as much rapidity as men in their circumstances were able to effect; and came up with the army on the evening of the 6th, just at the close of an action with the enemy near to Seedaseer. The regiment, after this, continued their route in conjunction with the army, and were almost daily engaged in skirmishing. They were, on more than one occasion, almost entirely surrounded by the whole of the enemy's cavalry, and had to encounter many difficulties before their arrival in the neighbourhood of Seringapatam. Here, and during the progress of the campaign, Col. Marshall had frequently the command of a brigade; and by his skill, prudence, and gallantry, contributed in no small degree to the success which attended the British arms in that quarter. He shared largely in the toils and dangers of that ever memorable siege, and participated in the honour which was so nobly acquired by the assault and capture of the regal seat of Tippoo Sultaun.

Col. Marshall, to the courage and intrepidity which are so essential to the character of a soldier, joined a coolness and presence of mind that were particularly striking; and which, in very critical scenes, and amid dangers of no ordinary nature, never deserted him. On the first day of the siege, while leading on his regiment to take up a position, preparatory to breaking ground for the trenches before Seringapatam, he was preceded by his chair-bearer a few paces; and being exposed to the fire from the enemy's batteries, a cannon-shot struck the head of the poor fellow, scattering the mangled fragments of his skull and brains all over the Colonel; but he continued to march on as if nothing had happened, and succeeded in gaining the position he had in view, which afforded a tolerable shelter to his men, being in some degree under cover from the guns of the citadel.

At another time, some few days afterwards, while the men were busily proceeding with the works, and erecting batteries for their own protection and the annoyance of the enemy, the Colonel, and two of the youngest officers of his corps—the late Col. Imlack, C.B. and Capt. Marshall,—were sitting near to, and looking over the working party, the former at one of the doors of his palanquin, and the other two on his right and left on the ground, when a shot from the fortifications fell directly between them, which completely covered the whole party with dust, overturning the Colonel into his palanquin, and nearly forcing him out at the opposite door. The only expression which proceeded from him at this narrow escape was, " Well, a miss is better than a hit; and these fellows, though they seem to aim pretty accurately, have not yet killed us!" And this he uttered in so jocular a manner, that it clearly evinced how well he retained his self-possession, which was the means of communicating a similar coolness to all around him, and of exciting to redoubled exertions in the work in hand.

His was a truly happy disposition, combining the most exalted courage with the greatest softness of manners, and the warmest of feelings, which naturally gained him the respect and love of all to whom he was known; and by none could he be more esteemed than by those composing his own regiment, who, both officers and men, looked up to him as to a father. The Native soldiers always designated him by that endearing appellation. In all their dangers he had a full share; and no one was more inclined to despise personal suffering, or more ready to afford relief to the distress of those around him, than Col. Marshall. In him was conspicuous every noble and every amiable quality. But, while his natural disposition was of a fascinating cast, he was by no means inattentive to the duties of his station; and he required the most scrupulous attention to all military regulations, and to every necessary duty. Perhaps some of his men, who were more attached to their ease than to the details of military tactics, might consider him as over rigid in his discipline; but as he never enjoined any duty, in the fatigue of which he did not participate equally with the meanest soldier in his corps, his commands were always obeyed with alacrity and pleasure.

His playful and open manner caused him to be highly beloved by his officers; and the greatest harmony prevailed in his regiment. On forming parade one morning, when the corps was expected to be very actively employed, he accosted one of his officers with,— " Well, I ——— I hope you have made a hearty breakfast this morning, and taken something to qualify it, for it is likely we shall have warm work to-day!" By such observations as these, and an example of the brightest description, he obtained so great an influence over those who acted under him, that they would at any time, with the greatest cheerfulness, have followed him to the cannon's mouth, or encountered any peril when he led the way.

After the capture of Seringapatam, and the overthrow of Tippoo's power, the army employed in the campaign dispersed, and Colonel Marshall returned, with his corps, to the Malabar coast, and subsequently marched to Mangalore in Canara; whence the regiment was ordered to proceed to Goa, a Portuguese settlement, to join the British forces assembling there, under the command of the late M.-Gen. Sir W. Clarke, His Majesty's 84th reg. To this station the 2d batt. 2d reg. was conducted by its gallant commander; and here, in 1800, he remained, justly enjoying the respect and esteem of those under his authority, and of all who knew his worth.

About 1801, Col. Marshall, deeming himself possessed of a competency, obtained a furlough to England, with the view of eventually retiring from the service. He had remitted his fortune to a kinsman, to be placed in the English funds; and there he supposed it was placed, he continuing for a year or two to receive the dividends regularly through the hands of his said kinsman. Some circumstances, not necessary to mention, made him suspect that all was not exactly right; following up the enquiry which this led to, he had the mortification to find that he had no stock, and never had had any; and that his ungrateful kinsman had purloined and wasted the whole, or very nearly the whole, of his property; the savings of the care and economy of 30 years' service in India!

But this severe stroke did not ruffle the serenity of this good man's mind. Its severity he could not but feel keenly; but he suffered no bitterness of reproach to escape his lips towards his unhappy kinsman, who absconded. The delinquent had an amiable wife and daughter, now destitute: these were received into the family of the injured man, and treated, like all his other guests, with the greatest attention and kindness. Returning to his duty in India, with his excellent wife, was now the object of Lieut.-Col. Marshall; and this he cheerfully set about preparing to do. Unexpectedly, however, by some augmentation of the army, or other casualty, he obtained the rank of Colonel and the command of a regiment, the emoluments of which enabled him to remain in England, and to live in a style of respectability befitting his rank, though not in so extended or elegant a style of hospitality as the continuation of his former circumstances and his own habits would have warranted and inclined him to.

Col. Marshall attained to the higher ranks of the army, and became senior officer of that of Bombay, in regular succession; continuing in the exercise of all the kindnesses, charities, and benevolences, of the real good, and pious Christian.

A few years ago, four or five, perhaps, he had the misfortune to fall and break his thigh: he was then about 75 years old. The long and painful confinement incident to this calamity, he bore, as he had done others, including acute paroxysms of gout, without repining, complaint, or impatience. His numerous friends in London, witnessed his manly resignation under this affliction, of the effects of which he never entirely recovered, with respect and admiration. Their regret and veneration accompanied him to his tomb, full of years and honours, in a measure not often attained, in May 1824 *.

* The following note has been communicated to the Editor, by a distinguished brother officer of Lieut.-Gen. Marshall:—Few officers have passed through the service for a

CAPTAIN WILLIAM MARSHALL.

(Bombay Establishment.)

THIS officer was an infantry cadet of the year 1797. He arrived at Bombay on the 21st Sept. 1798, and being the same day promoted to the rank of Ensign, was posted to the 2d batt. 2d reg. N. I., commanded by L.-Col. (the late Lieut.-Gen.) Thomas Marshall.

period of nearly half a century, with more credit than the subject of this memoir; none more respected or beloved by the service, or in society: thoroughly acquainted with his duty as an officer, he passed through every grade with great credit, and when he rose to command, shewed he was well qualified for the situation. His loss to society will not easily be replaced. He was well known to the author of this note, both as an officer, and as a member of society, and he feels happy in the opportunity afforded him of testifying his respect to his memory.

Lieut.-General, then Capt. Marshall, was for many years town-major of Bombay: the kindness, protection, and hospitality, he shewed to the young and friendless, who arrived there from Europe, will long be remembered. In the exercise of these virtues, he was warmly seconded by his amiable wife; and it would be an injustice to his memory, not to detail an action of his, which shewed a rightness of feeling not often met with.

Mrs. Marshall brought to her husband a considerable fortune, the produce of which, on being remitted to Europe, was, as they supposed, placed in the public funds, but on their arrival in England, and making enquiries, it was found that no such sum appeared in the books. This heavy blow fell upon this worthy couple when they had retired from India, both advanced in life, to pass with comfort and in affluence the remainder of their days: the blow was so heavy, as considerably to shorten, it was supposed, Mrs. Marshall's life. The General bore the loss with manly fortitude, and immediately resolved so to reduce his expenditure, as to make up to her expecting relatives the loss they had sustained. This, previous to his death, he accomplished to the uttermost farthing, preserving at the same time, respectable appearances suitable to his rank; and, to a few friends, gratifying his natural disposition to hospitality.

During the many years he was town-major of Bombay, he often delighted the society of that place by his very superior talents on the stage. In face, in person, and in figure, he was not unlike our great favourite Munden, and played in the same cast of characters. There was, however, this difference in their acting: when Capt. Marshall gave, what is called in theatrical language, "a point," he never looked to the audience for applause, but kept his eye steadily fixed on the person he was acting with, and the business of the scene, appearing perfectly unconscious that he was before an audience.

His look from under the table, when discovered in Corinna's lodgings, in the Citizen, can never be forgotten by those who witnessed it, as did the author of this note, and another gentleman, well known in East India circles, who, strange to relate, played the part of Corinna in the same piece—"Sic transit gloria mundi," &c.   E. N.

The battalion at this period was quartered at Anjarrypur, in the Cotiote country, Malabar, then in a state of rebellion. This officer immediately embarked for Calicut, and proceeded to join the head-quarters of his corps. In the course of eight days after joining the regiment, Ensign Marshall, owing to the want of officers for duty, and the detached state of the battalion, was ordered to march, in command of a detachment of grenadiers, against a party of the rebels, who had risen at no great distance from Anjarrypur; on which occasion he was completely successful. Some short time afterwards, his commanding officer received instructions to call in all his detached parties; to select 700 men, with a suitable proportion of officers, and to join the army then assembling at Cananore, destined for the Mysore country, under the immediate directions of the Com.-in-Chief, the late General James Stuart. This officer was appointed to accompany the head-quarters of his regiment, while that part of the corps, which was not required for the above service, remained at Anjarrypur, under the command of the late Colonel, then Major, Burrows.

During the march of the army towards Seringapatam, information was privately received, of an attack being meditated by a party of freebooters, or armed banditti, on the post of Stoney River, (near the foot of the Poodicherrum ghaut, in the Cotiote Rajah's dominions), where there was a depôt of stores and provisions, for the use of the united army. The 2d batt. 2d reg. were in consequence suddenly ordered, about 1 o'clock A. M., on the 4th March 1799, to proceed with all possible dispatch, and take possession of this station. The corps commenced their march in this direction accordingly, which they prosecuted with the utmost expedition; but did not reach the top of the mountain until about 6 o'clock in the evening. The majority of the regiment were completely worn out with fatigue, and could advance no further; it was therefore found necessary to select 100 men from the flank companies, with Lieut. Lock, (late Major,) and the same number from the battalion companies, with this officer, the whole under the command of Captain (late Colonel) Heath.

This party was ordered to proceed to the bottom of the pass, and occupy the post of Stoney River, near the foot of the ghaut. It was not, however, until about 4 o'clock next morning, that the detachment arrived within a few hundred yards of their destination, where they made a halt; and, conjecturing from certain appearances, that the station was already in possession of the marauders, immediate arrangements were made for an assault. At day-break the party rushed in, but instead of finding the enemy, to their surprise and horror, perceived that a most cruel massacre had taken place. Considering the depôt to be perfectly secure, it was guarded only by one officer, a commissary of stores, a purvoe belonging to the commissary, and 20 or 30 sepoys, besides a few recovered European soldiers, on their march to join their respective corps with the army. This handful of men, dreaming of nothing but safety and repose, had been unexpectedly attacked by the armed banditti alluded to, who put every one of them, both European and Native, to the sword, and plundered the stores.

The party had scarcely completed the melancholy duty of disposing of the dead, when Lieut. Imlack, (late Lieut.-Colonel, and C. B.) arrived, about noon, with a detachment from head-quarters, to relieve the two companies, who were directed immediately to join the regiment. Near 3 o'clock they began their march, but only Lieut. Lock and this officer, with about 20 men, succeeded in reaching the top of the ghaut the following morning, a few hours before day-break, at which time the battalion was to march for the purpose of uniting with the army. At the hour appointed, these officers, with the few men above-mentioned, fell in with their respective companies, and joined the army the same evening. Capt. Heath, and nearly 180 of the men had, from excessive fatigue, dropped down during their progress up the mountain. Many of them did not join the regiment for several days after *.

* A march on foot for nearly three days and three nights, with only an occasional halt of an hour or two, in such a climate as India, and in so mountainous a district as that alluded to, although it may not be considered an achievement of much enterprise, is ne-

The movement to Stoney River was made, as has been already observed, with a view to afford speedy assistance to the detachment stationed there, and the rapid return of the battalion to the army was ordered in consequence of an extensive encampment of Tippoo's troops having been unexpectedly observed from the hill of Seedaseer, forming near the fort of Periapatam.

On the arrival of the army before Seringapatam, and during the whole time of the siege, Ensign Marshall was, on all occasions, at the head of the company of which he had charge, and was present in the various engagements and skirmishes when his regiment was employed. From the deficiency of officers in the 2d batt. 2d reg. (one having died on the march, two having been wounded the first day of the siege, and the sickness of others,) Ensign Marshall, at a very early age, and while yet only a few months in the country, had generally the command of a number of men, equal to two companies, nearly the whole period of that eventful campaign. He was actively engaged all the time of the siege, either in the trenches, or at the out-posts of the Bombay army, and received one of the honorary medals. After the fall of Seringapatam, he returned with his regiment to the Malabar coast, and subsequently marched to Mangalore, in Canara; and from thence to Goa, a Portuguese settlement, to join the British force assembling there under the command of the late Major-Gen. Sir W. Clarke, His Majesty's 84th regiment.

Regimental rank having taken place at the end of 1799, Ensign Marshall was removed to the Bombay European reg., then stationed at Cochin, under the command of L.-Col. (the late L.-Gen.) Wiseman, which he immediately joined. About this period an augmentation

---

vertheless a most arduous and harassing task. Indeed, in marching and counter-marching, a greater degree of native courage and firm resolution are required, and in such cases more frequently displayed, than what prompts to brave the stormy front of battle: in the one case, there is an excitement that rouses to ardour, and stimulates to exertion; in the other, nothing exists but what is calculated to damp the energy, and repress the activity of the most zealous and intrepid. The particulars of the above service would not have been so minutely detailed here, were it not supposed, that of all those employed on that toilsome duty, the subject of this memoir is now the only survivor.

was made to the army, by raising the 7th and 8th regiments N. I., and he was promoted to the rank of Lieutenant, commission dated 6th March 1800, and transferred to the 2d batt. 4th reg., at that time quartered at Hullihall, in the Soordah country.

On proceeding to join the latter corps, after a march of nearly a month, he arrived at the top of the Bilghie ghaut. Here he was informed, that it would be highly dangerous for himself alone to pursue the route to Hullihall, and almost impossible to succeed, if he made the attempt, as the country between Bilghie and that place was infested by the followers of the rebel chief Doondia Waugh, all the hill forts on the direct road being also in their possession. This intelligence induced him to remain for a few days at the Bilghie palace with Lieut. Prother* (late Lieut.-Col. and C. B.), who commanded the small detachment there; but learning that the flank companies of the 2d batt. 2d reg., and 2d batt. 4th reg., were in the immediate neighbourhood, under the charge of the late Capt. Maxwell, he forthwith joined that force, and did duty with it until its arrival at Hullihall.

Soon after this, Lieut. Marshall volunteered (with the sanction of the late Lieut.-Col. Lauriston†, its commander) to join the 1st batt. 7th reg., then under orders to embark for Egypt. His application, however, was not acceded to, as the late Lieut.-Gen. Nicholson‡, to whom he had made the request, was pleased to say, that he had some other object in view for him. And, on the 19th Dec. 1801, he was, through the kindness of Gen. Nicholson, appointed to the situation of Adjutant and Quarter-Master to the 4th N. I. This appointment was soon afterwards abolished, both in the Madras and Bombay army. But, at the recommendation of the Commander-in-Chief, he was, on the 10th Nov. 1802, nominated by government, Adjutant of the 2d batt. of the same reg. The battalion, previous to this, had left Hullihall for Cundapore, in Canara. Symptoms of disaffection being again exhibited in the Cotiote country, the corps embarked for Tellichery, and were for some time actively employed against the rebels.

* Services, vol. i. p. 304-7. † Vol. i. p. 226-8. ‡ Vol. ii. p. 256.

In 1803, it was deemed necessary to re-assemble a British force at Goa, to which quarter the battalion was ordered, along with H. M.'s 77th reg. and 2d batt. 2d reg. N. I. Towards the close of the same year a further increase was made in the Bombay army, and the 9th N. I. was raised, to which corps Lieut. Marshall was transferred. On the recommendation of Gen. Oliver Nicholls*, H. M.'s 66th foot, then Commander-in-Chief at Bombay, he was appointed Adjutant to the 2d batt., and ordered to the presidency where it had been embodied. In the course of the following year this battalion proved fit for field service, and, under the command of Lieut.-Col. Mason, was ordered to embark for Broach, in the Gulph of Cambay, and from thence to march to Baroda, in Guzerat.

On various occasions, while attached to this corps, Lieut. Marshall acted as Major of Brigade to the officer commanding the Northern Division of Guzerat. But, with respect to his services in the 9th reg., it is only necessary to mention the opinion of the Commander of the forces, and that of his own commanding officer, under whom he acted from 1804 to the end of 1807, without noticing the various favourable division orders issued by the late Col. Woodington.

Extract of a Letter from Major-General J. Bellasis, Commanding Officer of the Forces, to the Honourable Jonathan Duncan, President and Governor in Council, dated 10th of August 1807.

" I have further to recommend, that you will be pleased to appoint Lieut. Marshall, Adjutant of the 2d batt. 9th N. I., to the situation of Barrack Master at Goa, as a reward for that officer's zealous and meritorious exertions, under the authority of Lieut.-Col. Mason, in bringing that corps to the high state of discipline, so honourably recorded in Lieut.-Col. Woodington's station orders, after the review of the battalion at Baroda, previous to its proceeding to the presidency.

(Signed) " ROBERT GORDON, Adj.-Gen."

The following is an extract of a letter from his immediate commanding officer, Lieut.-Colonel Mason :—

* Services, Royal Military Calendar, vol. ii. p. 9-10. 3d edit.

" At the various reviews and inspections, you were invariably complimented by the reviewing officers for the zeal and ability you had displayed, whilst acting under my authority, in bringing the regiment to the highest state of discipline, and for which the Commander-in-Chief rewarded you with the first staff appointment in his gift.

    (Signed)   " WILLIAM MASON."

In consequence of the recommendation of Maj.-Gen. Bellasis*, Lieut. Marshall obtained the appointment of Barrack Master at Goa, to which place he proceeded on the first opportunity, and assumed the charge of the barrack department. On the 14th March 1809, he was promoted to the rank of Captain-Lieutenant, and on the 18th June, in the same year, to Captain of a company.

The Governor in Council having revised and new modelled the system for paying the troops on the Bombay establishment, nominated, on the 8th Dec. 1809, this officer to officiate as Paymaster at Goa, inclusive of the situation of Garrison Storekeeper, and with permission to retain his appointment as Barrack Master. A very short time after his entering on those arduous and complicated duties, the Governor-General in Council (the late Earl Minto) issued a government general order, dated Fort St. George, 3d Jan. 1810, directing the transfer of the troops serving at Goa, to the Madras presidency; and further, that all returns and reports should be made to the regular authorities at that presidency, from and after the 1st March following. But by a subsequent order, this latter regulation was not to take effect until the 1st May 1810. These instructions had not been many days promulgated when another Government general order arrived, directing the removal of the whole of the Bombay staff, and appointing officers of the Madras army as their successors. The officer in command of the British troops at Goa, strongly recommended that the Major of Brigade (Major Cockburn, H. M.'s 84th reg.) and Capt. Marshall, should be continued in their situations; but the recommendation was not attended

---

* Services, vol. ii. pp. 85, 86.

with the desired result. The late Lieut.-Col. Smyth (then Military Secretary to the Commander-in-Chief at Madras) was appointed Barrack Master, and Capt. (now Lieut.-Col.) Ahmuty*, Paymaster and Garrison Storekeeper, in room of this officer. Before Captain Marshall, however, had been relieved from the duties of one of his appointments, he had the satisfaction to receive an official letter from the Adjutant-General of the Bombay army, of which the following are extracts:—

" *To Captain Marshall.*
" *Bombay, 4th May* 1810.

" The Commander-in-Chief (the late Gen. Sir John Abercromby, G.C.B.) proposing to form a Cadet establishment on a revised plan, and the Hon. the Governor in Council having attended to his recommendations on that subject, he requests to know, as you have lately been deprived of a staff appointment, if it would be acceptable to you to take charge of that department. (Here follows the plan of the institution, &c. &c.)

" Should you accept of the situation, the Commander-in-Chief wishes you to come to the presidency with the least possible delay, as the first Cadets of the season will arrive by the China ships early in June. Should you decline the appointment, the Commander-in-Chief requests your early reply, in order that time may be given for the selection of another officer for the proposed situation before the setting in of the monsoon.

(Signed) " ROBERT GORDON†, Adj.-Gen."

Considering the very handsome manner in which this appointment was offered, Capt. Marshall accepted of the situation, and answered the Adjutant-General to that effect. The season being far advanced, and only one pattamar boat remaining at Goa, bound for Bombay before the commencement of the monsoon, and wishing to take his passage in that vessel, he, immediately on the receipt of the above letter, waited on the officer in command, and solicited permission to proceed to Bombay; his request was instantly complied with, and the order, from which the following is an extract, was issued on this occasion:—

* Services in this vol. p. 82. † Services, vol. ii. p. 312-321.

Extract from Station orders.

"*Goa Cabo*, 17*th May*, 1810.

" Captain Marshall being about to proceed to Bombay, Lieut. Molesworth, of the 1st batt. 18th reg., (now Lord Viscount Molesworth), will take charge of the barrack department. Lieut. White, of the artillery, (now Captain) of the Engineer department. And the pay and provision department will remain in charge of Mr. Fernandez. Lieut.-Col. Adams feels called on, to notice the regular and attentive manner in which Capt. Marshall has carried on the complicated duties of the different departments under his charge.

(Signed) " R. COCKBURN, Major of Brigade."

With a view to meet the wishes of the Com.-in-Chief, Capt. Marshall lost no time in getting forward to the presidency, and on his arrival at Bombay, the following government order appeared, relative to his appointment to the Cadet establishment :—

" *Bombay, Tuesday*, 5*th June*, 1810.—*By the Hon. the Governor in Council.*

"*Bombay Castle*, 3*d June*, 1810.

" The hon. the Governor in Council, is pleased to appoint Capt. Marshall of the 2d batt. 9th reg. Native infantry, to take charge of the Cadet establishment, which has been formed at this presidency, under the directions of the Hon. the Com.-in-Chief. The appointment of Captain Marshall is to have effect from the 13th of last month.

(Signed) " F. WARDEN, Chief Secretary."

During the period he remained in this situation, he had the high satisfaction to meet the approbation of the Commander-in-Chief, as frequently notified to him, and as publicly expressed in orders :—

Extract.

" *Bombay*, 2*d May*, 1811.

" Lieut.-Gen. Abercromby avails himself of the same opportunity to express to Captain Marshall his entire approbation of the zeal manifested by him to attain the object which the Com.-in-Chief had in view, in recommending to government the formation of the establishment placed under that officer's directions. And Lieut.-Gen. Abercromby, from the experience of last year, is led to entertain sanguine expectations that it will prove, to a certain extent, beneficial to the young gentlemen who may hereafter receive appointments on the military establishment of this presidency.

(Signed) "ROBERT GORDON, Adj.-General."

Gen. Abercromby having been appointed Governor at Madras, he left Bombay in 1813, on which occasion, in addressing a private letter to this officer, he says: " I can feel no difficulty in bearing ample testimony to the zeal and attention which regulated your conduct, during the time you held the difficult and responsible situation of superintendant of the Cadet establishment," &c.

Captain Marshall's private affairs had, before this period, urgently called for his return to Europe, and the declining state of his health, (occasioned by extreme anxiety of mind, from the circumstance of the non-adjustment of his accounts, as pay-master at Goa), had contributed to render a change of climate not only desirable, but absolutely necessary. He was in consequence, under the painful necessity of tendering the resignation of his appointment, and soliciting leave of absence to go to Europe, on both which points his wishes were attended to. Having it in view, however, to make application to the Court of Directors, for employment on his arrival in England, he had, previously to resigning the Cadet establishment, communicated his intentions to the Adjdtant-General of the army, and some time prior to his quitting India, he was honoured with a letter from that gentleman, of which the following is an extract:—

" *To Captain Marshall.*

" *Bombay,* 1813.

" As I have known you, for the greater part of the time you have been in the service, I have much satisfaction in saying, that your conduct as an officer, has at all times met with my approbation; and I may venture to say, with the approbation of Lieut.-Gen. Nicholls, Major-Generals Nicholson, Bellasis, and Jones, and of Lieut.-Gen. Abercromby, the officers who have commanded the army at the periods referred to; and I shall be very glad if this declaration, to which you are entitled, assists your future views in life.

(Signed) "ROBERT GORDON, Adj.-Gen."

About the middle of May, 1814, this officer arrived in London, and immediately applied at the India House, for employment on the recruiting service, during the period of his furlough. The offer made of his services was accepted, and he had the honour, the same month, to be appointed Recruiting Officer, in the Edinburgh district.

In 1817, his health, which had been but indifferent since his return to this country, became so unsteady, that he was strongly urged by his medical attendants, to give up all idea of returning to the east; and, through their representations and advice, he was, unwillingly, induced to address the Court of Directors, soliciting permission to retire, on half-pay, from the service in India; at the same time stating his anxiety to be continued in the duty on which he was then employed. The prayer of his application was granted, by permitting him to retire on half-pay, and confirming him in his situation as Recruiting Officer, for the Hon. Company in North Britain, which appointment he still continues to hold.

Thus was this officer compelled, with the utmost reluctance, to relinquish a service, to which it is well known, he was as ardently attached as any officer in the Bombay army. He has now been twenty-seven years actively employed at home and abroad, without intermission; and it is worthy of remark, that he has not, in all that length of time, been more than *two months* absent from duty. It is upwards of eleven years, since he entered on his present situation, and the duties connected with it have been carried on in a manner alike creditable to himself, and beneficial to the interests of his honourable employers. He has been repeatedly honoured with the approbation of the various officers, under whom he has acted, both of his Majesty's and the Company's service. But without entering into particulars, an extract of a letter addressed to him, by Col. Hastings, the inspecting field-officer in North Britain, who has presided over the recruiting department in Scotland during the whole of the time this officer has been employed on that service, sufficiently evinces his zealous and sedulous attention to the duties of his office.

" It gives me great pleasure to express the sense I entertain of your meritorious exertions in the service in which you are employed; and of your unremitting attention and zeal in the discharge of the troublesome duties attending it. And the liberality evinced by you, for promoting the success of your parties, by the application of pecuniary means, not incumbent on you to make, is a convincing proof how much you have the good of the service at heart.

(Signed) "C. H. HASTINGS, Lieut.-Col. I. F. O."

LIEUTENANT-COLONEL ROBERT J. HUDLESTON.

(Madras Establishment.)

THIS officer was appointed in 1782 a Cadet on the Madras establishment; he arrived in India in August of the following year, and received a Cornet's commission in the 1st reg. of Native cavalry, which corps he joined at the Mount, where the army then lay encamped. Lieut.-Col. Dugald Campbell commanded the 1st regiment, and was the senior officer of the Company's corps of cavalry, which then consisted of four regiments only. In the course of March 1784, on the conclusion of peace with Tippoo Sultaun, the army was broken up; the cavalry moved to Arcot, and was permanently cantoned on the north bank of the Palar, in the neighbourhood of the city.

In January 1786, he was promoted to Lieutenant, and posted to the 2d regiment, commanded by Major Jourdan. In the beginning of November 1787, a fifth regiment of cavalry was raised at Arcot, by drafts from the other four. About the end of December following, Major Jourdan resigned, and soon after returned to England, when Major Darley was appointed to the command of the regiment; and in the course of some months after, a change in the numbers of the several regiments took place, and Major Darley's regiment was numbered the fifth, although by no means the youngest, whilst the new regiment, raised about a year before, was, by orders, designated the first.

Early in January 1790, preparations were made for taking the field against Tippoo. The army assembled on the plains of Trichinopoly. On the 15th of that month, the 5th Native Calvalry marched singly from Arcot in that direction: at Trincomalee it was joined by H. M.'s 36th regiment, two battalions of Native infantry, and some artillery; and the whole joined the troops at Trichinopoly, about the middle of February. On Col. Floyd's arrival, at the end of April, with the 19th light dragoons, the 2d, 3d, and 4th Native cavalry, the whole formed a brigade, of which he was appointed to the command.

In consequence of the appearance of greater numbers of the enemy, and a better order of cavalry than had yet shewed itself, commanded by Seid Saib, Tippoo Sultaun's kinsman, Col. Floyd, with very inferior numbers, commenced against this corps a series of well combined and active operations, creditable to his professional address, and to the spirit and energy of the European and Native cavalry; and Seid Saib, incessantly kept on the alert, found it expedient to place his corps to the northward of the Bhowanny, a river running from west to east, and occasionally fordable at a few points; but finding himself exposed in that situation also to the enterprize of the British, and restricted for space between that river and the hills, ultimately ascended for safety above the ghauts. Tippoo was justly enraged at this weak and unskilful proceeding. Seid Saib, as he observed, ought never to have crossed the Bhowanny; but, on Col. Floyd's approach, to have dispersed into small bodies, to have ranged round his rear and flanks, to have occupied in a desultory warfare every detachment on the line of communication with Trichinopoly, and to have straitened the supplies of those appointed to distinct services, particularly that which afterwards reduced Dindigul and Palgaut, and subsisted exclusively on the country through which it marched*.

* See Historical Sketches of the South of India.

The events that immediately followed, have been briefly narrated in other parts of this work*. The following statement is principally from the able pen of Col. Wilks:—

Sattimungul, on the north bank of the Bhowanny, was reduced and occupied by a battalion from Col. Floyd's corps, whose general operations were confined to the south of that river, looking to that depôt as his main object. At this period the British possessed a chain of depôts, commencing with Tanjore and Trichinopoly, and including Caroor, Eroad, and Sattimungul, in a good line for advancing provisions and stores to the pass of Gujelhutty, which the Com.-in-Chief, Gen. Medows, expected to ascend early in October; but, unfortunately, even Caroor could scarcely be deemed a good depôt; Eroad was better qualified to contain than protect stores, and Sattimungul was ill adapted to either purpose. Exclusively of minor detachments, and a respectable corps of cavalry and infantry employed, with all the spare carriage, in escorting provisions and stores, to be successively advanced, the army might be considered as separated into three divisions, very different in their composition, but not far from equality in actual strength: the division 60 miles in advance, under Col. Floyd; the head-quarters of the army at Coimbetoor, and the division under Col. Stuart, 30 miles in the rear, engaged in the siege of Palgaut; making a distance of about 90 miles between the extreme corps.

About 15 miles further up the river than Sattimungul, is the fort of Denaickencota, still in the Sultaun's possession. This fort is about 7 miles south from Gujelhutty, the foot of the pass, which by the most direct road, does not exceed 18 miles from Sattimungul. About 4 miles below Denaickencota, is the ford of Poongar, now occasionally practicable; and at a greater distance below Sattimungul, a better ford at Gopalchittypoliam. The river was every where passable in basket-boats, of which a considerable number

---

* See the Services of the late Gen. Sir John Floyd, vol. ii. p. 330, *et seq.*, with which will be found his celebrated letter to Col. Stuart, describing the contest of Sattimungul.

was collected at Denaickencota, and other points. The Sultaun early in the month of Sept., leaving his heavy stores and baggage at the summit of the ghaut under Poornea, commenced the descent of this most difficult pass of the whole eastern range. The horse, which had last ascended, were first made to descend; and the English cavalry, recognizing their former antagonists, drew no particular inference from their return, but attacked and defeated them wherever they approached a patrole or a detachment. Col. Floyd, however, had early intelligence of the Sultaun's proceedings; it was indisputably confirmed, by the desertion of a Native officer, formerly in the English service, who gave a circumstantial account of the number of guns which had descended, and the number still to descend. This successive intelligence, and this individual to be examined, were dispatched, express, to head-quarters; with a suggestion, founded on the dispersed state of the army, which has been described, that the advanced corps should fall back upon the head-quarters of the army; but there the intelligence was disbelieved, and the Colonel was ordered to maintain his advanced position. His encampment, consisting of H. M.'s 19th dragoons, of 6 troops; 16 troops of Native cavalry; H. M.'s 36th foot; and 4 battalions of sepoys; including the garrison of Sattimungul, and 11 guns, was exactly opposite that post.

Among his arrangements of precaution was a daily examination of the ford of Poongar, and its vicinity. On the morning of the 12th, after the return of one of these detachments, Tippoo commenced the passage of the river, at the ford, and in basket-boats above it; and, before night, had passed a large portion of his army, and encamped some miles to the south of the ford; the remainder was ordered to descend by the north bank, to operate by cannonade across the river, to seize Sattimungul, and eventually to cross by the lower or upper ford, or by boats, according to circumstances. The intelligence and appearances of the two preceding days, indicated that the descent had been nearly accomplished. On the 13th, an hour and a half before daylight, three troops of the 19th dragoons were sent in advance, to reconnoitre the ford, and a regiment of Native cavalry was ordered out at daylight to support them. There are two roads to the ford, one winding by the river side, and another more direct: the advanced body, after charging and driving into the river some cavalry they had met, returned by the river side; the Native regiment was meanwhile moving by the direct road, and had only proceeded a few miles, when it was suddenly met by larger bodies than had hitherto been observed*. The regiment instantly charged, and overthrew its immediate opponents; but perceiving heavy bodies of cavalry in every direction, the officer commanding determined to take post in a favourable spot, which presented itself, formed partly by the fences, and to send intelligence to Col. Floyd, in order that time might be given for the requisite dispositions, as well as for his own support. It was rather a position for infantry than cavalry; but if he had attempted to retreat, the consequences must have been more unfavourable. Nearly an hour elapsed before support arrived, during which time he was surrounded, and hard pressed in every direction; and had expended his carbine ammunition. His earliest support was another regiment of Native cavalry, which in the first instance relieved him in the defensive post, and left his regiment free, to the use of their swords, in conjunction with the 19th dragoons, which regiment, including the returning detachment, attracted by the firing, and the remaining four troops of Native cavalry, immediately followed the supporting regiment.

The Mysoreans, in surrounding the regiment which had taken post, had very improvidently entangled themselves among the enclosures; in one of these, from which there was no retreat, between 4 and 500 of the Sultaun's stable-horse, were charged by two troops of the 19th dragoons, and every man put to the sword: in other directions the charges of the European and the Native cavalry, were perfectly successful; the field was completely cleared of every opponent, and the whole cavalry returned to camp.

* The country is intersected by high and generally impenetrable enclosures, chiefly composed of various kinds of euphorbia and opuntia.

They had scarcely dismounted, however, before a large body was perceived descending the northern bank of the river, and about ten o'clock opened some guns on the grand guard, which was immediately ordered to join the line; the Sultaun's columns were at the same time perceived rapidly approaching from the west, in a direction which threatened to turn the left, and a change of front was promptly executed, which placed the infantry in a position difficult to be outflanked, and the cavalry imperfectly covered by a low hill. The Sultaun's army drew up in a corresponding order, seeking, but failing, to obtain an enfilading fire, and opened a distant, but efficient cannonade from 19 guns, besides those to the north of the river: this was answered by the English eleven, but not with great vivacity, as well on account of the distance, as the limited store of ammunition. At distances much exceeding point blank, a few discharges are generally necessary to ascertain the range: when this was found, every shot carried off a file; and to distract the enemy's aim, the corps frequently receded or advanced a short distance; these movements were executed by the sepoys with the most perfect steadiness. Col. Floyd in passing along the line, when the casualties were most frequent, expressed regret to the Native officers, and cheered them with the hope of retaliation in due time; the answer was nearly uniform, " We have eaten the Company's revenue (salt); our lives are at their disposal, and God forbid that we should mind a few casualties." The cannonade only terminated with the day*.

Of the English guns, 2 12-pounders and a 6 were disabled; the casualties had been serious among the troops, the horses, and the draught oxen; and this last equipment had suffered still more severely in the desertion of most of the drivers, during the cannonade. A council of war determined on retreat; and although the two

---

* Lieut.-Col. Charles Deare who commanded the Bengal artillery, was killed early in the day, by a shot from the enemy's guns; and his second in command, Captain Sampson, desperately wounded in the head. Lieut.-Col. Deare served many years as major of brigade to the corps of artillery, and was with it in all Sir Eyre Coote's campaigns against Hyder Ally. He proceeded with a detachment of it to the coast, and joined Gen. Floyd near Denaickencota, and soon after terminated his career as above related.

twelves had been restored soon after midnight, by the active and intelligent exertions of an officer of his staff*, the causes which have

* "Brigade Maj. Dallas, who is always active and fertile in expedients, got timber from the fort," &c. &c. (See Col. Floyd's Letter in this work, vol. ii. p. 330.) He had been foremost in every charge by day, and acted the artificer by night.

In reference to the earlier career of this officer, now a Lieut.-General, and a Knight Commander of the order of the Bath, it may in this place be observed, that in the cavalry of Hyder Ally, the officers were fond of exhibiting a chivalrous spirit, which induced them frequently to approach, individually, within speaking distance of the flanking parties of the British, and give a general challenge to single combat: and the following anecdote, from Col. Wilks's work, will shew the manner in which these challenges were answered and silenced. The young cavalry officer alluded to, is the present Sir Thomas Dallas.

"There was in Sir Eyre Coote's body guard, a young cavalry officer, distinguished for superior military address; on ordinary service always foremost, to the very verge of prudence, but never beyond it; of physical strength, seldom equalled; on foot, a figure for a sculptor; when mounted—

> ———— ' He grew unto his seat,
> And to such wond'rous doing brought his horse
> As he had been incorpsed and demi-natured
> With the brave beast.'

"In common with the rest of the army, this officer had smiled at the recital of these absurd challenges; but, while reconnoitring on the flank of the column of march, one of them was personally addressed to himself by a horseman, who from dress and appearance, seemed to be of some distinction. He accepted the invitation, and the requisite precautions were mutually acceded to: they fought, and he slew his antagonist. After this incident, the challenges were frequently addressed, not, as formerly, to the whole army, but to *Dallas*, whose name became speedily known to them; and, whenever his duty admitted, and his favourite horse was sufficiently fresh, the invitations were accepted, until the Mysoreans became weary of repetition. With a single exception the result was uniform. On that one occasion, the combatants, after several rounds, feeling a respect for each other, made a significant pause, mutually saluted, and retired. As a fashion among the aspiring young officers, these adventures were not calculated for general adoption: it was found, that in single combat, the address of a Native horseman is seldom equalled by an European."

The favourite horse above referred to, " besides the common duty of carrying his rider, exercised when required, and sometimes spontaneously, all the aggressive force with which he was furnished by nature; and the Mysoreans, whose imaginations had added to the evidence of sight, would make inquiry regarding the extraordinary phenomenon of a gigantic figure mounted on a furious black horse, of enormous size and destructive powers; the stature of the man being just 6 feet, and that of the horse 14 hands, three inches, and a half."— Vol. ii. p. 391-2.

The following extract from General Harris' despatch, dated Seringapatam, 13th May, 1799, to the Governor-General, is an honourable testimonial of this officer's later services:—

been noticed, compelled him to leave on the ground one 18-pounder, one 12, and one 6. After some blameable delay, in executing the orders for abandoning the untenable post of Sattimungul, with its provisions, the battalion crossed in basket-boats, and the whole corps commenced its march at eight in the morning; the infantry and cavalry in separate columns, and the baggage in a third. For about 12 miles, an open country admitted that order of march; but at Oocâra, a country intersected by enclosures compelled the adoption of a single column, the cavalry, with Col. Floyd, leading; and the infantry, from that period, " entirely conducted, and most judiciously managed, by Lieut.-Col. Oldham, his second *."

Tippoo had, on the preceding night, drawn off his army, at the close of day, to a position distant six miles, which he had previously appointed, but the army overtaken by the night, and by torrents of rain not felt in the English position, unable to find their places in the line, were scattered over the country without order or connexion. If this state of things had been known to Col. Floyd, there can be no doubt, that even with his inferior numbers, and after the fatigues of such a day, he would have attempted, and probably succeeded in a decisive enterprise by night. There was no indication of movement until the English troops were in actual march, and it was of course between eight and nine before intelligence could reach the Sultaun, whose arrangements were prepared for a renewal of the cannonade, with an augmented artillery, about noon. He instantly ordered the great drum to be beaten, and verbal orders to be circulated for immediate march, and he hastened, with such cavalry

---

" Major Dallas has strong claims to be particularly recommended to your Lordship's notice: the readiness with which he came forward to exert his personal influence with the principal natives in the bullock department, at a period when it seemed scarcely possible to move forward the public stores; the effectual aid which he gave to the store department, by his personal assistance in its arrangements; and the duty, equally important and laborious, which he voluntarily took upon himself, of seeking and securing forage for the public cattle, during the marches of the army, are amongst the many instances in which his zeal has been distinguished, and which entitle him to the attention of government."

* See Col. Floyd's letter, p. 331, vol. ii. of this work.

as were ready, to reconnoitre, and to send back instructions regarding the route to be pursued. The Sultaun's sepoys had, in general, fasted a day and night, and were busily employed among the hedges in dressing their food. It was the custom of the army on ordinary occasions, to beat two preparatory sounds of the great drum, and march on the third: a portion of the dispersed army was really unacquainted with the orders for immediate march; another portion did not choose to understand them; the officers were directed to move without a moment's delay, and did so, with whatever men they could collect; but it is supposed that the whole force of every arm really collected for action on that day, did not exceed 15,000 men *, and certainly did not amount to 20,000: they were, however, flushed with the intelligence of the abandoned guns, and the elation of pursuit, and behaved with considerable firmness and spirit. It was past two o'clock before Tippoo could bring any of his infantry into action. The column of English infantry marched on the main road, which was now in most places bounded by thick hedges; and the enemy's cavalry, infantry and guns, bore directly on the rear, and diagonally on both flanks, compelling the column occasionally to halt and return the cannonade, with various success, making as much progress as was consistent with the successive means, very skilfully employed, for keeping the pursuers at a distance. In these operations, three more guns were disabled and abandoned, the number remaining being reduced to five 6-pounders. About five o'clock the Sultaun had advanced his whole force so close, as to compel Col. Oldham to halt, and form the whole infantry in a strong position; a select body of cavalry made a rapid detour, and charged, with considerable spirit, the rear of the position, while the infantry in front was prepared to take advantage of the expected confusion; the English line, only two deep, faced about to receive the cavalry, and repulsed them with great loss, many of the horsemen falling by the bayonet.

* The more general estimate is 10,000, but we must consider that it is the calculation of disappointed men.

The English cavalry had by this time advanced near to the village of Shawoor, (or Cheyoor), about two miles in front; the small portion of baggage that remained, was ordered into the village; ground was selected for the encampment; the cavalry had begun to forage; and a troop which had been ordered to examine and make the detour of the village, appeared on its opposite side, on the road leading from Coimbetoor. Some of the followers called out that it was Gen. Medows' personal guard, and the head of his column; and Col. Floyd, who had at the same moment received from Col. Oldham a report of his situation, seizing the fortunate error, caused it to be announced to the cavalry, who, throwing down their forage, formed, and returned to the scene of action, proclaiming, with three huzzas, the arrival of Medows, which was instantly greeted by a similar cheer along the infantry ranks. It was almost at the same critical period, that the Sultaun's army had rushed to the close of a fancied triumph, with a general shout, but were checked in the first instance, by the admirable conduct of the infantry, and in the next, by the exulting intelligence of succour. In this state of wavering, they were charged by the British cavalry, who pursued on both flanks of the position, and completely cleared the field.

The Sultaun received at once the report of the death of his favourite kinsman, Burhan-u-Deen, (who had fallen in a gallant attempt to force one of the fences which have been described) and of the supposed arrival of the English General: authentic information had placed his division on a different route, but believing for an instant his intelligence to be erroneous, he drew off his army in disappointment and indignation, at the escape of a prey deemed to be within his grasp *.

* Ascribing this disappointment chiefly to the inclosures which we have mentioned, he some years afterwards ordered them to be entirely levelled, over the whole face of the district; and it is a curious fact, that he was materially aided in this operation, by an almost invisible agent. The prickly pear, or straight-thorned opuntia, (*cactus ficus Indica*, Lin.—Ainslie), is the chief material of these fences; and the silvester cochineal insect, introduced into Coromandel shortly after the order had been given, devoured not only the leaves,

On the disappearance of the Sultaun's army, Col. Floyd, about seven o'clock, occupied the ground near the village, which he had previously examined. He had, during the action, received a despatch from head-quarters, dated on the preceding day; it related to promotions and matters of detail; and a postcript was added, stating, that the General would march on the 14th, for Velladi; a piece of intelligence which he had carefully concealed *.

Accordingly, at two o'clock, Col. Floyd moved to join Gen. Medows; at daylight he heard and answered three signal guns. Gen. Medows had also heard the firing of the preceding day, and three guns fired at eight at night, to indicate the situation of the detachment; but distant sounds are referred with little accuracy to their true directions, and had not enabled him to determine the situation of the detachment. Col. Floyd pursued his march, and arrived at Velladi, at eight at night, without seeing an enemy, the troop having been three days without eating. In the course of the march, however, he had met two Native horsemen of the General's bodyguard, who, in the anxiety produced by the firing, and the uncertainty of its direction, had been sent as a sort of forlorn hope, on the preceding evening, to endeavour to discover the detachment,

but the root of that plant, with such avidity as nearly to have terminated its existence in the south-eastern provinces, while the "*cactus tuna*," or awl-thorned opuntia, remained untouched by the insect.

* This measure appears to have been adopted by the General, on the tardy persuasion that the reiterated intelligence of the Sultaun's descent was not entirely unfounded. Velladi is on the nearest road from the pass by Denaickencota to Coimbetoor, but the direct road to the same place from Sattimungul, 15 miles lower down the river, is that on which Col. Floyd was marching, and had been invariably used by every convoy and detachment for the last month. To cross from Cheyoor, his present ground, to Velladi, was nearly 20 miles: the Sultaun as soon as he had time to examine his intelligence at leisure, caused a report to be circulated, that he had moved to an intermediate position towards that place, in the hope that Col. Floyd might be induced to pursue his route to Coimbetoor, and leave Gen. Medows' division without support; but this intelligence had an effect exactly the reverse of that it was intended to produce, by impressing on the mind of Col. Floyd, the absolute necessity of attempting, at all risks, to force the junction, as the only chance for the ultimate preservation of the army: and, if the report were true, it afforded the further hope of entangling the enemy between two fires.

and communicate the requisite intelligence. From them he ascertained that Gen. Medows had marched that morning through Velladi to Denaickencota, and a reciprocal anxiety was excited on his account. The two men and their horses were quite exhausted; it was obvious that no fresh horse or man was to be found in the detachment; but the vital importance was still more obvious, of stopping the further advance of the General; and Brigade-Maj. Dallas, volunteered and executed alone this essential service. He found the army ten miles in advance of Velladi, and reported the existence and the wants of the detachment. The most urgent was that of surgeons for the wounded, (two surgeons having been killed) and an immediate refreshment of biscuit and spirits for the Europeans—the sepoys being already occupied in dressing the rice, which they always carried on their backs: these wants were supplied in the course of the night, and the next morning, the General* retraced his steps to Velladi.

In all the preceding operations, and until the return of the army to Madras, in January 1791, the 5th Native cavalry, to which Lieut. Hudleston belonged, bore a distinguished part.

Lord Cornwallis had arrived from Bengal a few days before, resolved to conduct future operations in person, and to ascend the ghauts, leading to Seringapatam, by the Amboor Pass. The army, therefore, commenced their march on the 7th Feb., accompanied, as before, by Col. Floyd and the cavalry brigade, of which the 5th regiment formed a part. From the great deficiency of horses in the several regiments, it was thought expedient to leave behind 300 dismounted troopers, with a proportion of Native commissioned and non-commissioned officers, the whole under a subaltern; and to remain doing duty at Madras. Happening to be the next on the roster for detachment, Lieut. Hudleston was ordered to take charge of the party, and accordingly he repaired to Fort St. George, where he

* His reception of Col. Floyd was a noble example of candour: "My dear Colonel, your's is the feat, and mine the defeat." The General was fond of epigram, and it was usually well pointed.—*Sketches of the South of India*, vol. iii. p. 91.

continued until the 6th May, when, by a government order, he marched with the details, about 25 horses lately purchased, and half a lac of rupees; and on the 12th reached Velore; delivered the treasure over to the paymaster, and the horses, with the detail of the 1st regiment, to Major Murray, the Commandant of that corps. In a few days after, agreeably to instructions, he proceeded with the remaining dismounted men, to do duty at Arnee, under the orders of Capt. Robert Mackay *, commanding the garrison.

About the end of July, Col. Floyd and the cavalry returned from the Mysore country into the Carnatic to refit; having suffered much during the last very active campaign. Major Darley had resigned, and Major Orr† was appointed to command the 5th regiment. The dismounted details had now rejoined their respective regiments, and in Sept. Lieut. Hudleston rejoined the 5th, then at Arcot. On the 26th Oct. the office of adjutant became temporarily vacant, and so continued until the 4th of Feb. following, during which interval, and at the request of the Commandant, Lieutenant Hudleston officiated as Adjutant.

In the course of October the cavalry brigade, with Col. Floyd and the 19th light dragoons, had re-united, and by the 23d Dec. had re-entered the Mysore country, by the Padnadurgum Pass. About the 14th Jan. 1792, it rejoined the grand army near Maghery, and on the 26th the whole moved forward. By the 5th the army arrived in sight of Seringapatam, and encamped within three or four miles of it. On the evening of the 6th, when Lord Cornwallis made the memorable attack on Tippoo's lines under the walls of Seringapatam, the cavalry brigade, and the reserve, under Col. Duff‡, were drawn up in front of the encampment, to protect the park, baggage, &c. where it remained under arms all night.

From this period to the 25th, when hostilities ceased, the cavalry were actively employed in marching to meet and facilitate the junc-

---

* Now Lieutenant-General. Services, vol. i. p. 37-49.
† Now Lieutenant-General. Services, vol. i. p. 272-3.
‡ Services, vol. ii. p. 250.

tion of the Bombay troops, under Gen. Abercromby, which was effected on the 16th, and afterwards the brigade detached two or three marches, to re-inforce and bring up Major Stevenson's * detachment, having in charge a large body of Brinjarries.

* The estimation in which this officer was held by the Indian army, is shewn by the accompanying address. The Company's officers on duty at Madras, had resolved to attend him to the beach on his embarkation, in 1804, for Europe; and there to present him the address; but owing to his embarking at an earlier hour than was expected, the address was forwarded to him, through the senior officer, on board the Ceylon, in the Roads.

"*To Colonel James Stevenson.*

" Sir,—Unwarped by interest, uninfluenced by authority, unbiassed by power, we are assembled here, by the dictates of grateful and admiring minds, to show towards you, the only token of our reverence and esteem, which the suddenness of your departure from India leaves it in our power to offer.

" In parting with you, Sir, we part with an officer whose private character and public conduct have, for a series of years, added a bright lustre to the name of this army; and been greatly instrumental in advancing its credit and reputation, beyond its former limits.

" It never has been in your power to confer on us individual rewards or favours; but insensible should we be, not to perceive, and ungrateful indeed, not to acknowledge, the manifold advantages and lasting benefits we derive from many glorious exertions of your superior talents, and the noble sacrifices you have made at the shrine of your public duty; exertions and sacrifices by which both our individual interests and public character have been advanced and extended. When we shall have long been deprived of your animating presence; when your unerring counsel shall no longer avail us; when your frame shall long have mingled with your parent earth, the zeal your example has created,—the spirit your conduct has excited,—will continue to invigorate and adorn this army; and, with emulous pride, preserve in our minds, you once were one of us: with our memories,—our gratitude, esteem, and admiration will last, and part only with our lives.

" In these feelings and sentiments, we readily anticipate the cordial concurrence and participation of all our brother officers; and the lively pain those will experience, who, by the suddenness of your departure, have lost this opportunity of doing willing, but unequal, homage, to your private virtues and public merits.

" Although we hope and trust your absence from these shores will be but short, and with lively pleasure anticipate your speedy return, yet, Sir, we would not willingly allow any opportunity to pass, without offering you some token of those sentiments, which never cease to actuate our minds and feelings towards you.

" Wishing you a safe and pleasant passage to your native country,—that country in whose service you have devoted so many years of your life; whose interests you have been so greatly instrumental in advancing, and for whose public good your zeal knows no limits, we now take a painful but temporary leave, with our most fervent wishes, that its salubrious air may speedily restore you to a state of rendering it further services."

(Signed by the officers of the Honourable Company's service on duty at Madras.)

For some time past, Lieut. Hudleston's health had suffered considerably, and a peace with Tippoo being shortly after concluded, he returned, in the Northumberland, on sick certificate, to Europe, which vessel also carried home the definitive treaty.

Lieut. Hudleston again repaired to Madras in Sept. 1795, and in October he was re-appointed to, and joined his former regiment, the 5th, under Major Orr, in cantonments, near Cudalore. In Jan. 1796, he was detached, with a party, to Trichinopoly, to receive some remount horses; and in March he rejoined his corps, with 174 horses.

The new regulations for the Company's troops arriving in this year, 1796, from Europe, this officer was included in the consequent promotion, and obtained the rank of Captain.

The 5th regiment remained near Cudalore, until April 1798, when it was removed to cantonments, near Trichinopoly, where it again joined the 19th light dragoons, under Col. Floyd, who commanded that district. In July following, the 5th regiment was ordered to Vellout, near Pondamallee, where it arrived in the middle of August. Early in January 1799, Col. Orr proceeded to Madras, in order to return to Europe, and the command of the regiment devolved on Major, the Hon. A. Sentleger*. About this time, agreeably to instructions from Europe, arrangements were made for reducing one of the five regiments of cavalry, whereby the number of Capt. Hudleston's corps, was changed from the 5th to the 3d.

Preparations for the field, in contemplation of hostilities with Tippoo, were made in Jan. 1799, and by the 6th February, the four regiments, with H. M.'s 25th and 19th light dragoons, joined the troops assembling near Velore, headed by Gen. Harris, the Com.-in-Chief; Col. Floyd, as before, commanding the cavalry. By the 22d Feb. the army had ascended the ghauts, and encamped near Vaniambady, on the road leading to Seringapatam.

The subsequent marches and proceedings of the army, to the 27th March, when the action at Malavilly took place, and to the 5th April, when the British took up their ground near Seringapatam,

* The late Major-General. Services, vol. i. p. 78-84.

have been referred to in various parts of this work. The cavalry, however, at Malavilly, so greatly distinguished themselves, that a detailed account of that gallant action cannot be unacceptable to military readers.

On the 27th, the English army, on preparing to take up its ground of encampment, to the westward of Malavilly, distinctly perceived the Sultaun's army drawn up on a height, little exceeding two miles from the intended encampment. The great object of the English General was, to escort in safety to the spot in which they were to be used, the effective means of reducing the capital, and not to seek for serious action until that object should be attained. He accordingly ordered the ground of encampment to be marked, and the troops to continue their march in such order as should admit either of encampment or action; the principal division, under his own orders, being destined to form the right, and the column under the Hon. Col. Wellesley, the extreme left, and eventually to turn the enemy's right. The troops intended for the advanced picquets, under Col. Sherbrooke*, moved out, as usual, to examine their ground, and they were soon threatened by large bodies of the enemy. After some manœuvring, they took post with their right to a village, and the support of these troops eventually brought on the action. The column of the principal division, or right wing of the army, successively deployed into line on the left of the picquets, and when formed, advanced on the enemy. An interval between two brigades, caused by the nature of the ground, seemed to present an opportunity for an effort of cavalry, which the Sultaun himself directed and accompanied, till in the very act to charge. The charge was prepared with deliberate coolness, and executed with great spirit; it was purposely directed against the Europeans; and although many horsemen fell on the bayonets, was completely repelled, without causing the slightest disorder in the ranks; and the advance of the line being continued, in a direction outflanking the

* Now a Lieut.-General, and a Grand Cross of the Order of the Bath, &c.—Services, Royal Military Calendar, vol. ii. p. 193-6, 3rd edit.

enemy's left, the Sultaun's guns began soon afterwards to be withdrawn from the heights.

In the meanwhile, the division under Col. Wellesley, moved in echellon of corps, to turn the enemy's right, supported on his right by a brigade of cavalry, under Col. Floyd. The English centre being entirely refused, and Col. Floyd being prepared to act with either attack, as circumstances might require: the remainder of the cavalry was on the right, keeping in check a body of horse, which threatened, by a circuitous route, to attack the baggage. As Col. Wellesley approached his object, the Sultaun's cushoons advanced in very creditable style in front of their guns, against the 33d, which was the leading corps, giving their fire, and receiving that of the 33d, together with a discharge of grape, till within 60 yards, when the regiment, continuing to advance with a quickened step, they gave way; and Col. Floyd, availing himself of the critical instant, charged and destroyed them to a man. The guns now began to be withdrawn from this flank also, and an appearance of making a stand on another height, occupied by the second line of the Mysoreans, was only intended to cover their retreat. The result to the Sultaun of this injudicious affair, was the loss of upwards of a thousand men, and to the English of 69 only *.

On the 6th, the 19th light dragoons, 1st, 3d, and 4th Native cavalry, and a considerably infantry force, the whole under Col. Floyd, were detached to Periapatam, near 40 miles, to meet the Bombay troops, under Gen. Stuart, which they did on the 10th, and the next day the whole commenced returning to Seringapatam, accompanied and harassed most of the way by large bodies of horse hanging on their flanks and rear, and much annoying the stores and baggage. On the 14th, they rejoined the camp before Seringapatam; and on the 16th, the cavalry brigade, with three or four infantry corps, again marched away, and about the 5th May, at Hunnoor, were joined by detachments under Cols. Brown † and Read, coming up

* Sketches of the South of India, vol. iii. p. 410.
† The late Lieutenant-General. Services, vol. ii. p. 207, *et seq*. This distinguished officer died in London, on the 4th May 1825.

from the Baramahal; the whole then marched back, and rejoined the army on the 11th. Seringapatam had been stormed, and Tippoo killed on the 4th.

In a few days after, a force of five battalions, and the 3d regiment of cavalry, was detached, under Col. Dalrymple, and formed a subsidiary division for the protection of the Nizam's country, and of the districts now ceded to him. The detachment left camp on the 19th, and passed by Bangalore on the 6th June, and reached Ryacotah on the 10th. The 3d reg. was ordered to march back to Bangalore, which it reached on the 15th; it remained there till the 5th July, and was then ordered to Pedibalapore, a walled village 26 miles distant, and about 10 miles from Nundydroog.

From the latter place, Capt. Hudleston was detached, on the 4th of August, with a troop and a 6-pounder, to join Capt. Greenhill, who, with five or six companies, was marching in various directions through the ceded districts. On the 2d Sept., Capt. Greenhill's detachment having returned to Nundydroog, Capt. Hudleston rejoined his regiment.

In September, two new regiments of cavalry, the 5th and 6th, were raised; to command the former, Lieut.-Col. (the late Maj.-Gen.) Macalister, was removed from the 3d; and the senior Captain, Rumley, was promoted to the Majority and command of the 3d.

On the 25th Sept. the regiment left Pedibalapore, and continued marching about with few halting days, until the 2d Nov., when, at Cannaghery, near the Toombuddra, it joined Col. Halyburton with some of the subsidiary force.

On the 4th Jan. 1800, the 3d reg., with Col. Halyburton's party, arrived at Hyderabad. Here the corps remained until the middle of June, when a detachment of flank companies, and the 3d reg. of cavalry, were ordered out for the purpose of co-operating with the force under Gen. Wellesley, against Doondia Waugh, in the Dooaub. Early in July the detachment had reached the Toombuddra, about

14 miles from Rachore: here the orders of Government were received, directing the raising of two new battalions of infantry, and a seventh regiment of cavalry, to be commanded by Lieut.-Colonel Sheriff, and promoting Capt. Hudleston to the majority of the new regiment: he, however, continued doing duty with the 3d. The detachment kept marching in various directions, crossing and recrossing the Toombuddra and Mulpurba rivers, dependant on Doondia's movements, until the 10th Sept., when Gen. Wellesley's division came up with him: a total defeat and dispersion of his party ensued; and Doondia himself was killed in the engagement.

This service being concluded, the 3d reg. and the detachment, marched towards Hyderabad, which they reached by the end of November.

On the 15th Jan. 1801, Major Hudleston quitted the 3d reg. and Hyderabad, setting out for Arcot, where Col. Sheriff was stationed, and occupied in raising the 7th reg., and whom he joined on the 20th February.

On the 7th April 1802, Col. Sheriff died at Madras, and the command of the regiment and of the cantonment devolved on Major Hudleston until the end of June, when Lieut.-Col. Pogson, who had been appointed to the command of the corps, joined. The regiment being soon after ordered to be stationed at Sera, it left Arcot on the 12th July, and by the end of that month arrived at its destination. On the 15th Nov. orders were received for the regiment to prepare for field service. In the beginning of December, Lieut.-Col. Pogson was removed from the 7th to command the 3d, and Lieut.-Col. Orr appointed to the 7th. The latter officer being in Europe, Major Hudleston was continued in command of the corps.

The rupture with the Mahrattas now approached, and by directions from Gen. Wellesley, who was assembling troops at Banawar, Major Hudleston joined him there on the 17th Feb. 1803. The regiment was reviewed in a few days after its arrival, and met the approbation of the General.

On the 6th March, Gen. Wellesley's party arrived at Hurryhur, where the main army, under the Com.-in-Chief, Gen. Stuart, was assembled. The cavalry brigade attached to the division under Gen. Wellesley, consisted of the 19th light dragoons, the 4th, 5th, and 7th regiments of Native Cavalry, the whole under Lieut.-Colonel Dallas.

The progress of Gen. Wellesley's division, which separated from the main army on the 8th, through the Mahratta states, to the 19th April, when, accompanied by the cavalry, the General made the memorable night march to Poona, to save that place from plunder by Amrut Row; the capture of Ahmednuggur on the 12th August; and the subsequent movements of this force, to the 23d Sept., when the battle of Assaye took place, have been already referred to in this work, and will also be found noticed in the Memoirs of the illustrious Duke of Wellington. It is, therefore, only necessary to state, in this place, that the 7th reg., with the rest of the cavalry brigade under Lieut.-Col. Maxwell (for Lieut.-Col. Dallas, from ill health, had departed to Bombay four months before), shared in the operations of that day, when, towards the evening, Lieut.-Col. Maxwell fell in the general charge made by the brigade which contributed to save the remains of the gallant 74th reg.*, which had lost nearly all their men, and all, except two or three, of their officers. The loss among the several cavalry regiments was pretty equal: the 7th had about 110 horses killed and wounded, and about 30 men; among them was Captain Macgregor, mortally.

About the 24th Nov., Major Leonard, of the 5th reg, became dangerously ill, and Major Hudleston succeeded to the command of the brigade.

* The regiment lost at Assaye, Captains D. Aytone, Andrew Dyce, Roderick Macleod, John Maxwell; Lieutenants John Campbell, John Morshead Campbell, Lorn Campbell, James Grant, J. Morris, Robert Neilson; Volunteer Moore; 9 serjeants, 7 drummers, and 127 rank and file killed. Major Samuel Swinton; Captains Norman Moore, Matthew Shaw, John Alexander Mien, Robert Macmurdo, J. Longland; Ensign Kierman; 11 serjeants, 7 drummers, and 270 rank and file wounded.

On the 29th, Col. Stevenson's division, with whom were the 3d and 6th cavalry, under Lieut.-Colonels Sentleger and Pogson, joined the 7th on the march towards Argaum, near which place the corps fell in with the Berar Rajah's army. In the disposition for the attack, which commenced about four o'clock, the cavalry of both divisions were united. Lieut.-Col. Sentleger was placed in command of four regiments, while the 5th and 7th formed a second line under Major Hudleston.

The Rajah's troops, unsupported by Scindia's (who was then negotiating a separate treaty with Gen. Wellesley), gave way in a little time and fled, as did his cavalry on the left, pursued by the whole of the British to a very considerable distance; but the immense clouds of dust, and their own fleetness, kept them from the view of the British, who did not return to their former ground till near eleven o'clock.

In a day or two afterwards, the two divisions (Gen. Wellesley's and Col. Stevenson's) moved towards Gawilghur, a strong hill fort, about 10 miles from Ellichpoor. Here, on the 5th Dec., a number of the sick, and among them Major Leonard, were placed under medical care: that officer died very shortly after.

By the 8th, the divisions had approached Gawilghur, and positions were taken up for the siege; the cavalry reconnoitring under Col. Sentleger, as a covering party, about four miles distant. The place was taken by storm on the 15th. On the 17th, Col. Sentleger, with his two regiments, rejoined his own division, Col. Stevenson's. On the 23d, a treaty of peace with the Berar Rajah was signed; and on the 5th Jan. 1804, a similar treaty was concluded with Scindia.

On the 15th Jan. Major Kennedy, of the 19th light dragoons, was promoted to Lieut.-Colonel, *vice* Lieut.-Colonel Maxwell, killed at Assaye; and as senior officer the command of the cavalry brigade devolved on him. By the 23d Feb. the division had arrived near Porinda, when Gen. Wellesley left it to proceed to Poona, leaving Colonel Wallace, of H. M.'s 74th regiment, in command.

Early in April, Col. Wallace marched the division near to Poona, where it remained till June. Early in May, the government orders were published, raising the 8th reg. of cavalry, and promoting Major Hudleston to the Lieut.-Colonelcy of the 7th, from the 1st May.

On the 25th June, the 19th light dragoons and 4th reg. cavalry left this division, and proceeded towards the Mysore country.

About the 22d August, a rupture with Holkar having some time commenced, Col. Wallace and the division left Poona, to march towards his country. The division reached the Godaveri, near Toka, on the 29th Sept. and was joined by the 3d and 6th regiments of cavalry, at which period Colonels Sentleger and Pogson had left those corps from ill health. In a division order by Col. Wallace, the four regiments were formed into one brigade, and Lieut.-Col. Hudleston appointed to the command of it.

On the 8th October, the division reached Chandoor, a hill fort, which surrendered on the 12th: the British quitted it on the 17th, and on the 21st encamped near Gaulnah, another hill fort, which, after two days' battering, surrendered on terms; and on the 3d of Nov. the division quitted it, leaving a small party as a garrison.

On the 8th of May, 1805, the division being then at Ahmednuggur, it was joined by the 1st reg. of cavalry, under Major Neale. The division left Ahmednuggur on 24th May, resuming a northern direction, and by the 10th of June arrived at Palood, near 40 miles beyond Aurungabad. Here, in consequence of instructions that day received by Col. Wallace, from Bengal, he issued orders for the 1st, 5th, and 7th regts. of cavalry, with H. M.'s 74th reg. and six of the park guns, to march back to Ahmednuggur, and named Lieut.-Col. Hudleston, as senior officer, to command the detachment. The latter accordingly moved next day, and on the 24th arrived at Ahmednuggur. In a few days after, he received orders from the Adjutant General, that all the horses most fit for service in the 5th and 7th regts. should be selected and drafted among the 1st, 3d, and 6th regts., and that being done, the two former regts. were to proceed, *via.* Poona, to the

Carnatic. By this arrangement, upwards of 200 horses from the 7th, and about the same number from the 5th, were given over to Major Neale, of the 1st reg. The two regiments commenced their march from Ahmednuggur on the 8th July, and by the 14th of October arrived at the cantonments at Arcot. Here they were stationed to refit and renew the various articles of equipment, in which they had unavoidably become deficient, including horses, of which they had only about 50 remaining, and those unfit for service.

The corps continued at this station to the end of the year 1808; long before which, it had recovered its former efficient state. The health and constitution of Lieut.-Col. Hudleston had for some time suffered very considerably, and in October 1808, he sailed for England on sick certificate. Finding, in 1813, his health not sufficiently re-established to allow of his returning to India, in a state equal to further effective service, and the period having arrived when by the regulations it became necessary to decide, he retired on the allowance of his rank, to which his length of service had entitled him.

THE LATE MAJOR JOHN CANNING.

(Bengal Establishment.)

This officer entered the Bengal army, about the year 1796. He became a Captain in the 27th reg. of Native infantry on the establishment of that presidency, in 1816. He was subsequently appointed Political Agent at Aurungabad; and on the 20th March, 1824, was nominated to accompany the expedition, destined against the territories of the King of Ava, in the same capacity of Political Agent to the Governor General, who appointed Capt. Canning his Aid-de-camp.

Upon the new organization of the Bengal Army in May 1825, this officer attained the rank of Major.

He accompanied Sir Archibald Campbell to Rangoon, and it is

understood, was the medium of some important communications from the court of Ava.

Major Canning had been but a short time at Rangoon before he was attacked by illness: he persevered, however, in the fulfillment of his duties, till he conceived his visit to Calcutta, for change of air, would be attended with the advantage of enabling him to afford information to the Bengal government respecting the war. He died the 2d Sept., only 18 hours after he landed at Calcutta, in a very emaciated state. His age was 49.

The distinguished talents and services of this valuable officer, afforded a pledge, that his country would have derived great benefit from his discharge of the important post which he filled; and justify the terms of regret in which his loss is spoken of in the despatch from the Government of Bengal, of 6th Sept. 1824. His goodness of heart and kindness of disposition, are recorded by his contemporaries, as qualities which secured to him the esteem and affection of all who knew him.

A numerous and respectable assemblage attended the removal of his remains from Tank Square to the Roman Catholic church, to which the Major belonged; including part of the Staff of the Governor-General, and the principal civil and military officers of government, as well as the most respectable members of the chief Roman Catholic church in Calcutta.

CAPTAIN A. G. FISHER.

(Bombay Establishment.)

In 1791, this officer went out to India as a Cadet, and joined the artillery of the army under Gen. Abercromby, near Seringapatam, during the cessation of hostilities, that terminated in the peace of 1792. He served at the capture of Cochin, in Malabar, in October 1795, and at that of Columbo, in Ceylon, in February following.

He joined the Bombay army under Gen. Stuart, and served with it at the siege and capture of Seringapatam, (for which he has received the medal): he was also at the reduction of Sadashewghur, in 1799. He next served on the ordnance staff, with the British force at Goa, until the Mahratta war, when he joined the force under Gen. Wellesley, and continued with it, until after the capture of Ahmednuggur, where he was, for some time, stationed as commissary of ordnance, and commanding the artillery.

He then joined the force under the late Col. Wallace, and served with it at the capture of Chandore and Gaulna, where his health suffered so much, as to compel him to leave India, in 1805, and subsequently to give up his prospects in the service, by retiring, 9th Dec. 1807, on half-pay, with most flattering testimonials from Sir Arthur Wellesley, and other officers under whose command he had served.

The following are the dates of this officer's commissions: Lieut. fire-worker, 30th Nov., 1791; Lieutenant, 8th Jan., 1796; and Captain, 10th Nov. 1800.

THE LATE COLONEL CHARLES FREDERICK*.

(Bombay Establishment.)

THIS officer was the son of the Hon. Sir Charles Frederick †, K.B. who died in Dec. 1786. He entered the East India Company's

---

* Incidental mention is made of this gallant officer in pages 248, 279, and 340, of vol. i., and in p. 488 of vol. ii. of this work.

† Sir Charles was third son of Sir Thomas Frederick, F.R.S. and A.S. Governor of Madras. Sir Charles was born in 1709: he married Lucy, daughter of Viscount Falmouth, by whom he had one son (Col. C. F., born in 1748) and three daughters. The second daughter, Augusta, born in 1747, married Thomas Prescott, Esq. in 1771. The present worthy East India Director of that name, is their son. Sir Charles was eminently distinguished for his taste, and for his skill in drawing. He was M. P. for Stoneham, in 1746; and was Surveyor-General and Comptroller of the Ordnance. He directed the splendid exhibition of fire-works in the Green Park, on the peace in 1749—an exhibition not, perhaps, outshone, except by that in the same place on the peace with France in 1814.

service, as a Captain, about the year 1776; previous to which period he was in his Majesty's army, and served on the Continent.

In 1778, he served as Major in the campaign against the Mahrattas, which terminated in the affair at Telligaum. It is recollected, among the old officers of the Bombay army, that Major Frederick's exertions on that occasion, and in others of that discreditable* campaign, were deserving of more commendation and eclat than were extended to them.

In 1790, having intermediately been Commandant of the garrison of Surat, and promoted to the rank of Colonel, he left Bombay with the European regiment, and the 9th battalion N. I., to reinforce a weak brigade of the Bombay army, serving with the Mahrattas, under Purseram Bhow. The Mahrattas were then besieging Darwar; but seemed to make slow progress, from the vigour of the defence. Col. Frederick superseded Capt. Little† in the command of the Bombay brigade, which now consisted of the Bombay European regiment, a company of artillery, and three battalions (the 8th, 9th, and 11th) of Native infantry.

He fell a sacrifice to the ardour of his feelings at the failure of an assault on the fort of Darwar. Lieut. Moor ‡, in his "Narrative of the Operations of Capt. Little's Detachment," thus mentions the death of his lamented friend and commander:—

"We were this morning much surprised to hear of the death of our much-respected Colonel, for none but the medical gentlemen had any idea of its being so near; they, however, had long seen he could not recover. Actuated by the ardour of a soldier, his enterprising spirit could not brook the procrastinations to which he was obliged to submit; and losing, with the unsuccessful attempt of the 7th of Feb., all expectation of an honourable conquest of the fort, he had from that time been on the decline. No event could have been more acute to his detachment, for with them he was universally beloved; nor could the Bombay army, of which he was at the

---

* See Treaty of Worgaum, vol. ii. p. 78-9.
† Services in this volume.   ‡ Now Major. Services, vol. i. p. 339-48.

head, have sustained a severer loss, for he was truly a good soldier, and a soldier's friend. As a husband, his kindness and tenderness were exemplary; and as a father, his affection could not be exceeded: his amiable widow will, as far as possible, supply the place of a father to a large family, several of whom are yet too young to feel the irreparable loss they have sustained. It must be admitted he had many enemies, for his pride would not admit his stooping to soften their enmities: such persons, perhaps, will not agree in the assertion, that his honourable employers lost in him one of the best of their servants; but all impartial people will confirm the declaration; and we cannot, in justice to our conviction and feelings, say less, when speaking of the late Col. Frederick, our protector, our patron, and our friend."

Col. Frederick, as already stated, was of a family distinguished for rank and talent, and was himself an honourable descendant. His education had been of a description very superior to that usual with the officers who had then attained rank in the Indian army. He was most gentlemanly in his manners, and an excellent soldier. He died at the age of 53 *.

* The Editor has very great pleasure in introducing the following note, written by a highly valued friend and officer of distinguished service in the Indian army:—

"Col. F. was well known to the author of this note. Although a man of hasty temper, he had very superior talents as an officer. From the station he had filled, as adjutant in the guards, no man understood the theory better, or had more knowledge of the practical and parade duties of the profession. He was, in fact, a great martinet; severely insisting on the strict performance of duty in all ranks in the European regiment under his command. He was not disliked by the men; for, though severe, he was just, and always encouraged, in the interval of parade duties, all sorts of the native country sports, in which he joined, and was himself no mean proficient.

"Of his talents in the field, the writer of this article had but one opportunity of judging; but that was on a most memorable and trying occasion—on the 12th Jan. 1779, in the retreat from Telligaum, which was followed by the Convention of Worgaum.

"The distance between Telligaum and Worgaum is about fifteen miles, and the ground, as that near Waterloo is described to be, undulated by small eminences. The road leading at no great distance from a range of hills, which protected the left flank of the retreating army, and gave protection to the baggage and followers, who moved on between the line and the hills. The retreat commenced under circumstances calculated to raise the spirits of the pursuing army, and to depress those of the pursued. The heavy artillery, sto of

Col. Frederick left a numerous family. His eldest daughter, Matilda, married Doctor Robert Stewart, President of the Medical Board at Bombay. The second, Augusta, is the widow of the late

all kinds, in short, every thing that could obstruct a march, were destroyed previous to quitting Telligaum; and these circumstances being well known to the enemy, they were perfectly prepared to obstruct the retreat. Of course the army had to fight for every inch of ground they gained; and by the time the line was clear of its encampment, it was almost immediately attacked. The pressure was most severe on the rear-guard, six flank companies of sepoys, commanded by Capt. (afterwards M.-Gen. Hartley). He defended himself with great gallantry for two hours, but the number of men and officers he had lost obliged him to send for support. Those who knew Gen. Hartley, will easily judge how harassing the occasion must have been. The European regiment was sent to his support, and the command of them, of course, devolved on Col. (then Major) Frederick. The left being the most assailable part of the eminence, became the station of the Europeans. The artillery, four 6-pounders, on the flanks, and the sepoys on the right. This eminence, emphatically called by the soldiers "Bloody-bank," had not even a shrub to protect the occupants from the unceasing fire of the enemy's artillery and sharp-shooters. The officers and men, to render them less exposed, were directed to sit down—a position they did not enjoy for long intervals, being frequently obliged to stand to their arms to repel the many attempts made by the cavalry to charge up the eminence. In this situation they remained, under a dreadful carnage, for nearly four hours, when orders were received to join the line. During the whole of this time, Major Frederick and Capt. Hartley were moving about, observing every motion of the enemy, and evincing a degree of coolness and courage which was the admiration of all who beheld it. It may be said that this was merely passive valour; but let it be recollected, that it was to passive valour, to the patient endurance of a most murdering conflict, that we are indebted for the glorious and immortal victory at Waterloo. On this occasion, considering the numbers engaged, the loss was not less severe; of near 1000 men that occupied the hill, not above 600 left it bearing their arms. The retreat, a most critical operation, was conducted by these two officers with consummate skill; and had it been recorded in the official despatches would, no doubt, have excited the same admiration as the heroic defence of Captain, the late Lieut.-Col. Staunton (Services, vol. i. p. 95-106, and in this volume,) on ground not far distant.

"It is painful to relate the sequel of this well-fought action, as far as respected Col. Frederick. No man knew better, or could more fully appreciate the merits of the late Gen. Hartley, than the writer of this article; but it would be a contradiction to his own feelings, were he to approve the act by which he was raised over the heads of many deserving officers, and, among others, of the subject of this memoir, who, instead of meeting the reward his gallant conduct merited, found himself, on his return to Bombay, superseded in rank by the very officers who had been under his command on this memorable occasion. His high spirit could not submit to such degradation. He immediately resigned the service, returned to England, and, on representing his case to the Court of Directors, he was restored to his proper rank, and returned to the service. In the zealous discharge of his duty, he fell a sacrifice (as already stated), leaving behind him a very high character as an

eminent physician, Helenus Scott*. The third, Lucy, married Col. Sir William Young, Bart. His two sons are field officers in the Bombay army.

CAPTAIN HENRY RALFE.

(Bengal Establishment.)

This officer joined the regiment of Bengal artillery in 1810, and accompanied a detachment of that corps on the expedition to Java, where he was engaged in every affair, from the troops first landing, on the 4th August, till the day the island was finally ceded to the English.

In March of the following year, he proceeded, in command of a detachment of his regiment, with the force employed against Palambang, under the late Gen. Gillespie; after the capture of which he was appointed Commandant of artillery, and Commissary of ordnance on the island of Banca.

In Sept. of the same year, he commanded a detachment of artillery in an attack upon an enemy's post, about 200 miles up the river of Palambang, and in which the late Major Meares, of the Madras army, who commanded the force, was mortally wounded.

Being obliged to leave Banca the following Jan., on account of his health, Capt. Ralfe returned to Java, and was appointed to the command of the artillery in the Bantam district; from which he removed, in July following, in order to take the command of a detachment of artillery directed to proceed with the force sent against Palambang, under Lieut.-Col. M'Gregor, of H. M.'s 59th reg.; and on his return from thence with the despatches of the surrender of that place, he was again appointed to command the artillery in Bantam.

officer, which the Editor of the East India Military Calendar has great merit in rescuing, with that of many other gallant men, from oblivion.

"E. N."

* See p. 97 of this volume.

In March 1815, Capt. Ralfe was obliged, on account of ill health, to proceed to Europe. He again, in March 1818, left England for Bengal; and in the following Nov. was selected for the command of a detachment of artillery, and directed to place himself at the disposal of Sir T. S. Raffles.

He, accordingly, left Bengal, under the orders of that eminent character, and by whom he was subsequently appointed to the command of the artillery, Assistant Engineer, and to the charge of the military stores at the settlement formed on the island of Singapore, where he remained till Nov. 1821, when he was permitted, on account of ill health, to return to Bengal, from whence, in a few months, he was, from the same cause, obliged to proceed to England.

CAPTAIN JAMES TILLYER BLUNT.

(Bengal Establishment.)

This officer was appointed a Cadet in 1782, and was admitted upon the Bengal establishment in Sept. 1783. He was selected for the engineer corps with five others, who were qualified for commissions in that branch of the service, under the instruction of the late Mr. Reuben Burrow, and was appointed an Ensign in the corps of engineers on the Bengal establishment, in Jan. 1785. In the same year, he was ordered to proceed to the relief of the engineer officers on duty at the field station of Caunpoor. In 1786, he was made a supernumerary Ensign, the corps of engineers being reduced.

In 1787, he was appointed assistant to Mr. Reuben Burrow, in the execution of an extensive survey for determining the latitudes and longitudes of many of the principal places in India. A fever and ague, acquired by continued exposure to the damps at night while making astronomical observations at Dacca, amidst the low, flat, and marshy country of Bengal, compelled him to relinquish that service, and proceed to Mongheer for the recovery of his health; at which station he was appointed assistant Engineer, during the construction of the buildings for the establishment of a magazine for military stores at Mongheer.

In Nov. 1791, he joined the grand army under Lord Cornwallis, in the Mysore country, and served with it until the conclusion of peace with Tippoo Sultaun, in 1792. During this service, he was present at the siege and storming of the hill fort of Savendroog, and taking of Ootradroog. The scaling ladders attached to the advance guard of the centre column, on the night of the 6th Feb. 1792, under the personal command of Lord Cornwallis, were placed under this officer's charge. The advanced guard, consisting of six flank companies from his Majesty's regiments, under the command of Lieut.-Col. Knox, of the 36th, forced a passage through the bound hedge to Sibbald's Redoubt, through the enemy's camp, then standing to the river Cavery, and crossed the river to the Sultaun's palace, in the Dowlut Bang. At this place the troops composing the advance guard were much separated; Ensign Blunt, with the ladders, accompanied a part of the troops under the command of Capt. Russell, of the 74th: they proceeded to the fort, and were fired upon from the fortifications, from which they retired to the pettah of Shere Ganjam, and there found the streets of the pettah crowded with loaded cattle, carrying the camp equipage and baggage of the Sultaun's army. At this time there were only Capt. Russell, a wounded officer, and Ensign Blunt, with this part of the troops, about 75 men that had separated from the advance guard, under the command of Lieut.-Col. Knox; meeting with a Frenchman in the habit of a mussulman, as a practitioner of medicine, he conducted the party to the prison where the English prisoners were confined: a high palisade gate was scaled with the ladders, the guard over the prisoners put to flight, and the prisoners released, the most pitiful emaciated objects. The party under Capt. Russell proceeded, carrying away the prisoners through the main street in the pettah, to the river Cavery, and there found the fortifications upon the bank of the river occupied, in considerable force, by the troops of Tippoo Sultaun. The party collected and attacked the nearest round tower, which was soon cleared of the enemy, and they took post therein, defending themselves for some time from the attempts of the enemy to retake it, but the 7th batt. Bengal Native infantry, that were observed to be crossing the river, were, by the assistance of the ladders, enabled to ascend into the fortifications, and soon dispersed the enemy. Other corps soon joining, the whole, under the command of then Lieut.-Col., and subsequently Lieut.-Gen., Stuart, compelled the enemy to retire, and as day light appeared, on the morning of the 7th Feb., the Lolbang, the palace, and Hyder's mausoleum, with all that part of the island of Seringapatam, were soon occupied by the British troops, the enemy being driven into the pettah, and under the walls of the fort of Seringapatam.

Ensign Blunt served during the siege, and, until the peace in May 1792, when he was employed on a survey, and accompanied the Nizam's army to Hyderabad, where he remained until October 1792, and then proceeded through the Nizam's country to Neermul, on the Godaveri river, to Mahore, Ellichpoor, to Hussungabad, on the Nerbudda river, through Bhilsah, Bhopaul, Saugor, and part of Bundlecund, to Culpee, on the river Jumna, to Caunpoor, where the survey in which he was employed terminated. Ensign Blunt was subsequently appointed to the station of Dinapore, to superintend the constructing and repairing of the public buildings at that place, and in October 1793 was appointed to assist in a survey, under the late Lieut. Gen. Reynolds*, then Capt. Reynolds, of the Bombay army, in surveying the North-west frontier of Hindostan, and joined Capt. R. at Allahabad, in Dec. 1793. This survey extended to the north-west, as far as Panniput, and to the north-east to the Hurdwar, and terminated through Rohilcund to Lucknow, in May 1794, when the party acting together on this survey, were dispersed, and ordered to different stations, Capt. Reynolds proceeding to Surat.

Ensign Blunt rejoined the station of Dinapore, and from thence was removed to Fort William, and in Oct. 1795 was employed on an ex-

* Services, p. 87.

tensive survey to explore the country situated to the southward of Chunarghur, on the Ganges, towards the northern Circars, a narrative of which arduous service is published in the transactions* of the Asiatic Society of Calcutta. This survey was completed in January 1796.

Ensign Blunt was promoted to the rank of Lieutenant in 1796, having served as Cadet and Ensign about 14 years; he was promoted to the rank of Brevet Captain in 1797, and was employed in the office of the Surveyor General in Bengal, and in the Arsenal, under the Commissary of Stores; and in 1798 was appointed Barrack-master of Fort William.

In 1803 he was employed in the conquest of the province of Cuttack†, under the command of Lieut.-Col., the late Sir Alexander

---

* Vide Asiatic Researches, vol. vii. p. 57-169.

† An account of the conquest of Cuttack has been published in the Asiatic Journal for Jan. 1818. It will be sufficient to introduce in this place the orders issued on the capture of Koordah, which are not in that work:—

Public Thanks.---Head-Quarters, Camp, near Koordah, 6th Dec. 1804.

" *Morning Orders, by Col. Harcourt.*

" Col. Harcourt begs to acknowledge, with sincere gratitude, the able and gallant conduct Major Fletcher yesterday evinced in the assault and capture of Koordah; nothing short of the intrepid valour, fortitude, and promptness, with which every officer and man conducted himself, who was employed in the attack, could have rendered it so completely successful.

" Major Fletcher, has announced to the Colonel his applause of the good conduct of the co-operating detachment, under Captains Hookland and Itory.

" Where the general good conduct of all has been so manifest, it would appear needless to particularize individual merit; but Col. Harcourt cannot pass over, in silence, the spirited conduct of Capt. Greenhill, of the 17th reg. in leading his company to the assault, though suffering under the effect of the severe wound he so recently received; or that of Lieut. Palmer, of the Madras European regiment, whose gallantry in escalading the walls of the enemy's last retreat, demands, from Col. Harcourt, the expressions of his respect and applause.

" To the memory of that gallant officer, Lieut. Bryan, every sentiment of admiration and respect is due from Col. Harcourt: he volunteered his services on the assault, and the same spirit that dictated his exemplary conduct, led him foremost in the rank of honour. It affords some consolation, under the affliction which his loss occasions, to advert to his distinguished gallantry and valour; but as he lived in the regard and affection of all his brother officers, so is his death to be lamented.

" The events of yesterday calling on Col. Harcourt to particularize part of the detachment, he cannot omit the opportunity of noticing the general spirit, discipline, and zeal.

Campbell, Lieut.-Gen. Commander-in-Chief at Madras, and subsequently, upon that officer's disability from severe illness, under Lieut.-Col., since the late Major Gen., Harcourt, until June 1805, when the province was delivered over to the civil authorities, and Captain Blunt returned to the barrack department in Fort William. In 1807, after almost 24 years service in India without furlough, his constitution being greatly debilitated, he obtained permission to proceed to Europe on furlough.

In 1807 he was promoted to the rank of full Captain in the Bengal corps of engineers, and in 1809, (perceiving that all further promotion was almost hopeless, and which has since been verified, for Capt. Blunt would only have been a supernumerary Major in the Bengal corps of engineers had he remained in it to this date, 1825,) he retired from the service.

This officer was also employed by the Governor-General in Council, with the late Capt. Cook, of the Royal Navy, then in command of His Majesty's ship, Sybille, and the late Mr. Golledge, Assistant Master Attendant, in surveying and reporting to the Government the most efficient measures to be adopted in the defence of the port and city of Calcutta, in the event of invasion from the sea; accounts having then been received of the sailing of the French armament from Toulon, and its destination for Egypt at that time not being ascertained.

---

which has animated the whole force under his command, and on the continuance of which every public benefit and individual advantage must arise.

" To Capt. Blunt, for the energy, zeal, and ability, with which he has uniformly conducted himself, the Colonel offers his very great acknowledgments.

" By reports received from Major Fletcher, since the issue of the morning orders, the conduct of the artillerymen, and gun lascars, with the six-pounders, and the Madras European regiment, under Capt. Custance, has been stated to Col. Harcourt, as conspicuous for spirit and gallantry: the Colonel has infinite satisfaction in expressing his high sense of their merits on all occasions.

" Extra batta to be issued to all the troops in camp."

LIEUT.-COLONEL J. A. PAUL MAC GREGOR.

(Bengal Establishment.)

This officer was appointed a Cadet on the Bengal establishment of the Hon. East India Company's service, in 1795; he arrived in India, 4th Feb. 1797; was promoted to Ensign, 15th Oct. 1796; to Lieutenant, 30th Oct. 1797; to Captain, 21st Sept. 1804; to Major, 4th June, 1814; and to Lieut.-Colonel, 12th Aug. 1818.

He served the whole of the campaign of 1799, in Mysore, against the late Tippoo Sultaun, and the rebel chieftain Doondia; he was present at the battle of Malavilly, 27th March 1799; also, at the siege of Seringapatam, and in the attack and capture of the entrenchments before that fortress, on the 21st and 26th of April following. He next served with a detachment of Bengal volunteers, under the command of Lieut.-Col. Gardiner *, in the Northern Circars, and was present at the capture of the fort of Polaveram, and two stockaded positions of the enemy, in April 1800.

He served in the campaigns of 1803, 4, and 5, with the grand army, under the personal command of the late Gen. Lord Lake, and was present at the battles of Delhi and Deeg, 11th Sept. 1803, and 13th Nov. 1804. He had one horse killed, and another wounded under him in the latter engagement; and owing to circumstances, which precluded the officer commanding the 1st batt. 2d reg. from being with it soon after the commencement of the action, viz. having been stunned by a cannon-shot, that killed the Major's orderly by his side, it fell to the lot of this officer, then Capt. Mac Gregor, as the next senior officer, being adjutant at the same time, to lead the corps out of the village, whence the British column debouched into action; on which occasion it captured some of the enemy's artillery, in their first line, which were turned by his orders, against their second, before he was relieved from the charge of the battalion, by the arrival on the ground of his superior officer.

* Services, vol. ii. p. 303.

He was next present at the seige of fort Sossing, and repulse of a sortie of the garrison; at the siege of Catchoura, Agra, Deeg*, and Bhurtpoor, and at the second assault of the latter fortress.

This officer served as adjutant of the 2d batt. of Bengal volunteers, and of the 1st batt. 2d reg. N. I., for six years and one month, chiefly during war; he was major of brigade, with the army, at the siege of Bhurtpoor, for four months; aid-de-camp to the Right Hon. Lord Minto, Governor-General, for three years and four months; and fort-adjutant of Fort-William, eight months. He was appointed deputy-military-auditor-general, in March 1813, which situation he holds at the present time.

From Jan. 1819, to the 1st of Jan. 1820, he officiated as Auditor-General; and his services in that capacity were approved of by the Governor-General in Council, as promulgated in the following general orders, dated Fort-William, 1st January 1820:—

"Lieut.-Col. Mac Gregor, Officiating-Military-Auditor-General, having furnished the prescribed certificate, from the pay department, has permission to proceed to Fort St. George, on urgent private affairs, and to be absent for four months from this date. The Most Noble the Gov.-Gen. in Council, feels much gratification in recording the sense which government entertains of the satisfactory manner in which Lieut.-Col. Mac Gregor conducted the duties of that important office, during the period it was under his charge.

(Signed)   "W. CASEMENT, L.-Col., Sec. to Gov. Mil. Dept."

THE LATE COL. JOHN A. BANNERMAN.
(Madras Establishment.)

THIS officer entered the East India Company's Military service, at the age of 17, and in the various stations which he successively

---

* Lieut.-Col. Mac Gregor having personally ascertained that the enemy had withdrawn from Deeg, entered that fortress, attended by his orderly, and was the first to send notice of its evacuation to head-quarters. On this occasion, when exploring the place, he was so fortunate as to discover treasure to a large amount, which in consequence of his exertions, and report to the Commander-in-Chief, was secured for the benefit of the capturing troops.

filled, both as a distinguished soldier, and an eminent member of the civil service, he rose by the decisive character of his merits alone.

In October 1789, he was appointed Resident at Travancore, and instructed to stimulate the Rajah to prepare troops for any eventual service, and to give every encouragement to brinjarries and bazarmen, to join the Bombay army : to restrain the Rajah from committing premature hostilities; to urge him to dismiss from his service and dominions all French and other foreigners; and to inform him, that if he desired it, they should be replaced by British subjects*. This service he executed to the entire satisfaction of Government.

During a long period of service, as an officer of the Madras army, which army he ever continued to regard with feelings of pride and attachment, he acquired high honour by his able and successful conduct, both in military and political capacities. He afterwards sat in Parliament for a short time; and was for many years an eminent member of the Court of Directors of the East India Company. In 1817, he retired from the Direction, and was, on the death of Mr. Petrie, appointed Governor of Prince of Wales' Island.

In the latter situation, he exercised the power with which he was entrusted in a manner worthy of his former reputation. With that active public spirit and inflexible integrity, which belonged to his character, he steadily pursued, under circumstances of uncommon difficulty, the course of proceeding which he firmly believed to be demanded, by the honour and true interests of his country.

Col. Bannerman's abilities were of a superior order: penetrating and sagacious, rapid in execution, yet guided by a judgment matured by long experience, he passed the various gradations of the service, with equal honour to himself and advantage to the Company. But distinguished as have been his public services, it is

* Beatson's "View of the Origin and Conduct of the War with Tippoo Sultaun."

chiefly in the recollection of his private virtues that the memories of his friends will love to dwell. His mind was endowed with every exalted sentiment, his heart filled with every amiable affection by which human nature is capable of being ennobled or adorned.

In the mingled language of eulogy and regret, the general order, dated Fort Cornwallis, 9th August 1819, issued on his decease, at the age of 61, records—

" That he was one whose zeal and anxiety to promote the public welfare were ardent and unceasing, and whose useful and honourable labours, marked alike by integrity and every manly virtue, were not confined to the sphere of this Presidency, but have been exemplified, and often publicly appreciated, during a period of upwards of 43 years, passed in the service of the Hon. East India Company, in various stations of difficulty, honour, and responsibility.'

THE LATE LIEUT.-COLONEL THOMAS SALKELD.

(Bengal Establishment.)

In 1780, this officer was appointed to an Ensigncy on the Bengal establishment; promoted to Lieutenant, 16th July 1781; to Captain, 7th January 1796; to Major, 21st September 1804; and to Lieut-Col., 1st January 1810.

After serving in some subordinate appointments, he succeeded to that of Quarter-Master-General to the Bengal army; and served under Lord Lake, in all his memorable campaigns in the Dooaub; and his admirable activity in that very important situation became the theme of praise of the whole army: no dangers or exertions repressed his zeal or sense of public duty.

The peculiar merits, however, of this valuable staff-officer, cannot be better exemplified than in the following general order, dated Fort William, February 17th 1807, on his returning to Europe:—

"The departure for Europe of Lieut-Col. Salkeld, Quarter-Master-General of the Bengal army, affords to the Commander-in-Chief an opportunity, which he embraces with sincere pleasure, for recording, in the general orders of this army, the character and conduct of that officer, which his Lordship with confidence recommends, as an example worthy of being emulated by all who are following in the same career of military exertion and renown.

"From the commencement until the close of the late war, Lieut.-Col. Salkeld filled one of the most important situations on the general staff of the army in the field, under his Lordship's personal command; during which extended period, the unabating zeal, indefatigable and laborious exertion, and the active spirit of gallantry invariably manifested by him on all occasions, not only in the discharge of the arduous duties of the Quarter-Master-General's department, but on several other duties on which he was employed, and, especially, in the superintendance of the guide and intelligence department,* which required peculiar ability, temper, and discernment, have not only established the pre-eminent claims of Lieut.-Col. Salkeld to the highest praise, and the most grateful acknowledgments which the Commander-in-Chief can bestow, but also entitle him to the honour of having his name recorded with those of the most meritorious officers who have zealously and faithfully served their country and the Hon. Company in this remote quarter of the globe."

Lieut.-Col. Salkeld retired from the service, 2d January 1810.

* It may here be remarked, that important objects and much success in India campaigns may frequently depend on paying liberally for correct intelligence, and the ingenious contrivances resorted to for obtaining accounts of the motions of an enemy in India. A penurious hand is ill suited for such occasions.

THE LATE MAJOR THOMAS BOLTON.

(Bengal Establishment.)

In 1767, this officer was appointed a Cadet on the Bengal establishment; Ensign, in 1768; Lieutenant, in 1770; and rose to the rank of Major, in 1784.

He commanded the 18th Native battalion, and which he brought to a high state of discipline*. This corps was with the force employed under Sir Robert Abercromby, in 1794, and was selected by him to form part of the reserve, with the European battalion, and the 13th Native infantry; which was posted on the right of the line in the battle which was fought on the 26th October in that year. The misbehaviour of the commanding officer † of the cavalry on that day, threw those fine corps into confusion; and the enemy's horse and foot getting in among them at the same time, a dreadful slaughter was the consequence; the enemy charged in wedges twenty deep.

Major Bolton being a very powerful man, cut down four of the enemy, when his sword breaking at the hilt, he was overpowered, and killed.

Major Bolton's battalion lost in this action 200 men killed and wounded. Such was their steadiness under arms, that it was observed, the killed and wounded were lying in their ranks, as regular as when drawn up on parade ‡.

---

* A friend of the Editor was with Lord Cornwallis at the review of Major Bolton's battalion, and he never saw more pleasure depicted on any countenance than on his Lordship's, on witnessing the admirable discipline of this distinguished corps.

† This officer made his escape from Rohilcund, entered the French service, and was in the Commissariat of Buonaparte's army. It is a singular fact, that during the whole of General Goddard's campaigns he served with distinction.

‡ See Williams's Bengal Army, p. 153.

THE LATE COLONEL PRIMROSE GALLIEZ.
(Bengal Establishment.)

This officer came a Captain into the Bengal army in 1764, from the Madras establishment, where he had previously served with much distinction. He was the particular friend of Vincent Row Berkie, who formerly commanded the troops of Mysore in the campaigns against Chunda Saheb.

Colonel Galliez, on his promotion, commanded the 2d Bengal brigade, with which he marched against the Rohillas, and served in the army under the command of Colonel Champion *, at the famous battle of St. George. In 1776, he resigned his command; and retiring to England, lived, much respected by a numerous circle of friends, beyond the age of fourscore, when he became so weak as to render it necessary to be always attended by a servant, lest he might fall into the fire. This really occurred: the servant stepping for something out of the room, on his return found the Colonel dead. He had fallen upon his head on the grate:—his head was burnt to a cinder.

CAPTAIN ALURED GIBSON.
(Madras Establishment.)

In August 1798, this officer landed at Madras, and obtained a commission in the 2d batt. of artillery on that establishment. When the army for prosecuting the war against Tippoo Sultaun was forming, under Gen. Harris, he joined it with his corps. Shortly after taking the field, the office of Quarter-master becoming vacant, he was appointed to that Staff situation, though then only about six months in the service. And during the march to Seringapatam, and so long after as the army continued together, he discharged the

* Services, vol. ii. p. 86-92.

duties of Brigade Quarter-master to the artillery; a service of considerable responsibility, and great fatigue, as it comprised the duties of the park. During the siege of Seringapatam, though labouring under a severe illness, he was included for duty, and was one of those who composed the left attack of the storming party. The greater part of this division forced its way into the body of the town; and the small portion that remained on the walls, from being vigorously opposed, soon lost all their officers and many men; and this officer was left, with about fifty soldiers only of H. M.'s service, to resist the whole body of the enemy; as those who fled from the right attack concentrated themselves against this position.

In this trying situation the men had expended the whole of their ammunition, and were on the point of falling back, when, knowing how fatal such a movement might prove, this officer called to them to maintain their ground, and to avail themselves of the ammunition of their dead and disabled companions, at the same time ordering the drummer to beat the grenadier's march, and pointing out to them the British flag, which had been hoisted by the British troops on the right attack. These had the desired effect; and they succeeded in restraining the enemy's advance until reinforcements came up, under the command of Capt. Lambton*, Major of brigade to General Baird†.

The two attacks having joined, Capt. Gibson was ordered, by Gen. Baird in person, to turn the guns of the fort on the flying enemy;

* Services, p. 100.

† Services, vol. ii. p. 60-75, Royal Military Calendar, 3d edit.; to which may be added the following very correct observation of Col. Stewart, in his Historical Sketches of the Highlands of Scotland:—

" History has seldom produced a more striking difference in the fortunes and circumstances of a man's life than in the case of this officer. He now entered as a conqueror within the walls of a town where he had been led in as a prisoner, and kept in chains for three years, suffering under the most cruel treatment. As a conqueror, he shewed a bright example of the difference between ferocious and generous minds. His revenge, when retaliation was in his power, was shewn by endeavouring to save the now prostrate enemy, and the inhabitants, from the fury of his troops, who knew what he and his brave fellow-sufferers had been made to endure, and were, consequently, more than usually exasperated."

and the first gun fired from Seringapatam on its late possessors, was pointed by this officer.

Capt. Gibson received one of the silver medals bestowed by the East India Company on the officers of their army employed on this service.

In 1802, he again accompanied his corps with the army under General Stuart, to the banks of the Toombuddra; whence the army, under Col. Wellesley, was sent forward to Poona. The invasion of the province of Cuttack was at the same time determined on; and Capt. Gibson was appointed to Ganjam, as Deputy Commissary of ordnance, to prepare the equipments for the troops, assembling there from Bengal and Madras, destined for that service. This garrison had been long neglected, and the arsenal consequently utterly deficient in many of the most important articles; however, by much individual exertion, every requisite was completed before the other departments were in readiness. At this time, Col. (late Sir Alex.) Campbell, commanded the northern division of the Madras army; and he was pleased to compliment Capt. Gibson, exclusively, in division orders, by his approbation of his zealous and efficient services.

Capt. Gibson accompanied the troops in charge of the ordnance departments, and succeeded in bringing up the whole of the ammunition and stores, without a single instance of loss or damage, to the walls of Cuttack, although the other departments suffered to a great extent from the deeply inundated state of the country the troops marched over. Of his services on this occasion, Col. Harcourt, who commanded, made favourable reports to the government of Madras; and to these testimonies may be attributed his appointment, in 1803, to the Commissaryship of ordnance at Masulipatam. In this situation he continued until 1811, when, from the increasing effects of bad health, which he suffered under uninterruptedly from his first arrival in India, he was compelled to return to England, where his hopes of re-establishing his health failing, he was, in 1813, induced, with great reluctance, to relinquish all thoughts of returning to India, and consequently retired on half-pay.

CAPTAIN MARSHAL CLARKE.

(Madras Establishment.)

This officer entered the service as a Cadet on the Madras establishment in 1807. He witnessed some of the turbulent scenes in the unhappy differences of 1809; served to the eastward, at Malacca, as Fort Adjutant in 1812 and 1813; at the new and sickly settlement of Banca, in 1814, 15, and 16, as Superintendent of public works, with from 300 to 400 Chinese, Malays, and Javanese, under his charge, encouraged and supported by Major Court*, the Resident. He constructed all the public buildings in brick and tiles there; formed roads, cleared the country, and rendered Mintao, the chief seat, a charming and healthy spot.

In 1817 he rejoined his regiment, Banca being ceded to the Dutch. He served during 1817, 18, and 19, under Sir Thomas Hislop, and was present at the battle of Mehidpoor, 21st Dec. 1817, and at the last affair, the capture of Asseerghur, under Brig.-Gen. (now Sir John) Doveton. In these campaigns he was personally engaged in repulsing two smart sorties of Arabs; at Malligawm in May 1818, and at Asserghur in March 1819; in the former of which, Lieut. Davies, a most valuable officer in the Madras engineers, fell; and in the latter, Lieut.-Col. Fraser, of the 1st foot, or Royals, with a few privates. In both of these affairs the decided nerve and superiority of European troops were proved.

Broken down in health, this officer returned to England early in 1820, and published the " Summary of the War in India," the chief heads of which may be thus classed:—" The treachery and weakness of the native princes; the feebleness and mildness of the human character

* Services, vol. i. p. 237-8.

in India. In nerve and vigour, generally speaking, unfit for hardy occupations; in military life, easily managed and trained, but easily shaken and routed. Importance of European troops in India; greater care in clothes, and diet in the field and hospital, required; paucity of European officers to corps—many taken away improperly upon trifling servic s, thereby injuring their regiments; mistaken policy in having introduced the native commissioned officers; mistaken lenity to some of those officers and sepoys found guilty of revolt and conspiracy in Java, and sentenced to death, but pardoned by Marquess Hastings, in 1815. Irregular troops of our allies, generally a rabble, and would be, if they durst, looties or maurauders. Danger and unfitness, in its present state, of the liberty of the press in India; greater danger from the rashness of missionary speculations and tampering; imprudence of allowing the power of ordaining native christians to the Bishop of Calcutta."

CAPTAIN JOSEPH JONES.

(Bombay Establishment.)

In 1808, this officer was employed with the grenadier battalion (in which he was Lieutenant) with the Poona subsidiary force under Col. Wallace, in the Bheer district, and at the capture of Sakrooda.

In 1812, he was employed with the 2d battalion 1st regiment during a commotion at Baroda, and the securing of Cannojee: in 1813, with his regiment in the Sunkeera district, keeping in check a body of Scindians, who disturbed the tranquillity of Baroda. In 1814, he accompanied his regiment, with the force under Col. George Holmes, from Baroda to Pahlunpoor, which was taken possession of by the British, and one wing of the 2d batt. 1st reg. left to garrison it.

In 1817, he served with his regiment at Poona, when the brigade quitted the old cantonments, and took up a position at Kirkee, and this officer was left in the old cantonments with 100 men, from the 1st Nov. till the morning of the 5th, when he was relieved; and shortly after arriving in the new camp, the Peishwa's army drew out in front, was attacked, and defeated by the force under Lieut.-Colonel Burr*.

The 2d batt. 1st reg. was immediately after ordered to form part of the force under Brig.-Gen. Lionel Smith, to pursue the Peishwa's retreating army to the southward, and after some marching returned to Seroor.

On the 31st Dec. this officer marched from Seroor at nine at night for Poona, with the 2d batt. 1st reg. under Capt. Staunton †, to whom he was next senior officer. They fell in with the Peishwa's army at Corygaum, which attacked them, but eventually was compelled to retreat.

Captain Jones retired from the service 3d September 1823.

THE LATE MAJOR GIDEON HUTCHINSON.

(Bombay Establishment.)

THIS officer entered the East India Company's military service in 1801. He was soon distinguished as a promising young officer, and became, at an early period of his residence in India, better acquainted than most men in that country, with the language, customs, and religion of the inhabitants of the East. At the time he was thus studiously employed, he did not forget he was a military servant of the Company's; and although he never had an opportunity of displaying his military talent in command, he was on many occasions, and particularly in the late Mahratta war, actively employed in the field, and stood appointed, during the campaign in the S. Concan,

* Services, vol. i. p. 350-65.

† Statement of Services, vol. i. p. 95-106, in which the particulars of the gallant action of Corygaum, and the general and division orders issued thereon, will be found, and which contain honourable mention of this officer.

in 1818, Interpreter to the force under the command of the late Col. David Prother, C. B.*, where he rendered most essential service, as he had it in his power, from his perfect knowledge of the Mahratta language, and local information, to procure intelligence highly useful to the Colonel, and creditable to himself. Indeed, owing to the favourable report which Col. Prother made of the useful talent of Major Hutchinson, the Gov.-in-Council was induced, on the completion of the service, to nominate him to a staff situation in the force, which was then about to quit Bombay, under the command of Major-Gen. Sir William Kier Grant †, to act against the troops of the Ranee of Sawant Warree, in Malwan, and ultimately appointed him to take charge of the political duties at that court: there he gave such satisfaction, that on the employment of a resident at Sawant Warree being thought no longer necessary, soon after his return to Bombay, Major Hutchinson was offered the residency at Mocha, which holding out a fair field for his abilities in the political line, and of making a handsome provision for his family, he accepted.

Major Hutchinson had been in delicate health for some time, and was urged to give up the above appointment, which he declined, still persevering in the execution of the Hon. Company's interest, and thus falling an early sacrifice to over zeal and anxiety, to do well the duties entrusted to his charge, leaving a widow ‡ and four children to mourn for their heavy loss.

CAPTAIN JOHN G. WILLIM.

(Bengal Establishment.)

IN 1798, this officer went to India a cadet; he served under different officers, and relieved the late Lieut.-Gen. Sir Ewen Baillie, in the

---

* Services, vol. i. p. 304-7. † Services, Royal Mil. Cal. vol. iii. p. 267-9, 3d edit.

‡ The widow of Major Hutchinson, accompanied by some European friends, went to the village where he died, and saw performed the last melancholy offices to her deceased husband, and afterwards followed his lamented remains to Tais, where they were interred.

command of Azimghur, a military cantonment and extensive city. He joined the division of the army employed in the reduction of the Bundlecund district, and commanded the 2d batt. 18th reg. N. I. He commanded five companies in the pettah before Fort Bursat, and after its surrender, he commanded the fortress. In this service he was honoured with the public thanks, in general orders, of the Commander-in-Chief, the late General Lord Lake.

He was next employed, under the late Lieut.-Gen. Sir Henry White, K. C. B.*, at the siege of Fort Gwalior, a certificate of whose approval of his service, he sent to the Court of Directors, as well as an authenticated certificate from the Staff officers who served in the division in Bundlecund, of his having received the thanks of Lord Lake, referred to above, in order to incline the Court to allow his return to India, he having repaired to England, in 1807, and, owing to illness, exceeded the maximum of leave, five years, allowed by act of Parliament: this request was refused, on the ground that his resignation had been sent to India, and that he had received his half-pay.

THE LATE LIEUT.-COLONEL WILLIAM FLINT.

(Madras Establishment.)

Whilst a Cadet, this officer was selected by Col. Braithwaite to obtain possession of Wandewash: he moved, on the night of the 10th of Aug. 1780, with one hundred firelocks, and after a fatiguing march, by deviating to unfrequented paths, he arrived, without interruption, in the vicinity of the fort, late in the forenoon of the 11th. After ascertaining that the place was still in possession of Mahommed Ally's troops, he sent a message to the killedar, announcing his approach, but was answered, that he should be fired at if he attempted to come within the range of his guns, and met a picquet to stop him at the verge of the esplanade. He had the address to per-

* Services, vol. i. p. 24-37.

suade the officer, that he had misapprehended his orders, which could only have been to stop the party till he was satisfied they were friends, of which he could entertain no doubts; and during the remainder of the parley continued to advance, persuading every successive messenger to return with another reference, until within musket-shot of the ramparts, which were manned with troops, and the gates distinctly seen to be shut. Here he halted, announced that he had a letter from the Newaub Mahomed Ally to the killedar, which he was ordered to deliver into his own hands, and demanded admission for that purpose with a few attendants: with this demand the killedar positively refused to comply, but at length agreed to receive the letter in the space between the gate and the barrier of the sortie. Lieut. Flint was admitted with four attendants, faithful and well-instructed sepoys, and found the killedar seated on a carpet, attended by several men of rank; thirty swordsmen, his usual guard, and 100 sepoys drawn up to protect him. After the first compliments, Lieut. Flint avowed that he had no letter from Mahomed Ally, but possessed that, which in the exigency of the times ought to be deemed equivalent, the order of his own government, written in communication with Mahomed Ally: this order the killedar treated with the utmost contempt, and his arguments with derision; desired him to return to the place he came from; and to the proposition of impossibility, from the increased distance of the corps from which he was detached, and the country being in possession of the enemy, he was answered with fresh sarcasm. He mildly replied, that he was placed in a desperate situation, and as the killedar rose to depart, he suddenly seized him, and announced his instant death if any person moved a hand for his rescue; the bayonets of the four sepoys were in the same instant at his breast, and their countenances announced a firm decision to share the fate of their officer. The consternation of the moment afforded time for the remainder of the detachment to rush in at the concerted signal, and effectually secure the killedar. Lieut. Flint then addressed the troops in the language of conciliation, explained the conditions on which the killedar should retain all the honours of command, while he himself should provide effectually for the defence of the fort; and, finally, the gates were opened, and the whole party entered together as friends.

The instrument for surrendering the place to Hyder Ally had been prepared, and was to receive the seal of the killedar on that very day, and during the interval in which Lieut. Flint awaited the authority of his government to exclude him from the fort, the killedar's incessant efforts at counteraction, were foiled by the address of the new commandant, who found means gradually and effectually to secure the attachment of the better portion of the garrison from the 12th August 1780, to the 12th February 1783*.

Lieut. Flint rose to the rank of Lieut.-Colonel in the Hon. Company's service: he retired from the service, 27th June 1798, and died in London in 1820.

THE LATE COLONEL COLIN MACKENZIE, C.B.
(Madras Establishment.)

THIS much-distinguished officer, and eminently scientific character, died on the 8th May 1821, at Chowringhee, near Calcutta, aged 68 years, 40 of which were passed in the Company's service, and rendered useful to his employers and to science in general, by the most active and indefatigable researches into the history and antiquities of India. The merits of Col. M., and the devotion of his whole time and fortune to the advancement of science, were rewarded

* Lieut. Flint's conduct during the siege of this place by Hyder has before been noticed, vide note, vol. i. p. 245-6, to which it may be added, that it is to be regretted, that the constitution of the Company in its Directorial and Proprietary capacity, has not admitted of stated Court Days, when every General and Field officer coming home on furlough, might be publicly received, and thanked personally, for important services in India. The Royal Commander-in-Chief has his fixed days for receiving officers, whether on public business or for ceremonious reception; and it may be truly said, that even for the latter cause, officers feel a gratification in being noticed for past services by the Head of the army. The want of these official public attentions at the India House is much felt by officers of the Honourable Company's army.

a few years since by his honourable employers, when they united the Surveyor-Generalship of the three Presidencies into one office, for all India, and appointed him to fill it. His disinterested friendship, high sense of honor, and singularly mild disposition, endeared him to all who knew him; the Highlands may justly consider him one of their brightest ornaments, for to the qualities of a gallant soldier and gentleman, he united the attainments of a man of profound science.

On the extension of the Order of the Bath, in June 1815, to the officers of the Company's army, Col. Mackenzie was appointed a Companion of the Order.

The following interesting letter, addressed by this officer to the Hon. Sir Alex. Johnstone, knt., at Ceylon, and dated Madras, Feb. 1st, 1817, contains an epitome of his life:—

"No one can have a fairer claim than yourself, to expect some account, however concise, of the nature of those inquiries, in which you are aware, my curiosity, if not my attachment to useful research, has induced me to embark, for much of the term of a continued residence in India, for several years. On the chief predisposing causes of a course so foreign to the general habits of military men, and for which I was so little prepared by early instruction, it were unnecessary for me to enlarge; I must, however, attribute some part to the early seeds of passion, for discovery and acquisition of knowledge, and to ideas first implanted in my native isle. To these, I may add a further stimulus, in the contemplation of the opportunities too often neglected, or passed over in doubt, for want of conviction of the utility of efforts, that if steadily directed, might in many instances, acquire and preserve a body of information, useful to the more regular process of investigation, conducted on more permanent principles. That in the midst of camps and the bustle of war, and of travel and voyages, the human mind may be exercised to advantage, has been long known and acknowledged; and although all " that a Cæsar wrote, or a Camoens sung," may not be reached by every military adventurer, it is nevertheless universally acknowledged, as a celebrated sage of antiquity (Tacitus) writes, " that the human mind can expand to the occasion." That science may derive helps, and knowledge be diffused in the leisure moments of camps and voyages, is no new discovery; but in complying with your wish, I am also desirous of proving, that in the vacant moments of an Indian sojourn and campaign (for what is the life of an Indian adventurer, but one continued campaign on a most extensive scale?) the collected observations of leisure time, and vacant moments, may be found useful, at least, in directing the observation of those more fortunately gifted, to matters of utility, if not to record facts important to philosophy and science. The first 13 years of my life in India, from 1783 to 1796, may be fairly considered as of little moment to the objects pursued latterly, in collecting observations and notices of Hindoo manners, of geography, and of history. With every attachment to this pursuit, to which my attention was engaged before I left England, and not devoid of opportunities in India; yet the circumscribed means of a subaltern officer, a limited knowledge of men in power or office, and the necessity of prompt attention to military and professional duties, would not admit of that undeviating attention, which is so necessary to the success of any pursuit at all times, much more so, to what must be extracted from the various languages, dialects, and characters, of the peninsula of India. In particular, a knowledge of the native languages, so essentially requisite, could never be regularly cultivated, in consequence of the frequent changes and removals, from province to province, from garrison to camp, and from one desultory duty to another. Proper encouragement to study the languages of the vast countries that have come under our domination, since my arrival in India, were reserved for more happy times, and for those who might be more fortunate in having leisure for their cultivation; from the evils of famine, penury, and war, the land was then slowly emerging; and long struggling under miseries of bad management, before the immediate administration of the south, came under the benign influence of the British government. In the whole of this period, in which I have marched or wandered over most of the provinces south of the Kistna, I look back with regret to objects now known to exist, that might have been then examined, and to traits of customs and of institutions that might have been explained, had time or means admitted of the inquiry.

" It was only after my return from the expedition to Ceylon in 1796, that accident, rather than design, (though ever searching for lights that were denied to my situation) threw in my way those means that I have since unceasingly pursued, (not without some success, I hope) of penetrating beyond the common surface of the antiquities, the history, and the institutions of the south of India.

" The connexion I then formed with one person, a native and a Brahmin *, was the first step of my introduction into the portal of Indian knowledge. Devoid of any knowledge of the languages myself, I owe to the happy genius of this individual, the encouragement and the means of obtaining what I had so long sought. In the 10th page of the enclosed papers, you will observe that fifteen different dialects, and twenty-one characters, were necessary for this purpose. On the reduction of Seringapatam, in 1799, not one of our people could translate from the Canarese alone; at present we have these translations made not only from the modern characters, but the more obscure, I had almost said obsolete characters of the Sassanums, (or inscriptions in Canarese and in Tamul); beside what have been made from the Sancrit, of which, in my first years in India, I could scarcely obtain any information. From the moment the talents of the lamented Boria were applied, a new avenue to Hindoo knowledge was opened; and though I was deprived of him at an early age, his example and instructions were so happily followed up by his brethren and disciples, that an establishment was gradually formed, by which the whole of our provinces might be

---

* The lamented C. V. Boria, a Brahmin, then almost a youth, of the quickest genius and disposition, possessing that conciliatory turn of mind, that soon reconciled all sects and all tribes to the course of inquiry followed in these surveys. After seven years service, he was suddenly taken off from these labours, but not before he had formed his younger brothers, and several other useful persons of all castes, Brahmins, Jains, and Malabars, to the investigations that have since been satisfactorily followed.

analyzed, on the method thus fortuitously begun, and successfully followed so far. Of the claims of these individuals, and the superior merits of some, a special representation has lain before this Government, since the 26th September last, yet unanswered; how they are to be disposed of, on my departure for Bengal, is still in doubt. The attachment existing, and increased during the space of from eighteen to twenty years, leaves me no room to doubt that some will adhere to my fortune; but it is to be confessed, that there will be some hazard in exchanging a state of moderate comfort with their families, for a state of dependance in a distant country; and this uncertainty of an adequate provision for these useful people, renders my situation at present more uncomfortable than I wish to say. For these 13 years, therefore, there is little to shew beyond the journals and notes of an officer employed in all the campaigns of the time; first, towards the close of the war of 1783, in the provinces of Coimbetoor, and of Dindigul; afterwards on professional duties in the provinces of Madras, Nellore, and Goontoor; throughout the whole of the war from 1790 to 1792 in Mysore; and in the countries ceded to the Nizam by the peace of 1792; and from that period engaged in the first attempts to methodize and embody the geography of the Deccan; attempts that were unfortunately thwarted or impeded by measures not necessary to be here detailed. The voyage and campaign in Ceylon (1795-6), may be noticed as introductory to part of what followed, on my return to resume the geography of the Deccan in 1797.

"Some voluntary efforts for these purposes at last excited the notice of a few friends in the field, in the campaigns in Mysore, too partial, perhaps, to my slender talents, and my ardour for the pursuit; and in 1792, after the peace of Seringapatam, I was sent a subaltern from the army in Mysore, by the desire of the late revered Lord Cornwallis, with the small detachment first employed in the Nizam's dominions, for the purpose of acquiring some information of the geography of these countries, and of the relative boundaries of the several states, then assuming a new form and new limits. From 1792 to 1799, it were tedious to relate the difficulties, the accidents, and the discouragements, that impeded the progress of this design; the slender means allotted, from the necessity of a rigid (no doubt a just) economy; the doubts and the hindrances ever attendant on new attempts; difficulties arising from the nature of the climate, of the country, and of the government; from conflicting interests, passions, and prejudices difficult to contend with, and unpleasant to recollect. In the year 1796, a general map of the Nizam's dominions was submitted to Government for the first time, compiled and digested from various materials, and from various authorities, described in a memoir that accompanied it, and chiefly designed as a specimen for future correction, and to shew what was wanting, as well as what was done. It had, however, the use of bringing the subject into one point of view. Further inquiry improved its supplements in 1798-9, and some encouragement was then held forth that induced perseverance, though little effectual assistance was given. My removal from any share in the direction of the Deccan surveys, in 1806, put a stop to the further improvement of this map; yet the subject has not been neglected, and it is hoped that it will one day be resumed, on the revisal of the materials since collected, though on a more circumscribed scale than was at first intended.

"On returning to Hyderabad, in 1798, for the third time, to resume the investigations of Deccan geography, measures were proposed, and in part methodized, for describing the whole Deccan; and before 1799, considerable help was attained by obtaining a copy of the regular official dufter of the Deccan, in its provincial and even minuter divisions. This document has been since translated from the Persian, as well as certain MSS. of authority, which were proposed as the basis of the plan to be followed in the inquiry and description. The Deccan was, in fact, then a *terra incognita*, of which no authentic evidence existed, excepting in some uncertain notices and mutilated sketches of the marches of Bussy, and in the Travels of Tavernier and Thevenot, which convey but little satisfaction to the philosophical accuracy of modern times. This plan, in its bud, was nearly overset by the new war with Tippoo, in 1799.

It may be satisfactory, however, to know that the attempts then made were not without use, both in a military light (as described more fully in official reports) and in anticipating measures that have since, or may be still, advantageously followed, in arranging the history, antiquities, and statistics of that interesting country.

" After the reduction of Mysore, in 1799, and in the arrangements that followed, I was employed in assisting the commissioners with geographical information, as well as in the general arrangement, and in the acquisition of a correct knowledge of the subject of partition. On my return to Madras, the Gov.-General, the Earl of Mornington, being justly of opinion that a more complete knowledge of these countries was indispensably necessary for the information of Government, was pleased, in the handsomest manner, without solicitation or any personal knowledge, to appoint me to survey Mysore. I was provided, however, with an establishment suited rather to an economical scale of expenditure, than to so extensive an undertaking, to be carried through a country as yet so little known, that the positions of some of the provinces, ceded by the treaty of partition, could not be ascertained*, till this survey was advanced, under peculiar circumstances of embarrassment. Consonant to my original ideas, I considered this occasion favourable for arranging a scheme of survey, embracing the statistics and history of the country, as well as its geography; and submitted a plan for this purpose, which was approved by this government. Three assistants and a naturalist† were then, for the first time, attached to me; yet this moderate establishment was immediately after disapproved in England, and a design that had originated in the most enlightened principles, was nearly crushed by the rigorous application of orders too hastily issued, received in India about the end of the year 1801, when I had, at very considerable hazard to my health, just completed the survey of the northern and eastern frontier of Mysore. How far the idea

* For instance, Hollallkaira ceded to the Mahrattas, Goodicatta on the N. W. of Chittledroog, mistaken for a small port north of Colar, in the east of Mysore; and many other instances, whence some knowledge of the country rendered a survey indispensable.

† Mr. Mather, Lieutenants Warren and Arthur, Assistant Surveyors, and Dr. Heyne, Surgeon and Naturalist.

suggested was fulfilled, it is not for me to say. From adverse circumstances, one part was nearly defeated, and the natural history was never analyzed in the manner I proposed and expected, in concert with the survey. The suspense I was placed in from the reduction of the slender stipend allotted to myself, both for my salary and to provide for increasing contingencies, was not only sufficiently mortifying, but involved the overthrow of the establishment first arranged for the work. The effects of these measures on the public mind, and on the energies of my assistants, contributed to paralyze every effort for the completion of my undertaking. Notwithstanding these difficulties, the success attending the first researches, and a conviction of the utility of the work, induced me to persevere till 1807, in investigating the geography of the provinces of Mysore in the minutest degree, over 40,000 square miles of territory. Considerable materials were also acquired illustrative of statistics, and of the history of that country; and the basis was laid for obtaining a general knowlege of the whole peninsula, on a plan undeviatingly followed up ever since. Much of the materials collected on this occasion were transmitted home in seven folio volumes, with general and provincial maps; but it is proper to observe, that still more considerable materials for the history of the south are in reserve, not literally belonging to the Mysore survey, though springing from the same. It is also proper to notice, that in the course of these investigations, and notwithstanding the embarrassments of the work, the first lights were thrown on the history of the country below the ghauts, which have been since enlarged by materials constantly increasing, and confirming the information acquired in the upper country. Among various interesting subjects may be mentioned—1. The discovery of the Jain religion and philosophy, and its distinction from that of Boudh*. 2. The ancient different sects of religion in this country,

* In allowing just credit to Col. Mackenzie on this subject, it is proper to observe, that much of the discovery respecting the Jains being a distinct class from the Baudkas and the orthodox Hindoos, together with other important facts relating to them, is to be attributed to the profound researches of that distinguished gentleman and first Oriental scholar in Europe, Mr. Colebrooke, the Director of the Royal Asiatic Society of Great Britain and Ireland.

and their subdivisions: the Lingavunt, the Saivam, and Pandarum Mutts, &c. &c. 3. The nature and use of the sassanums, or inscriptions on stone and copper, and their utility in throwing light on the important subject of Hindoo tenures; confirmed by upwards of 3,000 authentic inscriptions, collected since 1800; always hitherto overlooked. 4. The design and nature of the monumental stones and trophies found in various parts of the country, from Cape Comorin to Delhi, called Veeracull and Maastee-cull; which illustrate the ancient customs of the early inhabitants, and perhaps of the early western nations. 5. The sepulchral tumuli, mounds, and burrows of the early tribes, similar to those found throughout the continent of Asia and of Europe, illustrated by drawings and various other notices of antiquities and institutions.

" On the conclusion of the field duties of the Mysore survey, the compilations resulting from it have, at different times, occupied much attention since. An office was conferred on me in Mysore, which was afterwards confirmed by the Court of Directors' favourable opinion, for the purpose of following up the investigations, and digesting and improving these materials in some tranquillity; but, on a reform of some branches of the military establishment, in 1810, that department was entirely new modelled, and my appointment ceased, without any compensation in salary or otherwise for what I then lost. The Hon. Court, in that order, had signified their approbation of what had been done, and even issued orders encouraging the further pursuit.

" About the end of 1810, the Government of Madras, on a review of the sudden increase of the expense of surveys in the last five years, and of the unconnected, confused manner in which these works were executed, without any general fixed system, found it necessary to create an office of Surveyor General, as already established at the other presidencies; and were pleased to appoint me (without any previous communication with me) to this charge, for reasons that I had in vain attempted to shew the advantage of for fourteen years previously. In consequence of the little countenance given to these propositions in Europe, I had, on the completion of the Mysore survey, relinquished all view of conducting what would have been gratifying to early habits, and more appropriate to my health and time of life some years before; and I only undertook the charge at this time, in the hope of being able to assist in giving shape and order to what I had long considered might be useful to the public, and beneficial, in an economical view, to the East India Company.

"In March 1811, I became employed in arranging this office, proposed 14 years before, for carrying on these duties in future, and for combining the execution and results of the several works on one general systematic plan; with measures for preserving and digesting the various materials resulting from the labours of several years back, in concert with a very considerable reduction * of expences; when, from the exigencies of the military service, my professional attendance on the expedition to Java was required, by the concurring authorities of government; and I had only time to deposit the materials then collected into office, and to submit the mode of its direction, during my absence, my attention being called, as above stated, to the pressing calls of the expedition. Of that service, wherein I embarked with all alacrity, in submissive obedience to the wishes and orders of my superiors, several detailed reports were submitted to the government in India, to which my friends need have no scruple in referring; although a copy, which was sent to this presidency in June 1813, appears not to have been brought on record, as, in justice to me, I conceive it should have been long ago. It may not be improper here to observe, that the plan proposed for the Surveyor-General's department in 1810, besides the very considerable reduction of the expense incurred of late years, for various widely unconnected, and I may add inefficient establishments of survey, embraced (at the same time with a gradual extension on one regular

* In the very first year ending 1st Dec. 1810, the annual expence was reduced from 85 or rather 100,000 pagodas per annum, to 55,000 pagodas, by the operation of the plan submitted, and this with more effect, than in the former unconnected system, as appears from a table of five years' expence presented to government, on 30th April 1816.

system, together with the usual objects of goegraphical delineation) a body of statistical and historical materials, added to the mass of geographical and military surveys, then collected and deposited by me in one office, for the first time, before my departure. Among these is a copy of the memoirs of the statistical and geographical survey of the Mysore country, with the original sections, charts, and maps, constructed from them on various scales, from one to twenty-four miles, which were among the first of the official documents delivered into the office of the Surveyor-General, under the inspection of a special committee, early in 1811.

"Of the Mysore survey the detailed reports stand on the records of the government of Fort St. George, and copies are sent home to England. Respecting the opinions of the authorities at home, on the close of that work, the annexed extract is referred to, (Letter, page 328.) On its final completion, in March 1809, the remaining establishment of Native surveyors was sent, on my special representation, to the ceded districts, which have been since surveyed; thereby almost completing an entire survey of all the dominions of the late sovereignty of Mysore, as it existed a few years ago, in the plenitude of its power and territory. This work adds 30,000 square miles to the 40,000 formerly reported on (Letter, page 328); being altogether 70,000 square miles minutely analyzed. The direction of this survey of the ceded districts was voluntarily conducted in Oct. 1808, without any particular compensation, until it fell into the general superintendence of the Surveyor-General's office, in Dec. 1810, which arrangement is now again reversed, and the duty transferred to the Surveyor-General of India.

"While these works were in progress, the collection of materials on the history, antiquities, and statistics of the country, was extended throughout the whole of the provinces under the presidency of Fort St. George, formed on the basis of the lights originally obtained on the Mysore survey, by natives trained and instructed by me for this purpose; and with the only burthen to government of the postage being franked, and the aid of some of the native writers: but all the purchases have been entirely at my private expence, as well as the collection of MSS. throughout the Carnatic, Malabar, the southern Provinces, the Circars, and the Deccan. The papers annexed*, explain the progress of this branch during the period of my absence in Java. I regret that I cannot at present recur to other documents, more fully explanatory of the extent and nature of these researches into the ancient history and present state of the south of India, as the greatest part of the collection has been sent on to Calcutta, to wait my arrival at that Presidency.

"A detailed view of the origin and progress of that work alone (the Historical Investigations) would more properly be the subject of a separate Memoir. A concise view of a similar attempt made in Java† is annexed‡. Effected under limitations of time and means, regu-

---

* See " Brief View of the Collection of Notes, Observations, and Journals, of 34 years; and of Collections of MSS. Inscriptions, Drawings, &c. for the last 19 years, made by Col. Mackenzie in India; exclusive of a considerable Collection of Native MSS. in all languages," published in the Asiatic Journal for April 1822. Our limits prevent the insertion of this interesting document, and we must therefore refer our readers to that miscellany of Asiatic intelligence.

† For his services in Java, Col. Mackenzie had the honour of receiving the medal conferred for the attack and capture in August and September 1811.

‡ *General View of the Results of Investigations into Geography, History, Antiquities, and Literature, in the Island of Java, by Col. Mackenzie, in the years* 1811, 1812, *and* 1813. (*Extracted from a short View of Researches in Java.*)

1. In the geographical and hydrographical branches, complete registers have been taken of the numerous atlasses, plans, charts, and memoirs, belonging to the Dutch government, since its establishment, from 1612 till the year 1811. Among these are to be found detailed regular surveys of several of the Eastern provinces, on a plan which Col. Mackenzie recommended to our government in Java, to be gradually carried on at no great expense. This was intended to be the subject of a particular report, which he proposed to accompany with a detailed register§ of these documents, and of numerous charts of different descriptions supposed to be in depôt with the present government.

II. Of military plans, numerous pieces exist still, though some of them, particularly connected with the views of the late government, are unattainable, and supposed to be lost in the confusion attending the victory and retreat of Cornelis: those remaining appear in the register. There is reason to think that much of the contents of the depôts at the *Bureau de Génie*, and the plans of military movements, were lost at the period referred to, or carried off.

III. Of the resources and revenues of the island: the whole, it is believed, are saved of the

---

§ This register was presented to the government of Fort William on the 18th Feb. 1815.

lated by local circumstances; but under a liberal degree of encouragement and protection, both from the local government there and

numerous memoirs, reports, and productions, arising from the discussions and plans of reform of late years, where the opinions and sentiments of the most intelligent and experienced men in India and Holland are to be found, the result of their reasoning, with a vast body of information in memoirs, reports, and documents* in the depôts of archives, which, previous to the late government of Marshal Daendels, were preserved on a regular systematic plan. The indexes, or rather abstracts, of the proceedings and resolutions of the government from its first establishment, were particularly curious: under the heads *Realia*, *Secret Realia*, *Personalia*, and *Miscellanea*, reference might be made with ease to any subject that had ever occupied the deliberations and orders of government. There is reason to believe the *Miscellanea*, consisting of eight volumes, were lost; at least they could not be found on inquiry, since the reduction of Java.

2. The reports of the Committee of Archives, translations of which it is believed have been sent to India, will fully explain the number and description. Col. Mackenzie, confining himself more particularly to the geographical and hydrographical parts, only brought copies of the reports relating to them, and of the register of reports and memoirs from the dependencies, particularly such as regarded India.

3. It may be proper here to notice, that in the course of inspection of the archives and library of the late government, he casually lighted on a series of memoirs or reports of the Dutch governors and directors in Coromandel, from 1612 to 1771, carried regularly on from one director or governor to another. One of the most material to us, is a collection or register of all treaties, contracts, perwannas, and grants, between the Dutch government and the Native powers of the south of India: a copy † of this volume was taken, as it was conceived to be useful in fixing dates, facts, privileges, and claims. The other volumes, besides the instructions of the first governors, give a view of the nature of the commerce, and concise views of the political state of the different countries at the time, though not all equally interesting—as the memoirs or reports of the governors or directors of Ceylon, Surat, and Hoogly in Bengal, and of the Spice Islands, &c. &c.

4. In the same deposits are a complete series of the despatches and letters of the government of Batavia to Europe, consisting of many volumes, which undoubtedly contain many interesting facts and documents regarding the policy and history of these once opulent establishments. As these volumes are in the Bibliothèque, and it is doubtful whether they are included in the report of the Committee of Archives, they are particularly adverted to here. It was a peculiar trait of the Dutch government that complete memoirs, or memories,

* The whole of the voluminous minutes, correspondence, and proceedings, of the Commission sent from Holland in 1793, of which Mr. Nedenburg was President, and which terminated in 1800, are deposited in a great Almyra, or cabinet. Mr. Nedenburg afterwards returned to Holland, and was one of the leading members of the Secret Committee on India affairs that sat at the Hague, whose final report, in 1807, seems to have been the basis on which the plans adopted by the late government of Holland for their Oriental colonies was founded.

† This is one of the works translated at Serampoor since January last, and sent to government, April 1816.

from two successive Governors-General of British India, and without any expense to government on that account, the success of these

were usually given in by the Governors-General, and those of the dependencies, to their successors, on being relieved; and as the whole of them were furnished with very complete indexes, reference was ready and easy to any particular subject or fact before the archives were thrown into confusion, and many lost on their removal from the castle of Batavia in 1808; and afterwards, from the events attending the reduction of Java. To restore them to some order, would be desirable to the future historian of Oriental commerce and possessions; if not, in a political point of view, to the British supreme government of India.

IV. Of the history and antiquities of the island of Java considerable materials have been obtained by Col. Mackenzie's immediate exertions. Little indeed had been done in Java by Europeans in regard to such inquiries, since the time that Valentyn published his useful but voluminous work on the Dutch East India Company's settlements, in six folio volumes, in 1724; and although a society of sciences had been established a few years previous to our's in 1780, but little progress had been made in developing the history of the Eastern islands, and the society itself had fallen into decline (although not absolutely extinct) since the commencement of the revolution. Of the laudable efforts to revive it since the British government was established, this may not be the appropriate place to speak. Under the patronage of the supreme government, should Java remain a British colony, it may be hoped still to contribute essentially to the general culture of science, of commercial economy, and of useful knowledge in these parts.

2. Col. Mackenzie's first efforts were particularly directed to this object of investigation, the progress and actual state of knowledge, and of the history and antiquities of the island; and it is due, in justice to several respectable individuals in Java, British and Dutch, to say, that much ready and cordial aid was furnished in the prosecution of these researches.

3. Some of the colonists, who had paid attention to these subjects, a circumstance not very general in Java, very readily communicated the aid of their knowledge and experience in directing the pursuit, and pointing out the sources and individuals that could further assist. To conciliate the minds of men, and remove difficulties arising from prejudices of education and religion, and from the variety of languages, the experience acquired in India was found of great advantage: but the powerful aid of the penetrating acute genius of the Brahmins, which had been of such importance in India, was here wanting; and the languages presented obstacles of no common degree. It was necessary not only to employ translators from the Dutch, French, and Malay, but it was extremely rare to find persons capable of rendering Javanese MSS.* into either of these languages previous to an English version. The difficulty of procuring any of the colonists capable of acting as interpreters, was considerable, from the rarity of these necessary qualifications, and from a repugnance to travelling and fatigue, arising from indolence, and from habits widely dissimilar from our's. In the interior, the Malay language was of little use, and the Javanese, in its several dialects, had been little studied by the European colonists in Java. These few

* An ingenious native of Java has since this accompanied Col. Mackenzie to India, and has already made some progress in translating from the Javanese.

investigations justify the hope, that considerable advantage may be derived from following up the same plan of research, wherever the

were in the service of government, and there were but few on the island capable of rendering a letter from the Javanese into Dutch.

4. Notwithstanding these obstacles, and the discouraging prospect held out by those who had the best pretensions, from long residence, to know the native character and their literary attainments, it is satisfactory to observe, that the conclusion of this journey produced an accession of knowledge and of lights that had been by no means hoped for, even in the most sanguine expectations.

5. The colonists were found willing to assist and produce their stores, and the Natives were soon reconciled, even the class whose interests might be presumed to traverse, if not oppose these inquiries. The Regents and their dependents were, though at first shy, ultimately cordial assistants in regard to the objects of investigation; and on the eve of leaving the eastern districts, and to the last moment of Col. Mackenzie's stay at Batavia, materials, MSS. and memoirs, in copy or original, with letters in reply to the questions circulated, were transmitted from the most distant parts: in fact, as in Mysore, and other parts of India, the same causes had the same effects. Inquiries before little known, and at first held in suspicion, being found to have no other object than a laudable research into history, laws, customs, and literature, to assist the rulers to protect the subjects, and ameliorate their condition, by a more perfect knowledge of their own institutions; all ranks appeared to concur in supporting what they found attended by no deviation from good faith, and tending to conciliate their feelings and prejudices.

To conclude: what is intended is a general view of the results of these inquiries, until the arrangement of the materials enable a more detailed report to be made up. The following may be considered an abstract of a collection of materials formed for illustrating the history, antiquities, and institutions of Java.

One hundred and seventy-one sections[*], rather than volumes, of paper MSS., written in characters of Java and of the Malay, but all in the Javanese language. Catalogues of them are made out; but difficulties occur in getting them translated, that can only be removed by the interposition of government. Most of them are on paper: some were saved from the wreck of the Sultaun's library at the storm of the Craten of Djocjacarta, by the permission of the prize agents, and the concurrence, indeed, of all the military present. Others were purchased and collected on the tour through the island. Some were presented by Dutch colonists and by Regents, and others are transcripts by Javanese writers, employed by Col. Mackenzie to copy them from the originals in the hands of Regents, and with their permission. Several of these are historical. A few of the lesser and more curious tracts, were translated into the European languages during his stay in Java. A considerable number of papers, containing a series of Voyangs, or Javanese dramas, which are still a popular and expensive subject of exhibition with the native chiefs of Java.

Twenty-four MSS., written on Cadjan leaves in the Hindoo manner: most of them are

[*] Several of these here enumerated are in paper sections, quarto and octavo; and Col. Mackenzie has got them bound up, at Calcutta, into portable volumes for their better preservation: probably the whole may amount to forty volumes.

influence of the British government affords the same facilities, in the intervals of military occupations.

in the Javanese character, and some are in a character yet undeciphered. From explanations of the titles of some, they appear to belong to the ancient (or Dewa) religion of these islands; but though a native of superior intelligence was found capable of reading them, the prejudices of religion prevented any further information of the contents of books supposed to be adverse to the Mahomedan tenets. This difficulty might, however, have been got over. These MSS. are apparently ancient, and were brought by the civility of a Regent from a long deserted house in the distant forests, where they had lain neglected for years.

Thirty-five volumes of Dutch MSS., in folio, quarto, and octavo, consisting of historical works, memoirs, and reports; some translated from the Javanese into Dutch. Some of these are original; others were copied, by permission, from MSS. in the hands of private individuals, and a few of the most valuable were purchased *. Some of the most remarkable of them are, 1st. A complete History of Java, in three quarto volumes, translated into Dutch; giving its history from the first colonization to the year 1807; the original apparently written by a native. This is now nearly translated into English. 2. Ancient History of Java; containing its fabulous history, in two volumes quarto, in Dutch. This appears to have been compiled from the ancient Mythological Poems, Voyages, or Dramas, of Java; and communicated by the liberality of a Dutch gentleman, by whose desire they were translated. 3. A Dictionary † of the Javanese language into Dutch, communicated by its author, still living at Samarang. 4. Several other abridged memoirs and historical materials, relating to Java; descriptions and reports relating to Batavia, and to the island in general, and its climate; with memoirs on commercial and political subjects. 5. Copy of a Grammar in the ancient Tamul, in Grundum character, written in India, with copies of some ancient inscriptions, transcribed from the original in the library of the Society of Sciences at Batavia; and a variety of memoirs illustrative of the statistics and geography of Java, composed at Col. Mackenzie's request. 6. Extracts and copies of some memoirs and abridgments addressed to the Hon. the Lieut.-Gov., Mr. Raffles, who liberally communicated them. They are in answer to queries and suggestions recommended to particular persons more conversant in the customs and history of the country, by Colonel Mackenzie.

Ancient Inscriptions, Coins, and *Sculptures*, in every country, assist materially in developing the ancient history and origin of nations, of institutions, and of the arts and sciences. In India the pursuit has been so successful that it could scarcely be omitted in Java.

* It is necessary to observe, that all these are exclusive of the Memoirs and Reports belonging to the Committee of Tenures, which are official, and belong to Government, though every liberal indulgence was granted by the Governor, Mr. Raffles, and access given to official records. The collection here specified is wholly distinct from these, and entirely private property.

† Attempts are making to form a Javanese and English dictionary from this, but for want of assistants this work is delayed; Col. Mackenzie brought one Javanese with him, who has been assisting to render it, by means of the Malay, into the English language.

" On my return to this presidency, in 1815, I found the office of Surveyor-General at Madras was ordered to be abolished; and before I could well go into the revisal and completion of the review of

Inscriptions.—Setting modern inscriptions out of the question, about twenty inscriptions or sassanums in ancient characters have been discovered in Java, only one of which had been noticed, and that slightly, by European authors (the *Batoo Toolis*)*. Fac-similes have been taken of them, and copies are intended to be communicated to the Society at Calcutta, and to any other desirous of the communication. Three different characters are used in them, all yet undeciphered. One alone, in the Deva Nagri character, was found on the visit to Prambana.

Ancient Coins.—A small collection has been made. A few are Chinese and Japanese; most of them of a kind hitherto unnoticed by any European collector, perforated in the centre by a square opening, and bearing a variety of figures, resembling those of the Voyangs or Javanese plays: none of these coins are to be found, even in the collection of the Batavian Society. They are usually dug up, with other vestiges of antiquities, near places that have been destroyed by volcanic eruptions. It is singular, that a few coins of the same Chinese kind were found some years ago in a distant part of the Mysore country; and one also among the ancient coins recently discovered at Mavelliporam, near Madras, a circumstance that points at early commercial communication between the Oriental islands and continents with India.

Ancient Sculptures and images are frequently met with in Java; some indicating the existence of the Hindoo mythology at a certain period: most of them relate to the Baudhist and Jain doctrines. Some few specimens of the small copper images dug up were obtained, and drawings have been taken of all the remains of architecture and sculpture that were discovered in the tract of this tour. Several of these drawings relate to the interesting remains of Prambana, said to be a very early, and the most ancient capital of the dominion, arts, and literature of Java; a particular memoir of its present state was communicated to the Society of Batavia, and has been published in the seventh volume of their transactions, but without the drawings of curious sculptures, as no engraver was to be found at Batavia.

Col. Mackenzie has thus attempted to convey a hasty, but, he trusts, correct idea of some of the objects that have occupied much of his time in Java; for besides those observations, in a military and political view, that might be expected from his professional situation on the late expedition, it was also necessary to pay attention to the inquiries and objects of the commission on tenures and lands, &c. in Java, to which he was appointed in Jan. 1812, when on the journey to the eastward.

In conclusion, he apprehends that ample materials are collected to give a pretty clear view of the present state of Java; and if the materials, now considerably increased, should assist in affording any illustration of the ancient history and geography of that island, it will be gratifying if his exertions have in the least degree contributed to such result, or should yet stir up a spirit of inquiry, that may be usefully applied to fill up the outlines he has ventured to trace.

Fort William, Nov. 10, 1813.

* Thunberg's Voyages.

the survey department commenced in 1811, and which had been discontinued in consequence of my being sent on foreign service, I was honoured with the appointment of the office of Surveyor-General of India on a new system, which requires residence at Calcutta or Fort William. My attention has, in consequence, been chiefly turned to that object ever since, with the view of fulfilling the Hon. Court's intentions in an appointment which I must ever consider an honourable mark of their distinction, that justly demands efforts that I had no longer in contemplation.

" In this place it would be foreign, perhaps, to make any remarks on this particular subject, or the cause of my detention hitherto here, particularly since October last. Viewing it on public grounds, if the East India Company are benefitted, the consequences, though very detrimental to my personal convenience and interests, may be less matter of regret; and I may be permitted to hope, that the continued close application of my time, at this period of life, and its effects on my health, will be ultimately viewed with more consideration than I have hitherto found in the present administration of Madras. I will only further notice the effect of this removal on the inquiries and collection here described. The individuals reared by me for several years, being Natives of the coast, or the southern provinces, and almost as great strangers to Bengal and Hindostan as Europeans, their removal to Calcutta is either impracticable, or where a few, from personal and long attachment (as my head Brahmin Jain, translator, and others) are willing to give this last proof of their fidelity, yet, still it is attended with considerable expense; and without that assistance, most of what I had proposed to condense and translate from the originals in the languages of this country, could not be conveniently, or at all, effected at Calcutta. I mean, however, to attempt it; and I hope in this last stage, preparatory to my return to Europe, to effect a condensed view of the whole collection, and a catalogue *raisonnée* of the native manuscripts and books, &c., and to give the translated materials such form as may at least facilitate the production of some parts, should they ever appear to the public, by persons better qualified, if the grateful task be not permitted to my years, or to my state of health. I regret exceedingly, that the pressures of this moment will not permit of my adding further to this hasty sketch. It would require an actual inspection of, and reference to, the originals themselves, to give you any tolerable idea of their nature, and of the interest my partiality may attach to them. I hope, however, that it will appear to all considerate men, that some leisure and tranquil exclusive application to an arrangement of these, would be at least necessary to one who has now resided thirty-four years in this climate, without the benefit of once going to Europe, or even to any of our other presidencies, on account of health or private affairs.

   (Signed)   "Colin Mackenzie."

The opinion entertained by the Court of Directors of the scientific and literary labours of Col. Mackenzie, will be seen by the following extracts from their letter to the government of Fort St. George, dated 9th February, 1810:—

" 2. In our despatch of the 11th Feb. 1809, written in the regular course of reply to letters from you in this department, we were prevented by the pressure of other affairs, from entering into the consideration of the subject which occupied your letter of the 14th March 1807, namely, the services of Lieut.-Col. C. Mackenzie, in the survey of Mysore, and certain provinces adjacent to it.

" 3. Having now reviewed with attention the whole of that subject, as it is detailed in the letter just mentioned, and the papers which accompanied it, and in the various documents which are referred to in your subsequent advices of the 29th Feb., 21st, 24th, and 26th Oct. 1808, we feel it to be due to Lieut.-Col. M., and it is great pleasure to us to bestow our unqualified and warm commendation upon his long continued, indefatigable, and zealous exertions in the arduous pursuits in which he was employed, and upon the works which those exertions have produced. He has not confined his labours to the leading object of his original appointment, in itself a very difficult one, the obtaining of an accurate geographical knowledge of the extensive territories which came under the dominion or protection of the Company, in consequence of the fall of Tippoo Sultaun in 1799; but has carried his researches into two other very important branches, the statistics and the history of those countries; and in all of them he has succeeded to an extent which could not have been contemplated at the commencement of his undertaking.

"4. The actual survey, upon geometrical principles, of a region containing above 40,000 square miles *, generally of an extremely difficult surface, full of hills and wildernesses, presenting few facilities or accommodations for such a work, and never before explored by European science, in a climate very insalubrious, is itself no common performance, and the minute divisions and details of places of every description, given in the memoirs of the survey, with the masterly execution, upon a large scale, of the general map, and its striking discrimination of different objects, rarely equalled by any thing of the same nature that has come under our observation, form altogether an achievement of extraordinary merit, adding most materially to the stores of Indian geography, and of information useful for military, financial, and commercial purposes. For such purposes we shall wish the many materials furnished by Lieut.-Col. M. to be used by our government, and a set of his memoirs ought, with that view, to be lodged in some of the public departments, particularly that of the Revenue Board, together with the sections of his map, which he purposes to form into an atlas. But, desirous as we are that the public at large should have the gratification, and himself the credit, which would result from a general knowledge of his work, we entertain considerable doubts of the propriety of publishing it† at this time, and would wish no measure to that end to be taken without our further consideration and authority; therefore no copy of his map, or of the division of it, further than for the public offices just mentioned, ought to be permitted to be taken.

"5. On a full review of these labours, and of others which were not so

---

* In addition to this, the ceded districts have since been completed on the same plan, containing about 30,000 square miles, with maps, &c., and sent home to England in January 1816.

† Col. M. did not intend such a publication, without some prospect of encouragement to so extensive a work, but materials have been since added, that will nearly complete the peninsula. He conceived, however, that the publication of the work would be ultimately economical to the East India Company, exclusive of its advantage to the public and to science. The great expense incurred by the Company of late years, in copying maps without end, for their several departments in India, would be saved by the publication of an atlas of this kind, of which Col. M. submitted specimens in 1808.

immediately within the scope of Lieut.-Col. M.'s commission, we must admit that his merits have not been merely confined to the duties of a geographical surveyor, and finding that his representations on the subject of the inadequacy of his allowances are seconded by very strong recommendations from you, we direct that you present him with the sum of nine thousand (9,000) pagodas, as full remuneration for his past labours, and as a mark of our approbation of his work.

" 6. We next proceed to notice the Statistical Researches, in which also Lieut.-Col. M. employed himself. These are nearly allied to inquiries of a geographical kind, and answer the same end in an improved degree; they have, too, the merit of being in India much more uncommon, and though they were adverted to in the original instructions given to Lieut.-Col. M., the ample and successful manner in which he has pursued them, in the midst of other arduous labours, proves the zeal by which he has been actuated, and adds to the value of his services and his discoveries.

" 7. This observation applies, with at least equal propriety, to his superadded inquiries into the *History*, the *Religion*, and the *Antiquities* of the country; objects pointed out, indeed, in our general instructions to India, but to which, if he had not been prompted by his own public spirit, his other fatiguing avocations might have been pleaded as an excuse for not attending.

" 8. Real history and chronology have hitherto been desiderata in the literature of India, and from the genius of the people, and their past government, as well as the little success of the inquiries hitherto made by Europeans, there has been a disposition to believe that the Hindoos possess few authentic records. Lieut.-Col. M. has certainly taken the most effectual way, though one of excessive labour, to explore any evidence which may yet exist of remote eras and events, by recurring to remaining monuments, inscriptions, and grants, preserved either on metals or on paper; and his success in this way is far beyond what could have been expected. The numerous collections of materials * he has made under the different heads above noted, must be highly interesting and curious, and the specimens he has adduced in the manuscript volumes he has sent us, abundantly answer this character. Whether the grants, which are generally of lands to Brahmins,

* This collection has been augmented in a quadruple proportion since 1808, both in the peninsula and Hindostan, and ultimately extended to a new field, the Oriental islands, seas, and coasts of Asia.

are all authentic *, (which we mention not to assert a doubt, but to suggest a reasonable point of inquiry,) or whether the whole of the materials shall be found to form a connected series of historical facts, respecting a country which seems to have been always subject to commotions and changes, and unfavourable to the preservation of political records; still it must be allowed that this effort promises the fairest of any which has yet been made to bring from obscurity any scattered fragments which exist of true history, and undoubtedly encourages the expectation of obtaining, at length, both considerable insight into the state of the country and its governments, in more modern periods, and some satisfactory indications of its original institutions and earlier revolutions. We are therefore very desirous that Lieut.-Col. M. should himself digest and improve the materials he has collected; and we hope the office † which you have conferred on him in Mysore, will afford him leisure for this work. After he has accomplished it, the original materials are to be transmitted to us, to be deposited in our Oriental Museum. In the meantime, we wish to indemnify him for the disbursements he has made in procuring this collection of materials, trusting that it will not amount to any large sum; and we desire that he will state to us an account of it; which, from his character, we are persuaded will be correctly done: but, not to suspend all payment till the arrival of such an account, we permit you, on receipt of the present letter, to make him a reasonable advance on this score."

THE LATE CAPTAIN DANIEL CARPENTER.
(Bombay Establishment.)

CAPTAIN CARPENTER was among the early and intimate friends of that much esteemed and distinguished officer the late Major-General James Hartley ‡, with whom he shared in the confidence of Governor Hornby, whose talents in discriminating the character of the

---

* There can be no doubt of their authenticity; not an instance of forgery has been discovered, or even suspected, save one, (and that rather assists history:) as they are all previous to 1620, there is no inducement to fraud, and no one has yet adduced any claims upon them.
† This office was done away by the time this order arrived in India.
‡ Services, vol. ii. p. 102.

individuals whom he selected for employment in the public service, have never been disputed. Capt. Carpenter, while yet a subaltern, was employed to raise and discipline the old 2d, or Blue* battalion of Bombay N. I., to the command of which he succeeded on the demise of the senior officer; and with this corps he became most actively and conspicuously engaged in a variety of arduous services along the Mahratta territory, in the Concan, and in Guzerat.

Capt. Carpenter served on the expedition to Baroche, under Brigadier-Gen. Wedderburn. When the force left Bombay, on the unfortunate expedition to Telligaum†, under Brigadier-Gen. Egerton, in Nov. 1778, he was appointed Quarter-Master to the army,

---

* Second, or Blue Battalion.—The Native corps of the Indian army having been so often broken up on reduction, and on reformations, have now entirely lost, and, perhaps, wholly forgotten, their original designations. They were, probably, at all the three presidencies, at first named after colours. The first regularly disciplined, armed, and cloathed corps, raised in Bengal, (about 1760) was called the *Lal Pultun,* or *red regiment ;* probably from the colour of their coats; and having once so began, other colours were used to distinguish the corps next raised. Their facings, and, eventually, their regimental colours, may have corresponded. *Pultun* is, we believe, not a Hindoo word, but merely a corruption of *battalion.* The writer of this note can recollect, in the Bombay army, the *Lal,* the *Kala,* the *Peela,* and the *Leela Pultuns*; that is, the *red,* (or *ruby,*) the *black,* the *yellow,* and the *green* battalions; though he has forgotten which were so named. Their facings, however, did not correspond. All the battalions of the Bombay army, except the marine battalion, had blue facings, until the breaking up and reforming of it, in 1788, by Gen. Medows. The distinctions of *Lal, Kala,* &c., were not disused among the sepoys until then.

It may be further noted, that the change then made in the facings of the army, from blue to yellow, was galling to many officers of the Bombay army—among others, to the writer of this note. The army had somewhat plumed itself on partaking more of royalty than the armies of either of the other presidencies, and looked at their facings with some self-complacency. The circumstance of Bombay not being the absolute property in fee of the East India Company, like Bengal and Madras, but actually appertaining to the crown, and only rented by the Company, gave a sort of ground for such assumption. It was strengthened by the recognition of Royal Supremacy in the public acts of the government, which, at the time we speak of, and always before, were, and, perhaps, still are, designated as of " His Majesty's Island and Castle of Bombay." In the year 1788, two of H. M.'s regiments, the 75th and 77th, were raised for the Indian service, and attached to the Bombay army. These were the first so attached; and Gen. Medows was the first King's Governor and Com.-in-Chief. The facings of these two regiments were yellow, and the alteration of the facings of the Company's Bombay battalions from their favourite blue, had probably its origin in a feeling not unfelt, though unavowed, by the authority whence it emanated. E. M.

† Or Tullagaum, a large town about 18 miles from Poona, on the Bombay road.

discharging all the duties of Quarter-Master-General; no such Staff appointment being then allowed.

In Jan. 1780, he was appointed to the command of the 2d batt. of sepoys, which he held until his departure from India, in July 1787.

In Sept. 1780, he was sent to reinforce the garrison of Callian, then besieged by a very superior force of the Mahratta confederacy, where his services were eminently useful in defending that place until the arrival of Lieut.-Col. Hartley with a further augmentation of the forces. Lieut.-Col. Hartley, the moment the season permitted, took the field and drove the enemy up the ghauts; and Capt. Carpenter, with his battalion, assisted in this operation, and stood very high in the opinion of Col. Hartley, for his conduct as an officer on that occasion.

The 1st batt. of sepoys, under Capt. Abington, had for some time been employed in the siege of Bawamullen *, a hill fort of extraordinary strength; and the battalion having suffered severely from casualties and the climate, Capt. Carpenter, with the 2d battalion, was ordered to relieve him. No effort that art or courage could employ, was left untried by Capt. Carpenter; and it was supposed he would have succeeded in capturing the fort; but the situation of the army in the Concan, under Lieut.-Col. Hartley, obliged him to send orders to Capt. Carpenter to raise the siege and join him. Capt. Carpenter effected this junction, and displayed the highest qualities as an officer in so doing.

Three days after this junction, he was with his corps in the division under the command of his friend Col. Hartley, in the valley near Vizrabhoy, emphatically denominated " Hartley's trap," where the division, surrounded on all sides by an overwhelming force of the enemy, was critically relieved from its embarrassment by the death of Gunnees Punt, the Mahratta chief in command, who was killed † by a shot from one of the 6-pounders attached to Capt. Carpenter's battalion, laid by Lieut. Whitman‡. The discipline of

---

* A stupendous fortified rock in sight from Bombay, to the N. E.   † See vol. ii. p. 3.
‡ Charles Henry Whitman, or Witman, was promoted to Captain, by brevet, in 1784.

Capt. Carpenter's battalion, and his own personal conduct on this occasion, were highly commended by Col. Hartley.

Not long after this, Capt. Carpenter, with his battalion, proceeded down the Malabar coast, with the force under Major Abington, destined to raise the long-protracted siege of of Tellichery*, so gallantly defended against the troops of Hyder Ally, under one of his most distinguished generals. This was in the early part of 1782; and the result of this expedition was pre-eminently brilliant and successful. The garrison, reinforced by the division from the presidency, attacked the besiegers in their extensive lines, and completely routed and dispersed them, with the loss of all their artillery and stores, and the capture of their general, who died of his wounds shortly afterwards, because he would not submit to amputation. The exertions of Capt. Carpenter were eminently conspicuous on this occasion; and the career of the victors was not suspended, until crowned in the capture of Calicut, the reduction of which was accelerated by the explosion † of a magazine.

The following extract from a letter written by Capt. Carpenter,

* At an early period of the war in 1780, an adequate force had been allotted, and successively increased, for the reduction of Tellichery, the only possession of the English on that coast; a mere mercantile factory, fortified according to the early practice of European nations, against the ordinary insults of banditti. But as the population had increased from the superior protection experienced by the inhabitants, an extensive but indefensible line surrounded the limits of the town. The English troops were entirely inadequate in numbers, to furnish even sentinels for such a line; but a timely reinforcement conveyed from Bombay, by Sir Edward Hughes, and the zeal of the inhabitants and adjacent chiefs, who detested the Mysorean rule, enabled them to continue a protracted and highly meritorious defence, deserving a more ample description than the records afford, until the early part of this year, when the arrival of reinforcements under Major Abington, enabled them, by a determined sortie, to raise the siege, by the capture of all the enemy's cannon, amounting to 60 pieces, with the whole of their baggage equipments. The Mysorean General, Sirdar Khân, was wounded and taken prisoner, with about 1200 men, who failed in effecting their retreat; and in a few days afterwards, the remaining fugitives who had taken post at the dismantled French settlement of Mâhe, surrendered at discretion.—*See Wilks' Historical Sketches*, vol. ii. p. 359.

† It is a remarkable fact, that the report of this explosion, although at the distance of between thirty and forty miles, was distinctly heard on board a ship in Tellichery roads, where an officer, to whom the Editor is much indebted for some of the statements in this memoir, had just arrived on his way to Bombay.

at this period, furnishes some of the details of the above proceedings:—

" I left Bombay the 22d of December, with seven complete companies of my battalion, with Jameson, who had seven companies of his battalion, and 40 artillery, commanded by Hawkes*, with two 6-pounder field pieces.

" We arrived at Tellichery the 29th, at night, and all the troops landed the next day, in full expectation to attack the enemy immediately; but our commanding officer was in hopes the enemy would walk off when they knew the force that was arrived. The advanced guard consisted of a company of Europeans, 4 grenadier companies of the 10th and 11th battalions, and 2 companies of regular tivies, and two 1-pounder field pieces. Jameson's battalion and mine followed in columns from the centre, with our grenadiers in front; two 6-pounder field pieces were to have been attached to our battalions, but they were too heavy to carry, and the artillery, under Hawkes, acted as infantry, and marched in front of the advanced corps, which was commanded by Capt. Whippy. This party was to storm Putney Hill, which was the rear of the enemy's batteries, against Mile End, and commanded all the others. The 2d and 8th battalions were to cover them in this attack, and as soon as the place was taken, to march on and attack the enemy's camp, which was about a mile beyond Putney; Capt. Whippy was to reduce all the enemy's batteries, assisted by Capt. Lindrum, who was in Mile End fort, with six companies of sepoys, and was to attack the enemy's trenches when a good opportunity offered: exclusive of these troops, about 1000 irregulars marched out of the lines. At 12 o'clock at night of the 7th Jan., the troops were ordered under arms, and about two o'clock in the morning arrived at the brass pagoda, and marched from thence a little after three o'clock, through

* Afterwards Major Jeremiah Hawkes, Commissary of Stores at Bombay. He was drowned in the narrow channel, between Bombay and Colaba, when returning to his house on the latter island, to the great regret of a large circle of friends.

an opening made in our lines; our route lay over the batty fields, and about 500 yards in our front there was a small nullah, which we threw a bridge over without being perceived by the enemy's picquets, though they had two a little way in front, and what is more extraordinary, the whole army passed between them within 50 yards, though some of the people were awake, and the road from the nullah to the high road, was nearly up to the calf of the leg in mud and water. Fortune conducted us to the foot of Putney Hill at day-break, and some of the enemy who were posted there, were killed by our bayonets before a shot was fired.

"The enemy were very alert when they discovered us, and got the gun turned towards us, but they had no time to level, so no one was hurt by it, and the place taken with the loss of three men wounded, and those, I believe, by our own people. The battery upon Bench hill, was immediately evacuated by the enemy. The two battalions remained formed upon the road which led to the enemy's camp, till Putney was taken: but we did not know of the success of our party till some time after, owing to the Staff being entirely ignorant of their duty. When it came to my knowledge, a few of the enemy appeared in our front, and the commanding officer not being to be found, I took upon me to order the troops to advance, and we drove the enemy before us to a hill, where they seemed determined to make a stand; seeing which, I sent Jameson's battalion to attack them upon their right flank, while mine attempted to mount the hill in front, and along the road, to attack their left: there was a small nullah full of water, which ran close under the foot of the hill, and difficult to get over every where but along the road, and at this place it was up to the waist in water, and near 50 yards over. Lieut. Wheldon was in front with his company. Sirdar Caun was by this time upon the hill, mounted, and encouraging his men to stand, but Wheldon pushed through the water under a heavy fire of musketry, and soon got possession of the hill. Sirdar Caun's horse was wounded, and himself thrown to the ground, before his people gave way: just after this, Major Abington joined me.

"The enemy's camp was between this hill and Coorachee, which is about a mile; here Sirdar Caun had his head-quarters and a strong post. Not the least halt was made by the troops, but we followed the enemy through their camp to Coorachee, close under which was another piece of water to pass like the former; the house was itself a strong post, and there was a redoubt upon the right, and another on the left, both difficult of access; but so little time had the enemy to recollect themselves, that they never occupied the one upon their right, where there were two brass 3-pounder field pieces, and that on their left was taken in a few minutes, by Lieuts. Hawkes, Hodges, and M'Lane, who marched along the beach in pursuit of the enemy, that had been driven out of Putney and Bench hill: they had time only to fire the 6-pounder that was in this redoubt twice, and that without any execution. Sirdar Caun was here wounded, and I never saw men so obstinate, as a few of the enemy were at this place. Jameson's battalion passed the house to the left, and some of mine with Wheldon in pursuit of the enemy, towards Fort George and Mâhe, not knowing the house was fortified till they got near a mile beyond it; when, hearing a smart fire, they halted: Jameson went on so far, and that with so few people, that the enemy faced about, and he took post on the top of a hill, where he collected his people; but this he was positively ordered to do, by one of the Major's staff, at the request of Engineer Christie. This being perceived by some of our sepoys at Coorachee, and a small party returning for ammunition, a report spread that our people were retreating, which was not improbable, as the enemy still kept their colours flying on the house, and sounding their trumpets. I ordered the long roll to beat, and collected the people together under Coorachee hill: soon after this, the detachment from the vessels landed, and Mr. Sparkes informing me that the troops in front wanted ammunition, I sent the marines with 10 boxes to reinforce them, as Major Abington was not then to be found, and pointed out a gun to Lieut. Pruen, I wished to have made use of against the house: Pruen shewed himself an active officer, and would soon have made a breach, if he had had plenty of ammunition, but we were obliged to send on board the ships for it. Soon after the house took fire, which I believe was occasioned by one of their rockets. They had been repeatedly desired to surrender, and their lives should be saved, but to no purpose; nay, after the house was on fire, they continued to fire upon us, and at last, all who were able, endeavoured to run away, by which many lost their lives. It was a terrible sight to see a number of fine women darting out of the flames, and the sepoys firing upon them, which at first it was impossible to prevent: numbers of wounded men and children perished in the flames, without a possibility of assistance: and had we not been stopped at Coorachee, some thousands would have been drowned in the river; as it was, their terror was so great, that one elephant, and nearly 500 men, women, and children perished, and numbers of bodies were thrown upon the beach. Fort George surrendered that night, and Mâhe the next morning. The enemy kept possession of their trenches till the firing ceased at Coorachee, when they surrendered.

" The commanding officer, Sirdar Caun, was wounded and taken prisoner, in Coorachee house, and all his family: about 1700 prisoners were taken, 13 elephants, and all the guns, amounting to 100 at least, with all the stores, ammunition, and baggage, &c. *

* The following notice of these events, is extracted from a work, entitled " Transactions in India," &c., published in 1786:—" Major Abington having arrived from Bombay, with a considerable reinforcement of troops, determined to attempt the dislodgement of the enemy, and open a communication of the town with the country. His movements deceived the enemy into such a state of security, as considerably facilitated his designs. Having drawn such part of the garrison as could be spared, without notice, into his camp, he surprised and carried their several posts before day, on the morning of the 8th of Jan. 1782. Not allowing a moment for the enemy to recover their confusion, he stormed their camp as soon as it was light, and completely routed them. Sirdar Caun, their commander, retired with his family, and a chosen party of his friends and best troops, into a castle scooped on the side of a hill, and possessed of no other walls than such as were formed of the living rock. Notwithstanding a vigorous and manly defence, this brave man and his party were torn from their asylum, though bomb-proof, and made prisoners. These operations produced considerable spoil, consisting of artillery, military stores, and several elephants. The town was relieved, and the coast, for several miles on both sides, entirely cleared of the enemy."

"We marched from Mâhe plain the 10th Feb., and encamped the 12th, in the afternoon, within three miles of Calicut: a few of the enemy appeared upon the beach, and 200 or 300 horse about a mile in front of our advanced picquet. Our force was 1600 regulars and four 6-pounder field pieces, 1000 irregulars, and 600 Nyars.

"It was not till late in the evening that the Major determined to march as the next morning; and all I could say could not persuade him to order the Drake and boats to sail that evening in order to get close to Calicut, which the wind would not permit them to do in the morning. We marched at sun-rise along the beach, my battalion in front, and a company of Europeans, with two 6-pounders; the Major intended not to attempt the town, but to encamp at a little distance, but never gave any positive orders: when the front got within about 600 yards of the north side of the town, the enemy hoisted French colours upon the French flag-staff, and fired a shot from one of their batteries, which ran along the flank of our column; as the Major was not to be seen I desired one of his staff would incline the column to the left into the cocoa-nut parts, as we should be then under cover: this being done, I sent one of the staff to look for the Major, with my compliments, to desire the 6-pounders might be left behind, and that I might attack the batteries and town with my battalion and the European company; and while the messenger was gone, I made the disposition for the attack, as we were too far advanced to think of any thing else. Lieut. Lighton, having the advanced guard, led the attack; Capt. Brownrigg*, with the Europeans, and Hodges, with his grenadier company, supported him, and the battalion followed. The front was got near the battery when one of the staff returned from the Major, who said, I might act as I thought proper: the battery was immediately attacked, and carried without the loss of a man, though they fired several shot and a great deal of musketry. Just before our people got to the battery, about 300 horse made their appearance on the plain, and made as if they

---

* Afterwards Major-General, and commanding officer of the forces at Bombay.

intended to take us in flank, which obliged me to wheel up two companies and front them; but they retired on seeing their people run from the batteries. The enemy evacuated all their batteries along the beach and the town, and retired under the fort walls. We were obliged to wait some time for guides to shew us the way to the fort, which gave time for some of the irregulars to get before us, and the Major to come up. We soon saw which route to take, by the enemy driving some of our irregulars before them down the street. Here we had some smart work, and upwards of 40 of my battalion were killed and wounded before we could establish our posts, which we did within 120 yards of the fort. Vanrayne, Hawkes, Hodges, Wheldon, and Lighton, behaved very well, as did Christie and all that were in action. My battalion were under arms the whole day, and a constant fire was kept up from the fort, but we were so well covered, that little harm was done. In the afternoon, the 8th battalion was ordered to relieve mine, as the Major supposed it must be much fatigued; but at my request he permitted it to remain.

"About 7 o'clock in the evening, we got three small mortars up, and threw about 300 shells during the night. The battery was began about 10, for three 18-pounders: my battalion and some of the 8th, worked at it the whole night; but it was not finished in the morning; if it had, not a gun was on shore to put in it, for all the boat people, though they had been idle all the fore part of the day, could not work at night. We had a plan of the fort, and knew where the magazine was; and about 9 o'clock in the morning, Lieut. Tredeneck threw an 8-inch shell into it, and blew it up. While the smoke and dust continued, the enemy kept up a smart fire from their works, and I prepared my battalion to storm the place, expecting to see a breach; but the wall appeared perfect on the sides next us, and we began to play away again with our mortars, when two of our marine officers, who were prisoners in the fort, came running out with a white cloth displayed, and two or three of the enemy with them. The latter offered to give up the place if we would give them their lives and cloaths; but the explosion brought up one or two of the staff, and I sent them to the Major. As there was a large breach made on the east face of the fort, they were afraid the Nyars would enter, and cut them to pieces; some of them came out and desired I would prevent this disaster. In the interim, I sent Hodges down to the Major to tell him what they wanted; yet, notwithstanding, he would have given them every thing in the fort, if they had not been afraid of the Nyars, and I got possession of it before any terms were made. The Major did me the honour to order that my battalion only should take possession of the fort. When I got in, a terrible scene of havock presented itself,—men, women, and children—horses and bullocks,—lay scattered about, mangled and torn in a shocking manner; large trees torn from their roots, and thrown to a great distance; an elephant was thrown over a large tank, and struck the top of the parapet. I got 1 elephant colour and 12 stand of foot colours; 2500 prisoners were taken, 9 elephants, and about 30 horses; 300 of the enemy's horse marched off on the morning the place was taken: upwards of 100 guns were mounted in this fort.

"Colonel Humberstone arrived soon after the place was taken, and landed 1000 Europeans."

Capt. Carpenter appears to have passed the rainy season of 1782, during a period of inactivity, at the presidency; since, at the close of the year, he accompanied the force which proceeded under the brave, but unfortunate General Mathews, to the invasion of Canara; which, however disastrous in the issue to a great part of the troops employed, succeeded most effectually in drawing the armies of the Mysore Sultaun from the Carnatic. On this occasion several subalterns attached to Capt. Carpenter's battalion, landed with the principal force near Rajahmundroog, which was taken by assault, after a slight resistance. The main body of the 2d battalion arrived shortly afterwards with the troops under Colonel Norman M'Leod, from Paniana, before the lines of which place a chosen body of troops, under Tippoo in person, was signally repulsed, and, in a great measure, through the distinguished bravery of the gallant Major

Campbell, of H. M.'s 42d, who attacked the assailing column in flank.

It had, for a short interval, been in contemplation to attack the then respectable fort of Mirjee, a few miles up the river from Rajahmundroog; but, on more mature reflection, this design was abandoned by the General, although the flank corps of the army had been actually embarked for the purpose. The resolution was adopted without further delay, to invest the more important fortress of Onore*. Capt. Carpenter, with his battalion, was left in charge of Rajahmundroog, and to check any hostile demonstrations on the part of the garrison of Mirjee.

On the subsequent capture of Onore, by storm, Gen. Mathews, with the army, proceeding southward to Cundapoor, and finally forcing the Hyderghur ghaut towards Bednore, Captain Carpenter received instructions to traverse the districts within land of Onore, and to cover that place against any attempt on the part of the enemy.

"*To Captain Carpenter.*

"Sir,—It is necessary that an active, although small party, should remain in the field, and I have thought of you to command it. You will therefore proceed to Chundoor or Comptah, and collect your partizan force. It will at first consist of two iron three-pounders, drawn by bullocks, and the ammunition carried by men. And whatever men of the European artillery and lascars as can be drawn from Rajahmundroog and Onore, and as many sepoys as can be spared from each place, that is, from the immediate service and security of both garrisons. If you get 15 Europeans, and 150 sepoys, it will be reckoned a small army. The object is to protect the country from plunder and conflagration, and by seizing with spirit and judgment every opportunity of attacking the enemy, you may drive them from the frontiers of this district. It will be a fortunate circumstance if you can approach either the fort of Bilghie or Gurripah pass, as it may serve to keep the enemy at a distance, and alarm them for fear that you should really ascend the hills. The garrison of Mirjee also deserves your attention, and you should endea-

* Afterwards so heroically defended by its feeble garrison, commanded by the late Major (then Captain) J. S. Torriano, of the Bombay artillery, as detailed in vol. ii. of this work.

vour to keep them on the north side of the river. Being lightly equipped, and without tents or baggage, your movements may be as rapid as your sense may render them judicious. In short, all the country between the rivers of Mirjee and Onore, are under your protection; and Capt. Torriano, who commands the garrison of Onore, has orders to supply you with every thing you may want, and to send all recovered officers and men, whether European or Native, to join you. You will strictly observe to keep this one material point constantly in view, which is, the safety of Onore, on account of our stores, provisions, and many *etceteras:* Capt. Torriano has orders to detain no more sepoys than the necessary guards. When we begin to act to the southward, the enemy may draw off part of their force; then will be your time to make an impression, and I have hopes of hearing that the fort of Bilghie will, in a fortnight or three weeks, be in your possession. Capt. Torriano will send 2 three-pounders, and 2 artillery-men, with a few Europeans and what sepoys can be spared. You will keep up a constant correspondence with Capt. Torriano, who will occasionally acquaint me of your motions. Your command will be separate from his, unless he finds it necessary to call your party into Onore, for its apparent security, in which case only, you are to act under his orders. I wish you health and success.

(Signed) "R. MATHEWS.

" *Onore, 12th Jan.* 1783."

In the course of his operations, Capt. Carpenter being compelled to subsist the sepoys by threshing the rice from the straw, wherever it could be found, his advanced guard, under Lieut. Wheldon, while in part thus employed, was fired upon by the enemy; but as it was probably a small party sent to explore, it was repulsed without difficulty. The same evening, after the sun had set, the grenadier and light companies of the battalion, recently concentrated into one by a regulation of Gen. Mathews, marched under Lieuts. Hodges and Wheldon, with Ensign David Price*, attached for the purpose of surprising the Bilghie ghaut. This pass, defended by an advanced work, and two gateways flanked with towers, and mounted

---

* Now Major, on the retired list. Services, vol. i. p. 282. Major Price is the author of "The Retrospect of Mahommedan History," in four volumes, 4to., and of the "History of Arabia," one vol. 4to.; works of great research and value, selected and translated from Arabic and Persian authorities.

with cannon, was carried about three in the morning, after a slight resistance; the officers entering successively through the embrazures and over the tiled roofs. On this occasion a French gunner was taken prisoner, and assisted in opening the gates for the sepoys. A bazaar, abundantly supplied with all sorts of provisions, was taken possession of about two miles within the pass. Capt. Carpenter, with the remainder of the corps, now joined, and with that promptitude, which was a distinguishing feature in his character, availing himself of the panic which seemed to have taken possession of the enemy in this quarter, determined to make a push for the town of Bilghie, about 12 or 15 miles from the head of the ghaut. This design was carried into immediate execution, and in another night-march, accomplished with little difficulty; the enemy retiring, after merely discharging their matchlocks at the entrance of the town.

The extreme neatness and cleanliness of this little place, and the verdant and romantic scenery through which they passed on the occasion, left the most pleasing impressions on the minds of the officers of the detachment. In the palace of the Rajah was found moreover a considerable booty, in rich dresses, shawls, &c. which was divided on the spot; but what would have been of more solid advantage, an immense deposit of copper, and brass furniture and utensils of various descriptions, was necessarily left untouched. The vicinity of a superior force of the enemy on the side of Gootty*, which was pointed out among the hills to the eastward, rendered it expedient to withdraw, before the numerical inferiority of the detachment, certainly not more than 300 rank and file, should be discovered.

The next morning but one, long before daylight, while the detachment were getting under arms for departure, and the officers were standing round a large fire, in the outward court of the palace, a note was put into the hands of Capt. Carpenter, from Gen. Mathews, announcing that he was in possession of Bednore, and that Hyat

---

* This could not, however, be the strong fortress of that name, to the eastward of Bellary.

Saheb, the Governor of the province, had delivered himself up to him; at the same time, Capt. Carpenter was directed to proceed immediately with the detachment under his orders to the reduction of the different fortified places of the enemy to the northward, between Onore and the Portuguese districts dependant on Goa.

Leaving a small party of 30 men only, under Lieut. David Laurence, in possession of Bilghie, Capt. Carpenter, with the remainder of his force, returned to the territory below the Ghauts, and proceeded towards Mirjee, which was promptly delivered up to Lieut. Young. From Mirjee, Capt. Carpenter continued his march to Ancola, before which, with the officers of the detachment standing round, he narrowly escaped destruction, from a perfidious discharge of the guns of the fort, while attending to a message sent out by the petty Killedar, with proposals of submission. After keeping up an ineffectual fire, the place was, however, evacuated the same night, and taken possession of by Lieut. Ross, who had been posted not far from the gates of the fort.

The object which next engaged the attention of Capt. Carpenter, was the subjugation of Sadashewghur, a post of considerable strength on the north side of the entrance of the river leading to the large village of Carwar, when, on crossing the extremity of the hill range, pointing towards the Portuguese Island of Anjadeiva, the place came within view of the detachment. The outline of the works was indeed sufficiently imposing; but the resolution of Capt. Carpenter was not to be easily shaken; and he accordingly led the detachment across the plain in sight of the fort, to the imperial factory on the south side of the river, a little higher up, and there encamped. Having secured some of the river craft, in the course of the same night, he crossed with his determined little band to the opposite side, and took post under some cocoa-nut trees, within distant gunshot of the enemy's works*.

---

* The boldness of this undertaking, when we consider the smallness of his force, must reflect upon Capt. Carpenter a distinguished character for intrepidity and vigour of mind; and it is but an act of justice to record in this place, the names of the officers who accom-

The following day was occupied in examining the works of the place, and preparing ladders for an escalade. It was determined to attack the first that night, to the left of the right hand, or eastern tower of the gateway. Lieutenants Hodges, Wheldon, and Laurence, who had recently rejoined, were selected to lead the storming party, which consisted, indeed, of the greater part of the detachment; Ensigns Morris and Price, with two small parties, of about 30 each, being employed to draw the attention of the enemy on opposite points; Capt. Carpenter, with the remainder, in reserve. Having reached the first gateway, without material resistance, and expecting, as at Bilghie, to enter the embrasures, or port holes, at the heels of the enemy, the storming party, instead of taking its course, as had been intended, to the left of the right hand tower, and attacking in the angle where it joins the long curtain, pushed to the wall between the two towers; unfortunately placing the two ladders exactly before the circular openings, or holes in the wall, at the very mouth of the guns. The three officers who had ascended the ladders at the head of the file, were of course swept to the ground at the first discharge. Lieut. Hodges was killed on the spot, his head being completely laid open by the grape and langridge; and Lieutenants Wheldon and Laurence being both at the same time blinded and disabled by the explosion of the guns, succeeded, with considerable difficulty, in exploring their way out of the ditch, and were brought safe off, the party having been withdrawn by the Serjeant-Major, (Cahill) an excellent soldier, after sustaining a severe loss *.

panied him: there were Lieutenants John Hodges, Thomas Wheldon, Thomas Fyfe, (Adjutant); and David Laurence, and Ensigns William Morris, Charles Lonsdale, and David Price. Lieut. Ross had been left in command at Ancola.

* It is here a melancholy satisfaction to place upon record, the names of two most gallant and distinguished young men, whose bright career of excellence was destined to terminate, before they had indeed well passed the threshold of manhood. Handsome, accomplished, ardent, and brave, Lieut. Hodges, the senior, although scarcely three and twenty, had already acquired a moderate competency in fortune, was an Aid-de-Camp in the family of the Governor of Bombay, and had, on many former occasions, greatly distinguished himself in presence of the enemy. Preferring, however, the glorious excitements of his profession in the field, to the luxuries, ease, and abundance, of the Government House,

On the following morning, a message was sent into the place to demand the body of Lieut. Hodges, accompanied with a hint from Capt. Carpenter to the Killedar, that having been pretty close to him the night before, he should find him still closer in a few hours. The hint was not without its effect, as the body was immediately sent out, nothing having been abstracted from the person of the gallant deceased but his gold watch and epaulettes; and that very night, moreover, rather than tarry the result of another conflict, the garrison evacuated the fort. Ensign Price, who was posted at the entrance of the bazaar, below the gateway, and who received immediate information of what had taken place, entered on one side, while the enemy was withdrawing on the other*.

he hastened to join his corps, and thus prematurely fell, in the path of duty and honour, at Sadashewghur. Lieut. Wheldon, still younger, for he was scarcely one and twenty, equally accomplished, mild, and intrepid, of a carriage less impetuous, more sedate, but not less keen, than his gallant associate, had displayed, on many occasions, a steadiness far beyond his years; had frequently been left in command of the battalion, and so distinguished himself on every occasion, that he was become a terror to the enemy wherever he was known, under the appellation of the *Butchah Serdaur*, or Boy Captain. He recovered, however, from his wounds before Sadashewghur, to renew, as will be seen, for a short time, his exemplary career. But, at a subsequent period, ordered away for the known purpose of being placed with the army under Gen. M'Leod, in a situation more worthy of his conspicuous merit, he was cast away in the fatal gale of the 5th Nov. 1783, on the territory of the Queen of Cananore, by whom he was delivered up, to her own future cost, to the Mysorean monarch. It is generally understood, that not long afterwards he was seen to be conducted to a wood near Bednore, where he was murdered in cold blood, by direction of that ferocious and inflexible barbarian, at the very moment probably that he was in treaty for peace with the British government. At all events, nothing further was ever heard of this most valuable young soldier. Two and forty years are now elapsed since their separation; but the writer of this note still looks back with veneration to the many estimable qualities of Lieut. Wheldon, whose cool discretion and tempered valour, suited him in an eminent degree to the highest situations of difficulty, trust, and danger.

Lieut. Laurence survived for many years, and although with qualifications less brilliant, proved himself, nevertheless, on many occasions, a very deserving and meritorious officer.

It cannot but reflect the highest credit on Capt. Carpenter's memory, that he should have been able to attach to his corps, men of such distinguished proof as those whose names we have thus endeavoured to rescue from oblivion.

* In this place it may be proper to state, that at the period under consideration, so deplorably was the service provided with medical aid, no surgeon was to be found nearer than Onore, a distance of nearly 30 miles; to which place it became therefore necessary to

The following extract of a letter from B.-Gen. Mathews, to the Select Committee of Bombay, dated Camp before Mangalore, 4th March 1783, refers to the above operations :—

" My last informed you of the surrender of Bednore, and I am happy to find, by private letters from Bombay, that you had received authentic accounts of that fortunate event : I have now the honour to inform you, that Capt. Carpenter has taken Sadashewghur, otherwise Carwar, thus completing his reduction of all the forts in the low country, which are now in his possession. Your Honours should consult the map, and take into your serious consideration, the great scope of country that I have already gained, extending from Carwar to Mangalore, and the number of garrisons that must of course be occupied until the country is settled, and peace secured with the hostile nations that surround us. To begin with the Portuguese, for they too lay a claim to Carwar : if it had not been for the activity and prudence of Capt. Carpenter, which I cannot sufficiently applaud, they would certainly have got possession of this fortress, (which is the same they call the Peer,) from the Nabob's Killedar, and thus effectually have prevented us from hoisting our colours upon it; for on the 19th ultimo, it was but a few minutes after the colours of the enemy had been hauled down, that a Portuguese vessel and three boats appeared in sight of Corrum Gurr, but Hyder's colours not being hoisted, they sheered off; comparing this fact then, with the intelligence sent to Capt. Carpenter by Mr. Crommelin, and communicated by the former to me, (copy of which is inclosed,) it appears that three companies of their best sepoys were embarked in these boats, whom the Killedar wanted to admit into the fort, in order to protect it against our arms ; nor am I satisfied that they have not, by this time, attempted to retake it by force, as Capt. Carpenter, in a letter I received from him of the 19th, advises me, that a Portuguese Colonel, and 5 or 600 men, had arrived that day on their frontiers, within three miles of the place. I ordered him not to give an inch of ground, and was sorry I could not send him any reinforcement at present. If then the kingdom of Soundah should not become a source of contention between us and the Portuguese, it is owing to the zeal and success of that officer."

convey the wounded officers and men from Sadashewghur, before their wounds could be properly attended to. But the often fatal deficiency here complained of, has long since been removed by the paternal care of government, in the ample supply of Medical Staff attached to the three presidencies.

After some few days devoted to his arrangements for the security of Sadashewghur, on the extensive works of which, it is to be observed, that there were found from 40 to 50 pieces of mounted iron ordnance, Capt. Carpenter proceeded, with the major part of the detachment, in pursuit of the fugitive garrison, which was understood to have retired to the precincts of the Portuguese districts, some miles to the northward of the then compact and neat little fortress of Sewisser. The enemy, under their Killedar, Luxman Naik, were discovered in considerable numbers, on the outskirts of a deep wood, or forest, which proved to be the conventional boundary of the Portuguese territory. At all events, on the dispersion of the enemy, when assailed on different points, by Capt. Carpenter's detachment, a guard of sepoys, under a Portuguese European officer, drawn up in the rear, were completely run over in the ardour of the pursuit. Several palanquins, umbrellas, and other trophies, and some few horses, fell into the hands of the pursuers, with which they returned towards Sewisser and Sadashewghur.

The attention of Capt. Carpenter being now attracted towards the districts of the province of Soundah, above the Souppah Ghaut, the fortress of Sadashewghur, as furnishing a very respectable supply of stores and ordnance, was very properly chosen as the head-quarters of the corps, and the basis of his future operations. It possessed, moreover, the paramount advantage of commanding a communication with the sea, by the mouth of Carwar river, within reach of its guns. Before he could, however, prudently engage in any distant operation, it became necessary to obtain possession of Koorumghur, a fortified island opposite the mouth of the river, at a very short distance. Lieut. Young, accompanied by Ensign Price, was sent over to summons the Killedar, a respectable old Patan, of the name of Murad Beg. After a delay, which occasioned some anxiety, he was prevailed upon to surrender his post the same evening; and it was accordingly taken possession of, without further difficulty.

Thus relieved from an embarrassment of some weight, Capt. Carpenter considered that he was now at liberty to extend his views, and a part of his already small force, was accordingly detached, shortly afterwards, under Lieutenants Fyfe and Ross, to ascend the Souppah Ghaut, about 18 miles to the eastward, with orders to attack the fort of the same name, if they found it practicable, some distance in the interior of the pass. The service was executed with distinguished gallantry by those brave officers; the fort of Souppah being carried by assault, after a very obstinate resistance on the part of the small garrison, probably encouraged by the still inferior numbers of their assailants, with whom they combated hand to hand, from beneath the sloping roof, which covered the ramparts all round *.

Lieut. Wheldon, who had been conveyed to Onore for recovery from the injuries received in the attack of Sadashewghur, had now rejoined his corps; and about the period under consideration, being ordered to take command of the detachment in the Souppah district, soon availed himself of an opportunity for the display of that ardent spirit of zeal and enterprise, which so early distinguished this gallant young officer.

A detachment of the enemy, consisting of horse and foot, was understood to have taken post in considerable force, at the pagoda of Hurryhall, at the extremity of the district, overlooking the spacious plains to the eastward, a view of which, from the avenue in its front, it commands to a great extent. Having possessed himself of the requisite information, relative to the position of the enemy, Lieut. Wheldon at once determined to beat up their quarters; and marching,

* These minor details may perhaps appear trivial to some fastidious readers; but there are those, and not a few indeed, who must remember that detached services, of the nature here described, afford opportunities for individual prowess and exertion, not often attainable with the main body of an army. Neither should they, in truth, be ever entrusted, but to men of sterling ability and tried experience. At all events, justice to the memory of two most deserving and gallant officers, seemed to demand that an action should have some place in this record, which, like many others in the same quarter, might otherwise be suffered to perish in oblivion.

under cover of the night, from his ground near Souppah, a distance at which they might perhaps have considered themselves sufficiently secure against sudden attack, he took them so completely by surprise, that they dispersed in the utmost consternation, almost without resistance; leaving a number of horses, of a superior description, with several flags and other trophies, in the hands of the detachment*.

Long previous to the rainy season of 1783, intelligence poured in from different quarters, that the unfortunate Gen. Mathews was surrounded at Bednore†, by the armies of Tippoo, under the immediate command of the Sultaun; and Capt. Carpenter had early perceived the expediency of calling in his small detachments, without delay.

Having gradually withdrawn his small detachments from the Souppah districts, and along the course of the river, to Sadashewghur, Capt. Carpenter, about the commencement of the rainy season, despatched orders to Lieut. Ross, to undermine the different towers of the fort of Ancola, preparatory to the dismantlement of that place; and a party was now marched from Sadashewghur, to the support of

---

* Such was the last service which Lieut. Wheldon was permitted to perform; but so completely had he discharged the country in that quarter, of every appearance of an enemy, that the writer of this Note, on his way to join him at Hurryhall, not many days afterwards, traversed the district for 18 or 20 miles, with no other protector than a single sepoy, orderly. But this day of bright prosperity was destined shortly to terminate in disappointment, depression, and gloom.

† In the event, it seemed indeed most unfortunate, that the General should have been led by whatever motives, with such inadequate means of defence, and at such a distance from all rational hope of support, to the fatal resolution of remaining at Bednore, instead of receding in time to concentrate his force below the ghauts; where the memorable defence made by an inferior garrison at Mangalore, under the gallant Major Campbell, as well as on a minor scale, under the able conduct of Major Torriano, (Services, vol. ii. p. 117,) of the Bombay artillery, at Onore, afforded, at a subsequent period, such distinguished proofs how completely the superior force of the enemy, aided by European skill and tactics, could be set at nought, even with far diminished numbers. In justice to Gen. Mathews, it may, however, be alleged, that having as yet experienced no proof of that flagrant perfidy to which both he and so many other gallant officers were subsequently destined to be the victims, and having accomplished the primary object of the expedition, in relieving the Carnatic from the long protracted horrors of a barbarous invasion, he might have conceived that a capitulation solemnly guaranteed, would have protected him and the excellent body of troops under his command to the sea coast, where their services would be available.

Lieut. Ross, in case he should be molested by the enemy on his retreat. In the meantime, that brave and deserving officer, had, by a rapid movement to the southward, effectually succeeded in destroying a large vessel, nearly finished on the stocks, at Tudree, on the river of Mirjee, just opposite to Rajamundroog, and said to be designed for a fifty-gun ship in the Sultaun's projected marine. Lieut. Ross then blowing up the towers of Ancola, brought off his garrison to the westward of the Terring, a small post on a point projecting into the sea, where, at a small village on the shore, he met his reinforcement, and with which, the next day, he proceeded without accident to join the head-quarters at Sadashewghur.

The rainy season from May to October, 1783, was busily occupied at Sadashuguhr, in making every preparation to resist any attack on the part of the enemy. A considerable body of recruits, raised for the particular service of the district, was armed, clothed, and disciplined to act with the batt. Lieut. Galbraith Tredenick, an experienced and intelligent officer of the Bombay artillery, who had been severely wounded in the defence of the lines at Paniana, had recently joined the detachment, and was now usefully employed in refitting the small equipment of field artillery attached to the corps. It was towards the breaking up of the monsoon, that a small party, under a subaltern officer, Ensign Bunbury, was despatched by sea to open a communication with the garrison of Onore, long since besieged by the enemy. Having passed the bar of the river at Onore, with considerable hazard, that officer succeeded in joining the garrison; but the subsequent conduct of this unhappy young man*, in going over to the enemy, in whose service he continued for several years, has left a stigma upon his name from which he can never be vindicated.

The season had, however, no sooner become sufficiently open, than the main part of the detachment was encamped near a pagoda, on the strand, in the rear of the pass looking towards Anjadeiva. Intelligence being received that the enemy proposed to enter the district, parties were stationed both at the summit of that pass, and the head

* See siege of Onore, vol. ii. p. 154, 182, &c.

of the Hyderghaut on the same range of hills, about eight or nine miles to the eastward, on the direct road to Ancola. It was at this crisis, that Capt. Carpenter received orders to detach Lieut. Wheldon from his corps, to join the troops proceeding down the coast, under Brig.-Gen. M'Leod, as it was supposed, to the relief of Mangalore. In the destructive gale of wind that occurred about the 5th of Nov. 1783, he was, as formerly intimated, cast away somewhere in the neighbourhood of Cannanore, and wickedly delivered up to Tippoo, by the Ranee; which furnished just occasion for that retribution which instantly followed, in the siege and capture of her capital, by the force under General M'Leod.

Towards the close of the month of November, or early in December, 1783, the main body of the detachment encamped, under Capt. Carpenter, in a position nearly centrical between the two advanced posts, so as to be at equal distance for the support of either, in case of attack. The post on Hyderghaut to the left, had been once previously menaced with an attack from the enemy, who had, however, retired without firing a shot, on the arrival of a reinforcement. But not many days afterwards, the party at Hyderghaut, thus reinforced to the number of 70 or 80 rank and file, a great proportion of them recruits, under Lieut. Ross and Ensign Price, was seriously attacked by the enemy, to the number of some thousands, pressing hard upon the post from the jungles on all sides, to within the distance of 30 or 40 yards. The steadiness of the sepoys, encouraged by the exertions of their officers, succeeded in baffling every attempt, and the enemy were compelled to retire, after suffering a heavy loss in killed and wounded, on the approach of the reinforcement under Lieut. Fyfe, between one and two in the afternoon. The attack commenced about seven in the morning*.

From the decision inherent in the character of Capt. Carpenter, it could not be very difficult to predict the measure that would follow:

* The conduct of the officers was mentioned with sufficient applause on the occasion by Capt. Carpenter; and, in truth, their situation was extremely critical for many hours: Lieut. Ross was wounded in the loins by a matchlock ball; but he survived many years to distinguish

and accordingly, when some days had been devoted to complete his arrangements, he determined to retaliate upon the enemy in their camp, the attempt, in which they had been so shamefully foiled, by such a handful of men in an open post, exposed on every side to the jungle. The enemy had been long observed, to have taken up a permanent position at the village on the strand westward of the Terring, formerly noticed; and their movements in the vicinity, could be pretty clearly distinguished from the post on Hyderghaut with the aid of a telescope. Having therefore made every preparation that his means afforded, and completed the troops for the attack, to about 600 rank and file at the utmost, Capt. Carpenter marched from the top of Hyderghaut, before daybreak one morning, directing his course along the road immediately towards the enemy; leaving Mrs. Carpenter at the head of the ghaut, under the protection of a trusty jemedar, with thirty sepoys.

In compliment to their recent behaviour, the column was led by the two officers who had so fortunately defended the pass. About eight in the morning, they came upon the picquets in front of the enemy's position. These seemed to be completely electrified when they perceived the scarlet uniform of the sepoys, issuing from amidst the verdure of the jungles; and they snatched up their clothes and matchlocks, and fled to the main body, without even discharging their pieces. The enemy had evidently been prepared for flight at a moment's warning; for the advanced parties of the attacking column had scarcely topped the sandhills, on the verge of the brook to the right of the enemy's camp, when they found themselves within pistol-shot of a very dense column, marching with rapid steps along the strand, for the Terring. On these a sharp fire was immediately opened by our snipers; but the march of the retreating enemy was not to be retarded for an instant, although it was an object so desirable

---

himself on a variety of occasions, and fell gloriously in action, on the 29th of December 1792, at the battle of Gadjnoor, near Simoga. He was then Major of Brigade, to Capt. (since Col.) Little's detachment of the Bombay army, serving with the Mahratta army under Purseram Bhow. (See Moor's Narrative, and Dirom's Narrative.) His coadjutor is still living to tell the tale.

to us, in order to allow of the main body, or some part of it, being brought up, with our six-pounder and grasshopper. The line of march had, however, become so extended, by the narrowness of the road through the jungles, that this could not be accomplished until the enemy had spread themselves in swarms along the brow of the hill, adjoining to the little post of the Terring on the left. The grasshopper was then brought to bear upon them; while the advanced party, now reinforced by Lieuts. Fyfe and Laurence, pushed through the Terring at one side, just as the enemy were receding at the other; part pushing immediately along the strand for the ferrying-place towards Ancola, and part taking the plain to the left, skirted by a large grove of cocoa-nut trees. From thence, they kept up an occasional fire upon that division of their pursuers, that diverged in the same direction; but their movements continued so rapid, as to baffle every exertion to overtake them; and the pursuit accordingly terminated on the bank of the river or creek, which bounds the district of Ancola to the westward. The loss of the enemy on this occasion could never be ascertained, as the dead bodies scattered over the strand, were washed away by the receding tide after high water; and on the side of the victors this signal advantage was obtained, as far as recollection serves, without the slightest loss.

After collecting together the force of his detachment, which had become thus considerably dissevered, Capt. Carpenter withdrew the same afternoon from the Terring, to the position lately occupied by the enemy. The day following, it was determined to take up a permanent position at a little distance off, in the rear of a small pagoda and tank, effectually commanding both the roads leading from Ancola to the Carwar districts. Here the detachment continued stationary for many weeks, without experiencing from the enemy the slightest further molestation, nor indeed during the whole of the remaining period of hostilities.

At the subsequent pacification, the whole of the captured territory on the Malabar coast being ceded back to the Sultaun, Sadashewghur, with the post dependent on it, was also delivered up to a small detachment of the Sultaun's troops, in the month of April 1784; Lieut. Ross and Ensign Price, after starting a large quantity of powder into the river, being the last to quit the place.

Capt. Carpenter having, according to stipulation, discharged about 400 of the recruits raised for the service of the district a few days before his departure from Sadashewghur, reached the presidency of Bombay, with his corps, previous to the setting in of the rains. He continued at the presidency until the close of 1784, when he was ordered up with his battalion, now completed, to form part of the garrison of Surat, and at that station they continued for a period of two years of profound peace.

Towards the conclusion of 1786, or commencement of 1787, the corps returned to the presidency; and during the rainy season of the latter year, there being under the then existing system, no leave of absence, Capt. Carpenter took final leave of the service, to proceed to England, by way of China; his paternal attention, and most liberal hospitality, being long remembered with regret, esteem, and gratitude, by every officer of the corps.

Extract from General Orders.

"*Bombay, 7th July*, 1787.

" Capt. Daniel Carpenter is permitted to proceed to Europe, by the way of China, agreeably to his request, contained in his letter to the President and Council of the 3d inst.; and will be suitably recommended to the Hon. the Court of Directors.

(Signed) " T. MARSHALL, Town Major."

Copy of the 59th paragraph of the General Letter, from Bombay, dated 28th July, 1787.

" Capt. D. Carpenter having likewise requested the same permission, as per copy of his letter, No. 29 in the packet, has obtained our leave; and we feel a satisfaction in recommending him to your notice, as a zealous and active officer, requesting that you will be pleased to permit of his return with his rank, should he hereafter apply for that indulgence."

The following are copies of letters, from Governor Hornby and Major Gen. Hartley, to this officer:—

"*London, 6th April,* 1798.

"Sir,—Agreeable to your request, I have read your memorials, and sincerely wish you success in your application. With respect to what you have set forth in your memorial of 1796, I am ready to bear testimony to what is set forth as to military merit, of your being selected on occasions of service, in which you ever acquitted yourself as deserving the high opinion had of you, as an active officer, and particularly at Carwar, where your exertions in recruiting a large force, and making the supplies you did, when the presidency could not assist you.

"I am, with esteem, &c.
(Signed) "W. Hornby."

"*Weymouth Street, 28th Oct.* 1796.

"Dear Sir,—I have attentively perused your memorial to the Court of Directors, and most heartily wish success to your application; for I shall derive infinite satisfaction in having you return to the army, on the Bombay establishment. The reference you have made to me, gives me great pleasure, for should it be thought necessary to follow up that reference, by an application to me, I shall be extremely glad of the opportunity of bearing public testimony of the experience I have had, for a length of years, of your great merits as an officer, and to certify that on all occasions of service, you have ever been selected as worthy of particular distinction, and that invariably you have ever acquitted yourself as truly deserving the high opinion entertained of you. The facts you have stated as ground of military merit in your memorial, I am happy in declaring to you are fairly and justly set forth.

(Signed) "J. Hartley."

This memoir furnishes an instance of the important commands, formerly entrusted to officers, of no higher rank than Captain in the East India Company's service. Capt. Carpenter, with a single battalion of sepoys, absolutely conquered, and for above a twelvemonth kept possession, of the extensive province of Carwar, and was left to his own resources, to raise troops and furnish them with supplies, and subsistence. These operations he conducted in a manner that will always reflect great honor on his memory, and holds out a bright example for the service.

THE LATE LIEUTENANT-COLONEL WILLIAM LANE.

(Bengal Establishment.)

This officer was appointed a Cadet on the Bengal establishment in 1767; and in 1781, he commanded a battalion of sepoys under Major Popham, at the capture of Beetabur and Bidzighur; shortly after which he returned to England for the benefit of his health. Some years afterwards, he was appointed Deputy-Governor of St. Helena, and was detached, with four companies of that garrison, to serve as marines in the fleet under Sir Home Popham, and subsequently, at the capture of Buenos Ayres. He returned, after the latter service, to England, and retired upon full pay. He died in Ireland, where he had some years previously married a sister of Lieutenant-Colonel Jacob Camac*.

He was an excellent officer and worthy man.

CAPTAIN JOHN SUTHERLAND.

(Bombay Establishment.)

This officer entered the Company's service in 1810, as a Cadet of Infantry on the Bombay establishment, and served in 1811 and 1812 in garrison at Guzerat.

In 1813, he repelled, near Ahmednuggur, in company with Capt. Burton, of the 4th regiment, and with a havildar's party of infantry, an

---

* Services, vol. ii. p. 101.

attack of a body of 500 Pindarries, under Sheik Dallah: they fought their way, surrounded by those plunderers, for about a mile, to a small hill, where they took post, and of which they kept possession, the Pindarries, after a time, retiring. On this occasion, the party received the applause of the Hon. Mr. Elphinstone, the Resident at Poona.

In April 1817, this officer was appointed by the Supreme Government, on the recommendation of Major Davies, to the command of a risala of His Highness the Nizam's reformed horse, organized under that officer for service against the Pindarries; and consisting of 4500 men, three of the risala's being each 1000, and the fourth 1500 strong.

In the latter end of 1817, when employed with a detachment of the army of the Deccan, this officer overtook and cut up, with his risala, the retreating garrison of Newassa, which maintained a desultory action across a plain and in a ravine. His conduct received the thanks of Sir Thomas Hislop, G. C. B., Com.-in-Chief of the army, and those of Col. Deacon, C. B., commanding the detachment.

He next joined, with the head-quarters of the reformed brigade, Sir Lionel Smith's division, and was employed in the service in pursuit of the Peishwa: he was present with his risala when Chimajee Apah, the Peishwa's brother, and Apah Dessae Nipanekur, with 3000 horse, surrendered to the brigade under the command of Major Davies, in May 1818.

In July of the same year, he was detached, in command of a risala of the brigade, in pursuit of Dhurmajee Purtaub Rao, and who he surrounded in the small ghuree of Dhabé, on the morning of the 30th July; dismounted and stormed the place at two points in the afternoon of the same day, and carried it with the loss of a jemedar, and nine men killed, and upwards of twenty wounded. Capt. Sutherland received several wounds in the assault.

In the Marquess of Hastings' General Orders to the Indian army, on the termination of the war, the above affair is noticed in these words:—

"Captain Sutherland, of the same corps, has distinguished himself by a gallant and well-conducted movement, against a noted predatory leader, and by assaulting, sword in hand, a ghuree, where the banditti had taken post."

In January 1819, Capt. Sutherland was employed with his risala, under Lieut.-Col. Pitman, in the siege of Nowah. On the place being stormed and carried by the infantry, on the 31st of the same month, a great portion of the Arab garrison sallied, with the view of cutting its way to a neighbouring hill and jungle. His risala charged with the rest of the cavalry, led by Major Davies; the garrison was annihilated, and Capt. Sutherland was wounded in the affair.

In the end of 1819, and until May 1820, Capt. Sutherland was employed in a desultory and nearly useless service, against a body of Bheels, in the Adjunta range of hills, in which, in addition to his risala, he had also at one time a battalion of infantry under his command.

In the end of 1820, and for some months of 1821, Capt. Sutherland was employed, under the orders of Sir Charles Metcalfe, the Resident at the court of Hyderabad, in command of a detachment of cavalry and infantry, with some ordnance, in the reduction of six or eight forts and ghurees, held by persons in rebellion against the Nizam's government. In some instances the garrisons resisted, in others, evacuated during the night, or laid down their arms. In one of these, Capt. Sutherland had an opportunity of charging on the plain, with 100 horse, a considerable portion of the garrison of Sooleale, in which the enemy suffered severely, and Capt. Sutherland had only two men and some horses wounded. The proceedings of the detachment, on all occasions, met with the approbation of Sir Charles Metcalfe, and in several instances it was honored with his thanks.

In 1821, this officer was appointed a Captain-Commandant in his Highness the Nizam's service.

Since this period, Capt. Sutherland has been chiefly employed in the civil branch of the Nizam's service, superintending, under the instructions of Sir Charles Metcalfe, the affairs of an extensive district.

In March 1824, he was appointed by the Supreme Government to the political branch of the Company's service, as an extra-assistant to the Resident at Hyderabad, and permitted to hold his command in the Nizam's army.

In May of the same year, Capt. Sutherland obtained a troop in the 3d reg. of light cavalry, having, on an augmentation, been transferred to this branch of the service by Sir Charles Colville*, G.C.B., Com.-in-Chief of the army; an exception to a rule, which required that all officers should join and do duty with their regiments for two years, having been made by His Excellency, in the case of this officer.

LIEUT.-COL. COMMANDANT WILLIAM TURNER.

(Bombay Establishment.)

This officer left England as a cadet for Bombay in 1797, and arrived in Bombay in Feb. 1798. He was appointed to an Ensigncy in the Bombay European regiment, on the 1st, and to a Lieutenancy on the 30th Jan. 1798; he joined his regiment at Cannanore in April of the same year, and was posted to the light company.

Lieut. Turner was present with his company during the whole of the siege of Seringapatam, and the service connected therewith, at the close of which his regiment returned to Cannanore, from whence it was soon afterwards removed to Cochin.

On the new organization of the army in 1800, Lieut. Turner was removed from the European to the 3d reg. N. I. and posted to the 1st batt. (or kaulee pultun,) which he had joined at Cundapore, in the province of Canara. He was not long with his new regiment before he was appointed Adjutant, which situation he held till his promotion to Captain, in 1805.

* Services, vol. iii. p. 16-19, Royal Military Calendar, 3rd edit.

Whilst in Canara, Lieut. Turner was detached, by order of L.-Col. Williamson, commanding the regiment, in pursuit of the Bilghie Rajah, who had escaped from confinement in Seringapatam. He also was entrusted with the command of a detachment stationed in the fort of Backell, on the sea coast, between Mangalore and Cananore.

During this time, the well known rebel Timnaick*, surprised and took the strong hill fort of Jemaulabad; but, being afterwards so hard pressed, by the force sent to retake it, as to induce him to make his escape over the walls, he betook himself to the jungles, where, if allowed to remain long, he might, by collecting fresh strength, have caused greater disturbances in that province; so that the seizure of his person became an object of considerable importance.

Lieut. Turner hearing that the rebel chief was somewhere in the neighbourhood of his post, instantly set about using every exertion to apprehend him; and, at last, by adopting several stratagems, was fortunate enough to secure him, and have him safely lodged in the fort of Backell, from whence he was soon after sent, under a strong escort, to the head-quarters of the province, and there blown from a gun.

For the performance of the above service, Lieut. Turner had the thanks of Colonel Mignan, commanding the province.

Lieut Turner and his detachment rejoined his battalion, and marched with it from Cundapore, and had proceeded as far as Mangalore, on the route to join Gen. Wellesley, who was then in command of a force in pursuit of the Boolum Rajah, but that service being over before the 1st. batt. 3d reg. reached, it was ordered into garrison at Goa, where it remained nearly twelve months.

Towards the close of the year 1802, Lieut. Turner accompanied his battalion to Bombay, where it had not remained a month when it was ordered to Bassein, in the northern Concan, as a guard to Bajee Rao, the Peishwa, who had previously left his capital in consequence of the disturbances at the court of Poona at that period.

A small force was formed at Bassein, consisting of H. M.'s 78th

* See Services of Capt. Thomas Grant, p. 172-4, of this volume.

and 84th regts., the 1st batt. 3d reg., part of the 1st batt. 7th reg., and a detail of foot artillery, under the command of Col. Murray, for the purpose of escorting his Highness to Poona, and reinstating him on the musnud. On its march, however, and before ascending the ghaut, this little force was employed against the fort of Kurnella, till then considered impregnable, but which was soon carried by assault, in the most gallant style, when the troops continued their route to Poona, and then joined Gen. Wellesley. The Bombay part of the force there assembled, was left during the rains, for the protection of the city.

At the close of the monsoon the 1st batt. 3d reg. was selected, with part of the 1st batt. 7th reg., and a detail of artillery, for the purpose of taking the strong hill fort of Poonadur, then in the possession of a refractory sirdar, who surrendered soon after operations had commenced against him. The detachment then returned to Poona, leaving a detail in the fort, until the Peishwa's troops should arrive to take charge.

In March 1803, Lieut. Turner accompanied the 1st batt. 3d reg. from Poona, to join Col. Murray, who was collecting a large force on the borders of Guzerat, for service in Hindostan. Previous to quitting the Deccan, that regiment was employed in taking the hill fort of Lowghur, situated near the top of the ghauts; which being effected, the battalion continued its march to Copperwanjee, the point of junction with the force then forming. It subsequently moved to Oogein, where it was supposed the whole of Col. Murray's force would remain for the rains; before the close of which, however, (in the month of August,) it was found necessary to take possession of Indore, and some small forts in its neighbourhood: the 1st batt. 3d reg. was ordered, along with H. M.'s 65th and 86th regiments, and another Native battalion, the whole under the immediate command of Col. Murray, for the performance of that service; and when completed, they again joined the main body of the army, which had moved from Oogein to meet them. The army encamped between two branches of the Siprah, and after experiencing the greatest hardships*, it returned to Oogein, where it was obliged to remain until provided with new equipments. It then moved on, by way of Rutlam, Kotah, &c. &c. to Bhurtpoor, where it joined Gen. Lake, who had sat down, with the troops from Bengal, before that fort.

Lieut. Turner was with his battalion during the whole of the siege of Bhurtpoor, and in which the 1st batt. 3d reg. suffered severely.

The siege being raised, the army moved off to Dholpore, where it remained some time.

In May 1804, the Bombay division of the grand army was ordered into monsoon quarters at Tonk Rampoora, which place it reached on the 4th of June, having again suffered severely on the march from want of water and the extreme heat of the weather.

The 1st batt. of the 3d reg. was not allowed to rest long. Early in July it was detached in the direction of Agra, to reinforce an escort, proceeding with provisions and military stores for the Bombay division; and during this trip of one month, this battalion was again doomed to the endurance of severe hardships. The whole of the march, the rain fell in torrents; the roads, always very bad, were, from the accumulation of water, rendered almost impassable, and the rivers being swollen, the whole of the stores, had, at each successive river and nullah, to be taken from the backs of the carriage cattle, and transported across by the sepoys.

In September of the same year, the Bombay division quitted its winter quarters, and proceeded towards Delhi; and after moving in different directions in that neighbourhood for a considerable time, was at last ordered to return to its own presidency. It arrived at Baroda in the beginning of 1806, where it was broken up; and the 1st batt. of the 3d reg. pursued its route to Bombay, and was quartered there during the monsoon.

Here again it was not allowed to rest long without employment; for as soon as the rains were over, its services were called for in the Deccan; and it again took the field. It quitted Bombay about the

---

* The extreme sufferings of the army on this occasion, owing to the severity of the weather, have been already fully described. See p. 124, and p. 178-9, of this volume.

middle of November, and joined the field force in camp at Seroor, under Colonel W. Wallace, of H. M.'s 74th regiment, and continued under his command for a period of more than two years; all that time actively employed; principally in the reduction of refractory chieftains, such as Sukroodhur, Mhyput Ram, Bungush Khan, and Dadan Khan.

In this place it may be proper to mention, that in consequence of Major East, (see p. 192 of this volume) the senior officer with the 1st batt. 3d reg., obtaining the command of a brigade, Captain Turner, as next senior, succeeded to the charge of the battalion, and during the period of the operations above alluded to, the 1st of the 3d was especially selected at different times, for the performance of services, where the greatest promptitude was requisite, and which were always performed to the entire satisfaction of the officer commanding the force.

Capt. Turner accompanied his regiment from the Deccan to Surat, in November 1809, where it was employed in garrisoning that place, and at the outposts in the districts, without any thing particular occurring till the end of 1812; when the Pindarries made an incursion into the Atteveessy. Capt. Turner, with his company, (the light) and the grenadiers of the regiment, both under Capt. W. W. Steuart, were ordered out in pursuit, where they continued until recalled to join the head quarters of their regiment, then under orders for the Deccan.

The regiment reached Seroor in May 1813: it was immediately employed in bringing to subjection Neepunkur, a Jaghiredar of the Peishwa; which occupied it till the middle of October.

About this period, Colonel L. Smith, of H. M.'s 65th reg., commanding the subsidiary force of the Peishwa, feeling the want of a body of light troops, which he could employ on all occasions where celerity of movement was requisite, and the Bombay establishment having no army of that description, the Colonel determined on concentrating all the light infantry companies belonging to the

Native corps under his command, and placing them under an active intelligent officer. Unasked and unsolicited, he did Capt. Turner the honour to offer him this enviable situation, which, of course, was readily accepted.

In pursuance of this measure, about the middle of 1814, the whole of the light companies were assembled at Seroor, when Captain Turner found himself in command of a body of between 7 and 800 of the finest troops in the Poona force, which he immediately set about organizing and drilling as a battalion of light infantry*. In two months after the formation of the battalion, it was reviewed by Colonel Smith, both in open and in close order, as a light infantry battalion, and also as a battalion of the line, and acquitted itself so well in all three situations as to call forth the Colonel's most unqualified approbation and praise.

Captain Turner's battalion was most actively and conspicuously employed (under the title of the light battalion) in every service within the Poona division, during the Pindarry war; and, from the manner it was trained, armed, and equipped, proved of the greatest use on all occasions.

The city of Poona was taken possession of by the force under Gen. Smith, on the 17th November 1817. After getting possession, the General received information of the whole of the enemy's light guns being drawn off towards the hill fort of Seooghur: in consequence, a detachment was ordered, composed of a brigade of horse artillery guns, 2 companies 65th reg., 2 companies Bombay

* This was a task of no small magnitude. Many of the men were not acquainted with a single sound of the bugle, and many more, who did know something of it, were obliged to be exchanged, in consequence of age or infirmities, which unfitted them for such active duty. When it is considered that such a corps was entirely new on the establishment, that neither officers nor men had ever been accustomed to move in battalion as light troops, and that so many men had to be taught individually, not only the movements, but the sounds of the bugle by which they were to move, and these men natives too, it may well be concluded that much temperate patience, much diligence, and, what is more, much good sound judgment and system, must have been displayed, to effect the end required; and which it appears crowned Captain Turner's labours with the most happy success.

European reg., 2 companies 1st batt. 4th reg. N. I., and the light battalion, to proceed in pursuit; and Capt. Turner was selected by the Brigadier-General for the command.

Capt. Turner marched in the afternoon of the 18th, came up with the enemy after sunset, strongly posted in three different batteries, on the ridges of Seooghur hill, and under the guns of the fort. On observing their situation, Capt. Turner made his dispositions accordingly. As he approached, the enemy's guns opened, but, from being placed on an elevated situation, did little execution. The infantry advanced under cover of the fire of the horse artillery, and on reaching the bottom of the hill, came to the charge, and pushed forward with such impetuosity, that the batteries were successively carried at the point of the bayonet, with scarcely any loss on the part of the detachment. The number of guns captured on this occasion was 21, of different calibres.

About this period, the Bombay government found it expedient to raise two regiments of cavalry, a perfectly new arm to that presidency, and which was officered by transfers from the infantry. Capt. Turner was, in consequence, promoted to a Majority in that line of the service, and posted to the 2d regiment.

He continued with Gen. Smith's force during the first pursuit of the Peishwa to the southward, and in the end of December was ordered to proceed to Guzerat, to join his new regiment; but being detained some time in Bombay, collecting horses, he did not reach head quarters till the beginning of March 1818.

In October of the same year, Major Turner was detached with a squadron of his regiment to accompany a small force under the command of Col. L. Stanhope, of the 17th dragoons, for service on the Mihie Kaunta. During this service, which was in the reduction of refractory zemindars, the squadron was actively employed, but not without several casualties, both in men and horses.

The object for which the force was sent out being attained, Major Turner accompanied his regiment to Mhow, in Malwa, where it remained inactive for ten months; at the expiration of which it was ordered into Kattywar, and from thence to Cutch, to join a large force then forming under the personal command of his Excellency the Commander-in-Chief, with the view of entering the Scind territories; but, about the close of the year, (1820) matters with these states being amicably adjusted, the force was broken up.

Major Turner was promoted to the rank of Lieut.-Col. on the 4th of May of this year (1820); and as part of the above-mentioned force was ordered, under the command of Col. Stanhope, for the reduction of the fort of Dwarka, and several others, in Okamundel, Col. Turner volunteered his services for the command of the 2d batt. 3d reg. N. I.; and was present at the taking of all these places. At Dwarka, he commanded the centre attack of the escalade; and received his due meed of praise from Col. Stanhope for his conduct on the occasion.

After matters were settled in Okamundel, Col. Turner continued in command of his infantry battalion, employed on a very harassing and fatiguing service in Kattywar, against a horde of freebooters that were plundering the country, and which occupied him about six months.

He was next ordered to Baroda, and appointed to the command of a brigade for field service, for the purpose of bringing to subjection several refractory zemindars in the Mihie Kaunta; and having satisfactorily performed that duty, his brigade returned to Baroda for the rains.

At the opening of the next fair season, the Lieut.-Col. was again appointed to command another brigade for a similar purpose, which was attended with equal success.

On the close of the last-mentioned service, Lieut.-Col. Turner marched, with part of his brigade, to Kattywar; and on his arrival (June 1822) was appointed to the Lieut.-Colonelcy of the 1st reg. light cavalry, then stationed at Rajcote. He remained there eighteen months, when his regiment was ordered to Kaira, for the purpose of being reviewed by the Com.-in-Chief in brigade, with the horse artillery, the 4th dragoons, and the 2d reg. light cavalry. On this occasion, Lieut.-Col. Turner received the most flattering compliments from the Com.-in-Chief, as well as from Col. Dalbiac*, inspecting officer of cavalry, for the high state of discipline in which they found the 1st regiment.

From Karia the regiment was ordered to the station of Deesa. Here Lieut.-Col. Turner was promoted to Lieut.-Col. Commandant of the 1st regiment.

After an uninterrupted service of nearly 27 years, without being one day absent from his corps, towards the close of 1824, finding his health beginning to break, Col. Turner was forced to seek for change of climate, and quitted his regiment with the view of returning to England. He left Bombay on the 15th Dec. 1824, with furlough to the Cape of Good Hope, and eventually to England.

MAJOR JOSEPH GARNER.
(Bengal Establishment.)

HAVING first arrived in India the latter part of 1804, this officer was ordered up to the army in the field, under Lord Lake. He joined the 1st batt. 15th reg. (then commanded by Lieut.-Colonel Robert Haldane, the present Major-General) in the early part of 1805, being one of the battalions under the personal command of his Lordship, then acting against the Mahratta confederates. With this regiment he remained until the conclusion of the war; and in 1806, the corps was ordered into cantonments at Benares. On the general relief taking place in 1808, the battalion was ordered to Calcutta; and in June of the same year, he commanded a company with the expedition sent by Lord Minto to China†, where the troops remained until the differences which subsisted between the British government and the Chinese were finally adjusted. The volunteers returned to Bengal in 1809, when they were highly complimented by government for the hardships and privations they had undergone.

* Services, Royal Military Calendar, vol. iv. p. 211-12, 3d edit.
† See vol. ii. p. 182-7, of this work.

In 1810, government again requiring volunteers for secret and foreign service, the regiment to which this officer belonged was again selected for this duty, and he was appointed to the command of a company in the 1st Bengal volunteer battalion. He proceeded with the force under General Abercromby, and was present at the capture of the Isle of France, where the Bengal division remained, and, ultimately, returned to Bengal in 1812. In June, the volunteers were broke up, and he rejoined his former corps in the latter end of that year.

In March 1813, the regiment got orders to prepare for field service, and in April, marched to join the field force assembling in Rewah; where, after a most irksome campaign, in the severest season of the year, they were ordered, by forced marches, to Mirzapore, to save that city from being burnt by the Pindarries, who had entered the district with 2,500 irregular horse; and by moving 20 miles a-day, the regiment just arrived in time to prevent the meditated destruction of the city.

In 1814, the Marquess of Hastings was pleased to appoint this officer adjutant to the 2d batt. of his regiment, then stationed at Dinapore. The corps being ordered for service, against the state of Nepaul, it marched from Dinapore in Nov. 1814; and it remained in the field until the peace of Muckwanpoor, in 1816. In the second campaign against the Nepaulese, this officer had the honour of commanding the flank companies of his regiment in forcing the pass in the Chowriaghatee range of hills, the key to Muckwanpoor and Khutmhandoo, their capital. This battalion was one of the 4th brigade, of which such honourable mention is made in Sir David Ochterlony's division orders*, dated in Camp, at Dooreeah, 5th April, 1816.

* The following are extracts from those orders, as well as from the Marquess of Hastings' orders on the close of the war, and conduct of the Dinapore division:—

Extract of General Orders by the Right Honourable the Governor-General in Council, Fort William, 20th March, 1816.

"The military operations against the state of Nepaul having been brought to a triumphant close, the Governor-General in Council has peculiar pleasure in offering a public

About six months after the termination of hostilities, this officer was seized with the terrai fever, or "owl"; and, after struggling for acknowledgment of the merits of those by whom the campaign has been so speedily and decisively terminated. The zeal, the judgment, and the energy of Major-Gen. Sir David Ochterlony, have been brilliantly conspicuous; in the late operations, he has afforded a fresh and most instructive lesson to the troops, that vigour, united with science, regards no obstacle as embarrassing, but will, with ease and security, master difficulties which, to a superficial view, appear insurmountable. To particularize others, when all have merited applause so highly, would entail the objection, that wheresoever the discrimination should stop, those not named might appear to have deserved less. The Governor-General in Council, therefore, entreats the staff, the officers, Native as well as European, the non-commissioned officers, and the soldiers of the Dinapore division, to be persuaded, that he contemplates, with admiration, the patience under uncommon fatigues, the cheerful endurance of unusual privations, and the animated courage manifested by all descriptions in the division.

"The whole of that force may indulge the gratifying reflection of having worthily fulfilled their duty to the state, and they will necessarily retain a proud confidence in their own powers.

"The nature of the country and the climate were so novel to the Native troops, that a greater degree of merit must be attached to intrepidity, under such circumstances; at the same time, that a testimonial of exemplary behaviour, in such a service, must have more than ordinary value to those on whom it may be bestowed, Government has therefere determined, that silver medals shall be presented to every Native officer who actually served within the hills, and to as many of the non-commissioned officers and privates as shall be recommended by the commanders of their respective battalions, for distinguished zeal and gallantry, in the course of that duty.

"By command of his Excellency the Governor-General in Council,
(Signed) "J. ADAM, Secretary to Government."

Extract.—Division Orders by Major-General Sir David Ochterlony, K.C.B.; Camp, Dooreeah, 5th April, 1816.

"In publishing the above general orders, the Major-General is apprehensive of diminishing their value, by any expression of his own sentiments, but to be wholly silent would denote an ungrateful insensibility to the merits of the gallant army which he had lately the honour to command, and to whose exertions he feels himself indebted for the distinguished honour he has received. In an appeal to arms made solely to resent injury, and vindicate the national honour, the speedy submission of the enemy, and early re-establishment of peace, are just objects of exultation and desire. Those objects have been attained: an enemy confident in their courage, and in the natural strength of their country, have been reduced to implore the acceptance of a treaty they had recently delayed or rejected; and it has been the proud fortune of this army to evince the superiority of British valour only to display in stronger colours British moderation and liberality. To the zeal, perseverance, patriotism, and intrepidity, of those he had the honour to command, the Major-General ascribes the approbation which has been bestowed on his humble efforts, and in offering his acknowledgments, he requests they will accept his most sincere congratulations on the

two years, was compelled to seek change of air in England: until this period he had never been unwell, or one hour absent from his duty. He returned, and joined the 2d batt. 15th reg. at Juanpore, and shortly after was promoted to a majority, and posted to the 1st battalion of the regiment (now the 30th) then at Chittagong, where he joined it; but owing to unusual sickness and mortality in the corps, it was sent into cantonments at Midnapore; and in the month following Major Garner was again reappointed to the 2d battalion, (now the 31st regiment).

Major Garner has had the honour to serve with the united forces of His Majesty and the Hon. Company, who on three successive occasions received the thanks of both Houses of Parliament; viz. 1st. with the army under the late Lord Lake, in 1805. 2d. with Gen. Abercromby, at the taking of the Isle of France, in 1810. 3d. with Sir David Ochterlony, in the Nepaul war, in 1814-15-16.

CAPT. A. WOGAN BROWNE.

(Bombay Establishment.)

This officer, son of the Hon. Col. Anthony Browne, late of the Saxon service, was appointed a Cadet on the Bombay establishment in the year 1803, and arrived at that presidency on the 20th June 1805. He was sent to the Hon. Company's College, at Mahim, to acquire a knowledge of the Oriental languages; on leaving

---

well-merited encomiums they have received. The 3d and 4th brigades, under the personal command of the Major-General, have the strongest claims on his entire approbation: Lieut.-Cols. Miller and Burnett are entitled to his warmest thanks, for the active discharge of their separate and arduous duties, from the 14th to the 28th February. Under the influence of grateful recollections, which he could not restrain, the Major-General has entered into longer and more particular details than he originally designed, and more perhaps than were requisite, where all had such claims to his unqualified approbation and praise.

" To all then, individually and collectively, he begs to repeat his thanks, and in the word ' Farewell,' to offer his sincere wishes for their health, prosperity, and success."

which, he was attached to the 3d reg. N. I., then doing duty in the garrison of Bombay.

He was afterwards posted to the 2d batt. 6th reg. N. I., with which he remained until the 15th May 1809, when he was selected to serve in the troop of Native cavalry, then commanded by Capt. Henry Roome *, and the only regular cavalry at that time on the Bombay establishment. He was with that distinguished corps on the many and arduous services where it was engaged, from that period until 1816, when most urgent private affairs obliged him to proceed to Europe. During his absence, two regiments of cavalry were raised, and he was thereby deprived of the reasonable expectations, which he so long entertained, of being permanently posted to that branch of the service, and to which an uninterrupted and laborious attendance of seven years to that line of duty, gave him no small claims.

He was present with the cavalry at the capture of Mallia, under Col. Walker †, in 1809, upon which occasion the officers and corps were made honourable mention of, in the field detachment orders.

In 1810, he was employed in the memorable campaign in Guzerat and Cutch; and in 1811, he commanded an advanced detachment of cavalry at Khanpore, on the Mihie, to prevent the incursions of the predatory chieftain Narbhoy.

In 1812, he served at the siege of Newanuggur, where he received a wound from a spent ball, in the wrist, whilst advancing with the cavalry pickets, which were attacked in force by the enemy. On this occasion, the corps and officers were thanked in field detachment orders, by Major-General Sir Lionel Smith, K.C.B.

He commanded, in 1813, a detachment of cavalry and horse-artillery, at Songhur; and in 1814, he served the campaign under Colonel East, and was employed at the taking of Anjar, and various other places: also, at the reduction of the provinces of Cutch and Waugur.

In the following year, 1815, he commanded a detachment of ca-

* Services, p. 114 16 of this volume. † Services, vol. i. p. 425-460.

valry and infantry, to protect the south-west frontier of Guzerat from the hitherto frequent incursions of the Jhuts and Waugurs, in which he succeeded most completely, by the accurate information he managed to procure, and the celerity of his movements to the points threatened. He received thanks for saving the flourishing town of Dollerah, (then filled with Company's cotton, and other goods, to a large amount) from being plundered and burned, by the speed with which he performed a long forced march, and arrived in time to prevent the meditated attack.

He served the campaign of 1816 *, in Cutch, under Colonel East, at the conclusion of which he went to Europe.

This officer obtained the brevet of Captain, 1st January 1818; he returned to India in 1819, and was soon after promoted to Captain of a Company, and appointed to the command of the fort and garrison of Sholapore. In 1820, he was appointed Barrack-Master of the Surat division of the army; in 1822, Major of Brigade at Poona; in 1823, Inspector of hill forts in the Deccan; and was directed to put into a state of repair the hill forts in the Poona division of the army.

MAJOR EDMUND HARDY.

(Bombay Establishment.)

This officer was a Cadet in the Royal Military Academy, Woolwich, on the East India Company's establishment, in 1801; he joined the artillery at Bombay, as 1st Lieutenant, May 24th 1804; and the field army at Baroda, under Lieut.-Col. Woodington, in 1805. He was on field service in Kattywar, under Lieut.-Col. Alex. Walker, in 1807; and was present at the reduction of Kundoorna Ranaka;

* The troop to which this officer belonged was for this year attached to that excellent regiment, H. M.'s 17th light dragoons, then commanded by the Hon. Col. Lincoln Stanhope.

and, in 1809, at the storm and capture of Mallia. Subsequently in the same year, he was employed on a survey round the coast of Kattywar, and constructed a map of that country for government.

In 1810, he was appointed Quarter-Master and Acting Adjutant of the artillery at Bombay. In 1811, he was employed on field service in Kattywar, under Lieut.-Col. East; and was present at the siege and capture of Chiah, commanding the artillery, and as Commissary of Stores. In 1812, he served, as Commissary of Stores, under Lieut.-Col. (now Maj.-Gen.) Sir Lionel Smith, at the siege of Noanuggur.

From 1813 to 1819, he served in the Poona division of the army, under Maj.-Gen. Sir Lionel Smith. He was appointed to the horse artillery in 1815; and removed, on his promotion to a company, in 1817. He was present at the attack of the Peishwa's army before Poona, in 1817; at the siege and reduction of the hill forts of Seooghur, Poorunder, Wapoota, and others, under Maj.-Gen. Sir Theophilus Pritzler, K.C.B.[*]; of the hill forts of Ioodhur, Joonur, and others, under Major W. Eldridge [†] of the Bombay European regiment; and at the capture of Mallegaum, under Lieut.-Colonel M'Dougal.

In 1819, he acted as Military Secretary to Maj.-Gen. Baillie [‡], commanding the forces at Bombay; and in 1820, he commanded the Artillery, and served, as Commissary of Stores, under Maj.-Gen. Sir W. Keir Grant [§], K.C.B. and K.C.H. in the Persian gulf; and was present at the siege and capture of Rhas ul Kyma.

He was promoted in 1821, to the rank of Major; and in 1824, appointed Acting Director of the Artillery Depôt of Instruction.

[*] Services, Royal Military Calendar, vol. iv. p. 174, 3d edit.
[†] Died at Poona, 7th October, 1818.   [‡] Services, vol. i. p. 244-50.
[§] Services, Royal Military Calendar, vol. iii. p. 267-9, 3d edit.

LIEUTENANT-COLONEL H. E. GILBERT COOPER.

(Bengal Establishment.)

This officer went out to India as a Cadet, in 1801, and joined the old 15th regiment in 1802. He was present with the corps in every action, storm, assault, &c. during the campaigns of Gen. Lord Lake, in 1803, 4, and 5, including the capture of Allyghur, battle of Delhi, taking of Agra, battle of Lasswarree, battle of Deeg, and two out of the four storms of Bhurtpoor. He also served with the 15th in the Nepaul war, and continued with that corps till his promotion to Lieut.-Colonel, and was then posted to the 63d reg., which he now commands.

Lieut.-Col. Cooper has held the following staff situations:—Adjutant of his regiment; Brigade-Major at Penang; Brigade-Major to Maj.-Gen. L. Burrell*, at Lucknow; Barrack Master at Agra; and Superintendent and Director of telegraphic communications.

LIEUTENANT-COLONEL WILLIAM GARRARD.

(Madras Establishment.)

In 1796, this officer was appointed a Cadet: he went through a course of study at Woolwich, in order to be qualified for the corps of engineers, to which he now belongs; sailed for India in March 1797, and arrived at Madras in August following; but as the present regulations regarding Cadets for the engineer and artillery corps were not then in existence, he was, on his landing, appointed an Ensign of native infantry, and continued as such several months, during which time, however, he was permitted to do duty in Fort St. George, under Maj.-Gen. Ross, the chief engineer; and after-

---

* Services, vol. ii. p. 213-29.

wards, having undergone an examination, he was appointed to the corps of engineers.

He was attached to the grand army under Gen. Harris, in the war against Tippoo Sultaun, in 1799; but, on the march towards Seringapatam, engineer officers being much wanted with the Nizam's subsidiary force, then commanded by Colonel Wellesley (now Duke of Wellington), he and another officer, of the name of Rowley, were detached to it, and placed under the orders of Capt. Mackenzie, the senior engineer with that force. Their ordinary duties were to survey every day's line of march and encampment, and regularly to prepare, immediately after coming on the ground, and furnish to the commanding officer, drawings of the same, including the relative position of the head-quarter flag of the grand army; and to superintend the removal of all obstructions, whether to the march or to the free communication between the two camps.

He was engaged in the battle of Malavilly, and had a principal share in bringing up, by means of bildars, the brigade of guns attached to H. M.'s 33d reg., after the cattle had broke away from them, which guns did great execution.

On arriving before Seringapatam, he was immediately employed in converting a considerable village, abandoned by the enemy, into a secure post; which, being on commanding ground and on the right flank of the camp, became an important position. He also surveyed the principal nullah between the encampments and the fort, and which winded round what was called the engineer's tope. This survey he, unaccompanied by any one, extended to a very considerable distance beyond the extreme outposts on the right of the line, and for which he obtained the marked approbation of Colonel Wellesley.

So soon as the general plan of the siege was decided on, Ensign Garrard rejoined the grand army, and was appointed to the 2d brigade of engineers, under Capt. Johnson, who, after the fall of the place, made a very honourable report of his conduct to the chief engineer. He accompanied his Brigadier to the assault, and entered the fort through the breach, with the European grenadiers.

As soon as the army could move from Seringapatam, its march was directed towards the formidable hill fort of Chittledroog, whose killedar refused to surrender. A captain and subaltern of engineers were ordered to proceed with it; and Ensign Garrard, although but partially recovered from a severe dysentery, occasioned by fatigue and privation during the siege, was selected by Col. Gent, the chief engineer, as the subaltern for the occasion. On the arrival, however, of the army before the place, it surrendered, and the two engineer officers were ordered to march, on the following morning, with a force under Col. Dalrymple, in pursuit of Doondia Waugh, who was in considerable force, and ravaging the country; this was a very harrassing service, from the season of the year (as the rains had set in), from the great length of the marches, and from the nature of the roads and country in general.

The fort of Hoonelly, on the left bank of the river Toombuddra, was first attacked, and speedily taken, notwithstanding the difficulty of crossing that river, which was quite full, and running a most rapid stream. The activity of the engineer department, aided by the labours of the pioneers, soon furnished the means of passing over, on which occasion the engineer officers, perceiving the comparative tardiness and inefficiency of the common round basket boats, in such a case of emergency, with the enemy on the opposite bank, had a barge of bamboo-work constructed and covered with raw hides, in the same manner as the round basket boats were, no other hides being procurable; to which a sail, mast, and rudder, being affixed, Ensign Garrard volunteered to steer it across, laden with a mounted 6-pounder, complete in all its parts, some gunners, lascars, and others. This hazardous undertaking succeeded completely, and the barge made several expeditious trips before it failed, and then without the loss or hurt of any one.

The battery, which was constructed immediately opposite the fort, did such good work, that when the escalade took place it was found to be entirely abandoned by the garrison. Immediately after this affair the detachment made a night march of about 25 miles, to Shicarpoor, where Doondia was with his whole force. An action took place close to the walls; the gate was blown open, and the fort taken by assault, at the same time that the enemy was completely defeated, with great loss, on the outside. After this victory, the detachment marched 59 miles in pursuit of the fugitives, and had the mortification to be close at their heels just as they had taken shelter in the S. Mahratta territory, and were, consequently, out of its reach.

On the return of the detachment from this service, Capt. Blair and Ensign Garrard were ordered by the Hon. Maj.-Gen. Wellesley, who then had succeeded Gen. Harris in the command of the army, to proceed to the northern frontier of the Mysore territory, for the purpose of visiting and surveying six forts, which were described by Poorneah, the regent, to be of great importance; they were also to prepare a sketch survey and report of that part of the country in general.

The unhealthy season had set in; the greater part of the country was an impenetrable jungle; the roads of the very worst description, and in many places quite impassable until much labour had been bestowed on them. Both these officers, and Ensign Garrard in particular, were attacked by the jungle fever; they were destitute, both of medicine and medical aid, in a part of the country never before explored by Europeans, and their followers were dying fast around them. The force with them consisted merely of a havildar's or of a jemedar's guard; yet, notwithstanding all these disadvantages, they performed the duty required of them. Ensign Garrard, during the intermissions of his fever, surveyed and completed drawings and reports of four of the forts (the other two were found to be completely demolished). On their return to Chittledroog, quite worn out by sickness, they were gratified by the receipt of a letter of praise from the Hon. Gen. Wellesley, for their services.

All field duties being now at an end, Ensign Garrard was directed to proceed to the head-quarters of his corps at Fort St. George, but on reaching Bangalore, he was so completely exhausted by his illness (the jungle fever) that he could proceed no further. Colonel Campbell (the late Sir Alexander Campbell, Commander-in-Chief at Madras) at that time commanded there; he received him with parental kindness, kept him under his roof until he became convalescent, and afterwards, on his own removal, took him with him to Madras.

On Ensign Garrard's arrival at Madras, Maj.-Gen. Ross, in consideration of his services, recommended him for the Adjutancy of the corps, then vacant, which was immediately conferred on him; but he could enjoy this only a short time, as the fever would not quit him, and his constitution became so much impaired that he was obliged to return to England on sick certificate, in July 1800. Whilst in England, an invasion from France being apprehended, he applied to the Court of Directors for permission to offer his services to Government, which was granted immediately, with the expression of the Court's high approbation of his employing the remaining period of his furlough "in so spirited and patriotic a manner." He accordingly made the offer to Lord Sidmouth, one of His Majesty's ministers, and received an assurance that it should be accepted if the invasion were attempted; but the peace of Amiens followed almost immediately afterwards.

In Sept. 1805, he was again compelled to return to England on sick certificate, and the ship in which he embarked touching at Fernanda Noronia, instead of at St. Helena, he took the opportunity of making drawings and a sketch plan of the side of the island off which the ship was anchored; which, with a report, he, on his arrival in England, transmitted to the Court of Directors, and received their acknowledgments for the same.

He was appointed Adjutant of engineers on the expedition against the island of Java, in 1811; and, soon after his return from thence, was, at the especial desire of Sir Samuel Auchmuty, the Commander-in-Chief, appointed, as a reward for his services on that expedition, Superintending Engineer of the Mysore division.

Whilst on his passage to Java, he prepared a trigonometrical table for military surveys, on the principle of the traverse table used in navigation; or, in other words, he adapted the latter to the scale of the perambulator. On its being afterwards submitted to the Madras Government, many copies were printed, by order, and distributed amongst the officers employed on survey. For this Capt. Garrard received the approbation of the Government of Fort St. George, and afterwards that of the Court of Directors.

In the year 1812, a force, under Lt.-Col. Dowse, was ordered into the S. Mahratta states, and Capt. Garrard was, by Sir S. Auchmuty, specially appointed the commanding engineer to it. The immediate object of this force was the attack of the Fort of Kooshgul, the garrison of which was in rebellion against the Peishwa. It, however, surrendered to Col. Dowse at discretion, and nothing further of any moment was executed.

This officer has, within the last three years, been obliged, for the third time, to repair to England on sick certificate, but contemplates returning to India at midsummer 1826.

He was, in April 1825, promoted to the Majority of his corps, and in June following he became a Lieutenant-Colonel.

LIEUTENANT-COLONEL JOHN PESTER.

(Bengal Establishment.)

IN 1800, this officer went to India as a Cadet: he was appointed Ensign on his arrival; joined the 1st batt. 2d reg. at Futtehghur, in June 1801; and in December following proceeded with it to occupy the advanced post of Shekevabad, in the then ceded provinces.

In August following, Lieut. Pester was detached, with his company, against a rebel force assembled in the Shekevabad district, the chief of which had set the civil authorities at defiance. After a night march of ten hours, across a country, the greater part of which, at this season, was under water, the detachment arrived at the strong walled village and ghurry (or small mud fort) of Khomney, which was immediately attacked and carried; but so determined was the resistance, that great numbers of the rebels fell fighting hand to hand with the sepoys in the streets. The detachment also suffered severely, principally from the fire to which it was exposed, before the gates of the village could be forced. On this occasion, Lieut. Pester (who was ably supported by Ensign Marston) received, through his commanding-officer, letters expressive of the fullest approbation of his Excellency Gen. Lake, and the Hon. Mr. Wellesley, Lieutenant-Governor of the provinces.

In November following, the 1st batt. 2d reg. formed part of a strong detachment employed for the reduction of certain refractory chiefs in the ceded districts, and Lieut. Pester was present with his corps at the taking of the forts of Phurrah, Sasnee, Catchoura, and Tateah. At Sasnee, where General Lake assumed the command, Lieut. Pester was honoured with his Excellency's personal thanks for having, under a cannonade from the garrison, moved out of the trenches with his company, and dislodged a considerable body of the enemy, who had taken possession of a jungle with a view to annoy the troops in the trenches.

In the storm of Sasnee, Lieut. Pester had the good fortune to save the life of his gallant and much-esteemed Captain (Sinclair), by shooting a man who was in the act of spearing Capt. Sinclair as he ascended the ladders to the assault.

At the close of this campaign Lieut. Pester obtained one month's leave on his private affairs, the only absence, in the course of twenty-five years, that he ever solicited from his corps or station, except in cases of certified sickness.

In June following the Sasnee campaign, Lieut. Pester, with the grenadiers of the 2d, formed part of a detachment from the corps employed against the small, but strong fort of Buddoon, which was taken after a smart resistance.

In August of the same year, Lieut. Pester marched with his corps from Shekevabad to join the grand army assembling at Secundrapore to oppose Scindia; and when the troops were brigaded, he was appointed Acting Quarter-Master to the regiment, and holding that appointment, he was present with the advanced guard and pickets in the action at Coel, of the 29th August; the capture of Allyghur, by assault; the battle of Delhi; siege and taking of Agra.

On the fall of Agra, the 2d regiment was ordered to garrison the place; but Lieut. Pester was permitted by the Commander-in-Chief to proceed with the army in pursuit of Scindia's force, and was, by his Excellency, the same day appointed Major of Brigade to the 4th brigade of infantry, which, immediately subsequent to the battle of Lasswarree, was detached to obtain possession of the fortress of Gwalior: this was effected after an arduous siege of some weeks. Brigade Major Pester was, with the officer commanding*, at the head of the column employed in the night of the 2d January in occupying the town and storming the pettah; and for his conduct on this occasion, and in wholly managing the details of the division, and performing the various other duties which devolved on him during the siege, he received the repeated thanks of the Brigadier. His Excellency the Commander-in-Chief was also pleased, in a letter penned by himself, to signify his satisfaction of the reports made to head-quarters, of Captain Pester's conduct, by the Brigadier commanding.

In Sept. 1804, the 1st batt. 2d reg. being one of the battalions selected to join the grand army assembling at Secundra, Capt. Pester was permitted, at his own request, to quit his Staff appointment at Gwalior, and join his corps; and when the nomination of prize agents took place, he was elected, by his brother officers, their agent for captured property; and on the first vacancy was re-appointed, by the Commander-in-Chief, Major of Brigade to the 2d infantry brigade, which situation he held until the conclusion of the Deeg and Bhurtpoor campaigns; and on the breaking up of Lord Lake's army on

---

* The late Maj.-Gen. Sir Henry White, K. C. B. Services, vol. i. p. 24-37.

the banks of the Chumbul, his health, which had been long and seriously impaired, compelled him to proceed to the presidency, and thence, as his only alternative, to Europe.

With his health but imperfectly re-established, Captain Pester returned to his duty in Bengal, and, shortly after his arrival, was appointed by his Excellency, Sir George Nugent, a permanent Brigade Major on the establishment, posted to the station of Benares, and thence removed, in 1817, to Dinapore; and when Brig.-Gen. Toone's division moved from the latter station for the protection of the frontier, during Lord Hastings' campaign, Brigade-Major Pester was directed to accompany it, and was appointed by his Lordship to the responsible duties of Assistant Quarter-Master-General, with charge of the guide and intelligence department of the south-west frontier division, which appointments he continued to hold until the breaking up of the different divisions in the hot weather of the ensuing year.

Brigade-Major Pester continued to fulfil the duties of his station until 1823, when he was compelled by severe indisposition to re-visit Europe.

In July 1823, this officer obtained his Majority, and in December of the following year was promoted to the rank of Lieut.-Colonel.

LIEUTENANT-COLONEL JAMES ROBERTSON.

(Bengal Establishment.)

This officer was a Cadet of the year 1796: he arrived at Fort William, Bengal, on the 27th January 1798; was promoted to the rank of Ensign, and posted to the 2d European regiment, then at the presidency; a few months following, to Lieutenant, and removed to the 8th reg. N. I. at Chunar, which corps he joined, and did duty with, until December, when he was removed to the 2d N. I. at Allahabad. He joined the latter regiment, and did duty until regimental rank took place, when he was removed to the 11th Native infantry.

He joined the 1st battalion then at Midnapore, and marched up the country with the corps to Chunar, where it formed part of a detachmen under the command of Maj.-Gen. Sir Ewen Baillie, which assembled at Benares, and, immediately after formation, marched with the detachment to Sultaunpore Oude, where it was cantoned.

In 1801, Lieut. Robertson marched with his regiment to Caunpoor, where it was stationed. In June following he was appointed to the general staff of the army, and held the appointment of Cantonment-Adjutant and Quarter-Master to the cavalry cantonment at Ghazeepore*. In this situation he continued until 1810, when he was promoted to the rank of Captain, which obliged him to rejoin his regiment at Sultaunpore Oude, with which he did duty until 1812, and escorted a state prisoner (who was supposed to have assassinated Mr. Cherry) to Benares.

Capt. Robertson proceeded to Europe on furlough, in Feb. 1812, and returned to India in Nov. 1814, about which time the disturbances in Nepaul were breaking out. He proceeded immediately from Calcutta by dawk, and joined his regiment at Seerora in Oude, 700 miles from Fort William, where he was appointed to the command of five companies of his regiment, and two brigades of guns, and detached to Bulrampoor in Oude, to protect and prevent the incursions of the Nepaulese, on the frontier of His Majesty the King of Oude's dominions, and at the same time to co-operate and obey all instructions he might receive from Major-General Sullivan Wood, who was then in command of an army against Nepaul, on the eastern frontier.

Capt. Robertson remained at Bulrampoor, with his detachment, for the space of three months, constantly harassed and threatened to be overpowered by the enemy, (two detachments of the same strength, under the command of Capt. Sibley and Blackney, between him and Maj.-Gen. Wood's army, having been completely cut

* The late Marquess Cornwallis, Governor-General, died in Lieut. Robertson's bungalow at Ghazeepore. Memoir in this volume.

up and destroyed); after which he was ordered, by Maj.-Gen. Wood, to join the main body of the army with his detachment, about 200 miles to the eastward, from Bulrampoor, which he effected with great difficulty, from the enemy being in strong force all along the frontier.

After having joined Gen. Wood, Capt. Robertson marched with his detachment to the attack of Butevool, a town situated close to a pass into the Nepaul territory, where the enemy were so strong in number, that this small army, under M.-Gen. Wood, after battering the town, were obliged to retire; and as the rainy season was now approaching, this force was broke up, and each detachment returned to its respective cantonments.

Capt. Robertson's detachment escorted the park and field train, towards cantonments; and on his reaching Seerora, the head-quarters of his regiment, the death of the Bhow Begum, took place at Fyzabad, (in Oude) in that vicinity, when a detachment of eight companies was formed at Fyzabad, for the protection of his treasure and property; Capt. Robertson was appointed to the command, and received instructions from the British Resident at Lucknow, to superintend the reckoning and arrangement of the treasure of his highness the late Bhow Begum, in which duty he was engaged for the space of three months, the treasure having been buried and concealed in different places. In and about the palace, one million of coin, in gold and silver, was found, besides a large quantity of valuable jewellery, the value of which could not be ascertained, but was supposed to be about one million more. Capt. Robertson escorted the whole of the treasure and jewellery to Lucknow, and delivered over the same to His Majesty the King of Oude, who, as a mark of his approbation of the duty performed, presented him, in presence of his Court and the British Resident, with a valuable sword; in addition to which, Capt. Robertson received the approbation of government, as per annexed extract of a letter from the secretary to government in the political department, addressed to the British resident at Lucknow:—

"*To R. Strachey, Esq., Resident at Lucknow.—Political Department.*

"SIR,—I have had the honour to receive your despatch, No. 71, dated the

8th instant. The testimony borne by you to the laborious nature of the duty in which Capt. Robertson has been engaged, in superintending, by your direction, the reckoning and arrangement of the treasure of his Highness the late Bhow Begum, and the satisfactory manner in which he discharged it, have impressed the Governor-General in Council with a favourable sense of Capt. Robertson's services on that occasion. I am accordingly directed to request, you will assure Captain Robertson of the favourable opinion entertained by the Governor-General in Council, of his services at Fyzabad.

"J. ADAM, Sec. to Government.
"*Fort William, 31st August,* 1816."

Capt. Robertson was promoted to the rank of Major, in February 1821; and to Lieut.-Colonel, in May 1824, and is now (1826) in command of the 17th regiment Bengal Native infantry, and the troops at the frontier part of Bhopalpore, bordering with Scindia and Holkar's territories.

MAJOR CHARLES HENRY BAINES.

(Bengal Establishment.)

THIS officer joined the 6th reg. N. I., as an Ensign, in Nov. 1799: he volunteered to serve with the expedition to Egypt, in 1800, but was rejected on the score of youth, by Lieut.-Col. (now Lieut.-Gen.) B. Marley, the commanding officer of his corps.

In 1801, he joined the 1st batt. 7th reg., at Futtehghur, and was present in the assault, by escalade, of the fort Dustempoor, in the Vizier's dominions, under command of Lieut.-Col. (the late Major-Gen.) Morris, on which service he lost 60 men, out of a battery guard consisting of 90 men, and was himself slightly wounded.

In May 1801, he joined the 2d batt. 13th reg., and in 1803, was present at the siege, and on the storm of the fort of Chowkundie, in Bogulcund, serving with two companies of the 2d batt. 13th reg., commanded by Lieut. (now Lieut.-Col. Commandant) W. Thomas *, co-operating with the 2d batt. 6th reg. under the general command of Major Hefferman.

In 1804, on a call for volunteers for distant service, Ensign Baines sent in his name, but being on command, the name of another officer was forwarded by his commanding officer, Lieut.-Col. (now Lieut.-Gen.) Martindell, before his could arrive.

In the same year, 1804, a command devolved on Ensign Baines, consisting of 2 companies and 200 irregular horse, posted on the Rewah frontier, which was exposed to the constant incursions and depredations of a marauding chief; and who, previous to the call for troops, consequent to hostilities breaking out with the Mahrattas, had for a considerable time engaged the attention of five companies, a squadron of cavalry, and a brigade of gallopers, under Capt. (now Col.) Worsley, C.B.†, but having, after consulting with the judge and magistrate of Allahabad, determined on pursuing him beyond the Company's frontier, he succeeded in capturing him, the first time he presented himself, after a pursuit of 12 hours. This service was acknowledged in the following letter:—

" *To Lieut. Baines, commanding a Detachment at Barre.*

" SIR,—I have derived very great satisfaction from the information contained in your letter of the 1st inst., and beg you will immediately direct the person you have apprehended, to be conducted to Allahabad, under a proper guard. I shall not fail to notice the zeal and activity displayed by you on this occasion, to his Excellency the Most Noble the Governor-General in Council, and his Excellency the Commander-in-Chief, as the object effected by you may certainly tend to discourage, if not operate as a final check, to the depredations of the Bagailahs.

(Signed) " W. T. SMITH, Magistrate.
" *Zillah, Allahabad, the 2d May,* 1804."

In October 1805, Ensign Baines marched from Lucknow, with

* Services, vol. i. p. 162-7.
† Services, vol. i. p. 130-9. See also p. 78, and p 424 of this volume, which contain further notices of this distinguished officer and most amiable character.

treasure to a considerable amount, and escorted by one company, for the grand army, under Lord Lake, while in pursuit of Holkar's force, and having orders to proceed with all possible dispatch, he passed Muttra, before Lord Lake's orders arrived for his being relieved at that station by five companies, as that part of the country was infested by hordes of Mahratta banditti.

Ensign Baines joined the Commander-in-Chief's camp, within two marches of Delhi, after a march of 20 days from Lucknow, and for the last ten days skirmishing the whole of the way; and on thi occasion his Lordship was pleased to observe, that nothing but such extreme vigilance, and zealous exertions, as had been displayed by Ensign Baines, could have effected the safe arrival of the treasure entrusted to his charge, for which he had begun to entertain great fears, on finding one company alone had been suffered to continue with it from Muttra.

Ensign Baines experienced a very severe and obstinate attack of the liver complaint, in consequence of the exposure and fatigue he had undergone on the above occasion, and for his recovery therefrom, a voyage to Europe became necessary, but after an absence of 14 months, he rejoined his corps at Banellie.

In 1809, he was present with the army that advanced to the Sutlej, under Major-General St. Leger, serving with the 2d battalion of light infantry.

In Feb. 1809, he was at his own request, and through the interest of Sir John Malcolm*, appointed to the corps of pioneers, and on the breaking up of Major-General St. Leger's division, in March of that year, he joined the same as second in command, and which station he held until Feb. 1818, when he was again compelled by ill health, to repair to Europe.

In July 1809, he proceeded in command of three companies of pioneers, with a detachment employed in the Hurriannah district, under Lieut.-Col. Ball, and on the 29th August, joined in the capture (by assault), of the town of Bhowanny, and for his conduct on that

* Services, vol. i. p. 468-500.

occasion, Col. Ball * in public orders†, expressed himself in the most flattering manner, which orders were confirmed by the Com.-in-Chief, the Supreme Government, and the Court of Directors.

Lieut. Baines commanded the pioneers, employed with Col. Adam's detachment, in 1810, against the Bhuttees, and at the surrender of the forts of Futteabad and Rahneeah.

In Feb. 1811, on a call for volunteers for distant service, Col. (now Brig.-Gen.) Adams, Lieut. Baines's immediate commandant, sent in his name, with a strong recommendation that his services should be accepted, and in anticipation of their being so accepted, he obtained that officer's, and the general of division, M.-Gen. Fuller's, permission to proceed, but on the march he received orders from Gen. Champagné, commanding in the field, to return to Hanse, and which he was compelled to do, under the mortification of witnessing his then junior officer, Lieut. Baddely (now a Lieutenant-Colonel) preferred to the command of three companies of the corps in which he had been distinguished, and was second in command of, and this, on the plea of having received an advance of a few thousand rupees for the repairs of a fort ditch. Lieut. Baines thus lost his share in the glorious triumph over a European power, by which the operations of the army on the island of Java were crowned.

* Services, vol. ii. p. 355-7, 563; and 418-426 of this volume.

Extract of detachment orders, issued by Lieut.-Col. Ball, commanding the troops employed against the town of Bhowanny, in Hurriannah, under date 1st Sept. 1809.

" The Commanding Officer having now received from Lieut.-Col. Magrath and Major Smith, detailed accounts of the proceedings of their respective columns, on the 29th ultimo, is most happy to find that their reports of the gallantry, steadiness, and perseverance, of the troops employed on the assault of Bhowanny, fully corresponds with the high opinion he has expressed of their conduct, formed upon his own personal observation.

" The pioneer companies, under the command of Lieut. Baines, have deservedly obtained a just tribute of praise, for their unwearied exertions. The conduct of Lieut. Baines, and of the whole of the officers attached, who volunteered to accompany the storming party, proceeded with the heads of the columns, planted their ladders in the face of a determined and desperate resistance, and afterwards continued to remove all obstructions that impeded the progress of the troops through the town, till it was completely in our possession, reflects the highest credit on the pioneer detachment, and upon Lieut. Baines, its immediate commanding officer."

In a letter from the Assistant Secretary to the Military Board, to the address of Lieut.-Col. Adams, commanding at Hanse, it was stated with reference to the works above alluded to:—" That the Hon. the Vice President in Council had been pleased to notice with great satisfaction, the highly important benefits received from Lieut. Baines's active and meritorious exertions."

In November 1813, this officer served with the pioneer corps, in the campaign of Ulwur, the Row Rajah's country, under the command of the late Major-General Sir D. Marshall.

On the 27th October, 1814, he took the command of the pioneer detachment, attached to Brigadier Ochterlony's division of the army, preparing to invade the country occupied by the troops of Nepaul, under Ummer Sing Toppah, in the mountains of Hindoos, and during a campaign of seven months' incessant labour and exposure to climate, &c., in which four forts were breached and captured, and an attack by the whole of Ummer Sing's force, repulsed by a small detachment to which Lieut. Baines belonged, commanded by Col. Thompson, the Major General's and Commander-in-Chief's approbation of his conduct was recorded in public orders on each of the above occasions, and on the latter most particularly and exclusively so.

Extract.—Detachment Orders, issued by Major-General D. Ochterlony, dated Camp, at Bhutoo, 13th January 1815.

" The Commanding Officer has much pleasure in publishing to the troops, the Right Hon. the Com.-in-Chief's entire approbation of the conduct of Lieut.-Col. Thompson, the officers and men under his command, on the 28th and 29th ult., with his Excellency's best thanks to the Lieut.-Col. and the troops under his orders, for the steadiness and gallantry they evinced in the repulse of the enemy. His Excellency directs the Commanding Officer to offer his particular thanks to Capt. Baines, and the pioneers under his orders, for the indefatigable and laborious services of the detachment of that valuable corps on the above occasion."

On the 4th Oct. 1815, this officer received a communication from

Capt. (now Lieut.-Col.) Cartwright, informing him, that M.-Gen. Ochterlony had been called to the command of the army destined to act against Ratmandoo, and that he wished to have the benefit of his experience and services with the pioneers thereof, but that he made it optional with him, from knowing how severely his health had suffered from the preceding campaign. Capt. Baines immediately availed himself of this handsome compliment; and his services, and those of his company, in removing the difficulties to the passage of a small corps of the division over the Chowriaghattee range, which led to the battle, and defeat of the Ghoorka army, on the heights of Muckwanpoor, and to the termination of the war, were acknowledged by Sir David Ochterlony in public orders.

Soon after the completion of this service, Capt. Baines repaired to England. He returned to India in Dec. 1824, in a very delicate state of health, and received from Lord Hastings the most flattering assurance* of a strong desire to place him in a situation of ease and emolument, proportionate to his Lordship's sense of his deserts; and a month after his arrival he was appointed Acting Fort Adjutant of Buxar, and subsequently a temporary Sub-Assistant in the stud, in which latter appointment he continued from Sept. 1821 to Aug. 1822, when he succeeded to the temporary command of the Furruckabad provincial battalion.

On the 1st May, on the re-organization of the army, he was promoted to a Majority, and joined his regt. (the 27th), on the Chittagong frontier, in Sept. 1824, and took the command, the Colonel being a Brigadier, and the Lieutenant-Colonel on furlough.

* "*Barrackpoor, 29th June* 1822.

"Sir,—I have had the honour of receiving your letter of the 18th inst., and of presenting that which it enclosed to the Governor-General. It were superfluous here to repeat expressions of the high opinion entertained by his Excellency of those services which have already been distinguished by his public acknowledgment, but I am commanded to say, that his Lordship will feel satisfaction in an opportunity of more substantially marking his sense of your deserts, and he has directed me with that view, to communicate the general application conveyed in your letter now before me, to the military Secretary, to the Commander in Chief.

" To Capt. C. H. Baines."   (Signed)   " J. M. M'Nabb, P. S.

MAJOR EDMUND F. WATERS.

(Bengal Establishment.)

In 1799, this officer was appointed a Cadet: he arrived in India in 1800, and joined the army as an Ensign.

In 1803, war was declared against the confederated Mahratta princes, and the corps to which Ensign Waters belonged formed part of the grand army, under the personal command of Lord Lake. He served during the two campaigns, and was with the storming party that assaulted the strong fortress of Allyghur, which place was taken after two hours' severe exposure and fighting: he was also with the small force of 5000 men that defended Delhi, under the late Major-General Burne*, in 1804-5.

In 1804, he had obtained the rank of Lieutenant; and in 1805, he was appointed to a regimental Staff situation, which he held till 1814, when he vacated it on his promotion to the rank of Captain. In the interim, he served with his regiment, and was on service against the Goorkahs in the Nepaul war.

In 1821, he was appointed to the command of a frontier battalion, and in 1823, obtained his majority.

In 1824, war was declared against the Burmese empire, and Major Waters was destined to act with his battalion in the division of the army, commanded by Brigadier Alfred Richards, that has conquered the petty kingdom of Assam.

In the 2d campaign of the Burmese war, Major Waters was detached, with the disposable part of his battalion, from the main force, and for his exertions and services on this occasion †, he received the thanks of the highest military authorities.

Major Waters, with the head-quarters of the Dinagepoor batta-

---

* See volume ii. p.496-500.

† Every circumstance relating to the Burmese war being of high interest at this period, the Editor has introduced a particular statement of the progress of the force under Major Waters, from its quitting Gowahutty.

lion, amounting, in effective strength, to about 250 men, and a brigade of gun-boats, mounting pounder cannonades, quitted the post of Gowahutty on the 19th Oct., for the purpose of surprising and dislodging the enemy on the line of the river Kullung, and of occupying the position of Raha Chokey, a centrical point, keeping in check the main body of the enemy stockaded at Noagong, and also commanding the mountain passes leading from Cachar. On the second day the division arrived at the mouth of the Kullung, at its confluence with the Sonage and the Brahmaputra, distant from Gowahutty about 15 miles; and the following day, with the advantage of a favourable wind, passed the deserted post of Kejlee-chokey, and overtook the advanced party, under Lieut. Jones, of the 46th regiment, temporarily attached to the command (60 men).

For many succeeding days the progress of the division was extremely slow and tedious, owing to the rapidity of the current, in a channel peculiarly winding and tortuous, and the nature of the banks, which were overgrown with high and impervious reed jungle, and did not admit of the usual mode of tacking. On the 26th, the division reached the village of Jaghee, now nearly depopulated; and about that time Major Waters received intelligence of a party of the enemy being stationed at a village inland, called Hautgong, or Saut-gong, where they were committing plunder and ravage upon the surrounding district. On the following morning, the division passed the deserted village, and the same evening reached a point of the river opposite the village of Moree Kullung, from whence the road to Hautgong branched off, and reported to be a distance of eight or nine miles. In consequence of confirmed intelligence of the strength and position of the enemy's party, Major Waters determined on giving them an alert; and disembarked at midnight with one hundred men for that purpose: after marching (officers, as well as men, on foot) for about four miles, they reached the village of Moree Kullung on the edge of a broad and deep jeel, which the detachment crossed by rafts. At this time there commenced heavy rain, which continued, with little intermission, during the whole of the march.

The road, for the first ten miles, was practicable, and though occasionally passing through tracts partly inundated, did not generally offer much difficulty. The distance, however, proved to be nearly double that previously estimated; and, in addition, the fatigue was much increased by the nature of the country, the last eight miles being through rice-fields, almost entirely knee, and sometimes waist, deep in water. The heavy rain and mist, however, aided the surprise; and the detachment arrived, at about 8 o'clock, unperceived, on the enemy's position, into which it immediately dashed. The slaughter, however, was comparatively small, owing to the numerous outlets from the village favouring the escape of the enemy, and the depth of the surrounding jungle: many Burmese fell, and some women and plunder were captured in returning from the pursuit. The former were released, on being claimed by their families. By following mistaken information, the detachment, on its return to the fleet, experienced added fatigue and difficulty in a bad and circuitous route, and did not reach the boats till the following morning, having been compelled to bivouac in a small village for the night. The distance traversed cannot be estimated at less than from thirty-five to forty miles. On the 30th, the division resumed its progress up the Kullung, meeting with rather more favourable ground for tacking, and less strength of current, though in a channel equally devious and winding. Major Waters, of course, deemed that the knowledge of his advance upon Raha Chokey could no longer be concealed from the enemy, after the alarm excited by the attack on Hautgong; but on approaching that post, he had reason to believe that their attention had rather been diverted to the line of the great river, in which Major Cooper was then proceeding; and that they attributed the alert to a detachment from that quarter. He, in consequence, made arrangements for surprising them; and having pushed in, with a party of 200 men in the gun and light boats, landed a little below their post at Raha Chokey, and succeeded in reaching it, unperceived, by early day-break. Major Waters, having taken a rapid view of the place, divided his party into two, and immediately attacked the position by separate entrances. This arrangement was attended with complete success; the party on the right entering by the open road falling on the principal body, who, with loss, were driven on the left division, by whom they were received with great slaughter; and the pursuit becoming general, the enemy were followed for a considerable distance, leaving many killed and wounded in the jungles in their flight: their loss was estimated at about one-third, but subsequent accounts gave reason to suppose it far greater. There were captured several stand of arms, (English muskets) numerous swords, many of which belonged to chiefs, and all their baggage and plunder. Major Waters had previously received information that the preceding day a party of Burmese had been detached from the body at Raha Chokey to ascertain the real circumstances attending the attack of Hautgong, on the 28th; and as the great guns had not been brought into play, he formed hopes that they might remain unconscious of the defeat of their main body, and that he might be able to surprise and cut them off in their return: the event proved the justness of his expectations, and about mid-day, information was given of their approach. Major Waters accordingly ordered out a party, and took post with it in a concealed position, in jungle, on the skirts of a village, distant from Raha Chokey about two miles, and through which the road of the enemy passed. The measure was most successful, as the enemy advanced on the party unawares, and were suddenly attacked with very heavy loss: they made one feeble attempt at returning the fire, with jingals, &c., and took to a precipitate flight through the streets and lanes of the village, closely followed by the troops, and falling in considerable numbers, not one half could be considered to escape, of whom many were wounded. The fugitives in both cases took the direction of Noagong, in which town were established the head-quarters and main body of the Burmese army, under their governor the Baoraor Mogaum Rajah, the Deakah Rajah, 2d in command, and various other phookuns, or chiefs. They were known to be in a stockade, or fortified position, of considerable strength, and amounting to about 1,000 or 1,500 men. Early on the following morning (the 4th), Major Waters received intelligence that the Rajah with his force had quitted his stockade, and had taken post on the road towards Roha, either with intention of anticipating an attack, or of seeking safety in flight. He accordingly ordered out a strong party, and leaving a sufficient protection for the guns and fleet, proceeded immediately in the direction of Noagong, said to be about twenty or twenty-four miles distant. It proved, however, much further, and he did not reach the stockade until the next morning, when he found it entirely evacuated by the enemy. By the accounts gathered from the inhabitants, he learnt that immediately on the arrival of the fugitives and wounded from Raha Chokey, &c., the panic of the enemy became general, and the Boora Rajah and chiefs determined on instant and precipitate flight, as Major Waters was said to be in close pursuit. They effected their escape to the hills in the utmost consternation and confusion, abandoning their artillery *, baggage, plunder, military stores, and war-boat; taking with them only their women and children, and the gold which they were able to carry about their persons. Unfortunately, they had already gained so much ground, that Major Waters was obliged to give up all hopes of pursuing them with infantry, and on the morning of the 5th Nov. took possession of their stockade.

On the 29th Jan. 1825, Brigadier Richards's force marched to the attack of the stockades and fortified posts around the capital of Upper Assam (Rungpore.)

During the assault, the gallant Brigadier was wounded whilst leading on the men, and Major Waters succeeded to the temporary command of the force. The day terminated by the expulsion of the enemy from all their strong holds, and they were compelled to seek shelter in the town or fort.

The result was highly beneficial, as the loss the enemy sustained so alarmed them, that 3 days afterwards they capitulated and gave up the fort of Rungpore, which contained 400 guns of various cali-

* Captured 24 swivels (1 and 2 pounders.)

bres. The thanks of government were individually expressed to Major Waters, and to all commanders of corps, for their services.

The 2d campaign being at an end, Major Waters is now, 1826, serving with his corps in Assam.

LIEUTENANT-COLONEL POWELL THOMAS COMYN.

(Bengal Establishment.)

THIS officer was appointed a Cadet on the Bengal establishment in 1798, and arrived in India in November of the following year. In 1807, he was sent with a detachment against a caste of people, the Garrows, who had infested to a great degree the Cunibarree country, and committed numerous depredations and great havoc amongst the ryotts of the district. After a few months' exertion and determined perseverance, the enemy were expelled from the Company's dominions.

Early in 1811, he was employed against a large force, under the noted freebooter, Dulgimjun Sing, who was the terror and dread of the poor inhabitants of the Company's territories in the district of Allahabad, bordering on the Mhow, Burdee, and Reewah countries. In the course of time, every success attended his detachment, by making a capture of the Sirdar, and many of his people, and small as the action was, it intimidated the enemy, and they quickly absconded to a distant retreat.

In 1814-15, this officer served with his regiment, under M.-Gen. Sir D. Ochterlony, against the Goorkahs, under the personal command of Ummer Sing, during the Nepaul war.

In 1817-18-19, he was with his regiment, which formed part of the reserve, under Sir D. Ochterlony, when employed on service in the Ragpootana states, against Meer Khan, Scindia, and the Jeypoor Rajah, and other disaffected independent parties. He has subsequently served in the Burmese war.

The following are the dates of this officer's commissions: Ensign, 22d Oct. 1799; Lieutenant, 28th Oct. 1799; Captain, 2d Jan. 1810; Major, 7th Oct. 1821; and Lieutenant-Colonel, 1st May, 1824.

LIEUTENANT-COLONEL T. H. SMITH.

(Madras Establishment.)

This officer received a Cadetship in the East India Company's service in 1797: he landed at Madras, 15th Aug. 1798, and embarked in Dec. of the same year on board the Dublin East Indiaman, with 2 companies of the 2d batt. 10th reg.; landed at Vizagapatam, and immediately joined a force near Chicacoli, formed to proceed against the refractory zemindars. He was engaged in numerous actions with the enemy, among the hills in the northern Circars, during the year 1799, and was present at the taking of the forts of Kimedy, Coladah, Vizianagur, &c. In 1800, he joined the 1st batt. 9th reg. N. I. to which he stood appointed, and was in various actions among the Polaveram Hills in the Rajahmundry district. In 1801-2, he was on constant service in the hills in the Ganjam district. He joined the force assembled at Ganjam in 1803, under the command of Col. Harcourt; was present at different actions with the Mahrattas at the taking of the Cuttack province; also at the storming of Fort Barabatty, and with the storming party at the assault and capture of the Hill Fort of Koordah, December 5, 1804.

In 1805, he joined the Hyderabad subsidiary force. In 1806, he served with a brigade in the field at Bassum. In 1809, he joined Gen. Conran's force at Akowlah. In 1810-11, he was in the field against the Pindarries. In 1812, he joined the Poona force in the field, and was appointed Brigade-Major to the Madras brigade. In 1813, he was appointed to the 2d batt. 9th reg. N. I. at Cannanore. In 1815, he joined the army of reserve, under the command of Sir

Thomas Hislop on the banks of the Toombuddra. In 1816-17-18, he was at Kurnool, and in the field to prevent the incursions of the Pindarries into the ceded districts.

In Feb. 1818, he joined the reserve division of the army, under the command of Sir Thomas Munro, in the southern Mahratta country, and was present at the storming of Badamy and siege of Belgaum, and personally on the assault and capture of the fortified pettah of Sholapore.

Lieut.-Col. Smith is now, 1825, at Prome, commanding a brigade, (H. M. 89th reg. and 43d Madras N. I.) serving with the British army, under the command of Sir A. Campbell, against the King of Ava.

The following are the dates of this officer's commissions:—Ensign, 1st Aug. 1798; Lieutenant, 26th Dec. 1798; Capt.-Lieutenant, 21st Sept. 1804; Captain, 2d July 1806; Brevet-Major, 4th June 1814; Regimentally, 1st Sept. 1818; Lieutenant-Colonel, 1st May 1824.

MAJOR JOHN ALFORD SAY.

(Madras Establishment.)

This officer landed at Madras 19th July 1804, and proceeded with the cadets of the season to Tripassore, where he learned the usual military duties, and joined his corps, 1st batt. 16th reg., 8th March 1805, at Velore. In May he proceeded with his regiment to Bellary, at which place an army of reserve, composed of the 22d light dragoons, 8th reg. Native cavalry, H. M.'s 34th reg., the 5th, 8th, 16th, and 19th regiments, N. I., had been directed to assemble. On the conclusion of peace, in October or November, this army was broken up, and Major Say proceeded with his regiment to the garrison of Gooty.

In February 1806, he escorted treasure to Madras. In October of the same year he marched with his regiment to Hyderabad, and in December following, he accompanied his regiment, which formed part of a brigade, under the command of Col. O'Reilly, to

Bassum, as an escort to the Rajah, Govend Buksh*, who had been appointed by the Nizam to the government of Berar. This was the origin of the advanced force stationed at Jaulnah.

In November 1807, his regiment was relieved, and he returned with it to Hyderabad.

In February 1808, Major Say proceeded with his regiment, which formed part of the force † that marched under the command of

---

* In the latter end of 1806, the court of Hyderabad came to the resolution of removing Rajah Myaput Row from the government of Berar, and appointing Rajah Govend Buksh to succeed him. These two Rajahs, from their politics, were personal enemies, and the circumstance of one being appointed to supersede the other added to their enmity. Both were known to be errant cowards. From their having hitherto filled civil appointments, they had no knowledge of military affairs, and not much beyond the mere official intercourse in government, of military men: but in this respect Myaput Row had the advantage of Govend Buksh; and Seedaput Row, Myaput Row's nephew, commanded a body of foreign troops, composed of Arabs, Scinds, &c. all of whom were devoted to his service, and ready, like their leader, to enter on the most desperate enterprise. These circumstances, together with a report that was generally believed, that Myaput Row would not relinquish his government without being compelled to do so, operated strongly on the mind of Govend Buksh, and induced him to declare he would not proceed without a body of the Company's troops. Two regiments of cavalry, and one of infantry, were accordingly ordered, but after moving out, the cavalry were countermanded, and another regiment of infantry substituted, under the command of Col. O'Reilly. This was the origin of the advanced force at Jaulnah. After some little delay the troops marched, and proceeded to Bassum without opposition, Myaput Row having moved off sometime previously with his foreign troops, towards Sholapoor, his jaghire.

† This light force, consisting of two regiments of Native cavalry, six companies of H. M.'s 33d regiment, a brigade of Native infantry, a proportion of artillery, and a party of Nizam's cavalry, marched from Hyderabad on field service, towards Sholapoor. The cause of this movement was the rebellion of Rajah Myaput Row, the same person who had been superseded in the government of Berar the year before. In consequence of his not having settled his jaghire accounts with the government of Hyderabad, the Nizam sent a body of his own troops, composed of cavalry and infantry, the latter under the command of Major Palmer, to enforce his demands. The Rajah moved out to meet them: the Nizam's cavalry at the moment of attack, fled, and left the infantry to their fate, who were cut up almost to a man. Major Palmer was the only officer who escaped; the rest, who were not cut down in action, were barbarously murdered after all was over. These acts of contempt of government demanded instant and exemplary chastisement, for which purpose application was made to the British resident, and the above detachment, under the officer commanding the subsidiary force, Col. Montresor, H. M.'s 22d light dragoons, proceeded so far on the direct road as Undercherry, towards Sholapoor, by easy marches: at this place information

Col. Montresor, H. M.'s 22d light dragoons, who commanded the Hyderabad subsidiary force, in pursuit of Myaput Row, a Hindoo chief, who had rebelled against the Hyderabad government, and who had cut up a detachment of its troops. The enemy was driven into Hindostan without bringing him to action; the pursuit ceased, and the force returned to Hyderabad, having marched 1201 miles in little more than three months.

In February 1809, Major Say accompanied a light detachment, composed of the 1st regiment Native cavalry, and the flank companies of the 5th, 10th, 16th, and 21st regiments, under the command of Major Neale, in the direction of Neermul, after a body of Pindarries, which had made its appearance on the Nizam's north-east frontier, but on its returning to the northward, the detachment retraced its steps to Hyderabad.

In Oct. 1809, Major Say marched with his regiment under the command of Col. (the late Sir Barry) Close, to Jaulnah, and thence with the army to Seronge, in Hindostan. On its return to the Nerbudda, the 16th reg. formed part of a detachment, commanded by Lieut.-Colonel Hare, H. M.'s 22d dragoons, and returned with it to Hyderabad, where the 16th received further instructions to proceed to Samulcottah in the Circars. On its arrival, Major Say was detached to Coringa, where he commanded for 13 months, when he was appointed Adjutant of the regiment, and rejoined the headquarters at Samulcottah. In October 1811, he marched with the regiment to Ellore. In October 1812, the 16th reg. was one of those selected to form the light infantry brigade, and marched in that month to Bangalore, where, this officer accompanied it, to be instructed in the light infantry drill. In March 1814, he moved with the regiment to Jaulnah, remained there during the monsoon, and then proceeded with the force under Colonel, now Sir J. Doveton, to oppose the Pindarries.

He continued with Sir John Doveton's force till June 1816, when

was received that the Rajah had fled northward, and a pursuit was commenced, by turning north, to the large town of Mulkair, thence to the ancient capital of Calberger.

he accompanied his regiment as part of the Nagpore subsidiary force, under the command of L.-Col. Walker, to the vicinity of Nagpore.

Major Say's health being very much impaired, he was removed, in October 1816, for its restoration, to the 2d batt. 16th reg., which he joined at Harponnelly, on field service, guarding the passes of the Toombuddra into Mysore: he was detached to Holul, but the Pindarries having quitted that part of the country early in March 1817, the corps was directed to return to Chittledroog. His health still declining, he was sent in December, on sick certificate, to Mangalore, on the Malabar coast; from thence he proceeded by sea to Madras, where he landed in March 1818, after an absence of 12 years. There being no prospect of his regaining his health in India, he embarked, July 14, 1818, for England.

In 1822, Major Say returned to India, and joined the 2d batt. 16th reg. at Hyderabad: in 1824 the corps marched to Madras, and in October of that year he was honoured with the command of it by Sir A. Campbell, late Com.-in-Chief, which he held to the day of his embarkation, on his return to Europe on sick certificate.

The following are the dates of this officer's commissions: Ensign, 18th July 1804; Lieutenant, 21st Sept. 1804; Adjutant, 16th July 1811; Captain, 1st Jan. 1818; and Major, 1st May 1824.

MAJOR-GEN. SIR THOMAS MUNRO, Bart. & *K.C.B.*

(Madras Establishment.)

This distinguished officer, after attracting, by his services, the notice of Government during Lord Cornwallis's Mysore war, was nominated by that nobleman to be one of the assistants to Col. Read in settling and governing the provinces conquered from Tippoo. After the fall of Seringapatam he was appointed, jointly with Captain (now Maj.-Gen. Sir John) Malcolm, Secretary to the Commissioners, to whom was confided the adjustment of the affairs, and division of the territories of Mysore, and the investment of the young Rajah with the government of that country.

In 1799, he was selected by Lord Wellesley (to whom he was personally unknown) to administer the government of Canara, to which the province of Malabar was afterwards annexed. After rendering important services in this situation, he was appointed, by the same illustrious statesman, to a similar office in the extensive and valuable provinces ceded by the Nizam, in 1801, in commutation of his subsidy; and his conduct in that situation not only gained general applause, but was equally beneficial to the inhabitants and to the Company.

He obtained the rank of Lieut.-Colonel in 1804, of Colonel in 1813, and of Major-General 12th August 1819.

He returned to England in 1808, and, on the renewal of the Company's charter, was for many days consecutively examined for several hours before the House of Commons, when his evidence excited the surprise and even the admiration of all parties in the house*.

He was next sent to Madras (to which establishment he belongs), by the Court of Directors, on an important duty, connected with the permanent settlement of the revenues of that presidency.

In 1817, Colonel Munro being in the neighbourhood of Soondoor, where he had been sent as Commissioner to take charge of the districts ceded to the East India Company by the Peishwa, he was appointed by Lieut.-Gen. Sir Thomas Hislop, to undertake the reduction of the rebellious feudatory of Soondoor; and he was shortly

---

* "Few governments had servants better qualified for diplomatic missions, by general understanding and local experience, by perfect knowledge of the interest of their own and the neighbouring states, and by familiarity with the languages, manners, and character of the countries to which they were to be sent. Some of these accomplished gentlemen have since distinguished themselves in European diplomacy. Others have, by valuable works, enabled the public to estimate their talents; some have displayed the minds and the knowledge of lawgivers and statesmen, in their examination before both houses of Parliament, at the renewal of the Company's privilege."—*Edinburgh Review*, vol. xxv. p. 403.

after vested with a separate command of the reserve, and the rank of Brigadier-General, under orders from the Marquess of Hastings. The place was surrendered on this officer's approach, towards the end of October.

That illustrious and eloquent statesman, Mr. Canning, on the 4th March 1819, in moving the thanks of the House of Commons to the noble Marquess of Hastings, and the army in India, for the splendid services in the Pindarry * and Mahratta war, describes the conduct of this officer, then Colonel Munro, in this command :—

* In the speech above referred to, Mr. Canning paints the character of the Pindarries, and the necessity of their extirpation, in the following energetic language :—

" Nothing can be imagined more dreadful than the irruptions of the Pindarries. There is no excess of lawless violence which they did not perpetrate; no degree of human suffering which they were not in the habit of inflicting. Rapine, murder, in all its shapes, torture, rape, and conflagration, were not rare and accidental occurrences in their progress, but the uniform and constant objects of their every enterprise, and the concomitants of every success. After ravaging tracts of country of all visible wealth, they inflicted torture on innocence, helplessness, and age, for the purpose of extorting the avowal and indication of hidden treasure. There were instances where the whole female population of a village precipitated themselves into the wells, as the only refuge from these brutal and barbarous spoilers; where, at their approach, fathers of families surrounded their own dwellings with fuel, and perished with their children, in the flames kindled by their own hands. If it were not a shame to add to such details any thing like a calculation of pecuniary loss, it might be added, that this last invasion was calculated to have cost, in booty and in wanton waste, scarcely less than a million sterling. No wonder, then, that the Government of India had resolved to avenge and chastise such unparalleled atrocities, so soon as the season for taking the field should arrive, even had they not received any previous sanction from England. No wonder that the Government at home had not hesitated to revoke its interdicts of war, and to qualify its injunctions for forbearance, upon receipt of details so afflicting to every feeling of human nature.

" It is obvious, from what I have already stated, that a war once excited in India might draw into its vortex many whom fear of our power only kept at peace. With respect to the Pindarries themselves, the difficulty was to find an opportunity of striking a decisive blow. Attacked, routed, scattered in all directions, they would speedily collect and congregate again; as a globule of quicksilver, dispersing for a moment under the pressure of the finger, re-unites as soon as that pressure is withdrawn. But the Pindarries had, also, chances of external support. They had many of them been trained to arms in the service of Scindia, the greatest among the native princes, who maintain an independent rule; in the service of Holkar, long the rival of Scindia for preponderance in the Mahratta confederacy; and in that of Meer Khan, a Mahomedan adventurer, who, originally employed as an auxiliary by Holkar, had the address to render himself, for a time, master of the government which he

"To give some notion of the extent of country over which these actions were distributed, the distance between the most northern and most southern of the captured fortresses is not less than 700 miles. At the southern extremity of this long line of operations, and in a part of the campaign carried on in a district far from public gaze, and without the opportunities of early and special notice, was employed a man whose name I should indeed have been sorry to have passed over in silence; I allude to Col. Thomas Munro; a gentleman whose rare qualifications the late House of Commons had opportunities of judging when he was examined at their bar on the renewal of the East India Company's charter; and than whom England never produced a more accomplished statesman, nor India, fertile as it is in heroes, a more skilful soldier. This gentleman, whose occupations, for some time past, have been rather of a civil and administrative, than a military nature, was called early in the war to exercise abilities which, though dormant, had not rusted from disuse. He went into the field with not more than 500 or 600 men, of whom a very small proportion were Europeans; and marched into the Mahratta territories to take possession of the country which had been ceded to us by the treaty of Poona. The population which he subdued by arms, he managed with such address, equity, and wisdom, that he established an empire over their hearts and feelings. Nine forts were surrendered to him, or taken by assault on his way; and at the end of a silent and scarcely observed progress, he emerged from a territory, heretofore hostile to the British interest, with an accession, instead of a diminution, of force, leaving every thing secure and tranquil behind him. This result speaks more than could be told by any minute and extended commentary."

was called on to support, and to carve out for himself, in return for his abdication of that influence, a substantive and independent sovereignty. However contemptible, therefore, in themselves, when compared with the numerous and well-trained armies of the British Government; yet, as the fragments of bands that had been led by formidable chieftains, to whom they still professed allegiance, these vagrant hordes might be the means of calling into action powers of greater magnitude and resources—Scindia, Holkar, and lastly, Meer Khan himself, essentially a predatory power, and the leader only of more regular and disciplined Pindarries. Nor was this the utmost extent of danger to be apprehended. Suspicions might also be naturally entertained, that the other Mahratta powers were not displeased to see the British authority, against which they had more than once combined, with all their forces, in vain, weakened in effect and opinion by the unavenged attack of such despicable antagonists; and that when the occasion should ripen, they might not be disinclined to avenge and retrieve their former defeats."

In the general orders of the Governor-General in Council, Lord Hastings, dated 29th Aug. 1818, his Lordship observes—

" Brigadier-General Munro has splendidly exhibited how a force, apparently insufficient, may be rendered adequate by judgment and energy ; his subjugation of fortress after fortress, and his securing every acquisition, with numbers so unproportioned to the extent of his endeavours, is the most unquestionable evidence of his talents."

In the same general order his Lordship further observes—

" The approaching retirement from active duty of Brig.-Gen. Munro is a subject of deep regret to the Governor-General in Council, whose mind will retain a lasting impression of his singular merits and services through a long and distinguished career."

The retirement alluded to by his Lordship, was the nomination of this officer to the high office of Governor of Madras, and which is the first instance of a Company's military officer being so exalted, and should be a source of exultation and emulation to every officer in the Indian army. Sir Thomas Munro took his seat as Governor on the 10th June 1820.

In June 1820, the following letter was addressed by the King of England to the Newaub of the Carnatic. It is here introduced, as it contains a just tribute to the merits of Sir Thomas Munro.

" George the Fourth, by the grace of God, King of the United Kingdom of Great Britain and Ireland, defender of the Christian faith, King of Hanover, &c. &c. to his Highness the Prince Auzum Jah Omdut-ool Omrah, Mokhtai-ool-Moolk, Roshun-ool-Dowlah, Mahomed Moonmour Khan Bahadoor, Bahadoor Jung, Nabob Subadar of the Carnatic. It is with much concern, that we received intelligence of the death of your Highness's father, the Nabob Azeemul Dowlah, whose well tried fidelity, and excellent character, were fully known to us, and had long secured him our sincere respect and esteem. Deeply suffering in mind under the recent privation of several of our nearest and dearest relations, and more especially of a beloved and highly revered father, who but a few weeks ago was removed from this transitory state, to receive a happier and ever-during life, the reward of virtues which will endear his memory to the latest posterity, we are the better enabled to sympathize and condole with your Highness on the occasion of your own loss. It is, however, vain to repine at the ordinances of the Almighty, who, in his infinite wisdom, has appointed a narrow limit to human life; it rather behoves us, to imitate the bright examples of our departed parents. We congratulate your highness on your peaceable and undisputed succession to the station and dignities of your illustrious ancestors. Your highness will doubtless be highly gratified at the appointment of our trusty and beloved Sir Thomas Munro, Knight Commander of our most honourable military Order of the Bath, and a Major-General in our army, to the important office of Governor of Fort St. George, for which he has been selected, as well on account of his meritorious services in India, as under a firm persuasion, that from his many excellent qualities, and chiefly the kind disposition which, in a more subordinate situation, he uniformly manifested towards our Indian subjects, no one was better calculated to ensure their attachment to our rule and Government. We are convinced, that in all his transactions with your highness it will be the constant endeavour of Sir Thomas Munro to promote your highness's comfort; and we trust that your highness will repose the utmost confidence in his wisdom and friendship, and ever conform to his advice, which your highness may be assured will on no occasion have any other object than to preserve unimpaired the harmony which so happily subsisted between the British government and your highness's father, the late Nabob of the Carnatic. We heartily pray that your highness, enjoying the inestimable blessing of health, may long continue to fill your present exalted station; and so we bid you farewell. We are your affectionate friend,

(Signed)   " GEORGE R.

" Given at our Palace of Carlton House, the 29th day of May 1820, in the first year of our reign.

(Signed)   " GEORGE CANNING."

The annexed Government general order, is not less flattering to than merited by the important services of this officer :—

" *Fort St. George, 10th May* 1825.

" In obedience to the commands of the honourable the Court of Directors, the honourable the Gov.-in-Council is pleased to publish the following despatch received from the honourable court :—

" *Our Governor in Council, Fort St. George.*

Par. 1. " Our last letter to you in this department was dated the 8th inst.

2. " Our chairman has acquainted us that he has received from the Governor of Fort St. George two communications, under dates the 3d March and 19th July last, in both of which Sir Thomas Munro states the reasons which would have induced him to have withheld the intimation of his wish to be relieved from the office of governor of Madras, made known to us in his address of Sept. 1823, and expresses his intention to remain till the arrival of his successor. The right hon. the President of the Board of Commissioners has likewise made known to our Chairman a letter to the same effect which he received from your president, under date the 8th July last.

3. " We have derived the most sincere satisfaction from the foregoing communications. We consider Sir Thomas Munro to have evinced the same high public spirit and ardent zeal to promote the interests committed to his charge on the present, as on all past occasions, thoughout his long and honourable course of public service. As no arrangement has yet been made for the appointment of a successor to the Governor of Madras, we are happy to signify to you our unanimous desire to avail ourselves of an extension of Sir Thomas Munro's services in that high station, at a period when his distinguished talents and peculiar qualifications cannot fail of being eminently beneficial to the country under your government, as well as to our interests; and we have accordingly unanimously resolved to abstain from nominating any successor to Sir Thomas Munro until we shall have received from you an acknowledgment of this communication, and an intimation of his wishes in consequence.

4. " With the view of making known to the service, and to the public, the sentiments which we entertain regarding Sir Thomas Munro, we direct that this despatch be published in the Government Gazette.

" We are, &c.

" *London, 10th Dec.* 1824."

In further illustration of the noble and good feelings which direct the policy of this distinguished soldier and statesman, we shall here quote a passage from Col. Wilks's History of the South of India:—

" I will not deny myself the pleasure of stating an incident related to me by a respectable public servant of the government of Mysore, who was sent, in 1807, to assist in the adjustment of a disputed boundary between that territory and the district in charge of this collector. A violent dispute occurred in his presence between some villagers, and the party aggrieved threatened to go to Anantpoor and complain to their *father*. He perceived that Colonel Munro was meant, and found upon inquiry, that he was generally distinguished throughout the district by that appellation."—Vol. i. p. 210-11.

It may finally be observed of this officer, as of Sir John Malcolm, and without disparagement to others, that in talents and character he is inferior to no officer of the Indian army, that with great mental powers he embraces practical skill, (as noticed in the extract from Mr. Canning's speech,) in the difficult art of administering the government of large provinces, in times of confusion and danger, both with advantage to the governed, and to the authorities by whom he is employed.

On the extension of the order of the Bath to the Company's army, this officer was appointed a Companion; and on the 26th November, 1819, he received the dignity of a Knight Commander. The King has been also graciously pleased to create Sir Thomas Munro a Baronet, as a further testimony of the high opinion his Majesty entertains of his distinguished character and services.

LIEUTENANT-COLONEL JOHN ROSE.

(Bengal Establishment.)

This officer was appointed a Cadet in 1795; and Ensign, 5th October 1796: he arrived in India 6th March 1797; was promoted to Lieutenant, 30th October following; to Captain, 6th June 1806; to Major, 1st May 1813: and to Lieutenant-Colonel, 4th November 1817.

He served the campaign in Mysore; was present at the siege of Seringapatam in 1799, and in the expedition from India to Egypt.

He subsequently served during the whole of Lord Lake's campaigns, was severely wounded at the action under the walls of Agra, 10th October 1803; and although only then a Lieutenant in the army, he was specially thanked in general orders *.

He acted as Brigade-Major to Colonel, the late Major-Gen. Burn †, during three years of Lord Lake's campaigns, and in that situation rendered such essential service as to excite the approbation of the Commander-in-Chief on many occasions; particularly in his general orders of the 24th October 1804 ‡, wherein it is mentioned that—

" His Excellency remarks with peculiar pleasure the decision, spirit, and judgment, with which the sortie on the enemy's works was conducted by Lieutenant John Rose."

This sortie was from the city of Delhi, which was then besieged by the whole of the troops of Holkar, amounting to about 18,000 men, chiefly infantry, the artillery consisting of upwards of 100 guns, while the regular troops capable of forming the defence of the place, did not exceed 2,000 men, then under Col. Burn's command. Lieut. Rose was selected by Col. Burn to command the party for the destruction of the enemy's batteries, which had made a breach in the walls of the town. On the evening of the 10th October 1804, about 200 men, under this officer, in a sortie from the city, succeeded in driving the enemy from their battery, taking and spiking their guns: it was conducted with so much promptitude and judgment, that the enemy precipitately fled with great loss, caused by the spirited and sudden attack made on them; the result was, that the enemy withdrew his troops altogether from a position whence he had greatly annoyed the British.

The siege of Delhi being finally raised, Col. Burn was ordered by Lord Lake, the Commander-in-Chief, to march with his detachment to the relief of Saharunpoor, then besieged by the Seiks. On his

---

* See vol. ii. p. 307.   † Services, vol. ii. p. 495-517.   ‡ See vol. ii. p. 501.

route thither he was overtaken and surrounded by Jesswunt Rao Holkar, with the whole of his cavalry, upwards of 20,000, near the town of Shamlie. In this position, Col. Burn received numerous attacks from the enemy, during a day and a night when on the plain. Early in the morning of the 2d day, he passed the enemy's outposts, and retired to a position where the detachment remained exposed several days to the utmost privations from the want of food. It became requisite to adopt every means to relieve the necessities of the troops, and Col Burn therefore appointed Lieut. Rose to the command of a foraging party, when his conduct was such as again to procure him the thanks of his Excellency the Commander-in-Chief; who finally relieved the detachment from their extreme distress. The fidelity and courage of the Native troops were never more put to the test than at this period, as they underwent the greatest personal sufferings.

In the further progress of this war, Col. Burn was employed against the Seiks, who were in considerable force in the upper part of the Dooaub, and having succeeded in defeating them, he was called to Rohilcund to act against Ameer Khan; who, with a large force, had long infested and plundered that country; and on coming up with him on the 10th March 1805, after a sudden and forced march of eight and twenty miles, he was so fortunate as to put his army to flight. On the following morning, Col. Burn detached Lieut. Rose, with the irregular cavalry belonging to the detachment, in pursuit of the enemy. The Lieutenant came up with their bazars, baggage, &c. under a convoy of 2,000 horse and foot, and succeeded in capturing the principal part of the bazars and the cattle, and in killing and wounding a great number of the enemy.

The Commander-in-Chief, in a letter to Col. Burn, of the 20th March 1805, expressed his highest obligations for the very gallant conduct of Lieut. Rose.

Success still attending Col. Burn's operations, he marched into the Seik country, conquered a considerable part of it, and made peace with all the chiefs on the left bank of the Sutlej, and in performing this duty he had many opportunities of noticing Lieut. Rose's services.

Lieut.-Col. Rose served during the Pindarry war with the division under the command of the late M.-Gen. Sir Dyson Marshall.

Lieutenant-Colonel Rose was on furlough to Europe in 1808, and again in 1824.

MAJOR PATRICK DUNBAR.

(Bengal Establishment.)

IN 1798, this officer was appointed a Cavalry Cadet on the Bengal establishment, and in 1799 commenced his military career, by joining a battalion of the 13th N. I., with which corps he continued until June 1800, when the 5th and 6th regiments of cavalry were ordered to be raised at Ghazeepoor, and he was directed to join and do duty with the latter corps. He continued with it until the adjustment of rank of the cadets of 1798, when he was permanently posted to the 3d light cavalry, as Cornet, and joined, in Aug. 1801, at Caunpoor.

At this station the corps remained until the beginning of 1802, when it was ordered to form part of the escort selected to attend the Marquess Wellesley, on his visit to the late Newaub of Oude. The regiment proceeded to Lucknow, and afterwards escorted his Lordship down the country, as far as the zillah of Juanpore, where the services of the corps were dispensed with, and it was ordered to Rohilcund. It was stationed at Barreilly until the disturbances with Bauguan Sing, and other chiefs in the Dooaub, in the end of 1802, occasioned a force to be assembled for their subjection and the reduction of their forts. The 3d cavalry was one of the corps employed on the service; and this officer was present at the sieges of Sasnee, Catchoura, &c.

In 1803, the war broke out with the Mahrattas: the grand army under the Com.-in-Chief, the late Lord Lake, took the field, and the 3d light cavalry was one of the first corps that joined it. Cornet Dunbar was present at Gen. Perron's defeat near Coel, 29th Aug. 1803; at the capture of Allyghur, 4th September; at the battle near Delhi, 11th September; at the siege and fall of Agra, 18th October; and at the hard-fought battle of Laswarree, 1st November. He was also at the capture of Tonk Rampoora; at the battle and siege of Deeg; at two of the storms of Bhurtpoor; and with Gen. Smith's division, in pursuit of Ameer Khan, when that chieftain invaded Rohilcund.

At the termination of the latter campaign, the 3d cavalry was cantoned at Muttra, and after having remained for some time at that station, this officer was detached with his troop to Bundlecund, and employed under various commanders in that troublesome province, and particularly with Col. Arnold * above the Ghauts. On leaving Bundlecund, he was sent into the province of Oude, where he was employed at the reduction of many of the mud forts. He was with the army under the late Gen. Marshall †, at the bombardment and capture of the fort of Hattrass, in the Dooaub; with the grand army assembled under the personal command of the Marquess of Hastings, and subsequently detached from his Lordship's camp, and proceeded with Maj.-Gen. Sir Thomas Brown's ‡ light division, towards the south, and was present at the attacks made on the fortified towns of Rampoora and Jawud §; he was afterwards sent to join the Neemuch field force, under the late Lieutenant-Colonel Ludlow, C.B.

Major Dunbar had the honour of commanding his regiment for a short time, when Lieutenant; he held the command of it a second time, when Captain; and got the command a third time, when Major. He joined in 1801, and continued with the corps till September 1821, when he returned to his native country.

The 11th March 1805, he obtained the rank of Lieutenant; he was promoted to Brevet-Captain, 8th January 1816, and regimentally, 1st Sept. 1818; and to Major, 8th May 1821.

* Services, p. 1 of this volume.
† Vol. i. p. 395-7.
‡ Vol. i. p. 253-8.
§ See p. 105.

LIEUTENANT-COLONEL JOHN SWINTON.

(Bengal Establishment.)

THE 17th Sept. 1799, this officer was appointed to an Ensigncy on the Bengal establishment; and promoted to Lieutenant, on the 28th of the following month. He joined in 1800, the 1st batt. 11th Bengal N. I., and marched, under the command of Capt. Hodgson of the same corps, with a company of sepoys, against Zubbur Sing (a refractory zemindar in the Newaub of Oude's district): they came up with, attacked, and effectually routed the enemy. In the same year, Lieut. Swinton marched with a large detachment, under the command of Col. Vanas, for the purpose of disbanding 10 of the Newaub of Oude's battalions, which was readily accomplished.

In 1801, Lieut. Swinton was posted to the 12th N. I., and marched, in 1802, under the command of Col. Blair*, by whom, on the 14th December, he was appointed Assistant-Engineer, under Captain Wood. He made the batteries before the fort of Sasnee; was in the trenches when they were attacked, and carried the ladders to the breach; in storming which, he was wounded in the foot.

This officer was also present at the siege of Bejighur, and having made the batteries and trenches, he commanded, by order of Lord Lake, a chosen party of 12 Europeans, from His Majesty's 76th, and stormed a small work within the Rowney, (or outer fort) which commanded the breach and gateway. The enemy abandoned the fort just before the storm took place, having done all the mischief in their power, by putting a slow match in the powder magazine, which blew up just as this officer entered, and killed about 300 natives, together with Colonel Gordon of the artillery.

He next served at the storm of Catchoura, which place he was left behind to destroy, together with several other forts.

Mr. Claud Russell, then Gov.-General's agent, having directed

---

* Now Lieut.-General Sir Robert Blair, K.C.B.—Services, vol. ii. p. 288.

Lieut. Swinton to reconnoitre a small fort near Catchoura, supposed to have been very strong, he succeeded in taking it with the reconnoitring party, consisting of a jemedar and 20 men.

In 1803, Lieut. Swinton joined the grand army under Lord Lake, and was appointed to the pioneer corps, on its formation, in August of the same year. On the 29th of the same month, he was at the battle of Coel; and on the 4th Sept. 1803, he carried the ladders at the storm of Allyghur, and was the first who entered the wicket at the last gateway; he was also at the battle of Delhi in the same month; at the taking of the fort of Agra; and in the trenches during the whole of the siege.

On the 1st Nov., Lieut. Swinton was at the battle of Laswarree; and marched from the grand army, with Col. White's* detachment, against Gualior, in December 1803, with whom he continued during the siege.

In 1804, he rejoined the grand army, and remained with it to the end of the campaign, in June 1804. He was removed to the 21st N. I. on its formation, and marched to Muttra, against Holkar and the Mahratta confederates in September, (commanding the corps of pioneers;) and subsequently marched with the army to the relief of Delhi. In Nov. of the same year, Lieut. Swinton was at the battle and siege of Deeg; made the batteries and trenches before the fort, and carried the ladders to the storm, where he received a severe wound through the thigh from a cannon-ball, which has lamed him for life. He received praise in general orders, from Lord Lake; quitted the army for a short time on account of his wound, and joined again at Bhurtpoor, in the beginning of 1805. He was in the last attack made on Holkar's camp near Bhurtpoor, and remained with the army till it broke up in 1805.

Lientenant Swinton marched, under Lord Lake, in pursuit of Holkar, as far as the Beah (Hyphasis) river, in the punjaub, and returned to Muttra in 1806. He again marched with the pioneer corps against Fort Jarkee, which was abandoned on his approach. Lieut.

---

* The late Major-Gen. Sir Henry White, K.C.B.—Services, vol. i. p. 24.

Swinton moved, in October 1807, with Major-Gen. Richard Mark Dickens, (H. M.'s service) against Fort Comona; was severely wounded in the head by a matchlock ball while making the trenches; and received praise from Gen. Dickens, in general orders, for his conduct throughout the siege. He was at the taking of Fort Ganowrie, which, with the several forts ceded to the army on that occasion, he was left behind to destroy. In 1808, he proceeded with the pioneer corps to Caunpoor, where it was increased from 3 companies to 8, when he marched thence to Karnaul, where he was stationed. The 8th Sept. 1809, he obtained the rank of Captain.

In Oct. 1810, he took the field with Col. (the late Lieut.-Gen. Sir Dyson) Marshall's detachment, against some refractory Seik chiefs. In June 1812, he was employed, with Col. Hodgson's army, against the Shekawut chief; and in Oct. 1813, with Gen. Marshall's army, against the Rao Rajah of Alwa.

Capt. Swinton proceeded from Agra to Dinapore (by water) in Sept. 1814, and joined M.-Gen. Bennet Marley's army against the Goorkahs, on which service he continued in the field till March 1815. In Jan. 1816, he joined Gen. Ochterlony's army, went up the pass with him, and was left behind with his pioneers to make it practicable for elephants, which, though a work of great labour, he accomplished in four days.

Capt. Swinton again joined the army, and moved on with it to Muckwanpoor; was in the battle fought on the hill; and when the campaign was brought to a termination, Sir D. Ochterlony was pleased to mention his name, in a most handsome and flattering manner, in his letter of thanks to the army.

In Feb. and March 1817, he joined the army under Gen. Marshall, and was at the taking of the fort of Hattrass*. In 1818, he was with the army under the personal command of the Marquess of Hastings, and received praise in general orders for making a bridge of boats over the river Jumna.

This officer succeeded to a Majority in 1823; and the 13th Jan.

* See commendation of pioneer corps, vol. i. p. 396.

1825, was promoted to Lieut.-Colonel. At his own request he has been lately tranferred to the Invalid establishment, and has succeeded to a good appointment in that branch of the service.

THE LATE LIEUTENANT-COLONEL GEORGE BALL*.

(Bengal Establishment.)

This officer was appointed a Cadet in 1777, and arrived in India the end of that year: he was promoted to Ensign, in Jan. 1778; to Lieutenant, Sept. 1778; to Captain, 1795; to Major, 1799; and to Lieutenant-Colonel, January 1803.

We cannot now exactly ascertain what corps this officer first joined on his arrival in India; but in the year 1781, he belonged, we believe, to the 6th reg. of sepoys, at the time of the Rajah Cheyt Sing's revolt and insurrection in the province of Benares. Lieut. Ball was engaged, and wounded, with the 1st batt. of that reg. and other details, at the unfortunate attack of the town of Ramnagur, in Aug. 1781, which, with a misapplied zeal, was rashly undertaken, contrary to orders, by the officer in command of the detachment, who lost his life, with many of his brave troops, on the occasion. (See p. 215.)

On the assembling of troops under the command of Major (late Lieut.-Gen.) W. Popham, for putting down the insurrection, Lieut. Ball was selected for the staff situation of Brigade-Major, and in that office conducted the details at the attack and capture of the strong hill fort of Bidzighur, which surrendered on the 10th of Nov. 1781, yielding to Major Popham, as observed by Mr. Hastings, " the pe-

---

* A brief notice of this officer will be found in vol. ii. p. 355, together with the general orders on the capture of Bhowanny; and also, p. 563, the government orders on his death. The importance, however, of his services, has induced the Editor to avail himself of the kind assistance of a distinguished officer of the Bengal army, through whose means he is now enabled to present a detailed statement of the military career of this bright ornament of the Indian army.

culiar credit of having surmounted all the obstacles which nature and art opposed to the conquest of two of the fortresses of Hindostan, which had been before universally deemed impregnable."

On the cessation of warfare in the zemeedary of Benares, Chunarghur became a principal station for a division of the army, and the illustrious Warren Hastings, who was on the spot, actuated by the desire of rewarding, as far as he could, the officers who had distinguished themselves during that arduous and evenful crisis, caused the several Staff appointments, created on the occasion, to be filled by those who were brought to his notice; when Lieut. Ball was appointed Station Major of Brigade. He continued in that situation until 1784, when reforms and reductions, consequent to the general peace, caused the office to be abolished, and Lieut. Ball was posted to the 34th regiment of sepoys.

On the reduction of that corps in 1785, Lieut. Ball was appointed to the 20th reg. of sepoys at Chunar; and whilst attached to that corps, he was employed with a detachment from it, with other troops, at the siege and capture of the fort of Bujjerah, in the province of Furruckabad, in 1786.

During the interval of peace which followed, Lieut. Ball was distinguished for a zealous attention to his professional duties, and to the study of the Persian and Hindostannie languages, in which he attained excellent proficiency.

The next occasion of service that offered for the corps to which Lieut. Ball belonged, (the 20th batt.) was the disputed succession and fratricide which occurred on the death of Fyzoolah Khan, the Rohilla chieftain of Rampoor, and the consequent battle of Bætoorah, on the plains of Rohilcund, the 26th Oct. 1794, between the Hon. Company's forces, under the personal command of Gen. Sir Robert Abercromby, the then Com.-in-Chief in India, and the Rohilla tribes, under Gholam Mahomed, who had caused the lawful successor to be assassinated. The 20th battalion was one of the corps of the left wing, and did not suffer much in the action.

When the army advanced in pursuit of the enemy towards the

hills, Lieut. Ball was selected by the Com.-in-Chief, to occupy the city of Bareilly with a small detachment, for the especial purpose of superintending the care of the sick and numerous wounded officers and men of our own, and of the enemy's forces. In the discharge of that duty, Lieut. Ball evinced great professional assiduity, and a generous spirit of philanthropy and kindness by which his character was peculiarly distinguished.

After the return of the troops to cantonments, a considerable interval of peace afforded no opportunity for professional emulation beyond that of attention to discipline, conciliation, and improvement of the Native troops, in which Lieut. Ball was always prominently engaged.

On the re-organization of the army into regiments in 1796, we find Capt. Ball posted to the 3d reg. of European infantry; subsequent to which, either by exchange, or other army arrangements, Capt. Ball was removed to the 8th reg. N. I., and in the command of the 1st batt. of that reg. as Major and Lieut.-Colonel, we find that officer's career corroborated the warmest augury of his numerous friends, and fully justified the favourable opinion which his progressive character in the service had invariably indicated.

When the Com.-in-Chief took the field in 1802-3, the 1st batt. 8th reg., under Lieutenant-Colonel Ball's command, was one of the corps employed against the fort of Sasnee, and on the fall of that place, Lieut.-Col. Ball was selected, with his corps, for the command and garrison of it.

On the approach of hostilities with Dowlut Rao Scindia, in the autumn of 1803, Lieut.-Col. Ball was still in command of Sasnee, then become of more importance, from its proximity to the positions occupied by the European commanders, and organized forces in the service of that chieftain.

As soon, however, as Sasnee ceased to be a frontier post, by the advance of the army under the Com.-in-Chief, followed by the fall of Allyghur and the battle of Delhi; Lieut.-Col. Ball, with his batt.

(the 1st of the 8th) was called into the field, and, in the command of a detachment of regular and irregular troops, was employed on the south-west frontier of Delhi, in subduing the forts of Narnole, Kanoon, and others, in the possession of the enemy in that quarter. In the performance of the service entrusted to Lieut.-Col. Ball's execution and judgment, under circumstances which required much discrimination, combined with conciliatory disposition and professional skill, to overcome the difficulties arising from a very limited proportion of troops, and a still greater paucity of materials and means for the attack of fortified places, Lieut.-Col. Ball was eminently successful; and after a series of arduous exertion and enterprize, the enemy was completely expelled, and the districts thus brought under the authority of the Hon. Company's government, were, by Lieut.-Col. B.'s judicious arrangements, soon restored to order and tranquillity; for which he was honoured with the cordial applause of the Com.-in-Chief, and the marked approbation of the government.

When the main army under the Com.-in-Chief, advanced into the Jeypoor territories, to oppose the hostile demonstrations of Holkar, early in 1804, Lieut.-Col. Ball was ordered, with a strong detachment, to advance on the Shekawatty frontier, and occupy positions to prevent the inroads of the enemy in that quarter. In the execution of that service too, Lieut.-Col. B. fully accomplished the Com.-in-Chief's expectations, and was again honoured with his particular thanks.

After the main army retired for the rainy season of 1804, leaving Col. Monson's detachment in advance, Lieut.-Col. Ball was continued in the field, on the Rewarry frontier, with the view of acting in concert with Col. Monson's force, in the event of the enemy attempting to provoke hostilities, or to penetrate in that direction.

On the retreat of Col. Monson's detachment, Lieut.-Col. Ball was ordered to leave garrisons in the forts captured in 1803, on the Delhi frontier, retiring with his battalion to join the troops concentrating at Muttra, to oppose the incursions of Jesswunt Rao Holkar; whence those troops afterwards retired on Agra. Lieut.-Col. Ball's battalion now became one of the corps comprising the main army, under the personal command of the Com.-in-Chief, Lord Lake, and accordingly partook in the operations, which were resumed on His Excellency's repairing to Agra, in Sept. 1804.

After marching to the relief of Delhi, the army divided; one division, under the Com.-in-Chief, to pursue Holkar's cavalry in the Dooaub; the other, under Major-General Fraser, in pursuit of the enemy's infantry and guns, which took up a position under the walls of Deeg. There they were attacked, and defeated by Gen. Fraser, on the 13th Nov. 1804, after as obstinate and hard-fought action as any that occurred during the war. In that battle, Lieut.-Col. Ball commanded the 3d infantry brigade; and though left at first to protect the camp, baggage, and stores, soon brought his brigade into action, by moving down to the support of the cavalry and other corps, which were obstinately opposed, and suffered severely from the determined bravery and firmness of the enemy. The result of that day's contest and victory needs not to be recounted in this place. It was followed up by the siege and capture of Deeg, as soon as the Com.-in-Chief arrived with the troops under his personal command, to give effect to those operations, in which Lieut.-Col. Ball's battalion was prominently engaged, and that valuable officer was severely wounded, by which his corps and the army were deprived of his services for the remainder of the campaign.

Lieut.-Col. Ball rejoined his corps during the rains of 1805, preparatory to the renewal of operations, as soon as the season permitted; and when the Com.-in-Chief advanced into the Punjaub, in pursuit of Holkar, Lieut.-Col. Ball, with his battalion, and some other troops, was again ordered to the Delhi and Rewarry frontier, to cover the imperial city, and protect the adjoining country.

On the conclusion of peace, in 1806, Lieut.-Col. Ball was ordered by the Com.-in-Chief to establish a permanent cantonment, or station, in the neighbourhood of Rewarry, to the command of which he was nominated, with a very respectable force, consisting of several corps of infantry, with cavalry and artillery details.

Lieutenant-Colonel Ball was continued in that important situation for several years.

During the years 1808-9, the warlike and turbulent tribes inhabiting the country of Hurrianah, which fell into the possession of the Hon. Company by right of conquest, from Dowlut Rao Scindia, evinced a very restless and predatory disposition, and in some instances plundered the supplies and baggage of our troops employed in that quarter, which led to the necessity of their being coerced into respect for authority and lawful government. Measures were accordingly ordered to be adopted for that purpose, as soon as practicable, with reference, more especially, to the rainy season, when alone, it was understood, military operations could be carried on in that country, owing to the want of water, which is no where to be permanently found, except within their fortified towns and villages.

Lieut.-Col. Ball was fixed on for the execution of that difficult service; and in the spring of 1809, was directed to make the necessary preparations so as to be in readiness to take the field as soon as the periodical rains should obviate the difficulty in regard to water; and in order to leave nothing to chance that could be guarded against, leathern bags, or pukkauls, for the conveyance of water on camels, hired for the purpose, were amply provided, and every other means, combined with a very handsome force, were placed at Lieut.-Col. Ball's disposal, for the accomplishment of the service in prospect, which was undertaken with every possible precaution, to guard against failure; a result that public opinion among the Natives anticipated, from the traditionary belief that these hardy tribes had never been subdued by force, owing to the difficulties of their country for regular military operations.

In the month of August 1809, Lieut.-Col. Ball commenced his march from Rewarry toward Bhowanny, the head-quarters of the turbulent chieftains, who had intermediately rejected all the overtures at conciliation which had been proposed to them by the resident of Delhi; (one of the most conciliatory and beneficent characters that ever adorned public life, the late Archibald Seton, of the Hon. Company's Bengal civil service); but, faithless themselves, they could not repose any confidence in others, and boldly resolved to measure spears with the British government, as they had often successfully done with the authorities to which they had formerly yielded nominal subjection.

When arrived within a few miles of their fortified town, Lieut.-Col. Ball sent them a summons, renewing, in the name of the government, the tenders that had been previously made to them by the resident, with a promise of oblivion in regard to the past, provided they would attend at Delhi, and enter into engagements for their future good conduct and submission to the authority of government. All was of no avail; they seemed to prefer death to the relinquishment of their rude and predatory habits, or at least to try the chance of being able to maintain them. They refused to listen to any negociation whatsoever. Lieut.-Col. Ball then took up a position before their fortified town of Bhowanny, and after battering the walls for a few hours, directed his troops to advance to the assault at noon day. The enemy met them in the breach, and defended their houses and strong holds for some time, but, at length, yielded to superior prowess and discipline, with considerable loss on both sides. The orders and communication on the subject from the Governor-General, (who was then at Madras,) mark the sense entertained by government, and his Excellency the Com.-in-Chief, of " the brilliant and important achievement." (See vol. ii. p. 355.)

Lieut.-Col. Ball resumed his command at Rewarry, in which he continued until the beginning of 1810, when, on Lieut.-Col. Worsley's * resignation of the office of Adjutant-General, Lieut.-Col. Ball

---

* Services, vol. i. p. 180-9. The following is a copy of one of the addresses to Lieut.-Col. Worsley, on his relinquishing the office of Adjutant-General of the Bengal army:—

" SIR,—We, the undersigned Officers and Staff, serving under the Bengal presidency, feel the deepest sorrow and regret on the occasion of ill health having obliged you to relin-

was called from his important command to fill that laborious office, for which, as emphatically expressed on a subsequent melancholy occasion, " he was selected from an innate knowledge which his Excellency the Com.-in-Chief possessed of Lieut.-Col. Ball's zeal, talents, and individual worth."

The Bengal government and army did not long benefit by the services of Lieut.-Col. Ball in the distinguished situation to which he had been called. His constitution soon yielded to the change of climate, (from the upper provinces to Calcutta), and the arduous, sedentary duties of his office; and towards the end of 1811, he prematurely closed his honourable career, esteemed and lamented by the government;—(see general orders on the occasion, vol. ii. p. 563) beloved and regretted by the army, European and Native, to whom his name was endeared by the exemplary conduct which had always marked his character through the several gradations of the service.

As an officer and a gentleman, Lieut.-Col. Ball was an ornament

---

quish the appointment of Adjutant-General, which you filled with such brilliant ability and success.

" His Excellency the Vice-President in Council, has been pleased to publish the most honourable testimonies of the services you have rendered to government, and of the loss the public interests will sustain from your retirement; and we, equally lamenting your loss, feel the utmost gratification in recording, that your love and regard for the army has ever gone hand-in-hand with your inflexible adherence to the public interests.

" Those who trace back your earliest steps in life see most to admire. The brilliancy of your career was then universally pronounced, and hitherto it has been amply fulfilled.

" If the assurances that your brother officers have, and ever will retain, the warmest regard and esteem for you, founded on the most desirable points of character,—such as distinguished talents,—invincible zeal and ardour in the discharge of public duties,—a firm adherence to the strictest principles of integrity and impartiality,—together with universal philanthropy, are objects of your wishes; we entreat your acceptance of such assurances, as the most suitable tribute we can bestow on such transcendant worth, in a brother officer; the tender of which has been the chief object of this address: to which we add our best wishes and fervent prayers, that your health may be speedily re-established, and that you may long, very long, enjoy the utmost happiness to the end of so valuable a life.

" We beg leave to subscribe ourselves, Sir, your most sincere friends and faithful servants,
(Signed by the officers of one of the divisions of the army.)

" *Karnaul, 23d Feb.* 1810."

to his profession, and an enviable example of all the social relations of private life; and though it behoves us not to repine at the decrees of Providence, we may be permitted to express regret, that this excellent character was not spared to render further service to the state, and to participate in the national honours, and the advantages of the service, which have subsequently been extended to the Hon. Company's army.

LIEUT.-COLONEL COMMANDANT WILLIAM LAMB.

(Bengal Establishment.)

THIS officer was a Cadet of 1793; was appointed to an Ensigncy in October 1794; and arrived in India in February 1795; he was promoted to Lieutenant, in July 1796; to Captain, 21st September 1804; to Major, by brevet, 4th June 1814; regimentally, 16th Dec. following; to Lieut.-Colonel, 1st July 1819; and to Lieut.-Colonel Commandant, 1st May 1824.

In 1801, Lieut. Lamb accompanied the escort to Sir Home Popham, ambassador to the Arabian states, which proceeded to Mocha, in the Red Sea, from whence he went with the Secretary to Sannaa, the capital of Arabia Felix, and returned to Bengal in July 1803.

In December 1809, Capt. Lamb was appointed Commissary of Supplies to Col. Martindell's detachment, which office he held till the detachment was broken up in May 1810.

On his promotion to a Majority, in Dec. 1814, he was appointed to the command of a grenadier battalion, with which he served in 1817, at the siege of Hattrass.

In April of that year, the grenadier battalion having been broken up, Major Lamb rejoined the 51st N. I.*, which he has commanded

---

* The 51st Bengal N. I. was raised in 1804, as the 1st batt. 26th reg. In 1809, it was at the siege of Adjeeghur, in Bundlecund; in 1810, with the forces under Col. Martindell; in 1817, it formed part of the left division of the army, under Major-Gen. Marshall, against

from that period, and to which he has belonged since it was first raised, in 1804.

LIEUTENANT-COLONEL THOMAS NEWTON.

(Bengal Establishment.)

This officer arrived in India, at the age of sixteen, 9th December 1800; in March 1801, he was posted as Lieutenant to the 1st batt. 10th, now 14th N. I., which corps he joined at Lucknow, in August. The 10th performed duties at Caunpoor and Lucknow, alternately, until September 1805, when it marched to Muttra, and there joined Gen. Dowdeswell, who commanded an army of observation, which ultimately broke up at Chilkanah. In December, the 1st-10th, marched to Karnaul, and assisted with other corps under Col. Burn, at Panniput, in preserving tranquillity on that side of the Jumna, and in affording escorts for treasure, stores, &c. procceding to Lord Lake's army, then beyond the Sutlej, in pursuit of Holkar. In April 1806, the 1st and 2d-10th, 4th cavalry, and some artillery, marched to and cantoned at Munt. In May 1807, the 1st-10th were suddenly called to Delhi, to assist in quelling a serious disturbance in which many of the inhabitants had fallen. By forced marches, the battalion arrived in time to prevent more serious consequences; and precautionary measures being deemed necessary, the 1st-10th was detained at the imperial city. In June, the 1st battalion, with one gun, marched from Delhi, under the command of Major, the late Col. Mac Grath, attended by Mr. (now Sir Charles) Metcalfe, and accomplished a march of 35 miles without halting, to

the Pindarries, until December, when it was ordered to join the centre division, under the Marquess of Hastings. In Feb. 1818, it was ordered to rejoin Gen. Marshall's division, and continued employed with that force, in the Saugor and Oornutwarra districts, till Feb. 1820, when it proceeded to Delhi, by the route of Kotah and Jeypore, and in Nov. 1821, took the same route, and Hussungabad to Nagpore, where it continued to the end of May 1824. On the 1st of May 1824, the corps was numbered the 51st.

subdue about 20 refractory villages on the Panniput road. On the night of their arrival, their camp was fired upon, but no mischief done, and on the following day Lieut. Newton was ordered, with two companies and a gun, to force the gate of a small ghurry in the neighbourhood, which he accomplished without loss. The earnestness of the Commissioners' proceedings had a salutary effect, for during that day Capt., now Lieut.-Col., Bowen proceeded with one detachment, and Lieut. Newton with another, both under the direction of Major Mac Grath, and disarmed the whole of the refractory villagers, and brought their arms into camp, without firing a shot.

Towards the end of 1808, as senior officer of light infantry, Lieut. Newton was ordered to proceed with five light companies of the Delhi and Rewarry force, to Muttra, where on their arrival they were joined by three other companies, and formed into a battalion, designated the 3d light infantry, commanded by L.-Col. (the late Gen.) Hardyman, and in company with H. M.'s 17th foot, 24th dragoons, 8th Native cavalry, 2d light infantry battalion, and a proportion of horse and foot artillery, 23d N. I. &c., the whole commanded by General St. Leger, they proceeded on to Pyle, where they encamped as an army of observation, and remained for five or six weeks, while negociations were carrying on with Ringit Sing, the Seik chief.

At the commencement of the hot season of 1809, the army broke up, and the corps proceeded to their several destinations. Lieut. Newton returned and joined his battalion at Delhi, immediately after which, in July, Prince Jehangeen, one of the King's favourite sons, and a particular favourite of the household troops, became, from an immoderate fondness for liquor, unmanageable, and committed so many excesses within the interior of the palace, that the King, failing in his paternal admonitions, called upon Mr. Seton, the resident, to suggest plans to prevent access of spirits to him. A guard of sepoys, under European officers, at the outer square, between the two gates of the principal entrances to the fort or palace, was proposed and acceded to by his Majesty; and it fell to

Lieut. Newton's lot to be posted with Capt. Bowen and Lieut. Gabb, at the Delhi gate of the fort, whilst Capt. D. M'Pherson, with a similar party, commanded at the Lahore gate.

Mr. Seton had not left Lieut. Newton's party an hour before the Prince came down towards his post, leading a large body of the King's troops, himself mounted, with his sword drawn, and the troops armed. He instantly formed line, primed, and loaded. The double sentries at the inner gate were driven in from their post, and the the inner and outer gate closed at the same moment. The situation of the party became critical. Lieut. Newton fortunately found a man, at the outer gate, who he despatched, with Capt. Bowen's permission, to Mr. Seton, in whose absence they were close prisoners in the outer yard of the palace, enduring all the abusive epithets to be found in the vocabulary of the Hindostannie tongue, and menaced with a 9-pounder in the upper apartment of the inner gate, loaded to the muzzle with grape, and hundreds of loaded matchlocks from the upper works presented at them, with matches lighted. Within a reasonable time, Mr. Seton arrived, and by some means got admission at the wicket: he had no sooner entered, than a shot from the upper story of the gate was fired at him; luckily the shot was too high, passed directly over his head, and went through the cap of Capt. Bowen's orderly, standing immediately behind Mr. Seton. Without a moment's hesitation, Mr. Seton directed Capt. Bowen to move out, and take up a position outside, there to wait until the arrival of all the troops in garrison, which at that time amounted to about 2000, besides the 6th reg. of cavalry, with its gallopers. In less than an hour two columns were formed, and moved down with a gun each to the two gateways, the cavalry keeping the streets of the city clear, while the gallopers were employed in taking off the defences from the walls of the fort. A sharp but ill-directed fire was kept up from the walls, while the columns advanced. The gates, though as strong as gates could well be made with wood, iron, brass, and copper, were soon blown open. The garrison suffered severely; the British had none killed, but about 17 wounded, mostly with small-shot. The King and most of the royal family got out by the river side, and the Prince was taken by the cavalry, whilst attempting to escape over the plain.

Connected with the palace is a strong, though small fort, called Selinghur; the communication of one to the other is by means of a small bridge across a branch of the Jumna, and to this place about 200 of the garrison escaped, after the British entered the gates of the palace. Lieut. Newton was deputed by Mr. Seton to march against it; and Lieut. Munt, of the 1st N. I., volunteered, and accompanied him. On arriving at the bridge he summoned the garrison to surrender and deliver up their arms; they immediately opened the gate, marched out, and, when on the bridge, threw their arms into the Jumna. Lieut. Newton then took quiet possession of the fort, and remained there until he was relieved to proceed with the detachment of light infantry grenadiers, and the 6th cavalry, to join Colonel Ball's force, with which he was present at the siege of Bhowanny.

In 1809, the 1st batt. 10th reg. marched to Karnaul, from which place they had a short campaign, under Sir Dyson Marshall, against some refractory zemindars, who, one after the other, upon the appearance of the force, became peaceable. Towards the end of 1811 the corps marched into Oude.

In 1813, this officer was promoted to Captain, and in May 1816 he joined the 2d-10th N. I. at Futtehghur, from which place, in November, the battalion proceeded towards Culpee, and joined the Nagpore subsidiary force under Col. Adams. Capt. Newton was soon after detached, in command of the grenadier companies of the force, to a ghaut, 40 miles to the N. W. of the camp, to intercept a body of Pindarries, supposed to be proceeding by that pass. This march, agreeable to instructions, was performed without halting. On ascertaining that the enemy had not taken that route, he was recalled, and directed to join the force on its march to Subbulpore.

In Feb. 1817, this officer was employed on detachment duty, and in April he joined his corps, which was cantoned at Hussungabad, with a part of the subsidiary force, Colonel Adams having there established his head-quarters.

In November, Colonel Adams, with part of the force, crossed the Nerbudda in the common cause against the Pindarries, while the 6th cavalry, and the 22d N. I., proceeded towards Nagpore; and the 1st, 10th, and the heavy artillery, with some irregular horse, under Major M'Pherson, remained for the protection of Hussungabad. Shortly after, Captain Newton was detached, with two companies and some irregular horse, to escort provisions and ammunition to the troops at Nagpore. After the action with the enemy on the heights of Seetabuldee, and ten days after Capt. Newton's return to Hussungabad, he was again ordered to Nagpore, with the battering train, for the reduction of the Rajah's palace; but, although he made forced marches, the service was completed before he could join, and he was consequently remanded by the Resident. On his return, and when within two marches of Hussungabad, he received an express from Major M'Pherson, directing him to bring the guns across the country, and join him at Sewny, distant south-west of Hussungabad about 24 miles. On arriving at the head-quarters of the detachment, the 18-pounders were set up against the fort, at the distance of 300 yards, and Captain Newton was ordered to remain in readiness with the grenadier companies of the detachment, and to storm the moment a breach was practicable. The guns opened about two hours before sunset, and nearly effected a breach; shortly after, at night-fall, the garrison, who from their incessant firing, had threatened serious resistance, vacated the place, and the British took quiet possession.

On the following night, hearing that the fugitive garrison had obtained possession of the small ghurry, at Bainsadah, distant only 16 miles due north of Sewny, and near the Nerbudda, Capt. Newton volunteered to go in pursuit, with 150 of Capt. Roberts' irregular horse; his services were accepted, and, accompanied by Lieut. Mac Queen of the 23d N. I., he proceeded at 11 P.M., taking with him two guides, who had watched the refractory zemindar's motions.

They were favoured with a bright moon, and when within half a mile of the enemy's post, being then 2 A. M. of the 17th January 1818, Capt. Newton sent forward the hircarrahs, with an intelligent trooper dismounted, to ascertain the strength of the place, the number of the enemy, and the nearest and best road. In half an hour they returned, reporting that there were 250 in the fort, who were regaling, as if at a marriage ceremony; that there was a picket of 12 men at the south gate, apparently not watchful; and the road was good, but led close under the walls. Captain Newton immediately moved forward, preserving all possible quiet, but when within twelve paces of the picket, the sentry gave the alarm, upon which the advance, about a dozen men, faced about, leaped the thorn fence, surrounding the picket, and pistolled nearly the whole of them. The confusion inside was very apparent, but presently a fire from all the faces of the fort was opened; the detachment was on the south face, and Capt. Newton immediately ordered Lieutenant Mac Queen to the gateway, to the eastward, with half of the party, while he remained at the one on the west face.

It was soon ascertained that the enemy's firing was of little avail, and as the men were dismounting to prepare to escalade, the walls being low, a rush was heard towards the east gate, from which they attempted to escape, and immediately after a sharp firing on the plain commenced. The rout became general very soon, and all hands were instantly engaged. Lieut. Mac Queen executed his orders with much credit to himself; and Capt. Newton had the satisfaction to report 85 of the enemy killed and wounded, besides bringing in the head man, his son, and family, as prisoners to the Major's camp, capturing some camels, a state carriage, and forty horses, saddled, and every way equipped for service.

Captain Newton's exertions on the above occasion, received the thanks of the Commander-in-Chief, his immediate commanding officer, and the commanding officer of the forces.

Shortly after his return to Hussungabad, he volunteered to command a detachment of four grenadier companies, to accompany Col.

Adams, which offer being accepted, he proceeded with the Colonel to Chanda*; and after the fall of that place, Capt. Newton returned with the force to Hussungabad; and in July, he was again detached in command of three flank companies and two guns, into the Baitool valley, which had now become the theatre of war, and unheard-of barbarity †.

When Appah Saheb had succeeded in effecting his escape from the escort which was conducting him to Allahabad, he immediately (either under a previous arrangement, or from instant necessity) threw himself on the protection of the Goand chieftains, inhabiting the extensive range called the Mahadeo hills, by whom he was well received and heartily assisted; and he had soon the satisfaction of seeing great numbers of those Arab and Hindostannies who formerly served him, again flocking to his standard, and zealous in his cause.

Capt. Sparkes had been, for a long time, in charge of the Baitool valley, and had under him two companies from the 2d batt. 10th, but he had not been at all molested, till after Col. Adam's return from Nagpore to cantonments, when rumours were circulated of the assembling of troops and the disaffection of the neighbouring districts. He communicated these reports to Col. Adams, who thought it advisable to reinforce him by sending out three companies of the 2d batt. 23d reg., on the 18th and 19th July, but before these could reach Baitool, Capt. Sparkes had an unsuccessful action with the enemy, the result of which was the defeat and brutal massacre of himself and all his party ‡!

---

* On the way to Chanda, they turned off the road to watch the motions of the Peishwa, who was at the head of a large army, which they fell in with, and totally routed at the village of Sewny, on the 18th April, 1817, after a march of 35 miles; his loss in killed and wounded was immense, and the whole of his baggage was captured.

† The Editor is principally indebted to Lieut. M'Naughton's Memoirs, for the operations of the Nerbudda subsidiary force, at this period.

‡ It appeared that being informed of the occupation of the town of Mooltye (distant 27 miles from Baitool) by a body of the enemy, Capt. Sparkes proceeded with one company on the 19th for the purpose of dispersing them; and on arriving at Mooltye on the 20th, he was told that the body in question was at a village a little further on. He continued his

As soon as intelligence reached Colonel Adams of the above, he ordered out a squadron of the 7th cavalry, and the 2d batt. 10th march till he very suddenly found himself in front of about 2,000 horse and foot, strongly posted, and well equipped. This being a force infinitely greater than his intelligence had led him to expect, and his other company being too distant to give him any hopes of being able to procure its assistance, he found himself in a situation of unusual peril, and from which he could have had but little hopes of being extricated. He, however, very gallantly resolved to stand firm, and having secured a good post in the bed of a nullah, he commenced a brisk fire upon the enemy, who returned it very determinedly, seeing the smallness of his party, and the necessity he was under of occupying a defensive position. Notwithstanding the immense superiority of their numbers, his opposers had not the resolution to attack him closely in that situation, but began to surround him, in the first instance; which he perceiving, quitted the nullah and retreated to a height a short way in the rear. Here he maintained the fight with great undauntedness, till more than half his party had fallen, and his ammunition was nearly expended—he had been likewise himself wounded in his retreat to the hill, and most of the survivors were similarly situated. In this desperate situation he repelled several of the enemy's charges up the height, and his men evinced the most determined bravery; but seeing not even the slightest hopes of success, or the means of retreat, he displayed a flag of truce—that last resource and acknowledged safeguard of every enemy. Here, however, it was not only disregarded, but allowed to increase the ferocity of the barbarians, to whom it served as an undoubted sign of the forlorn condition of the British detachment, instead of an irresistible claim to mercy, and it was pressed still more closely than before. Capt. Sparkes then resolved, as a last effort, to gain possession of another and more tenable eminence, at a little distance to the left of that he occupied, and proceeded towards it accordingly; but while on the point of gaining this new position, he was mortally wounded, and his fall bereft his few remaining sepoys of all hopes, and encouraged his savage enemy to make another charge, in which they succeeded, and cut, or thought they cut, every man in pieces. Our brave fellows fought with desperate fury in this last attack, as if disdaining to call a second time for quarter, and revenged their deaths on numbers of their assailants. The Subadar fought with most heroic gallantry, and though repeatedly wounded, he "kept both foes and fate at bay" till his sword broke in the conflict. Even then, when a *courageous* horseman advanced to spear him, he threw his turban in the coward's face, and in the momentary stoppage which this occasioned, succeeded in laying hold of another sword, with which he maintained the fight, till, weakened by loss of blood, and overwhelmed by increasing numbers, he fell on the very spot he had so resolutely defended, and was literally hacked to pieces! The body of Capt. Sparkes was afterwards found, but dreadfully disfigured, and one or two of the sepoys who had been left for dead, but afterwards recovered, were all who remained to give the particulars of this lamentable catastrophe.

It is to be regretted that Captain Sparkes had not received more accurate information of the strength of this body, (which consisted of Arabs and Hindostannies proceeding to join the ex-Rajah) or that he had not deferred going against it till he had been joined by the reinforcements for which he had sent in expresses to Hussungabad, and which arrived at Baitool not many hours after he had left it. Or if, on the other hand, the haste of his de-

(with the exception of the flank companies) to proceed immediately to Baitool under Major M'Pherson; and two days afterwards the flank companies followed under Capt. Newton, together with a brigade of six-pounders. Alarming intelligence (but exaggerated, as subsequently appeared,) of the great and augmenting force of the enemy, still continuing to arrive, another squadron of the 7th cavalry, 4 companies 1st batt. 19th, and a brigade of Native horse artillery, the whole under Major Cumming, of the 7th, followed the before-named detachments on the 27th of the same month, (July)*.

The first accounts from Major M'Pherson were not of a nature which served to dissipate Col. Adam's anxiety regarding the state of affairs in that quarter; for they informed him of intelligence having reached the Major of the plunder of Shahpore, (a village between Hussungabad and Baitool) and the slaughter of eighteen sepoys who had been left there from inability to proceed. Another body of the enemy had posted themselves near Mooltye, upon which place they had made a requisition for supplies; and Major M'Pherson expressed his fears of not being able to protect the country by establishing a line of communication, owing to the numbers of hostile troops appearing from all quarters, and the weakness of his own detachment rendering a separation highly injudicious.

---

parture was owing to false ideas of military honour, or the fear of shame for lying inactively so near an enemy, it is equally to be lamented, that such an exuberance of martial feeling should have overcome his better judgment, and led to so melancholy and detrimental a result as is here recorded.

* Hostilities were for some time carried on in the valley under more mortifying circumstances to the British troops than they had usually been in the habits of experiencing; but many unfavourable and unavoidable occurrences had joined to render the situation of the detachments more difficult and trying than those in which they are commonly used to be placed; for the enemy were very strong, and the bad success of Capt. Sparkes had given them a great occasion of confidence; the rains were continual, and heavier than the oldest inhabitants remembered ever to have seen; the country, situated in the middle of hills and jungles, was most distressingly unhealthy to the troops, who could not possibly succeed in getting their camp equipage over the ghauts, and cut up roads through which they had themselves to pass. The Goands and Arabs were familiarly acquainted with the retreats and all the localities of the field of warfare, and they had succeeded in destroying one or two more small parties of our troops, and in plundering some villages.

Capt. Newton's party had not been heard of, and there was a force of 1500 Arabs at Julpie Ammer, only fifteen coss from Mehlghaut, situated between Shahpore and Baitool. These were accounts far from satisfactory; but others from Major Cumming, who had in the interim advanced near to Mooltye, giving a detail of a very spirited and successful affair with the enemy, who had got possession of that town and ghurry, gave fresh hopes of speedy success*— for its ultimate attainment was never despaired of.

On the 20th, Major Cumming and Major M'Pherson arrived before Mooltye; but they found the enemy in such force and confidence, that the former, considering the weak state of his detachment, was of opinion it would be imprudent to risk an assault, as a failure, in his unsupported state, would be attended with the most fatal consequences; and in this opinion Major M'Pherson coincided. Judging from what he saw on the morning of his arrival, Major Cumming conceived that the enemy's force could not be less than between 1,000 and 1,200 men, for when his detachment arrived within half a mile of the place, about 300 horse, and a large body of

* In consequence of having been informed that the Arabs, &c. had collected in force at Mooltye, Major Cumming deemed it advisable to reinforce a detachment he had pushed on to Synkerah, (a village only six coss from it) and accordingly marched himself on the 15th August with a squadron of his regiment, and fifty sepoys of the 2d batt. 23d N. I., and wishing to procure more certain intelligence of the enemy's strength and situation than he had hitherto received, he dispatched Capt. Ker and Cornet Duffin with a troop, for the purpose of reconnoitring the town. Capt. Ker came in sight of Mooltye a little after daybreak on the 16th, and succeeded in surprising a mounted picket, which he pursued under the very walls of the fort, and cut up to a man; but by this time the alarm having been given, a body of about 400 horse, and 500 infantry, sallied out of the town to attack the troop, (amounting to no more than 60 men) and not doubting of being able to annihilate it. Capt. Ker, with great judgment, feigned a retreat, in order to induce the horse to pursue, and by that means separate themselves from the infantry, which manœuvre completely succeeded; and as soon as he got them to a convenient distance, Capt. Ker halted and charged them repeatedly, with great slaughter; continuing to retreat slowly after every charge till he reached Synkerah, which he did with the trifling loss of one trooper, and four horses killed, and one havildar and one horse wounded. He also took twenty horses, but having no means of bringing them to camp, he subsequently abandoned them. Capt. Ker spoke in the highest terms of the gallant conduct of Cornet Duffin and the rest of the troop; but the simple detail of so very spirited and ably conducted an affair requires no comment to set forth its brilliancy.

infantry, came out against him. The former were soon defeated, with the loss of thirty killed, and the latter were dispersed and driven back into the town by a few well-directed rounds from a 6-pounder. Both officers were, therefore, of opinion, that a considerable reinforcement would be absolutely necessary to enable the attack to be made with any probability of success; and concurred in strongly recommending a battalion of Native infantry, with at least two squadrons of cavalry, and a proportion of artillery, being sent out with the least possible delay. Col. Adams had no sooner received these accounts, than he determined to proceed, in person, to Mooltye, and accordingly ordered a suitable force to be in readiness to march on the 26th August, under his own command; but this movement was fortunately rendered unnecessary by the arrival of intermediate expresses notifying the evacuation of that place by the Arabs. This occurred during the night of the 22d, but Major Cumming was not apprised of it till the following morning, when he immediately took possession of the town, and likewise sent off a squadron and some infantry in pursuit of the garrison. The complete success of the pursuing party, under Capt. Newton, compensated amply for previous disappointments. That officer came upon the enemy about day-break, on the 24th, after a march of 21 miles; as they lay encamped about 300 yards on the further side of the Bheal river, a very rapid stream, and so deep, that in some places the cavalry and infantry were obliged to swim. The surprise was, notwithstanding this obstacle, very complete, and till the cavalry had formed under Lieut. John Lane, and were preparing for the charge (which Captain Newton immediately directed) they could have no idea of the detachment's proximity.

Their number amounted to 150 horse and 200 Arabs, out of which not more than half escaped, as 117 dead bodies were counted on the field; and among the slain, the sepoys recognized the person of one of the men, who had deserted with the ex-Rajah, on his escape from Captain Browne's detachment. Several of the sebundies, who proved unfaithful to the British government, in whose service they were, by giving up without resistance the town of Mooltye to the Arabs, were likewise among the slain; and the whole party were of the number of those who cut up Captain Sparkes and his company.

The loss of the party was trifling, being but five men and six horses killed and wounded; so that every thing concurred to render this one of the most dashing and destructive affairs, that happened in the course of these operations, and to entitle Captain Newton and those under him to very great praise*.

There being no more of the enemy in the vicinity of Mooltye, Major Cumming returned to Synkerah on the 1st Sept.; but not without extreme difficulty, owing to the fatigued state of his men, and the heavy and incessant rain having rendered the country an entire swamp. In consequence of information, after his return to Synkerah, of a considerable body of the enemy having possessed themselves of the fort of Omlah, not very far distant, he detached Capt. John Jones of the 7th cavalry, with one squadron, and 150 sepoys towards that place; who, on arriving before it early the next morning, was joined by a detachment from Mooltye, consisting of a troop from the 6th battalion cavalry, and 150 Madras sepoys.

* Another successful attack was made by Capt. Ker much about the same time, on a party of the enemy, which Major Cumming had heard was at a village six coss from Mooltye, and immediately sent a troop and company under the above named gallant and truly zealous officer, in quest of them. After a fatiguing march, Captain Ker came up, and found the enemy posted in a small ghurry, near which (since he had not the means of dislodging them) he proceeded to take up a position till he could be reinforced from camp; but this party, amounting to about 300 horse and Arabs, not thinking themselves perfectly secure in their present situation, made a sudden and precipitate retreat; which observing, Capt. Ker immediately took up the pursuit. The enemy crossed a nullah about half a mile from their first post, and there endeavoured to oppose the advance of our detachment; but a well directed fire from the infantry, soon put them to flight, and Capt. Ker instantly crossed the nullah. The fugitives then made for another small fort, into which the horse and part of the foot succeeded in getting, but with the loss of 50 killed; and Cornet Duffin, who was detached for that purpose, destroyed several straggling parties of their infantry, after which Capt. Ker returned to camp with three men and two horses wounded. This party likewise proved to have been part of the body who killed Capt. Sparkes; as several of his things were re-taken, as well as two doolies of the 2d batt. 10th, to which his unfortunate company belonged.

Capt. Jones found the fort of Omlah so strong, as to prevent the possibility of his getting into it without scaling ladders, which, however, he could not procure of sufficient length; but being informed that the opposite side of the place to that on which he was posted, presented less insuperable difficulties to an attempt at escalade, he moved round, and at the same time divided his cavalry so as completely to invest the fort. An attempt was then made by the infantry under Lieutenants Dunn, of the Madras, and Cruikshank, of the Bengal establishment; but on their approach they not only found that the walls were too high for the ladders, but likewise double, and very strong; in consequence of which, they relinquished the enterprise, and Capt Jones was compelled by the swampy nature of the ground, and the want of provisions, to draw off his detachment to a distance from the fort, when the garrison, aided by the inhabitants of the district, escaped during the following night, having had altogether about 20 of their number killed.

The next affair of any consequence, which occurred during these hostilities, and the first in able management and importance, took place under the guidance of Lieut. Cruikshank, of the 24th regiment, but then doing duty with the 2d 10th *.

From the 25th till the 27th September, Capt. Newton was engaged in a series of operations, which, although not remarkable for the *eclât* produced by former affairs, were yet very destructive and injurious to the enemy, by driving them from their places of shelter, and compelling them to seek refuge in the woods. That officer marched from Baitool on the 25th, taking with him a force of 300 men, including a squadron of the 7th cavalry; and, in the course of the day, arrived at Ninda Gunda, the head-quarters and cantonments of Purtaub Sing, Luchman Sing, and another Goand leader, situated a few miles from, and rather to the S. W. of Raneepoor, in a dell formed by two ranges of hills, and having two nullahs, one running E. and W. round the front, and the other N. and S. The cantonments were situated in the centre, strongly stockaded, and

* See Lieut. M'Naughton's Memoirs.

guarded by numerous and well-posted pickets, who descried Capt. Newton's detachment while yet at a considerable distance; and, in consequence of this discovery, he immediately pushed on to the attack in the following order:—

Lieut. Cruikshank, with sixty men, was sent to the right, and Lieut. Mac Queen, with a like number, to the left; while Capt. Newton, with the remaining eighty infantry, pushed on to the front followed by the squadron, which was destined to pursue the enemy across the valley. On the detachment ascending the principal stockade, a sharp, but ill-directed fire, was opened on it by the Goands, who immediately afterwards "fled (as the despatch expresses it) with the agility of monkeys, up the mountains in every direction, so that it was impossible to close with them." The party succeeded, however, in killing nine, and wounding about thirty of the fugitives; besides having had the gratification of destroying two very fine cantonments, and four large villages, the plunder of which, with 150 head of cattle, Capt. Newton gave to the detachment. After having in vain pursued the enemy for several miles, through a country frequently intersected by deep nullahs, and over hills very thickly wooded, Capt. Newton struck off towards Raneepoor; on arriving at which place he was joined by sixty men of the 1st batt. 19th reg. who had (by his orders) proceeded there from Shahpoor, with a brigade of gallopers, under Lieutenant Orr.

Information was here received of the principal cantonment of Kulloo Bair Thakoor, to which place the Goands had fled from Ninda Gunda, and where Capt. Newton accordingly resolved to proceed; but just as he had finished his arrangements, and was preparing to march, word was brought to him that Gubha had returned to Bakoor. Fearing that this chief would again depart, (after the rough manner in which he had been handled by Lieut. Cruikshank) if he heard of the vicinity of his detachment, Capt. Newton resolved to go and attack him in the first instance; and accordingly marched at 11 A.M. the next day, by which he expected to reach Bakoor at day-break on the 27th. When he came within four miles of the place, he pushed on with the cavalry, (taking Lieut. Cruikshank - as a guide) and when at the distance of 1000 yards from their post, he discovered a large body of Goands in the village at the foot of a high mountain. He instantly charged with the squadron, but his progress was unfortunately impeded by a nullah, which proved the cause of his being discovered by the enemy, who fled immediately up the hills, from which they fired, but without the least effect, upon the detachment. Having scoured the village, Capt. Newton dismounted the skirmishers, whom he sent up the hills under Cornet Allen, while himself and Lieut. Cruikshank continued the pursuit as far as Jewah Ghurry, distant four miles east. In this affair eleven more were killed, and a good many wounded, but these latter endeavoured to conceal themselves so as to elude discovery, which the nature of the country facilitated their doing*.

A heavy fall of rain having prevented his march on the morning of the 28th, Capt. Newton moved on the evening of that day in quest of the cantonment, to which, as has been already stated, the return of Gubha, to Bakoor, induced him to defer proceeding on the 26th. In the course of his approach, he observed a number of goands hastily driving their cattle up the hills in every direction, and pursued them with the cavalry till nightfall—killing only one goand, but taking 50 head of cattle. The next morning Capt. Newton continued his progress to Kulloo's cantonment, but his guide having missed the road, and being unable to recover it, he was compelled to retrace his steps; particularly as Maj. M'Pherson had, by orders from Lieut.-Col. Munt, recalled him to Baitool. While on his return, he was met by a number of villagers, who informed him that Kulloo having left his canton-

---

* Several other articles which belonged to Capt. Sparks, were found with the above body, from which it may be inferred, that they also were present at his destruction, and thus doubly deserved the severe punishment which now fell upon them; for the loss of their villages, goods, but particularly their cattle, was the most irremediable hardship that could have befallen them; as the inclemency of the season proved fatal to great numbers of the wanderers, and the natural sterility of their country rendered them entirely dependent for sustenance on the cattle which they plundered yearly from the valleys.

ment, was then with 100 matchlockmen, and a few horse, in the hills leading to Asseer (a fort about four coss from Raneepoor) and their intelligence assumed so much the appearance of authenticity, by their pressing their services as guides to the detachment, that Capt. Newton was induced to defer his return to Baitool, and proceeded in quest of that chief and his party. He accordingly took 80 sepoys, the command of whom he gave to Lieut. Cruikshank, who had volunteered his services; and, as cavalry was recommended by the guides, he directed the squadron to accompany him, but left all sick and lame men behind. He moved off at 11 P. M. and after having surmounted as many difficulties as were ever presented to a detachment—moving over hills 1,500 and 2,000 feet high, unassisted by a moon, and the rain falling all night—they were fully rewarded by the success of a complete surprise of the enemy at 8 A. M., insomuch that with the exception of Kulloo's brother (a boy about seven years of age, who was unfortunately wounded in the attack) his mother and younger brother at the breast, not another soul was spared to tell the story*."

In these several attacks upon the goands Capt. Newton had only one man wounded, and he returned to Baitool, after having, with his party, undergone very great fatigue, and done proportionate damage to the enemy; but he informed Col. Adams that had he not been so hastily recalled by Lieut.-Col. Munt, (then in command of the Baitool valley), he had no doubt, that from the information he was every day obtaining, he should in the space of a week, have succeeded in exterminating every goand in that part of the country†.

* Kulloo was represented as an uncommonly handsome young man, 22 years old, and nearly as fair as a European; and as he had before succeeded in cutting up a small party of sepoys at Shahpoor, nothing could exceed the joy of Capt. Newton's detachment, (composed chiefly of sepoys from the 2d-10th) at the opportunity this surprise gave them, of revenging the fate of their comrades; and they declared themselves better rewarded for all their exertions, than they could have been by "any amount of plunder."

† No subsequent operations worthy of particular notice, were carried on by the Hussungabad detachments, who were recalled towards the breaking up of the rains, on being relieved by the Bengal and Madras troops from Nagpore, the former being the 1st-23d, under Lieut.-Col. Popham, (who was invested with the general command of the valley) and part of the 6th cavalry. The Hussungabad parties returned to cantonments totally exhausted from constant

At the conclusion of this campaign, Capt. Newton was seized with a fever that carried off numbers of his brother officers and men, and he did not recover until his corps was ordered, in April 1819, into the provinces, and Maj. M'Pherson being appointed to a civil situation, Captain Newton proceeded to Benares in command of his battalion *.

In Nov. 1820, Capt. Newton went in command of two companies of the 1st batt. 10th reg. with H. M.'s 87th reg. to the presidency, and in Feb. 1821, joined the 1st batt. 10th reg. at Barrackpore. In July 1823, he was promoted to Major, and in October following he proceeded with his corps to Dacca. On the 5th Nov. he was ordered on express service with the left wing of his regiment, to Sylhet, which place he reached on the 22d, and found the inhabi-

---

exposure to the wet, and consequent sickness, so that but a very small portion of them indeed were fit for ordinary duty, and numerous deaths had greatly reduced their original numbers. Nor did the officers, who were all equally exposed, return in a much better state; for almost all of them had been attacked by sickness, and several had fallen victims to the jungle fever, which was inseparable from the arduous and protracted service they were sent to perform; so that, upon the whole, no troops ever underwent more hardships, nor bore them with greater cheerfulness, than those of whom we are now speaking. Heavier rains, or of longer duration, than those of 1818, were not in the memory of the oldest inhabitants; and the whole country, as far as the eye could reach, was completely inundated by the overflow of the Nerbuddah, Towah, and all the inferior streams.

Hills and jungles are at all times fatal to our troops, but in so dreadful a season as the above, they were ruinously unhealthy—not so much from the rains merely, as from the continual exposure to them of the several detachments, who found it altogether impracticable to bring on their camp equipage. But all these severities were unavoidable, for the Baitool valley must either have been defended, and cleared of its ferocious and accumulating enemies, or (to our eternal shame,) have been plundered, and actually re-taken, by the deposed and infamous Rajah, in the very sight of our principal stations; and an act of almost unparralleled atrocity, the massacre of a British detachment in defiance of a flag of truce, have been allowed to pass by unheeded and unavenged, and its perpetrators to triumph in the impunity with which it was committed! Appah Saheb himself was not in the Mahadeo hills during these operations, for he had left the Goand chiefs to go and seek for aid and adherents about Asseergurh, and the adjacent country; he subsequently returned to Purhmurry, and before Col. Adams's invasion of the hills.

* This fine corps had, in 1816, marched with the force, 1100 strong, and 11 officers: it arrived at Benares in June 1819, mustering only 480 men and 3 officers—one of the many proofs that might be adduced of the insufficiency of the number of European officers to Native corps.

tants of the country under the greatest alarm, at the approach of large divisions of the Burmese army. He was joined at Sylhet by four companies of the Rungpore light infantry, and in December he was reinforced with three companies of the 23d N. I., under Capt. Johnston. He was also led to expect he should find four guns, with a detail of artillery, at the post; but was disappointed.

The report of a large Burmese force being on the march, for the purpose of invading Cachar, being confirmed, Major Newton proceeded on a tour of inspection of the passes accessible to the enemy across the mountains, and established posts at the most convenient and commanding positions on the frontier; which done, the protection of the civil station of Sylhet became a necessary consideration, and to which he gave his attention. Thus employed, he accidentally found five old iron guns laying in a shed, half buried in the earth, and of which no person had the least idea. Aided by Mr. Turquand, the magistrate, he obtained carriages and ammunition; and also 30 sets of entrenching tools of all descriptions; conceiving that he would have occasion for entrenching his detached parties, and to enable him to throw up works in case of necessity. With the assistance of the quarter-master-serjeant of the corps, and a discharged Golandauze entertained for the occasion, Major Newton trained 25 sepoys of the left wing of the 1st batt. 10th reg. to the exercise of the guns, and he had the satisfaction, in less than a month, of seeing them perfect in their evolutions. He sent off two of the guns to Budderpore, to be placed in the works he threw up there; and caused a small mud ghurry to be erected opposite the Mootagool pass, and midway between Sylhet and Budderpore, to which place he detached a company of the Rungpore battalion. Early in Jan. he detached Capt. Johnston, with five companies in advance, to Telain, a commanding position, distant from Budderpore, due east, about 20 miles. On the 17th, hearing of the near approach of about 5000 Burmese, and of their having had an action with the Rajah of Cachar, Gumbeer Sing, in which they were successful, and obliged him to retreat before them, Major Newton deemed it necessary to reconnoitre the road, on the Cachar side of the river, leading to Telain; to ascertain the practicability, or otherwise, of marching with his guns, should he deem it proper to form a junction with Capt. Johnston's detachment, not judging it prudent to relinquish so advantageous a position as Telain, by ordering him to fall back. For this purpose, Major Newton desired Lieut. Fisher, of the quarter-master-general's department, a jemedar, and 20 sepoys, to accompany him. They set out at one P. M. of the 17th, and at four P. M., when half-way between Budderpore and Telain, Major Newton received information of another force of about 4000 of the Assamese and Burmese having actually crossed the hills to the northward, and being then busily stockading at the village of Bickranpore. At the time of receiving this information, Major Newton's attention was drawn towards the spot, by thousands of poor inhabitants coming towards him from that direction, with their baggage on their heads: thus situated between two armies, and between his own detachment, he resolved instantly to recross the Surma, and order both detachments to join him. He crossed the river at Juttrypore, two miles in advance, obtained possession of all the ferry-boats, and dispatched orders to Capt. Johnston at Telain, and Capt. Bowes at Budderpore, to join him at Juttrypore. Capt. Johnston's detachment arrived at 11 P. M., and Capt. Bowes' at 1 A. M. of the 18th, and at 2 o'clock the whole moved forward towards Bickranpore. The force consisted of five companies of the 1st battalion 10th regiment, three of the 23d regiment, and 3 of the Rungpore light infantry, in all 800 men. The road lay through an almost impervious jungle, intersected by numerous nullahs. At 8 A. M. they broke into a comparatively open space, where the enemy discovered themselves by firing on the advanced guard. Major Newton's force immediately formed in two columns, and moved towards the enemy's position, which was well chosen, on the banks of a nullah, and stockaded. Capt. Johnston's column came first into action, whilst Capt. Bowes' was employed in cutting off the retreat of the enemy towards the hills. The Assamese, shortly after the commencement of the action, fled, losing a number in killed and wounded. They left only 40 odd Burmese to defend the stockade, which they did most gallantly for near two hours, when the British succeeded in storming and killing every Burmah in the place.

Major Newton's loss on this occasion was 11 killed and 10 wounded. After destroying the enemy's stockade, he returned with the detachment to Budderpore, resolved to attack the force, on the following day, that had defeated Gumbeer Sing, and for which purpose, on hearing of their arrival at Juttrypore, he embarked the guns in boats to cross them over the river; but the commissioners thought the attempt would be too hazardous, as the enemy were so numerous, and requested he would defer further operations until the arrival of Mr. Scott, the Governor-General's agent. Mr. Scott arrived on the following day; and on seeing how affairs stood, made a requisition upon Dacca for troops and guns, and recommended acting on the defensive until the arrival of the reinforcement. On the 14th Feb. Lieut.-Col. Bowen, of the 1st-10th, arrived with the right wing of that corps, and, as senior officer, assumed the command of the force, and instantly detached Major Newton and Lieut. Armstrong, with 200 men, to occupy the enemy's stockades at Juttrypore, which they had that day vacated. On the day following, the Lieut.-Colonel arrived with the remainder of the force, from which time nothing material occurred until the 21st of Feb., when Major Newton and Lieut. Armstrong joined the head-quarters, immediately after which the force proceeded and attacked the enemy in their stockade at Doodpatlee. After being before the place five hours, incapable, by every exertion of officers and men, to drive the enemy from their position, Lieut.-Col. Bowen resolved on a retreat, but afterwards altered his intention, formed the troops in line, and ordered them to charge the west face of the stockade. The line advanced gallantly to within forty paces of the works, when they were brought up by a very formidable ditch, thickly studded with bamboo spikes, from six to forty inches long, to the distance of thirty-five paces in front, on arriving at which the enemy opened a most destructive fire, which, with the obstacles just mentioned, obliged the line to retreat and fall back on the guns, and ultimately, the same evening, to re-embark and retrograde to Juttrypore. The British loss, on this occasion, was Lieut. Armstrong, killed; Capt. Johnston, of the 23d, severely wounded; Ensign C. S. Barberie, leg amputated; and Lieut. H. M. Graves, 10th reg., slightly wounded; and 166 native officers and men killed and wounded. The day after their return to Juttrypore they were joined by Brigadier Innis, and a battalion of the 19th, and some guns. Lieut.-Colonel Bowen, of the 10th, being reported sick, the command of that corps devolved on Major Newton, who proceeded with it and the 19th and guns, under Col. Innes, to renew the attack upon Doodpatlee; but, on arriving at Telain, it was found that the enemy had evacuated the position. Seven days afterwards, Lieut.-Col. Bowen rejoined the 10th. Major Newton, after making over the command to that officer, was desired to proceed with a detachment to Budderpore, and shortly after the whole force fell back for the purpose of cantoning at Sylhet.

On the 15th April, Major Newton was removed to the 2d-10th, and proceeded to join it at Barrackpore. In Sept. following he was promoted to a Lieutenant-Colonelcy in the 48th N. I., which corps he joined at Saugor, in July 1825.

THE LATE CAPTAIN JAMES CRAWFORD.

(Bengal Establishment.)

THE brilliant talents of this officer, and his capacity for civil employment, together with the coincidence of his commanding a corps of the same number as Cæsar's favourite one, the 10th legion, obtained for him, throughout the Indian army, the appellation of "Cæsar Crawford."

On the assembling of a force, in 1778, at Allahabad, which was destined to march, under the command of Col. M. Leslie, across the peninsula, and co-operate with the Bombay government, in hostilities against the Mahrattas, the 10th battalion, under Captain Crawford, formed a component part.

The severe sufferings which were experienced, both by officers and men, from the intense heat of the weather, the want of water and due information respecting the roads and nature of the country through which they were marching, have already been referred to in this work. (See vol. ii. p. 418-20). In this service, Captain James Crawford died raving mad; and the following account is from the pen of an officer of the Bengal army:—

"Proceeding from Culpee, the detachment lost, on the second day's march, one of its most valuable officers, Captain James Crawford, commanding the 4th battalion, who died from a stroke of the sun. Connected with that unfortunate event, the following relation of facts will doubtless be read with unfeigned sympathy and admiration.

"Captain Crawford had acquired the character of an excellent sepoy officer, and the battalion which he commanded was considered one of the finest corps in the service.

"The appellation of 'Crawford,' by which the 4th battalion was called by the men of the corps, and the Natives in general, was an exception to the practice that generally prevailed, in former times, of calling corps by the name of the officer by whom they were formed, or that of the place at which they were raised. Capt. Crawford was considered by the men as a rigid and, perhaps, severe disciplinarian; yet that excellent officer so happily blended, with the strictest principles of military discipline and arrangement, the practice of the most inflexible integrity and impartial justice, in the general exercise of the influence and powers of authority, combined with considerate and manly indulgence, in regard to the religious habits, the customs, and prejudices of the men under his command, that, of Capt. Crawford, it may with truth be affirmed he had the good fortune to verify what ought to be the emulation and object of every military man, with regard to those under his command—the enviable distinction of commanding their lives through the medium of their affections.

"It is a fact no less creditable to Capt. Crawford's memory than it is honourable to the character of the men whom he commanded, that during the halt of the detachment at the encampment where he was buried (which continued for several days, owing to the severity of the weather, and waiting the arrival of stores, &c. from Caunpoor), all the individuals of the corps, native officers and men, went from time to time to render their tribute of grateful attachment and affection, by making their obeisance, after the manner of their country, at the grave of their lamented commander. And on the day the detachment moved forward from that encampment, the grateful and sorrowing 'Crawford,' or 4th battalion, after it had been told off, preparatory to the march, requested leave to pile their arms, and to be permitted, collectively, to go and express their last benedictory farewell over the remains of their respected commander, protector, and friend *.

---

* *Ext. of a Letter from a Field Officer to the Editor of the East India Military Calendar.*

"Thus much I have often heard asserted, that he (**Capt. Crawford**) was held in the highest esteem by all under him, as well as by his brother officers; and to show the veneration he inspired in the Natives, I have to relate the following anecdote:—he died on the first day's march from Culpee, after the army had crossed the Jumna, in a district then held by Allee Behauder, a great enemy of our's; yet, notwithstanding that, the Natives established a perpetual light to be kept up at his tomb, 'to keep quiet the spirit of the hero;' and a faqueer and his wife were stationed there to watch over it. In 1808, when I commanded a battalion at Etawah, I found the faqueer had died; but his wife waited upon me ostensibly to announce she had been left in charge, but in reality to obtain a present, which, of course, I gave her. Let me also add, on the subject of the tomb, that when I dispatched three companies from Etawah, with treasure, they had to pass by and encamped at the spot, when all the commissioned native officers, both Hindoo and Mussulman, entered the holy circle drawn round his tomb, and performed their services to the dead.

"On the day Col. Leslie's army marched from Culpee it was the hottest period of the hot winds. Misled by the guides (supposed wilfully), they were very late in the day before they reached their ground; in consequence, the sepoys began to droop, and several remained behind, from being entirely exhausted with thirst and fatigue, which, when perceived by Capt. Crawford, he dismounted, and nothing could persuade him to mount again, and thus encouraged, his own men (almost all) reached the encampment. On the line of march he distributed every drop of water that was carried by his servants, for his own use, among his

"What soldier can read this without being inspired with a resolution to emulate the example, and aspire to the honour which distinguished the character and exalted the memory of Capt. Crawford! or emphatically to exclaim, in the language of Scripture, ' May my last end be like his.'"

To the preceding statement we must add the following extract from the journal of Lieut. Duncan Stewart*, a companion in arms of the gallant Captain Crawford:—

"June 3, 1778—Marched at length from Culpee, on the Jumna, leaving Major Baillie, of the Bengal artillery, with the 2d and 5th battalions, the one for the purpose of bringing us a supply of provisions, and the other to accompany the magazine.

sepoys; they did not arrive till 10 o'clock, A. M., and from this extra fatigue, and the excessiveness of the heat, he only lived till four."

* Lieut. Duncan Stewart, late of the Bengal establishment, was born in North Britain, in 1756, and left England as a midshipman, on board the Duke of Albany, East Indiaman, in February 1772. This vessel was wrecked on the long sands at the mouth of the river Hoogley, in the Bay of Bengal, in July of the same year. On his arrival at Calcutta, Mr. Stewart was received into the family of the late Gen. Sir Archibald Campbell, K. B. (late Governor and Commander-in-Chief of Madras), then Colonel commanding the corps of engineers, in Bengal; and, through his interest, was appointed a Cadet on the Bengal establishment, and an assistant engineer in his, Sir Archibald Campbell's, own corps.

In the year 1774, Mr. Stewart joined the 17th battalion (sepoys) as a volunteer, on that corps being ordered on an expedition to reduce the hilly country westward of Midnapore, in which he served with great credit during that and the following year, when a fever, caught through the unwholesomeness of the climate, obliged him to proceed to Bombay for the recovery of his health.

In 1776, he returned with his health re-established, and having been promoted during his absence to the rank of Ensign, he was appointed as such to the 10th batt. of sepoys, commanded by Capt. James Crawford, which was stationed at Patcome, and had co-operated with the corps above-mentioned, at the time he served in it, in the reduction of the hilly country. He continued to serve in this battalion, with whose commander he had formed the most intimate friendship, till that service was accomplished.

In the following year, on the death of Lieut. Col. Fordnam, field engineer to that army, Lieut. Caldwell, surveyor, having succeeded to his situation, Lieut. Stewart was promoted to the office vacated by the latter; but he did not live long to enjoy the fruits of this promotion. The fever, contracted through the unhealthiness of the climate, in the jungle, in the early part of his services, returning upon him, unfortunately terminated his existence on the banks of the Scind, in 1799; when, as a last proof of the long friendship that had subsisted between him and the present Col. Sir John Kennaway, he bequeathed his property and papers to that officer, then a subaltern, serving with the Bengal army in the Carnatic.

"We struck our tents at 2 in the morning, but what with the weakness of the draft bullocks, badness of the roads, and other untoward circumstances, it was day-light before the rear-guard marched off the ground.

"We had not proceeded far before a mistake of the guides caused one half of the line to separate from the other; this occasioned a long delay; the sun now became hot, the troops to want water, of which there was only on the line of march, what could be supplied from a few scattered wells.

"Towards 10 o'clock, the thirst of the men became excessive, and no sooner did a Beastey (water carrier) make his appearance, than they broke from their ranks, and in an instant swallowed up every supply that could be brought. Such distress I never before saw: men, women, children, and even dogs, dropping down for want of water.

"Having that day had the baggage guard, I was every moment a spectator of the miseries of some poor object or other; and I then had an opportunity of seeing how necessity will, in a case of this kind, prevail over the scruples of the poor bigotted Hindoos, for many of them eagerly swallowed water from my own flask: a few indeed would not, but these I observed were not reduced to the greatest degree of distress.

"At 11, the line encamped at the village of Meergoow, having been 9 hours in performing a march of 10 or 12 miles. At 1, I arrived with my guard, when I was informed of the indisposition of my friend Capt. Crawford: the heat of the sun, and the sufferings of his troops, so preyed on his mind, and affected him so severely, that he died in three hours after coming to the ground. All other distresses are nothing to this; nor can words describe the extreme anguish I felt, and still feel, for the loss of that worthiest of men. Hard, indeed, was his fate to be thus cut off in the bloom of life, just as a field opened for the display of his superior abilities: had he died as a soldier ought, at the head of his troops, in the field of battle, it would not have been so deplorable; to be torn from us in this manner, and to have his last hours embittered with the sufferings of his soldiers, makes me almost wish that I had never lived to see this day. Poor fellow! a few minutes before he expired, he burst into tears, lamenting the miseries of the sepoys; his soul was too great to bear, with proper moderation, the observations he made on the conduct of the expedition. Never can I see his fellow! his equal is not in the army! what a stroke to the service—to the detachment—to all that ever knew him, and particularly to his friends! In him I lost a father, brother, and every thing that was dear to me! May I never again experience any loss like this; life with such alloys is almost insupportable."

THE LATE MAJOR CHARLES ARMSTRONG.

(Madras Establishment.)

This officer was descended of very respectable parents in Ireland, whom he quitted at an early period, and enlisted as a private soldier in H. M.'s 101st regiment, with which corps he proceeded to India, and, consequently, served during the Bednore campaign, under the unfortunate Gen. Mathews. He was present at the siege of Cudalore, and it is probable he was shortly after transferred to the Hon. Company's service. He served under Lord Cornwallis during the Mysore campaigns of 1791 and 1792; he was present with the army under General, now Lord, Harris, at the siege and storming of Seringapatam, in 1799, and he was then, or soon after, chosen by the army one of its prize agents.

A Cadet establishment was formed by the Madras government, in 1800, at Chingleput, which Major (then Captain) Armstrong was selected as a person highly qualified to command. This appointment, however, he requested permission to resign in 1802 or 1803, and joined his corps, the 1st batt. 16th reg., then in garrison at Madras. In 1804, he marched in command of the regiment, which, with the flank companies of one of the King's regiments, and the 4th N.I., under the command of Col. Moneypenny, of His Majesty's service, proceeded against the Chittoor, Vincatagherry, and Bumrauze Poligars, who had risen in arms against the civil authorities. This force was afterwards joined by the 5th and 19th regiments, Native infantry, and the 4th reg. Native cavalry. The service, which lasted but a few months only, was exceedingly fatiguing; but upon all occasions Capt. Armstrong acquitted himself highly to the satisfaction of the officer commanding the detachment.

Colonel M. Grant, arriving from Europe, superseded Capt. Armstrong in the command of the 16th regiment; but the command of the 5th extra regiment, directed to be raised at Tanjore, was immediately conferred on him. Early in 1805, this regiment was drafted into the line; and Capt. Armstrong, being promoted, rejoined and took the command of the 16th regiment shortly after its arrival at Bellary, to form part of the army of reserve. On the army being broken up, at the latter end of the year, Major Armstrong proceeded with his regiment to Gooty, where, in 1806, he had a severe attack of fever: his medical friends advised his proceeding instantly to the coast, and to return to Europe as soon as possible, and which he purposed doing. He arrived on the glacis of Velore the night of the unfortunate mutiny, and was challenged by the mutineers from the ramparts. On giving his name he received a volley of musketry, which broke both his legs, or thighs, and a fakeer shortly after, in a most inhuman manner, closed an honourable life, which he had devoted to the service of his country, and the welfare of his companions in arms.

COLONEL HOPETOUN S. SCOTT*, C. B.

(Madras Establishment.)

Extract of a letter from Mr. Adam, Secretary to the Supreme Government, to the Resident at Nagpore, under date Fort William, the 18th June, 1818:—

" Adverting to the nature, extent, and importance, of the command of the force, the Governor-General is decidedly of opinion, that the Commanding Officer should be placed in point of allowances, on the footing of the officers commanding the other established subsidiary forces, and they will be fixed on that principle accordingly, from the date of Sir Thomas Hislop's order for forming the force on its present scale.

" In confirming Lieut.-Col. Scott in this command, the Governor-General experiences the most cordial gratification, in the opportunity it affords of expressing his high sense of the merit of that distinguished officer, throughout

---

* A statement of this officer's services will be found in vol. ii. p. 525, &c. The papers here introduced are honourable additions to that statement; and they will, it is presumed, be acceptable to the several officers and corps mentioned.

the late service in Nagpore, from the day of the glorious defence of Seetabuldee, to the concluding operation of the campaign, the gallant assault of Chanda, which was led by Lieut.-Col. Scott in person."

Supplement to the London Gazette of Tuesday, July 14th, 1818.

" *India Board, July* 13*th*, 1818.

" Extract from a despatch from Lieut.-General Sir Thomas Hislop, to the Governor-General and Commander-in-Chief, dated Headquarters of the army of the Deccan, Camp at Pan Behar, seven miles north of Oogein, 19th December 1817 :—

" It is now with additional pleasure, that I have to lay before your Lordship, the detailed accounts of a most brilliant action at Nagpore, in which the British interests at that capital have been gloriously maintained, by the undaunted courage and perseverance of a small detachment of the 5th division of the army, headed by Lieut.-Col. H. S. Scott, of the Madras establishment.

" The general order published to the army on this most gratifying occasion, will shew to your Lordship the sense I entertain of the admirable conduct of the troops engaged. Whether, indeed, I regard the vast superiority of the enemy's numbers and artillery, or the length of time during which our brave soldiers had fought, until they repulsed the army of Nagpore, I feel assured that your Lordship will consider the actions of the 26th and 27th November as worthy of being recorded in the brightest page of our Indian annals, and the gallant troops who achieved the exploit entitled to the warmest gratitude and admiration of their government. It were endless, on such an occasion, to enumerate the names of those officers, whose situations enabled them particularly to distinguish themselves. The success which attended the efforts of his soldiers, speaks more in proof of the intrepidity and conduct of their commander, Lieut.-Col. Scott, than any expression of praise, however unqualified, can convey; and the spirited exertions of Major Mackenzie, of the 1st battalion, 20th regiment of Madras Native infantry, have also been such as to deserve and to receive my best thanks and applause. I can, however, neither deny myself the satisfaction, nor Capt. Fitzgerald the justice, of bringing to your Lordship's particular notice the undaunted and judicious charge made by three troops of the 6th regiment of Bengal cavalry, led on by that officer, against an immense body of the enemy's horse, which were defeated, and their guns turned against them, at a moment the most critical to the result of the day.

"Your Lordship will perceive by the returns of killed and wounded, that our loss has been severe; and I have to lament the fate of several brave officers, who have fallen with honour in the cause of their country.

"I cannot, in this place, but state to your Lordship my decided opinion that there never has been an instance in which not only the courage, but the allegiance of the Native troops, have been put to a severer test, and been displayed in a more brilliant result, than on the present occasion. It required, indeed, no common exercise of both qualities, to enable these intrepid men to maintain their position, at a time when they saw their wives and children exposed, and suffering under the same fire, which was thinning their own ranks: such a trial was greater than falls in general to the lot of soldiers, and it has been gloriously met and supported at Nagpore.

"On a full consideration of this memorable engagement, I feel that I should be doing less than my duty, were I to refrain from expressing a hope, that the 1st battalion of the 20th and 24th regiments of Madras infantry, may receive some signal and lasting memorial of their gallant deeds, from the government they have served so well: the claim of the detachment of Bengal cavalry to a similar honour, will not, I am confident, escape your Lordship's attention."

"*Head-quarters of the Army of the Deccan.*
"*Camp at Gunny, 14th Dec.* 1817.

"The Commander-in-Chief has now the pleasing duty of publishing to the army, a further instance of the admirable conduct of a detachment of the distinguished army he has the honour to command.

"Official reports (see p. 163) have reached his Excellency from Lieut.-Col. H. S. Scott, commanding the detachment of the 5th division at Nagpore, of a most brilliant and decisive action, which took place at that capital, between the British troops, and the whole of those belonging to His Highness the Rajah of Berar, on the 26th and 27th ultimo.

"The detachment under Lieut.-Col. Scott's command, previous to the treacherous attack made upon it, by a chief with whom we were on terms of friendly alliance, did not exceed the total amount of 1350 rank and file, and with this small and gallant band, an action of 18 hours in continuance was maintained, with a degree of perseverance, determined courage, and unconquerable bravery, which has never on any occasion been surpassed.

"It is a peculiarly gratifying part of the Commander-in-Chief's duty to offer his most grateful tribute of unqualified praise and admiration, to Lieut.-Col

Scott, and the officers and men of his detachment, for their excellent conduct upon this memorable occasion, and his Excellency may with truth assert, that there never has occurred an occasion where praise has been better earned or more justly merited than this.

" The gallant perseverance and devoted courage of the small brigade of infantry, consisting of the 1st battalion of the 20th and 24th regiments Madras Native infantry, (weakened by a large proportion of sick in hospital) place those corps in the enviable possession of the applause of their superiors, and the admiration of their brother soldiers.

" The pressure of the attack was sustained by the 1st battalion 24th Native infantry, and his Excellency feels no common pride and satisfaction, in declaring his most unqualified praise, not only of its gallantry, enterprise, and steadiness, but of the high and honourable feelings which have since been manifested by the corps, in the unanimous request which has been made, that their original number in the army and facings may again be restored, in preference to any reward which could be conferred upon them, and which his Excellency feels it due to the corps to acknowledge, through the medium of this public record, of their distinguished gallantry and brilliant services.

" The feelings which have dictated this request are so highly honourable to the character of the corps, that his Excellency would be guilty of great self-denial were he to conceal the pride and gratification he will experience in submitting their petition to the favourable notice of his Excellency, the Most Noble the Governor-General and Commander-in-Chief; and Lieut.-General Sir T. Hislop ventures to assure the 1st battalion, 24th Native infantry, that his Lordship, in considering their petition, will not allow it to diminish their claims upon his approbation and favourable consideration.

" The three troops of the 6th regiment, Bengal cavalry, under Capt. Fitzgerald, reinforced by a small detail of the Madras body guard, have established a claim to the highest commendation. The judgment and decision displayed by Capt. Fitzgerald, in seizing the happy moment for attack, will ever speak the high eulogium on that officer's professional skill and ability ; and the gallantry and perseverance of this small but formidable body, place its merits and services in the most distinguished rank, nor is it too much to add, that the arduous contest which had been supported for 18 hours by the persevering gallantry of the infantry, was decided by the discipline and enterprise of this gallant detachment, led on by Capt. Fitzgerald.

" The conduct of the small detachment of the Madras artillery and pioneers has been eminently conspicuous, and has added another instance of courage and discipline, to the well established reputation of the corps to which they belong.

"The important results of this action speak forcibly the praise of every individual officer and soldier engaged, and the Com.-in-Chief feels that all have an equal claim to his grateful approbation, but the fortune of war frequently presents opportunities particularly claiming distinction, and His Excellency feels it an imperative duty to record the names of the following officers, who with the most honourable zeal, have been so fortunate as to benefit by the favourable occasions which presented themselves during this arduous struggle :—

Major JOHN M'KENZIE, commanding 1st battalion, 20th Madras N. I.,
Capt. LLOYD, Bengal infantry, commanding the Resident's escort,
Capt. FITZGERALD, commanding detachment, 6th Bengal cavalry,
Capt. CHARLESWORTH, commanding 1st battalion, 24th Madras N. I.,
Lieut. JENKINS, Bengal establishment, commanding Nagpore battalion,
Lieut. MAXWELL, commanding detachment, Madras artillery, and
Cornet SMITH, Bengal cavalry.

"The pleasing duty Lieut.-Gen. Sir T. Hislop has had to perform of publishing his sentiments of approbation and thanks to this gallant detachment, equally imposes upon him the melancholy duty of paying a just tribute to the memory of those who have gloriously fallen on this memorable occasion. The severe loss in killed and wounded is a subject of deep regret; but it will be a considerable consolation to the relations and friends of those brave men who have fallen, to remember that they have died in the most devoted and honourable struggle, for the interests of their country, and the glory of her arms; and that their memory will be handed down to posterity with honour and grateful respect.

"The following are the names of the officers who have fallen:—Captain Sadler, commanding 1st batt. 25th reg. Madras N. I.; Lieut. and Adjutant Grant, 1st batt. 24th reg. Madras N. I.; Lieut. Clarke, 1st batt. 20th reg. Madras N. I.; Assistant Surgeon Niven, unattached. The sufferings of the families of the Native corps during the action were unavoidably great, and many, it is deeply feared, have perished from their exposed situation, and the inveterate cruelty of the enemy. The Com.-in-Chief deeply deplores this melancholy event, and assures the Native army that the widows and orphans left destitute shall have his immediate attention and consideration, and that he will recommend them in the strongest terms to the generous protection of the government, which is ever watchful to reward merit, and relieve the wants and distresses of its faithful soldiers: Lieut.-Col. Scott will be pleased immediately to form a committee of experienced officers, to ascertain the persons who have a claim to pensions, &c. and will lose no time in transmitting the proceedings to the Adjutant-General of the army.

(Signed) " T. H. S. CONWAY, Adj.-Gen. of the army."

General Orders, by His Excellency the Governor-General.

" The Governor-General experiences the most lively satisfaction in announcing the repulse and entire defeat, by the British troops at Nagpore, of an immensely superior force of the Rajah of Nagpore, by which they were attacked without any previous declaration of hostilities, or the slightest act of aggression on the part of our government or troops.

" The conduct of the Rajah having afforded decided indications of a hostile design, the brigade of British troops, consisting of two weak battalions, 1st-20th and the 1st-24th of Madras N. I., and three troops of the 6th reg. of Native cavalry, the whole amounting to not more than 1,200 fighting men, took post at the residency on the 25th November, and, during that and the following day, occupied themselves in strengthening their position. On the evening of the 26th, they were attacked by the enemy, with a force computed at upwards of 20,000 men, who assailed them at all points with cavalry, infantry, and artillery. The action lasted eighteen hours, and the repeated charges of the enemy were sustained with the greatest gallantry and perseverance by our troops, who succeeded, after a most desperate contest, in completely repulsing and defeating the enemy with great loss, capturing eight of their guns. Capt. Fitzgerald, of the 6th Bengal Native cavalry, is reported as having particularly distinguished himself in a most spirited charge against the enemy's cavalry, in which he captured four of their guns, and immediately turned them against the enemy, with great and decisive effect. At this period the enemy appeared to be thrown into confusion by the blowing up of a tumbril. The advantageous moment was nobly seized; our troops charged and broke the enemy, and pursued their success until the fortune of the day was completely decided in their favour. Our loss was considerable, but the amount has not been exactly ascertained. After the action the Rajah sent in vakeels to sue for a suspension of hostilities, but the Resident, Mr. Jenkins, refused to communicate with him until all the troops were withdrawn from the vicinity of the residency, which was accordingly done. Reinforcements are on their march to Nagpore from several quarters, and a considerable British force will shortly be assembled there.

" His Excellency the Commander-in-Chief is requested to direct a royal salute to be fired from the artillery park.

" By command of his Excellency the Governor-General,

(Signed) " J. ADAM, Sec. to the Gov.-Gen.
" JAS. NICOL, Adj.-Gen. of the army."

To Lieutenant-Colonel Scott, &c.

" SIR,—After an action so arduous and glorious in its termination to the British name, as that of the 26th and 27th inst., I should neither be doing justice to my own feelings, nor to the situation I hold, were I not to express to you the high admiration with which I witnessed the events of those memorable days.

" With such a handful of men opposed to the whole military power of the state of Nagpore, nothing but the most devoted courage and conduct on the part both of officers and men could have secured the happy result which has attended their efforts. In the midst of so much to admire, and such universal claims to praise, it is quite unnecessary for me to say more, than to offer to yourself and the whole of the officers and men, individually and collectively, in the name of the Governor-General, my sincerest thanks; but I cannot also help adding my unfeigned admiration of the conduct of the three troops of the 6th Bengal cavalry, under Capt. Fitzgerald, in the charge which they made on so superior a body of cavalry, supported by infantry and guns, the success of which, at the critical moment in which it happened, may be said to have decided the fate of the battle.

(Signed) " R. JENKINS, Resident.
" *Nagpore, 30th November,* 1817."

THE LATE L.-COL. FRANCIS FRENCH STAUNTON, C.B.*

(Bombay Establishment.)

Extract from the Bombay Gazette, of 5th January, 1820.

Account of the ceremony of the presentation of the sword voted to this officer, by the Honourable the Court of Directors.

" *Bombay, January 5th,* 1820.

" The Governor's levee, on New-year's-day, was crowded; amongst the company present were his Excellency Sir Charles Colville, G. C. B., Com.-in-Chief, Admiral Sir Richard King, the Hon. the Recorder, the Members of Council, and all the principal civil, naval, and military officers at the presidency. The day was also memorable, as being the second anniversary of the battle of Corygaum, and rendered particularly interesting, as having been fixed on for presenting to the gallant officer who so nobly distinguished himself, the tribute so justly his due, in the public presentation of the sword sent to him by the Court of Directors, as a token of their approbation. Mr. Elphinstone, receiving the sword from the Chief Secretary to Government, addressed the gallant officer as follows :—

" MAJOR STAUNTON,—I am commanded by the Honourable the Court of Directors to present you with this sword, as a testimony of the sense they entertain of the bravery and undaunted perseverance evinced by you in the defence of Corygaum. I am happy it has fallen to my lot, to communicate to you the sentiments of the Court, and to add my own congratulation on the well-merited distinction conferred on you. I need say little of the conflict which has obtained you this honourable acknowledgment: it is already well known to all who take an interest in the achievements of the British arms in the East: all know the situation in which your detachment was placed, surrounded by numerous and implacable enemies, cut off from all hope of succour, and sinking under the pressure of thirst, exhaustion, and fatigue: in that hour of difficulty and danger, it was your firmness that

---

* The documents here introduced, relative to the career of this highly-distinguished officer, are necessary additions to the statement of his services given in the 1st vol. of this work, p. 95-106.

afforded to your brave companions an opportunity of displaying that devotion and gallantry which terminated in their triumph over the vast force opposed to them, and not only established for ever their own reputation, but threw a lustre over the character of their establishment, and added to the glory of the Indian army: it is therefore with feelings of no common satisfaction, that I present you with this sword; I hope that you may long wear it with honour, and, I doubt not, that if an opportunity should again occur, you will use it with the same valour with which it was gained."

Extract of the account of the ceremony of the laying of the first stone of the monument erected by order of the Bombay government, to commemorate the victory of Corygaum.

"*Bombay, April 7th*, 1821.

" The foundation stone of the monument destined to perpetuate the defence of Corygaum, was laid by Col. Huskison, on behalf of Major-Gen. Smith, on Monday the 26th ult. This interesting ceremony took place at half-past five in the evening, in presence of the chief civil and military authorities of the Deccan. The party assembled in an adjoining suite of tents, and marched in procession to the spot, where they were received, under a general salute, by a detachment of artillery, two companies of grenadiers, from the 1st or Corygaum regiment, and the band of H. M.'s 47th regiment.

" A brass plate, with the following inscription :—

' This foundation stone was laid, Anno Domini 1821, the Most Noble the MARQUESS of HASTINGS, Governor-General of India, and the Hon. MOUNTSTUART ELPHINSTONE, Governor of Bombay,' was then deposited in the foundation-stone, with a few British coins, and a scroll of parchment, containing the names of the persons present at the ceremony. The Colonel then ascertained, with true masonic precision, the correctness of the level, when three vollies of musquetry, and a royal salute from the artillery, announced the termination of the ceremony."

Letter from Mr. Adam, on his succeeding to the general government.

"*Barrackpore, March 3d*, 1823.

" MY DEAR SIR,—I have this day had the gratification to announce in public orders, your appointment to be one of my Honorary Aides-de-Camp. In taking this step, without a previous communication with you, I have ventured to assume, that an arrangement which is intended to mark, in the most public manner, my cordial participation in those sentiments of admiration of your conduct, and that of your brave companions in arms, which was so warmly felt by the preceding government, will not be unacceptable to you, or your fellow soldiers. Assuring you of my sincere good wishes, I have the honour to be, &c.

" *To Major Staunton.*" (Signed) " J. ADAM.

Letter from Lord Amherst, on his Lordship's assumption of the Supreme Government of India.

" *Calcutta, 4th August,* 1823.

" SIR,—On Lord Amherst's assumption of the Supreme Government of India, His Lordship naturally recurred to the brilliant events of the late war, by which the British power in this country has been so much exalted and secured; and among the distinguished names of those who then contributed to the success of our arms, your's prominently presented itself to his Lordship's recollection. In order, accordingly, to manifest the high sense which his Lordship entertains of the eminent services rendered by you at Corygaum, he has been pleased to appoint you to be an Honorary Aid-de-Camp to the Governor-General.

" *To Major Staunton.*" (Signed) " C. LUSHINGTON, P. S.

In 1818, Lieut.-Col. Staunton was appointed permanent Commandant of Ahmednuggur, which was made, on that occasion, as a special mark of favour to him, a separate and distinct command.

Early in 1825, the rapid decline of his health, previously much impaired by his long residence and arduous services in India, compelled him most reluctantly to apply for permission to retire from the service, and to return to England, on which occasion, the Hon. the Court of Directors evinced their sense of his meritorious services, by the grant of a pension of £500 a-year, with the option of returning to India at the expiration of five years, with such advancement of rank as he might in that time obtain. In April, Lieut.-Col. Staunton embarked for England, in so very infirm a state of health, as to preclude all hope of his recovery, a melancholy anticipation, too fatally verified, for before he could reach his native land, death closed his bright career, and deprived the service of one of its most distinguished officers. He died off the Cape of Good Hope, on the 25th June 1825, deeply regretted.

LIEUTENANT-GENERAL GEORGE HARDYMAN*.

(Bengal Establishment.)

ON this officer's arrival in India, he was immediately ordered to join a party of Cadets, proceeding by water to General Sir Robert Barker's army at Ramgaut; and he was appointed (1773) to that distinguished corps, the Select Picket, consisting of gentlemen, who were formed into a company. This picket was posted on the right of the advanced guard of the army in the field.

Orders were received for the army to march down into the Company's provinces, to their different destinations; and in 1774, general orders were issued for an army to be formed with the 2d brigade, and the Cadet corps to hold themselves in readiness to take the field.

This officer served in the expedition against the Rohillas, under Col. Champion, who commanded the army. The battle was fought at Cuttra, on St. George's day, (23d April) when the enemy met with great loss, and their chief Affashamit was killed. It required a halt for three days to bury the dead. The army then marched to Bussola, to canton for the rainy season. In the latter end of that year the army broke up, and marched to Belgrom, and remained there till the year 1777, when it marched down to Barrackpore. Ensign Hardyman then was appointed by the Com.-in-Chief to the 1st reg. Native cavalry, stationed at Futtehghur. In 1779, the station was ordered to march, under the command of Col. Muir, to assist in opposing the Mahrattas, against the Rannah of Gohud. In 1782, the army returned to Futtehghur, and soon after was ordered again to march to Anoopsheher, under the command of Sir John Cummins. In 1796, the army was formed under the command of Gen. Sir James Craig,

* See vol. i. p. 271-2.

to give check to Zemaun Shaw, King of Cabul, but who declined the contest. In 1799, Major Hardyman was ordered, with his regiment of cavalry, to Sultanpore, to assist in disbanding the Nabob's troops; which service being accomplished, he received instructions, in 1800, from Gen. Sir James Craig, to march and join the station at Caunpoor, where his regiment was inspected, and its appearance and conduct approved in general orders. A few days after, Lieut.-Col. Hardyman received orders to march to Futtehghur, and to be under the command of Gen. Robert Stewart. The General left that station in 1802, and the command devolved on Colonel Hardyman.

THE LATE M.-GEN. SIR D. OCHTERLONY, Bt. & G.C.B.

(Bengal Establishment.)

The services of this gallant and accomplished soldier, down to the year 1822, have already been given in this work, (vol. i. p. 379-387*).

* The following document was omitted in the volume referred to:—

"*Fort William, June 5,* 1806.

"The Governor-General in Council is pleased to appoint Lieut.-Col. D. Ochterlony to the command of the fortress and station of Allahabad. Ordered,—that Lieut.-Col. Ochterlony's appointment to the command of the fortress and station of Allahabad be published in general orders, together with the following testimony of the services rendered by that officer to government, during the time that he has held the situation of Acting Resident and Resident at Delhi.

"The Governor-General in council avails himself of the occasion to express the high sense which government entertains of the merits and services of Lieut.-Col. Ochterlony. The zeal, integrity, and ability, uniformly manifested by Lieut.-Col. Ochterlony, in conducting the arduous duties of Resident at Delhi, and especially the firmness, energy, and activity, displayed by him during that crisis of difficulty and danger, when the city of Delhi was besieged by the collective force of Jeswunt Rao Holkar, commanded by that chieftain in person, and during the prevalence of warfare, tumult, and disorder, in the surrounding districts, establish that valuable officer's claim to the recorded approbation of the British government; and the Governor-General in Council discharges a satisfactory part of his duty in combining with the notification of Lieut.-Col. Ochterlony's appointment to the command of Allahabad, this public acknowledgment of the value of his services, and of the distinguished merits of his character and conduct.

Towards the close of the year 1824, political dissensions in Jeypoor obliged him to take the field, in order to restore tranquillity, but which was accomplished without hostilities.

In June 1825, the state of his health (after nearly fifty years of uninterrupted residence and active service in India) obliged him to resign his appointment as Resident and Political Agent in Malwa and Rajpootana, with the intention of repairing to the Presidency, and thence to this country. He went, for the benefit of change of air, to Meerut, where, in his 68th year, he died, on the 15th July 1825.

The annexed division and general orders offer a just tribute to the memory of one of the brightest ornaments of the Indian army; an officer universally respected, both on account of his high talents and amiable qualities; and who, from his thorough acquaintance with the character of the Natives of India, his attention to their prejudices, and conciliating* deportment to all classes, and to all

---

" The Governor-General in Council is pleased to direct, that the head-quarters of one of the battalions of Native invalids be transferred from Allahabad to Chunar.

(Signed) "THOMAS HILL, Acting Sec. Mil. Dep."

* " As conquerors, we have to dread the explosion of fresh conspiracies against our newly-acquired authority; and when we consider that there is not, in any part of India, above *one European* to *fifty thousand Natives;* and that, in many parts, the proportion is much smaller—this disparity presents, it must be confessed, strong temptations to rebel; and it is only by the greatest moderation and justice that we can avoid this danger. In the capacity of legislators, the greatest danger arises from our ignorance and inexperience in the local usages of the country; in consequence of which, with the best intentions, we may commit the greatest errors, and agitate the country with the dread of dangerous innovations on manners and customs, interwoven with the very frame of the Indian community."— *Edinburgh Review*, vol. xl. p. 281-2.

" The countries subject to the British authority in India, ever since the acquisition of the Dewanny, require and deserve the full attention of government to preserve. Those watered by the Ganges alone, embrace a population of thirty millions of souls, or twice that of Great Britain and Ireland. History furnishes no example of so extensive and populous a nation continuing long subject to another, placed at so immense a distance, and with a population so much inferior. Government, founded on opinion every where, cannot here repose on an opinion that the strength of the governing body is physically competent to enforce obedience. The distance, the climate, and the limited population of Britain, must at all times prevent the supporting an European military force, capable of being opposed to Native numbers. Those Native troops who have fought and bled in our cause, are, nevertheless, taken from the mass of the inhabitants; imbued with the same prejudices; animated

ranks of the army, had acquired the enthusiastic attachment of the Native, as well as of the European troops.

Extract of Division Orders, by Major-General Reynell, C. B., commanding Meerut Division:—

" *Head-Quarters, Meerut, July* 15, 1825.

" It is with feelings of unfeigned sorrow that Major-Gen. Reynell announces to the division the death of Major-Gen. Sir David Ochterlony, Bart. and G. C. B., Resident in Malwa and Rajpootanna, and commanding the Western Division of the army, which took place last night about ten o'clock, and in 14 hours after his arrival at Meerut, from Deblee.

" The important services rendered to our eastern empire by this gallant, highly-gifted, and most meritorious officer, have been noticed and rewarded by the strongest proofs of his Sovereign's approbation, and are recorded in some of the brightest pages of our military history in India, rendering imperishable the fame of Sir David Ochterlony, as an officer and a statesman; while the virtues of his heart, and the many amiable social qualities he possessed, will long preserve his memory unfaded in the recollection of those who had the happiness to enjoy his friendship and confidence. A division order is not the most suitable place to panegyrize such a character, and the Major-General will therefore conclude this brief and imperfect tribute of respect, by repeating his own sincere regret for the irreparable loss thus sustained by the Bengal army, and expressing his full conviction that every officer and soldier of the Meerut division will participate in his feelings, and regret with him in deploring the death of the gallant veteran, Sir David Ochterlony.

" The funeral will take place this evening, at six o'clock, under detailed instructions, which will be issued by Brigadier M'Combe, in the station orders.

by kindred sentiments; and exposed to the influence of all the causes which may eventually excite a general spirit of discontent. The permanence of a government thus circumstanced, must, therefore, unquestionably rest on an opinion, that it is a *wise* and *beneficent* one; and that it is for the general interest to submit to its authority. But a people whose calculating habits render them uncommonly clear-sighted, where their own interest is concerned, cannot easily be either deceived or satisfied in this particular. To appear good, the government must really be so; and that, not merely in our view of it, but in theirs also. Besides preserving inviolate the great maxims of justice and humanity, it must be, in a certain degree, accommodated to the prejudices and opinions of its subjects."—*Ibid.* vol. xv. p. 261-2.

"Nine 6-pounders of the horse brigade, three squadrons of his Majesty's 11th light dragoons, his Majesty's 14th foot, and 35th reg. of N. I., will be under arms, and furnished with blank ammunition required for the occasion: the whole under the immediate command of Brigadier M'Combe. The dismounted artillery and dragoons to attend, and all officers of the general staff of the army, generally, at Meerut, are to attend—every body in his full dress uniform."

General Order, by the Right Hon. the Governor-General in Council.

"*Political Department, July* 28, 1825.

"The Right Hon. the Governor-General in Council has learnt with great sorrow, the demise of Major-Gen. Sir David Ochterlony, Resident in Malwa and Rajpootanna. This melancholy event took place on the morning of the 15th inst. at Meerut, whither he had proceeded for the benefit of change of air. On the eminent military services of Major-Gen. Ochterlony it would be superfluous to dilate: they have been acknowledged in terms of the highest praise by successive governments; they justly earned a special and substantial reward from the Hon. East India Company; they have been recognized with expressions of admiration and applause by the British Parliament, and they have been honoured with signal marks of the approbation of his Sovereign. With the name of Sir David Ochterlony are associated many of the proudest recollections of the Bengal army; and to the renown of splendid achievements, he added, by the attainment of the highest honour of the military Order of the Bath, the singular felicity of opening to his gallant companions an access to those tokens of Royal favour which are the dearest object of a soldier's ambition. The diplomatic qualifications of Sir David Ochterlony were not less conspicuous than his military talents: to an admirably vigorous intellect, and consummate address, he united the essential requisites of an intimate knowledge of the Native character, language, and manners. The confidence which the government reposed in an individual gifted with such rare endowments, was evinced by the high and responsible situations which he successively filled, and the duties of which he discharged with eminent ability and advantage to the public interests."

MAJOR CHARLES WILLIAM ELWOOD.

(Bombay Establishment.)

The services of this officer have been already stated in this work, (vol. ii. p. 344-6). The following extract of a letter from the Hon. Lieut.-Col. Lincoln Stanhope, dated 20th November 1821, is an honourable testimonial of his conduct, when Political Assistant to the Colonel at the reduction of the province of Okamundel:—

" I cannot close my letter without again making a tender of my best acknowledgements and warmest thanks, for your zealous exertions when serving under me, as well in a military as a political capacity, by which the service was greatly forwarded. Indeed, from your general acquaintance with the political relations of the country, and intimate local knowledge, your services were truly useful.

(Signed) "Lincoln Stanhope."

THE LATE COLONEL JOHN LITTLE.

(Bombay Establishment.)

At the defence of Mangalore*, in 1782-3, this officer, then Lieut. Little, was Adjutant of the 8th battalion of sepoys †.

---

* That defence was one of the most gallant achievements of modern times; and may be well placed in the same page of history with its compeer, the defence of Gibraltar. Considering, indeed, the means of defence, a doubt may be reasonably entertained, if the defence of Mangalore was not the most heroic of the two. But see the difference—how few persons, be they where they may, have not heard of Gibraltar and the gallant Elliot; how few, except the East Indian class, ever heard of Mangalore, and the equally gallant Campbell!—of Mangalore, which the Bombay army ought to " stand a tiptoe" at the mention of.

† The following general order, by the Bombay government, under date the 23d Nov. 1823, marks a high sense of the merits of this corps, especially when we recollect, that the civil governments of that day were not prone to *encomia* on the armies of India:—

" The 8th battalion of sepoys having been composed originally of grenadiers, and always distinguished themselves by the most steady and exemplary valour and discipline, and their good behaviour during the late siege of Mangalore having been highly commended

He continued Adjutant of the grenadier battalion, under the gallant Capt Dunn, till the death of that excellent officer, who too soon followed his gallant commander, Colonel Campbell. Their death was probably hastened by the fatigues and privations of the siege of Mangalore, with which their names ought to be for ever associated.

In 1790, this officer, who had arrived at the rank of Captain, was selected by the Bombay government, to command a detachment of two battalions of Native infantry, (his own, the 8th, and Capt. Alexander M'Donald's, the 11th), and a company of artillery, which, by treaty, was formed to co-operate with the Mahratta army, under General Purseram Bhow, against Tippoo Sultaun. With this army Captain Little's detachment continued to serve, until the conclusion of the war in 1792. The siege of Darwar was among the earliest of its services; and owing to the inactivity and strange tactics of our Mahratta allies, on whom the detachment wholly relied for material, this siege was protracted to a duration of upwards of six months, yielding many occasions for Captain Little's detachment to act in all the varieties of operations, including breach and storm, of such a service.

The siege and storm of Hooly Honore, and of Simoga, and the attack and defeat, and dispersion, with capture of all the ordnance, of an army of 10,000 men, under Reza Sahib, one

---

by General M'Leod and Colonel Campbell, the Hon. the President and Select Committee have been pleased to direct, in consideration of their good services, that they be again established into a grenadier corps, to be called 'the Bombay grenadiers,' and that Captain George Dunn, whose gallantry and good conduct have been particularly noticed by Colonel Campbell, be confirmed in the command of them."

The above extract is taken from Maj. Moor's compilation of "Bombay Military Orders and Regulations." See vol. i. p. 343. The following note is appended to the above:—"This corps, which still exists with undiminished reputation, under the denomination of the 1st, or grenadier battalion, of the 1st regiment of Bombay Native infantry, was formed at the presidency, by general orders of 12th Nov. 1779, of a complete grenadier company, of the then 1st, 2d, 3d, 4th, 5th, and 6th battalions of sepoys, and of two complete companies of the marine battalion."

We may add, that this distinguished corps still exists, with augmented reputation, as the Grenadier, or 1st Bombay regiment. See General Order in this work, vol. ii. p. 490.

of Tippoo's most esteemed generals, were among the more brilliant operations of Captain Little's detachment. (See Services of Major Moor*, vol. i. of this work, p. 341, &c.)

We might fill many pages with the distinguished services of Capt. Little, while holding this delicate and important command. But a volume having been published expressly thereon, under the title of " Narrative of the Operations of Capt. Little's Detachment, and of

---

* Major Moor, as already observed in the first volume, is the author of several highly interesting works relating to India; and he is, moreover, a warm supporter of the interests of his brother officers of the Indian army. It may most justly be observed, that those gallant officers, Maj.-Gen. Sir John Malcolm and Colonel Worsley (the names of other distinguished individuals might be added), are warm friends and supporters of those interests; but at the same time the Editor cannot avoid offering an opinion, and not a singular one, that if all officers who have acquired interest and amassed wealth by service under the Hon. East India Company's government, would, in their retirement, reflect on the advantage that their support might afford to their less fortunate brethren, a greater number of distinctions (sought after, in the words of Mr. Canning, " with intense and laudable eagerness,") might very naturally be expected for the Indian army, than they at present enjoy.

When officers of the Hon. East India Company's service were first admitted to the national honour of the Order of the Bath, it was declared, in the name of His Majesty, that the number of Knights Commanders should be confined to fifteen. Without any similar authority of announcement, it is now understood that it is restricted to twelve! There was no positive limitation, expressed or implied, as to the number of Companions, but it is believed, that it is the intention to limit the number to about *fifty*, for an army of about 200,000, or more, men; and further, that none are now eligible but for services rendered in the rank of Field Officers, all previous services being thus of no avail, though they may be admitted into the scale of comparative claims.

Captains in the Hon. East India Company's army, as most fully shown in this work, often perform duties, and exercise responsibility and command, equal to Field or General officers in other services. Thus, such a scale of measurement would seem quite inapplicable, and calculated to blast that emulation which it was the object of the distinction to excite and reward.

Surely, therefore, the Editor may again observe, that those officers of the Indian army who have arrived at high rank and fortune, and returned to this country, or quitted the service, will not remain indifferent to the advancement of their less fortunate companions in arms, and that they will employ their influence in a matter of such vital importance.

The President of the Board of Controul is too highly gifted a public character not to hearken to a fair exposition of this subject; and the munificent Sovereign, who most graciously extended this high honour to the Indian army, will, it may confidently be asserted, accord the further boon of rendering the scale comparatively equal to the proportion the officers of the Indian service bears to that of the British navy and army.

the Mahratta Army, commanded by Purseram Bhow," 4to. 1794, we shall not indulge in such line of narration. One important fact must, however, not be passed over. The circumstances are well known of Lord Cornwallis's brilliant victory over Tippoo's army on the 15th May; and of the subsequent necessity for destroying the battering-train, and the heavy stores in the artillery department. A great mortality among the cattle had so far reduced their numbers, as to render dragging the guns back to Bangalore impracticable, and an alarming scarcity in the article of grain threatened a real want of that essential before the probable period of the army's arrival in the neighbourhood of its own magazines. The want of grain, if not caused, seemed greatly forwarded, by the inactivity of the Nizam's army, who, instead of furnishing the British with grain and forage, as from their number in horse might have been expected, were actually inefficient to their own support, without daily drains upon the British bazaars for grain. Under these unauspicious circumstances, one day's melancholy march was heavily marched toward Bangalore, when the critical junction of Captain Little's detachment, and the Mahrattas, unexpectedly relieved the British army from the apprehensions of increasing scarcity, as the Bhow's bazaars were amply stored with grain; and the immense number of cattle following his army, promised a speedy removal of the deficiencies in the bullock department.

At the conclusion of that war of confederates against Tippoo, Capt. Little was appointed to the command of Surat garrison, then one of importance. He was afterwards appointed Quarter-Master General of the Bombay army, and held that situation till his death, which happened in or about the year 1800. He was, however, intermediately, again selected to command a force to act with the Mahrattas, in the campaigns which ended in the capture of Seringapatam and death of Tippoo, respecting which we can only add, that the mode in which he conducted the operations of that force, was such as to fully justify the selection of its commander, and to demand the entire approbation of those who made that judicious selection.

In compliance with the wishes of some distinguished Officers of the Indian Army, whose valuable assistance has encouraged the Editor to complete the East India Military Calendar, *by the publication of this Volume, Sketches of the Military Career, in India, of the Marquess Cornwallis, Duke of Wellington, Lord Lake, and the Marquess of Hastings, are here introduced.*

THE LATE GEN. CHARLES MARQUESS CORNWALLIS*, K. G.

In 1790, war commenced with Tippoo Sultaun; and in May, a large army was assembled at Trichinopoly, of which Maj.-Gen. Medows assumed and held the command during the whole of the campaign of that year.

Lord Cornwallis, as Commander-in-Chief, joined the army early in 1791. The whole was immediately put in motion, and, after several marches, encamped close to Bangalore, on the 5th March. On the 21st, his Lordship finished his preparations for an assault of that place, and which was accomplished with little loss.

On the 13th April, the forces of the Nizam, amounting, nominally, to 15,000, but in reality to 10,000 cavalry, well mounted, joined the army; and on the 8th, a detachment of European troops, from the Carnatic, had also joined. The army, thus reinforced, commenced, on the 4th May, its march on Seringapatam, and on the 13th came within sight of the enemy, drawn up a few miles from the town, their right resting on the river, and their left on the Carigut heights. On the following night, the troops were put in motion with a view to surprise the enemy, but owing to the unfavourable state of the weather, almost impassable roads, and the exhausted state of the

---

* The copy of the monumental inscription which accompanies this service, states, generally, the career in India of the noble Marquess: it will, therefore, be sufficient for our purpose, to narrate briefly his campaigns; and for his conduct of which he was raised, 15th August 1792, to the dignity of Marquess.

draught cattle, the troops were unable to accomplish their object in time. Next day, however, after great exertion and fatigue, the troops were brought into action, drove the enemy from a strong position, and forced them across the river into the island upon which the capital stands.

Lord Cornwallis was, however, notwithstanding this partial advantage, compelled, from the advanced state of the season, the impossibility of procuring a sufficient supply of provisions, incessant rains, and the exhausted condition of the cattle, to relinquish the attempt. His Lordship, consequently, determined to retire to Bangalore, and wait a more favourable opportunity. In the retreat* the troops suffered considerably from the inclemency of the season, and in the early part of it, from the want of an adequate supply of provisions. The latter distress was relieved by the junction, as before stated in this work (see p. 471), of Purseram Bhow's army supplies †.

Soon after his arrival at Bangalore, Lord Cornwallis detached Major Gowdie against Nundydroog, a granite rock of great height, which had been fortified with such care as to make regular approaches necessary ‡.

* The cause of this retreat is thus stated by Major Dirom:—"The Mahratta armies having advanced to Seringapatam, in May 1791, later than the appointed period, their delay, and other unfortunate circumstances, reduced Earl Cornwallis to the necessity of destroying his battering train, after having defeated Tippoo Sultaun on the 15th of that month, in a pitched battle; and obliged his Lordship to lead back his victorious army, leaving the siege of the enemy's capital to be the object of another campaign."

† The famished followers of our army now ran to the Mahratta camp in thousands, and were happy to purchase grain at any rate. Luckily, the want of money was none of our difficulties, else we should have profited little by this supply; for the chiefs being the proprietors of the grain, which they had brought from their own, or collected as plunder in the enemy's country, did not permit their joy to operate to the prejudice of their interest, and sold every thing at the most exorbitant rate. Three seers (quarts) of rice, and six of raggy, or gram, for a rupee, was the common, and, in general, the lowest price; so that the wages of the black servants could not provide them with grain, and the pay of a subaltern would scarcely feed his horse. But grain was now worth its weight in gold; and, while this lasted, there was no hesitation in making the exchange.—See *Dirom's Narrative.*

‡ The rock was inaccessible on every point except one, which was strengthened by a

After fourteen days labour, batteries were formed and breaches made, one on the re-entering angle of the outwork, and another in the curtain of the outer wall: the inner wall could not be reached by the shot.

Lord Cornwallis, with his whole army, on the 18th October, made a movement towards Nundydroog; and the same evening preparations were made for an assault. Both breaches were to be stormed. The assault commenced at moonlight on the morning of the 19th. The preparations for resistance had been made with great care and labour: enormous masses of granite had been prepared, and preserved till the moment the troops should begin to ascend, when the stones were to be rolled down the rock with an effect which, it was hoped, would prove irresistible. But although the enemy were on the alert, the ardour and intrepidity of the assailants surmounted every obstacle; a lodgement was made within one hundred yards of the breach, the enemy were driven from the outward rocks, and so closely pushed as to prevent their barricading the gate of the inner rampart, which, after some delay, was forced, and the place carried with the loss of only thirty men killed and wounded; principally from the stones tumbled down the rock.

Lord Cornwallis, keeping in view the capture of the Sultaun's capital, determined to attempt the possession of all the intermediate strong holds that might interrupt his communications. The most formidable of these, and the strongest in Mysore, was Savendroog*. This place had been reconnoitred, and deemed inaccessible; but the success at Nundydroog, and other places, encouraged the English general to attempt adding this to the number, judging that, if successful against this, the strongest of all, the rest would easily be reduced.

double line of ramparts; a third had been recently commenced, and an outwork covered the gate by a flanking fire. The whole had every appearance of being impregnable. Yet Nundydroog, however high and steep, was still approachable, but not without immense fatigue and labour in dragging up guns, and constructing batteries on the face of a craggy precipice.

* See description of Savendroog, vol. i. p. 26.

After the usual preparations and attempts to batter some of the outworks, the 21st of December was fixed upon for the assault. At eleven in the forenoon, the band of the 52d regiment, playing " Britons strike home," the troops selected for this service, ascended the rock, clambering up a precipice, which, after the service was over, the men were afraid to descend.

The eastern citadel was soon carried. This was followed by the surrender of the whole in succession, each post being deserted or surrendered when approached; and the fortress, so formidable in appearance, and indeed impregnable if defended by a resolute enemy, was taken in less than an hour, in open day, " without the loss of a man, only one private soldier having been wounded in the assault."

Ootradroog, Ram Gurry, and Sheria Gurry, or Sheva Gunga, all fell in the same manner. Tippoo having relied on the natural strength * of those places, left his worst troops to garrison them.

Lord Cornwallis, in Jan. 1792, again put his army in motion for Seringapatam; and on the 5th of February, his Lordship was once more in sight of that capital. On the evening of the 6th, the army was formed into three columns; the right column † being under Gen. Medows, the centre under Lord Cornwallis, with Lieut.-Col. James Stuart, and the left ‡ under Lieut.-Col. Maxwell.

General Medows was to penetrate the enemy's left, and directing every effort towards the centre, to endeavour to open and preserve the communication with Lord Cornwallis's division. A part of this division, under Col. Stuart, was directed to pierce through the centre of the enemy's camp, and thence attempt the works on the island;

---

* " The Sultaun, sensible of the advantages of Savendroog, was reported to have congratulated his army on the infatuation of the English, in having engaged in an enterprise that must terminate in their disgrace; as half the Europeans, he was pleased to assert, would die of sickness, and the other half be killed in this attack."—*Dirom's Narrative.*

† See Capt., now M.-Gen., Beatson's Report of the operations of the right column, in this work, vol. ii. p. 395-401, and Appendix of this volume.

‡ The centre consisted of the 52d, 71st, and 74th; the right, of the 36th and 76th; and the left, of the 72d regiment: the Native troops were divided in proportion to each column.

whilst Col. Maxwell*, with the left wing, was ordered to force the works on Carigut hill, to descend, turn the right of the enemy's position, and unite with Colonel Stuart.

At eight o'clock in the evening, the three columns were in motion; the head of the centre, after twice crossing the Lockani, which covered the right wing of the enemy, came in contact with their first line, which was instantly driven across the north branch of the Cavery, at the foot of the glacis of the fort of Seringapatam. Capt. Lindsay, with the grenadiers of the 71st, attempted to push into the body of the place, but was prevented by the raising of the drawbridge, a few minutes before he advanced. He was here joined by some grenadiers and light infantry of the 52d and 76th regiments, and with this united force, he pushed down to the Loll Baug, where he was fiercely attacked by a body of the enemy, which he quickly drove back with the bayonet. His numbers were soon afterwards increased by the grenadier company of the 74th, when he attempted to force his way into the pettah, but was opposed by such overwhelming numbers, that he did not succeed. He then took post in a small redoubt, where he maintained himself till morning, when he moved to the north bank of the river, and joined Lieut.-Colonels Knox and Baird, and the troops who formed the left of the attack. During these operations, the battalion companies of the 52d, 71st, and 72d regiments, with the 7th and 14th Bengal sepoys †, forced their way across the river to the island, over-

---

* This able and high-spirited officer died at Cudalore, in 1794. He was son of Sir William Maxwell, of Monreith. At an early age he was appointed to a company in Fraser's highlanders, in which regiment he served during the whole of the American war, with a degree of approbation which his later conduct proved he so well merited, and which shewed that he was one of those whose premature death their country has reason to deplore."—*Stewart's Sketches of the Highlanders*, vol. ii. p. 168.

† The 14th Bengal battalion followed H. M.'s 52d foot, in the centre column of attack. In passing the bound hedge, the advance of the troops was considerably impeded, and the previous order of march, (by half companies from the right,) necessarily disconcerted, from the troops being obliged to pass by Indian files, through the narrow openings or paths through the hedge. Capt. Archdeacon, who commanded the 14th batt., was killed; and in the confusion to which all night operations are liable, (but which, in the present instance, was solely ascribable to the circumstances above stated,) the wings of the 14th batt. be-

powering all that opposed them. At this moment Captain Archdeacon*, commanding a battalion of Bengal sepoys, (the 14th) was killed: this threw the corps into some confusion, and caused it to fall back on the 71st, at the moment that Major Dalrymple was preparing to attack the Sultaun's redoubt, and thus impeded his movement. However, the redoubt was attacked, and instantly carried. The command of it was given to Captain Sibbald, who had led the attack with his company of the 71st. The animating example and courage of this officer made the men equally irresistible in attack, and firm in the defence of the post they had

came separated; and the right wing of that corps, led by Lieut. White, (the late Major-Gen. Sir Henry, K. C. B., Services, vol. i.) having joined the battalion companies of H. M.'s 52d reg., they resumed the order of march by half companies, and pushing through the enemy's camp, directed their march on the Derriah Dowlut Baug palace on the island. Approaching the river, they fell in with a body of the enemy's horse, which they charged, after having formed and fired a volley, and dispersed them. They then forded the river, and took possession of the palace, where they continued some time; but not finding any other divisions of the centre column, fording the river at that part, the senior officer, Capt. Hunter, of H. M.'s 52d reg., resolved to repass the river, with the view of rejoining the corps of the column. Most of these had, in the mean time, pushed across the river at other fords, and the party from the Derriah Dowlut Baug returned through the enemy's camp to the Sultaun's redoubt, then commanded by Capt. Sibbald, by whose name it was afterwards designated. After remaining there some time, without being able to learn any thing of Lord Cornwallis's situation, or that of the other corps of the column, an aid-de-camp arrived from his Lordship, and reported the want of assistance, as the enemy's left wing, not having been dispersed, were moving in force upon the position his Lordship had taken with H. M.'s 74th foot, for the purpose of observing the general operations of the troops. The party from the Derriah Dowlut Baug had expended all their ammunition; but luckily, whilst halted at Sibbald's redoubt, the spare ammunition, carried on bullocks, of the 28th Bengal battalion, having been left behind, was brought to the redoubt. The companies of the 52d, and 14th Bengal battalion, were supplied from that source, and instantly got in motion to join Lord Cornwallis, where they arrived just as several fresh cushoons of the enemy were approaching; who, observing the advance of this party, took it for the advance of the columns of the army, and halted. Capt. Dugald Campbell, who commanded H. M.'s 74th, availed himself of this juncture, with admirable promptitude and decision; and the moment the companies of the 52d, and 14th Bengal battalion, joined H. M.'s 74th, they formed up into line, charged, and defeated the enemy. Lord Cornwallis was slightly wounded; but by this timely aid, perhaps, his Lordship, and the small reserve with him, were rescued from defeat or capture.

* See vol. i. p. 30 and 181.

gained. The enemy made several vain attempts to retake it, in one of which Capt. Sibbald was killed. The command of this post was assumed by Major Skelly, of the 74th regiment, who had gone up with orders from the Commander-in-Chief, and remained there after the death of Capt. Sibbald. The Sultaun seemed determined to recover this redoubt, distinguished by his own name, and directed the French European corps to attack it; but they met with no better success than the former, notwithstanding their superior discipline, and having failed in all his attacks he withdrew his troops, and retired within the garrison. The British loss on this occasion was 535 killed and wounded; that of the enemy was estimated at 4000 men, and 80 pieces of cannon *.

* The writer of this note was present on that glorious occasion; and although thirty-four years are since past and gone, the grandeur and magnificence of the scenes of that night made such an impression on his mind, that they are as fresh in his memory, at this moment, as if they had occurred only as many weeks or months ago. Lord Cornwallis was out the greater part of the day, reconnoitring the enemy's position, and returned to camp late in the afternoon. The corps had had their usual evening parade, and officers and men were retired to their tents without any idea of being called out. The order and plan of attack was communicated late in the evening, to the commanding officers of wings and brigades only. As soon as it was dark, the troops fell in, and formed into three columns; the centre commanded by Lord Cornwallis in person; the right, by General Medows; and the left, by Lieutenant-Colonel Maxwell.

About eight P. M. the columns advanced at a steady pace, and in awful silence, towards the enemy, from whose position the British camp was four or five miles distant. The sky was serene and clear, the moon was near its full, and its rays were reflected from thousands of glittering bayonets and muskets. Approaching the bound hedge, rockets from the enemy's advanced posts were flying over and around the columns; then the blaze of musketry, the roar of cannon from the Sultaun's batteries, the Ead Gah, and other redoubts, thicker and louder as the conflict at those points prevailed, followed by intervals of awful stillness, denoting where the conflict had partially ceased, and of many gallant spirits having fled to the silence of the grave. Advancing through the enemy's camp and lines, the cannon from the fort and city ramparts blazed forth their thundering voice, whilst the re-echoing of peals of musketry from the Carigut hills on the enemy's right flank, denoted the spirited attack on that position by the left column, and which soon paused in victory. The moon still shining in all its brightness, combined with the cannon's blaze, to show, like enchantment, the gold-capt towers, the gorgeous palaces of the Sultaun's capital. Wading through the rocky bed of the Cavery, and reaching the island, we there again beheld the majestic dome of Hyder's mausoleum, in the Loll Baug, amidst the solemn gloom and grandeur of many rows of noble cypress trees. Again attention was attracted by sheets of musketry

On the 9th Feb. a final position was taken for the siege of Seringapatam, and immediate operations commenced. Major-Gen. Robert Abercromby, with the army from Bombay, consisting of the 73d, 75th, and 77th regiments, besides several Native corps, joined the same day. On the 18th, Major Dalrymple, with the 71st, crossed the Cavery, at 9 o'clock at night, and surprised and routed a camp of Tippoo's horse. This movement was intended as a cover to the opening of the trenches, which took place at the same moment, 800 yards from the garrison. During the 19th, 20th, and 21st, traverses were finished, and the advances carried on with spirit and energy.

On the 22d, a sharp conflict took place between part of the Bombay army, under Gen. Abercromby, and the enemy, which terminated in the defeat of the latter. This was the last attempt of the enemy, and the repulse being complete, it led to negociations which ended in a cessation of hostilities *.

Thus terminated a war in which the East India Company and their allies captured seventy forts, or fortified places, and 800 pieces of cannon, and obtained the cession of nearly one-half of the Sultaun's dominions.

Lord Cornwallis returned to his seat of government in Bengal, and again embarked, in 1793, for the attack of Pondicherry, on the breaking out of the revolutionary war with France, and after the fall of that place, his Lordship proceeded to England, attended by the veneration and gratitude of all classes who had served under him

---

fire, in the direction of the enemy's late camp, more distinctly seen than heard, (the moon having now set) from the position in which the centre column had established itself in the Loll Baug and pettah, which proved to be the attack made by the enemy on Lord Cornwallis alluded to above, combined, in all its features, with victory in our train, such a display of magnificient scenery and awful grandeur, as, perhaps, was seldom, if ever, equalled on any similar occasion whatsoever. The parole that day was "England," and the orders and plan of attack which were penned with admirable brevity and precision, were prefaced with the following animating sentence:—

"The army marches in three divisions this evening to attack the enemy's camp and lines."

* Lord Cornwallis and General Medows gave up their shares of prize-money in the campaigns of 1790-2 to the army. The prize-money and gratuity which his Lordship relinquished amounted to £47,244; General Medows's to £14,997.

in the field, or enjoyed the benefit of his paternal administration in the united offices of Governor-General and Comander-in-Chief for a period of seven years.

The following extract from Lord Wellesley's answer to the address from the inhabitants of Calcutta, on the successful termination of the war with Tippoo Sultaun, pays a just tribute to the career of the Marquess Cornwallis:—

" In reviewing the more immediate causes of our success, I cannot repress a tribute of gratitude to him who laid the foundations of that strength which it has been my lot to call into action. The name of the Marquess Cornwallis is inseparably connected with the fame and power of Great Britain in this quarter of the globe; and will continue to be an object of affection and reverence as long as wisdom, fortitude, and integrity, shall be respected, or any sense retained of justice, clemency, benevolence, public faith, or military glory. The final conquest of Mysore recalls the memory of that glorious war, in which the first shock was given to the hostile power of Tippoo Sultaun. It must never be forgotten, that under the auspices of the Marquess Cornwallis in that war, the supply and movement of our armies in Mysore were first reduced to a system of regularity and order; and our officers acquired that experience and skill so conspicuous in the able and masterly operations of the late campaign: under the same auspices, the whole system of our defensive alliances in the peninsula of India was founded; and the national faith was maintained in a degree of purity and lustre which inspired a general confidence in the British government, and disposed the Native powers to strengthen and cement their connexion with the Company on the solid basis of reciprocal interest and mutual security. This favourable disposition was confirmed by the prudence, integrity, and honour, of my immediate predecessor; and in the important negociations which it has been my duty to conduct, I have derived considerable assistance from the advantageous impressions of the British character, which I found deeply fixed in the minds of our allies."

Inscription.

Sacred to the Memory of Charles, Marquess Cornwallis;
Knight of the Most Noble Order of the Garter;
General in His Majesty's army;
Governor-General and Commander-in-Chief in India, &c.
His first administration,
Commencing in Sept. 1786, and terminating in Oct. 1793, was not
less distinguished by the successful operations of war, and
by the forbearance and moderation with which he dictated
the terms of peace, than by the just and liberal principles which marked his internal government.
He regulated the remuneration of the servants of the State on a
scale calculated to ensure the purity of their conduct. He laid
the foundation of a system of revenue, which, while it limited
and defined the claims of government, was intended to
confirm hereditary rights to the proprietors, and to
give security to the cultivators of the soil.
He framed a system of judicature, which restrained within strict
bounds the power of public functionaries, and extended to the
population of India the effective protection of laws adapted
to their usages, and promulgated in their own languages.
Invited in Dec. 1804, to resume the important station, he did not
hesitate, though in advanced age, to obey the call of his country.
During the short term of his last administration he was occupied in
forming a plan for the pacification of India, which, having the
sanction of his high authority, was carried into effect
by his successor.
He died near this spot*, where his remains are deposited, on the
5th day of October 1805, in the 67th year of his age†.
This monument, erected by the British inhabitants of Calcutta,
attests their sense of those virtues which will live in the remembrance of grateful millions long after this memorial of them
shall have mouldered into dust.

* Ghazepore, Benares district. † Born December 31, 1738.

FIELD MARSHAL HIS GRACE THE DUKE OF WELLINGTON, *K.G., G.C.B.*, &c. &c.*

In 1797, the Marquess Wellesley, then Lord Mornington, was nominated Governor-General, and in the same year his brother the Duke of Wellington, then Col. Wellesley, went out to India with his regt. the 33d foot; and on the 22d Feb. 1799, Lord Wellesley published a declaration of the causes that precipitated the necessity of an open declaration of hostilities with Tippoo Sultaun.

The most active military preparations immediately commenced. A well-appointed army was soon formed and put in motion, and the chief command bestowed upon Lieut.-Gen., now Lord, Harris. A subsidiary force was supplied by the Nizam, composed of Native troops, and with a view to give to those troops a more effective energy in the field, the Governor-General not only strengthened them with some of the Company's battalions, but appointed the 33d reg. to join them, thus placing that part of the British forces† under the command of Col. Wellesley.

The plan of this campaign was to advance to Seringapatam by the rout of Talgautporam and Cankanelli. The march commenced at day-break on the 10th March 1799; the cavalry in advance, the baggage on the right, and the detachment under Col. Wellesley, which had marched by the left, moved parallel, at some distance, on the right flank of the army. Their progress was soon impeded by the vigilance of the enemy, whose cavalry harassed them, by destroying the forage and villages in their course; they even attacked Col.

---

* The military career of this illustrious General will be found narrated in the 1st vol. of the Royal Military Calendar, 3d edition. In this place it will be sufficient to sketch his masterly operations in India.

† The amount of this force consisted of the whole of the Nizam's detachment, forming the reserve of the army; Col. Wellesley's own reg. the 33d; the 11th; part of the 2d and 4th; two battalions of the 1st Bengal reg.; two brigades of artillery; the Nizam's infantry, commanded by Capt. Malcolm, and the cavalry of the same Prince, commanded by their own Native officer, Meer Allum. The aggregate force under the command of General Harris was returned at 36,959 effective men.

Wellesley's rear-guard, and 20 sepoys were killed in the skirmish and several wounded.

As Col. Wellesley and his advance approached Sultaunpettah, early on the morning of the 23d, a cloud of dust to the westward indicated the vicinity of Tippoo's army, and subsequently it appeared that he had just quitted his position on the western bank of the Maddoor river, and encamped at Malavilly. Pursuing their march, the right wing, the cavalry, and the detachment under Col. Wellesley, halted on the 25th, and were joined by the left wing and the battering train. On the 26th the whole moved in compact order, and encamped five miles to the east of Malavilly. The ground which they had taken was open; and as it was known that Tippoo had declared his determination to attack the army whenever it should move out of the jungles, or thick forests through which it had to pass, every preparation was now made for his reception.

On the 27th was fought the battle of Malavilly*, in which Colonel Wellesley's division had a conspicuous share. The feeble resistance of the enemy on this occasion, constituted nearly the whole that was offered till the British arrived, on the 3d April, in sight of Seringapatam. On the 5th, the army took up its ground opposite the west face of the fort of Seringapatam, at the distance of 3,500 yards, the left being to the river Cavery, while Col. Wellesley with his division was encamped to the right of the whole.

In front of the British camp there were several ruined villages and rocky eminences, besides an aqueduct, which passing from the left of the camp takes there an easterly direction till it approaches within 1,700 yards of the fort, where it winds off to the right, to a large grove of cocoa-trees and bamboos, called the Sultaunpettah tope. These positions afforded cover for the enemy's infantry and rocket men so near the camp, that many of the rockets which were thrown fell among the tents. It was of the highest importance to dislodge the enemy's troops from these retreats, and to Col. Wellesley was entrusted the difficult service. He received orders on the evening of the 5th, to

* A full account of this battle has already been given, p. 276-7.

have the 33d reg. and 2d Bengal reg. in readiness at sunset: similar instructions were also given to Col. Shaw, with the 12th and two batts. of sepoys, with their guns. The former were to scour the Sultaunpettah tope, while the latter was to attack the posts at the aqueduct. It was nearly dark before these detachments began to advance, which much impeded their operations. Col. Shaw succeeded in securing a ruined village about 40 yards from the aqueduct, but he could not dislodge the enemy. Col. Wellesley's detachment, the moment it entered the tope, was assailed on every side by a hot fire of musketry and rockets; but to retreat was even at this period a manœuvre not familiar to him, though the darkness of the night, the uncertainty of the enemy's position, and the severity of the attack, would have almost justified it. He could not indeed accomplish the precise object intended, but by persevering created a diversion which was of no mean importance.

On the following morning it was judged necessary both for the safety of Col. Shaw's position, and that of the camp itself, to obtain possession of the Sultaunpettah tope; and three distinct but simultaneous attacks, therefore, along the whole of the enemy's outposts, were determined upon. That which was directed chiefly against the tope, was again entrusted to Col. Wellesley, supported by the co-operations of Cols. Shaw and Wallace. Col. Wellesley at the appointed hour, nine o'clock, advanced to the attack with the Scotch brigade, two battalions of sepoys, and four guns. By a series of well-concerted movements, which the enemy did not anticipate, they were soon thrown into confusion and forced to retire precipitately. The possession of the aqueduct was obtained, and a strong line of posts secured, extending from the river to the tope, a distance of about two miles.

The siege continued with great activity, and many instances of gallantry occurred on the part of the British troops. On the 14th, the Bombay army, under Gen. Stuart, crossed the Cavery, and took a strong position on its northern bank. This river was now almost dry, and its bed a naked rock. The allied armies had thus formed a complete junction; the enemy's advanced works beyond the river were taken; and the British continued to draw their lines of circumvallation closer and closer around Tippoo's citadel.

A practicable breach having been made in the walls of the fortress, on the evening of the 3d May, the troops destined for the assault were stationed in the trenches before day-break on the 4th, that no extraordinary movement might occasion alarm; and, in order to take the enemy by surprise, it was determined to make the attempt in the heat of the day, when the Sultaun's troops would probably have surrendered themselves to indolence and repose. Col. Wellesley was ordered to take the command of the reserve in the advanced works, and to act as circumstances might require. About half-past 1, P. M., every preliminary arrangement being concluded, Gen. Baird stept out of the trench, drew his sword, and with animated heroism exclaimed to the troops, " Come, my brave fellows, follow me, and prove yourselves worthy of the name of British soldiers!" This gallant appeal was not without effect; they rushed forward into the trenches, and entered the bed of the river, under cover of the fire from their own batteries; but being discovered by the enemy, they were immediately assailed by rockets and musketry. Every obstacle, however, which could be opposed to their progress was surmounted by the valour of the troops, and in a short time the British colours were displayed on the summit of the breach.

Col. Wellesley's services during the siege and storming of Seringapatam, acquired for him the public thanks of Gen. Harris; and Lord Mornington, in his congratulatory address to that general, and the allied armies, stated, that the successes surpassed the most sanguine expectations that were previously formed, and had raised the reputation of the British arms in India, to a degree of splendour and glory, unrivalled in the military history of that quarter of the globe. " The lustre of the victory," he added, " could be equalled only by the substantial advantages which it promised to establish by restoring the peace and safety of the British possessions in India on a durable condition of genuine security."

Col. Wellesley was appointed governor of Seringapatam two days after its capture (May 6th), an office of equal labour and delicacy. He had to new model a conquered kingdom; he had to determine on the precise manner both of rigour and lenity with which the people should be treated; he had to mould it into the other possessions of the company; he had to awe, to conciliate, to punish, to reward, to satisfy, a victorious army *, and yet not to annihilate all property and right in a conquered people. In this arduous capacity he exhibited firmness, moderation, and sagacity: he anxiously laboured to prevent every kind of excess, and issued a notice that exemplary punishment would follow the transgression of the strict line of duty. To restore confidence to the inhabitants, he went himself into all the principal houses where the real, or supposed accumulations of wealth, might most likely tempt to plunder, and placed guards to protect the property, and so successful were his exertions, that those who had fled in terror returned in a few days to their houses; the bazaars were opened, traffic resumed its activity, and the appearance of the city denoted nothing that could be considered as part of those calamities which attend upon a place taken by assault.

In the commission which was afterwards appointed for the purpose of settling the future condition of the conquered territories, determining what portion should revert to the family of the former sovereigns of Mysore dispossessed by Hyder Ally, and what should belong to the East India Company and its allies, Col. Wellesley acted a distinguished part. The Commissioners nominated were Gen. Harris, Lieut.-Col. Close, Col. Wellesley, the Hon. Henry Wellesley, and Lieut.-Col. Kirkpatrick †, but the active execution of the commission devolved chiefly upon the last three.

---

* Upwards of 10 lacs of rupees worth of jewels, and the amount of 500 camel loads of muslin, shawls, rich cloths, and various kind of merchandize, became the prize of the captors.

† The late Major-Gen. William Kirkpatrick. The services of this officer will be found in the 2d volume of this work, (page 454.) To which it may be added, that in 1811 he published his " Embassy to Nepaul," and in the same year, " Select Letters of the late

On the termination of Col. Wellesley's active duties as a Commissioner, the Governor-General appointed him to the permanent command of Seringapatam, in which office he had already been provisionally placed*.

In 1800, the tranquillity of Mysore being threatened by the incursions of Doondia Waugh, Colonel Wellesley was called from his government of Seringapatam to take the command of a force against this freebooter. He accordingly took the field on the 3d Sept. 1800, and after much skirmishing between the troops of the marauder and those of the Company, Doondia retired, on the 10th, to a strong position called Conaghull. Here he made a stand, and Col. Wellesley having pursued him with his cavalry, leaving his infantry far behind in the rear, he suddenly found himself in front of him with a very unequal force. At this critical moment, aware that it would be in vain to wait the coming up of the infantry, and so arranging his operations that the enemy could not bring all his superiority of numbers † to bear at once, he rushed onwards to the assault. The intrepidity of the British soldiers signally manifested itself. After a sharp conflict, the enemy fell back in confusion: Doondia himself was among the slain, and the remains of his army were dispersed in small parties over the country.

Part of the enemy's baggage still remained in his camp, about three

---

Tippoo Sultaun," works in high estimation among orientalists. His admirable notes to the last work, and the interesting nature of the late Sultaun's letters, make us regret that more of the letters of that unwearied penman were not similarly given to the public. We cannot help thinking, that if one or more of the many competent officers on the Hon. Company's retired list, would occupy their leisure in translating, elucidating, and publishing a further selection from Tippoo's letters, that such a work would be exceedingly well received by the public. Such manuscript letters, we imagine, would be readily accessible on proper application.

* " The command of Seringapatam," observed Lord Mornington, in a despatch to the Court of Directors, ' will remain in the hands of Col. Wellesley. It is a trust of great delicacy and importance, which it is my duty to repose in a person of approved military talents and integrity, and to superintend with peculiar vigilance and care."

† The enemy's force was 5000, which Col. Wellesley attacked with his slittle band, consisting of only the 19th and 25th dragoons, and the 1st and 2d regiments of Native cavalry.

miles from Conaghull, to which Col. Wellesley returned, and obtained possession of all the elephants, camels, &c.

In the government orders issued on this occassion, the Governor-General observes—

"Though the implicit confidence reposed in the talents of that officer, (Col. Wellesley) caannot be strengthened by the successful events of the campaign, his lordship will feel the greatest pleasure in reporting to the Hon. Court of Directors, the solid and extensive advantages derived to the affairs of the Hon. Company by the able and spirited conduct of the war entrusted to Colonel Wellesley."

The death of Doondia, and the complete dispersion of his troops, once more restored peace to India *. (See also p. 378-9.)

* "*Head-Quarters, Choultry Plain, 24th September,* 1800.
"*General Orders by Major-General Braithwaite.*

"The operations of the force employed under the Hon. Col. Wellesley, on the frontier of Mysore have been frequently marked by circumstances which demanded and obtained the applause of the Com.-in Chief of the army, but in no instance has judgment in the plan, and gallantry in the execution of a military movement, been so eminently conspicuous as in the conclusion of the campaign on the 10th instant, when the rebel chief, Doondia Waugh, baffled by the judicious disposition of Col. Stevenson's detachment, in his attempt to escape in a northern direction, was intercepted in his retreat at Conaghull, by Col. Wellesley, with the cavalry of his division only, and forced to a decisive action, which terminated in his total defeat and death; Col. Stevenson's detachment on the same day, dispersing the remnant of his force, then employed in crossing the Kistna, near Deodroog, and seizing the remaining cannon and baggage of the rebel army. M.-Gen. Braithwaite requests that Col. Wellesley will accept his public thanks for the judgment with which his measures have been planned, and the vigour which has marked every movement of his force. He has particular satisfaction in publishing to the army at large, the very honourable report Col. Wellesley has made of Col. Stevenson's conduct, and the activity of the detachment under his command, to which that officer attributes the occurrence of the opportunity he seized, of forcing Doondia to a decisive action; and the Commander-in-Chief of the Army is happy to record, in honour of H. M.'s 19th and 25th regiments of light dragoons, and the 1st and 2d regiments of Native cavalry, that those corps, under Col. Pater, Majors Patterson and Blaquiere, and Captains Doveton and Price, composed the line, whose rapid charge, upon a body of 5000 horse, formed to receive them, achieved this glorious conclusion to a campaign, distinguished throughout every stage of its operations by peculiar and progressive energy.

"The Hon. Col. Wellesley has expressed his obligation to Lieut.-Col. Bowser, for his services with his detachment from the subsidiary force; and reported, in the warmest terms of praise, the uniform good conduct of the troops in general, under circumstances of uncommon fatigue and difficulty, incident to the nature of the recent service. The advan-

Col. Wellesley was next appointed second in command to Gen. Baird, in the projected expedition for the conquest of Batavia. Some misconception however of Admiral Rayner, who then commanded in the Indian seas, as to the extent of the Governor-General's powers to undertake the expedition, occasioned the plan to be discontinued, and the disposable force, under Gen. Baird, amounting to 5000 men, was ordered to proceed to Egypt*, to co-operate with the English army, under Sir Ralph Abercromby. Colonel Wellesley, however, was directed by the Governor-General to return to his command at Seringapatam.

The Mahratta states having commenced hostilities against the British government in India, an army was forthwith assembled at Hurryhur, under Lieut.-General Stuart, amounting to 3581 European and Native cavalry, 390 artillery, 2845 European infantry, including the 33d regiment, and 1212 Native infantry, together with 40 field pieces, besides smaller guns, and a battering train. On the 27th Feb. 1803, General Stuart was directed to adopt the necessary measures, for the march of the British troops in the Mahratta territory, and to detach † such a force under General Wellesley, as he thought sufficient for that purpose.

---

tages derived from the able arrangements of the gentlemen charged with the department of supply, have been pointed out to the particular notice of the Com.-in-Chief of the Army; and he is happy in adding this record of their merits, to the general expression of his thanks to the Hon. Col. Wellesley, and the army employed under his orders on the recent service on the frontiers of Mysore."

* In this expedition it seems to have been the intention of government that Col. Wellesley should have participated, for he was actually gazetted on the 25th July 1801, as Brigadier-General in that country. That he did not proceed thither is certain; yet that a confident expectation of his arrival was entertained is evident, from the fact, that Lord Elgin, in a letter which he wrote to this country, dated 5th June 1801, stated, that Lord Keith had received a despatch from Admiral Blanket, of 6th May, announcing the arrival of General Baird and Colonel Wellesley with the Indian army.

† The high opinion which the Governor-General had formed of his brother's talents now displayed itself, for we are told, in the memoir drawn up by the Marquess himself, that the command of this detachment necessarily required the united exertion of considerable military talent, and of great political experience and discretion. No one, however, appeared so fit to assume it as Major-Gen. Wellesley, not only in the estimation of the Governor-

On the 3d March, General Wellesley advanced from Hurryhur, and arrived at the Toombuddra river on the 12th, which he then crossed. In the whole line of his march through the Mahratta territory, the British troops were received as friends, and many of the chieftains joined him with their forces and accompanied him to Poona.

Poona, the capital of the western Mahrattas, was threatened with immediate devastation, by Amrut Rao, (an officer of Holkar's army) upon the approach of the British to its relief. Holkar himself was at Chandore, about 130 miles to the north east of Poona, and Rao was left in the latter city with about 1500 men. To save this place from the ruin that impended over it, became an important, but, at the same time, a difficult object, because there was reason to apprehend, that any means taken for its safety, would in fact hasten its destruction. One only course presented itself, which was to advance with the British army to within the distance of a forced march, and then, by the sudden appearance of the British cavalry, and the Mahratta troops before the city, to take Amrut Rao by surprise. This scheme was accordingly executed by Gen. Wellesley with admirable rapidity and effect, and produced precisely the result that was perhaps rather hoped for than expected. Amrut Rao, alarmed and disconcerted by the appearance of so large a force, abandoned the place before he had time to perpetrate his meditated vengeance on it, whilst Gen. Wellesley and his gallant few (for only

---

General, but in that also of Lord Clive, then Governor of the Madras Presidency, and within whose Government the army was formed, who expressed his conviction that the extensive local knowledge of Gen. Wellesley, and his personal influence among the Mahratta chieftains, obtained by his conduct in the command of the Mysore, and his victories over Doondia, as well as his military skill, peculiarly qualified him to carry on the future important operations in a manner best calculated to ensure the ends of government. Instructions to this effect were consequently given by Lord Clive, to Lieut.-Gen. Stuart, and a detachment from the main army, amounting to 9707 infantry, with about 2500 of the Rajah of Mysore's cavalry, was placed under the command of Gen. Wellesley, for the purpose of advancing into the Mahratta territory. This force consisted of one European and three Native regiments of cavalry, two regiments of European, and six battalions of Native infantry.

a small portion of the whole army had been brought up) were welcomed as deliverers by the inhabitants who still remained.

The capital of the Peishwa, thus rescued from usurpation, by the masterly operations of Gen. Wellesley, the Peishwa himself returned to it on the 13th May, under an escort from Bombay, and resumed his seat upon the musnud, with the usual ceremonies.

Scindia was now in arms, with the ostensible view of opposing Holkar, but his sincerity was justly doubted by the Governor-General, who suspected that a confederacy actually existed between those chiefs and the Rajah of Berar. It became necessary, therefore, in the opinion of the Marquess, to unite the control of all political affairs in the Deccan, connected with the negotiations then going on, and with the movements of the army, under a distinct local authority, subject indeed to the Governor-General in Council, but possessing full power to conclude upon the spot whatever arrangements might become necessary, either for the final settlement of peace, or for the active prosecution of the war. It was obvious, also, that these powers ought to be held by the commanding officer of the troops: and, therefore, according to the statement of the Marquess himself, he determined to vest them in Major-General Wellesley, whose already established influence among the Mahratta chiefs, and intimate knowledge of his sentiments, concerning the British interests in the Mahratta empire, eminently qualified him for discharging the arduous trust, in a way most beneficial to the public welfare.

Strengthened with these united powers, and authorized either to win the desired object by force or negociation, as circumstances might suggest, Gen. Wellesley addressed a letter on the 18th July, to the British resident, directing him to state both to Scindia and the Berar Rajah, the anxious desire of the English government for peace, at the same time observing, that the only proof which could be accepted of their amicable professions, would be the immediate disbanding of their armies, and their return from the Nizam's frontier to their own capital. If these terms were not complied with, Scindia was to be informed that our resident had orders to quit his camp immediately.

After various evasive attempts to elude the conditions of this proposal, the two chieftains sent an answer, professing their willingness to retire from their position, provided Gen. Wellesley would also return, with his army, to its usual stations; and adding, that on the same day the British troops reached Bombay, Madras, and Seringapatam (the relative distances of which places differed from 1049 to 321 miles) the Mahratta confederates would encamp their united forces at Burhampoor, a city belonging to Scindia, and not more than 50 miles distant from the Nizam's frontier. This foolish or insidious proposal was promptly rejected, as were several others which sprung from obvious artifice.

The army opposed to Gen. Wellesley, under the immediate command of Scindia and the Rajah of Berar, amounted to about 38,000 cavalry, 10,500 regular infantry, 500 matchlock men, 500 rocket men, and 100 pieces of ordnance. In addition to these forces, Scindia had an advanced party of a few thousand horse, dispersed through the surrounding hills. The artillery was served by French officers. The immediate advance of our troops was prevented by a very heavy rain, which lasted three days; but when that ceased, it proceeded, and Gen. Wellesley dispatched a messenger to the killedar of Ahmednuggur, a place 30 miles distant from Poona, requiring him to surrender the fort. On arriving in the vicinity of the pettah, General Wellesley offered protection to the inhabitants; but this was peremptorily refused, because implicit reliance was placed upon its means of defence. No alternative then remained, but to storm the pettah, which was accordingly done in three separate, but simultaneous attacks, under the respective commands of Lieut.-Col. Harness, Lieut.-Col. Wallace, and Capt. Vesey. Much gallantry was displayed both by the officers and men; the wall surrounding the pettah was lofty, and defended by towers, but it had no ramparts, so that when the troops had ascended by the scaling ladders, no footing presented itself upon which they could easily follow up their advantages. Notwithstanding this great impediment, they soon made themselves masters of the place, though the garrison, which consisted partly of Arabs, offered a most brave resistance.

Gen. Wellesley immediately began to reconnoitre the ground in the vicinity of the fort, after having so far established his troops by the successful assault on the pettah. An advantageous position was soon discovered and taken possession of on the 9th, by a detachment under Col. Wallace. In the course of the night, a battery of four guns was erected, to take off the defences on the side where it was intended to make the principal attack. At dawn on the following morning, this battery was opened, and continued such an effective fire, that the killedar proposed a temporary suspension of operations to afford time for capitulating. Gen. Wellesley, knowing the fraudulent expedients by which Asiatic morality accomplishes a desired end, replied, that the firing should not cease until he had either taken the fort by arms, or that it was surrendered to him: meanwhile, however, he was willing to receive any proposals that might safely terminate the attack. There was no alternative left, therefore, but to fight or yield, and the former being hopeless, the latter became inevitable. Accordingly, on the morning of the 11th, two commissioners came to the General, and proposed a surrender upon condition of being allowed to depart with the garrison, and to have private property secured. These terms were acceded to; but, notwithstanding this virtual arrangement, the firing was continued till the moment that hostages arrived in the British camp, as a security for the fair and full performance of the stipulations. On the 12th August 1803, the killedar marched out with a garrison of 1400 men, and the British took immediate possession of the fort. The General proceeded to take charge of all the districts dependent upon it, yielding a revenue of 650,000 rupees.

The eminent services performed by General Wellesley, and the officers and soldiers under him, in the above successful operation, were warmly acknowledged in the general orders issued by the Bengal government.

No sooner had General Wellesley stationed a garrison in Ahmednuggur, sufficient for its protection, than he proceeded, 24th August, to cross the Godaveri, with his whole army; and, having arrived at Aurungabad on the 29th, entered the territories of the Nizam by the Adjuntee ghaut, with a large body of horse. They had actually passed between Col. Stevenson's corps, which had moved to the eastward, towards the Badowley ghaut and Aurungabad, and had proceeded as far as Jaulnapoor, a small fort, the capital of a district of the same name, about 40 miles east of that city; but no sooner did they hear of the arrival of the British troops, than they moved to the south-east, with the reported intention of crossing the Godaveri and marching upon Hyderabad, the metropolis of the Nizam's territory. In consequence of this, Gen. Wellesley immediately marched to the left bank of the Godaveri, and continued by that route to the eastward, a line of march that effectually interposed his army between Hyderabad and that of the enemy. Thus, disappointed by the celerity and skill of the General's movements, they retraced their steps and proceeded to the northward of Jaulnapoor. Col. Stevenson, in the meanwhile, returned from the eastward, and, on the 2d September, attacked and carried the fort of Jaulnapoor.

These rapid movements of General Wellesley's little army completely preserved the territories of the Nizam from any depredatory incursion, and the confederated chieftains finding their usual mode of desultory warfare not attended with its customary success, resolved to carry on operations in a different manner. They accordingly crossed over to the northward, towards the Adjuntee pass, where they were reinforced by a detachment of regular infantry, commanded by Messrs. Pohlman and Dupont, consisting of sixteen battalions, with a numerous and well-equipped train of artillery. The whole of this force was collected in the vicinity of Bokerdum and Jaffierabad.

On the 21st Sept. the two corps of General Wellesley and Colonel Stevenson effected a junction near Bednapoor, when it was determined to move forward in separate bodies, and attack the enemy on the morning of the 24th. Having arrived at Naulnia on the 23d, and there receiving a report that Scindia and the Rajah of Berar had moved off in the morning with their cavalry, and that the infantry were about to follow, but were still in camp, at the distance of about six miles from the ground on which he had intended to encamp, Gen. Wellesley resolved at once to march to the attack*.

When the British army moved on towards the confederates they found them posted between and along the course of the two rivers, the Kaitna and the Juah, towards their junction. Their line extended, east and west, along the north side of the Kaitna river, the banks of which are high and rocky, and impassable for guns, except at places close to the villages. The enemy's right, consisting entirely of cavalry, was posted in the vicinity of Bokerdum, and extended to their line of infantry, which was encamped in a manner somewhat resembling a European entrenched camp, near the fortified village of Assaye. There was a fearful difference in the numbers of the respective armies. The forces of the confederates amounted altogether to about 40,000 men, while those of General Wellesley did not exceed 5000, and of which not more than 2000 were Europeans. The skill of his arrangements, and the valour of his men, were all that he had to counterbalance this inequality. These, however, proved sufficient. Col. Stevenson, with the troops of the Nizam, had not arrived, though he was hourly expected.

A river flowed nearly in front of the enemy's position. The General forded it, and drew up his infantry in two lines, with the British cavalry behind them, as a third line in reserve. His intention was to attack the right of the Mahrattas, it being his great object to avoid their artillery, which was on the left, and to turn their right, knowing, that if he defeated the infantry, the guns must

* A determination, to use the words of the Marquess Wellesley, " dictated both by prudence and courage." Delay would have permitted the enemy to retreat during the night, and thus have extended till a still further period the opportunity of deciding the conflict; or, on the other hand, it might have exposed the General to difficulties and loss by enabling Scindia to ascertain the precise position of his baggage, stores, &c., which are necessarily excessive in an Indian army.

follow as a matter of course. His orders were, however, either misconceived or disobeyed. The officer commanding the pickets, which were on the right of the first line, moved upon the enemy's left. This immediately made a gap in the first line. The 74th, which was on the right of the second line, naturally followed the pickets, and Gen. Wellesley was therefore obliged to bring the whole of his force into one line. The consequence was, as he had anticipated; the right of his line was exposed to the fire of upwards of 100 pieces of artillery, and was nearly destroyed. Nothing, however, could surpass the promptitude and skill with which his operations were conducted, when he found himself compelled to alter, instantaneously, the whole plan of attack, in consequence of that officer's disobedience or error*.

A circumstance now occurred which, when the numerical inferiority of the English army is considered, might justly have excited alarm and dismay in any commander who did not possess the firmest reliance upon the resources of his own genius. It was discovered that the artillery, of which there was but little, could not be brought into use, while the numerous cannon of the enemy, served by French officers and engineers, were placed so as to do the greatest execution. Gen. Wellesley, with that intuitive perception

* "The order of battle was now formed; and the pickets being named as the battalions of direction, the General ordered the line to advance in a quick pace, without firing a shot, but to trust all to the bayonet. This order was received with cheers, and instantly obeyed. It was soon perceived, however, that the leading battalion, composed of the pickets, had diverged from the line of direction, which made it necessary to halt the whole front line. This was a critical moment. The troops had got to the summit of a swell of the ground which had previously sheltered their advance; and the enemy believing that the halt proceeded from timidity, redoubled their efforts, firing chain shot and every missile they could bring to bear on the line. Gen. Wellesley, dreading the influence of this momentary halt on the ardour of the troops, rode up in front of a Native battalion, and, taking off his hat, cheered them in their own language, and gave the word to advance again. This was also received with cheers, and instantly put in execution. When the 78th was within 150 yards of the enemy, they advanced in quick time and charged. At this instant, some European officers, in the service of the enemy, were observed to mount their horses and fly. The infantry, thus deserted by their officers, broke, and fled with such speed, that few were overtaken by the bayonet; but the gunners held firm to their guns; many were bayoneted in the act of loading, and none gave way till closed upon by the bayonet."—*Stewart's Sketches of the Highlanders*, vol. ii. p. 193.

of the precise course to be adopted in any exigency, immediately gave orders to abandon his guns, and come to close combat. He took his own station of peril and command, at the head of the whole line; and having placed Col. Maxwell, with the cavalry, so as to cover his right (being secure on his left, from the nature of the ground and relative position of the enemy) he advanced to battle.

The Mahrattas were astonished and dismayed at the firm, unbroken, and dauntless band that opposed itself to their hosts; but after a few minutes they rallied from their consternation, and their tremendous cannon opened a murderous fire upon the assailants. English courage, however, led on by Gen. Wellesley, was not to be intimidated. Our soldiers had recourse to the bayonet—a powerful and resistless weapon in their hands; the Mahratta troops for a while sustained the shock; presently the first line gave way, but they rallied again, as if struck by a sense of shame that such an inferior force should subdue them: it was a momentary vigour; they again gave way, and fell back upon their second line, which was posted on the river Juah.

Meanwhile the Mahratta horse, who hung upon the adjacent hills in numerous cohorts, made a furious attack on the 74th, being a part of that force which Gen. Wellesley had posted on his right to secure his rear and flanks. The 74th received the onset with an undaunted front. The British cavalry, led on by Col. Maxwell, rushed to their assistance, followed the Mahratta horse up the hills, and achieved a conquest with immense slaughter.

The second line of the enemy yet remained entire, and an attack was now directed against it. This line had been thrown into some confusion by the incorporation of the first with it, which fled before the fierce assault of our bayonets.

The cavalry, under Col. Maxwell, and the infantry, headed by Gen. Wellesley, made a furious charge upon them all at once; unable to withstand it, they fled in all directions; and the British, deeming victory complete, followed the fugitives with all the ardour of conquest. But this impetuosity had nearly proved fatal; and the discretion of Gen. Wellesley, aided by the intrepid bravery of Col. Maxwell, alone prevented it from robbing our army of all the fruits of its glorious labours. A considerable number of the Mahrattas, who had thrown themselves on the ground, as if slain, were passed unnoticed by the British troops, in the pursuit of the flying enemy; but suddenly they arose, seized the cannon which had been left in the rear by our army, and began to open upon them a fierce and destructive cannonade. The British, scattered by pursuit, could not effectively act against them in a mass. The Mahratta infantry seeing this, and encouraged by our confusion, began to re-form themselves, and faced about upon their pursuers.

The British were thus placed between two fires, and were besides divided into small bodies, from the pursuit which they had commenced. The whole battle was now to be fought over again; and Gen. Wellesley seeing at once the imminent danger in which his army was placed, put himself at the head of the 78th, and a battalion of sepoys, and charging the Mahrattas, who had seized the guns, after a bloody and perilous contest, in which a horse was shot under him, and his personal danger was very great, he routed and put them to flight. At the same time, Colonel Maxwell charging the enemy's infantry, at the head of the 19th dragoons, completed the victory with the loss of his own life, adding one name more to the list of those heroes whose memories are embalmed in the grateful tears of an admiring nation. The slaughter was great. The Mahratta soldiers fought with the fury of men stung with the deep sense of shame in yielding to an inferior force; while the British, partly stimulated by their conscious inferiority, and partly incensed by the snare that had nearly proved so fatal, displayed even more than their wonted valour and fortitude.

The consequences of this memorable victory were great and important. The complete defeat of the confederate armies was accomplished; an irreparable blow to the strength and efficiency of their military resources, especially of their artillery in the Deccan, was struck; a hostile and predatory force was expelled from the territory of our ally, the Nizam; and a seasonable and effectual check was interposed to the ambition, pride, and rapacity of the enemy. As a mark of public distinction to the brave troops who won this well-fought victory, the Governor-General ordered, that honorary colours, with suitable devices, should be presented to the various corps employed on the occasion, and he directed also, that the names of the officers and men who fell in the battle, should be commemorated, with the circumstances of the action, upon the public monument to be erected at Calcutta, in perpetual remembrance of that glorious day.

After this decisive overthrow, the confederate chieftains began to think of peace, and wished that an accredited British agent should be sent to their camp; but as this proposal was made with some circumstances of ambiguity, Gen. Wellesley declined acceding to it, and proceeded to pursue his military operations against the enemy, who shewed a disposition to try the issue of further hostilities. These operations, combined with those which were carrying on in other parts of Hindostan, under Gen. Lake, whose army was on the north-west frontier of Oude, soon completed what the battle of Assaye had begun.

Scindia and the Rajah of Berar moved their army along the bank of the Taptee, to the westward, as if they meditated an attack on Poona, and Gen. Wellesley therefore determined to remain to the southward, in order to watch their motions. In execution of this system, he continued to harass their march for several weeks, constantly frustrating their plans by the admirable rapidity and sagacity of his own, but still unable to bring them to action. The day of Assaye was yet too fresh in their memories, and as often as they heard of the near approach of the British forces, so often did they retreat before them. A truce was even sought by Scindia, and granted by Gen. Wellesley, on the 23d November, but finding that the terms of this armistice were violated by the former, whenever such violation seemed expedient, it was resolved to prosecute hostilities with renewed vigour. Accordingly, on the 28th of November, the British troops came up with a considerable body of

Scindia's regular cavalry, accompanied by the greater part of the Berar infantry. The day was extremely hot, and the General felt inclined to postpone the further pursuit till the evening, but he had scarcely halted, when the dispositions manifested by the enemy compelled him to alter his resolution. Large bodies of their cavalry were noticed in advance, and the pickets being immediately pushed forward, the whole army of the confederates was distinctly perceived, formed in a long line of horse, foot, and artillery, presenting a front of five miles on the plains of Argaum. There was no time for deliberation. A moment so employed, would have been injudiciously employed. The enemy seemed resolved for action, and prompt measures were all that the crisis admitted. To Gen. Wellesley, such rapidity of conception and of action were natural. He instantly advanced with the whole army in one column, in a direction nearly parallel to the enemy's line. The British cavalry were in the van. As the two armies approached each other, a furious onset was made by a large body of Persian troops. The conflict was long, sanguinary, and, for a time, doubtful; but victory declared for the British, and the Persians were every one destroyed. While this engagement took place at one part of the extensive line presented by the enemy, a charge of Scindia's cavalry was made at anoher, and repulsed with dauntless intrepidity by the 1st batt. of the 68th; after which the whole line gave way, and fled with the utmost precipitation, leaving 38 pieces of cannon, and all their ammunition, in the hands of the conquerors.

The next operation of Gen. Wellesley was to invest the fortress of Gawilghur, a strong hold, containing such natural and artificial defences, as were deemed almost impregnable. By his skilful arrangements, however, it was soon forced to yield, after sustaining a vigorous assault, in which many were killed on both sides.

The result of these splendid triumphs soon manifested itself, in a way most conducive to the existing and permanent interests of our government in India. On the 17th December 1803, Gen. Wellesley concluded a treaty of peace with the Rajah of Berar, in his camp at

Deogaum, in which he renounced all adherence to the confederacy, ceded to the Company the provinces of Cuttack and Ballasore, and stipulated never to retain in his service the subjects of any state which might be at war with England.

This treaty, which thus deprived Scindia of a powerful confederate, was soon followed by another between that Chieftain and Gen. Wellesley, which was concluded on the 30th December 1803, and included many conditions highly favourable to the British interests in India. The subsequent events of the Mahratta war, including the defeat and subjection of Holkar, who still continued a sort of predatory hostility, belong rather to a history of India than a memoir of the Duke of Wellington; for though the army which he still commanded in the Deccan occasionally co-operated with the forces under Gen. Lake, yet no opportunity presented itself for General Wellesley to assume an active station.

In April 1804, Gen. Wellesley visited the presidency of Bombay, and was there received with all the distinction due to the conqueror of Assaye; and the most flattering and respectful addresses were presented to him, expressive of the high sense entertained of his important services.

In February 1804, the officers of his army agreed to present him with a vase of gold, worth 2000 guineas, of superior workmanship, with an inscription recording the battle of Assaye. This intention was notified to him by the committee appointed to carry it into execution, and he accepted the honourable memorial with those expressions of personal gratitude, and of commendation to the officers themselves, which the occasion so naturally suggested. A handsome sword, of the value of 1000 guineas, was also presented to him at Calcutta.

Nor was the government at home unmindful of what was due to such distinguished services. On the 3d May 1804, he received the thanks of both houses of Parliament, which were conveyed in the most flattering terms, and the King appointed him a Knight Companion of the most honourable Order of the Bath.

THE LATE GENERAL LORD VISCOUNT LAKE.

This illustrious nobleman was born 27th July 1744, and commenced his military career, in 1758, as an Ensign in the 1st foot guards. In 1760, he proceeded with the 2d batt. of that corps to Germany, where he served during the remainder of the seven years' war, and part of the time as Aid-de-Camp to Gen. Pearson. At the battle of Williamstadt, and on various occasions, during this early period of his military life, he displayed much of that spirit of enterprise, and decisive judgment, which so eminently characterized his maturer years.

The 16th Feb. 1781, he attained the rank of Colonel; 28th April 1790, that of Major-General; 26th January 1797, that of Lieut.-General; and 29th April 1802, that of General.

In 1781, he proceeded to America, and joined the brigade of guards serving under Lord Cornwallis. During the siege of York-town he distinguished himself by storming one of the enemy's batteries in so gallant a manner, as to obtain the warmest thanks of the Commander-in-Chief.

After the fall of York-town he returned to England, and, as a testimony of his Sovereign's approbation of his conduct in America, he was appointed Aid-de-Camp to His Majesty.

In 1793, he went to Holland, in command of the 1st brigade of guards. He was present at the siege of Valenciennes, and in most of the considerable actions of 1793-4; and perhaps the most brilliant exploit of the campaign, was the assault of Lincelles, by the brigade of guards under Major-Gen. Lake. His personal exertion at Bois d'Alkmaer materially contributed to the safety of his regiment.

In 1798, on the breaking out of the rebellion in Ireland, Lieut.-Gen. Lake was appointed to the Staff in that kingdom. At Vinegar Hill, he attacked, with great judgment and spirit, the collected force of the rebels, which he completely defeated; and followed up this success so rapidly, as to prevent their ever again assembling in any considerable number. Upon this occasion, as on all others in which he was engaged, he led on the troops in person, and had a horse killed under him.

The total suppression of the rebellion which the decisive action at Vinegar Hill gave reason to expect, was for a time retarded by the arrival of a French force under Gen. Humbert. At Castlebar, that officer obtained an advantage over the troops commanded by Gen. Lake; and, in the expectation of being joined by the disaffected in his progress, moved rapidly forwards to the capital. Reinforced by some fresh troops, Gen. Lake, after a most severe and fatiguing pursuit, came up with the enemy at Ballinamuck, and compelled the whole to surrender.

In 1800, he was nominated to the important situations of Com.-in-Chief of the King's and Company's forces in India, and second member of the Supreme Council of Bengal. He arrived at Calcutta in March 1801, and in July following proceeded to Caunpoor, where his whole attention was devoted to the improvement of the Bengal army, and especially of the Native cavalry, which, by his professional skill and indefatigable knowledge, was brought to the highest state of excellence.

For some time a negotiation had been carrying on with the Nabob Vizier, the object of which was to obtain a cession of territory in lieu of the subsidy which his Excellency paid for the troops employed in defence of his dominions.

This negotiation was brought to a successful termination in Nov. 1801, and owing to the judicious disposition which Gen. Lake had made of the troops under his command, the civil authorities were established without difficulty, over those extensive and valuable provinces, with the exception of Sasnee, Bejighur, and Catchoura, the zemindars of which refused to submit to those municipal arrangements of the Company, which had produced such benefits to the inhabitants of Bengal. Every conciliatory endeavour was unsuccessfully made to bring back the rajahs of those places to a sense of duty, but as they continued to resist the orders of government, Lord Lake was compelled, in the spring of 1802, to attack them with a military force: in the course of two months, he reduced the strong fortresses of Sasnee, Bejighur, and Catchoura, with no very considerable loss on our side, and by this means secured the tranquillity of the country.

The defeat of the armies of Scindia and the Peishwa, and the seizure of Poona, by Jeswunt Rao Holkar, in their consequences led to a subsidiary treaty between the Peishwa and the English government, and involved the latter in a war with Scindia and the Rajah of Berar. When negotiation had failed, and every effort been unavailingly tried to procure the continuance of peace, the noble Marquess Wellesley, then at the head of the Indian government, in defence of his ally, and for the safety of the dominions more immediately entrusted to his charge, was reluctantly compelled to resort to arms. (See Memoir of the Duke of Wellington.)

Gen. Lake, towards the middle of July 1803, received orders to take the field. At that time, the disposable force in Bengal was small, owing to the reduction which had taken place in the Native army, in obedience to orders from England each battalion having been reduced from 900 to 700 privates, and of the latter 100 were absent on leave. Every means was strained to supply the deficiencies of cattle, &c. and such were the indefatigable arrangements made by Gen. Lake that he was enabled, on the 5th August, to take the field in person, with a small but well-appointed army, and of which M-Gen. the Hon. Frederick St. John* was second in command.

---

* General the Hon. Frederick St. John entered the army in 1778, and served as a Subaltern in the West Indies until 1781; then as a Captain in Jersey and Guernsey, till the peace of 1783; as a Lieutenant-Colonel, he commanded the 2d, or Queen's regiment, in Gibraltar and in England, and subsequently as Brigadier and Major-General in Ireland throughout the rebellion. He received the rank of Colonel, the 21st Aug. 1795; and that of Major-General, the 18th June 1798. He commanded the stations at Clonmell and Cork, and the advanced post stationed at Bandon and Bantry Bay: he received the thanks of the Marquess Cornwallis, Gen. Hewitt, and also of all the persons of property in the county of Tipperary, both catholics and protestants, for his services in Ireland.

Subsequently, he served in India as a General officer: he was in command for 4 years of the principal depôt, Caunpoor; and where he formed the army for the field, by the most constant and unwearied instruction; and when that army was reviewed by the Marquess Wellesley, he received the most marked public thanks in general orders, for having rendered

On the 29th Aug., General Lake entered the Mahratta territories, where he found Gen. Perron, with from 12 to 15,000 horse, drawn up in a very strong position, near to Coel, prepared to receive him.

General Lake, at the head of the British cavalry, immediately attacked the enemy, and, after a short and desultory action, drove him from the field, and took possession of Coel.

On examining the fort of Allyghur, it was found to be so strongly fortified, that its reduction, by regular approaches, could not be looked for in less than six weeks, a loss of time which might have proved fatal to the success of the campaign, by allowing Scindia's regular brigades, then rapidly advancing from the Deccan and the Punjab, to form a junction.

Its possession was, however, deemed indispensably necessary, as, if left in the hands of the enemy, it would have cut off the communication of the army with the Company's provinces, whence our supplies were derived. General Lake, therefore, determined to at-

it efficient, both in movement and discipline, beyond his lordship's utmost hopes. He likewise served as second in command under Lord Lake, throughout the Mahratta campaigns, and commanded the left wing of the army. At the battle of Delhi, his services were of the highest importance. At a critical moment, he charged, with his wing of sepoys, the whole of the enemy's artillery, consisting of 100 pieces, (chiefly 18-pounder cannonades) and at the moment enfilading the British advance. Lord Lake, in his despatch to the Governor-General, observes, " Major-Gen. St. John was opposed to the enemy's right: the steadiness and ability displayed by the Honourable the Major-General, quickly surmounted every difficulty, and forced the enemy to retire with very heavy loss."

He was also present at the siege of Agra, where he was chosen to drive in a sortie made by the enemy. The Com.-in-Chief, in his despatch on this occasion, thus notices his services—" My thanks are due to the Hon. Major-Gen. St. John, for his spirited conduct in advancing at the head of the 2d batt. 2d N. I. which I found it necessary to order up to support the attack."

He likewise served at the battle of Laswarree, and at the taking of several other forts of minor importance.

In every instance the British were successful, and this officer received the public thanks of the Com.-in-Chief, the Governor-General Marquess Wellesley, and of both houses of Parliament, for his services to the close of the war in India. On the journals of Parliament it appears, that the vote was ordered to " Major-Gen. the Hon. Frederick St. John, for his courage and steadiness in supporting the attack of the Commander-in-Chief."

He returned to England, after a residence of six years in India, and soon after his arrival was promoted to the rank of Lieut.-General, 30th Oct. 1805, since which period he has remained unemployed. The 4th June 1814, he received the rank of General,

tempt to carry this important place by a coup-de-main. It was accordingly attacked on the morning of the 4th September; the three gates successively blown open by a 12-pounder, and after a gallant resistance from the garrison, it was carried.

This decisive and able operation enabled General Lake to move towards the main body of the enemy's force, and, on the 11th Sept. 1803, after a fatiguing march of 23 miles, in the warmest season of the year, his lordship engaged, and defeated with great slaughter, two of Perron's regular brigades, consisting of 16 battalions, a considerable body of horse, with upwards of 70 pieces of ordnance:—all the latter were taken.

In this brilliant action, which was fought on the plain opposite to Delhi, the British force was under 3000 firelocks, 3 weak regiments of cavalry, and a small proportion of artillery*.

* "General Orders by his Excellency the Most Noble the Governor-General in Council, Captain-General and Commander-in-Chief, of all the land forces serving in the East Indies:—

"*Fort William*, 1st *October*, 1803.

"The returns received by the Governor-General in Council of the ordnance taken on the field of battle, near Delhi, on the 11th Sept. 1803, have completed the official statement of the military operations conducted under the personal command of his Excellency General Lake, from the 29th of August to the 18th of September.

"In reviewing the rapid and brilliant success of our arms within that period of time, every loyal subject of the British empire must be animated by the most zealous emotions of just pride, national triumph, and public glory.

"The Governor-General in Council has already expressed the sentiments of gratitude and admiration with which he contemplates the conduct of his Excellency the Commander-in-Chief, and of the officers and troops under his Excellency's personal command, in the action of the 29th August, and in the gallant assault of the fortress of Allyghur, on the 4th of September.

"His Excellency in Council highly approves the judicious and early movement of the army, after that important success, towards the principal station of the enemy's infantry and artillery, and the position whence the most speedy relief might be afforded to the unfortunate representative of the house of Timur, and to his Majesty's Royal family.

"The decisive victory gained in the battle of Delhi, on the 11th of Sept., justified the firm confidence reposed by the Governor-General in Council, in the bravery, perseverance, and discipline, of the army, and in the skill, judgment, active spirit, and invincible intrepidity, of their illustrious Commander.

"The glory of that day is not surpassed by any recorded triumph of the British arms in India, and is attended by every circumstance calculated to elevate the fame of British valour, to illustrate the character of British humanity, and to secure the stability of the British empire in the east.

With his usual activity and zeal, General Lake led the troops into action, at the head of the 76th regiment, and had a horse killed under him in the advance.

"The Governor-General in Council acknowledges, with the most cordial satisfaction, the distinguished services of Major-General Ware, and of the Hon. Major-General St. John, in the action of the 11th of Sept.; and directs the Commander-in-Chief to signify his particular approbation of the conduct of Major-General Ware, in the command of the right wing of the British army, and of the conduct of the Hon. Major-Gen. St. John, in the ability and steadiness which he displayed in the command of the left wing, by surmounting every difficulty, and by forcing the right wing of the enemy to retire in disorder, with heavy loss.

"The Governor-General in Council also directs the Commander-in-Chief to notify to Colonel St. Leger, and to the corps of cavalry employed on this honourable occasion, the high approbation with which his Excellency in Council has received the report of their gallantry and firmness, and of the peculiar skill manifested under the able command of Colonel St. Leger, in their judicious, rapid, and decisive movements during the action, and after the flight of the enemy had commenced. His Excellency in Council contemplates with great satisfaction the advanced state of discipline of the Native cavalry of Bengal, and the splendid proofs which that corps has afforded of its efficiency in active service, against the numerous artillery of the enemy.

"The conduct of Capt. Boyce, and of His Majesty's 76th regiment, is noticed with the warmest applause, by the Governor-General in Council: the high reputation established by that respectable corps, in various services of difficulty and danger in India, appeared in the battle of Delhi, with a degree of lustre which has never been exceeded even by British troops. His Excellency in Council signifies his most distinguished approbation of the firmness and intrepidity of the officers and men of the Native infantry, who, with His Majesty's 76th regiment, at the point of the bayonet, forced an enemy, considerably superior in numbers, from a powerful and well-served artillery, and opened the way for the successful charge of the cavalry. The conduct of the Native troops on this memorable day reflects the highest honour upon the discipline of the army of Bengal, and confirms the confidence of the Governor-General in Council, in the diligence, skill, and courage, of the officers of this establishment, and in the eminent character of our Native soldiers.

"To Lieut.-Colonel Horsford, and the artillery, the Governor-General in Council repeats the public testimony of approbation, which that meritorious corps has uniformly deserved in every exigency of the service.

"To the Staff of the army, the Governor-General in Council is happy to express the satisfaction with which he learns, that they continue on all occasions to merit the warmest approbation of the Commander-in-Chief.

"The Governor-General in Council sincerely laments the loss of Major Middleton, Capt. MacGregor, Lieut. Hill, Lieut. Preston, Cornet Sanguine, and Quarter-Master Richardson; and the brave soldiers who fell in the exemplary exertion of deliberate valour and disciplined spirit, at the battle of Delhi. The names of these brave men will be commemorated with the glorious events of the day on which they fell, and will be honoured and revered, while the fame of that signal victory shall endure.

"In testimony of the peculiar honour acquired by the army, under the personal command of his Excellency General Lake, the Governor-General in Council is pleased to order, that honorary colours, with a device properly suited, to commemorate the reduction of the

On the 13th September, the army crossed the Jumna, and took possession of Delhi, the capital of the Mogul empire, where the General enjoyed the heartfelt satisfaction of relieving the aged and venerable Shah Alum, from the misery to which he had been so long exposed, from Mahratta and French oppression, and of restoring him to a situation of happiness and comfort.

The marked respect and veneration with which the Emperor was treated by his gallant deliverer, was particularly grateful to the feelings of that unfortunate prince, who testified his gratitude, by bestowing on Lord Lake the highest titles which could be conferred on such warriors as had rendered the most signal services to the state †.

---

fortress of Allyghur, on the 4th, and the victory obtained at Delhi, on the 11th September, be presented to the corps of cavalry and infantry, European and Native, respectively employed on those glorious occasions; and that a public monument be erected at Fort-William, to the memory of the brave officers and men, European and Native, who have fallen in the public service during the present campaign.

"The honorary colours granted by these orders, to his Majesty's 27th regiment of dragoons, and to the 76th regiment of foot, are to be used by those corps while they shall continue in India; or until His Majesty's most gracious pleasure be signified through his Excellency the Commander-in-Chief.

"In concluding his orders on this memorable occasion, the Governor-General in Council is pleased to direct that the public thanks of the Supreme Government of the British possessions in India be given to his Excellency General Lake, Commander-in-Chief of his Majesty's, and of the Hon. Company's forces in India, who, with unexampled alacrity, eminent judgment, and indefatigable courage, under extraordinary difficulties, has prepared the army of Bengal for the field; has conducted it, by a rapid succession of glorious victories, to the complete defeat of a powerful enemy; and has maintained the honour of the British name in India, by a humane attention towards the inhabitants of the conquered provinces, and by a due respect and reverence towards the unfortunate representative of the house of Timur, and towards his Majesty's Royal family.

"His Excellency the Most Noble the Governor-General in Council, Captain-General and Commander-in-Chief of all the land forces, serving in the East Indies, is pleased to direct, that these orders be publicly read to the troops under arms, at every station of the land-forces in the East Indies, and that the European officers of the Native corps do cause the same to be duly explained to the Native officers and troops.

"By command of his Excellency the most Noble the Governor-General in Council,
(Signed) " L. Hook, Secy. to the Gov. Mil. Dept.
"By command of his Excellency the Captain-General and Commander-in-Chief of the Land Forces,
(Signed) " J. Armstrong, Acting Mil. Sec."

† Titles conferred by the Emperor Shah Alum on General Lake, after the battle of Delhi, Sept. 1803:—Sum Saum ul Dowlah (Sword of the Empire); Ashghah ul Moolk (Bravest of the Country); Bahadoor Futteh Jung (Leader of Armies—Victorious in Battle); Khan Dowran Khan (the Valiant Lord of the Age). General Gerard Lake, Bahadoor.

Having provided for the security of the capital; for the Emperor's peaceful enjoyment of personal freedom, comfort, and dignity; and for the tranquillity of the surrounding country, General Lake hastened with the army to Agra, the " key of Hindostan," and which he reached in a few days.

The situation of the army before this place was such as to require the exercise of great prudence and enterprize. The garrison consisted of upwards of 5000 men. Four regular battalions, with 22 pieces of cannon, defended the ravines and approaches to the fort, and two of Perron's brigades, composed of 17 battalions, a considerable body of cavalry, and 82 pieces of field ordnance, arrived from the Deccan, and took a position about 20 miles in the rear of the besieging army.

The security of the Company's and Nabob's dominions, and the prosecution of future military operations, depending in a great measure upon the fall of Agra, these considerations determined General Lake to undertake the siege of that strong and very important place, and in the face of danger and difficulties, which might have deterred a less intrepid mind. The operations commenced on the 10th of October, by seizing the city of Agra, and defeating the force which occupied the ravines under the walls of the fortress, and terminated, on the 18th, by the capitulation of the fortress, after a vigorous but ineffectual resistance.

The capture of Agra secured a line of defence along the west bank of the Jumna, and left the British army at liberty to attack Scindia's remaining brigades. The pursuit accordingly commenced on the 28th Oct.; but the distance the enemy had gained in advance, and the celerity of his movements, soon shewed the little chance there was of overtaking him with the infantry.

Aware of the evils which would result to the public service, if this formidable body of troops was allowed to join Jeswunt Rao Holkar, then in great force on the borders of the Jeypore country, at 12 o'clock P. M. of the 31st Oct., Lord Lake pushed forward with the regular cavalry, and at sunrise, the 1st. Nov. 1803, came upon the enemy at Laswarree, whom he immediately charged and broke; but owing to the badness of the ground, and to the enemy's guns being linked by chains in extended order, by which the British cavalry were much broken and impeded in their charges on the enemy's lines, the advantage he first obtained could not be followed up.

When the infantry arrived and was refreshed, the enemy was again attacked, and after a severe contest, completely defeated; 82 pieces of cannon were taken, and a considerable portion of the infantry either killed or made prisoners.

In this memorable engagement, Lord Lake, who headed every charge, and whose personal exertions exceeded all his former exploits, had a horse shot under him, and was for some time exposed to the most imminent danger.

The small body of troops which accompanied him into action, after giving proofs of invincible courage, for a moment gave way to superior numbers, and the destructive fire of the enemy's artillery, and were on the point of being charged by the enemy's horse, when they were rallied by the personal exertions of his lordship. Encouraged by the arrival of the 29th dragoons, and animated by the presence of their beloved commander, they renewed the charge with an impetuosity that speedily decided the fate of the day. A small proportion only of the British force took an active part in this brilliant and decisive victory, which annihilated the whole of Scindia's regular army in Hindostan.

We cannot resist quoting in this place the observations of the Marquess Wellesley on this brilliant victory.

"The victory, however, must be principally attributed to the admirable skill, judgment, heroic valour, and activity, of the Com.-in-Chief, Gen. Lake, whose magnanimous example, together with the recollection of his achievments at Coel, Allyghur, Delhi, and Agra, inspired general confidence and emulation. In the morning, Gen. Lake led the charge of the cavalry; and in the afternoon, conducted in person, at the head of the 76th reg., all the different attacks on the enemy's line, and on their reserve, posted in and near the village of Mohaulpoor. On this day two horses were killed under the Com.-in-Chief. The shot showered around him in every direction. In the midst of the danger and slaughter which surrounded him, he displayed not only the most resolute fortitude and ardent valour, but the utmost degree of professional ability and knowledge, availing himself, with admirable promptitude, of every advantage presented by the enemy, and frustrating every effort of the enemy's obstinacy and boldness. His masterly plans of attack, during the action, were carried into instantaneous execution by his unrivalled personal activity; and he appeared, with matchless courage and alacrity, in front of every principal charge, which he had planned with eminent judgment and skill.

"The staff of the army distinguished themselves greatly, and merit the highest commendation. Among these, one of the most distinguished was Major G. A. F. Lake, of H. M.'s 94th reg., son to the Com.-in-Chief, who had attended his father in the capacity of Aid-de-Camp and Military Secretary throughout the whole campaign, and whose gallantry and activity in executing his father's orders, had been conspicuous in every service of difficulty and danger.

"This promising young officer constantly attended his father's person, and possessed the highest place in the Com.-in-Chief's confidence and esteem. In the heat of the action, the Com.-in-Chief's horse, pierced by several shot, fell dead under him. Major Lake, who was on horseback close to his father, dismounted, and offered his horse to the Com.-in-Chief, the Com.-in-Chief refused, but Major Lake's earnest solicitations prevailed. The Com.-in-Chief mounted his son's horse, and Major Lake mounted a horse from one of the troops of cavalry. In a moment, a shot struck Major Lake* and wounded him severely, in the presence of his affectionate father. At this instant the Com.-in-Chief found it necessary to lead the troops

---

* The Hon. George Augustus Frederick Lake, was subsequently Lieut.-Col. of the 29th regt. of foot, and lost his life in the glorious and gallant action of storming the strong pass of Roliea, in Portugal, on the 17th of August, 1808. He was killed while engaged with his regiment in forcing one of the passes, all of which were difficult of access. The pass was most obstinately disputed by the French, and he fell almost the very moment when they were forced to yield to that destructive weapon, the bayonet, which never fails in the hands of Englishmen.

against the enemy, and to leave his wounded son upon the field: a more affecting scene never was presented to the imagination, nor has providence ever exposed human fortitude to a more severe trial. Gen. Lake, in this dreadful and distracting moment, prosecuted his victory with unabated ardour. At the close of the battle, the Com.-in-Chief had the satisfaction to learn, that his son's wound, although extremely severe, was not likely to prove dangerous *."

Too much praise cannot be bestowed on the talents and ability which were exhibited by Gen. Lake in the conduct of this arduous and difficult campaign, when it is considered he had to contend with troops long accustomed to victory, vastly superior in number, disciplined by French officers, and furnished with a formidable train of artillery, which was admirably served in every action. His own force did at no time exceed 5000 infantry, 2,500 cavalry, and a small proportion of artillery; yet with these seemingly inadequate means did he, in less than three months from the opening of the campaign, defeat the enemy at Coel, Delhi, and Laswarree, take the strong fortress of Agra and Allyghur, and reduce the whole of Scindia's dominions east of the river Chumbul. In this rapid and victorious career, 39 of Gen. Perron's regular battalions were destroyed, upwards of 480 pieces of artillery taken in the field, and nearly 600 in garrisons.

In addition to these military operations, Lord Lake rendered essential service in the conduct of various political arrangements of great importance, and in the settlement of the conquered provinces.

Towards the close of the year, a treaty of defensive alliance was concluded with the Rajah of Jeypoor; and in Feb. 1804, Gen. Lake entered the Rajah's country, then threatened by Jeswunt Rao Holkar. While lying there, the strong forts of Gualior and Rampoora were reduced under his orders, by detachments from the British army.

In the middle of May 1804, the inclemency of the weather, and difficulty of procuring supplies, compelled the Com.-in-Chief to with-

* Transactions in the Mahratta Empire.

draw the greatest part of the army into the Company's provinces, leaving five battalions to cover the Jeypore country during the absence of the army; a force which was deemed fully adequate to that purpose.

Unfortunately, this detachment venturing too far in pursuit of Holkar, was overtaken by the rains, and not being able, in consequence, to procure supplies, was attacked and pursued by his collected forces, and after undergoing great fatigues and privations was driven under the walls of Agra, with the loss of all its artillery, camp-equipage, stores, &c.* and more than half of its original number. The war, by this unexpected misfortune, was brought home to the Company's provinces; and the diminution of forces which had been made by the defeat of this detachment was severely felt at this crisis of affairs.

In Sept. 1804, Gen. Lake joined the troops assembled at Agra; but an immediate movement against the enemy was retarded by causes as new as unexpected, arising out of the defection of the Rajah of Bhurtpoor, and the insubordination which, through the intrigues of that chieftain, and of the emissaries of Holkar, generally pervaded the ceded and conquered provinces, and in their consequences operated as a serious impediment to procuring provisions and supplies.

At length, Gen. Lake was enabled to put the army in motion, and it reached Delhi on the 17th Oct. The enemy's infantry had ineffectually besieged this place; and on the 15th Oct. they were repulsed in a general assault with great loss, and immediately afterwards retreated towards the river Bennee.

Anxious as the Com.-in-Chief was to bring the war to a speedy termination, by the destruction of this body of troops, the want of provisions rendered their pursuit totally impracticable, and compelled the army to halt until this most essential requisite could be supplied.

On the 31st Oct., Lord Lake, with three regiments of British, and

* See Narrative of the retreat of the detachment under the command of B.-Gen. Monson, vol. ii. of this work, p. 538-560.

three regiments of Native cavalry, two European flank companies, and two battalions and a half of Native infantry, followed Holkar, who had entered the Dooaub, and threatened to lay waste the whole country.

After a march unequal for celerity, Gen. Lake, on the morning of the 17th Nov., surprised the enemy's camp at Furruckabad, and defeated him, with the loss of nearly 5000 men left on the field. Holkar's army was estimated at 15,000 horse, while the British cavalry did not exceed 1800 mounted men, who engaged under the disadvantage of having marched fifty-eight miles within the twenty-four hours preceding the action. Holkar himself escaped with great difficulty.

This signal and decisive victory proved of incalculable advantage to the public interests; it saved the whole of the Dooaub from being laid waste; it evinced the superiority of the British arms; and shewed to the Natives that the boasted rapidity of the Mahratta horse could be outdone by our cavalry.

When the cavalry had, in two days' halt, recovered in some degree from the fatigue it had so lately undergone, Gen. Lake proceeded to join the army at Muttra, which, during his absence, had, under a combined and masterly operation, most skilfully planned by General Lake, and carried into effect by the gallant Gen. Fraser, defeated the enemy's infantry under the walls of Deeg, and taken most of his guns.

The siege of Deeg was begun as soon as the battering-train arrived. In the beginning of December, a practicable breach being made in one of the bastions, it was stormed and carried, and on the following day the fort was evacuated.

Bhurtpoor, to which the remains of Holkar's army had retreated on the fall of Deeg, was the only place of consequence which now remained in the hands of the enemy. It was invested early in Jan. 1805, and the siege was protracted to the beginning of March, during which interval it was stormed four times unsuccessfully, and with very considerable loss to the besiegers.

Notwithstanding these failures, arising from the great population of Bhurtpoor, the natural difficulties of that extensive fortress, but principally from the extreme deficiency of the means which the besieging army possessed, the Rajah foresaw that the place must ultimately be taken, and accordingly, early in March, he sued for peace, which was granted by Lord Lake on terms highly honourable to the English government.

Deeply as the miscarriage at Bhurtpoor was to be deplored, the enemy had little cause to exult. During the siege, almost the whole of what remained of Holkar's infantry, and also Meer Khan's, (which were strongly entrenched under the walls outside the town,) were destroyed, and their artillery taken; nor was the loss of the garrison, composed of the whole strength of the Bhurtpoor dominions, and a large addition of mercenaries, inconsiderable *.

Upon the conclusion of the treaty with the Rajah of Bhurtpoor, Holkar and Meer Khan retreated with the horse that still remained

* The want of complete success in the attack of Bhurtpoor continues to be occasionally adverted to, and the propriety of the attempt called in question, tending to implicate the character or conduct of the Com.-in-Chief, and others engaged in that arduous war. No person at all acquainted with the actual circumstances and state of affairs at that period, can for a moment doubt but that the measure was indispensably necessary, even under all the disadvantages of a very inadequate equipment, and an army, though flushed with victory †, yet, greatly reduced and worn down by the casualties and hardships of the previous campaigns; for so long as Bhurtpoor remained a rallying point, and afforded assistance and shelter to the discomfited, but not dispersed, forces of Holkar, Meer Khan, &c., (with Dowlut Rao Scindia, in great force on the Chumbul, watching the opportunity, as was actually evinced, of renewing operations against us) on the very threshold of our frontier, our own possessions were completely at the mercy of their predatory incursions, for carrying fire and sword, or exciting insurrection throughout our provinces.

The operations before Bhurtpoor, though failing as to its actual capture, did achieve the important and indispensably necessary object of causing, by their result, and the treaty consequent thereto, the retreat of all the Mahratta forces within their own territories, and thereby secured the safety and tranquillity of our own.

Much, too, has been said, and blame vaguely scattered around, as to the causes of that failure. They are justly and impartially, we believe, briefly explained by a note in our second volume, p. 224; viz. the paucity which prevailed far and near of all the materials requisite for such operations.

† This, however, is to be received with qualification; for the time was only a very few months after the defeat of Col. Monson's detachment (which spread dismay throughout our dominions,) when one battalion was nearly annihilated, and several others rendered unfit for service till re-organized.

to them; and as the country was now cleared of enemies, General Lake was enabled to put the troops into quarters on the Jumna, during the remaining part of the hot season and the rains.

He was not, however, permitted to indulge long in repose. Towards the close of 1805, Holkar and Meer Khan again appeared in considerable force in the countries north-west of Delhi.

Although their armies possessed no solid strength, nor were calculated to make any serious impression, being principally composed of predatory horse; yet still, if not timely checked, they might have caused great mischief, by laying waste the country, and destroying the villages. When, therefore, Lord Lake received money sufficient to relieve the immediate wants of the troops, who, from unavoidable causes, were in considerable arrears, he moved against the enemy with his usual promptitude and celerity, and pursued them so closely as compelled them to take refuge in the Lahore territories, at no great distance from the banks of the river Indus.

In this long and fatiguing march, Lord Lake traversed nearly the whole of the Punjab, a country hitherto very imperfectly known to the English, and the knowledge of which, on this occasion, was obtained of it, and of the powers who possess it, must be considered of great value, and eventually may become of the highest importance.

No prospect of escape remaining to Holkar, he sued for peace, which was concluded by Lord Lake in February 1806.

From this period, until his Lordship left India, in Feb. 1807, Lord Lake was successfully employed in completing all the various arrangements connected with the distribution of the army, the reduction of the irregular troops, and the final settlement and security of our invaluable conquests. His departure from India was accompanied by the regret both of the European and Native inhabitants of Bengal, and by the most public testimonials of respect, esteem, and gratitude. He arrived in England in the following September, after an absence of seven years, and was received by his King and his country with that attention his eminent services so well deserved.

In testimony of the generous spirit with which Lord Lake recognized the services of the army, his Lordship's farewell orders are here introduced:—

"*General Orders by the Commander-in-Chief.—Head-quarters, on board the Hon. Company's ship, Walthamstow.*

"*Saugur Roads, 24th Feb.* 1807.

"The Right Hon. Lord Lake having taken his departure from Fort William for the purpose of returning to Europe, feels himself now called upon to perform the last act of public duty in his situation of Commander-in-Chief in India, by recording his final testimony of the character and conduct of the army of India, and of all the officers and soldiers who have served under his command.

"In attempting the discharge of that duty, his Lordship feels it difficult either to do justice to them or to his own feelings, under the mixed sensations of pride and regret, inseparable from the occasion of contemplating their merits, and of bidding adieu to officers and men, collectively and individually endeared to him by habits of intercourse and the mutual exertions of the spirit of professional enterprize, during the long period of six years, for the most part passed amidst the vicissitudes of climate and the laborious duties of the field, in the service of their King and country. The merits and the services of the army, and of all the officers and troops engaged in the late arduous war in India, have been so repeatedly and emphatically expressed, and recorded by the Supreme Government of the British possessions in Asia, and the gratitude and applause of the Com.-in-Chief have been so frequently called forth to express his admiration of the gallant spirit of enterprize and exertions of the officers, the steady discipline and undaunted valour of the troops, that the Com.-in-Chief feels any endeavour of his to add to their reputation would only tend to lessen its estimation, in proportion as the attempt must fall short of the praise which it deserves.

"It therefore only remains for his Lordship to express once more, his most sincere and hearty thanks for the distinguished honour which he has derived from the gallant exertions and splendid successes of the British army in India; and to record that testimony which personal observance and experience during the period of six years entitles him to pronounce—that the approbation which has been bestowed on them has been most eminently deserved, and that they have established a just and undoubted claim to the best rewards which can be conferred on them by a grateful government.

"The Com.-in-Chief feels, that to ascribe any peculiar merit to the conduct by which the officers and soldiers, his countrymen, have been actuated, beyond what might attach to their distinguished valour and noble perseverance during a long and arduous war, would be felt only as a negative compliment. But he finds it difficult to do justice to the merits of our Native soldiers, who have encountered every danger with the most exemplary valour; who have submitted to every hardship and privation with the utmost fortitude and perseverance; and, who, to promote the cause in which they were engaged, have on many occasions made a ready and cheerful sacrifice of every habit and prejudice which they had been taught to regard as dear and inviolable.

"If any weight can attach to his success, or any influence be derived from the acknowledged national benefits that have been justly ascribed to the fortitude and valour of the British army in India, during the period of his command, the Com.-in-Chief will esteem it the greatest honour and the highest gratification of his life, to employ that weight and influence in promoting the interests and exalting the character of that gallant army to which he now subscribes his affectionate farewell. The remainder of his days will be enlivened by the recollection of those public services which obtained for him the approbation of his King and country; and his Lordship will never cease to cherish the affectionate remembrance of the companions of his glory, and the promoters of his success, during the eventful period of his long command in India.

(Signed) "HENRY WORSLEY, Lieut.-Col. Adj.-Gen. Bengal army."

When the result of the campaign of 1803-4 was known in England, Gen. Lake received the thanks of Parliament for his eminent services; and his Majesty, to mark the high sense which he entertained of his meritorious services, as well as to commemorate the recollection of those glorious achievements, created him a British Baron, by the title of Lord Lake of Delhi and Laswarree; and, soon after his return to Europe, raised him to the dignity of a Viscount, and conferred on him the government of Plymouth.

These honours his Lordship enjoyed but a short period; his valuable life terminated on the 21st Feb. 1808, after a short illness.

Few men were ever endowed with qualifications calculated to form an able commander, in a superior degree to the late Lord Lake. To judgment and quickness of conception, he united undaunted courage, great decision, and uncommon capability of undergoing fatigue. He possessed, in an eminent degree, the happy gift of conciliating the confidence and attachment, and of exciting the zealous exertions of those under his command. His attention to promote the comforts of the soldier, and reward the zeal of officers and men, who distinguished themselves in the service*, together with the constant exposure of his person in the midst of danger, could not fail to secure the devotion and attachment of the army.

A further trait in Lord Lake's character, is no less creditable to the beneficence of his mind, than it is worthy of the imitation of all officers who are destined to military command. Pending and subsequent to the war in which his Lordship was engaged in India, he availed himself of the patronage vested in him, as Com.-in-Chief, to confer staff-appointments, either by his own nomination, or by recommendation to the government, on every officer who was wounded during that war, within the scope of his command, and the extent of his patronage.

GENERAL FRANCIS MARQUESS OF HASTINGS, K. G., G. C. B. †, &c. &c.

In June 1812, his Lordship was created a Knight of the most noble Order of the Garter; and in Dec., he was appointed Gov.-Gen. and Com.-in-Chief of the British territories in India. He landed at Cal-

---

* A striking instance of this disposition has been given at p. 79. Many others might be offered, but it will be sufficient to observe, that as there was no provision in the Bengal Native army for the widows and orphans of Native officers and men, his Lordship was always happy to authorize the sons of Native officers who fell in the service, to be enrolled as privates, until of age to carry arms.

† The services of this gallant soldier, and accomplished nobleman, are given in the Royal Military Calendar, vol. i. p. 326-46, 3d edition. His Lordship's brilliant career, from the period of his appointment as Governor-General of India, is here briefly sketched.

cutta on the 4th Oct. 1813, and had scarcely been allowed sufficient space of time to become familiar with the scene of his new duties, when he was called upon to commence a war with the Goorkhas, who possessed the kingdom of Nepaul. Their insults towards the British had become so serious and intolerable, that his Lordship, however averse from inclination, as well as duty, to commence a war, determined upon hostilities, without waiting for a sanction from home; and accordingly he proceeded to the Upper Provinces, to be more immediately in communication with the troops employed in the field.

Four divisions were fitted to take the field, and before the close of Oct. 1814, the Goorkha Rajah was invaded in his *penetralia*, where he esteemed himself secure and inaccessible. The decisive operations of Gen. Ochterlony soon reduced him to submission, and a treaty was ratified in March 1816, when nearly the whole of the Ghoorka territories were left in our possession.

In 1816, his Lordship was created Viscount Loudon, Earl Rawdon, and Marquess of Hastings. In addition to this high mark of Royal favour, the thanks of both Houses of Parliament were voted to his Lordship, " for his judicious arrangements in the plan and direction of the military operations against Nepaul, by which the war was brought to a successful issue, and peace established on just and honourable terms." A vote of thanks was also passed to him by a Court of Directors of the East India Company, which was confirmed by the unanimous consent of a Court of Proprietors.

He directed, in 1817-18, the operations of the Mahratta war. This war was commenced upon a scale far surpassing any that had hitherto tasked the powers of a Governor of India, and before which the dimensions of an European campaign shrink in comparison. The punishment of a band of freebooters, who, under the denomination of Pindarries, ravaged Central India, and the adjoining British provinces, had convulsed the continent, and every Native power was upon the watch to profit by any miscarriage or misfortune of the British army, which had, moreover, to protect a frontier of not less than 2,500 miles in extent. But great as were the dangers of this crisis, the talents which were developed by Lord Hastings, were fully equal to them. Foresight and circumspection, sagacity and promptitude, on the part of him by whom the complicated system was conceived, and the gallantry of the troops employed, ensured success under the blessing of Providence *.

The military results of the campaign may be summed up in few words. Between Nov. 1817, and June 1818, *twenty-eight* actions were fought in the field, and *one hundred and twenty* forts, many scarcely accessible, some deemed impregnable, fell by surrender, siege, or storm. For the " promptitude and vigour" displayed by the Noble Marquess† in this eventful struggle, the thanks of Parliament, and also that of the East India Company, were voted to him.

* " If Lord Clive made India, Lord Hastings has preserved it from imminent danger, consolidated its power, as far as human foresight can extend, for a long period, and in converting danger into security, has also done that which commercial men, at least, rarely overlook, converted poverty into wealth."—*Universal Review*, May 1824.

† We cannot avoid in this place, inserting the following just compliment to the fidelity of the Native troops:—

" Out of about 90,000 troops whom Lord Hastings brought into the field, 10,000 or thereabouts only were British: the remainder were the Native forces of the East India Company; trained, it is true, by European officers, and proving, by their obedience, their courage, their perseverance, their endurance, that in discipline and in achievements they were capable of rivalling their British instructors. In doing justice to the bravery of the Native troops, I must not overlook another virtue,—their fidelity. Many of the Bombay army had been recruited in the territories of the Peishwa; their property, their friends, their relatives, all that was valuable and dear to them, were still in that Prince's power. Previously to the commencement of hostilities, the Peishwa had spared no pains to seduce and corrupt these troops; he abstained from no threats to force them from their allegiance, but his utmost arts were vain. The Native officers and soldiers came to their British commanders with the proofs of these temptations in their hands, and renewed the pledges of their attachment. One man, (Sheick Houssein) a non-commissioned officer, brought to his captain the sum of 5,000 rupees, which had been presented to him by the Peishwa in person, as an earnest of reward for desertion. The vengeance denounced by the Peishwa was not an unmeaning menace; it did, in many instances, fall heavy on the relatives of those who resisted his threats and his entreaties; but the effect was rather to exasperate than to repress their ardour in the service to which they had sworn to adhere."—The President (*Mr. Canning*) of the Board of Controul's speech in the House of Commons, 4th March, 1819.

In 1818, his Lordship was nominated a Knight Grand Cross of the Order of the Bath.

On the 1st Jan. 1823, his Lordship resigned the government of India, and embarked for Europe. The Marquess relinquished his high office in consequence of the state of his health, and on account of domestic concerns, contrary to the earnest wishes of his employers. The addresses presented to him, previously to his departure for Europe, cannot be perused without awakening the feelings of the reader, and leaving behind a durable sense of the worth of him whose actions are therein commemorated. Amongst these, the address from the British inhabitants of Calcutta deserves notice, for its elegant and concise exposition of his Lordship's services, and that from the Natives of the same city, on account of its allusion to his efforts on behalf of their education, and moral improvement.

Finally, it may justly be observed, that Lord Hastings filled the united offices of Governor-General and Commander-in-Chief for a period of nearly ten years, with the most unwearied zeal and devotion to exalt the character of the service, and promote the welfare of the British possessions in Asia.

How well he succeeded is nobly testified by the public results, and by the grateful admiration and respect for his Lordship's character, with the regret for his loss, evinced by all who served under him, or enjoyed the benefit of his beneficent disposition, and the exalted principles of integrity, humanity, justice, and kindness, which marked the whole course of his patriarchal administration; and has left a name which continues to be re-echoed with invocations for his return, throughout the regions of Asia, where he so long promoted the welfare and happiness of the people, and exalted the honour and reputation of his King and country.

In 1824, his Lordship was appointed Governor and Commander-in-Chief of the island of Malta and its dependencies.

MAJOR ALEXANDER MACLEOD.

(Bengal Establishment.)

This officer was appointed Ensign, 19th March 1805; Lieut., 20th March 1805; Captain, 24th April 1816; and Major, 14th July 1825.

He arrived in India in March 1805; and was posted to the 12th reg. N. I., which he joined, and was shortly after detached with a company, in pursuit of a refractory zemindar of the Nabob of Oude. After chasing him some days, he traced him into a small mud-fort, which he immediately attacked and carried, with the loss of the subadar, jemadar, and 20 sepoys in killed and wounded.

He next served at the taking of several mud-forts in Oude, with the corps under Col. (the late Major-Gen.) Gregory. (Services, vol. ii. p. 441-7).

On the formation of light battalions, in the Bengal army, this officer was attached to the 12th, commanded by Major Kelly. He marched with it to join Gen. Martindell's force on service in Bundlecund, and was at the attack of Ruggoulee, and siege and capture of Adjeeghur.

When the 12th regiment came down the country to Barrackpore, this officer volunteered his services with the drafts for Java, where, on his arrival, he was posted to the Java light infantry battalion, commanded by Major Dalton. (Services, vol. ii. p. 348-354).

On his way to join, he met, at Samarang, the force under the command of Col. (now Major-Gen.) Watson, His Majesty's 14th foot, with which he served at the taking of Sambas, in Banca: this service being terminated, he joined the Java light battalion at Djojocata.

When Gen. Nightingall was preparing the expedition against the island of Balli, and the Rajah of Boni, at Macassar, this officer volunteered his services, with a European light corps, formed of the rifle and light companies of His Majesty's 59th and 78th foot, commanded by the late Capt. T. Cameron (78th), and was in the advance at the landing of Balli Baleling; and at the attack on the Rajah of Boni, near Macassar; and also on an expedition against a refractory chief, near Balacomba, which was successful, after several marches into the interior, to seize the chief.

He returned to Bengal, when Java was given up to the Dutch government; and was appointed second in command to the Cuttack legion, at the request of Capt. (now Lieut.-Col.) Simon Fraser, who was nominated commandant, and had the formation of that corps.

He was employed with the mounted squadron of the legion, and 120 men of the infantry, at the attack on the Lurkacoles in Singhboon, commanded by Col. W. Richards. He was ordered to enter the country at an opposite point to Col. Richards, and to join that officer on a certain day at Bendeah, in the centre of the country, attacking the enemy on his route as opportunities occurred. After several skirmishes, and destroying many of the enemy's positions, he arrived at the appointed place. Circumstances prevented Col. Richards joining him, and two days after arriving at Bendeah, he received instructions to offer terms to the Lurkacoles in that direction, settle the country, and attack any that might be refractory; all of which orders he accomplished to the entire satisfaction of Col. Richards, and the late Major Roughsedge, political agent, and received their thanks.

In 1823, on Major Fraser going to England, this officer succeeded to the command of the Cuttack legion.

When the Cuttack district was quiet, and no further danger apprehended from Jugbundoo, the chief that headed the rebellion in that province, the legion was ordered to the eastern frontier, and the corps was organized as a light infantry battalion, (the late Sylhet frontier battalion, and two companies of the Dinagepore battalion, were embodied with it) formed into 10 companies, and denominated the Rungpore light infantry; the mounted part of the corps was done away with. The cantonment of the corps was taken up at Jumalpore, where it remained until the breaking out of the Burmese war, when it was ordered to Gowalpara, to join the force collecting there to invade Assam, under the late Brigadier Macmorine, (services, vol. ii. p. 141-7); since which time Major Macleod has been on active service in Assam, with the Rungpore light infantry, and engaged, under the command of Brigadier Alfred Richards (who succeeded Brigadier Macmorine), in every action that took place with the enemy, as shewn by that officer's public despatches.

MAJOR HOWE DANIEL SHOWERS.

(Bengal Establishment.)

This officer obtained the rank of Ensign 10th Oct. 1801; of Lieutenant, 13th July 1803; of Captain, 1st October 1814; and of Major, in 1825.

He was with the 2d batt. 9th N. I., on service under the personal command of Lord Lake in the campaigns of 1803, 4, and 5, in the war with Scindia, Holkar, and the Mahratta confederates. He was employed in the storming of the town of Agra, on the 10th October 1803, and at the siege of the fort; at the battle of Laswarree, on the 1st November following; at the siege of Gwalior in January 1804; and in Col. Monson's retreat, (see Narrative in vol. ii.) in July and August 1804; he also served at the seige of Bhurtpoor, in January and February 1805, and received a wound in one of the storms.

CAPTAIN CHARLES SMITH.

(Bengal Establishment.)

This officer arrived in India on the 19th July 1809, and was appointed Lieutenant Fireworker on the 2d April in that year. His first service was at the latter end of 1814, when he commanded the foot artillery with the army under the orders of the late Sir R. Gillespie, and was present at the unsuccessful assault of Kalunga, on which occasion Gen. Gillespie met his death. He afterwards commanded the artillery with Col. Carpenter's force in the Deyrah Dhoon.

The 17th Feb. 1815, he obtained the rank of Lieutenant, and was present at the siege of Hattrass in the early part of 1817; and after the fall of that fort, he proceeded to Calcutta, which he again left by dawk in the latter end of the same year, and joined the centre division of the grand army under the Marquess of Hastings. On the breaking up of that division, in February 1818, he proceeded to join the reserve of the grand army in Rajpootana, under the command of the late Sir David Ochterlony; and was present at the taking of the town of Ajmere, and fort of Tarragurh, in June 1818. He was at the siege of Madarajpoorah, in August of the same year; and at the reduction of the fort of Nusreedah, in October following. He commanded the artillery with the detachment under the late Major Lowry, C. B., against the Meenahs, in the early part of 1819; and he again commanded the artillery with the force under Lieut.-Col. G. Maxwell, C. B., against the Meenahs in the latter end of 1820. In Feb. 1824, he left the presidency for the north-east frontier, and commanded the artillery with the force under the orders of Lieut.-Col. Innis, C. B., in Cachar, from March to December 1824.

The 1st May 1824, he obtained the rank of Captain.

APPENDIX.

Operations of the Right Column, in the attack upon Tippoo Sultaun's fortified Camp, on the night of the 6th February, 1792.
(See vol. ii. p. 395-401).

Extract of a Letter to Major-General Beatson, from Lieut.-Col. Sandys.

" I received the second volume of the *East India Military Calendar*, last month; and I read your Report of the Operations of the Right Column, in the attack upon Tippoo Sultaun's fortified camp, on the night of the 6th Feb. 1792, with no common interest.

" More than thirty-two years have elapsed; and the noble chiefs of the army are beyond the voice of man! and so are, perhaps, eight-tenths of that army!

" The mystery which covered the operations of the right column, and had nearly proved fatal to the British empire in India; and also to the mind and life of the brave Sir William Medows, is now unveiled.

" The mystery appears, in part, to be accounted for by you, in stating, that the right column turned to the right, instead of the left, upon entering ' the bound hedge: as well as from its having met with so much opposition, in the assault of the Ead-gah redoubt.'

" In order to clear up an hiatus in your Report on events in which I was personally concerned, I beg leave to request your perusal of the following plain and simple narrative of facts, as connected with the operations of the centre and right columns, on that memorable night, the 6th of February 1792,—when, perhaps, the British interests in India depended upon 8700 firelocks, the whole amount of the three columns of attack!

" I will first transcribe your own report, ' that it was not until about four o'clock in the morning, when the enemy rallied and attacked the reserve, with great resolution, that General Medows knew where Lord Cornwallis was; he then gave orders to move, but before the column was in motion his Lordship arrived at the Carigut Hill. When the musquetry became heavy and incessant, General Medows evinced the utmost degree of solicitude; he exclaimed in these words to Capt. Beatson, " Good God! I would at this moment give ten thousand pounds of my fortune, to know where Lord Cornwallis is."' See General Beatson's Report—*East India Military Calendar*, vol. ii. p. 395.

" Colonel Wilks says, that it was at three o'clock in the morning, that the furious attack was made by the enemy upon the reserve under Lord Cornwallis; I believe, that it was rather before than after three o'clock. You state yourself, that the right column arrived at the Carigut Hill at three in the morning.

" In the latitude of Seringapatam on the 7th of February: twilight began after five, and the sun rose after six; so that the right column was full three hours within musket range of one subdivision of the reserve, where stood the Commander-in-Chief with little more than three battalions, and the 74th regiment *en potence!*

" With as little egotism as the nature of the subject will admit, I will endeavour to fill up your hiatus; and to introduce some interesting circumstances, which may be useful to the future military historian, and enable him to pourtray from correct and impartial information, the character and conduct of the late most honourable and exalted Marquess Cornwallis, in the heat of battle.

" His Lordship never lost his coolness and distinctness of order, although his Adjutant-General and himself were wounded in the early part of the enemy's attack, and many fell around him. His difficulties were increased, not only by a total failure of his expected co-operation of the right column, but by an absolute ignorance of its fate or position, until I fortunately galloped on the spot under the Carigut Hill, about half-past five in the morning of the 7th, where stood Gen. Medows, Major Close, Deputy Adj.-Gen., Colonel (now Lord) Harris, Col. Cockerel, and Sir William's personal staff, and yourself.

" At my advanced age, and with my retired habits, I shall not, I trust, be accused of presumption, in supporting, by proof, the circumstances under the head of my services, as stated in the first volume of the *East India Military Calendar*, that I was employed by Lord Cornwallis, on the night of the 6th of February, chiefly in conveying his orders to the 74th reg. commanded by Capt. Dougald Campbell, and that I was the first officer who fell in with the right column.

"Neither the subaltern rank I held, nor the appointment of Agent for the Carriage of the Public Camp Equipage of the Army, together with the charge of all the extra cattle belonging to the Company, were likely to excite a hope of martial fame.

"I was attached to the Bengal volunteers until I was ordered up, about midnight, by Lieut.-Col. Kyd, from the breaching battery at Bangalore, to attend the foraging party the next morning. Lord Cornwallis then, after reprimanding me for being absent from my important charge, directed me to be struck off the strength of the corps; and ever afterwards, with the exception of the general action before the walls of Seringapatam, on the 15th May 1791, when I fell in with the Bengal volunteers, to which corps I had been Adjutant and Quarter-Master, I used to attend his Lordship, and, occasionally, to convey his orders.

"The above explanation appears to be requisite, since *no narrator* [*] of the military details of the night attack upon Tippoo Sultaun's fortified camp *has mentioned* my name, and stated, that Lieut. Sandys was fortunate enough on the morning of the 7th, to gallop into the very spot where stood Sir Wm. Medows, surrounded by his Staff, as shall be more particularly detailed. After dining with Capt. Archdeacon on the 6th February, I went up, with some brother officers, to the top of a hill on the right, to view the enemy's fortified camp, and to discover foraging ground.

"Upon coming down from the hill I met Colonel (now Lord) Harris, who gave me to understand that some movement might be expected. I hastened to head-quarters, and was shortly interrogated by Lord Cornwallis on what I had seen [†] on the line of the fortified camp; and I then followed in his Lordship's suite.

"A little after 11 o'clock at night, the centre column, under his Lordship, pierced the bound hedge: he gave orders to Col. (now General) Alexander Ross, to number the corps as they passed. His Lordship here took post, and employed his Aids-de-Camp on the requisite points.

[*] "For instance, Major Dirom, one of General Medows' staff, mentions every name but mine with Lord Cornwallis."

[†] "Especially, I remember, about a white building which I had described, and which afterwards proved to be the Sultaun's redoubt."

"The enemy made a formidable stand at first; and within the bound hedge the gallant Capt. Archdeacon* fell, while leading the 14th battalion Bengal sepoys. Shortly afterwards, I was sent by Lord Cornwallis to Capt. Dougald Campbell, commanding the gallant 74th Highland reg., with orders for him to maintain his post, and that he should be supported. From this beginning I was chiefly employed the whole night in conveying orders to that regiment.

"I shall omit the intermediate relation of events occurring in the reserve, until after a total cessation of firing, I suppose about two in the morning, when his Lordship and Staff were all dismounted, and reflected with the utmost anxiety on the profound silence on his right. In this awful silence and anxiety we all participated. I was sitting down on a bank with Doctor Laird and Mr. Cherry†, his Lordship's Persian interpreter, a cannon-shot passed behind my neck, as I was leaning forward, and before Mr. Cherry's face, who was fortunately reclining backward: it broke his hircarrah's thigh, and killed a trooper's horse. This was the commencement of the enemy's resolute, judicious, and weighty attack upon the reserve; and, I believe, a little before, rather than after, 3 o'clock in the morning. His Lordship immediately mounted his horse, and gave his orders with the utmost coolness amid a sheet of fire; while the balls of the enemy's musketry rang on the bayonets of the column of reserve, now at shouldered arms.

"In the most furious moment of the attack, I was standing by the shoulder of his Lordship's horse, to receive his orders. The Adjutant-Gen., Colonel Malcolm, was now wounded in the leg, and a ball struck the golden-headed cane with which his Lordship rode, and grazed the skin of his left thumb. Observing him to rub his hand with the cane, I said, 'Your Lordship is wounded!' His words of reply were, 'O, no: nothing, Sandys! Go to Campbell, and tell him to maintain his post to the last; he shall be soon supported ‡.' I delivered the important message to that gallant officer, passing

---

* "His last words to his orderlies were, in Hindoostanee, 'Go, and join your battalion, my brothers, my business is over.'"

† "Mr. Cherry, while Resident at Benares some years afterwards, had invited Vizier Ally to breakfast, who drew his poignard and stabbed Mr. Cherry to the heart; and his followers began a general massacre of the Europeans. It was at this time that the late Mr. Davis, afterwards Director of the East India Company, so gallantly saved the lives of his wife and children with his defence of a narrow, winding staircase, by a hog-spear."

‡ "'If General Medows be above ground,' said Lord Cornwallis to Colonel Ross, 'this will bring him!'"

between numerous wounded, who knew me, and called upon me, in vain, for assistance.

"Capt. Dougald Campbell was at that time gallantly closing the openings made in his regiment by the destructive fire of the enemy, who was closing, with fresh cushoons, upon the 74th, which being joined by some companies of the 52d, and the 14th battalion of Bengal sepoys, with the parole Bangalore, shouted by then Ensign, (now Lieut.-Col.) Sir Thomas Ramsay, Bart., this small reinforcement were fortunately mistaken by the enemy for the columns of the army*.

"Having made my report of having delivered my message to Capt. Campbell, and on what I had seen, his Lordship asked me if I knew the Sultaun's redoubt, where Capt. Sibbald commanded, to go and bid him defend it to the last. I replied, that I did not know. Here Major Skelly, his Lordship's aid-de-camp, came up from conveying other orders, and said that he did. We all know with what true gallantry that redoubt was defended. After Capt. Sibbald was killed, Major Skelly, not being able to return, as it was encompassed with the enemy, assumed the command, and continued its noble defence.

"This furious attack of the enemy upon the centre column being repelled, I was standing close by Lord Cornwallis and Colonel Ross, and heard his Lordship observe to him, 'We must not stay here, under the guns of the fort, when the day breaks; we must retire to the Carigut Hill.' Then turning to me, he said, 'Sandys, have you preserved your horse?'—'I don't know, my Lord; it was in the water-course with your Lordship's body-guard.'—'Go to Turner†; take with you as many troopers as you like, and ascertain whether the Carigut Hill is in possession of the enemy, to which we must retire, and advance cautiously.'

"I found my excellent horse with the body-guard, and taking two troopers, I advanced cautiously, but found much difficulty in tracing my way. The loom of the Carigut Hill I could now and then discover, from the flashes of the firing; but in crossing a ravine, I lost the troopers. Finding myself alone, I halted a few minutes to listen. The firing had now ceased, and twilight began to appear, which it did on that day at half-past 5; the sun rising much after 6. I advanced very cautiously, but it was so obscure,

* "On returning from the 74th at this moment, I had nearly mistaken a cushoon of the enemy for our own troops."
† "The officer commanding the body-guard."

that I got close to the hill before I well knew where I was. At this moment, I heard a sentry cough, about the middle of the hill, and I immediately challenged. No answer was returned; but a deadly silence reigned, although I repeated the challenge three times.

"I was now impressed with an idea that the hill was in possession of the enemy, for I was persuaded that it was the cough of a Native, and not of an European.

"Being well mounted, and ashamed to return, without ascertaining the object for which I was sent, and having a little open space before me, which I remembered seeing from the top of the hill, when foraging the year before, I resolved to risk the movement; and with my sword drawn, and pistol cocked, I spurred my horse, and advanced briskly. A deadly silence still reigned; when having asked in a loud voice, ' who commands?' *intending* that my voice should *reach* the *top* of the hill, and looking upwards, the reins of my horse were seized by the Deputy-Adjutant-General, Major Close, answering, ' Gen. Medows.' I found, that I had been so fortunate as to close upon the right column *, where stood Gen. Medows, Col. Cockerel, and several of the Staff, as before described. Gen. Medows asked me if Lord Cornwallis was well; and having answered a few more questions, and told Colonel Cockerel that our friend, Archdeacon, had fallen on the first onset, I was impatient to get back to Lord Cornwallis, and I galloped away.

"At this time the day had so far advanced, that a person might be discovered at 15 or 20 yards.

"I soon met Lord Cornwallis, and the reserve, retiring from under the guns of the fort towards the hill.

"I will now relate, word for word, what passed:—

" ' My Lord, I have found Gen. Medows' column.'

" ' Where, Sandys?'—' Under the Carigut Hill, my Lord.'—' It is impossible, Sandys.'—' It is true, my Lord. I have seen and spoken to Gen. Medows, and to Col. Cockerel, and Major Close.' His Lordship replied, ' It cannot be.' At this moment, Gen. Medows, who had followed me, came up; when his Lordship addressed him, ' Good God, my dear Medows where have you been! What a glorious opp——' but here his Lordship,

* " Major-General Beatson says, that the right column reached the Carigut Hill by three in the morning."

checked himself. 'However, it is well as it is: we have carried the island, and done great things.'

"Here I was interrogated by his Lordship's staff, and heard no more of their conversation.

"The reserve got to the Carigut Hill just before it was daylight; but not before the fort opened its fire upon the rear of the reserve; and Lieut.-Col. Alexander Kyd, and myself, were ordered by Lord Cornwallis, then on the hill, to go and quicken its movements, to get out of the line of fire.

"His Lordship ordered the troops on the island to be relieved; and, shortly afterwards the enemy commenced his attack upon Sibbald's redoubt, in full view from the hill, where our noble chiefs were seated, and over whose heads I saw a shot fly from the fort or outworks, from whence the distance of the hill from the fort and its defence may be judged.

"Having borne my personal testimony to the facts of some incidents, hitherto unnoticed, of this most important night, to the stability of the empire of Great Britain, in British India; then hanging under providence on the life of that great chief, warrior, and statesman, who commanded the whole,

"I remain,

"Your faithful friend, and servant,

(Signed) "W. SANDYS,

"Lieut.-Col. on the Bengal retired list, since Sept. 1805."

"The force of the columns of attack, as given by Colonel Wilks, are—

		Casualties.
Right	3,300	95
Centre, subdivided	3,700	342
Left	1,700	98
Firelocks	8,700	535

"A true copy, for the East India Military Calendar,

"W. SANDYS.

"*Lanarth, near Helston, 30th Dec. 1824.*"

Extract from Major-General Beatson's letter to Colonel Sandys, dated 20th March, 1825.

"The circumstances stated in your letter, are indeed very interesting to me; but, in respect to the hiatus in my narrative, I think, if you were here, I could convince you it is not so considerable as you make it.

"The right column countermarched to the outside of the hedge, about half an hour after the cannon and musketry had ceased; which *you say*, was about two in the morning. It halted about a quarter of an hour on the outside of the hedge, and then moved to get upon Lord Cornwallis's track, and continued its march to the Carigut Hill. The distance it had marched, from the time it countermarched from the position in the inside of the hedge to the Carigut Hill, was six thousand yards, or nearly four miles, (as you will find by Dirom's plan, in page 135) and there it had halted about half an hour before the attack upon Lord Cornwallis commenced.

"Now, if the cannon and musketry ceased at two in the morning, it will appear, from the following data of halts and movements, that the time of the attack upon Lord Cornwallis could not have been at *three*, but nearer to four in the morning, as I have stated in my report:—

	Hours.	Min.
"Suppose the musketry and cannon ceased at	2	0
Halting inside, and countermarching to outside of hedge	0	30
Halting on the outside	0	15
Marching to the Carigut Hill	1	0
Halting there, before the attack on Lord Cornwallis	0	30
Deduced time of the attack on Lord Cornwallis	4	15

"Hence, it seems probable, the cannon and musketry may have ceased a little before two in the morning, and that the attack on Lord Cornwallis began about two hours later, because the halts and movements above-mentioned *must have* fully occupied two hours.

"But after all, the anachronism which appears to you in my report, is of no consequence whatever. It rests wholly on contradictory statements of the *times* at which the two events took place. I may be right, or I may be wrong, and yet I am of opinion, I am not wide of the mark; I wrote from recollection —and not from hours and minutes noted by a watch."

GENERAL INDEX

TO THE

Principal Battles, Sieges, Events, &c. &c., and Names of Officers, mentioned in this Volume.

ANJAR, capture of, 373
Arnold, John, M.-Gen., *C. B.*, Bengal E., services, 1, 205, 414
Assam, conquest of, 393
Adjeeghur fort, 4, 426, 523
Aldrit, J., Lieut., 238, 240
Argaum, battle of, 29th Nov. 1803; 9, 86, 118, 281, 500
Amyat, Mr. 212
Asseerghur fort, seige and storm of, 9, 80, 118
Aire, J. R., Lieut., 206
Allyghur fort, taking of, 30, 78, 203, 376, 383, 393, 414, 416, 505
Allen, Lieut., murdered by Timnaick, 173
Allen, Henry, late Ensign, 236
Agra fort, capture of, 30, 32, 78, 168, 203, 296, 376, 383, 411, 414, 416, 422, 509
Abercromby, Sir Robert, late Gen., 300, 419, 479
Abercromby, Lieut.-Gen., 118
Abercromby, late Gen. Sir John, 196, 203, 210, 257-9, 274, 284, 370, 372
Adams, Brigadier, 34, 151, 389, 391, 430, 433, 437, 442
Abington, late Major, 334, 337, 338
Ahmedabad, reduction of, 90, 209
Arnauld, capture of, 90
Amherst, Lord, 462
Ambarah fort, capture of, 34
Ahmuty, T. A. S., L.-Col., Madras E., services, 82, 257
Armstrong, C., late Major, Bengal E., services, 4,52, 34
Arakerry, assault and capture of, 35
Assaye, battle of, 86, 280, 495
Armstrong, late Lieut., 446
Adam, Mr. John, 38, 461
Ahtour, assault of, 39
Archdeacon, Capt., late, 477, 529, 530
Agnew, L.-Col., 44, 47, 48, 49
Auchmuty, Sir S., late Gen. 70, 110, 380
Agnew, Lieut., 77
Ancola, capture of, 345
Ahmednuggur, reduction of, 86, 280, 285, 492
Arrowsmith, Lieut., 92
Alldin, J. J., L.-Col. Com., 185, 186
Anderson, the late Lieut.-Gen., 192
Arden, Capt., 206

Bednore, surrender of, 348
Bolton, Thomas, late Major, Bengal E., services, 300
Burrow, Mr. Reuben, 290
Bellasis, late M.-Gen., 255, 256
Banda, capture of, in 1810, 236
Bowen, Herbert, L.-Col., Bengal E., services, 109, 428, 446, 447

Bowie, Robert, late L.-Col., Bengal E., services 109, 111
Bombay army, 125, 332
Burrows, late Col., 251
Bhowanny, assault and capture of, 109, 389, 390. 424, 430
Burns, Lieut., 142
Blair, Sir Robert, *K. C. B.*, Lieut.-Gen., 415
Blair, late Col., 222
Ball, George, late L.-Col., Bengal E., services. 418, 109, 200, 389, 390
Burmese, irruption of, into Cachar, and war, 110, 237, 393, 398, 444, 445
Bond, late Major, 135
Bayley, Lieut., 153, 163
Brooke, C., Capt. (now L.-Col.), 159
Bridport, Lord, Admiral, 170
Bomangaum, attack and capture of, 180
Baines, C. H., Major, Bengal E., services, 387
Burr, the late L.-Col., *C. B.*, 193, 306
Bombay docks, 196
Brown, Sir G. S., *K. C. B.* L.-Gen., 198
Blackney, J. F., late Capt. 199, 200
Bidzighur, siege and capture of, 1792; 203, 358, 418
Butler, Major, 206
Blackney, Capt., 385
Baines, G V., late Major, 208
Bell, C. H., Capt., 208
Burns, J. G., Lieut., 208
Boscawen, Admiral, 212
Broome, Capt., 213
Blair, Capt., Bengal E., services, 214
Burke, Edmund, Right Hon., 213
Baillie, Lieut., 220
Bryan, Lieut., 293
Blunt, J. T., Capt., Bengal E., services, 290
Balloon captains, 244
Bright, G. A. C. Surgeon, 241
Barwell, Mr. 231
Birrell, Lieut., 216, 218, 219, 220
Buhul fort, 7
Baillie, John, Lieut.-Gen., 375
Bowser, Lieut.-Gen., 9, 488
Baillie, Sir Ewen, late L.-Gen., 31, 307, 385
Burton, Capt., 358
Barramgaum, attack at, 9
Blair, Capt., 379
Brown, Capt., 9
Baroda, siege of, 1803; 11, 115
Baddely, W. C., L.-Col., 390
Bangalore, capture of, in 1791; 82, 203
Broach, reduction of, 1803; 11, 90
Baillie, Major, 450
Burn, W., late M.-Gen., 81, 91, 93, 94, 393, 411, 427

Bellassis, John, M.-Gen., 11, 172, 259
Bowen, Lieut., 13
Burrell, L., M.-Gen., 376
Barclay, R. the late L.-Col., Bombay E., services, 22, 23, 25.
Bentinck, Lord W., G. C. B., Gen., 46, 47, 50-7
Bejighur fort, 30, 31, 203, 415, 504
Beatson, M.-Gen., 83, 297, 475, 527
Black, Col., 31
Braithwaite, M.-Gen., 488
Bannerman, late Col., Madras E., services, 296, 37
Blackburne, W., L.-Col., Madras E, ser., 42, 176
Barlow, Sir George, 45, 46, 57
Brown, A., late Lieut.-Gen., 67, 84, 116, 277
Baird, Sir D., G. C. B., Gen. 67, 101, 171, 203, 302, 476, 485, 489
Brodie, Serjeant, 74
Blaquiere, Major, 488
Baker, Benjamin, Capt., 76
Bhurtpoor, sieges of, 79, 127, 129, 145, 179, 192, 199, 203, 296, 364, 376, 383, 414, 416, 514, see note 515
Bassein, siege of, 90
Brown, Sir Thomas, K. C. B., M.-Gen., 98, 103, 105, 188, 189, 414
Blacker, Col., 104
Batavia, capture of, 108
Barton, E., Capt., now Major, 204
Bawamullen, siege of, 333
Brownrigg, late M.-Gen., 339
Bilghieghaut, surprise of, 343
Bunbury, Ensign, 352
Browne, A. W., Capt., services, Bombay E., 372
Burnet, John, L.-Col., 372
Barrabutty, storm of, 399
Badamy, storm of, 400
Belgaum, storm of, 400
Bujjerah fort, siege and capture of, 419
Bowe, Capt. 445
Barberie, C. S., Ensign, 447
Bath, Order of the, see note 470

Colebrooke, Henry T., Esq., F. R. S., &c., 317
Corygaum, battle of, 306, 460, 462
Cunstance, Capt., 294
Court, Major, 304
Cochin, capture of, 284
Cockburn, Major, H. M.'s 84th, 255
Cole, Captain, 236
Cummonagh, siege of, 111
Cavaye, Lieut., 143
Clark, Lieut., 143-4
Campbell, D., Col., 143
Chalmers, Lieut., 143
Colebrook, L.-Col., 149, 150
Close, the late Sir Barry, 151, 528
Charlesworth, Capt., 156, 157, 457
Clarke, late Lieut., 160, 457
Campbell, Lieut., 164
Coleman, Col., 175, 176
Capon, Col., 176
Caulfield, Capt., 186
Chowkundee, reduction of, 191, 203
Clark, late Adjutant, 190
China, expedition to, 369
Cunningham, J., L.-Col., 193

Cosby, L.-Col., 194
Cowper, W., the late L.-Col., Bombay E., ser. 195
Commissariat department, 196
Culpee, taking of, 1781; 202
Cockerell, late L.-Col., 203, 210, 528
Cutterah, battle of, 23d Oct. 1794; 203
Carstairs, Capt., 213
Camac, Jacob, late L.-Col., 214, 358
Crabb, Major, 221, 223, 226
Chowriaghatee Pass, 201, 370, 392, 417
Cuttack, conquest of, in 1803 ; 293, 303
Champion, late Col., 301, 463
Clarke, M., Capt., Madras E., services, 304
Cook, late Capt., R.N., 294
Canning, J., late Major, Bengal E., services, 283
Campbell, Dugald, L.-Col., 261
Campbell, Major, H. M.'s 42d, 342, 351
Chads, Capt., R.N., 240
Chittledroog, surrender of, 378
Craig, Sir James, Gen., 2, 40, 91, 211
Clarke, Sir A., Gen., 91, 101, 144, 210
Chooro fort, 7
Cornwallis, Marquess, memoir of, 472, 8, 90, 129, 203, 210, 272-3, 300, 314, 385, 527, 534
Chamberlain, Col., H. M.'s 24th inf., 201
Clive, Lord, 43, 212
Chandore, siege and capture of, 9, 69, 87, 118, 285
Clarke, Sir William, late M.-Gen., 116, 120, 121, 175, 248, 253
Carnac, J. R., Major, 15
Chiah, siege and capture of, 375
Campbell, Sir A., M.-Gen., K. C. B., 29, 237, 283, 400
Campbell, Gen., Sir Arch., K. B., 43, 450
Catchoura fort, 30, 31, 203, 296, 382, 413, 415, 504
Chouragurh, surrender of, 114
Christie, Engineer, 337, 340
Cumming, Alex., L.-Col., Bengal E., services 31, 435, 436
Calicut, capture of, 334
Coombs, J. M., L.-Col., Madras E., services, 34
Cooper, H. E. G., L.-Col. Bengal E., services, 376
Croker, M.-Gen., 36
Cuppage, Colonel, 39
Caharcoil, capture of, 47
Campbell, Dougald, late General, 530-1
Campbell, Sir A., late Gen., 65, 77, 293, 303, 380
Cornelis fort, capture of, 70, 108, 110
Candy, projected expedition to, in 1814; 76
Coel, action of, 78, 383, 505
Chanda, assault of, 454
Cudalore, battle of, in 1783 ; 80
Covriporam, capture of, 83
Clarke, Edward, Lieut.- Colonel, 91
Canning, Rt. Hon. George, 104, 165, 405
Cornwallis, Admiral, 109
Campbell, late Captain, 131-3
Columbo, capture of, 284
Carpenter, Colonel, 526
Carpenter, late Capt., Bombay E., services, 331
Crommelin, Mr., 348
Captain, important commands confided to officers of this rank in India, 357
Colville, Sir Charles, G. C. B., General, 361

INDEX.

Cartwright, Edmund, Lieut.-Colonel, 392
Champagné, General, 390
Cooper, Major, 395
Comyn, P. T., Lieut.-Colonel, 398
Close, the late Sir Barry, Colonel, 402, 486
Camona fort, 417
Cruikshank, Lieut., 439-442
Crawford, James, late Capt., services, 447
Campbell, John, late Colonel, 468, 469
Conaghull, action of, 487
Cherry, Mr., murder of, 530

Dalbiac, Colonel, 369
Dunbar, P., Major, Bengal E., services, 413
Dickens, R. M., Maj.-General, 417
Dunn, Lieut., 430
Dunn, George, late Captain, 469
Duffin, John, Lieut., 438
Doodpatlie, attack of, 446
Dowdeswell, General, 427
Dirom, Major, 473, 529
Dalrymple, Major, 477, 479
Dalton, D. H., Lieut.-Colonel, 523
Davis, Mr., late E. I. Director, 530
Darley, Major, 261, 273
Dallas, Sir Thomas, K. C. B., Lieut.-Gen., 267, 268, 272, 280
Darwar, siege of, 286, 469
Dwarka, reduction of, 368
Deacon, Charles, Colonel, C. B., 359
Davies, Major, 359
Dudrea fort, 7
Daraporam, capture of, 9
Delhi, battle of, 30, 78, 81, 92-3, 203, 295, 376, 383, 416, 506
Delhi, defence of, 198, 393, 411, 464, 513
Deig fort, capture of, 30, 80, 198, 203, 295, 296, 376, 383, 414, 416, 422, 514
Deccan surveys. See services of the late Colonel C. Mackenzie
Darke, Captain, 33
Doveton, Sir John, K. C. B., Maj.-Gen, 69, 87, 151, 304, 402, 488
Davies, Lieut., 304
Dyce, Lieut.-General, 76, 77
Desse, P., Lieut.-Colonel, 83
Duboy, attack on, 90
Davis, W. B., Lieut.-Colonel, 91
Downes, H. E., Major, Madras E., services, 118
Dalrymple, Colonel, 119, 278, 378
Don, Patrick, Colonel, 127
Dominicity, late Lient., 131-3
Dashwood, Lieut., 131
Dyson, Lieut.-Col. Commandant, 140-1
Dunn, George, Lieut., 156
De Boigné, M., 168, 178
Dudrenec, M., 168
Davies, David, Lieut., 175
Dawes, Captain, 178
Dararah, attack and capture of, 180
Deare, George, Major-Gen., 191
Deare, Charles, Lieut.-Col., 266
Davy, L. H., Captain, 199
Duncan, late Lieut., 200
Dowse, late Lieut.-Col., 381

Elrington, Colonel, 17, 18
Ely, late Lieut. H. M.'s 69th, 74

Everest, George, Capt., 103
Edwards, Major, 119
Erskine, John, late Maj.-General, Bengal E., services, 107
Elphinstone, the Hon. M., 149, 150, 193, 359, 460
Exmouth, Lord, 169
Elliot, late Major and C. B., 188
East, W., the late Col., C. B., Bombay E., services, 192, 365, 373, 374, 375
Eastment, T., Adjt. (now Lieut.) 241
Egerton, late B.-General, 332
Eldridge, W., late Major, 375
Elwood, C. W., Major, Bombay E., services, 468
Egypt, expedition to, 489
Frederick, Charles, late Colonel, Bombay E., services, 285
Farquhar, the late Sir Walter, 243
Fallon, Lieut. 216, 218, 220
Futteabad fort, 7
Forrest, W., Lieut.-Col., Bengal E., services, 29
Floyd, Sir John, late Gen., 40, 67, 167, 262, 272, 275, 277
Frederick, the Hon. Sir Charles, K. B., 285
Fancourt, late Colonel, 73
Franklin, J., Capt., Bengal E., services, 97, 189
Fletcher, Major, 293, 294
Fletcher, Colonel, 119
Futtehghur, defence of, Nov. 1804; 109, 198
Falconer, Captain, 142
Fawcett, Lieut., 144
Fitzgerald, M., Col., Bengal E., services, 144
Fitzgerald, C., Capt., 160, 163, 164, 454, 459
Ford, M. R., Capt., Bengal E., services, 167
Fortescue, Earl, 169, 171
Falozé, M., 178
Faithfull, H., L.-Col., Bengal E., services, 190
Frazer, Gen., 198, 422, 514
Forbes, Mr., 213
Fountain, Lieut., 231
Fisher, A. G., Capt, Bombay E., services, 284
Fraser, Lieut.-Col., 304
Flint, W., late L.-Col., Madras E., services, 308
Fyfe, Lieut., 346, 350, 353, 355
Fuller, Major-Gen., 390
Fordnam, Lieut.-Col., 450
Fraser, Simon, Lieut.-Col., 524

Gabb, Lieut., 429
Graves, H. M., Lieut., 447
Grant, M., Colonel, 452
Gent, Colonel, 378
Garner, Joseph, Major, services, 369
Gadjnoor, battle of, 354
Galliez, late Colonel, Bengal E., services, 301
Greenhill, Captain, 278, 293
Gunge Mahoodra ghaut, 2, 4
Gawelghur, siege and storm of, 9, 68, 86, 118, 281, 500
Gardiner, late Major-Gen., 295
Grant, Captain, 129
Gaulnah, siege and capture of, 9, 69, 87, 118, 282, 285
Gordon, Robert, Colonel, 257, 259
Grant, Sir W. K., Maj.-Gen., K.C.B. & K.C.H., 29, 307, 375
Gordon, Robert, Lieut., 241
Gwalior fort, capture of, 30, 308. 383, 416, 512

Gowen, Captain, 212
Gregory, R., late M.-Gen., *C. B.*, 32, 523
Gillespie, Sir R. R., late Major-Gen., *K. C. B.*, 32, 70, 71, 72-5, 289
Greenstreet, J., Lieut.-Col. Com., Bengal E., services, 78
Gowdie, General, 84
Goddard, late Major-Gen., 90, 129, 209
Gunnowrie, siege of, 111, 417
Goa, taken possession of by the British, 120
Garraway, Major, 128
Gaban, Lieut.-Colonel, 156
Grant, George, late Lieut., 161, 164, 457
Gordon, J., Surgeon, 162
Grant, Capt., Bombay E., services, 169, 362
Gordon, W., Major, Bombay E., services, 192
Griffiths, Hugh, Lieut.-Colonel, 199
Garstin, E., Ensign (now Captain), 206
Grant, Alexander, Captain, 213
Gibson, A., Captain, Madras E., services, 301
Garrard, W., L.-Col., Madras E., services, 376
Gordon, Colonel, 415

Huddleston, R. J., L.-Col., Madras E., serv., 261
Halyburton, Colonel, 278
Harcourt, late Major-Gen., 293, 294, 303, 399
Hornby, Governor, 331
Hughes, Sir Edward, 334
Hawkes, Jeremiah, late Major, 335, 337, 340
Hodges, Lieut., 337, 340, 343, 346
Humberstone, Colonel, 341
Haldane, Robert, Major-Gen., 369
Hefferman, Major, 388
Hautgong, attack of, 395
Hare, Lieut.-Colonel, H. M.'s 22d dragoons, 402
Hardyman, late General, 428
Hardyman, G., L.-Gen., Bengal E., services, 463
Hooly Honore, siege of, 469
Hunter, Captain, 477
Harness, Lieut.-Colonel, 492
Horsford, Sir John, late Major-Gen., *K. C. B.* 507
Hastings, C. H., Col., 260
Heath, late Col., 245, 251, 252
Hampton, Col., 1
Holmes, Sir G., late M.-Gen., *K. C. B.*, 12, 13, 14, 28, 122, 181, 193, 305
Hookland, Capt., 293
Holland, Lieut., 16, 18,
Hattrass fort, capture of, 32, 79, 113, 414, 417, 426
Hodgson, Capt. 415
Hodgson, Col. 417
Hastings, marquess of, Gen. &c., memoir of, 519, 32, 37, 69, 202
Hardy, Edmund, Maj., Bombay E., services, 374
Hurreehurpoor, attack of, 112
Howden, Lord, Gen. 35
Hobart, Lord, 40
Hislop, Sir Thomas, *G. C. B.* L.-Gen. 41, 76, 104, 119, 163, 164, 304, 359, 404, 453
Hewett, Sir George, Bart. Gen. 211, 231
Harris Lord, Gen. *G. C. B.* 41, 82, 167, 171, 210, 267, 275, 301, 377, 379, 452, 482, 486, 528
Harris, Mr. 51-6
Hindley, E., Major, Madras E., services, 86
Hartley, late M.-Gen., 90, 288, 331, 333, 357
Hay, A., L.-Col., Bombay E., services, 96
Hetzler, Robert, L.-Col. *C. B.* 113
Hall, Major, H. M.'s 89th
Hayes, John, Commodore, 146-9

Hearsay, J. B. Lieut. (now Capt.) 161
Hutchinson, the late Capt. 179, 180
Hutchinson, late Major, Bombay E. services, 306
Heron, F. Capt. Bengal E. services, 179
Howorth, H. late Capt. 187
Hickes, F. Capt. 193
Hall, Lieut. 206, 208
Hart, G. V., L.-Gen. 210
Hastings, Warren, Rt. Hon. 203, 217, 219, 220, 418

Iheend fort, 5
Irton, late Col. 67
Ironside, Col. 91
Indore, battle of, 1801, 178
Isle of France, reduction of, 179, 370
Imlack, late Col *C. B.* 247, 252
Itory, Captain, 293
Innis, Brigadier, 447, 526
Innovations, danger of in India, 465

Jenkins, Lieut. 457
Johnston, Capt. 444
Jaheereea fort, 7
Jones, Sir R., L.-Gen. *K. C. B.* Bombay E., services, 124, 11, 14, 117, 192, 195, 259
Jenkins, R., Esq.. 34, 151, 152, 154, 164, 165, 166, 459
Java, expedition to, in 1810, 70, 110, 289, 319, 380, 523
Java, geography, history, antiquities, and literature of, 321
Jaulnah, siege and fall of, 118
Jawud, storm and capture of, 105, 188, 189, 414
Jacobs, Lieut., 138
James, Lieut., 143
Jemaulabad, seized by Timnaick, 173
Johnson, Col. *C. B.* 195, 377
Jourdan, Major, 261
Jones, Capt. Bombay E., services, 305
Jones, Lieut., 394
Johnstone, Sir Alexander, 311
Jameson, Capt. 335-7
Jones, John, Capt. 438

Kenny, Lt.-Col. 9, 117
Khosas tribe, character of, 19; operations against, and annihilation, 20-6
Kellett Lieut. R. N. 238-9
Kalunga, capture of, &c. 32, 526
Karnaul, capture of, 81
Kirkee, battle of, 116
Kopsa, battle of, 108
Kelly, Brig. H. M.'s 24th foot, 112, 197, 201
Kurnella, capture of, 175, 363
Kurawal, attack and capture of, 180
King, C. P. Lieut., (now Capt.) 187
Kennedy, James, Capt. (now Major) 187
Knox, A. Brig. Bengal E., services, 202
Khytul, storm of, 203
Kemmendine, action of, 237, 243
Kennedy, Major, 281
Knox, L.-Col. 291
Koordah, orders on the capture of, 293
Khooshgal, surrender of, 381, 399
Ker, H. J., Capt. 438
Kanoon, reduction of, 421
Kenneway, Sir John, Bart., Col., 450
Knox, Hon., Col. 476

Kirkpatrick, William, late M.-Gen. 486
Kyd, Col. 529

Lindram, Capt. 335
Lonsdale, Ensign, 346
Ludlow, late L.-Col., and C. B. 414
Lamb, W., L.-Col.-Com., Bengal E., serv., 426
Lane, John, Lieut., (now Capt.) 437
Leslie, M., late Col. 447, 449
Lindsay, Capt. 476
Lowry, late Major, C. B. 526
Lake, the Hon. G. A. F. late L.-Col. 511
Levee-days at the India-House, proposed, 310
Lauriston, late L.-Col. 254
Lock, late Major, 245, 251
Luttufpoor, capture of, see services of Capt. Thomas Blair
Leadbeater, Capt. 4
Lindsey, Adam, Major, 8
Lasligaum fort, 9, 118
Lake, Lord, Gen., memoir of, 502, 30, 78-9, 126, 127, 129, 191, 198, 199, 499
Lane, W. late L.-Col. Bengal E., services, 358
Laswarree, battle of, 30, 32, 79, 145, 203, 376, 414, 416, 509
Lawrence, H. P., L.-Gen. 183-5
Lawrence, Stringer, the late M.-Gen. 62
Laurence, David, late Lieut. 345, 346, 347, 355
Limond, J., L.-Col. Madras E., services, 66
Lindsey, John, L.-Col., Madras E., services, 86
Leonard, late Major, 86, 280, 281
Lambton, W. late L.-Col., services, 100, 302
Lindsay, A., L.-Col., Bengal E., services, 110
Lloyd, Capt., 121
Lyons, Lieut., 132
Leighton, Capt., 142
Lighton, Lieut., 339, 340
Lukin, Lieut., 144
Laudon, Lieut., 144
Lloyd, W., Major, services, Bengal E., 146, 457
Lackerie, battle of, 168
Little, J., late Col., Bombay E., services, 468, 171, 286
Leeches, 174
Lowghur, capture of, 176, 363
Lane, J. T., Lieut., 182
Langslow, R., Capt. Bengal E., services, 197, 243
Lamba, capture of, 207
Laird, Surgeon, 219
Lurkas, history of, 228
Lindsay, Mr. 232

Marshall, T., late L.-Gen., Bombay E., services, 244, 250, 356
Molesworth, Viscount, Capt., 258
Mackay, Robert, L.-Gen., 273
Macalister, late M.-Gen., 278
Macgregor, late Capt., 280
M'Gregor, L.-Col. 289
Morison, W., Major, Bombay E., services, 120
Miller, L.-Col., 372
Montresor, Gen. 121, 193, 194, 401
M'Pherson, D., L.-Col.-Com., 429, 436, 441, 443
Monson, late B.-Gen. 129, 168, 198, 421, 513
Macan, late M.-Gen., services, 129
Miller, Capt. 132, 139
Muckee, expedition against, 1804, 146
M'Donald, J., Capt., 157, 164

Moxon, Capt., (now L.-Col.) 162, 164, 166
Macdonald, W. B., late Lieut., 164
Mackenzie, John, Major, (now L.-Col. and C. B.) 164, 454, 457
Mutiny at Spithead, 170
Maxwell, W. G., L.-Col., 189, 190, 526
Maxwell, late Col., 475, 476, 497, 498
Morse, J., L.-Col., Bombay E., services, 193
Morris, James, late M.-Gen. 387
Mansell, Major, 53d foot, 200
Mac Grath, late Col., 427
Muir, Granger, late Colonel, Bengal E., services, 212, 463
Myaffre, Maj., 215, 217
Morgan, late L.-Gen., 217
Malcolm, Lieut., 219
Maillard, Lieut., 228, 229
Minto, Lord. 231, 256, 296, 369
Marshall, W., Capt., Bombay E., services, 250, 245, 247
Moor, E., Major, 286, 354, 469, 470
Meares, late Major, 289
Mac Gregor, J. A. P., L.-Col., Bengal E., services, 295
Mackenzie, Colin, late Col. and C. B. Madras E., services, 310, 377
Mysore survey, see services of Col. C. Mackenzie, C. B.
Morris, Ensign, 346
Murray, Maj., 273
Marches in India, 252
Murray, Lieut., 216, 220
Mundelah, siege and capture of, 114
Murray, Sir John Mac Gregor, the late Col., 96
Mehidpoor, battle of, 104, 251, 304
Martindell, Sir G., L.-Gen., K. C. B., 98, 211
M'Dougal, L.-Col., 375
Mason, L.-Col., 255
Marshall, Sir D., late M.-Gen. K. C. B., 32, 33, 188, 417
Muckwanpoor, battle of, 79, 179, 417
Martin, George, Capt., 35
Martin, T., Capt., Bengal E., services, 91
Maloun fort, 6
Metcalfe, Sir Charles, 7, 360, 427
Miles, W., L.-Col., Bombay E., services, 10
Murray, Sir John, Bart., Gen., 122, 123, 124, 175
Michael, James, Capt., 58
Morris, J. W., M.-Gen., 18
Malcolm, Sir John, M.-General, G. C. B., &c. 32, 47, 104, 389, 403, 470, 482
Marley, B., L.-Gen., 112, 387, 417
Mathews, B.-Gen., 90, 341, 351, 452
Moultye fort, capture of, 34
Macdowall, Hay, late L.-Gen., 35, 36
M'Kerras, late Col., 74
M'Lane, Lieut., 337
Macpherson, Capt., 35
Munro, John, L.-Col., 36
Marriott, T., M.-Gen., Madras E., services, 39, 84, 85, 119
Maxwell, late L.-Col., 40, 280
Maxwell, late Capt., 254
Maxwell, Lieut., 457
Manilla, expedition, 40, 82
Macauley, M.-Gen. 45, 65
M'Leod, Norman, late M.-Gen. 341, 347, 353, 469

INDEX.

Munro, Sir Thos., M.-Gen., *K. C. B.*, Madras E., services, 403, 61-6, 77, 400
Marriott, Chas., Maj., Madras E., services, 84
Malavilly, battle of, 67, 84, 86, 167, 276-7, 295, 377, 483
Medows, Sir Wm., late Gen., *K. B.* 210, 263, 270, 272, 332, 475, 479, 527, 534
Moneypenny, Col., 72, 452
Mackonochie, G., L.-Col. Com., Bombay E., services, 116
Murray, Lieut., 218
Mâhe, surrender of, 338
Mignan, G. W., late L.-Col., 362
Mallia, capture of, 373, 375
Marston, Ensign, 382
Mac Queen, Lieut., 431, 432, 440
M'Naughton, Lieut. 432
Munt, Lieut.-Col. Commandant, 442
Mangalore, defence of, 468
Middleton, late Major, 507
Macleod, Alex., Maj., Bengal E., services, 523
Macmorine, late Brigadier, 525
Malcolm, Col., 530

Nugent, Sir George, Gen., *G. C. B.*, 5, 211, 384
Neale. Geo. late Maj., 282-3, 402
Nalghur fort, reduction of, 6
Nepean, Sir E., 18
Nairne, Robert, late Major, 31
Nixon, John, Major, 77
Native soldiery, 78, 521
Nichol, W., L.-Col., 92
Nairs, instance of their savage barbarity, 122
Nicolls, L.-Gen., 125, 259
Nott, Lieut., 148
Nagpore escort, 151, 166
Niven, Assistant Surgeon, 160, 457
Nugent, Lieut. 180, 182
Nixon, G. L., late Capt., 236
Nicholson, late L.-Gen., 254, 259
Nicholls, Oliver, Gen., 255
Noanuggur, siege of, 375
Newton, T., L.-Col., Bengal E., services, 427
Narnole, reduction of, 421
Nundydroog, siege of, 473
Nightingall, Sir M., Gen. *K. C. B.*, 523

Ochterlony, Sir D., late M.-Gen., *G. C. B.*, and Bart., Bengal E., services, 464, 94, 112, 201, 204-6, 209, 370, 371, 391, 392, 520
O'Donnell, Henry A., L.-Col., *C. B.*, 32
Oram, L.-Col., 82
Onore, siege of, 90, 342
Oogein, distress of the British army at, in 1804; 124, 178-9, 363
Osborne, Lieut. 132
Ootradroog, capture of, 1791; 203, 291, 475
Oakley, Mr. 231
Oldham, L.-Col., 268-9
Orr, L.-Gen., 273, 275, 279
O'Reilly, Col., 400, 401
Officers of the Company's army, great talents, 404; insufficiency of to Native corps, 443

Patterson, Major, 488
Price, Capt., 488
Plassey, battle of, 212
Purneire, reduction of, 192

Pateeta, action of, see services of Capt. T. Blair
Polhill, Lieut., 223
Pogson, L.-Col., 279, 281-2
Prescott, C. E. Esq., E. I. Director, 285
Palmer, Lieut., 293
Putney Hill, storm of, 335
Pruen, Lieut., 337
Pritzler, Sir Theophilus, *K. C. B.*, 375
Pester, I., L.-Col., Bengal E., services, 381
Palmer, Major, 401
Popham, L.-Col., 442
Pater, Colonel, 488
Price, David, Maj. 343, 346, 347, 349, 353, 356
Page, W. G., Capt., 239
Pickey, Mr., R. N., 239
Pondicherry, siege and capture, 1793; 8, 479
Pleydell, Mr., 212
Pawanghur, reduction of, 11, 12
Pahlunpoor, capture of, 16-18
Paton, Lieut., 188
Prother, D., late L.-Col., *C. B.*, 29, 136-9, 254, 307
Pindarries, history of, &c. 32-4, 69, 405
Petrie, Hon. W., 37, 297
Persian language, 58
Palembang, expedition against the Rajah of, 70-1, 289
Pearce, T. D., late Col., 80
Pedanargdurgum, capture of, 83
Purnell, Dr., 131
Pelly, Lieut., 144
Palmer, M.-Gen., 145
Pitman, R., Maj., (now L.-Col. Com,) 156, 360
Popham, late L.-Gen., 167, 216, 217, 219, 220, 221, 358, 418
Pellew, Sir I., Admiral, 169
Powell, Capt., 175
Poonadur, capture of, 176, 363
Polhman, Col., 182
Pierce, T., Maj., Bombay E., services, 183
Paterson, John, Capt., 188
Phillips, Robt. L.-Gen., 197
Pollock, late Lieut., 199
Powlett, Earl, 153
Pringle, D., Lieut., now Capt., 206, 208
Prole, G., M.-Gen., Bengal E., service, 209

Richards, W. Col., 524
Richards, Alfred, Brigadier, 393, 397, 525
Rungpore, attack of, 397
Raha Chokey, surprise of, 396
Rose, J. L.-Col., Bengal E., services, 410
Ramnagur, unfortunate attack of, 215, 418
Roberts, H. T., Major, 431
Ross, Alex., Gen., 529, 531
Ramsay, Sir Thos., Bart., L.-Col., 531
Robertson, J., L.-Col., Bengal E., services, 384
Rhas ul Kyma, siege and capture of, 375
Ross, Lieut., 345, 350-3, 356
Russell, Capt., H. M. 74th, 291
Romney, James, Capt., 114
Ranneea fort, 7
Richardson, J., Esq., 2
Run, description of the, 23
Rampoora fort, capture of, 30, 414, 512
Rennell, Major, 88, 89
Raffles, Sir Stamford, 38, 290
Richmond, Duke of, 39

INDEX.

Richardson, J. L., L.-Col. Com., Bengal E., services, 80, 92
Read, late L.-Col., 82, 84, 277, 403
Reynolds, C., late L.-Gen., Bombay E., services, 87, 292
Russel, Claud, Mr., 92
Roome, H., L.-Col. Com., Bombay E., services, 114, 373
Ridge, E. I., Major, C. B., Bengal E., services, 185, 106
Richards, W., Maj., Bengal E., services, 107
Ryghur, siege and capture of, 136
Rebenach, C. C., Lieut., 143-4
Ritchie, Lieut., 162
Read, late Lieut., 190
Richards, Goddard, Col., 201
Rumbold, Sir Thos., 213
Roughsedge, E., late Maj., Bengal E., services, 227, 230-5
Rehe, S. A., Capt., 237, 238
Robson, Thos., Capt., 237
Ryves, Capt., 239
Reynolds, O., Ensign, (now Lieut.,) 239
Rumley, Capt., 278
Ralph, H., Capt., Bengal E., services, 289
Ross, M.-Gen., 376, 380

Stanhope, L.-Col., 367-8, 374
Souppah fort, capture of, 350
St. George, battle of, 300, 301, 419, 463
Sossing, siege of, 296
Sherbrooke, Lieut.-Gen., and G. C. B., 276
Sattimungul, battle of, 263
Seedaseer, battle of, 6th March 1799; 115, 246
Staunton, late Lieut.-Col., C. B., Bombay E., services, 460, 117, 288, 306
Sinclair, Captain, 382
Sadashewghur, 120, 285, 349
Singapore, survey of, 106
Sibley, Captain, 385
Severndroog, expedition against, and capture of, 131-5, 184
Stevenson, Lieut., 131-3
Soppett, Capt., 131-3, 137, 140-1
Sandwith, Capt., 141
Sadler, late Capt., 156, 457
Smith, Cornet, 158, 162, 164, 457
Stone, W. Capt., 161, 162
Sotheby, Mr., 160, 164
Sutherland, Col., 178
Sneyd, E. C. Lieut., (now Capt.) 207
Skeene, W. Capt., 208
Sandys, William, L.-Col., 527, 534
Sandys, F. H. Capt., 208
Smyth, C. C. Capt., 208
Sparkes, Capt., 215, 216
Sinnock, H. Capt., Bengal E., services, 230, 228
Smith, G. A. Ensign, 239
Smyth, L.-Col., 257
Sampson, late Capt., 266
St. Leger, M.-Gen., 389, 428, 507
Sentleger, the Hon. A., late M.-Gen., 275, 281
Sheriff, late Col. 279
Stewart, Robert, Dr., 288
Savendroog, siege and storm of, 291, 474
Salkeld, T., late L.-Col., Bengal E., services, 298
Stewart, Col. 302
Stewart, W. W. Capt., 365

Surveys, India, encouragement given for, 99; and see services of Col. C. Mackenze, Capt. Franklin, L.-Col. Lambton, &c.
Sanwith, William, Dr., 97
Shelden, Lieut., 92
Shamlie, defence of the fort of, 93, 412
Seetabuldee, battle of, 1817, 87, 151-166, 453-459
Seiks, character and country, 81
Sandie fort, 2
Sehleehoo fort, 2, 3
Skinner, Capt., 5
Sirsah fort, 7
Shower, Capt., 4
Seedmook fort, 7
Surcella fort, 7
Soluckneer fort, 7
Swinton, A. Capt., 2
Sutherland, J. Capt., Bombay E., services, 358
Simons, Jer., M.-Gen., Madras E., services, 8
Shaw, Col. 484, 479
Seringapatam, siege of, 1792, 8, 203, 273, 291, 452, 475
Seringapatam, siege of, 1799, 67, 82, 84, 86, 101, 116, 171, 253, 295, 302, 313, 361, 377, 410, 452, 483
Scott, Helenus, Dr., 97, 289
Swinton, L.-Col., Bengal E., services, 415-30
Stevenson, Col., 9, 274, 281, 488, 494
Seooghur Hill, action of, 367, 375
Sodowick and Souraboya forts, capture of, 70
Sewree, action of, 12
Soondoor, reduction of, 404
Strover, S. R. Major, Bombay E., services, 28
Smith, Sir L. K. C. B., M.-Gen., 306, 365-7, 373
Sooligheri, capture of, 83
Sasnee fort, 30, 31, 382, 413, 415, 420, 504
Shee, Lieut.-Col., 35
Stewart, G. M., Major, Madras E., services, 71
Shuldham, M.-Gen., 37
Scott, Robert, Col. C. B., 65
Stuart, Gen., 263, 277, 280, 292, 475, 485, 489
Scindia, character of, 68
Scott, H. S. Col., C. B., Madras E., services, 453-87, 153, 163, 164, 165
Smith, T. H., L.-Col., Madras E., services, 399
Say, J. A., Maj., Madras E., services, 400
Seton, late Archibald, Esq., 424, 428, 429
Sparkes, late Capt., 433, 441
Stewart, D. late Lieut., Bengal E., services, 450
Sibbald, late Capt. 477, 531
Skelly, Major, 478
St. John, Gen. the Hon. Frederick, services, 504, 507
Showers, H. D. Major, Bengal E., services, 525
Smith, C. Capt. Bengal E., services, 525

Tatteah fort, 30, 382
Torin, Mr. 43
Tanjore Provinces, frauds in the government departments, 44-57
Thompson, Colonel, 76, 391
Thomson, Colonel, 119
Tippoo Sultaun, his death, 172; family, 41, 72-5. 85; letters, 487
Torriano, J. S. late Major, 90, 342, 343, 351
Teinmouth, Lord, 91
Thomas, Lewis, M.-Gen., 92
Thatcher, Lieut.-Col., 124

Taylor, Colonel, 127, 128
Tolcher, late Captain, 129
Taylor, R., Brigade Major, 164
Timnaick, a rebel, 172-4, 362
Thievish dexterity, anecdote of, 176
Turner, Lieutenant, 189
Titcher, late Lieutenant, 199
Taylor, Charles, Captain, 208
Toom, Sir W., K.C.B., late M.-Gen., 232, 233
Tidy, F. S., Colonel, 237
Telligaum, action of, 286-8, 332
Tellichery, siege of, 334
Tredenick, Galbraith, Lieutenant, 340, 352
Turner, W. L.-Col.-Com., Bombay E., serv., 361
Thomas, W. Lieut.-Col. Commandant, 388

Velore, mutiny, 41, 72-5, 85, 453
Vardon, Lieutenant, 144
Verelst, Mr., 212
Vanrayne, Lieut., 340
Vanas, Colonel, 415
Vesey, Colonel, 492

Wheldon, Lieut., 336, 340, 343, 346, 347, 350, 353
Willim, J. G., Capt., Bengal E., services, 307
White, Sir H., K.C.B., late M.-Gen., 308, 416, 477
Wandiwash, capture of, 308
Wedderburn, late Brigadier-Gen., 332
Whitman, C. H. Capt. 333
Whippy, Captain, 335
Williamson, Lieut.-Col., 362
Walker, A. Col. 374
Wood, Sullivan, Major-Gen., 385, 386
Waters, E. F., Major, Bengal E., services, 393
Ware, late M.-Gen , 507
Watson, M.-Gen., H. M.'s 14th foot, 523
Wilks, M. Col. 263, 267, 409, 528, 533
White, W. G. Capt , 258

Wiseman, the late Lieut.-Gen. 253
Walker, C. A. Major, (now Lieut.-Col.) 240
White, John, Col., 1
Wellington, Duke of, Field-Marshal, &c., memoir, 482, 9, 14, 68, 276, 280, 281, 285
Wood, Captain, 415
Watson, Admiral, 212
Wallace, Col., 9, 281, 282, 285, 484, 492
Warren, John, Mr. 101
Woodington, late Col., Bombay E., services, 10, 12, 117, 255, 374
Watson, R. A. C., late Lieut.-Col., 199, 200
Wilkinson, Lieut.-Gen. 37, 194
Webbe, J. Esq., 48, 49
Wallace, Mr., 50, 53, 69
Wellesley, Marquess, 57, 101, 316, 480, 482, 485
Waddington, late Capt., 129
Weltevreeden, battle of, 70
Worsley, H. Col., C. B., 78, 211, 388, 424, 470, 518
Walker, Patrick, late Col., 87, 151, 373
Warden, Francis, Esq., 90
Warde, Sir Henry, L.-Gen., K. C. B., 118
Waite, Captain, 142
Wade, Ensign, 143-4
Wade, Lieut., 219
Wilks, Lieut., 143
Whichelo, Ensign, 144
Watson, L. W. Lieut., (now Capt.) 164
Webb, Lieut.-Col., 191
Wood, Sir George, K. C. B., late M.-Gen., 200
Wilkie, James, Capt., 208
Weir, R. D. Ensign, (now Lieut.) 239

Yates, W. A. Lieut., (now Capt.) 182, 243
Yates, C. W. late Major, Madras E., services, 235
Yates, G. late Capt., Bengal E., services, 243
Yates, Frederick, Mr., 243
Young, Sir William, Col., 289
Young, Lieut., 345, 349

THE END.

W. WILSON, PRINTER, 57, SKINNER-STREET, LONDON.

www.ingramcontent.com/pod-product-compliance
Lightning Source LLC
Chambersburg PA
CBHW082018300426
44117CB00015B/2273